# Human-Computer Interaction Series

T0140591

Human-Computer Interaction is a multidisciplinary field focused on human aspects of the development of computer technology. As computer-based technology becomes increasingly pervasive-not just in developed countries, but worldwide-the need to take a human-centered approach in the design and development of this technology becomes ever more important. For roughly 30 years now, researchers and practitioners in computational and behavioral sciences have worked to identify theory and practice that influences the direction of these technologies, and this diverse work makes up the field of human-computer interaction.

Broadly speaking, it includes the study of what technology might be able to do for people and how people might interact with the technology.

In this series, we present work which advances the science and technology of developing systems which are both effective and satisfying for people in a wide variety of contexts. The human-computer interaction series will focus on theoretical perspectives (such as formal approaches drawn from a variety of behavioral sciences), practical approaches (such as the techniques for effectively integrating user needs in system development), and social issues (such as the determinants of utility, usability and acceptability).

Author guidelines: www.springer.com/authors/book+authors > Author Guidelines

For further volumes:
http://www.springer.com/series/6033

Niels Ole Bernsen · Laila Dybkjær

# Multimodal Usability

 Springer

Niels Ole Bernsen
NISLab
Copenhagen
Denmark
www.multimodalusability.dk

Laila Dybkjær
SKAT
Copenhagen
Denmark
www.multimodalusability.dk

ISSN 1571-5035
ISBN 978-1-4471-2517-4        e-ISBN 978-1-84882-553-6
DOI 10.1007/978-1-84882-553-6
Springer London Dordrecht Heidelberg New York

British Library Cataloguing in Publication Data
A catalogue record for this book is available from the British Library

Printed on acid-free paper

Springer is part of Springer Science+Business Media (www.springer.com)

# Preface

This preface tells the story of how *Multimodal Usability* responds to a special challenge. Chapter 1 describes the goals and structure of this book.

The idea of describing how to make multimodal computer systems usable arose in the European Network of Excellence SIMILAR – "Taskforce for creating human-machine interfaces SIMILAR to human-human communication", 2003–2007, www.similar.cc. SIMILAR brought together people from multimodal signal processing and usability with the aim of creating enabling technologies for new kinds of multimodal systems and demonstrating results in research prototypes. Most of our colleagues in the network were, in fact, busy extracting features and figuring out how to demonstrate progress in working interactive systems, while claiming not to have too much of a notion of usability in system development and evaluation. It was proposed that the authors support the usability of the many multimodal prototypes underway by researching and presenting a methodology for building usable multimodal systems.

We accepted the challenge, first and foremost, no doubt, because the formidable team spirit in SIMILAR could make people accept outrageous things. Second, having worked for nearly two decades on making multimodal systems usable, we were curious – curious at the opportunity to try to understand what happens to traditional usability work, that is, work in human–computer interaction centred around traditional graphical user interfaces (GUIs), when systems become as multimodal and as advanced in other ways as those we build in research today. Third, we were perhaps ready for a stab at making usability and human–system interaction intelligible to newcomers, having often wondered why this field seems so hard to some, including many graduate students and PhD students in computer science and engineering. Finally, of course, we grossly underestimated the effort required for trying to make sense of multimodal usability.

If you are curious, too, let's just say that we found that a lot changes when we pass from GUI-based usability to multimodal usability, from GUI-based human–computer interaction to multimodal human–computer interaction. Interestingly, these changes, which amount to a generalisation of the field of human–computer interaction, seem to make the field easier, rather than more difficult, to explain and

express in a general model, i.e. the one that underlies the structure and contents of
this book.

Niels Ole Bernsen                                              Copenhagen, Denmark
Laila Dybkjær                                                  Copenhagen, Denmark

# Acknowledgements

This book was initiated in the context of the EU SIMILAR network of excellence 2003–2007 (www.similar.cc). We gratefully acknowledge the support.

We would like to thank the colleagues in SIMILAR who took the time to read a draft version of the book and send us their comments and feedback: Ana C. Andrés del Valle, Suzanne Kieffer, Pablo Lamata, Andrey Ronzhin, Dimitrios Tzovaras, Jean Vanderdonckt, Jörg Voskamp and Olga Vybornova. Thanks also to Benoit Macq for enthusiastically pushing the book idea and to SIMILAR project reviewers Robert Damper, Vaclav Hlavac and Panagiotis Markopoulos for constructive questions to, and comments on, our progress.

We are grateful to Springer's three reviewers for many important comments and helpful suggestions on how the draft version could be improved.

Thanks are due to Kostas Moustakas for delivering the Treasure Hunt system for usability testing and for taking part in the test in Copenhagen. We thank the Institute for the Blind for hosting the user test and Flemming Berthelsen for recruiting the test subjects. We also wish to thank Cornelius Malerczyk and his students for revising and delivering the Sudoku system for usability testing and answering our questions about technical details; Torben Kruchov Madsen for technical support with the Sudoku system test; Svend Kiilerich for taking care of the subjects; and Thanos Tsakiris for creating the 3D head of Mae, the Maths system teacher.

Thanks also to Hans Dybkjær for comments on the pre-final version.

We are grateful to all those who gave us permission to reproduce or reprint material: Usability Professionals' Association (UPA) (Fig. 6.1), Gerry Stimson (Fig. 8.1), George Silverman (Fig. 9.1), Nigel Bevan (Fig. 9.2), Ben Shneiderman and Pearson Education, Inc. (Fig. 11.10), Jakob Nielsen (Fig. 11.11), the International Organization for Standardization (ISO) (Figs. 11.14, 11.15 and 11.16), Paul Ekman and Joseph C. Hager (Fig. 15.4), David McNeill and University of Chicago Press (Fig. 15.5) and Kostas Moustakas (Figs. 7.8, 7.9 and 7.10).

Finally, special thanks are owed to our spouses, Lone Adler and Hans Dybkjær, for their encouragement, support and patience throughout the writing of this book.

# Contents

# Chapter 1
# Structure, Usability, Readership

Overviews are useful, so we start this introduction by deriving the book's structure and scope from its goals and two simple models of how to work on usability. We then introduce multimodal usability and provide a reader's guide and tour map.

In more detail, Section 1.1 describes our goals of writing a practical introduction to usability with special focus on multimodal systems and transparent structure and progress of presentation. Section 1.2 models usability work as a series of CoMeDa – Concepts, Methods and Data handling – cycles integrated in the development life cycle. Section 1.3 describes CoMeDa cycles and shows how the overall book structure explains the CoMeDa components and, in special chapters called Intermezzi, illustrates them by means of three multimodal Cases. Section 1.4 defines usability and puts usability and its study in conceptual and historical perspective, explaining the need to generalise from standard usability to multimodal usability. Section 1.5 discusses how much usability matters. Section 1.6 describes the intended readership and shows a map of scenic routes through this book. Note also the book's web site at www.MultimodalUsability.dk and the list of abbreviations before the index at the end of the book.

## 1.1 Goals

This book has an overall goal, a special focus and a presentation goal.

Our *overall goal* is to present a clear, well-structured and practical introduction to interactive system usability. We want to tell what you need to know, find out and do to develop a usable system end to end. It is generally agreed that usability is best optimised, and usability problems best avoided, by integrating usability into the development process from day 1 until system completion. We would like to show why and describe how it is done.

Our *special focus* is on building usable multimodal systems. Although most advanced and innovative interactive systems today are multimodal, work on multimodal usability remains poorly understood and, to our knowledge, has not been systematically addressed before. Rather, usability has been addressed mainly in the multidisciplinary field of human–computer interaction (HCI) whose origins and tradition are firmly rooted in graphical user interfaces (GUIs).

To establish this book's special focus, we have analysed concepts, models and methods of mainstream HCI and found that multimodal usability is, in fact, a generalisation of traditional HCI in important respects and at all levels, from contents through methods to framework and theory. We have integrated those generalisations into the structure, contents and order of presentation of what follows, so that you can focus on multimodal usability without feeling caught up in a scholarly debate about paradigm shifts. Our scholarly view is that the future of interactive systems is multimodal and that future books on usability must generalise and transform HCI just like we are trying to do.

Our *presentation goal* is to make the book's structure and contents as transparent as possible from the start to the end, so that the reader can maintain a full overview of where to find what. We start right away to build an overview based on a couple of simple models and generally try to proceed from structure or model to contents, from less detail to more, from anticipation to expansion, so that when something new turns up in the text, you have already met it in a more sketchy form.

*Note on terminology*: since we view multimodal usability as a generalised and updated notion of usability, we will simply speak about "usability" unless specifically discussing traditional usability vs. multimodal usability.

## 1.2 How to Work on Usability – Two Simple Models

Working on usability becomes a lot easier when you have a firm grasp of its main components. Given that grasp and some practice, you will really know what you are doing.

### 1.2.1 Model 1: A Well-Stuffed Bag of Usability Information

Considering the system development process as a whole, including any evaluations that might be carried out, let's imagine that, out there, there is an *ideal bag* of information relevant for optimising your system's usability. Let us call its contents *usability information* and stipulate that, were you to get hold of this information and analyse it properly, you could optimise the usability of your system. To work on usability is to engage in a quest for that bag, so *your* task is to collect a good deal of its contents, our task is to help you.

In the real world, probably, no one ever gets hold of all there is in the bag. However, if you ignore the quest for usability information, chances are that your system's usability could fail completely. If you work hard to collect and exploit a well-stuffed bag, chances are that the system will be usable to some satisfactory degree. If, like everyone else, you have limited resources to spend on the quest, you must be extra careful to spend them right.

A final point about Model 1 is that the quest starts as soon as you define a first version of the development goal for your project, that is, typically even before requirements capture and analysis. At that stage, all you may have is a loose idea of the kind of system to build.

## 1.2.2 Model 2: Usability in the Software Engineering Life Cycle

Let's look at how to stuff an initially empty bag with usability information, taking a first look at how to work on usability. This work is an integral part of software engineering and we will mostly take knowledge about software engineering for granted – as a stage on which what we have to say plays out. If you need to read up on the subject, grab one of the many fine textbooks, e.g. (Sommerville 2007, Pressman 2005).

A key construct in software engineering is the *life cycle*, i.e. the structure and contents of the process of building a system from idea to plan to early version to maturity to face/body-lifts to wherever software goes when it is not being used any more. Ever since the linear and sequential "Waterfall" model of system development (Royce 1970), lots of other models have been proposed to help developers think clearly and in detail about what they do and need to do, including coordination and communication with customers, sponsors, colleagues and others. These models may be incremental process models, emphasising development by small increments (Mills 1980, Beck 1999), evolutionary models emphasising iteration and sometimes risk analysis (Boehm 1988), models emphasising both increments and iteration (Jacobson et al. 1999), etc. Some are aimed to provide a more adequate general life cycle model than their predecessors, others to model a particular type of development process.

Figure 1.1 shows, *above* the project or system start–finish timeline, an abstract general life cycle model that simply says that between project start and finish, and especially if the project is not aborted, things will happen that could be characterised as having a development goal, capturing requirements, analysing them, deciding on a set of them (specification of what to build), design of system and components, implementation or construction of these, system integration and evaluation. All of those "things" might happen more or less simultaneously or not. The order in which they happen may differ widely from one project to another. Some or all of them may happen several, or even many, times, such as having several development goal modifications, re-specifications, re-designs, re-implementations, re-integrations or re-evaluations. Most everything that happens may be carefully documented or, at the other extreme, exist solely in the minds of the developers. If this looks potentially too chaotic to be real, just think about some advanced multimodal systems research project in which it takes a great deal of exploratory programming to become clear about what the project's development goal should be in the first place. This high level of uncertainty and risk obviously does not characterise all projects, such as small run-of-the-mill commercial projects in which most issues are familiar from earlier, similar systems.

Note that Fig. 1.1 does not include the final life cycle phase of maintenance or evolution in which an already developed system gets modified. When a system idea goes all the way from advanced research to product, this maturation process typically involves development of several different system versions in different projects and hence several passes through the life cycle in the figure.

Focus *below* the start–finish line in Fig. 1.1 is on the usability work that forms part of the life cycle. This work can be viewed as a series of cycles, larger or smaller, sometimes overlapping or including other cycles, with a common structure, i.e. that of involving *C*oncepts, usability data collection *M*ethods and *D*ata handling. We call those cycles *CoMeDa cycles*, and the figure shows how the data collected with the methods goes into the bag, or box, described in Section 1.2.1. The dashed CoMeDa cycles illustrate usability work in some particular project.

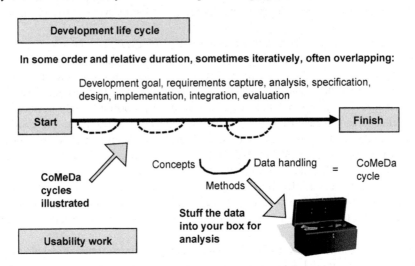

**Fig. 1.1**  Working on usability in the development life cycle

## 1.3  Structure and Scope of This Book

This section unfolds the overall book structure and its rationale by first getting inside CoMeDa and then describing the mechanisms we will be using to maintain links with development practice.

### *1.3.1  Concepts, Methods, Data Handling – Overall Book Structure*

Figure 1.2 shows what's inside CoMeDa. The *Concepts* part is our *AMITUDE model of use,* which claims that system use can be helpfully modelled as having the aspects *A*pplication type, *M*odalities, *I*nteraction, *T*ask or other activity, domain,

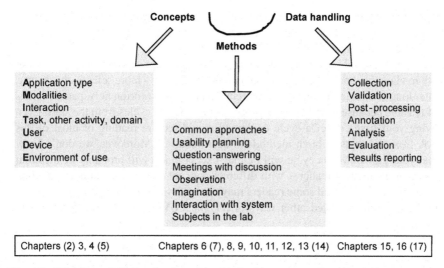

**Fig. 1.2** CoMeDa unfolded and reflected in this book's structure. Intermezzi chapters are in brackets and explained in Section 1.3.3

*U*ser, *D*evice and *E*nvironment of use. In addition to the notion of usability, AMI-TUDE is our main conceptual framework because, in order to create a usable system, the seven AMITUDE aspects must be analysed to some satisfactory extent during specification and design. AMITUDE is presented in Chapters 3 and 4.

Once we have the Concepts we need, the CoMeDa cycle requires that we select and apply some usability *Method or common approach* to gain usability information. Chapter 6 presents the *Common approaches*, listing them in Table 6.1 (Section 6.1), followed by discussion of usability planning. *Methods* are described in Chapters 8 (Question-Answering), 9 (Meetings with Discussion), 10 (Observation), 11 (Imagination) and 12 (Interaction). All methods are listed in Tables 6.2, 6.3, 6.4, 6.5 and 6.6. Chapter 13 addresses issues to do with working with users in the lab. Since many of the methods involve having users or subjects in the lab, it is efficient to present those issues in a horizontal chapter.

Having applied a common approach or, in particular, a method, we must do *Data handling* of the information collected. Figure 1.2 lists the data handling steps involved. These are described in Chapters 15 and 16.

## *1.3.2 Theory and Practice – Hen and Egg*

Let's summarise the message so far to show that it creates a problem for the practical goal of this book (Section 1.1): we work on system usability from day 1 until project end, executing CoMeDa cycles. In each cycle, we think in terms of the AMITUDE model of system use when applying some method or other approach to collect or generate usability information. This information is handled as data for evaluating or improving system model (Box 1.1) usability. The book's structure (Fig. 1.2) reflects the need to present those CoMeDa components. Where does this leave discussion of practice and examples of practical usability work?

Ideally, we would like you to develop your own system and make it usable along with reading this book. We believe that people read better – more selectively, deeper, better long-term retention – when practicing in parallel. Unfortunately, parallelism is not feasible because usability work proceeds in CoMeDa cycles from the start. Even having your first CoMeDa cycle explained would require reading of most of this book from concepts through methods to data handling. Moreover, we don't know what your first CoMeDa cycle will be like, except that it will probably be different from that of the next reader – with different concepts, methods and data handling techniques in focus. And some readers may not be developing any particular system at all. We obviously need other ways of relating CoMeDa to system development practice.

---

## Box 1.1  System vs. System Model

Whenever we use the term (interactive computer) "system", it is useful to think *system model* more generally. The reason is that the system model is there as soon as we have, say, a first tentative development goal, a first set of requirements or an interface sketch, and the system model is still there, possibly dramatically evolved, when the final system, duly implemented and tested, leaves the lab or gets commercially installed. The *system*, on the other hand, does not exist until the system model is realised in code running on some hardware. We consider AMITUDE, our model of system use, part of the system model.

---

### 1.3.3 Intermezzo, Case, Example, Overview, Exercise, Nerdy Stuff

We use a number of presentation mechanisms to integrate development practice into the fabric of this book, including intermezzi, Cases and other examples and look-ahead overviews that facilitate skipping to what's relevant to your own project. These mechanisms may be viewed as an overlay onto the book structure shown in Fig. 1.2. This overlay also includes several other presentation mechanisms to be described below.

An *intermezzo* is a chapter which keeps track of three worked interactive multi-modal system Cases that we follow from idea to, in one case, reporting on a controlled lab test with a representative user group. Intermezzi are bottom-up from Cases, whereas other chapters are top-down from some AMITUDE aspect, methodology, or otherwise, to examples used for illustration.

The *Cases* are introduced in Chapter 2 (Intermezzo 1) right after this chapter. These are relatively simple research prototype systems we have worked on recently ourselves, including a system for playing a familiar game using new modalities, a highly original multimodal game for the disabled and a multimodal affective tutoring system. We do Case requirements analysis in Chapters 3 and 4, illustrating AMITUDE work, and summarise results in Chapter 5 (Intermezzo 2). Chapter 7 (Intermezzo 3) presents a Case usability workplan and some Case design. Chapter 14 (Intermezzo 4) presents a Case usability method plan, and Chapter 17 (Intermezzo 5) reports a Case usability evaluation.

Since the Cases are insufficient for illustrating all important points made, we use other system development *examples* as well. The main difference is one of brevity: the Case descriptions are sufficiently detailed to be re-used for different purposes, whereas the examples are used to make specific points.

*Look-ahead overviews* may be exemplified by what you are reading right now.

We have included a small number of (six) *exercises* for the reader. In the first one, about usability in Section 1.4.7, we invite you to consider key implications of what has been said and present our own opinions for comparison. Our answers to the other five exercises can be easily accessed at this book's web site.

Finally, the *Nerdy stuff* idea is to announce, in the section heading, heavy stuff that may not be equally important to all readers.

## 1.4 What Is Usability

It is time to look at usability and the developments that call for generalisation from GUI-oriented usability to multimodal usability.

### 1.4.1 What Is Usability – The Short Answer

*System usability* is the goal of *making a system fit the bodies and minds of its users in context*. To better grasp what this definition means, let's put it in conceptual and historical perspective, look at its key components (terms and main issues) and discuss some implications.

### 1.4.2 Usability in Perspective – Systems and Other Artefacts

Conceptually, system usability is part of something far more general, namely, artefact usability. A system is an artefact just like the millions of other things humans design and build for various purposes. A pair of shoes, for instance, is an artefact typically meant to be worn by people when moving about on their feet. A usable pair of shoes fits the wearer's feet reasonably well, and it is an obvious goal for the producer to make usable shoes because they tend to sell better than ill-fitting shoes.

Generalising even more, would-be usable artefacts are produced not only for people but also for animals (cows' milking machines), virtual humans (in Second Life and elsewhere) and robots. In other words, usability came into the world when the first artefact – ignoring pieces of art – was created.

So what makes systems special compared to other artefacts as regards the goal of usability? The bottom line is that *systems aren't special*. Any category of artefacts raises more or less artefact-specific usability issues. However, let's consider two claims that systems are, indeed, special compared to other artefacts.

The first claim is that the difference is one of complexity. After all, usable shoes only have to fit a single body part whereas a usable system must fit the users' bodies *and* minds, right? Wrong! Ever heard of fashion? Fashion is mental and important to many people's choice of shoes, sometimes even to the point of overriding any other usability consideration.

Still, there are good reasons why computers emerged relatively late in the history of technology and why, on the whole, computer artefacts tend to surpass other artefacts in complexity. Thus, if 1st generation technology or 1 *GT* was artefacts directly manipulated by the human body (swords, shoes, door knobs, spades), 2 *GT* began to automate human muscle power (water and wind mills, steam engines), 3 *GT* began to automate human manipulation (weaving) and 4 *GT* began to automate process control (thermostats, cybernetics) – then computer systems represent 5 *GT* which is on its way to automate people more generally. In doing so, the argument says, interactive systems continue to raise a host of new issues of fitting people that have never been addressed before.

The second claim is that computer system usability is special because there is a science, would-be science or, perhaps rather, a science–craftsmanship conglomerate that focuses on interactive system usability. This book is about that conglomerate which today is called Human–Computer Interaction or (henceforth) HCI. For reasons we will not speculate about here, the usability of earlier technology generations has not become the subject of scientific study to nearly the same extent. The point is that they might have.

Let's briefly look at the origins of HCI for yet another perspective on usability and to inch closer to multimodal usability (this book's title).

The origins of usability studies in general and of HCI in particular may coincide. An often quoted origin of HCI has nothing to do with computers but rather concerns 1GT/2GT/3GT. During the pivotal battle of Britain in 1940, trained pilots were far more valuable than airplanes, so efforts were invested in cockpit (instrument) design to make aircraft control easier for the pilots by fitting their work environment to their mental and physical properties. Known as *human factors*, this kind of study received another boost during 4GT/5GT nuclear power plant control automation in the 1950s and 1960s, at which point the term *man–machine interaction* had taken root, soon to be replaced by *human–machine interaction* and, with proliferating computerisation, *human–computer interaction*. In other words, although mankind *might* have launched the scientific study of usability at the age of the flint stone or that of the bronze sword, it took a world war and the establishment of sciences, such as psychology, physiology and sociology, to succeed; and it took other mass safety-critical developments and events, such as the spread of nuclear power generation and accidents like the US Three Mile Island near-meltdown disaster in 1979, to help finance consolidation of this kind of study.

### 1.4.3  The Golden Age of HCI and After

It was the emergence of the PC in the 1980s that really established HCI as the multidisciplinary study of system usability, because, from then on, not only specialists but everyone became a system user, and systems spread from labs and control rooms to most workplaces and soon to homes as well. The HCI community avidly studied the interactive systems at the time, using theories and methods from its constituent disciplines as well as newly developed theories and methods, and succeeded in establishing a good deal of the conceptual apparatus, theoretical foundations and methods that are being applied today. This was the "golden age" of HCI, cf. the title of Section 1.1 in Carroll (2003).

The systems at the time, which revolutionised computing and interaction, had *Graphical User Interfaces* (GUIs) with the standard components *Windows, Icons, Menus* and *Pointing* (WIMP) and *WYSIWYG* (What You See Is What You Get) as interaction ideal, meaning that the graphical representation on the display would at any time more or less faithfully reflect the current state of the user's work. Pointing was done with a mouse device and the keyboard was standard, too. The classical GUI soon evolved into virtual reality, including 3D graphics and animation. The users were primarily anyone using the PC at work, and the usability issues of the day ranged from making the GUI intelligible to novice users in the first place, to enabling expert users carry out a rapidly growing range of work tasks easily and efficiently. Many of this book's topics were studied as forming the core of HCI: users were modelled, tasks analysed, task performance measured, learning-how-to-use studied, device usability analysed, usability methods established or rejected, conceptual frameworks worked and re-worked, thousands of usability guidelines proposed, how to involve users in development debated, etc.

A vigorous community by 1990, GUI-oriented HCI did not stop evolving between then and today. In this period of raw technological progress, GUI-based systems have come to serve a far larger range of human purposes than before. The Internet and, after some years, the World Wide Web presented a new set of usability challenges, with users becoming occasional visitors rather than long-term users. Mobile phone GUIs posed other challenges due to their small screen size and ubiquitous use. The abundance of computer games and other, more leisurely applications forcefully suggested that fitting systems to users has aspects other than ensuring easy and efficient task performance. On-line social and collaborative systems flourished, forcing analysis of multi-user system usability. And despite the failure of classical Artificial Intelligence (AI) in the 1980s, systems did become more intelligent as demonstrated by, e.g. abilities to adapt to simple user habits and preferences or to the user's geographical location. By the end of the 1990s, the usability vision had become one of usability for all, including children, elderly people, the disabled, the illiterate, those without electricity, the poor. In reality, however, the "for all" still read far too much like "for all who can use a PC or similar GUI-based system", not as truly universal usability.

At the same time, it was becoming obvious that classical GUI-based systems only provide a fraction of the value that computing offers: GUIs represent an interaction micro-cosmos within a far larger and far more diverse, multimodal space of opportunities.

## 1.4.4 Towards Multimodal Usability and Blending with People

A couple of trends that have gained strong momentum, particularly after year 2000, fit less well into mainstream GUI-oriented HCI. One is *multimodal interaction* which is often contrasted with GUI interaction as involving the use of modalities other than the GUI modalities, such as when people began to *speak* to systems rather than doing WIMP menu selection, or when systems began to *visually perceive* users instead of waiting for their next keyboard or mouse input. A related trend is *natural interaction* in which information is exchanged with the system in the same ways in which humans exchange information with one another, i.e. through speech, facial expression, gesture and so on. Natural interaction is multimodal by nature and, in practice, much but not all of what is going on in today's multimodal interaction R&D is natural interaction.

There is more. The prominent human-style communication aspects of natural and multimodal interaction come as part of an even larger package which also includes computational modelling of (i) *human perceptual functionality*, such as hearing, vision and touch sensing; (ii) *human central processing functionality*, such as goal structures, emotions or affects and situated reasoning; and (iii) *human action functionality*, such as walking or gesturing. Everything in this package is closely connected because we cannot model human-style communication without modelling the central processes behind it, the perceptual input that feeds the central processing and the actions that express it. The huge interactive systems potential of this package which we call *blending with people* (Box 1.2) is not restricted to stand-alone applications but is expected to transform Internet interaction from its current GUI dominance to something far more multimodal.

We call this book *Multimodal Usability* because we wish to include with multimodality the entire blending with people "package" within the scope of usable systems development. Formally, this is a generalisation of mainstream GUI-oriented *usability* and *HCI* to include far more modalities and far more complex interaction than the GUI modalities and GUI-based interaction. We do not aim to throw anything away but, rather, to include CoMeDa items of particular interest to developers of systems for blending with people and otherwise using non-standard GUI modalities. In Chapter 18, we review the nature and extent of the generalisation of HCI demonstrated in this book.

## Box 1.2 Blending with People

When trying to come up with a fresh name for the "package" described in this section and consisting of multimodality and its implications, we ran aground on scores of more or less worn, part-right, part-wrong candidates like "bionic", "clone", "anthropomorphic", "new AI".

Another way to think of what's happening is to start from the familiar GUI-age *desktop metaphor* – the idea that PC novices would immediately understand their graphical workspace far better and more intuitively if it resembles a desktop with iconic work items on it. Think about this great idea as that of *making systems blend in with familiar things*, an idea that later took other shapes which often went beyond the GUI world, including interaction paradigms from the 1990s, such as "Things That Think", "Wearables", "Ubiquitous Computing", "Pervasive Computing", "Ambient Intelligence" and "The Disappearing Computer". A large part of the new challenge to HCI and usability we are addressing may be viewed as the idea of *making systems that blend with people* as well. Interaction paradigms expressing this idea include "Spoken Dialogue Systems", "Affective Computing", "Embodied Conversational Agents", "Cognitive Systems", personal "Companions" and "Friends", "Bio-Interaction", "Humanoid Robots", "Internet 2" and others with no stable names yet, such as real-time virtual user manifestations.

*Note on terminology:* when speaking about the "standard or classical GUI" in this book, we refer to traditional WIMP-based systems equipped with screen, mouse and keyboard.

### 1.4.5 Decomposing "Usability": The Terminology

We have defined system usability as the goal of making a *system fit* the *bodies* and *minds* of its *users* in *context* (Section 1.4.1). Let's look at the *terms* of this definition.

By *system* we refer to an interactive system, one with which we exchange information in different modalities. The sense of *fit* is standard, as in "The shoes fit her feet but not her taste", which also illustrates how "fitting" may relate to both body and mind. Since the shoes may be RFID tagged or have a computer chip in them for some sports exercise, the example also fits a system development context. By *users* we primarily refer to people as *end users*. End users are those who actually use the system for its purpose as opposed to, e.g. the software developers who build or maintain the system and have very different usability requirements, such as clear and well-defined module interfaces. The plural of "users" is important, because a system is rarely developed for a single individual. The plural form signals that we must find out who the intended users are. Finally, the *context* part refers beyond the users' persons to the particular physical, social, etc. context of interaction involved. A usable system needs to fit these contextual aspects as well.

## 1.4.6 Decomposing Usability: The Substance of Fitting

*Fitting* is key to usability, so it would be helpful if we could analyse fitting, and hence usability, into a small number of informative *main issues*. This would provide some first concrete handles on usability, and we could use the issues to classify what we must look for when working on usability.

The early usability theorists spoke of a list of *human factors* (Section 1.4.2). As we shall see in Chapters 3 and 4, this list is neither small, nor closed, nor finite, so it is not the kind of decomposition of usability we are looking for. In the HCI of the 1980s, work on usability was primarily focused on enabling all those newcomers to computing to learn how to operate systems and then work efficiently. Another focus continued to be on professionals who need to work safely in high-risk environments. Common to these classical HCI areas are the main issues of *providing the user with the right functionality* and, in some very broad sense, *ensuring ease of use*. Since the 1980s, people have increasingly used computing for many other things than work, such as gaming or mobile phone chat using SMSs or voice. So far, the result has been addition of a third main issue, i.e. *user experience* – the primarily qualitative, positive or negative experiences produced by using a system, including pleasure of use, hardware aesthetics and fashion.

Table 1.1 generalises these observations into a small, would-be closed and finite model of usability decomposed. The heading should be read as claiming that *price and other costs* matter to users as much as anything else. So the overall message is that, if you really want to fit your system to users' minds and bodies, don't forget

**Table 1.1** Usability decomposed

What matters to users wrt your system (other than cost)?

| Main issues | Factors involved in a main issue |
|---|---|
| *Technical quality* | |
| *Technical quality:* does it work? *Normative:* it should work! | Bug-free, reliable, robust, real-time, stable, error tolerant, etc. |
| *User quality* | |
| *Functionality:* can it do the things you want to do? *Normative:* it should have the functionality which most users need or strongly want! | User's understanding of system purpose, needs and preferences, fashion, habits, etc. |
| *Ease of use:* can you manage to use it? *Normative:* is should be easy to learn and easy to operate! | Easy to learn to use, understandable, efficient, effective, fast, smooth, controlled, safe, easy to operate, etc. |
| *User experience:* how is the experience of using it? *Normative:* it should give positive user experiences! | Perceptual feel, pleasure of action, fashion, aesthetics, social and ethical values, intellectual pleasure, attraction, habits, personal preferences, etc. |

fitting their purses!Cost is not normally considered a component of usability but still tends to make itself felt in the large majority of development processes, for instance, as a constraint on how many and which CoMeDa cycles can be afforded by a particular project. The main usability issues in Table 1.1 are all to do with using the system in context as explained above. The left-hand column decomposes usability into *technical quality* and *user quality* and then further decomposes user quality into *functionality*, *ease of use* and *user experience*. Just as usability itself has the built-in norm "Make it usable!", the four main issues into which we decompose usability each have their own built-in norm stated in the column. The right-hand column illustrates factors involved in each main issue. We now explain each main issue in turn.

*Technical quality vs. user quality.* It may be surprising that technical quality is listed as one in four main usability issues. Many of us have the intuition that technical issues are one thing and usability is an entirely different kettle of fish! Table 1.1 honours the intuition by separating technical quality from user quality. Part of the intuition, we guess, is that technical quality is to some extent irrelevant to users, so that, in the extreme, a system could be technically superb but useless, or users may prefer technically poorer System A to technically superior System B. Another part is that someone may do a perfect technical job on the system without having a clue about usability. While all of this seems true, technical quality also has the role of being fundamental to user quality.

*Technical quality.* The technical quality main issue is fundamental to user quality issues in the straightforward sense that technical flaws can be more or less damaging to any and all other issues. For instance, if the speech synthesiser loops in a user test, this functionality gets a bad mark and so does ease of use, and user experience turns negative. Given a couple of annoying flaws or bugs, it may not even make sense to evaluate the system's user quality in, e.g. a user test. Similarly, a less usable solution is sometimes preferred when sufficient technical quality cannot be achieved for solutions that are more usable in other respects.

*Functionality.* To think clearly about functionality, assume that we have a technically perfect system. We probably don't, but the point is that then we will not mix up technical problems and functionality problems. In an interactive system, system functionality is what can be accomplished with the system through interaction. If that is what we want to do for any reason (work, fun, gadget fascination, whatever), we view the functionality positively in some way. Thus, if the functionality enables us to produce some desired result, like making friends on the net or feeling the texture of a virtual piece of cloth – we say that the functionality, and the system, is *useful*. If the functionality enables us to do some kind of activity which we like doing for its own sake, we rather tend to say that the functionality, and hence the system, is *fun* or *challenging*.

However, and this is key to understanding functionality as a main usability issue, we are not talking about *how*, more specifically, something can be accomplished with the system through interaction, only about that, in principle, something can be done using the system.

Functionality is closely related to *system purpose*. Unfortunately, however, the relationship rarely is so close as to be deductive. Had it been, then the system developers could have deduced the functionality the system should have from its purpose, and the users could have done the same, removing one large class of functionality problems. As it is, system functionality is what the developers have decided is necessary, important, good to have or relevant given the system's purpose. Users may think different: they may even have a different understanding of system purpose compared to the developers, and they often want different functionality. To try to find out which functionality users want, we must do a CoMeDa cycle, or several.

*Ease of use.* A way to think clearly about ease of use is to think about using a technically perfect system with perfectly satisfactory functionality for its purpose in context, and then ask what could go wrong about the interaction. In this case, there will be no technical problems and the system will have the functionality we want it to have, no more, no less. Remember, however, that having functionality F is one thing, how F is actually supposed to be made use of is quite another. Think about a 1GT (1st generation technology) spade: the fact that it has the right functionality only means that it can, in principle , be used for its purpose which is that of digging holes. But what if it's too heavy, large or small, the blade is too straight or curved, earth sticks to it and the shaft is slippery and moves in the hand while working, the material it's made of is too rigid or too elastic for you or you need special shoes for using it …? Or maybe the spade would have been great had the earth been moist or sandy, but when it's dry and hard we get nowhere. Or maybe the spade is fine in all those respects but is a fancy innovation which takes training and getting-used-to that might fail in our case. All these problems are *ease-of-use problems*, and we will meet numerous system problems of this kind later on. For now, we invite you to contemplate the fact that even a humble spade can have numerous usability problems of the ease-of-use kind.

*User experience* reflects the user's reaction to everything about the system, so it's about how the user perceives, likes, thinks about, feels about, etc. the system. A technical problem may cause frustration, a missing functionality annoyance, an ease-of-use problem more frustration, and all three together may cause the user to give up on the system, consider it unusable and describe the experience with it as a bad one. This example shows how, in a very real sense, user experience accumulates the effects of the three other kinds of problem. Conversely, if everything works fine technically and functionally, and the system is easy to use, the accumulating user experience may be neutral, respectful, or even one of joy. Important as this is, and especially the accumulation part, user experience has more to it.

A good way to think about user experience as more than a function of the other three main factors is to think about what could be wrong with the system even though the user has no technical, functionality or ease of use problems. This could be a lot of different things, such as that the game is boring, the conversation silly, the design ugly or the whole thing old-fashioned. Conversely, positive user experience might simply reflect the assumption just made, i.e. that there are no technical, functionality or ease of use problems. However, positive user experiences may also be caused by other system properties, such as that the game is challenging and fun, the conversation amazing, the design cool and the whole thing a must-use-again, even though there were technical, functionality and ease-of-use problems.

## *1.4.7 Implications – Seven Questions*

At this point, you might consider some key implications of what has been said about usability so far:

- *Q1*. Where do the norms in Table 1.1 come from? Why and when should we feel bound by them?
- *Q2*. Are the norms clear?
- *Q3*. Are the norms being complied with in familiar mass software products?
- *Q4*. By default, when would you prefer to do the CoMeDa cycles that can help improve the usability of your system model: early, mid-way or late in the life cycle? Why?
- *Q5*. Given the argument as it now stands, are you convinced that you should start thinking about usability from day 1 in your project?
- *Q6*. Why don't we replace Table 1.1 by just two main usability issues: (1) fitting the users' bodies and (2) fitting the users' minds? That's clear and simple!
- *Q7*. Should Table 1.1 have more main issues?

*Re Q1.* An artefact built for people has a purpose, so it better serve its purpose, that is, it better be usable by people. If usability decomposes into the four main issues described, then their attached norms describe what it means for the artefact to serve its purpose well. If it doesn't, people will be less happy with it and will prefer more usable alternatives. We all cherish our favourite bread knife that easily slices all kinds of bread, our favourite game or our favourite development environment. So, special arguments are needed to justify or, at least, explain why, for instance, the system has a technical flaw, is missing some functionality which most everybody needs, is difficult to learn or to operate or is hardly liked by anyone who used it. As for technical flaws, we typically cannot even argue to defend them and, at best, can only explain why they haven't been removed yet.

*Re Q2.* Clear enough for a start, but are far from precise. Making the norms more precise is the task of general and application-specific usability guidelines and standards. In fact, the norms in Table 1.1 are the mother of all usability guidelines and standards. We discuss guidelines in Section 11.4, standards in Section 11.5 and the evaluation hierarchy whose top is shown in Table 1.1 in Section 16.2.2.

*Re Q3.* No, finding a perfect system usability-wise is probably harder than finding a perfect bread knife. The big questions concern when users give up, choose a different product, stop recommending it, start criticising it harshly, etc.

*Re Q4.* As early as possible and meaningful, because having a well-founded and stable system model at an early stage can save a lot of effort that would otherwise be spent on revising requirements, design and code. Then according to need throughout development.

*Re Q5.* Yes, because even that early there might be a CoMeDa cycle to be done to collect, e.g. information on development goal and system functionality.

*Re Q6.* Try! It seems that fitting mind as well as body is involved in all our main issues, like when a hardware device fits the acting body so well as to cause a positive user experience. There is, in fact, a discipline which studies the fitting of artefacts to bodies. It's called *ergonomics* and we discuss it in Section 4.5.

*Re Q7.* Perhaps! In particular, we would like to replace *ease of use* with several main issues which include it *and* cover more territory. You might consider the problems involved by looking at the examples in Sections 11.4, 11.5 and 16.4.1.

## 1.5  Usability Matters – But How Much?

It's nice if we can even prove that usability matters, but the really important question is: *how much does usability matter in the real world*? This question has many interpretations and an enormous discussion to it. Let's just consider three examples, using the decomposition of usability in Table 1.1 to draw a couple of conclusions. We assume sufficient technical quality, ignore the cost issue and focus on relationships between functionality, ease of use and user experience.

*Example 1: Functionality is sometimes king.* This is when customers want the functionality so badly that ease of use hardly matters and positive user experience gets reduced to a bare "I got it [the artefact]! I can do it [whatever it is supposed to do]!" Standard mobile phones are not easy to learn to use or easy to operate. They are boxes loaded with unrelated or loosely related functionality obscured by a low-performance, small-size and only marginally intelligent GUI. Yet, since some of the functionality is just right – ubiquitous telephony and text messaging (SMS), voicemail, phone numbers indexed by names – most of us struggle to learn to use it and mostly succeed to some extent, leaving a smaller group behind who never gets it. They still possess a mobile phone for use as a last resort, at which time the phone is probably not at hand, the battery is flat or the pin code forgotten, resulting in yet another humiliating user experience. These tens of millions of people are likely to benefit from core functionality-only, easier-to-use mobile phones that are now finally coming on the market. This is a case for ease of use.

*Example 2: Even badly wanted functionality doesn't always win.* What happened to video conferencing and the electronic book? Video conferencing technology was developed in the 1970s, thousands of organisations bought it in the early 1980s, and then – POOF! Rather than help us save millions *and* time on travels, video conferencing rather seems to have become an extra bumpy version of phone conferencing. Until recently, the electronic book has shown a similar pattern, despite the enormous advantages of getting rid of print and paper and being able to download the most recent publications in seconds. What happened? A key problem may be that video conferencing still fails to provide personal presence, such as being able to look in the eye of a particular individual at the other end, or going to the pub together for a beer after the meeting. The electronic book has remained in conflict with human vision by the same causes – screen luminosity, contrast, resolution and update speed – why so many people still prefer to print out long documents instead of reading them off the graphical display, feeling that it is both faster and more pleasant to read a printed document. In both cases, the poverty of the *user experience* obstructs technology take-up. Note also that, contrary to videoconferencing and electronic books, the mobile phone (including the satellite phone) does not have any alternatives.

*Example 3: Sometimes it all comes together nicely.* iPod combines badly wanted *functionality, ease of use* and, for a large group of users, near-perfect *user experience* of being hot and trendy. Note that this is not a generic technology like those discussed in previous examples, but a particular model series which has lots of competitors. Would iPod have had the same success without the ease of use? Perhaps, due to the trendiness of its brand. But it might also have failed miserably, or its success among MP3 players might have been short-lived. The Google search page is another example of ease-of-use GUI-based technology.

The multimodal systems we will mostly be discussing in this book have barely reached the market, so what does the above tell their developers? Well, if you want to gauge user interest and market potential, these points are important:

- *Badly wanted or needed functionality with no competitors has a strong edge.* It may survive imposing a steep learning curve on users, difficult and unintuitive operation, frustration, and most, if not all, other negative user experiences – at least until more usable competitors arrive.
- *In the large majority of cases, having the right functionality is not enough* – and remember: identifying the right functionality is a main usability issue in itself. Arguably, most new system functionality has competitors – video conferencing has phone and face-to-face conferencing, the electronic book has the print world, iPod and Google have other products with similar functionality. This is when it becomes really important to make sure that a system's ease of use and the range of user experiences it offers do not make users favour the opposition. If they do, we might be able to identify, diagnose and fix those usability problems or soften up the users by adding new functionality, but, by then, the battle may be lost. New multimodal technology may be fancy and exciting, but the history of computing is replete with fancy technological monuments that failed to beat other ways of doing the same things.

## 1.6  Reader's Guide

This book assumes no previous knowledge about human–computer interaction and usability development. The book is written for everyone who wants an introduction to, or an update on, practical work on usability at this time of proliferation of multimodal and natural interactive systems and systems blending with people – professional developers; academics; students in computer science, engineering, usability, creative contents and design, media, and more; usability specialists; and marketing people who are beginning to market multimodal technologies, such as speech, vision, advanced haptics, embodied animated characters, bio-interaction.

**Table 1.2** Some lines – or scenic routes with points of interest – through this book

| CoMeDa/Lines | Case line | Planning line | Generalisation line | Nerdy line |
|---|---|---|---|---|
| Chapter 1 | Section 1.3.3 | Section 1.3.1 | Sections 1.1 and 1.4.4 | Section 1.3.3 |
| Concepts Chapters 2–5 | Chapter 2, Sections 3.2.2, 3.3.7, 3.4.6, 3.5.1, 3.6.3, 4.4.5 and 4.5.2, Chapter 5 | Section 3.1, Chapter 5 | Sections 3.1, 3.4.5, 3.6, 4.1, 4.2, 4.3 and 4.4 | Sections 3.4.7 and 4.2.2 |
| Methods Chapters 7–14 | Chapter 7, Sections 8.5, 8.6, 8.7, 8.8, 10.3, 10.4, 11.1, 11.2 and 12.1, Chapter 14 | Sections 6.2, 6.3, 6.4, 7.1, 13.2 and 13.3, Chapter 14 | Sections 6.2.2, 10.2, 10.3, 10.5 and 12.2 | |
| Data handling Chapters 15–17 | Chapter 17 | Section 15.1 | Chapters 15 and 16 | Section 16.3 |
| Chapter 18 | | | Sections 18.2 and 18.3 | Section 18.2 |

Table 1.2 describes four among many possible, special lines that readers might wish to follow – or avoid – out of practical or theoretical interest in this book's subject. The *Case Line* follows progress with our three Case systems: idea, AMITUDE analysis, usability requirements, planning, design, method illustrations, evaluation. The *Planning Line* lists the usability workplanning descriptions and illustrations provided in this book. The *Generalisation Line* seeks out key locations where we generalise from GUI-based to multimodal usability and multimodal HCI. The locations were identified based on the generalisation summary provided in Section 18.2. Finally, the *Nerdy Line* stops at the "nerdy" stuff presented in this book.

## 1.7 Key Points

At this point you are ready to use this book, armed with an overview of its structure, a stack of route maps and four tools that will be used throughout:

- *CoMeDa*: work on usability consists of CoMeDa cycles for collection – or generation – and data handing of usability information;
- *AMITUDE*: a central construct in all usability work is the part of the evolving system model that we call the AMITUDE model of use (for the application under development);

- *methods and other approaches*: collection and generation of usability data is done by applying a series of methods and other approaches;
- *usability*: all usability work aims at making the system fit users by complying with high-level norms, such as those stated in our decomposition of usability.

Before describing and illustrating AMITUDE analysis in Chapters 3 and 4, we must introduce this book's three multimodal development Cases in Chapter 2 (Intermezzo 1).

# References

Beck K (1999) Extreme programming explained. Embrace change. Addison-Wesley, Boston, MA.

Boehm B (1988) A spiral model of software development and enhancement. Computer 21/5: 61–72.

Carroll JM (2003) Introduction. In: Carroll JM (ed) HCI models, theories and frameworks. Towards a multidisciplinary science. Morgan Kaufmann, San Francisco, CA.

Jacobson I, Boosch G, Rumbaugh J (1999) The unified software development process. Addison-Wesley, Harlow.

Mills HD (1980) Incremental software development. IBM Systems Journal 19/4, 415–420.

Pressman RS (2005) Software engineering. A practitioner's approach, 6th edn. McGraw Hill, New York.

Royce WW (1970) Managing the development of large software systems. Proceedings of WESTCON, San Francisco, CA.

Sommerville I (2007) Software engineering, 8th edn. Addison-Wesley, Harlow.

# Chapter 2
# Intermezzo 1: Three Multimodal Cases

This first intermezzo introduces three multimodal interactive system development Cases, Sudoku, Treasure Hunt and Maths (Section 2.1), that will be frequently used to illustrate CoMeDa cycles and other usability development activities. Section 2.2 looks ahead.

## 2.1 Contents and Origins

Table 2.1 presents the Case ideas. These are, in fact, more or less precise development goals to be unfolded later on through analysis, specification, design, implementation and evaluation (Fig. 2.1). Where do these ideas come from?

All our multimodal Case systems are research prototypes. The *Sudoku game system* was developed in 2006–2007 by students at ZGDV in Darmstadt, Germany, under the supervision of Cornelius Malerczyk and evaluated with users by the authors in 2007. The *Treasure Hunt system* was developed in 2004–2007 by Kostas Moustakas and colleagues at ITI-CERTH in Thessaloniki, Greece (Moustakas et al. 2006, Argyropoulos et al. 2007, Moustakas et al. 2009), and evaluated with users by Kostas and the authors in 2007. The *Maths system* is being developed by one of the authors in parallel with writing this book and in collaboration with Thanos Tsakiris at ITI-CERTH on 3D facial animation.

We did not invent, specify and build the Sudoku and Treasure Hunt systems. Everything we say about their development processes – starting, in fact, with the development goal expressions in Table 2.1 – is for illustration of points we wish to make and only has accidental similarity with their actual development. However, unless otherwise indicated, our descriptions and illustrations relating to the evaluation of the two systems are real-life case material. The Maths system, on the other hand, has not been tested with target users yet but the documentation presented on its development is real-life case material unless otherwise indicated.

N.O. Bernsen, L. Dybkjær, *Multimodal Usability*, Human-Computer Interaction Series, DOI 10.1007/978-1-84882-553-6_2, © Springer-Verlag London Limited 2009

**Table 2.1** This book's three main Cases

| Name | Case idea: "Let's try to do a multimodal interactive system prototype . . ." |
|---|---|
| Sudoku | ". . .which can demonstrate the usefulness of camera-captured 3D gesture. How about a Sudoku game system in which the player points to the game board and inserts a number through speech?" |
| Treasure hunt | ". . .which shows how multimodal interaction can benefit different groups of disabled people and allow them to work together. This could be a game in which the blind and the deaf–mute help each other find something, like a treasure hunt for some ancient blueprint drawings which have suddenly become critically important to the town's survival." |
| Maths | ". . .for exploring the emergent paradigm of learning which goes beyond intelligent tutoring systems to incorporate affective learning. How about someone teaching maths to children more or less like a human teacher would do?" |

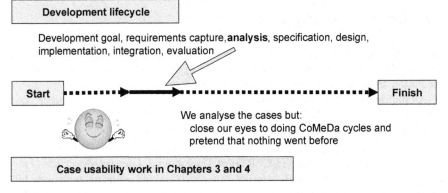

**Fig. 2.1** How we will start to work on the Cases

## 2.2 What's Next?

Our *first step* will be to specify AMITUDE requirements by creating and analysing a model of use per Case, starting from their preliminary development goals, i.e. the Case ideas. This we can set out to do now, no matter what we might have chosen to do had we had more knowledge about stuff to be presented later on, cf. Fig. 2.1. We will do it in Chapters 3 and 4 and summarise results in Chapter 5 (Intermezzo 2). Our *ultimate goal* is to optimise the usability of the three Case prototypes.

If you have your own project in mind, try to do the same for that one, or first skip to the methods and common approaches overviews in Chapter 6. This might help you getting started on requirements specification.

# References

Argyropoulos S, Moustakas K, Karpov A, Aran O, Tzovaras D, Tsakiris T, Varni G, Kwon B (2007) A multimodal framework for the communication of the disabled. Proceedings of eNTERFACE, Istanbul.

Moustakas K, Tzovaras D, Dybkjær L, Bernsen NO (2009) A modality replacement framework for the communication between blind and hearing impaired people. Proceedings of HCI.

Moustakas K, Nikolakis G, Tzovaras D, Deville B, Marras I, Pavlek J (2006) Multimodal tools and interfaces for the intercommunication between visually impaired and "deaf and mute" people. Proceedings of eNTERFACE. Dubrovnik.

# Chapter 3
# Creating a Model of Use

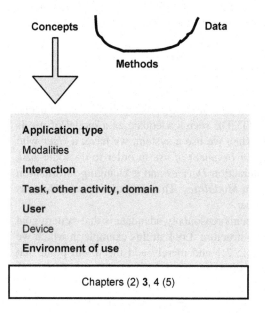

Chapters 3 and 4 share two tasks. The main task is to present concepts for creating a model of use of a system under development. We call this creation process AMITUDE analysis, and its result is a requirements specification of system use. The other task is to illustrate model of use creation by means of our Cases (Section 2.1) and other examples. Chapter 3 introduces AMITUDE as a generic model of use and presents the aspects: Application type, Interaction, Task, other activity, domain, User and Environment of use. Chapter 4 presents the two remaining aspects, Modalities and Device, with substantial coverage of modalities and multimodality. Each aspect presentation includes an aspect-specific analysis of the Cases.

Section 3.1 explains AMITUDE as a conceptual model of seven aspects of user–system interaction. Creating an AMITUDE analysis is a major step forward in system model development. Section 3.2 describes application type analysis. Section 3.3, on user analysis, reviews the many roles users and people have in development for usability. We present a 3-layered model of people and discuss how to do user profile analysis. Section 3.4 introduces tasks, other activities, and domain, and analyses a spoken dialogue system task. The analysis forms the basis of generalisations about task models and useful task classifiers. We argue that not all systems are task-oriented and discuss domain-oriented systems. Section 3.5 does Case use environment analysis and presents a checklist of use environment factors. Taking a look at the full scope of the "interaction" whose usability is the subject of this book, Section 3.6 generalises user−system interaction to user−system information representation and exchange, and makes generalisations from GUI-based interaction to multimodal interaction.


## 3.1  AMITUDE – A Model of System Use

This section describes the AMITUDE part of the system model and presents evidence for its adequacy. We look at how individual AMITUDE aspects have been charted rather unevenly in computing and HCI (Section 3.1.1), and use empirical data to show that it is when the abstract and formal AMITUDE model gets exposed to information about people that we start making the system usable (Section 3.1.2).


### 3.1.1  Unpacking AMITUDE

AMITUDE is *a model of use*, a generic model of the aspects involved when someone uses a system. One reason why AMITUDE seems adequate as a model of use is that we can state quite plainly that, when we use a system, we have: a *User* who *Interacts* with an *Application* in an *Environment of use* in order to do some *Task or other activity* by using certain interaction *Devices* and exchanging information with the system in certain input/output *Modalities*. This time the aspect order was UIAETDM! AMITUDE just looks nicer.

Another reason why AMITUDE seems reasonably adequate is that system goal expressions seem to have AMITUDE structure. Look at this example in which we take the Sudoku Case idea from Table 2.1 and merely add the trivial point that Sudoku must be played somewhere, getting:

(A:) a Sudoku (T:) gaming system to be used (E:) somewhere, in which (I:) ((U:) the player (M:) points to (D:) the game board and inserts a number through (M:) speech).

Thus, even in the simplest system goal expression, AMITUDE is already present. We expand the system goal when we create requirements and design specifications, which means that these include increasingly detailed AMITUDE models of use. AMITUDE is only a part of what we need to get right as developers, because what we need to get right is the system model (Section 1.3.2) and everything related to it, *including* the AMITUDE aspects. When working on system usability, however, it is primarily AMITUDE that matters. Everything else serves other purposes or can be viewed as means to the end of building a usable system, such as the technical issues that must be solved for the system to be usable (Section 1.4.6).

We will use AMITUDE as conceptual development-for-usability framework based on the hypothesis that AMITUDE describes all aspects of system use that must be taken into account when developing for usability. AMITUDE descriptions, from system goal description through requirements specification to elaborate design description, are hard-core factual descriptions of the intended system users, the task the system will support, the modalities involved, the environment in which the task will be done, etc. So what we will do in Chapters 3 and 4 is to describe in more detail the language, or the conceptual machinery, available for describing each AMITUDE aspect, and illustrate by describing requirements for this book's Cases and other examples. The resulting AMITUDE requirements specifications are summarised in Chapter 5 (Intermezzo 2).

Before presenting each AMITUDE aspect, it is useful to have an overview of the structural neatness of the concepts describing each aspect. Let's first compare with usability. In Section 1.4.6, Table 1.1 shows a high-level decomposition of usability. It's not perfect, but it is a common assumption that all or most other usability norms can be subsumed under its concepts, ideally creating a deep and complex, but well-structured usability evaluation hierarchy (Section 16.2.2). Unfortunately, what we have today is far from being as well-structured as we might wish.

Now look at the AMITUDE aspects. It would be great for each of them as well to have a complete and well-structured inheritance hierarchy, preferably one that has been proven complete from theory, or else a well-confirmed empirical one. Given that, we could, e.g. look up any particular application type, such as, to mention a highly particular one, "affective maths self-tutoring systems for children", or user profile, such as, to mention a more general one, "visually disabled adults and adolescents"; study its details and inherited properties; and even get advice on how to work with it in usability development. Unfortunately, this beautiful support system doesn't exist, and it is obvious why it is hard to establish: new *Application* types and *Devices* keep appearing as fast as ever, new *Tasks* and other activities become interactive, new *Modalities* are used in applications, applications are being used in new *Environments* and new properties of familiar environments become relevant to usability. Even our general model of *Interaction* continues to expand, and, if you think that the *User*, at least, remains a rather genetically fixed constant, the reality is that multimodality and blending systems with people (Section 1.4.4) calls for understanding of entire new classes of properties of people.

Despite attempts by people in computing and HCI, there are no would-be complete, well-established taxonomies of the AMITUDE aspects *Devices, Tasks* and other activities and *Environments* of use. There are open-ended lists and various attempts at creating sub-hierarchies, which may still be useful if you can find them out there. However, there *are* various would-be general taxonomies of *Application* types made by ICT (Information and Communication Technologies) member organisations and others, although they tend to miss out on advanced multimodal systems and haven't been created to support work on usability. *Users*, being people and having been studied for a long time, are well described in many respects, and, for *Interaction* and *Modalities*, we do have usability-oriented taxonomies and bodies of advice for usability work.

### 3.1.2  AMITUDE Unexposed vs. AMITUDE Exposed

We now come to a point crucial to work on system usability, which ties together everything said in this book, i.e. the two "sides" or "faces" of AMITUDE. So far, in Section 3.1.1, we have seen AMITUDE as a set of sets of concepts for expressing a model of use of the system under development as part of the requirements specification. Let's call this *AMITUDE unexposed* because it hasn't yet been exposed to users. It's just a description of a model of use for the system. Since the core of usability work is to anticipate and carry out exposure of the model of use to actual people, we absolutely need to explain *AMITUDE exposed*.

To do so, let's first tell a story about how a precursor to AMITUDE emerged from an empirical study of multimodal usability. Bernsen (1997) analysed and evaluated claims made in the literature about *speech functionality*, i.e. the properties of speech that make this modality usable or less usable for representing information, possibly in combination with other modalities. The claims analysed were the total number of 120 speech functionality claims identified in the 21 paper contributions in Baber and Noyes (1993). For instance, a researcher or practitioner would claim that "Spoken commands are useful in fighter cockpits because the pilot has hands and eyes occupied, and speech can be used even in heads-up, hands-occupied situations". In other words, someone would claim that a speech modality, or a modality combination including speech, is usable or less usable and justify the claim by reference to various factors and contexts.

**Table 3.1** Comparing AMITUDE and a precursor

| 1. 1997 paper | 2. Examples | 3. Relation | 4. AMITUDE |
|---|---|---|---|
| Generic system | Multimedia document, ATM | Equals | Application type |
| Modalities | Speech input, 2D static graphics output | Equals | Modalities |
| – Not addressed | – Not addressed | New | Interaction |
| Generic task and domain | Spatial manipulation, non-time-critical but critical command input | Part of | Task or other activity, domain |
| Communication act | Warning, instruction | Part of | |
| User group | Office workers, the blind who have not learnt Braille | Part of | User |
| Interactive device | Computer access over the phone, wireless device | Equals | Device |
| Environment of use | Public spaces, office | Equals | Environment of use |
| Performance parameter | Increased control, slower and less efficient | Out | – |
| Mental parameter | Attention-catching, burdens memory | Out | – |
| Learning parameter | No learning overhead, enhancement of long-term retention | Out | – |

All factors and contexts referred to in the claims were collected and organised in the two-level hierarchy shown in the left-hand part of Table 3.1. Column 1 shows a modified version of the classification's 9 top-level categories, each of which is illustrated, in Column 2, by two examples quoted from among the claims. Columns 3 and 4 show, for each category, its relationship to the corresponding AMITUDE aspect, if any. Comparison shows precursor equality for AMDE (Application, Modality, Device, Environment), generalisation for TU (Task, User) and novelty for I (Interaction). The generalisation from Generic task and domain + Communication act to *Task or other activity, domain* is due to a later discovery that not all interactions are task oriented (Bernsen and Dybkjær 2004). The generalisation from User group to *User* means that AMITUDE draws upon full description of people from which user groups can be defined.

The interesting question is why the three "parameter" categories (Performance, Mental, Learning) have no equivalent in AMITUDE. Where do these come from? Take a look at the full sets of parameter values in the claims data:

*Performance*: immediate response, more effective, better performance, fast, location free, mobile control, hands-and-eyes-free operation, ease of operation, increased control capabilities, user busy, safer, easier, workload conflicts, efficiency, avoids shorthand, faster, more accurate, better performance, slower and less efficient, effectiveness, slow and inefficient, delay, very difficult for cursor control and describing locations in the text, unsuited, difficult, speed, accuracy and ease of use, ease of review, attachment to right place in text.

*Mental* (cognitive and some emotive): attention-catching, be attended to, spatial and temporal distraction, setting a mood, persuasive, human discrimination capacities, reduction in visual workload, naturalness, unnatural, cognitive processing limitations, burdens memory, articulation impairment, irritating, annoying, acceptance.

*Learning*: interaction training time, no learning overhead, enhancement of long-term retention, elaboration options.

Seasoned readers might notice how these data points have an ancient feel to them, reflecting a time when speech was coming into its own in a GUI world. But what's special about them? Look again: something is attention-catching to someone, something gives someone control even when moving around, etc. The data points are *relational*, they always include, more or less explicitly, a user as one of the relata. And, since the study happened to be a study of modalities, there is always some modality involved, if only implicitly. In brief, the data points describe how modalities and sometimes other AMITUDE aspects fit users. That's why they do not belong in the AMITUDE-unexposed right-hand column of Table 3.1.

Now let's generalise.

Usability is about fitting systems to people. In more articulate AMITUDE terms, this means fitting AMITUDE, the model of system use, to people in real-life contexts. This implies that the relationship of fitting can have from two to eight relata, always with one of them, the user, at the centre; and from one to seven AMITUDE aspects at the periphery. Here is an example of a user-4-aspect relationship: You probably wouldn't develop a system with spoken input (*Modalities*) authentication for retrieving money (*Task*) from automated banking machines (*Application*) in the

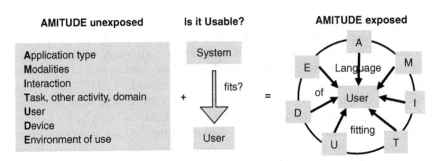

**Fig. 3.1** When the Amitude aspects of a system model are exposed to users, we get usability information expressed in the language of fitting

street (*Use Environment*). Why not? Because the users probably won't accept using this modality for this task with this application in this use environment!

Figure 3.1 summarises the discussion: AMITUDE is a model of use abstraction until it gets exposed to users in context by provision of any evidence of its usability or the opposite. Three points important to practical usability work follow from the Amitude-exposed part of Fig. 3.1.

The first point follows from having the real user and, implicitly, the real-life context, at the centre of the circle – the *U* in AMITUDE is merely the developer's idea or specification of the user. When working, from day 1, towards fitting each of the seven AMITUDE aspects to the real user at the centre, *you are constantly trying to grasp properties of the real users in context in order to make the fitting work.* When you cannot do that on your own because you've run out of knowledge and experience, you need to use a method or common approach to collect or otherwise generate usability information, as described in Chapters 6, 7, 8, 9, 10, 11, 12 and 13.

The second point concerns the circle connecting all AMITUDE aspects. We saw what it means in the bank teller machine example, but the point is worth making explicit. The circle means that, even if we may not like the implied complexity, *all AMITUDE aspects are interrelated, and some of the reasoning we need to do about them is holistic.* We will keep this in mind in Chapters 3 and 4 even if we have to describe the AMITUDE aspects sequentially. In fact, due to holism, it is sometimes arbitrary when we assign a particular conclusion about fitting to a particular AMITUDE aspect because that conclusion may involve several AMITUDE aspects.

Third, the *Language of fitting* in Fig. 3.1 is the language of usability and of the Performance, Mental and Learning data points above. This language is totally different from the language of AMITUDE specification that we will introduce in the following. How do we get a handle on the language of fitting in this book, i.e. some structure of concepts, anything useful on the relational information produced when AMITUDE is exposed to users in context? The language of fitting is the language of our usability Table 1.1, of usability requirements (Chapter 5), of usability guidelines (Section 11.4) and usability standards (Section 11.5), of data analysis and evaluation (Chapters 16–17) and this language is being used in many of this book's examples, so we are definitely going to meet the language of fitting. We will meet it in modest amounts in the Case requirements analyses in Chapters 3 and 4.

In summary, AMITUDE unexposed is an abstraction that allows specification and design of the most crazy systems from a usability point of view. It is by exposing AMITUDE to *usability information* that we begin to make a usable system.

Given the holism of AMITUDE reasoning, there is no particular order in which to present the AMITUDE aspects. We will start with Application type.

## 3.2  Application Type

In this section we look at advantages (Section 3.2.1) and issues involved in making application types explicit through application type analysis. There are many global classifications of software systems, application types, etc. on the web. However, since none of them may include exactly the types you need, this section focuses on defining project-specific types (Section 3.2.3). We illustrate with our Cases (Section 3.2.2).

### *3.2.1  The Notion of Application Type and Its Use*

By application type, the "A" in AMITUDE, we refer to the type of interactive system to be built. The application type notion is present in all but the most sketchy development goal statements. Thus, Table 2.1 describes the Sudoku Case as a Sudoku computer game, Treasure Hunt as a treasure hunt computer game and Maths as an affective maths tutoring system.

Trivial as this may seem, fixing the application type carries advantages for usability development in three ways. First, everything not related to the application type becomes irrelevant. Second, the application type name and description typically implies or suggests a series of assumptions about the system – functionality to add, usability requirements, issues that requires fixing of additional system model properties and other development activities that must be carried out in order to advance requirements specification or make other kinds of progress. Third, the application type provides a central clue on how to look for usability information and other information on similar systems. These advantages are multiplied by the easy-going behaviour of the notion of type because the system typically belongs to multiple application types at the same time.

### *3.2.2  The Cases as Application Types*

Let's try to advance our Case ideas by identifying their application types and using these in various ways.

*Sudoku.* The developers need to get the explicit and implicit rules of the Sudoku game straight because users will expect that. If the developers are not Sudoku players themselves, they can easily find the simple explicit game rules on the web. Implicit rules may be harder: are there any? What will happen during interaction if the system ignores them? The developers should take a close look at the electronic Sudoku games world on the web because this will give them a selection of Sudoku computer game functionality options to consider. Similarly, any common functionality among those web sites provides clues to functionality that all web Sudoku players are used to having. Any reviews of those web sites in games magazines or elsewhere would be interesting as well because these might contain usability evaluation points made on web-based Sudoku systems. Can you think of any reasons for or against looking at paper-based Sudoku games as well?

The Sudoku system is also of type *3D pointing gesture* system, "3D" meaning that pointing gesture is done in 3D space rather than onto a 2D surface like that of a touch screen (and even if the Sudoku gameboard is 2D). It is valuable to pursue this lead to look at existing systems and find out about any usability issues. Similarly, it is a must to look for systems *combining pointing gesture and speech for gaming or entertainment purposes*. Just as importantly, the general type *game* itself suggests that interaction should be fun and sufficiently challenging not to be boring, while not being prohibitively difficult either. The developers must work out how these basic principles of gaming apply to Sudoku.

*Treasure Hunt.* This system shares the general *game* requirements with the Sudoku system and looking into similar games might yield ideas about challenges that users must overcome to succeed. *Multi-user games* could also be of interest. Apart from this information, however, little else is available in the goal description in Table 2.1. Before we can get much further, the developers must do some creative thinking to specify, in particular, the interactive modalities that the blind and deaf—mute players are supposed to use. To collect food for thought on this problem, it could be useful to look into existing computer game products and prototypes *for the blind* and *for the deaf*, respectively. There might also, of course, already exist joint *games for the blind and the deaf*. When the modalities are being fixed, we will probably have yet other application types to look into.

*Maths.* Relevant application types include *affective computing* (Picard 1997) and *affective learning* (Picard et al. 2004). As a type, intelligent tutoring systems is far too broad to look into in general, but it might be worthwhile to look for *intelligent maths tutoring* systems and, in particular, *intelligent science* (including maths) *tutoring for children*. In fact, the idea of affective maths tutoring to kids is strongly suggestive of caring, motivation building, a pleasant atmosphere and more which could be elaborated into first requirements and into design as well. However, we need to do some creative thinking about interactive modalities and how we would teach maths to children "more or less like a human teacher would" before getting much further. If the maths teacher turns out to become an animated conversational character, the communities and literature on *spoken conversation for tutoring* (Luppicini 2008), *embodied conversational agents* (Cassell et al. 2000) and *companions* or *friends*, are obviously relevant. *Edutainment systems for children* might be of interest as well.

In conclusion, when you have a first application goal, you should identify and describe the system's application type(s), write down key implied and suggested facts, assumptions and questions, look for clearly relevant information, use it for expanding requirements — and you are in business doing requirements specification. Some developers build terse systematic lists, while others write application scenarios in lengthy prose.

### 3.2.3 Classifications of Application Types

Using the Cases as examples, we saw in Section 3.2.2 that it is very much up to the developers to extract the most useful types to which their system belongs. It is nearly always worthwhile to extract highly specific types, such as *affective intelligent tutoring of maths to children*, because if any other efforts of this kind exist and have even been accessibly documented with respect to usability, this information could be extremely useful. However, more general types can be useful as well, such as when the application type *game* is being looked into in order to collect information on default requirements to usable games.

The Cases constitute a small and special sample of all systems, and therefore don't call for many other important kinds of application types, such as safety-critical or high-security systems, but that doesn't affect the principles proposed above. The only usability-based distinction between system types that we can think of is the distinction between *walk-up-and-use* systems and all other systems. Walk-up-and-use is the idea of a system whose entire functionality can be used right away without any need for introduction, documentation, help, training or a special background of knowledge or experience. These are extremely demanding requirements to meet, and few systems do — arguably, the Google search page is one, and some spoken dialogue systems fall in this category as well. Among our Cases, Maths and Sudoku come closest.

Potentially, there is another approach to application types. This is to use more or less official, global classifications of interactive applications, systems or software types and find best matches. This is fine if you are developing a GUI-based system, but, if not, the problem is that global classifications are mostly based on existing products. Since most non-GUI multimodal systems are not at the product stage yet, they may not figure in those classifications. And then it's back to the research communities and their literature, conferences and demos.

## 3.3  Users and People

Since users are at the centre of usability work, including user profiling and usability information analysis, the notion of a user has many different roles in HCI. Section 3.3.1 sorts out a number of important roles. Just as central to HCI are the facts that individual people are both similar and different from each other in numerous respects. Sections 3.3.2, 3.3.3, 3.3.4 and 3.3.5 take a global tour around people, starting with the mind, then adding the body and then adding history, culture and gender. Section 3.3.6 introduces user profile analysis which is then applied to Case user profiling in Section 3.3.7.

### 3.3.1  Roles of Users and People in Development for Usability

Everything said so far indicates that "the user" has a key role in system development for usability. Usability itself is defined as *fitting the system to users*, implying that users are the target and purpose of all work on usability. Moreover, as we shall see throughout this book, multimodal usability adds new centre-stage roles to users in addition to those they always had in systems development.

Right now, let's try to prevent ambiguity and confusion later on due to the fact that several different notions of "user" are helpful to usability development. We will distinguish between three main "user" notions, one of which is a collection of several different ones, and describe what each of them is used for.

*People.* Basic to everything about "users" is *people*. The *user* at circle centre in Fig. 3.1 represents real people, potentially in their full individual and collective diversity. These are the ones we develop interactive systems for, whom we model in all the "user" models below and who may or may not appreciate our results. We use the language of fitting inside the circle in the figure to describe what real people do and say when exposed to our evolving AMITUDE model of system use. To understand and use that language, we need knowledge about people, i.e. usability information.

*Target users, user profile.* We typically don't develop a system for a single person nor for all possible people, but for something in between, that is, for a group of people called our target users, or our target user group. To steer development towards fitting the target users and be able to pick out individuals from among the target users, we specify them in a user profile. This is the $U$ on the circle circumference in Fig. 3.1. Typically, the user profile is a rather thin abstraction consisting of a small number or properties from among the thousands of properties real people have. A system can have several distinct target user groups, in which case it must be developed for each of them.

*People models.* We propose the term "people models" for a collection of five "user" notions, each of which plays a different role in usability development. People models draw on knowledge about people in different ways: (1) *Design-time user models* have been used for decades to specify and design systems in anticipation of how its target users will behave during interaction. This is like saying "Suppose we have a user who fits the specified user profile. Now let's call upon knowledge about real people in order to fit the system to the user's behaviour in more detail". (2) An *online user model*, on the other hand, is built on the fly during interaction in order to enable the system to adapt to individual users or sub-groups of users having particular characteristics. These models observe the user with the purpose of doing something based on the observations made, such as, in a GUI interface, modify menus to reflect the user's most recent functionality choices; in automated video surveillance, spot shop-lifting behaviour and call security; in mobile spoken in-car dialogue systems, identifying the driver's hotel preferences and location and offering reservation at a hotel fitting this information; or, indeed, in the Maths Case, observing the student and giving personalised advice. (3) A *people persona* is a detailed description of a particular target user and is used for more or less the same purposes as a user profile. What you do is trade the generality of the user profile for the detail of the people persona in order to help fit the system to the target users (cf. Section 11.2). (4) A *system persona* is a system – a virtual character or robot – behaving in some way like a real person and hence part of the blending with people agenda, cf. Box 1.2 and the Treasure Hunt and Maths Cases. Finally, (5) the notion of a *representative user group* is central to data reliability in many methods for collecting usability information, cf. Box 3.1.

## Box 3.1  Representative User Groups

What is a representative user? The answer may not matter much, because we are unlikely to ever meet a representative user, just like we will probably never meet the average mother. So let's talk about representative *user groups* instead. A representative user group is a group of people, all of whom are target users, whose composition proportionally reflects the composition of the group of all target users in important, specified respects.

*Example: Usability for school teachers.* Suppose that the target user group is school teachers teaching 1st–5th grade in Danish schools. It is relatively easy to determine several properties likely to be common to this group and relevant to system development, such as their minimum level of education, familiarity with the Danish school system, knowledge of the curriculum, fluent Danish speech and writing, etc. However, you might get things terribly wrong if you only look at what they have in common when selecting subjects or user representatives.

Suppose we select twenty 25–30-year-old male teachers who are all gung-ho about computer-supported learning. They all share the target user profile above. However, they do not at all reflect the enormous variation among the targeted school teachers. This is the variation we need to capture when selecting a representative group of subjects. How to do that? We look at the relevant, or potentially relevant, dimensions of variation in the target user population, such as age, gender, years of teaching experience, experience with computers in general and experience with systems similar to the one we are developing. We don't know if exactly this set of properties is the right one in this particular development case, but it is our job to find out through target user group analysis. It is often far easier to find out what the target users have in common than identifying those differences among them which end up causing usability problems.

To compose a representative user group, we must look at proportions in the target user population, asking, e.g. how many percent of the teachers already use computers in the classroom, how many of them are older than 50 years, how many of them are men, etc. As we work on target user group analysis, we might also discover that one of our initial assumptions is wrong, e.g. the assumption that the target users are all fluent in Danish speech and writing.

### 3.3.2 People, A Global Tour

In the following sections, we take a global tour around people. The primary purpose is to provide high-level concepts for user profile analysis, but these concepts are high-level components of any kind of usability information as well (Section 3.1.2).

### 3.3.3 Layer 1, the Mind: Cognition, Conation and Emotion, Attention and Awareness

The *mind* refers to human central processing as opposed to the study of how the human sensory and motor action apparatus works. At the highest level of abstraction, humans appear to have just three plus two main mental abilities. Humans possess and exercise all of them in parallel most of the time, except, perhaps, in dreamless sleep or if severely mentally disabled.

*Cognition* is everything to do with perceiving, recognising, understanding, knowing, guessing, hypothesizing, thinking, reasoning, imagining, mental modelling, deliberating, learning, intuiting, exploring, discovering, explaining, planning, remembering, being curious, knowledge, interpretation, truth and falsehood, certainty, probability, etc. Surprise is produced if reality is not as expected.

*Conation* is everything to do with desiring, wanting, wishing, willing, needing, preferring, striving, pursuing, hoping, goals, purposes, intentions, aims, etc. Goals are chosen with more or less decisiveness and are pursued with more or less determination. It is useful to view people as more or less organised and prioritised goal structures. Some goals, if fulfilled, go on hold until next time.

Cognition and conation are attributes of the mind so general that it can be hard to spot what all values of each of them have in common. Ordinary language has hundreds if not thousands of words denoting those values, primarily because there are a lot of them, all different, often subtly so.

A vivid explanation of what is common to all values of cognition and conation, respectively, and what makes cognition and conation basically different from each other, is due to Searle (1983): while cognition has *mind-to-world direction of fit*, conation has *world-to-mind direction of fit*. Since cognition is about what is the case in the world – that's what we perceive, learn about, etc. – cognition only succeeds if what it does "fits" the world or what is the case, or, in other words, what is true. An idea, or any other cognitive representation, is true if it corresponds to the world as is.

Conation, on the other hand, is about what humans *would like* to be the case – that's what we are hoping for, day-dreaming about, in need of, aspiring to become, striving to achieve, etc. – even though it may not be the case in the world as is. Conation only succeeds if the world fits, or comes to fit, how the mind would like it to be.

Given cognitive and conative abilities, we can construct the command centre of people in action, monitoring and trying to find out what the world is like, consulting conation for anything unwanted or missing, consulting cognition for an opportunity to change the world, and then trying to change things to fit their goals. So there seems to be a clear sense in which cognition and conation are active powers of the mind. But we are missing a crucial, third ability.

*Emotion* is everything to do with feeling or being happy, content, sad, angry, frustrated, joyous, envious, jealous, in a bad mood, etc. All emotions seem to be able to vary in strength. Emotion is often called affect, and it is easy to see why. Contrary to cognition and conation, emotion is basically reactive and dependent upon cognition and conation (Bernsen 1985). Emotion arises when we discover that reality either fits or does not fit how we would like it to be. Discovering that this is the case is a value of attribute cognition, and what we would like is a value of attribute conation.

Some discuss whether *moods*, being more long-term than emotions and not as evidently tied to particular events happening, are basically different from emotions. A plausible view is that moods are just deeper, more global and often longer-term reactions to states or events, which is why their causes can be more difficult to identify. It is a common assumption in most emotion research today that all emotions can be sorted in positive and negative emotions, e.g. Ortony and Turner (1990). This is exactly because emotions arise either because the world as we understand it behaves as we would like it to or because it doesn't.

There is a final and important point about emotion that we would like to make: emotion does not seem to be entirely passive. Some positive emotions appear to stimulate useful mental states, such as motivation and curiosity which are important for getting things done and learning new things (Picard et al. 2004). In fact, these insights are important to affective learning, the topic of our Maths Case (Table 2.1).

Is the cognition–conation–emotion theory true? We believe that it's the best in town. It explains emotion valence, i.e. that an emotion is positive or negative, and helps determine if a mental state is an emotion in the first place, which avoids confusion. If you want the system to recognise emotions, make sure that those states actually *are* emotions, e.g. desire (no!), curiosity (no!), anger (yes!). In fact, there only seems to be one alternative theory around. The cognition–conation–emotion model's claim that there are three basic mental abilities is due to 18th century German philosopher Mendelssohn. He developed the theory in response to Aristotle's claim that there are just two mental faculties, i.e. cognition and some mixture of conation and emotion. Aristotle's theory has supporters in the HCI community. For instance, it is assumed in Picard et al. (2004), Te'eni et al. (2007) and canvassed by a long-term front figure in HCI, Don Norman (2004).

*Awareness and attention* are like what is visible in a cone of light and what we actually look at among what's visible. They are at the service of cognition and are influenced by conation and emotion as well as by the concepts we have.

*Constructive notions: Personality.* Given the above mental abilities, it is possible to construct much of what we call a person's personality in terms of different capabilities and dispositions for cognition, conation, emotion, attention and awareness, and hence describe both similarities and some of the huge differences between individuals, including differences between not having and having mental disabilities to various degrees. People's different personalities manifest themselves in their observable behaviour and significantly determine their communication abilities and dispositions. Personality and the types of mental states above can be measured by the system from user behaviour observation and because the body is also a source of bio-sensed information. Personality differences have mattered to HCI all along. We develop customisation options to deal with a range of user preferences, try to make systems spot and act upon user needs, recognise user emotions and attitudes, support user learning, take users' background knowledge into account, make them enjoy gameplay, etc.

### 3.3.4  Layer 2, Adding the Body

Adding the body to the model, it appears that people, when not in dreamless sleep and in addition to the central processing they do, are in one or several of the following states.

*Sensing* by using the senses of vision, hearing, touch, smell and taste, respectively. These are the five classical "sensory modalities" by which people obtain sensory information about the state of the world. There are actually several other sensory modalities than these, including various internal senses for providing information about one's body, such as proprioception (the sense of the relative position of neighbouring parts of the body) and pain, and other external senses, such as the sensing of voltage and electrical fields. However, we shall stick to the five standard senses in this book.

*Acting* by using part or whole of the body for communicative action in speech, gesture, facial expression, etc., object manipulation (whether for communication purposes or otherwise), locomotion (might be for communication purposes as well), sensor orientation and solitary expression of emotion, mood and other central processing states. Action may be executed deliberately, through habit, using innate or trained skills, involuntarily, unawares, by physiological reflex, etc.

*Physical state:* humans can be well rested, wide awake, tired, drunk, drugged, sleepy, exhausted, panting, perspiring, fainted, in shock, etc. They may be physically fit or not, healthy or having health problems, physically disabled or not.

*Constructive notions: Users in action.* Given the mental and bodily properties of people mentioned so far, we can construct users in action and interacting with some system, including sensory and motor abilities and disabilities, and the physical states that users should be in when operating the system, physical states and behaviours to be monitored and reacted upon by the system, etc. This generates a new range of factors which help explain both similarities and differences among people as well as describe their states and activities during interaction.

### 3.3.5 Layer 3, History, Culture and Gender

To construct people in full, we need a third layer in addition to central abilities and dispositions for central processing, sensing, acting, physical state and condition. This third layer consists of history, culture and gender.

*Personal history* is what makes someone a novice or an expert in a task or domain, or in handling some particular system or computer systems in general. Personal history also contributes a great deal to users' expectations to, and attitudes towards, systems and creates habits and preferences which the system may or may not fit. Age is basic to personal history as well. A small child is someone who has a brief history, however eventful. Health is partly a function of personal history. Thus, our personal history modifies our central processing, sensing, acting and physical state and condition. Learning and training are systematic attempts to permanently change people in some respect.

*Culture* is a kind of personal history writ-large-and-with-omissions in the way it shapes personality in terms of knowledge and ignorance, religious beliefs, moral and other attitudes, habits, preferences, etiquette, politeness standards, sensitivities, etc. We might also include in the culture category the language the person speaks and, possibly, writes, including a wealth of more detailed items, such as measuring standards (weight, distance, etc.), date/time, address formats, etc.

*Gender* is also a variable in system development. Gender and gender/age values, such as man, woman, boy, girl, male or female teenager, may be relevant to development for usability because of showing statistical differences in interests and preferences, emotional dispositions, habits, etc. So if, e.g. we are developing an application to be used on a job known to be done largely by females, we might try to make it specifically fit female users.

*Constructive notions: Complete people.* Using the structure of people concepts described above, we can construct complete sketches of people, their similarities and differences, in which only the more fine-grained details are missing. We can also construct notions important to usability development based on all three layers reviewed above, such as *performance* on a task or other activity. The way a person performs with a system is a function of, among others, goals and motivation, intellectual capacity, current emotional state, attention and awareness (Layer 1), body condition, sensory-motor skills and physical state (Layer 2), personal history, culture and gender, including age, acquired knowledge and skills, attitudes, expectations, preferences and habits (Layer 3), as well as, of course, the AMITUDE model embodied by the system.

Since, when fitting a system to a user group, we may easily need more detail than provided above, the whole picture is a complex one. The developer's job is to focus on the properties of the target users that really matter and optimise the system's fitting of those. For that, we first develop a user profile.

## *3.3.6  User Profiles*

One of the key uses of knowledge about people (Sections 3.3.3, 3.3.4 and 3.3.5) in usability development is in specifying the target users for the system, or the *U* in AMITUDE, in a user profile (Section 3.3.1). In principle, any set of people properties can be used. Given this, and the huge and growing diversity of systems, there is no way for us to present a list of "main user profiles" or the like. You will have to do the user profiling yourself. Fortunately, what you will find is that, in practice, the user profile is constrained, sometimes strongly, by the other six AMITUDE aspects.

The purpose of user profile analysis is to identify and describe with reasonable reliability the group of people the system is meant to fit. User profile analysis has two steps and an optional step, depending on whether or not a representative user group is being specified. The *first step* is to specify the user profile that identifies the target users as everyone who fits the profile. The optional step is to specify a representative user group (Section 3.3.1). The *second step* is to analyse the people in the target user group or in the representative user group. For instance, suppose that either all target users are over 80 years old or that some proportion of a representative user group consists of the over eighties. In both cases, this important information is exploited in user profile analysis by asking: what's important about the over eighties with respect to the system we are going to develop? Depending upon the application, there may be a lot of things: the over eighties don't remember so well, they don't walk so well, etc., etc.: those are the properties our system must fit in order to be usable by the target users. Such properties aren't always so easy to identify, in which case user profile analysis may be supported by empirical investigation of the target user group in a CoMeDa cycle. We might investigate, e.g. if over eighties with dementia are able to interact reasonably with a system in their homes using speech or if some other modality or modality combination is required.

Some key points about user profile analysis are the following:


- *There is no such thing as a single interactive system for all possible users.* Ask yourself why. People are too different for that, right?
- *The development goal may suggest a single user profile where, in fact, there are several.* Suppose that the goal is to develop a system for increased comfort and security for the elderly in their homes. This may look like a system for a single user group. However, in addition to monitoring and advising the elderly person, the system will also be able to communicate with the nursing personnel and with the person's family members. How many target user groups does the system have? In most cases, the answer will probably be *three* groups, not just one, and it is therefore necessary to analyse and develop user−system interaction for three different user profiles. Why is that? It's because the three groups are so different in the context that interaction must be developed separately for each of them, even though the system is planned to eventually work as a single integrated one. In this example, it is Step 2 (cf. above) analysis that leads to the Step 1 conclusion that there are three user profiles, and the way it does so is by revealing

significant heterogeneity between the elderly, the family and the nursing staff.

- *Heterogeneity is a key issue in user profiling.* HCI would be infinitely simpler if all people were identical, because then the developer would only have to develop the system to fit him/herself. However, the point is both more subtle and more practical than that. It is that, even if we create a user profile in the first place in order not to aim at fitting everybody, but only a tiny fraction of all people, target user heterogeneity is likely to persist in many respects. So when, e.g. you want to create a system for the blind, the last thing you should do is assume that all blind people are identical. You need to analyse the group of blind target users in more detail and always with the following in mind, which can be expressed quite generally: when I identify heterogeneous sub-group UG(x), should I (a) ignore it, making my life as developer easier but maybe getting fewer people to use my system, or (b) develop for UG(x) as well, for instance by developing for several target user groups, offering customisation options, developing online adaptive user models for each group (Section 3.3.1), changing or extending the interactive modalities my system has, or . . ., etc.? For instance, since the percentage of school-age-and-above blind users who manage Braille reading and writing differs enormously from one country to another, changing from Braille input/output to speech input/output could make an important difference to the size of the target user group worldwide.
- *Whatever you do, your target user group will be heterogeneous* in many ways. This doesn't matter as long as the target group is homogeneous in the respects that matter.
- *45% of my target users don't like a particular system feature.* This is an empirical CoMeDa result, and if it shows serious dislike and shows that the 55% won't miss the feature, you might drop it. On the other hand, if the animated conversational character system does small talk in addition to help solve the task, and the introverts and the business minded among the users hate the small talk, whereas the extroverts love it, you face a problem rooted in different target user personalities and goal structures, and there is no easy solution.
- *Only 5% of my target users are likely to use a particular system feature.* This is another empirical CoMeDa finding that gives food for thought. For instance, why develop something as complex as spoken in-car hotel reservation dialogue if only 5% of all car drivers appear interested in using it (Bernsen 2003)?
- *I don't know who my target users are.* It is quite common in exploratory development not to know exactly how to specify the target users. The solution is to collect more usability information.
- *Your user profile may be wrong.* This is also quite possible, due to inadequate user profile analysis or insufficient CoMeDa work: you are aiming at the group of real folks over there all right, but your conception (= user profile analysis) of what they find usable is mistaken. The result is that there is either some other users who, unexpectedly, become users of the system or that no one does.
- *Ensure AMITUDE coherence.* Always try to ensure, as part of user profile analysis, that the specified user profile is consistent with all other AMITUDE aspects.

### 3.3.7 Case User Profile Analyses

It is interesting to note three general points about the following user profile analyses. First, we see the AMITUDE circle (Fig. 3.1) in action, e.g. when reasoning "holistically" about user age (*user*) and speech (*modality*). This helps avoid AMITUDE inconsistency. Second, we see how requirements analysis forms a continuum with design analysis. This reflects an iterative process of fixing everything down to the level of detail at which programming starts. Third, one can easily have several consecutive, operational user profiles in a life cycle.

*Sudoku.* At first sight, the user profile seems pretty easy to specify: why not go for everyone who is interested in playing the game, knows the rules, can stretch hand–arm–finger towards the displayed game board so that the stereo cameras can capture the finger's orientation and can speak the numbers and other commands? Potentially, this is a very large group of people, which reduces the risk of developing a system for no one.

On deeper analysis, several issues emerge. One is language. Linguistic interaction limits users to those who can communicate in the language chosen for interaction. Since we have no preferences one way or the other, we might as well go for a major international language, such as English. Offering a choice of several languages seems premature since what we are after is a test of concept. Another issue is user age and speech. Speech recognition for children is notoriously difficult to do compared to recognition of adult voices. Again, since we need proof of concept, we decide to avoid the extra work on fitting speech recognition to children, thus potentially limiting our core target users to adolescents and adults. A third issue is Sudoku novices who don't know the rules of the game. For simplicity, we decide to ignore this issue rather than making special precautions for novice users, such as making the system explain the rules on demand.

*Treasure Hunt.* This system is even more experimental and exploratory than the Sudoku system, so our user profile aims are correspondingly more modest. All we want are two groups of blind and deaf–mute users, respectively, who wish to test the system and provide as much feedback on it as possible. If the feedback is positive, we will use this and other usability information sources to build a more comprehensive user profile later on. Thus, we target blind and deaf–mute users who are preferably somewhat computer literate, experienced in playing computer games and interested in trying a new game technology. We want to avoid users who lack motivation and interest or might get stuck too easily in computer and equipment handling problems, because such users are less likely to give us the substantial data we need. Users will need basic English but we can help them if needed, and we can quickly teach them the little sign language they require. The blind user must have average levels of hearing, dexterity and force-feedback sensing. The deaf–mute user must have average levels of vision and dexterity.

*Maths.* To get a bit more precision into the user profile, let's specify that this system is aimed primarily at supplementing classroom teaching and training of basic multiplication. Secondarily, the system might act as maths teacher substitute. This means that the system targets children at the age when they start learning multiplication and have been taught some addition already. Depending on country and school system, the age would probably range from 6 or 7 to 9 years. This is a wide age range given the pace of child development, and we might narrow it later on after, e.g. having sought professional advice on whether there are compelling reasons for fixing a minimum user age. The language of interaction is English. Note that the nice simplicity of this user profile is due to the fact that we let it piggy-back upon the established school system, stipulating that, quite simply, system users will be those children who are admitted to perfectly ordinary schools.

## 3.4  Tasks and Other Activities, Domain

This section is about why interactive systems are being developed in the first place, i.e. because they enable people to *do* something by interacting with them. One useful classification of Application types is in terms of system purpose or what can be done with it (Section 3.2). People are at the centre as always, because it's a good idea to develop a system that many people need or strongly want, and a bad idea to develop a system that nobody wants. Section 3.4.1 explains tasks, other activities and domain. Section 3.4.2 illustrates task analysis, Section 3.4.3 generalises the results and Section 3.4.4 adds some useful task classifiers. Section 3.4.5 looks at non-task-oriented systems and Section 3.4.6 prepares Case task analysis. Section 3.4.7 is nerdy stuff on task notions.

### *3.4.1 Tasks, Other Activities, Domain*

We call what users do with the system *a user task* or *other activity*.

*User tasks.* Typically and traditionally, when users interact with a system, they carry out some *user task* or other. It is common in systems engineering to speak of a *system task*, meaning something a system or component must be able do, so a lot of system tasks are not user−system interactive. Let's stipulate that, in this book, "task"*means user task unless otherwise indicated.*

A task, then, is some specific real-life activity for which we might develop a system, such as playing Sudoku or learning maths. If you are trained in GUI-based, standard HCI task notions, read Section 3.4.7 now to avoid being confused by what we mean by a task.

*Task decomposition.* Tasks can be iteratively decomposed into subtasks which are eventually decomposed into something considered as individual user *actions*. The sub-task part is relatively straightforward, such as when *booking a return ticket to Rome* is a flight ticket booking sub-task and *describing the itinerary* is a sub-task of that sub-task. However, when it comes to defining individual user actions, we first need to specify the units we want to use. One useful unit is that of communicative act. So when you nod and say "Yes" to the animated travel agent character, you are doing a single communicative act of type confirmation. However, if we use a different type of unit, that single communicative act can be decomposed into *two* physical actions, i.e. nodding and saying "Yes". Even units at this level can often be further decomposed. The choice of units of task decomposition depends on purpose, and there are lots of unit types to choose from. This is not complicated, it's simply a matter of being clear and consistent about the units of decomposition used.

*Task goals.* Tasks have goals and it's only when the goal has been achieved that the task has been done, like when a Sudoku game has been completed or a flight ticket booked. Sub-tasks are typically steps towards achieving the task goal.

*Other activities.* We shall see that the task notion, although tricky, is often a great help to usability development. However, it is not evident that people always carry out *tasks* with interactive systems. If you are just having a nice chat with a friend, you probably wouldn't say that you are performing a task? Which task would it be? Or its goal? Did you achieve the goal? Thus we claim that some interactive activities are not tasks, because they have neither goals nor any structure of sub-tasks required for achieving the task. We call these *other activities.*

*Domains.* A domain is a more general contents area to which a user task or other activity belongs. Thus, if the task is *booking of flights within the US*, the corresponding domain could be *everything to do with US air travel*, including airline companies, their organisation and history, safety and other legal regulations, company policies, economy, aircraft and other technology, fine-print ticket sales conditions, etc. Often, the domain corresponding to a particular task or other activity is not terribly well circumscribed but normally that's not important.

The domain is important for two reasons. First, developers often need substantial knowledge about the domain in order to create a usable system, especially if the domain is familiar to the users prior to, and independently of, the system. The risk is that users may miss functionality, information or otherwise which they feel entitled to expect the system to possess; they may find downright errors in the domain knowledge reflected in the system; or there may be legal issues arising. An example of the latter is the question: could a system sell tickets over the phone without being able to notify users about the detailed ticket sales conditions? Second, in a large class of cases, developers must "carve out" the user task from the wider domain and try to get this right, cf. the next section.

### 3.4.2  User Task Analysis: A Spoken Dialogue System Example

When first looking at an interactive task to be developed for, the task often seems amorphous and hard to isolate from everything else. This is normal and, in fact, if, at first sight, the task appears clean, easy to grasp and well-structured, watch yourself! You are probably looking at your own preconceptions rather than at the task the users want to do. Let's look at a task analysis for a flight ticket reservation spoken dialogue system. The example is from the Danish Dialogue System project 1991–1996 and fully documented in Bernsen et al. (1998).

As a rule, task analysis has two distinct parts. The first is to "carve out" the task to be developed for from the surrounding domain, making the task a little interactive fragment of the domain. The second part is to analyse the carved-out chunk into sub-tasks, action units (Section 3.4.1) and other things. As usual in analysis, the two parts are done iteratively, and analysis is interspersed with decision making. The two-part rule just mentioned is not without exceptions. For instance, if the user task is being created from scratch, there is no carving out to be done. Task analysis, on the other hand, is mandatory: where there is a task, there is a task goal, and task analysis must find the ways in which the goal can and cannot be achieved.

*Domain.* The project's development goal was to build a world-first flight ticket booking system proof of concept using over-the-phone spoken user–system dialogue. We specialised the goal to Danish domestic flight ticket reservation and immediately faced the question of what should belong to the task and what should not. The domain was everything to do with Danish domestic flight travel, and we spent quite some time looking into rules about lost luggage, up to which age an infant does not require its own ticket, travelling with dogs, etc., wondering how much of this information, if any, the system should be able to provide. We also discussed things like whether the system should provide information about airport-to-nearest city distance and connections. We eventually chose to design for answering questions about check-in times, luggage, pets, infants, attendants accompanying young children, disabled and elderly, and pricing schemes for normal, group and standby fares and for reduced-price "red" and "green" departures. We could have provided the system with even more knowledge, or less, but this domain chunk seemed to give most travellers a fair chance of knowing what they were buying.

In fact, what the user does when asking for information of those kinds is an optional information-seeking task that must be linked to, and support, the main flight booking task. This latter task is not one of information seeking, it's making a commitment to buy a product.

*Basic task.* We then focused on analysing steps in flight booking for possible inclusion in the user task. In this crucial phase, it is good to start with a *basic task means-ends analysis.* This one always applies because a task has a goal or several. However, we need to keep in mind that tasks are often more complex than that. Typically, "the" basic task is an abstraction which few users might want to perform, and it may not be unique, so that we may actually start by analysing one particular basic task among several. Don't think that you are analysing *the* basic task when you are merely analysing *a* basic task. Think: "I'll first analyse *a* basic task and then ask what else".

In the present case, *a* basic task could be that the user provides information on two locations, departure airport and destination airport, and on date and time of departure. Given that there is a flight with a vacant seat fitting this 4-data-points description, all the user has to add is a "Yes, I'll take that one" to have succeeded in booking the desired flight. Simple, right? Now we ask *what else?* and use our common domain knowledge about air travel to advance the task analysis. However, we need to adjust to conditions back in 1991 with much higher airfares than today, paper tickets, paper invoices, few mobile phones and no web.

*What else?* We find that (1) there might not be a flight as specified by the user, or the specified flight might be fully booked, in which cases the user might want to select from a series of other flights offered by the system; (2) the user might want a return ticket, which requires two more data points on date and time; (3) the user might want a roundtrip ticket; (4) the user might want to book for several people; (5) these people might want to travel together or to go to different places, and might (not) want return tickets; (6) some or all might want the cheapest fare; (7) fare depends on age since children pay less and babies pay less still or nothing, so the user must specify whether the travellers are adults, children or babies; (8) fare also depends on departure date and time, so users might want to change date and time to get a cheaper fare; (9) the user might want to book tickets for a group, which implies lower fares for all; (10) payment requires an invoice, which requires some form of user id; (11) the user might want to pick up the ticket(s) at the airport rather than having them sent; (12) at some point during the dialogue, or by phoning later, the user might want to change some or all of the above.

There is more, but these 12 what-else points suffice to illustrate that we only get so far with basic task means-ends analysis. The points are all pretty straightforward and should all be included in the requirements specification because, if one or more of them are missing, or others added, we will build a very different system – for a different user profile and with different usability characteristics.

*Is that all?* No, but we are underway towards building a task model and will add more in the next sections. What we do not cover is the important part of task analysis that addresses what could go wrong in task performance, such as when the user's spoken input is not recognised or misrecognised, the user needs the system to clarify or repeat, the system needs the user to clarify or repeat, the user wants to cancel or change things in mid-stream, etc. See Bernsen et al. (1998).

### 3.4.3 Generalisation: Task Model Scope, Structure and Sharing

Let's use the Cases and the example in the previous section to illustrate a general model that may be helpful in early-task development for usability. Figure 3.2 shows, on the Y-axis, that tasks may be more or less structured, and, on the X-axis, that the task model may be shared more or less between developers and users. The Cases and the dialogue system sit at various positions in the space created. These positions are by no means exact quantitative ones but simply reflect our judgments about those examples.

*Task structure* is the extent to which the task has a sequential sub-task order. Order may be imposed by developers or may be one that users generally follow.

*Task model sharing* is the extent to which the task model is familiar to, and shared between, developers and users.

Task structure and task model sharing appear to be independent of one another. Thus, *Treasure Hunt* has a sequential structure fixed by the developers but unknown to first-time users because the task has been created from scratch (Section 3.4.6).

**Fig. 3.2** The task structure –
task model sharing
continuum

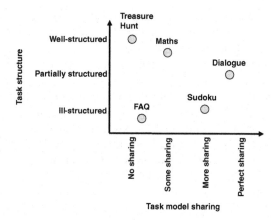

This means that users must probably be given clues to the task structure in order to be able to complete the game. The *Sudoku* task, on the other hand, is ill-structured because there does not seem to be any particular order of moves that facilitates success. For Sudoku developers, this means that they must make it equally easy to play the game in any possible sequence of moves because, otherwise, they risk designing against some population of users. The Sudoku evaluation will show why the task model turned out not to be fully shared by developers and users (Chapter 17). That's a task analysis problem.

The *Maths* system has a modest amount of task model sharing between developers and school children, simply because the latter have some familiarity with elementary classroom maths teaching, which, we hypothesise, has at least a modest degree of similarity from one teacher to another. Obviously, an empirical CoMeDa cycle is needed to verify this hypothesis. As for task structure, the Maths system has a pretty well-defined structure while allowing for some amount of free and unpredictable user initiative (Section 7.2.3). Finally, as we actually did find out empirically through a CoMeDa cycle (Section 10.2 example, Bernsen et al. 1998), the *Dialogue* flight ticket booking task does have a partial structure that's being followed by the primary user group, i.e. company secretaries used to booking flight tickets for their bosses. The secretaries (i) knew the core sub-tasks they had to do and (ii) these sub-tasks were partially ordered in their minds, starting with from where to where to go or with the number of people travelling and proceeding to the date and time information. In fact, (iii) they were also mostly happy with the way we had carved out the task from the domain. Another remarkable point about this task is that it may be assumed to be largely shared between developers and users, simply because almost everyone is familiar with public transportation in general and air travel in particular.

This is rich stuff because the large majority of systems are task-oriented. The following two mandatory rules (MR) and four rules of thumb (RT) summarise some implications:

- MR: Find out if the task is familiar to the target users.
- RT: If the task is familiar, find out which sub-tasks it includes in their minds and include those in the task model.
- MR: If the task is familiar, find out if the users structure the task and what the structure is.
- RT: If the task is familiar and is structured, model the structure.
- RT: If the task is unfamiliar, structure the task if possible and give the users sufficient clues to the task structure and the sub-tasks to be done.
- RT: If the task is ill-structured, only add structure if this does not conflict with user beliefs and preferences. Give the users sufficient clues to the task structure and the sub-tasks to be done.

If you still feel uncertain about what it means to model the task structure users already have, here's an example. When talking to a human travel agent over the phone, the users would start on the task by saying from where to where to go, and then move on to other sub-tasks. To model this in a spoken dialogue system, we might, e.g. let the system ask the user about departure and destination before asking about those other sub-tasks. This is what we did in the Danish system (Bernsen et al. 1998). See also Box 3.2.

## Box 3.2  Literal Fitting

You may have thought until now that the idea of usability as fitting the system to users is just a suggestive metaphor. Thus, while it is clear that a pair of shoes may or may not literally fit a pair of feet, it might seem fluffy how AMITUDE modelling could fit all the mental stuff in people (needs, wants, expectations, etc.). However, usability as fitting should be taken literally. In the present section on tasks, we are saying something like: if there are any patterns to users' thinking or behaviour on the task for which we want to develop a system, do model and implement those very patterns unless there are overwhelming reasons for doing something different. This user-oriented way of thinking may also be illustrated from the GUI HCI literature. For instance, a common and major web site usability error is to write everything there from the perspective of one's own organisation. The result of this navel-contemplation-made descriptive is that the frustrated visitors waste time and effort trying, and often failing, to get the information they want from a maze of irrelevance (Nielsen 1999).

Structuring ill-structured tasks is a hard problem, especially if the task is also unfamiliar to the target users. For example, information-seeking tasks, such as the auxiliary travel booking information task in Section 3.4.2, are typically ill-structured because a user may ask for any piece of information in any order. That task was small, however, and most of its information items could be assumed to be reasonably familiar to the users. In a different domain, one of the authors did a large spoken dialogue FAQ system together with a company (Prolog Development Center). The system would answer +50 questions in a complex bureaucratic domain that was mostly unfamiliar to the millions of users who, nevertheless, might have to call the system in order to obtain the information they need to get their holiday allowances paid to them before their holidays. In other words, as the user typically did not have a task model at all, this task would be close to the bottom left-hand corner of Fig. 3.2.

In a GUI-based system, we might present the +50 questions as an unordered list or impose some structure onto the list, possibly using menus. In a spoken dialogue system, a +50 item list is prohibitive and structure is required. The two problems of user unfamiliarity with the domain and an ill-structured task were solved as follows. (i) In its opening prompt, the system says that the user can use his/her own formulation of a question or choose from a spoken list of the four most frequently requested topics plus an offer to ask for additional options. (ii) If the user asks for more options, a list of 10–15 less frequently requested topics is presented. The user can interrupt the list anytime. (iii) Sometimes information provided in response to a question may be related to other information the user might want to have. In such cases, the system's response is followed by information about other topics that might be of interest. If, e.g. the user has asked about leave, the user gets information about this topic and is told that the system can also inform about who must sign the holiday allowance form when someone is on leave. For more detail, see Dybkjær and Dybkjær (2004). Thus, in this case, empirically identified question frequency was used as the sole principle for organising the questions hierarchically. Sometimes it is possible to find domain classifiers in the users' minds which can be used instead.

### 3.4.4 Other User Task Classifiers

This section lists, in alphabetical order, various standard task classifications that may help steer analysis in the right direction and remind of important issues.

*Economic import.* Tasks have smaller or larger economic import. If, by executing the task, users commit money or other valuables, this requires development effort on: feedback to users about economic commitments made, avoiding misuse, transaction security, ensuring and maintaining user trust, etc.

*Legal and ethical issues.* Some task ideas raise, or may cause, legal or ethical issues. These often concern privacy and information security (see below) but may concern IPR, human rights, protection of children and young people, and more.

*Number of tasks.* Systems may be single-task or multi-task. As exemplified by the flight booking task (Section 3.4.2), a multi-task system is one that's developed for a relatively homogenous user group and supports several interactive tasks, each of which requires separate task analysis. From a usability point of view, multi-task systems typically impose requirements to consistency of user–system interaction across tasks. Tasks in multi-task systems may be interdependent in various ways, such as when a task supports another (Section 3.4.2) or is interruptible by another task of higher priority and resumable afterwards, like when we interrupt spoken multimodal car navigation instructions in order to go looking for the nearest gas station. Tasks done with the system may also be related to tasks not done with the system.

*Number of users.* A task may be single-user or multi-user. The Treasure Hunt tasks are multi-user, involving two collaborating users. Multi-user tasks raise issues of coordination among concurrent users that have no counterpart in standard single-user tasks.

*Privacy.* Independently of their economic import, tasks are more or less private and intimate. This raises issues of privacy protection, information security and ensuring user trust.

*Safety.* Tasks are safety-critical when life, health or property is at stake. Good task performance can save lives or property, or avoid putting them at risk; bad task performance can cost lives or property, or fail to save them. Safety-critical tasks impose strong demands on developers in all life cycle phases, including everything to do with fitting the system to users and, not least, evaluation.

*Shared-goal tasks and others.* The standard task notion suggests that a task is shared-goal, i.e. user and system share the same goal of accomplishing the task. The flight booking task (Section 3.4.2) is shared-goal since both user and system are supposed to share the goal of making a flight reservation as quickly and efficiently as possible. You may consider it rather pompous to claim that the system "shares the user's goal" in this case, but, in fact, it turns out that shared-goal spoken dialogue has a number of characteristics that makes it different from conflicting-goal dialogue and that those characteristics are helpful for developing usable, shared-goal spoken dialogue (Section 11.4). The large majority of task-oriented systems are shared-goal even if involving some forms of negotiation. Thus, if we cannot get the departure we want because the flight is fully booked, we might settle for the second-best departure time after having negotiated with the spoken dialogue booking system. There is still the shared goal of optimisation according to the user's priorities.

A meeting place/date/time negotiation system is like a flight booking system except that the former may have, in addition, its own priorities as to when it would like to meet. In this case, even if there is still the shared goal of meeting at some point, priorities have to be traded off against one another. An example of a more sophisticated conflicting-goal system could be one in which the user has the task of persuading the system to do something it really does not want to do, like the colonel/doctor negotiation system in Traum et al. (2008). The human colonel's task is to persuade the conversational agent doctor to accept to move the field hospital that the doctor is in charge of. Of course, many computer games have a similar, antagonistic or competitive nature.

*Task complexity.* Tasks may be more or less complex, as measured through, e.g. number of sub-tasks, depth of task – sub-task hierarchy, number of actions or other basic units (Section 3.4.1) needed to carry out the task, task interrelationships in multi-task systems etc.

*Task classifications.* It would be nice to have an exhaustive taxonomy of all possible user tasks, complete with attributes like those listed above, and their detailed

AMITUDE requirements. In the 1980s, HCI and AI researchers dreamt of producing an exhaustive task taxonomy but failed. We doubt that this is a feasible scientific aim: how many goals do humans have; how many of those can form the basis of system development; how do we make them usefully generic; and how do we structure generic goals in some practically useful hierarchy? Today, there seem to be zillions of possible task-oriented systems and no easy way to generalise them, from document creation (*media creation tasks?*) through flight reservation (*reservation tasks? buy-a-product tasks?*), FAQs (*information-seeking tasks?*) and negotiation to reach a compromise (*conflicting-goal negotiation tasks?*) to jumping for fun to catch as many virtual pink elephants in flight as possible (*computer games?*). So we are back to our advice about application types, i.e. that you create your own abstractions for analysis and information-seeking (Section 3.2).

### 3.4.5  Beyond Task Orientation: Domain-Oriented Systems

User tasks have goals and sub-tasks, and, in interaction with a typical task-oriented system, the task goal is either achieved or not. Sometimes the goal takes long to achieve, like in writing this book, which takes a long series of word processor interactions. Sometimes there isn't any particular result of, or final end to, interaction at all, like with a physical exercise system that helps us exercise as much as we wish. The system may not have any notion of tests we could perform. Still, if it provides feedback on exercises one by one, each exercise may be viewed as a small interactive task.

Now that systems are beginning to blend with people (Box 1.2), we see interactive systems for which none of the above seems to hold. One such type of system is for having spoken conversation just for the fun of it, like the Hans Christian Andersen system (Bernsen et al. 2004). The system lets 10–18 years old children and youngsters have spoken and 2D pointing gesture conversation with the 3D animated fairytale author in his study. We call such systems domain-oriented because, as there is no task any more, all that's left are the domains about which the system makes conversation, such as Andersen's life, fairytales, person and physical presence, his study and the user. Note that the system is not a Q&A (question-answering) system because Andersen is a participant in conversation, not an answering machine; nor is it a story-telling machine that tells a story when prompted. What the system has is some conversational skills and some limited amount of knowledge about each of its domains.

### 3.4.6  Case Task Analyses

This section starts Case (Table 2.1) task analysis by discussing general issues of analysis and specification. We present the more detailed Case task analyses in Section 5.1.

*Sudoku.* The goal of this already existing task is to complete a Sudoku game. The domain is everything to do with Sudoku, in particular computer gaming.

Especially, if you play Sudoku, it may look as if Sudoku user task analysis is nearly as simple as can be. However, to believe that is to commit the most common error of all: it's simple because I don't see any problems right away! Think about how you would have discovered the following issues.

We may roughly distinguish four areas that must be carefully analysed, cf. Section 3.4.2. First, there is *core task analysis* which is simple in this case: the player tries to achieve the task goal by adding numbers onto a game board consistent with the game rules until the game board is full. In which order to fill the game board is a matter of individual user strategy and not an issue for the developers. The second area is *end-to-end system operation*: playing Sudoku also involves starting the system, selecting a game, e.g. according to difficulty, ending a game whether completed or not and closing the system. Third, *task delineation*, carving out the game task from the domain, is non-trivial. There is a wide range of support functionality that users may or may not want or expect to have, including online help, external memory support, score-keeping, ranking and time-keeping, customisation of these and various embellishments. Fourth, there is *error handling*, i.e. the general and often tricky issue of what to do when something goes wrong during interaction, such as when the user inserts a wrong number or the system fails to understand what the user says.

*Treasure Hunt.* The goal of this brand-new task is that the two-user team find the hidden blueprint drawings. As there is no pre-existent task of this kind, task analysis becomes *invention* of sub-goals, steps and actions, obstacles, etc., in a virtual environment. Initially, the domain is everything related to treasure hunting. What Treasure Hunt task analysis has to do is invent: (1) the task, making it challenging and fun; (2) end-to-end system operation; (3) task support functionality; (4) user coordination; and deal with (5) error handling in individual and collaborative gameplay.

*Maths.* The goal of this already existing task is to understand and master basic multiplication, and the domain is everything to do with teaching basic maths to kids. The task goal is basically different from those of the more standard Dialogue (Section 3.4.2), Sudoku, and Treasure Hunt tasks, because it raises two distinct, general usability issues and not just one like most other systems. The first issue is the same as for all other systems, i.e. to optimise technical quality and user quality (Table 1.1). If the Maths system's technical quality and user quality is good, this means, say, that children will have fun training with it and being taught by it. However, the second usability issue is specific to learning systems: do users actually learn what they are supposed to learn by using the system? Learning is a matter of long-term retention, of changing students so that what they are supposed to learn gets stuck with them for a long time. The interaction design that we do on a learning system is a means to the end of learning. Moreover, achievement of this end cannot be fully evaluated by evaluating technical quality and user quality. We need to do a separate evaluation of long-term retention as well.

Another difference between the Maths task and our other Cases is task complexity (Section 3.4.4). Few children would probably learn to master basic maths in a single session, so we must assume that students will use the system for weeks or months, doing multiple sessions and sub-tasks. Since the aim is to provide students with basic maths skills *and* understanding, we must assume that they will need both *teaching* for understanding purposes and skills *training*.

Maths task analysis must (1) define the maths to be learnt by carving it from the basic maths domain; (2) specify teaching and training tasks consistent with the idea of affective learning; (3) create end-to-end system operation; (4) keep track of individual students and their progress; (5) invent task support functionality; and (6) deal with error handling.

### 3.4.7 Nerdy Stuff: Different Task Notions

Classical HCI has a narrow task concept compared to the one used in this book. This is merely a granularity difference but it is potentially confusing. A classical user task is a relatively simple activity that users are meant to be able to do interactively, such as booking a flight from Pittsburgh to Boston with a meal en route, or changing font size in a word processor. A task in this sense can be analysed into a small sequence of actions constituting the unit steps (Section 3.4.1) the user is supposed to do to accomplish the task. To try this out, change the font size of a text bit and count the individual actions required. In the limit, a task *is* a single action unit. In our terminology, the flight booking and font size change examples are sub-tasks of the tasks of *booking flight tickets in the US* and *creating text documents*, respectively. The latter are tasks we develop systems for, whereas nobody in his right mind would develop a system for the Pittsburgh–Boston sub-task. It follows that user task analysis tends to be a far more complex activity than according to the classical HCI task notion.

Why did classical HCI use the narrow task notion? Explanation might refer to the fact that many GUI systems are unstructured "bags" of functionality supposed to be used in any order. To be sure, these systems do have a sort of conceptual structure announced by pull-down menus and otherwise, but this structure has little to do with task structure. Even if you might think that, e.g. there actually is a basic user task in something like this book's sense at the bottom of the enormous number of functionalities offered by a common word processor – such as the structured sequence: create document, type, edit, save, print, re-open document – there is no evidence that the word processor has been developed to facilitate this basic task in particular. This conflicts with the rules proposed in Section 3.4.3. Some claim that unstructured bags of functionality give users full freedom of interaction. This is true in the slightly scary and perverted sense in which chaos offers full freedom.

To be sure, GUI-based systems now include very many systems of a more structured nature, such as, in particular, form-filling applications whose structure resemble that of the Dialogue system in Section 3.4.2.

## 3.5  Use Environment

The purpose of use environment analysis is to specify the setting — physical, psychological, social — in which the system is to be used. We start with Case use environment analysis (Section 3.5.1) and then look at the general picture (Sections 3.5.2, 3.5.3 and 3.5.4).

### 3.5.1  Case Use Environment Analyses

*Sudoku.* Let's specify that gaming takes place in public indoor spaces, such as airports, exhibitions and other spacious areas where people are in transit and may have time to spare for a good game of Sudoku. In these locations there will be other people around, and some of them might want to watch the gameplay, creating a social environment around it. Given that, as well as the nature of 3D gesture, gameplay should preferably take place while standing on the floor. This requires some floor space of which there is often plenty in the kind of locations envisioned. Since numbers will be spoken, a limited-noise environment is required. Public indoor spaces are not perfect environments for spoken interaction, but it would seem that ways might be found to make interaction feasible, such as by an appropriate choice of microphone(s) and the assumption that, in general, spectators will politely refrain from speaking loudly close to the microphone. Similarly, it should be no problem avoiding extreme lighting conditions that might render the display unreadable for players and spectators. Ways must be found to protect the hardware from excessive damage and theft.

*Treasure Hunt.* This game can be played by players in the same room or over a network. For the time being, the game is somewhat heavy on equipment and would seem to fit best into (an) indoor location(s) with space to hold chairs for the two players and tables on which to put the hardware. As speech and non-speech sound will be used by the blind player, that player's environment must be relatively quiet. Extreme lighting must be avoided for the partner's environment because the deaf—mute player will have a graphics display.

*Maths.* The Maths system can be used both stand-alone and over the Internet. We will develop the system for use anywhere socially acceptable, quiet enough for spoken conversation, and without extreme lighting that might affect screen visibility.

The Cases show simple usability reasoning leading to decisions about which use environment(s) to develop for. We notice several common physical environment properties — public indoor spaces, floor space, tables and chairs – and reasoning aimed at ensuring consistency between modalities and use environment – graphics/lighting limits, 3D gesture/ample space, speech/environmental noise limits. Social environments frequently enter into the reasoning: Sudoku gaming will take place in a social environment of spectators; Treasure Hunt gaming creates its own social environment consisting of the two players; the ubiquity of use of the Maths system raises the issue of social acceptability of using spoken conversation when others are present; and social use may increase risks of theft and damage caused by misuse. Since it is not possible to develop for ubiquitous use in all possible environments, we choose the easy way out and pass on responsibility for proper use from developer to user. We also see compromise reasoning aimed not at use environment optimisation but at feasibly satisfying potentially conflicting goals: although Sudoku speech would work better in a strongly controlled environment, such as a quiet room with only the player present, we want to make it possible to use speech in a social environment.

### 3.5.2  Use Environment Factors Checklist

The Case use environment analyses in Section 3.5.1 only reveal a fraction of the use environmental factors that may have to be dealt with during analysis and specification. Here's a short list of different use environments to help widen our perspective:

> The office, the study, the beach, the simulator, the plant control room, the living room, the moon, the kindergarten, the street, the laboratory, the amusement park, the meeting room, the classroom, the operation theatre, the battlefield, the aircraft cockpit, the car driving seat, the production line, the theatre stage, the newsroom, the aircraft carrier deck, the conference site, the recording studio, the ambulance, the aircraft control room, the sunken ship in inky water, the soccer field, the windsurf board, the chat room, Second Life, . . .

This is a real diversity of use environments to which you might easily add many more. What is interesting about such lists is that one can start creating a checklist of use environment attribute/values which, if present in a particular development case, demand special analytical attention lest system usability may fail more or less seriously. Based on those examples, here follows a list of environmental factors that may affect interaction:

- *noise level high/low*, e.g. aircraft carrier deck vs. study. Noise levels change and can sometimes be controlled, sometimes not. An application may have to fit both values;
- *ambient light level high/low*, e.g. beach vs. sunken ship. Most ambient light levels change and can sometimes be controlled, sometimes not. An application may have to fit both values;
- *dangerous/non-dangerous* to user and others, e.g. car driving seat/simulator car driving seat. Danger levels change and often cannot be fully controlled;
- *stress and pressure level high/low*, e.g. aircraft control room vs. amusement park. Stress/pressure levels change and often cannot be fully controlled;
- *human error tolerance high/low*, e.g. living room vs. operation theatre;
- *external demands on user attention high/low*, e.g. aircraft cockpit vs. laboratory;
- *obstacles to human perception or action present/absent*, e.g. operating the application with protective clothing, gloves, etc., on the moon vs. most other use environments;
- *bystanders*, e.g. train vs. windsurf board. This often cannot be fully controlled;
- *spectators*, e.g. theatre stage vs. newsroom. This often cannot be fully controlled;
- *collaborators* depend on the task, cf. Section 3.4.4;

- *human backup present/absent*, i.e. can the user get help if there are interaction problems? Depends on task organisation;
- *risk of hardware damage, theft, etc., high/low*, e.g. street vs. some other use environments.

By now we are getting used to seeing the close interrelationships between all or most AMITUDE aspects whenever analysis is made of one of them. For instance, if there are collaborators, the use environment changes and so does the task or other activity, i.e. from single-user to multi-user, and the user profile may change as well if the collaborating users should or might have different profiles. Sometimes it is possible to control the environment, like when keeping everybody at a safe distance from a dangerous production robot; sometimes it's not, as in a car driving in the street, in which case the choice of modalities may reduce danger, for instance by replacing or supplementing on-board screens with spoken interaction.

### 3.5.3 Physical and Social Use Environments

To our knowledge, there are no useful comprehensive hierarchical classifications of use environments. As for application types (Section 3.2) and tasks (Section 3.4), it is hard to see how one could make a theory of use environment types, which is why we proposed an empirical factors checklist instead (Section 3.5.2). However, it may be useful to distinguish between two main use environments: the *physical environment* and the *social environment*. The examples listed in Section 3.5.2 show that, although most use environments are described physically in some way – the only exception being those that refer to virtual environments – nearly all of them are social environments as well, because other people may be around during interaction. The implication is that, in general, we should assume that both the physical and the social use environment must be analysed for any particular system under development.

While the notion of physical use environment is pretty self-explanatory, social use environments may have two layers, one direct and one indirect.

*Direct social use environments* must be analysed whenever other people are involved in actual system use, may affect it or be affected by it. They may be *spectators* as in the Sudoku system, *collaborators* like the blind and the deaf–mute in the Treasure Hunt system, or just *bystanders* who happen to be around so that they could adversely affect system use or be adversely affected by it.

*Indirect social use environments.* In a direct social use environment, other people are party to the interaction, even if only being disturbed by it. The contrast is to indirect social environments, or the organisational context being developed for, if any. Most systems are being developed to fit into some organisational context or other, if only in the minimal sense that, to use the system at all, the user must register with the producer. The Maths Case is aimed at a simple organisational context, too, i.e. one including a potentially large number of users who have system access and must be kept track of. Even these simple organisational contexts can make a user's life hard, as we know – with registration numbers, passwords, what-if-you-lose-them, delays in registration renewal, etc.

Another class of systems are more demanding as regards organisational context usability analysis. This is when, in order to fit the system to organisations, organisational contexts must be analysed in depth in terms of properties of organisations, such as organisational purpose, chain of command, work organisation, workflow, division of labour and responsibility, workplace collaboration, information sharing between different user groups, internal practices and standards and existing technology that must be taken into account.

Analysis of social use environments is often coupled with user profile analysis (Section 3.3.6), especially for collaborative and organisational systems. Thus, within the organisation, several user groups with different organisational roles and purposes, different education and expertise, may draw upon the information the system has; another group might do technical integration with existing systems, and system maintenance; a third may be responsible for updating information; a fourth may need privileged access to some of the information; a fifth may have to be convinced that acquiring the system is a good idea in the first place; a sixth may authorise its acquisition; a seventh may be closely involved in its development and evaluation; etc.

We will not address these issues any further in this book and refer to the HCI literature, e.g. Mayhew (1999), Preece et al. (1994) and Te'eni et al. (2007).

### 3.5.4 Environmental Responsibility

For systems bound to particular use environments, we can analyse those and use the results in our AMITUDE model of use specification. However, as computing becomes ubiquitous, systems are increasingly being used in multiple use environments, and not just in the sense that the system will have a physical, a direct social and an organisational environment, and sometimes a virtual environment as well – but in the sense that, right or wrong, it might be used most anywhere across differences among physical, social and virtual environments. Should development for usability take this into account and, if it should, how?

Arguably, we should (i) do our best to make systems fit one or several particular use environments and announce the "fits" clearly. A spoken dictation system, for instance, faces quite different use environments when used on the train, when driving a car, in a meeting room, on an aircraft carrier deck or in a quiet radio/TV broadcast back room where a translator dictates simultaneous translation and the resulting text appears on the TV viewers' screens. Depending on the use environment, executing the dictation task may be straightforward, socially embarrassing, socially annoying and disruptive, overly stressful or downright impossible. We recommend that the system be used in a quiet location and that care is taken not to disturb others when using it. The rest is the responsibility of the user. (ii) Supply environmentally helpful customisation functionality, such as that the mobile

phone can be customised to vibrating in the pocket instead of ringing out loud.
And (iii) prepare for a future with, e.g. handheld mobile phones that refuse to work
for the driver whilst driving, or cars refusing to be driven by drunken or drugged
drivers.

## 3.6  Interaction

"Interaction" is central to this book and to HCI because usability is making systems fit people when interacting with systems. In this section, we show that interaction has become far broader than the term "interaction" could possibly connote and
describe a more general model that fits multimodal usability.

In the 1980s, user interaction was essentially manual tools handling although
often described in loftier ways. All a standard GUI user does is use the manual tools
(keyboard and mouse) and watch (the screen) to see what the action results in. In
GUI speak this is called "dialogue" and it *is* a limiting case of user–system dialogue
to press labelled buttons and re-locate on-screen objects. This manner of system
operation comes close to handling second-, third- and fourth-generation technologies (Section 1.4.2) by means of knobs and dials and watching what happens, ensuring nice continuation with the pre-history of computing.

Already in the 1980s, interaction was evolving in new directions, and today we
need a comprehensive model for describing what is still commonly called "interaction". In fact, if taken to describe all human dealings with systems, the classical idea
of interaction became inadequate and potentially misleading decades ago.

Having presented a generalised model of interaction (Section 3.6.1), we discuss
(Section 3.6.2) how the core communication part of the model must be generalised
as well, when moving from GUI-based interaction to multimodality and blending
with people. The Cases are analysed in terms of the model in Section 3.6.3.

### 3.6.1  Generalising Interaction: Information Presentation
         and Exchange

Figure 3.3 shows a hierarchical model whose root is no longer interaction but something more basic and general, i.e. presentation and exchange of information between
user and system.

*Deliberate two-way communication.* To start with familiar historical roots of
"interaction", consider *deliberate two-way human-system communication* in the
model. This is classical interaction as in clicking on a link and getting a new web
page, typing a question to a Q&A (Question-Answering) system and getting the
answer, having spontaneous spoken dialogue with the system, or nodding at a virtual
character and having the nod correctly interpreted, as evidenced by the character's
output. Classical interaction clearly is a form of two-way communication. Moreover,
user interaction is basically deliberate: we think about what to input and then do it.
We think about the system's output before carrying on. We may get faster through
training and may automate our interactive behaviour so that we don't need to think

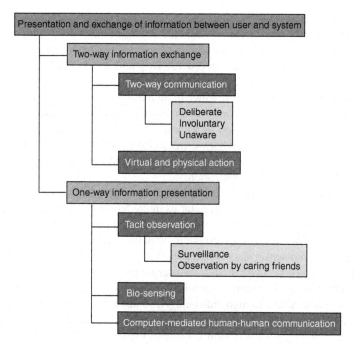

**Fig. 3.3** Varieties of human–system information exchange

about the details of what we are doing any more but just do them (Rasmussen 1983) – but that doesn't change the basics. What we do is still deliberate, and thinking and reasoning preserve a supervisory role, at least.

*Virtual and physical action.* Two-way communication has a single neighbour in the model, i.e. virtual and physical action. The reason for this distinction is that it seems less intuitively evident that we are into two-way *communication* with the system when, e.g. directly manipulating virtual, mixed reality or physical objects or dispatching clones in a Star Wars game. This seems as counterintuitive as considering the forming of a snowball a case of communicating with the snow. It may be less misleading to describe virtual and physical action as two-way exchange of information, not as communication. Future sex robots is another case in point because, intuitively, sexual intercourse is not primarily a form of communication.

*Beyond interaction.* Let's go back to classical interaction which, we want to show, is limited by the assumption that user information input is deliberate. In particular, three of the level-3 items in Fig. 3.3. – two-way communication, tacit observation and bio-sensing – include large parts of non-deliberate user input.

*Tacit observation.* Consider a camera surveillance system that captures a burglar dislodging a window pane. To the burglar, there is nothing deliberate about the information captured. He may be ignorant about the surveillance and would most likely not deliberately expose himself to being captured on camera. So the burglar is not interacting with the system in the classical sense nor is he communicating with the system (two-way). He is being tacitly observed. A more interesting, perhaps, and certainly more positive case of tacit observation is observation by caring friends. Friendly and caring systems are emerging and blend with people to unobtrusively capture information and learn about us, our habits, preferences, personalities, knowledge, skills, etc., in order to help and assist rather than getting us into trouble. The Maths Case is an example.

*Non-deliberate communication.* Much of human communication is, in fact, involuntary, and some of it we may not even be aware of producing, such as the quick glance of desire, the embarrassed or astonished facial expression, or the tone of voice that betrays by revealing what we would have preferred to keep to ourselves. Multimodal and natural interactive systems research has begun to deal with these important phenomena in communication.

*Bio-sensor data.* Multimodal interactive systems increasingly make use of physiological user data. In research, a popular example has been to wrap car drivers in bio-sensors, supposedly to find out if, e.g. the driver is distracted or falling asleep, at which point the system will do something to make the driver avoid imminent disaster. In general, bio-sensor data is probably best regarded as one-way information from human to machine, even though the user might be aware of some of it, or the machine may initiate communication with the user about it. In any case, most of this data isn't deliberate although, intriguingly, some of it is, such as when the physically disabled controls the wheelchair via EEG readings. The difference from tacit observation is that the user is typically aware of the fact that information of certain kinds is being presented to the system.

*Computer-mediated human–human communication.* Whether we chat on the Internet, are in video conference, visit Second Life or use the mobile phone, we primarily communicate with humans rather than with the system, which merely transmits the communication. Typically, we discover or are reminded that there is a system go-between when communication doesn't work or, due to inherent limitations (Section 1.5), the system fails to fully enable communication to come across to the human interlocutors. We suggest that the human–system interaction involved in the main part of computer-mediated human–human communication is one-way information to the system, because the system is not supposed to respond to the user's input but to simply pass it on to the human(s) at the other end. Of course, when we operate the system go-between to start or exit a video conference, or try to fix problems arising, we are back to deliberate two-way human–system communication.

*Two-way information exchange vs. one-way information presentation.* We now see that the core of this level-2 distinction in Fig. 3.3 is that, whether deliberately or not, in two-way information exchange, we actively make the system do something in response to our input. In one-way information presentation, we simply cause input to the system with which it will do whatever it has been developed to do – try to recognise the burglar and strike the alarm (tacit observation, surveillance), process the input for future helpful use (tacit observation, caring friends), analyse the signals for cues to act upon (bio-sensing) or transmit the signals (computer-mediated human–human communication).

In conclusion, it seems necessary to re-interpret Human–Computer Interaction (or HCI) in terms of the far more general notion of human–system information presentation and exchange. We will continue to use the terms "interaction" and "HCI" in this book but hope to have shown that they are historic relicts.

### 3.6.2 Generalising Two-Way Communication: Awareness, Initiative, Acts and Style

Section 3.6.1 describes "in-breadth" generalisation of interaction, trying to make sure that we face the full scope of the user–system dealings that could be involved in fitting systems to users – from pulse reading to virtual-clone-shooting or whichever the extremes in Fig. 3.3 might be. In this section, we focus on the traditional core of interaction, two-way communication, trying to generalise "in-depth" from GUI interaction to multimodal interaction and blending with people.

In general, GUI-based two-way communication relies on keyboard and mouse input while multimodal interaction may include full human-style communication input. In particular, we rarely use spontaneous natural human communication, such as spontaneous speech, as input to GUI-based systems. This means that standard GUI developers don't have to worry about processing spontaneous natural human communication input, whereas developers of multimodal systems and systems blending with people do. Let's look at what this means for multimodal usability.

*Involuntary and unaware user input.* We saw in Section 3.6.1 that two-way communication input can be either voluntary and deliberate or involuntary and unaware. In standard GUI-based two-way communication, the user produces keyboard and mouse input that is generally assumed to be deliberate and voluntary. However, natural human communication input is *both* voluntary, deliberate, involuntary and unaware.

Let us now look at generalisation needs with respect to three other aspects of two-way user–system communication: initiative, communication acts and communication style. It appears that, while the two latter are of little or no interest to GUI development, they are all of key importance to the development of usable multimodal interaction and systems blending with people.

*Initiative in communication* is about who drives communication forward or who must act for user–system communication to continue rather than hang, end or time out. This is a continuum, having 0% system initiative and 100% user initiative at one end, and 100% system initiative and 0% user initiative at the other. It's exactly the same in human–human communication, from which we also know that the balance of initiative may shift during communication, with, e.g. Interlocutor A taking most of the initiative at the start of the dialogue and Interlocutor B driving the dialogue towards the end. It is useful in practice to distinguish between three main stage posts, user–system communication being, wholly or largely, either:

- system-directed;
- user-directed;
- mixed-initiative.

*Most GUIs are user-directed*: the GUI output sits there offering a choice of input actions and waits until the user acts on one of them, whereupon the system responds. The user often needs a large amount of knowledge of system functionality to drive the task forward, cf. Section 3.4.7. For some tasks, this initiative distribution has turned out to be so unusable that the average user gives up in frustration. A common solution is form-filling, in which the system still waits for the user's next step, but guides each step through typed instructions, yes/no questions, * signs for mandatory input, requests for the user to correct something, continue buttons for viewing the next application window, etc. What happens is that, when the user has chosen to fill a form, communication switches from being user-directed to being system-directed. Mixed-initiative GUI-based communication also exists, mainly in computer games where the user competes with the system in some virtual world.

Switching to the world of multimodality, natural interaction and blending with people (Section 1.4.4), we see a different picture. Mixed-initiative human–human communication is an ideal, and a key research area is how to understand spontaneous natural communication input. However, most commercial spoken dialogue systems are still system-directed like GUI-based form-filling systems, cf. the Dialogue example in Section 3.4.2.

*Communication acts.* Some 60 years ago, it was discovered that communication is not just information exchange but action for a purpose, such as to get someone to do something, state some fact or express an emotion. An important early classification of communication acts is the speech acts taxonomy of Searle (1969), see Section 15.5.5.

GUIs include speech acts, such as questions and commands. That's one of the reasons why GUI interaction is communication. However, standard GUI developers don't worry about speech acts because all they need is humans who understand the system's output. What happens when the user clicks on a menu item, for instance, is hard-coded, so it doesn't really matter to anyone if what's on the menu item is a question, a command or something else.

In the world of multimodality and blending systems and people, on the other hand, the system must be able to identify and process speech acts and other items in spontaneous natural communication input. And there is more. Most work on speech acts so far has focused on spoken or typed language, looking at the acts we do when we speak or write. However, speech acts are parts of much larger natural communication acts which are intrinsically multimodal because they involve the entire body in communication. Future multimodal systems will have to process these "complete" acts of natural communication.

*Communication style* is characterised by attribute/values such as degree of politeness and verbosity vs. terseness. Communication style does have applications in standard GUI-based communication, like when the user is offered the choice between help and verbose help, or, more generally, in output message design. It is probably meaningless to speak about communication style in connection with *input* to standard GUI-based systems.

Again, things change as we turn to development for multimodality and blending with people. To blend with people, systems often need to understand natural human communication input in the form of speech or otherwise. As a general problem, this is one of the hardest in computing, so, as a developer, you do what you can to make the problem simpler. This is where the system's communication style can be of great help, because users tend to imitate the system's communication style. In spoken dialogue systems development, we call this phenomenon input control because it is possible, through system *output* design, to strongly influence the style in which users *input* information, making the system's task of understanding the input significantly easier. Thus, in practice, be careful not to make the system's communication overly polite because users will then embellish their input with expressions of politeness, making input understanding harder. Don't communicate verbosely because users will do the same. Be terse and to the point. Make sure that the system can understand the words, phrases and other constructs that it uses itself, because users will re-use them (Bernsen et al. 1998).

In this section we have looked at two-way user–system communication (Fig. 3.3). We found that user communication input is far more complex in multimodal interaction than in traditional GUI-based interaction. Multimodal interaction will eventually require the system to understand spontaneous natural communication through speech, facial expression, gesture, etc. This means that the two-way communication we must deal with when developing for multimodal usability is very different from, and far more general than, the two-way communication of GUI-based interaction.

### 3.6.3 Case Interaction

Let's use Fig. 3.3 to chart the information presentation and exchange involved in the Cases. It appears that the Cases essentially cover the entries in the figure.

*Sudoku.* AMITUDE specification focuses on usable deliberate two-way communication.

*Treasure Hunt.* This game must demonstrate usable deliberate two-way communication, virtual action and computer-mediated human–human communication.

*Maths.* Affective learning of basic maths requires usable deliberate and non-deliberate (involuntary, unaware) two-way communication, tacit observation by caring friends and bio-sensing.

## 3.7 Key Points

A major point of this chapter is demonstration of how holistic AMITUDE analysis works. We strongly believe that, to keep analysis under control, AMITUDE aspects should be analysed one by one and conclusions listed per aspect as in the Case specification summary in Section 5.1. Yet it is often clear that arriving at those conclusions is possible only after having analysed constraints arising from several different AMITUDE aspects.

We are well underway towards a first AMITUDE Case specification, having analysed five aspects with two more to go, and it is useful to start considering what has been done and how. AMITUDE itself provided first high-level support, stating that we have to analyse its seven aspects one by one but holistically. *Application type* analysis was an examination of the Case systems as belonging to various useful types to be looked into. *User profile* analysis was pretty straightforward but often strikes newcomers as surprisingly detailed and nitty−gritty. *Task analysis* was the more substantial of them all, even at this early pre-design stage. *Use environment* analysis was rather simple, especially compared to what it might have involved, but didn't − organisation analysis, hazards and danger analysis, etc. *Interaction analysis* was simply a classification of each Case in terms of a model.

We did it all as if by pure thinking based on experience and that's of course quite unrealistic. In a real project, we wouldn't have come this far without numerous team discussions, web and literature consultations, CoMeDa cycles, drafts and re-drafts, etc. Yet it is no bad approach to start by getting as far as one can by "pure thinking", in particular, if one more thing is being done which we haven't done above, i.e. to maintain and execute from an ever-growing list of things to investigate further before making a decision.

# References

Baber C, Noyes J (eds) (1993) Interactive speech technology. Taylor & Francis, London.

Bernsen NO (1985) Heidegger's theory of intentionality. Odense University Press, Odense.

Bernsen NO (1997) Towards a tool for predicting speech functionality. Speech Communication 23: 181–210.

Bernsen NO (2003) On-line user modelling in a mobile spoken dialogue system. In: Bourlard H (ed) Proceedings of Eurospeech'2003. International Speech Communication Association (ISCA), Bonn 1: 737–740.

Bernsen NO, Charfuelàn M, Corradini A, Dybkjær L, Hansen T, Kiilerich S, Kolodnytsky M, Kupkin D, Mehta M (2004) Conversational H. C. Andersen. First prototype description. In: André E, Dybkjær L, Minker W, Heisterkamp P (eds) Proceedings of the tutorial and research workshop on affective dialogue systems. Springer Verlag, Heidelberg: LNAI 3068: 305–308.

Bernsen NO, Dybkjær H, Dybkjær L (1998) Designing interactive speech systems: From first ideas to user testing. Springer Verlag, Berlin.

Bernsen NO, Dybkjær L (2004) Domain-oriented conversation with H.C. Andersen. In: André E, Dybkjær L, Minker W, Heisterkamp P (eds) Proceedings of the tutorial and research workshop on affective dialogue systems. Springer Verlag, Heidelberg: LNAI 3068: 142–153.

Cassell J, Sullivan J, Prevost S, Churchill E (2000) Embodied conversational agents. MIT Press, Cambridge, MA.

Dybkjær H, Dybkjær L (2004) Modeling complex spoken dialog. IEEE Computer August: 32–40.

Luppicini R (ed) (2008) Handbook of conversation design for instructional applications. Information Science Reference, USA.

Mayhew DJ (1999) The usability engineering life cycle. Morgan Kaufmann Publishers, San Francisco.

Nielsen J (1999) Designing web usability. New Riders, Indiana.

Norman DA (2004) Emotional design: why we love (or hate) everyday things. Basic Books, New York.

Ortony A, Turner TJ (1990) What's basic about basic emotions? Psychological Review 97/3: 315–331.

Picard, RW (1997) Affective computing. MIT Press, Cambridge.

Picard RW, Papert S, Bender W, Blumberg B, Breazeal C, Cavallo D, Machover T, Resnick M, Roy D, Stroehecker C (2004) Affective learning – a manifesto. BT Technology Journal 22/4: 253–269.

Preece J, Rogers Y, Sharp H, Benyon D, Holland S, Carey T (1994) Human–computer interaction. Addison-Wesley, Wokingham.

Rasmussen J (1983) Skills, rules and knowledge: signals, signs and symbols, and other distinctions in human performance models. IEEE Transactions on Systems, Man, and Cybernetics 13/3: 257–266.

Searle J (1969) Speech acts. Cambridge University Press, Cambridge.

Searle J (1983) Intentionality. Cambridge University Press, Cambridge.

Te'eni, D, Carey J, Zhang P (2007) Human computer interaction. Developing effective organizational information systems. John Wiley & Sons, Hoboken, NJ.

Traum D, Swartout W, Gratch J, Marsella S (2008) A virtual human dialogue model for non-team interaction. In: Dybkjær L, Minker W (eds) Recent trends in discourse and dialogue. Springer, Text, Speech and Language Technology Series 39: 45–67.

# Chapter 4
# Modalities and Devices

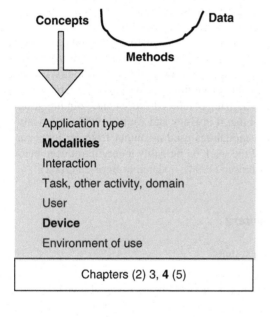

This chapter completes the presentation, begun in Chapter 3, of concepts for specifying an AMITUDE model of use. The concepts to be presented and illustrated through Case analysis relate to AMITUDE aspects *Modalities* and *Devices*. Modalities are covered extensively for several reasons. The obvious reason is that Modalities are key to this book's generalisation from GUI-dominated usability to multimodal usability. Second, modalities and multimodal systems tend to be poorly covered in standard HCI literature. Third, not even the notions of modality and multimodality are well understood, misunderstandings abound – you might share them, so prepare for surprises! Fourth, there is a large number of non-GUI modalities and a theory about them that we would like to introduce.

In more detail, Section 4.1 discusses some current views about multimodality and defines multimodal and unimodal systems in terms of information, sensor systems, physical information carriers, media and input/output. Section 4.2 presents a taxonomy of modalities. Section 4.3 presents modality properties. Section 4.4 introduces multimodal representation, discusses how to combine modalities and makes modality analyses of the Cases. Finally, Section 4.5 presents device analysis and makes Case device analyses.

N.O. Bernsen, L. Dybkjær, *Multimodal Usability*, Human-Computer Interaction Series, DOI 10.1007/978-1-84882-553-6_4, © Springer-Verlag London Limited 2009

## 4.1  What Is a Multimodal System?

Modalities are key to everything multimodal because something can only be *multi* modal if composed of several modalities, right? Let's say that if something – interaction, a system, whatever – is multimodal, it is composed of several *uni* modal modalities, that is, modalities which are not themselves multimodal. In fact, the vast majority of current systems are multimodal, and unimodal systems represent a limiting case rather than the standard case.

There are several explanations and definitions of multimodal systems around. Some exist in print, others are more like hunches about what to reply if asked what multimodality is and several don't take us very far. We discuss a couple of them in Section 4.1.1 before taking a systematic approach to media and modalities in Sections 4.1.2, 4.1.3, 4.1.4 and 4.1.5, based on the notion of interaction as representation and exchange of information introduced in Section 3.6.1.

The dictionary's term "modality" is not overly informative. One of its senses is to be *a manner of something*, another, the so-called *sensory modalities* of psychology (vision, hearing, etc.) that we met in Section 3.3.4. We don't know who first used the term "modality" to refer to the elements of multimodal systems. The term appears in Bolt's early paper on advantages of using combined speech and pointing gesture (Bolt 1980). One of the authors first met it in Hovy and Arens (1990) who mention written text and beeps as different modalities used as output from, or input to, a computer system. This paper set off the work on modality theory introduced below. A first comprehensive account is Bernsen (1994), updated in Bernsen (2002).

### 4.1.1  Some Views Lead Nowhere

Here's a definition of a multimodal system:

- A multimodal system is a system that somehow involves several modalities.

This is trivially true and quite uninformative about what multimodality actually is. It does, however, put a nice focus on the question: what are modalities? Here is another explanation that quite often seems to lurk in the background:

- A multimodal system is a system which takes us beyond the old and soon-to-become-obsolete GUI paradigm for interactive systems. Multimodal systems represent a new and more advanced paradigm. To quote Oviatt and Cohen (2000): "Multimodal systems are radically different than standard GUIs".

As an explanation of multimodality, this one is false and seriously misleading. Moreover, it's near-vacuous about what multimodality is, except for wrongly stating that multimodality has nothing to do with standard GUIs. We understand your surprise: haven't we presented this book as a necessary generalisation from GUI-based usability to multimodal usability? We have, but *we never said that GUI-based interaction is not multimodal.* That's where the claim above is so false that, if you accept it as an axiom, you will remain confused forever. GUI-based systems are heavily multimodal (see Section 4.3.1), so the point made in this book is a very different one. It is that there are far more, and far more diverse, multimodal and blending-with-people systems out there in reality, imagination or sheer potentiality than there are GUI-based systems; and these systems, we claim, pose new usability development issues that weren't addressed in the GUI tradition. In fact, there are unimodal systems that pose such issues as well, and these are, of course, within the scope of this book. Besides, GUI-based systems are not becoming obsolete. GUI-based interaction is a useful multimodal interaction paradigm which, because it came first historically, is just better explored, and more familiar to most people, than most other kinds of multimodal interaction.

## 4.1.2 Sensor Systems, Carriers, Media, Thresholds

Interacting with a system means that the system presents information to us, or we present information to it, or we exchange information with it (Section 3.6.1). It is important that this information is of many different kinds. For now, however, let's focus on the fact that exchange of information is ultimately a physical process.

Even though we are used to thinking and reasoning about information in abstract terms, we never exchange information in the abstract with people, animals or systems. When humans exchange information, the information is physically instantiated in some way – in sound waves, light or otherwise. Let's call these *physical carriers* of information. To physically capture the information conveyed, humans have sensor systems, including the five classical senses of sight, hearing, touch, smell and taste (Section 3.3.4). Each carrier corresponds to a different sensor system. When the information conveyed by a certain carrier gets picked up by the corresponding sense, what happens? Well, unless the physics of the event isn't up to this for some reason, what happens is that the entity doing the sensing perceives the information in the corresponding medium, such as graphics or acoustics. Thus we get the correspondences shown in Table 4.1.

**Table 4.1**   Medium–carrier–sense correspondences for the traditional "five human senses"

| Medium | Physical carrier | Sensor system |
| --- | --- | --- |
| Graphics | Light | Vision |
| Acoustics | Sound | Hearing |
| Haptics | Mechanical impact | Touch |
| Olfaction | Chemical impact | Smell |
| Gustation | Chemical impact | Taste |

See note on graphics in text.

In Table 4.1, graphics means everything visual or everything conveyed by elec-tromagnetic waves, acoustics means everything heard or everything conveyed by acoustic waves, etc. You may have to get used to thinking of everything visual as "graphics", particularly if you are a native English speaker used to thinking of graphics as the "pictorial" sub-set of everything visual. As we use the term, *graphics* refers to everything visual, including this typed text, and even if the text in some extraordinary experiment is being picked up by, say, radar.

For physically instantiated information to be perceived by a human recipient, the instantiation must respect the limitations of the human sensors. For instance, the human eye only perceives light in, approximately, the 400–700 nm wavelength band. Light intensity and other factors matter as well. The human ear can perceive sound in the 18–20,000 Hz frequency band and only if of sufficient intensity. Touch information, which is often collected by the hands, involving proprioception (Section 3.3.4), but can be collected by all body parts – must be above a certain mechanical force threshold to be perceived, and its perception also depends on the density of touch sensors in the part of human skin exposed to touch. Within these genetically determined limits, and due to a variety of factors, human thresholds dif-fer from one individual to another and over time as well.

If the information recipient is of a species different from humans, the threshold pattern is different, and the same is true if the recipient is a system. In other words, there is no threshold symmetry between the unaided human sensory system and the sensory systems of computers. Eventually, computers might become as good as, or better than, humans at sensing within the human sensory thresholds, and computers are already capable of receiving sensory information far beyond what the unaided human sensory system can do, such as when sensing gamma rays, infrared or ultra-sound. Moreover, computers can sense information represented in media to which humans have little or no unaided access, such as magnetic fields. In both cases, of course, humans can pick up the same information by transforming it to equivalent physically instantiated information that humans *can* access.

### 4.1.3  What Is a Modality? Modalities and Usability

Based on Section 4.1.2, we can define a modality in a very straightforward way:

- A modality, or, more explicitly, a modality of information representation, is a way of representing information in some medium.

Since the medium is linked to a particular physical carrier and to a particular kind of sensor system (Table 4.1), a modality is defined by its medium–carrier–sensor system triplet *and* its particular "way" of representation. It follows that a modality does not have to be perceptible by humans. Modalities don't even have to be represented in physical media accessible to humans. In what follows, however, we focus on modalities that are perceptible to humans unless otherwise stated.

What's the point of having these "ways" of representing information? In fact, if it were not for these different "ways", all we would need is Table 4.1. We need those "ways", or modalities, because humans use many and very different modalities for representing information in the same medium. We use, e.g. the graphics medium (everything visible) to represent text, images, facial expression, gesture and more. These are different modalities represented in the same medium.

This takes us directly to the reason why *modalities* is an AMITUDE aspect. This is because, in general, it makes large differences to usability whether abstract information items are being represented in one or another modality. Consider three simple examples of different granularity. (1) The blind cannot use any graphics modality as represented on a standard display. (2) The seeing can, but try to represent the contents of this sentence using images only, and no text. (3) This won't work, of course, but it is straightforward to read the sentence aloud for the blind. Now let's reconsider those examples in the context of AMITUDE analysis. In example (1), the use of graphics is excluded by the user profile (Section 3.3.6). In example (2), the graphics image modality is excluded because of the information contents to be represented, and the graphics text modality is chosen instead. In example (3), the same contents, i.e. that of the graphics text sentence above, are being represented in a very different modality, i.e. spoken language in order to fit the target user profile. This is a micro-cosmos of AMITUDE reasoning with multiple and quite familiar modalities.

Generalising, we get a familiar picture: when developing for usability, we do AMITUDE analysis, and one of its parts is modality analysis aimed at making a usable choice of modalities. Like all AMITUDE analysis, the reasoning required is holistic (Section 3.1.2) because the chosen modalities must be consistent with the user profile, the environment of use, the information to be exchanged in the task, etc.

## 4.1.4 Input and Output Modalities, Symmetry and Asymmetry

We saw that natural communication user input is far more complex than standard input to GUI-based systems (Section 3.6.2). More generally, as multimodal interaction may involve dramatic increases in input and output complexity, we need to maintain strict distinction between input and output modalities lest everything gets mixed up. For instance, what is a "spoken computer game"? It makes a big difference if the system takes speech input, produces speech output, or both. Moreover, since speech can be of different modalities, we quickly grow a small combinatorial tree and want to know where in this structure the "spoken computer game" sits, e.g. if we are doing application type analysis (Section 3.2).

We say that, during interaction, the user inputs *input* modalities to the system and the system outputs *output* modalities to the user. When humans communicate with each other, the input and output modalities are typically the same. This is called input/output modality symmetry. In today's human–system interaction, input/output modality asymmetry is the rule and symmetry the exception. Try to think of examples of both kinds.

### *4.1.5  Unimodal and Multimodal Systems*

We can now define a multimodal interactive system:

• A multimodal interactive system has both input and output, and uses at least two
  different modalities for input and/or output.

Thus, if *I* is input, *O* output and *Mn* is a specific modality *n*, then [IM1,
OM2], [IM1, IM2, OM1] and [IM1, OM1, OM2] are some minimal examples of
multimodal systems. For instance, [IM1, OM2] could be a spoken dictation
system that displays the recognised speech as text on the screen. Try to exemplify
the others! We can also define a unimodal interactive system:

• A unimodal interactive system has both input and output, and uses the same single
  modality for input and output, i.e. [IMn, OMn].

An over-the-phone spoken dialogue system is unimodal: we speak to it, it talks
back and that's it! Other examples are Braille text input/output chat or a system in
which an embodied agent moves as a function of the user's movements. There are
lots more, of course, but still the class of real and potential multimodal systems is
very much larger than the class of real and potential unimodal systems.


## 4.2  Which Modalities Exist? Taxonomy of Unimodal Modalities

A classical joke says "Great! Now we know the answer – but what was the question?" Table 4.2 answers the question in the heading above, but the answer will be a
lot clearer if we first make the question a bit more precise.

A modality is a particular way of representing information in a particular medium
(Section 4.1.3). Let's focus on modalities in three of the media shown in Table 4.1,
i.e. graphics, acoustics and haptics, ignoring olfaction (smell) and gustation (taste)
for now although these are appearing in multimodal interaction. Graphics, acoustics
and haptics are central to multimodal interaction today and in the near future. Our
question then becomes something like:

> Which are the graphic, acoustic and haptic modalities, and which among these are relevant
> to usability development?

Table 4.2 shows a taxonomy of all possible unimodal modalities in those media.
Some care has been taken to compact currently less relevant modalities, so the
table can be used as a toolbox of input/output modalities for constructing multimodal systems. We explain the table in steps, starting with its visible structure
(Section 4.2.1). Nerdy Section 4.2.2 explains origins and derivation of the taxonomy. Sections 4.2.3 and 4.2.4 present a walk-through of the taxonomy, and
Section 4.4.5 describes the elements of media, i.e. information channels. Space does

**Table 4.2** One view of the taxonomy of modalities

| Super level | Generic level | Atomic level | Sub-atomic level |
|---|---|---|---|
| Linguistic modalities → | 1. Sta. an. graphic ele. | | |
| | 2. Sta.-dyn. an. acoustic ele. | | |
| | 3. Sta.-dyn. an. haptic ele. | | |
| | 4. Dyn. an. graphic → | 4a. Sta.-dyn. gest. disc. | |
| | | 4b. Sta.-dyn. gest. lab. | |
| | | 4c. Sta.-dyn. gest. not. | |
| | 5. Sta. non-an. graphic → | 5a. Written text → | 5a1. Typed text |
| | | | 5a2. Hand-writ text |
| | | 5b. Written lab. → | 5b1. Typed lab. |
| | | | 5b2. Hand-writ lab. |
| | | 5c. Written not. → | 5c1. Typed not. |
| | | | 5c2. Hand-writ not. |
| | 6. Sta.-dyn. non-an. acoustic → | 6a. Spoken disc. | *Legend* |
| | | 6b. Spoken lab. | *an. = analogue* |
| | | 6c. Spoken not. | *compos. = compositional* |
| | | | *disc. = discourse* |
| | 7. Sta.-dyn. non-an. haptic → | 7a. Haptic text | *dyn. = dynamic* |
| | | 7b. Haptic lab. | *ele. = elements* |
| | | 7c. Haptic not. | *gest. = gesture* |
| | 8. Dyn. non-an. graphic → | 8a. Dyn. written text | *lab. = labels /keywords* |
| | | 8b. Dyn. written lab. | *non-an. = non-analogue* |
| | | 8c. Dyn. written not. | *not. = notation* |
| | | 8d. Sta.-dyn. spoken disc. | *sta. = static* |
| | | 8e. Sta.-dyn. spoken lab. | *writ. = written* |
| | | 8 f. Sta.-dyn. spoken not. | |
| Analogue modalities → | 9. Static graphic → | 9a. Images | |
| | | 9b. Maps | |
| | | 9c. Compos. diagrams | |
| | | 9d. Graphs | |
| | | 9e. Conceptual diagrams | |

**Table 4.2**  (Continued)

| Super level | Generic level | Atomic level | Sub-atomic level |
|---|---|---|---|
| | 10. Sta.-dyn. acoustic → | 10a. Images | |
| | | 10b. Maps | |
| | | 10c. Compos. diagrams | |
| | | 10d. Graphs | |
| | | 10e. Conceptual diagrams | |
| | 11. Sta.-dyn. haptic → | 11a. Images → | 11a1. Gesture |
| | | 11b. Maps | 11a2. Body action |
| | | 11c. Compos. diagrams | |
| | | 11d. Graphs | |
| | | 11e. Conceptual diagrams | |
| | 12. Dyn. graphic → | 12a. Images → | 12a1. Facial expression |
| | | 12b. Maps | 12a2. Gesture |
| | | 12c. Compos. diagrams | 12a3. Body action |
| | | 12d. Graphs | |
| | | 12e. Conceptual diagrams | |
| Arbitrary modalities ↑ | 13. Sta. graphic | | |
| | 14. Sta.-dyn. acoustic | | |
| | 15. Sta.-dyn. haptic | | |
| | 16. Dyn. graphic | | |
| Explicit structure modalities ↑ | 17. Sta. graphic | | |
| | 18. Sta.-dyn. acoustic | | |
| | 19. Sta.-dyn. haptic | | |
| | 20. Dyn. graphic | | |

not allow showing less compact taxonomy versions but there are clickable versions of several colourful views of the taxonomy at the book's web site.

### 4.2.1 Taxonomy Structure

This section describes the structure of Table 4.2. To read the table, use the legend inside it. To understand it, go to Section 4.2.3 or first read Section 4.2.2 to see about the basics.

The table shows a tree graph with four hierarchical levels, called super level, generic level, atomic level and sub-atomic level, respectively. As we move down-level, modalities become less generic, more specific and generally recognisable as belonging to a multimodal system developer's toolbox.

*Super level.* At the top super level, modalities are classified into four categories: *linguistic modalities*, i.e. ways of representing information based on language; *analogue modalities*, i.e. ways of representing information based on similarities between representation and what is being represented, like images resembling what they are images of; *arbitrary modalities*, i.e. use of something which does not have any specific meaning in advance but is given ad hoc meaning for some purpose, like when highlighting text to be discussed or deleted; and *explicit structure modalities*, i.e. something we insert to mark representational structure, like the line grid in common tables.

*Inheritance.* From the super level, each of the three following levels are generated from its predecessor using a common mechanism, i.e. that of adding distinctions in order to sub-divide the ancestor modality into different, more specific descendant modalities. For instance, the class of super-level analogue modalities is partitioned at generic level into, among other things, graphic, acoustic and haptic modalities, which is the distinction between the three media addressed in the taxonomy. This means that the taxonomy is an inheritance hierarchy, each modality inheriting the properties of its ancestors and having new properties of its own due to the distinctions used to generate it. One consequence is that sub-atomic-level modalities grow quite long and informative "names". Thus, you can verify in the table that the full "name" of 12a2 Gesture is Analogue Dynamic Graphic Image Gesture. The net result is that Table 4.2 shows modalities at different levels of abstraction. This is useful because people think like that. When doing modality analysis, for instance, it is sometimes useful to consider the properties of, say, linguistic modalities in general at super level, and sometimes useful to consider the details of, say, spoken discourse (6a) at atomic level. If a modality node in the tree has daughters, this is marked by "→" in the table.

*Numbering and colour.* Except for the super level, each modality is numbered between 1 and 20. This is because the generic level includes the original 20 different modalities that were generated from basics as described in Section 4.2.2. All modalities at lower levels are first numbered between 1 and 20 according to their generic-level ancestor, and then further distinguished from each other using simple alphanumerics. So if we start from, e.g. generic-level modality 5, we see that it has three daughters, 5a, 5b and 5c, each of which has two daughters at sub-atomic level, 5a1 and 5a2, 5b1 and 5b2 and 5c1 and 5c2, respectively. In this way, 20 numbered modality families have been generated, some comprising four generations and stretching from super level to sub-atomic level.

*Extensibility.* The number of modality family generations shown differs from two to four, counting a super-level ancestor as root. Two-generation families comprise families 1–3 and 13–20; three-generation families 4 and 6–10; and four-generation families 5 and 11–12. Why is that? This is because, apart from the original 20 generic-level modalities, we try to create new distinctions and extend a modality family one level down only when required by developers of usable multimodal systems. In some cases, especially generic-level modalities 1, 2 and 3, we don't believe that there will ever be a need, whereas this might easily be the case for some of modalities 13 through 20. In principle, the taxonomy has unlimited downwards extensibility. For an extension of 12a2, graphics gesture, see Section 15.5.5.

*Different views.* Why aren't the super level modalities numbered? As explained in Section 4.2.2, the backbone of the taxonomy is the generic level, and the super level shown in Table 4.2 is merely one among several possible classifications of the generic-level modalities. So if you prefer to work instead with a modality taxonomy organised by *medium* at super level, there is one at the book's web site. It has a different tree structure compared to the one in Table 4.2 but the contents are the same. A third super-level classification could be in terms of the distinction between static and dynamic modalities.

### 4.2.2  Nerdy Stuff: Origins of the Modality Taxonomy

The scope of the taxonomy is huge, it's "all of meaning" because computing will, or may, come to deal with all of meaning eventually. However, the taxonomy is not into olfactory meaning yet, for instance, and there are other limitations which will become apparent in this section. It is our claim that the taxonomy is exhaustive for modalities in graphics, acoustics and haptics, except that more fine-grained distinctions are due already in some cases, and others will be due as multimodal systems mature.

We now briefly describe the conceptual origins of the taxonomy and the principles of its derivation from those concepts. For more detail, see (Bernsen 2002).

Let's hypothesise that the meaning of physically instantiated information exchanged among humans or between humans and systems belongs to one of the categories shown in Fig. 4.1. The figure says (1) that modality theory currently addresses meaning represented in graphics, acoustics and haptics. (2) A meaning representation is either (a) *standard*, and hence either linguistic, analogue or explicit structures, (b) *arbitrary* or (c) *non-standard*. (3) Non-standard meaning is viewed as a result of applying some function to standard meaning, like the functions used to create metaphorical or metonymic meaning.

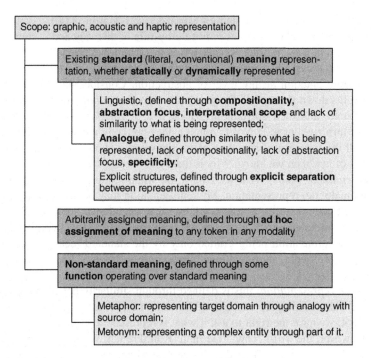

**Fig. 4.1**  Meaning representation tree. Boldface represents basic concepts

We now explain the concepts in Fig. 4.1 in order of appearance. This is uphill all the way, sorry, but central to the theory.

*Standard meaning*: standard meaning is (i) shared meaning in some (sub-)culture. Shared meaning is basic to communicative interaction because it allows us to represent information in some modality so that everyone in our (sub-)culture understands. Second, (ii) standard meaning is opposed to (shared but) *non*-standard meaning as explained below. Words in the vocabulary of some language, for instance, have standard meanings that are explained in dictionaries and thesauri.

*Static/dynamic*: this distinction is *not* defined in physical terms but, rather, as what the recipient of a representation can perceptually inspect for as long as it takes, such as standard GUI output, a blinking icon or an acoustic alarm that must be switched off before it stops – versus items that change beyond the control of the recipient, such as a ringing telephone that may stop ringing any moment. A static representation is one we must do something about to change it, whereas a dynamic representation changes on its own and, if you can make it stop changing and want to, you must do something, such as stopping dynamic text from scrolling across the screen. Thus, "static" includes all that is static in the ordinary sense plus short-term cyclic change which also allows freedom of perceptual inspection.

*Compositionality*: this is a standard concept in linguistic analysis, according to which linguistic meaning can be viewed, by way of approximation, at least, as built rule-by-rule from syntax to semantics (Jurafsky and Martin 2000). For instance, the sentence "Mary loves John" is built rule-by-rule in this way and systematically changes meaning if word order is reversed, as in "John loves Mary".

*Abstraction focus*: abstraction focus is the smart ability of language to focus meaning representation at any level of abstraction. Consider the sentence S: "A woman walks down the stairs". Do you know *who* she is, *how* she looks or walks, *what* the stairs and their surroundings look like or *whether* or not the stairs go straight or turn right or left? No! Language does perfectly meaningful abstractions like this all the time. But if someone paints the woman photo-realistically, or takes a snapshot of her, then we know. Why is that?

*Interpretational scope*: what we tend to do when reading S above is construct our own (analogue) representation. My representation may be different from yours and none of the two are substantiated by what declarative sentence S actually says. This is interpretational scope: we are both free to form our hypotheses about the details, interpretation being limited only by the standard meaning of the sentence. For more about interpretational scope and abstraction focus, see Bernsen (1995).

*Analogue representation*: this is defined through similarity between a representation and what is being represented. A drawing of a cow more or less resembles a cow – if not, we have the right to ask if what is represented in the drawing is really a cow. However, the *word* "cow" (German: Kuh, French: vache, Danish: ko) does not resemble a cow at all. Both drawing and word are representations rather than the real thing – remember Belgian painter Magritte's photo-realistic painting of a pipe titled "This is not a pipe"? He is right, it's not a pipe. The difference is that the painting is an analogue representation whereas the title is non-analogue.

Modality theory also addresses more tenuous analogue relationships than those of photo-realistic images to what they represent, such as between a raw sketch, a bar graph, the click-clicks of a Geiger counter or the acoustic signatures of the sonar, and what each of them represents.

*Specificity*: this is the inverse of interpretational scope: the more specific a representation, the less interpretational scope it offers. Language can conjure up an abstract staircase that is neither straight nor curved, or an unspecified colour, but the real world cannot. Its staircases are straight or curved and their colours specific. The same applies to our sensory imaginations. Analogue representation inherits specificity because it is being used to represent it.

*Explicit separation*: this notion may not look much. It's about what we often do when, e.g. creating tables or matrices, i.e. separating columns and rows using more or less straight lines. This can be useful for separation and grouping purposes, and GUIs, for instance, are replete with explicit structure – in windows having multi-layered explicit structures, in pull-down menus, etc. However, explicit structures are also useful in other modalities, such as when we use a beep to mark when the user can speak in a non-barge-in spoken dialogue system.

*Ad hoc assignment of meaning*: spies always used this trick to avoid that anyone else could understand their communication; kids use it when playing the game of saying "yes" when meaning "no" and vice versa until we flunk it; and we all do it when, e.g. assigning a particular meaning to coloured text. If ad hoc assigned meaning catches on, which is what happens when new phenomena get names in a language, it becomes standard meaning. Like boldface in text: it works like putting a linguistic stereotype next to the text, saying "This is important!"

*Non-standard meaning function*: although we tend not to realise, human communication is shot through with non-standard meaning (Johnson and Lakoff 1980, Lakoff 1987). The reason we tend not to realise is that, e.g. metaphors that began their career as attention-grabbing innovations, die or fade into dead metaphors like the "shoulder" of a mountain or the "head" of a noun phrase. Once dead, it takes a special focus to identify them, words behaving like conventional standard meanings just like most Chinese characters which began their careers as analogue signs. Typologies of non-standard meaning typically view each type as created from standard meaning using some particular function, such as *metaphor* ("He blew the top" – analogy with water cooling failure in a car) or *metonymy* ("The White House issued a statement saying . . ." – using the familiar physical entity of The White House as shortcut for the executive branch of the US government).

Based on those concepts, the generic level of the modality taxonomy was generated as follows: (i) Figure 4.1 introduces, by way of scientific hypothesis, a set of orthogonal distinctions aimed to capture the core of what it is to represent information in the physical media scoped by modality theory, i.e. graphics, acoustics and haptics. (ii) Each of the five distinctions linguistic/non-linguistic, analogue/non-analogue, static/dynamic, arbitrary/non-arbitrary and graphics/acoustics/haptics makes fundamental differences to usability in user–system interaction. (iii) Combining the distinctions yields a matrix of 48 potential modality profiles. (iv) Those that use established meaning arbitrarily are removed because they are incompatible with the purpose of clear presentation of standard meaning; and others with limited current relevance are combined or fusioned in a perfectly reversible way should they be needed later on. The results are the 20 generic-level modalities shown in Table 4.2. Got it? Else look at Bernsen (2002).

The taxonomy itself only addresses standard meaning, it does not account for famous interface metaphors, such as the desktop metaphor (Box 1.2), except as something derived from standard meaning, like a third dimension of Table 4.2. Had the table been 3D, you would have had the desktop metaphor sitting somewhere on an axis perpendicular to analogue static graphic image (9a).

### 4.2.3  Sharpening the Imagination

Using the taxonomy requires (1) understanding its structure (Section 4.2.1), (2) tuning the imagination, (3) understanding the "toolbox modalities" and (4) practice. We postpone practice until Case modality analysis in Section 4.4.5 and focus this section on imagination tuning and a walk-through of the modality taxonomy.

*Imagination*. The comprehensiveness of the taxonomy means that its representation in Table 4.2 is extremely compact. To "open it up", we will exercise the imagination by means of two examples and an exercise. Spatial dimensionality is an important property of graphic and haptic representation. Even acoustic representation (3D sound) can represent the three spatial dimensions (height, length, width). Choice of spatial dimensionality for a particular representation often makes a big difference to the purposes it can be used for. Yet we find no indication of spatial dimensionality in Table 4.2, which means that the taxonomy subsumes all representations in 1D, 2D and 3D. For instance, *analogue static graphic map* (9b) subsumes the 2D example shown in Fig. 4.2 as well as all other static graphic maps, whichever their spatial dimensionality. Of course, we could distinguish dimensions by creating three daughters of 9b at sub-atomic level as 9b1, 9b2 and 9b3, but we haven't. Time, on the other hand, is everywhere in the taxonomy due to the pervasive, user control-based distinction between *static* and *dynamic* representation, cf. the entry in Section 4.2.2. In a second example, the powerful *analogue image* modality is at 9a, 10a, 11a and 12a in Table 4.2. How can that be, given the fact that most of us are inclined to associate the term "image" with a reasonably realistic 2D static graphic picture, such as a photograph? The reason is that images can be either graphic, acoustic or haptic; any of those can be either static or dynamic, sketchy or realistic and both graphic and haptic images can be either 1D, 2D or 3D. If you work this out, you get 28 types of image modality compacted into just four in Table 4.2. Note that, like for spatial dimensionality, the taxonomy does not distinguish between sketchy and realistic representation, so both are covered, and we have to choose the type that best fits our representation purposes.

*Exercise.* As an imagination exercise, (1) try to imagine an example of each of those 28 image modality types. It *can* be done (probably takes some time). (2) For each of them, try to answer the question: might this representation serve a useful purpose in HCI? (3) Now let's try a different angle for which you might have to replace some examples with others: could all these types of image representation have been used, say, 2000 years ago? (4) How many of the 28 types of representation can be rendered on the pages of a book like this one? (5) Modify or

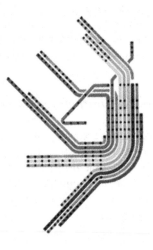

**Fig. 4.2**  Subway map

replace the four acoustic representations to also represent spatial dimensionality in 1D, 2D and 3D, bringing the total number of types to 36. Finally (6), answer Questions (2), (3) and (4) for all of the 12 acoustic modalities you have just generated. Our examples answering Questions (1) through (6) can be found at the book's web site.

## 4.2.4 A Toolbox of Modalities Walk-Through

Let's look at the modality families. Essentially, all modalities in the taxonomy, considered at all levels of abstraction, are potentially useful tools in a modality toolbox. The only probable exceptions are modalities 1, 2 and 3.

*Linguistic modality families 1, 2, 3.* Linguistic modalities are generally highly expressive modalities of key importance to multimodal interaction. Some written languages use signs that have analogue origins, such as Chinese characters and ancient Egyptian hieroglyphs. Moreover, all or most spoken languages include words having analogue origins, like the "slush, slush" we hear when walking through slush. However, these origins are irrelevant to the linguistic nature of modalities (Section 4.2.2), which is why we essentially ignore modalities 1, 2 and 3 in Table 4.2, i.e. the linguistic modalities using analogue signs as marked by "an". This, of course, should not prevent anyone from inventing analogue graphic, acoustic or haptic signs for some game or other purpose (or from killing our claim).

*Linguistic modality family 4.* Arguably, analogue signs are essential to modality 4, i.e. sign language or dynamic graphic language using analogue signs. Like spoken language, sign language is a situated language, primarily meant for use in situations where the interlocutors are co-present and share time, space and environment. The daughters of modality 4 are full-blown sign language (or gestural) discourse (4a), sign language labels/keywords (4b) and sign language notation, respectively. A label or keyword in any type of language is a meaningful expression, like a word or phrase, that's being used stand-alone. A notation is either a formal language or something more loosely defined, such as a somehow organised or restricted set of expressions developed for some purpose. The many sign languages in existence have been primarily developed for the hard-of-hearing and deaf-mute who can see. Work is ongoing to build increasingly powerful sign language understanding and generation systems, and it is already possible to understand and generate sign language labels/keywords and simple notations, as in our Treasure Hunt Case.

*Linguistic modality families 5, 6, 7, 8.* In addition to graphic sign language (4), the linguistic toolbox modalities are essentially static written language (5), spoken language (6), haptic language (7) and dynamic graphic language (8) that includes two very different families: dynamic graphic written language (8a–c), which is simply graphic written language represented dynamically, and visibly perceived spoken language (8d–f). We are all familiar with spoken language as perceived visually ("lip reading") and aurally, and with static and dynamic written language. Specialised haptic language has been developed for the visually impaired and there are haptic languages for communication with people who are both blind and deaf-mute. Like graphic sign language (4), spoken language, whether audio-only, visual-only or audiovisual, is a situated language, whereas written language and haptic languages like Braille are situation-independent languages developed for linguistic communication whose interlocutors do not share space, time and environment. There are important differences between situated and situation-independent linguistic representation, and we all sense the differences when engaging in communication using the many hybrids created by technology, from using telephone and voice messages over video-conferencing to instant messaging, on-line chat and SMS.

At atomic level, modalities 5 through 8 are expanded into (i) written text or discourse, (ii) labels/keywords and (iii) notation. Static graphic written language is expanded further at sub-atomic level into hand-written and typed varieties of text, labels/keywords and notation.

Among linguistic modalities 5 through 8 and their offspring – which, do you think, are currently and in future the most common in two-way human–computer communication (Fig. 3.3)? We have no objective figures, but ranking possible answers is interesting and useful as a way of getting a better understanding of the linguistic modalities and their multimodal combinations.

If we start from the least common modalities, the dynamic written language parts of modality 8 (8a–c), including scrolling language and other lively ways of presenting text, labels/keywords and notation, only appear usable for special reading purposes or by special users. From here on, however, estimation and prediction get much harder.

Although visual speech (8d–e) seems to have little use stand-alone, it has lots of uses in various multimodal combinations, such as for teaching lip reading, as part of sign language (4) which is, in fact, not pure gesture but includes elements of visual speech as well, and as part of audiovisual speech (6a–c + 8d–e). Audiovisual speech output is beginning to appear downstream from research not just in games but also at commercial web sites, to support hearing by the mildly hearing impaired or in noisy conditions, and in spoken dialogue applications. Audiovisual speech output may be all over the place in 5–10 years, whereas audiovisual speech input understanding is still mainly a research topic. Spoken language (6) is a proper part of multimodal audiovisual speech and has been around much longer. Text-to-speech synthesis has become quite good in some of the world's most spoken languages and is being used for many different output purposes just like pre-recorded speech still is. Spoken input is still more widespread than audiovisual speech input and is being used in a growing number of unimodal and multimodal spoken dialogue systems.

Haptic language (7) has many uses in all its varieties (7a–c), such as for the hard-of-seeing who master Braille. The problem of having to print the output to read it may be solved by the appearance of affordable dynamic Braille output touch pads. However, many hard-of-seeing do not master Braille, and there may be growing competition from acoustic speech-to-text input and text-to-speech output. But the real reason why haptic language is so widespread is that most people use it as input when typing on the keyboard and clicking with the mouse in the GUI environment.

Mouse clicking is, in fact, haptic notation (7c) input. The only reason we put up with it is that the mouse code is simple and relatively easy to learn. It is no problem to fully replace the keyboard by mouse-operated, extended Morse code but the learning challenge this would pose would be ghastly, not to speak of the time it would take to write a piece of text.

Finally, the classical GUI variety, static graphic written language (6) output still dominates the many other ways of representing linguistic system output. It is being used all over the place for representing text, labels/keywords and notation. For usability (legibility) reasons, among others, the typed varieties (5a1, 5b1, 5c1) dominate their hand-written cousins (5a2, 5b2, 5c2). In GUI-based linguistic interaction, we are most of the time being guided by output labels/keywords on menus and elsewhere, and primarily meet output written text in error messages or when trying to make sense of some help system.

*Analogue modality families 9, 10, 11, 12.* The analogue modality families have parallel structures at generic and atomic levels. At generic level, Table 4.2 separates the static (9) and dynamic (12) analogue graphic modalities and fusions static and dynamic analogue acoustics (10) and haptics (11). At atomic level, these all have five daughters, i.e. images (9a, 10a, 11a, 12a), maps (9b, 10b, 11b, 12b), compositional diagrams (9c, 10c, 11c, 12c), graphs (9d, 10d, 11d, 12d) and conceptual diagrams (9e, 10e, 11e, 12e). Haptic image (11a) and dynamic graphic image (12a) are extended to sub-atomic level, haptic image to haptic gesture (11a1) and haptic body action (11a2), dynamic graphic image to dynamic graphic facial expression (12a1), dynamic graphic gesture (12a2) and dynamic graphic body action (12a3). Let us first look at analogue representation at atomic level.

An *image* represents the perceptual appearance of something in any spatial dimensionality, in time or timelessly, sketchily or realistically. A *map* is, in fact, a special type of compositional diagram, but since the concept is so familiar, we have kept maps at atomic level rather than as a daughter of compositional diagram. A *compositional diagram* is an "analytic image", that is, an image which somehow takes the perceptual appearance of something apart. This may be done literally, like in the static graphic compositional diagram of an "exploded" wheelbarrow we find in the leaflet accompanying our brand new plastic-wrapped wheelbarrow, ready for assembly using the diagram as guide – or it may just be by naming various parts. To do its analytical job, the compositional diagram is typically at least bi-modal. Thus, if the compositional diagram is in static graphics, it would typically show an image of something, whether exploded or whole, and use labels/keywords to name various parts. The subway map in Fig. 4.2 is, in fact (maps being a kind of compositional diagram), the unimodal half of a subway compositional diagram complete with station names for the little black dots. A *graph* is a representation of quantitative data using spatial and temporal means of representation – or information channels, see Section 4.2.5. Finally, a *conceptual diagram* represents conceptual relationships using spatial and temporal means of representation, such as the AMITUDE "wheel" in Fig. 3.1.

Among those five types, images are central in at least four ways. First, the image modality is huge because there can be images of everything existing or imaginable in graphics, acoustics or haptics, and computers may eventually be able to understand and generate all of it. Second, the four other modalities are based on image elements, in opposite ways: in graphs and conceptual diagrams, we add image elements to render quantities and abstract concepts more comprehensible. In maps and compositional diagrams, we typically subtract image elements, or make images more sketchy and less realistic, to focus the information rendered. Third, while maps and other compositional diagrams, graphs and conceptual diagrams are human-made artefacts created to serve specific representation purposes, this is not necessarily the case for images. Fourth, images are less tied to language than maps and other compositional diagrams, and these are less tied to language than graphs and conceptual diagrams. In other words, many unimodal images make sense (and often many different senses) on their own, some compositional diagrams do, but hardly any graphs and conceptual diagrams do; and if a representation does not make sense without some kind of linguistic labelling or annotation, this representation is at least bimodal.

*Analogue graphics 9, 12.* We are thoroughly familiar with the classical, analogue static graphic varieties of images, maps, compositional diagrams, graphs – like bar graphs, pie graphs, line graphs, scatter plots – and conceptual diagrams, but it is worth remembering that there is a long history of invention and huge literatures behind the more or less usable forms we see every day in the media. Their analogue dynamic graphic cousins are much younger, however, and typically consist of video or creative animated output, showing, e.g. a young face morphing into an old one (image), a road growing on a static map (map), a diagrammatic car assembling itself from parts (compositional diagrams), bars growing and diminishing with time (graphs) or even conceptual trees growing from the root (conceptual diagrams). Static and dynamic image icons are common at the GUI interface.

*Analogue acoustics 10.* When leaving analogue graphics to turn to analogue acoustic modalities, things get less familiar to those of us who do not work in acoustics. We are familiar with acoustic image earcons and generally with acoustic images. Think about an acoustic image of a car engine running. If we somehow add linguistic annotation and maybe filter out irrelevant noise, we have an acoustic compositional diagram that could be used to train novice mechanics in engine fault diagnosis. An acoustic map might represent bird song typical of different parts of a country. It is easy to imagine many different uses of acoustic graphs (or data acoustics) that map data quantities into acoustic representations of, e.g. frequency or intensity. Film often uses acoustics – musical genre, rhythm, intensity, pitch – to reflect danger level, emotional intensity or emotional valence (positive vs. negative). Acoustic conceptual diagrams could be made using pauses and 3D sound; or think about the song by Tom Lehrer that has the periodic system as text.

*Analogue haptics 11.* Analogue haptic images, maps, compositional diagrams, graphs and conceptual diagrams all exist for use by the hard-of-seeing and others. These representations used to be mostly "flat 3D", sit in clumsy cardboard books, and made from materials with different texture to facilitate haptic exploration. However, 1D, 2D and 3D analogue haptic representations are emerging as computer output, as in our Treasure Hunt Case. Hapticons, i.e. little haptic output images corresponding to icons and earcons, exist. Analogue haptic output could have numerable uses for all users, such as enabling us to feel the fabric of a piece of cloth from its haptic image before purchasing clothes made from it over the Internet. System haptic input perception remains primitive.

*Arbitrary modalities 13, 14, 15, 16.* Arbitrary modalities can be used stand-alone or as part of other representations. Acoustic, haptic and graphic alerts and alarm signals are typical stand-alone uses whose point is to be effective in grabbing people's attention. A typical use as part of another representation is when we want to mark some part of a representation in any modality and medium for some purpose. In, e.g. static graphic Table 17.3, the use of shading in every second row serves the purpose of distinguishing between subjects in two different experimental conditions. There is nothing that connects the shading with this purpose, so its use is strictly arbitrary.

Some important guidelines for using arbitrary modalities are the following:

- Make sure that target users can easily perceive the arbitrary modality and distinguish it from everything else.
- Always explain what the modality means or does. Since it is arbitrary, this may not be evident and may even be difficult to guess. If not explained, the recipients of the representation may get it all wrong.
- Never use representations that have meaning already for arbitrary purposes. The likely result is confusion and error. It is hard to explain to people why, e.g. one chose the words "Stop the game" to start the game.

The main cost of using an arbitrary modality is the need to explain its meaning to those exposed to it. It is preferable, but not always possible or practical, to use a meaningful representation instead. Yet arbitrary representations sometimes manage to catch on and transform into representations with standard meanings, like the traffic light colours that mean something like "Go", "Prepare to stop or go" and "Stop". It might be argued that the red colour, in particular, is non-arbitrary and well chosen because red suggests danger in some cultures. This is true and important. The taxonomy addresses literal meaning only (Section 4.2.2) and the colour red does not literally *mean* danger, it's *associated* with danger but also with passion and probably much else in various cultures. However, it is good development practice to take non-literal meaning into account when designing representations.

*Explicit structure modalities 17, 18, 19, 20.* Across media, explicit structures may be illustrated by the horizontal and vertical lines in common tables (graphics output), the input listening area marked as a GUI button on a touch screen (graphics output, haptic input) or the pause in speech (acoustic input and output). Essentially, the meaning of an explicit structure is to mark separation of different entities and, by implication, to group similar entities.

*Modalities for situated natural communication 4, 6, 8d–f, 11a1–2, 12a1–3.* Situated natural human–system communication has a special role in multimodal systems and systems blending with people (Section 1.4.4), so it is useful to look at its constituent modalities at the end of this walk-through. There are actually two main varieties but they share a number of modalities. The first includes sign language (4), elements of visual speech (8d–f), analogue haptic gesture and body action (11a1–2) and analogue dynamic facial expression, gesture and body action (12a1–3). The second includes spoken language (6), visual speech (8d–f), analogue haptic gesture and body action (11a1–2) and analogue dynamic graphics facial expression, gesture and body action (12a1–3). We focus on the second multimodal combination in this book and refer readers interested in the first to the sign language literature.

If we want our system to generate or perceive part or whole of the communication acts of situated spoken conversation (Section 3.6.2), we must do usability development with some or all of these modalities: spoken language, visual speech, analogue haptic gesture and body action and analogue dynamic graphics facial expression, gesture and body action, either as input, output or both. There is a lot of research still to be done in this huge area, and it may appear early to even mention the need for a theory of complete natural communication acts. However, it's already possible to build such systems, and we consider their development an important part of future multimodal usability work. The only point we wish to make at this stage is that this kind of development involves a form of data handling unfamiliar to classical usability work. We call this data *micro-behaviour data* because we handle data on the actual physical behaviours of people when they, e.g. speak a particular phrase in a particular language with a particular accent, slap someone on the back or look concerned. We discuss micro-behaviour modalities in more detail in connection with data annotation in Chapter 15.

### *4.2.5 Information Channels*

Since a modality is a way of representing information in some medium, the medium acts as perceived physical substrate for all ways of representing information in it. Different media are different physical substrates: *haptic* representation has to do with force, hardness, texture, malleability, adhesiveness, liquidity, temperature, position, shape, size, dimensionality, spatial order, distance and orientation; and, when dynamic, with time of occurrence, velocity, duration or rhythm; *acoustic* representation with time of occurrence, pitch, intensity, duration, timbre, rhythm, temporal order and distance; *graphic* representation with position, shape, size, texture, colour, dimensionality, spatial order, distance and orientation, time of occurrence, velocity, duration and rhythm.

In this way we can describe each medium in terms of a set of elementary properties from which any representation in that medium is constructed. We call these properties information channels. No matter which modalities we distinguish in the graphics medium, for instance, these are all built from this medium's finite inventory of information channels. We can use colour to build graphic representations but not acoustic or haptic ones; colour has hue but cannot have timbre, whereas tones can have timbre but not hue; and force, although universal in physics, is only really relevant to haptic representation. Some information channels are cross-media: if you touch, look at, and listen to an anvil that's being hammered upon, you have truly multimodal access to the hammering rhythm: haptically, acoustically and graphically. In principle, within a particular medium, each modality must be perceptibly different from the others, but it is not always possible to tell the difference in an instant or when considering a single modality instance. It may take time to decide if a representation is static or dynamic; a speech sound in a foreign language may be mistaken for non-speech; and a schematic static graphic image may be part of an analogue sign language or "just" an image.

Information channels form the subject of multiple sciences and crafts, and some of the more applied among these already face usability issues at information channel level. Graphical design, for instance, has a discipline that creates readable things, such as new fonts and font styles. From there, it only takes a couple of steps upwards from elementary information channels through composite channels to work on the modalities in Table 4.2, such as work on data representation, diagrammatic representation or image representation, and this holds across our three media. Moreover, it holds for both input and output, so if acoustics design, for instance, is about output, or information presentation, signal processing is about recognising information channels and the modalities built from them.

We will not go into detail with information channels but focus on two points. The first is that modality analysis must occasionally descend to the level of detail of information channels. For instance, arbitrary modalities are often chosen from information channels, as when assigning different meanings to different colours or sounds. Or, an information channel may represent a variable to be modified to fit a particular user group, such as when doubling the speed of text-to-speech compared to standard speech in order to fit blind users, or replacing red and green to fit red-green colour blind people.

The second point is that natural human–system communication and blending with people requires developers to work on how, e.g. face and body use their information channels to express various kinds of information. These areas are far from being fully charted, and there are no design professions nor mature signal processing solutions. We discuss these issues in Section 15.5.5.

## 4.3  Practical Use of Modalities

In this section and in Section 4.4, we ask how knowledge about modalities can benefit practical work on multimodal usability. We need to do modality analysis of our Cases at some point and want to get as much support as we can.

In the following, Section 4.3.1 illustrates modality description based on the modality taxonomy in Table 4.2. Section 4.3.2 introduces modality properties as a handle on the complexity of reasoning about modalities and usability.

### 4.3.1 Modality Description: The Classical Multimodal GUI

A first use of modality theory in multimodal usability work is to enable succinct description of candidate modalities. Modality description based on the theory buys us three things: (1) A toolbox. The toolbox described in Section 4.2.4 shows which modalities there are to choose from and does not overlook any options, at least not as long as the toolbox is reasonably state-of-the-art complete. (2) Succinct description of the candidate multimodal input/output combinations we are considering. Precise description is also important in multimodal systems evaluation. (3) Conceptual hooks for collecting more usability information before making a decision. Everything else to do with modalities, multimodality and their usability builds upon the taxonomy and uses its formal terms or, preferably, toolbox terms. In this way, we can add knowledge on top of what we already have without getting lost.

As an example, let's do a modality description of classical (WIMP) GUI interaction. Since this involves all-haptic input and all-graphics output, interaction must be multimodal – it's even multimedia.

*GUI input*. There are two different generic-level haptic input modalities, cf. Table 4.2 to which numbers refer in the following.

The first generic-level modality is haptic language (7), most users inputting haptic text, labels/keywords and notation (7a, 7b, 7c) via some sort of keyboard and pointing device button. We typically type text for writing some kind of prose, including SMS jargon, type labels/keywords as part of form-filling and search, as well as when pressing the more informatively labelled (by means of words, abbreviated words, special characters and possibly image icons) keyboard function keys, and use notation when clicking the mouse button(s) or using key combinations. If a function key only has a number, this is an arbitrary modality (15). This means that, to interact using a classical GUI-based system, users must learn the meaning of a number of arbitrary modalities, mouse-click notation, what happens when hitting scores of labelled keywords and several key combination notations.

The second haptic input modality is analogue haptics (11) and, more specifically, 2D pointing gesture (11a1) which is used for navigation in the graphics output domain, putting the cursor where we want it by manipulating a pointing device. If you are wondering why the haptic text input above is not classified in the taxonomy as typed text (5a1), remember that modality family 5 is one of *graphics*. Graphic typed text input is something like showing a document to a system which looks at it, scans it in or even reads it.

*GUI output*. Classical GUI output is not only all-graphics, it's virtually all-static graphics (5, 9, 13, 17), even if the cursor keeps blinking. Assuming a screen, keyboard and mouse setup, the user will find static graphics in two places: on the screen and on the keyboard. The mouse is typically a black box. The screen holds the desktop (9a gone metaphorical) with labelled (5b) icons (9a) on it. Clicking on a standard application icon opens a window, which is a nested explicit structure (17), typically equipped with rows of labels/keywords (5b), unlabelled icons (9a), maybe some rare typed text (5a1), some boxy menu and text fields, scroll bars, etc. (17) and empty workspace (17). Colours are standard for the product range, and they, too, mean something, such as whether the window is active or not. Colours are thus arbitrary modalities (13). Open a couple of applications more, and you will see all descendants of the generic-level static graphics modalities in the taxonomy (5, 9, 13, 17), even hand-written notation (5c2). In fact, the scroll bar may be dynamic from time to time (20) when adapting to the amount of text present, and so may the text in the workspace if scrolled, but the latter is a case of pseudo-dynamic text because you hold the controls and can make it static at any time. The keyboard holds typed labels/keywords (5b1), including the little arrows and stuff which act as labels/keywords, some unlabelled icons (9a) and some arbitrary static graphics (13), such as function key numbers. The visible and tangible boundaries between keys serve as explicit structures in static graphics (17) and haptics (19), respectively.

Who said the standard GUI is not multimodal (Section 4.1.1)? In fact, multimodal interaction is older than the GUI and the computer. We do a small evaluation of the classical GUI in the next section.

### 4.3.2 Modality Properties

Can knowledge about modalities do more for modality analysis? We want to know about two topics: (1) how good is a candidate modality for its intended interactive role? And (2) how well does a candidate work with the other modality candidates we are considering? We look at (1) in this section and postpone (2) until Section 4.4.2.

A central part of work on modality theory is to analyse each modality in order to generate knowledge for usability development. We explored various approaches to this problem until the mid-1990s, always coming up short because of the complexity involved. It was only when discovering *modality properties* that we may have found a handle on complexity.

Each modality has a number of modality properties that follow from its nature. Suppose you do an empirical CoMeDa study and find that, when other people were present who were not involved in the interaction, and even turned their backs on it, they were distracted by the speech used for interaction with your system. Why is that? You think about it and find an important reason, i.e. that *speech is omnidirectional*. Then you notice from the video recordings that many non-speech sounds were as loud as what was spoken during interaction, yet the sounds didn't seem to distract anyone. On a hunch you consult the speech literature and end up concluding that the *speech was much more salient*, or intrusive, to the bystanders *than the non-speech*. The two italicised sentences above express, or reflect, modality properties of speech. In fact, the taxonomy (Table 4.2) makes it clear that the first of those modality properties is far more general: it is not only a property of speech but of all modalities in the acoustic medium.

From the point of view of AMITUDE analysis, modality properties have some interesting properties. First (1), they are straightforward to apply. What we do is consult the emerging AMITUDE analysis and check if acoustic input or output, or speech input or output, are candidate modalities. If any of them are, we check with our analysis of the other AMITUDE aspects if the sound, being omnidirectional, or the speech, being extremely salient, might cause problems. If they might, we better find out if they actually will, or we remove the risk in some other way. For instance, if we select an open space in an airport waiting area for playing Sudoku (Section 2.1), will waiting passengers be unduly disturbed by the gameplay? If we don't know, we might either make a field experiment in the airport to find out or we remove gameplay from the parts of the waiting areas where there is a risk.

This illustrates (2) that modality properties are predictive within limits: they can predict that there *may* be, or definitely *will* be, a problem that must be addressed, that choice of a particular modality will, or may, solve a problem that would otherwise exist, etc.

Third (3), modality properties are neutral. They express facts about modalities and do not pass any value judgment nor offer any specific advice. Thus, the omnidirectionality of acoustics may be negative when bystanders are being disturbed, but positive when a user who needs to move around at work can talk to the system without having to sit in front of it.

Fourth (4), modality properties are unconditional, they express rock-bottom science of modalities without any if's limiting their scope. This property made us wonder how powerful modality properties are in terms of scope because, obviously, it makes all the difference between *usable by most* and *nerdy specialty* whether usability developers need to access 100 or 10,000 modality properties. In the speech functionality study mentioned in Section 3.1.2, and in a follow-up study that looked at a cross-section of the literature on speech and multimodal interaction 1993–1998 (Bernsen and Dybkjær 1999a, b), we analysed a total of 273 claims made by researchers and developers about what particular modalities were suited or unsuited for. It turned out that +95% of those claims could be evaluated, and either justified, supported, found to have problems or rejected, by reference to just 25 modality properties. These are exemplified in Table 4.3. Moreover, even though speech in various multimodal combinations was the subject of rather few claims in the first study which evaluated 120 claims, and there were many more claims about speech in multimodal combinations among the 153 claims analysed in the second study, the number of modality properties used in evaluation only went up from 18 in the first study to 25 in the second study.

Of course, we might still need, e.g. ten times as many, that is, 250 modality properties to be reasonably well prepared for tackling common issues of modality choice for unimodal and multimodal systems, but given the size of the compact modality taxonomy itself, that's still a usable-by-most number.

So, refer to modality properties when doing modality analysis! Essentially, you will be addressing one or both of these questions:

- Is modality M1 useful and usable in the current AMITUDE context?
- Is M1 better than alternative modalities M2 ... Mn in the AMITUDE context?

**Table 4.3**  Modality properties, some examples. I means input, O means output

| No. | Modality | Modality property |
|-----|----------|-------------------|
| MP1 | Linguistic I/O | Linguistic I/O modalities have interpretational scope. They are therefore unsuited for specifying detailed information on spatial manipulation |
| MP3 | Arbitrary I/O | Arbitrary I/O modalities impose a learning overhead which increases with the number of arbitrary items to be learned |
| MP4 | Acoustic I/O | Acoustic I/O modalities are omnidirectional |
| MP5 | Acoustic I/O | Acoustic I/O modalities do not require limb (including haptic) or visual activity |
| MP6 | Acoustic O | Acoustic O modalities can be used to achieve saliency in low-acoustic environments |
| MP7 | Static graphics | Static graphic modalities allow the simultaneous representation of large amounts of information for free visual inspection |
| MP8 | Dynamic O | Dynamic O modalities, being temporal (serial and transient), do not offer the cognitive advantages (with respect to attention and memory) of freedom of perceptual inspection |
| MP11 | Speech I/O | Speech I/O modalities in native or known languages have very high saliency |
| MP15 | Discourse O | Discourse O modalities have strong rhetorical potential |
| MP16 | Discourse I/O | Discourse I/O modalities are situation-dependent |
| MP17 | Spontaneous spoken labels/keywords and discourse I/O | Spontaneous spoken labels/keywords and discourse I/O modalities are natural for humans in the sense that they are learnt from early on (by most people). Note that spontaneous keywords must be distinguished from designer-designed keywords which are not necessarily natural to the actual users |
| MP18 | Notation I/O | Notation I/O modalities impose a learning overhead that increases with the number of items to be learned |

As always, there might be helpful information in the literature about systems using similar modality combinations. However, unless we think in terms of modality properties when studying this information, all we may extract from it are lengthy and irrelevant conditionals. Let's express one of those on AMITUDE form, each parenthesis referring to AMITUDE aspect properties mentioned in this book or elsewhere: *If* A is (aa ... an), M is (ma ... mo), I is (ia ... ip), T is (ta ... tq), U is (ua ... ur), D is (da ... ds) and E is (ea ... et) *then* mb (modality b) might give a problem with x (could be almost anything). The chances that any such conditional, or multimodal design rule, would fit our AMITUDE analysis are slim indeed because the number of conditionals needed to cover multimodal systems is astronomical. At best, this rule-based approach is feasible for a minute fraction of all possible modalities and applications at a time, such as the tiny universe of spoken in-car navigation systems. Even then, this would be hard to do. That's why we have been looking for relatively small numbers somewhere.

Based on the modality properties illustrated in Table 4.3, we developed a usability development support tool called SMALTO (Speech Modality Auxiliary Tool)

(Luz and Bernsen 1999). SMALTO is a dynamic hypertext system which, in addition to a tutorial introduction to the tool and its basis in modality theory, includes a searchable database of claims about speech and multimodality. More recently, Sutcliffe et al. (2006) describe a multimedia design assistant tool that applies modality properties as well as aesthetic and other information as guidelines for media selection and design for attractiveness. The user test reported reveals a difficulty typical of early versions of theory-based development support tools, i.e. that most users had various difficulties mastering the concepts used in the tool.

*Exercise.* As an exercise in modality property thinking, let's see what the 12 modality properties in Table 4.3 can say about the classical GUI described in Section 4.3.1. Take a look at them and find out which ones are directly relevant to GUI evaluation. Which ones did you identify? What are their implications for GUIs?

We found four main properties: MPs 3, 7, 17 and 18. MP7 describes one of the main strengths of GUIs, i.e. that their static graphics output can display large amounts of complex information, available at all times for inspection and decision making. The main limitation on how much static information it is possible to represent is the combined size of the surfaces used to represent the information, such as the keyboard and screen of a standard mobile phone or desktop PC.

MPs 3, 17 and 18, on the other hand, expose some of the standard GUI's major usability problems.

MP3 raises the problem of learning what, e.g. 10–15 arbitrary keyboard function key numbers refer to. If users don't learn, they won't use the function keys, and we strongly suspect that most users don't use the keys much, just as we suspect that many users are oblivious to the colours indicating whether a window is active or not. In other words, arbitrary modalities tend to breed uncertainty, confusion and, ultimately, unused functionality. Do you know what happens if you press the right Shift key for more than 8 seconds on a Windows XP computer?

MP17, although about speech input/output, says that designer-designed keywords are not necessarily natural to users. Such keywords abound in GUI menus and on GUI buttons, and it is a thoroughly established fact that different people understand the words used in widely different ways. This again breeds uncertainty, confusion and, ultimately, unused functionality.

MP18 essentially says that notation is for specialists: it's not part of the natural language we read and speak; it requires special training; and we forget if we use notation infrequently. GUIs are shot through with notation "systems" for mouse clicking, use of key combinations and mode-menu combinations, but it is hard to find information on them, and the system does not train users in them. Once more, this breeds uncertainty, confusion and, ultimately, unused functionality.

Summarising, the four MPs show that the classical GUI, when used with many standard applications marketed for everyone, such as word processors, is for trained specialists and frequent use only. If we want to use the classical GUI for systems for a wider and less specialist user population, or for infrequent use, we must reduce the diversity of uses of mouse, keyboard, display output labels, notation and arbitrary modalities to the bare minimum and make this completely clear to users. Roughly, the less standard GUI functionality we retain, the more usable the system, like in the Google search interface or iPhone's 2D haptic input.

It is ironic to see how the dream of HCI in the 1980s, of solving the usability problems of GUI-based systems for ordinary users (Section 1.4.3), has failed miserably for large stand-alone applications, web sites and mobile applications. This does not mean that there has been a total lack of usability progress in GUI-based systems. It means that there are still plenty of usability problems for ordinary users faced with the majority of applications.

## 4.4  Multimodal Representation

Having studied individual modalities in Sections 4.2 and 4.3, it is time to look into relationships among modalities and how modalities can be combined to enable usable multimodal interaction. Multimodal interaction is not new: GUIs are multimodal, human–system interaction was always multimodal, even pre-computer age human–machine interaction was multimodal. Non-GUI-based and enhanced-GUI multimodal interaction has come to the forefront today because of the huge interactive potential of modalities that GUIs don't use at all, notably most input and output acoustic and haptic modalities, and all graphics *input* modalities. The sheer size of this potential poses an important problem. A lot is known about the classical GUI modalities and how they work together (cf. Section 4.3). However, even with the heavily condensed modality toolbox in Table 4.2, possible modality combinations run into millions of unimodal, bi-modal, tri-modal . . . 10-modal . . ., representations. As it is impractical to study modality relationships in each and every one of them, the problem is how to provide some useful handles – theoretical, experience-based or otherwise – on how to analyse any one amongst those millions of new multimodal combinations.

We address the problem from four angles. Section 4.4.1 introduces the notion of modality aptitude and proposes two rules – with variations – for how to select candidate modalities for an application in situations where different modality candidates are available. Section 4.4.2 describes seven common relationships between candidate modalities, which may be useful to consider during modality analysis. Section 4.4.3 lists a selection of stand-alone modality combinations of established usability with large groups of ordinary people and non-specialist users. Nerdy Section 4.4.4 confronts two opposing assumptions about modality combination: (a) that each new modality combination is a unique, non-analysable whole and (b) that the construction of multimodal representation from unimodal modalities is susceptible of analysis and prediction based on knowledge of the constituent modalities. At this point, we are finally in a position to do modality analysis of this book's Cases (Section 4.4.5).

### 4.4.1  How to Choose Modality Candidates, Modality Aptitude

A typical situation in AMITUDE analysis is that, as we accumulate information and make decisions about AITUDE (AMITUDE without Modalities) aspects, we gather constraints on which modalities to use and on the information to be exchanged between user and system. At some point we start identifying candidate modalities and try to work out which among them are most usable in context. This is when we meet the two following requirements to candidate modalities, which are necessary but not sufficient for making our modality choice optimally usable. Jointly, the candidate modalities must

1. be able to express the information to be exchanged between user and system;
2. express the information as aptly as possible.

Point (1) is pretty evident given the fact that different modalities often, but not always, have different expressiveness and hence can express different classes of information. Moreover, some modalities have high expressiveness, such as text, discourse and images, whereas others have low expressiveness, such as explicit structures or pointing gestures.

It makes little sense to choose modalities: (1a) for expressing information they cannot express; (1b) for expressing information that does not have to be expressed; or (1c) which cannot jointly express all the information that must be exchanged. So we don't choose explicit structure candidates for expressing a user's heart rate or blood pressure (1a), or images for expressing logical operators (1a). We don't choose compositional diagram candidates if we have no job for them (1b). But we do add a modality if the candidates listed already are not up to representing all the information we need them to represent (1c).

Points 1a, 1b and 1c above are the easier part of choosing modality candidates. Why? Because these points are based on whether or not a modality can represent some type of information *at all*. That's what makes those points evident but also unrealistic. In practical development, we have to take another crucial point into consideration, namely, that a modality can represent the information we want to present more or less well. This is what Point (2) is about.

We often have several modalities available that can express the information we wish expressed. For instance, all text modalities can express the same information no matter if they are static or dynamic, graphic or haptic (Table 4.2), or even acoustic, as in read-aloud text. However, modalities are not always equally *apt* at expressing what needs to be expressed. Some examples are the following: maps have developed to express certain kinds of spatial–geographical information as usefully and useably as possible; images have developed to express the perceptual appearance of things as usefully and useably as possible; mathematical notation has developed to express mathematical relationships as usefully and useably as possible; graphs have developed to express relationships among quantities as usefully and useably as possible. Let's say that those modalities are apt at expressing those particular kinds of information, i.e. (i) they can express the information; (ii) they do so usefully and useably overall; and (iii) they are the most useful and useable around for their respective purposes. Aptitude, in other words, refers to *apt pairs* consisting of a modality and a certain type of information to be expressed and is often the result of "natural (read: historical) selection" between competing representations in the same or different modalities. We cannot go into historical background here but, as an example, take a look at the wonderful literature on data graphics usability and its development from the 17th century (Tufte 1983, Bertin 1983).

Sometimes it is easy to choose between two candidates, both of which *can* express the information to be represented but one of which is far more apt than the other. Suppose that we succeed in exactly translating an apt photo-realistic image of a person into a multi-page text description from which the image can be reconstructed 100% (computers do it all the time). A picture is worth more than a thousand words, right? Still, the image is far more apt than the text for showing how the person looks. Grandparents wouldn't replace the photograph of their grand-daughter on the wall by a bunch of text pages. This is an extreme case, to be sure, because it shows information equivalence but hugely different aptitude. In many other cases, our choice is between modalities which can express the information more or less aptly but with no huge difference. For more on aptitude of individual modalities, see the book's web site.

In addition to apt individual modalities, there are many apt bi-modal, tri-modal, etc. combinations, such as static graphic text and images, graphs with labels/keywords and text explaining them. See also the paradigm list in Section 4.4.3. Thus,

2.1 unless other factors count against it, choose apt candidate modalities, if any exist, for expressing information to be exchanged between user and system.

*Sometimes several modalities are equally apt.* For instance, static graphic text, static haptic text and text-to-speech are, more or less, equally apt for expressing, say, a piece of story-telling. Then we look for other reasons for selecting between them, or we enable several of them.

*Sometimes a modality is apt on external conditions.* For instance, spoken output may be generally apt but the noise level may sometimes make hearing a bit difficult. A possible solution is to add a talking face to the spoken output, whose voice-mouth synchrony would help ensure correct recognition by users in all possible situations. In itself, the visual speech is less apt than the acoustic speech, but together they outperform visual and acoustic speech alone. Another solution is to offer text output for when the spoken output becomes hard to use. Thus:

2.2 if a modality is conditionally apt, either try to replace it with an uncondition-ally apt one or complement the modality with another, equally apt or less apt modality for which the condition is irrelevant.

*Sometimes there are no apt modalities.* A typical case is when the information to be represented is new or non-standard. Then we have to be as creative as we can, inventing, e.g. a new notation or a new hapticon, or choosing arbitrary modal-ities that are easier to remember than others because supported by an amount of metaphorical sense – like choosing green to mark the most healthy items on a food menu. Our inventions may not be all that apt, of course, but we do our best.

*Sometimes apt modalities cannot be used for one reason or another*. This is a large and important class of cases. Here are some example types:

- *User disabilities*. E.g. (1) Haptic text input via keyboard is apt but user's limbs are paralysed, so we choose eye gaze graphic text input. The user inputs text by fixating the gaze on a single letter at a time. (2) Spoken newspaper for the blind.
- *Lack of sources and resources*. E.g. a photo-realistic image of the suspect is apt but we only have an eyewitness description and cannot afford production of a phantom image, so we choose to circulate the description.
- *Technical limitations and unavailability*. E.g. high-resolution haptic output imagery via hapxels (haptic points analogous to pixels) (Mussio et al. 2001) would be apt but the technology isn't quite there yet.
- *Not enough output real estate available* on screen and keyboard. E.g. static text is apt for describing button functionality but we choose labels/keywords and/or image icons instead (cf. Section 4.3).
- *Challenge the users*. E.g. output spoken keywords are more apt but we want to make the game harder by forcing users to learn and remember arbitrary sounds.

We hypothesise that all AMITUDE aspects, as well as several other factors, such as the lack of sources and resources and the technical limitations mentioned in the list above, may enforce choice of less apt modalities. Moreover, as shown in the last example, developers might attempt to make games more challenging by favouring less apt modalities. The crucial point to be aware of is that choosing less apt modalities always puts an additional burden on the users, so:

2.3  if an apt modality cannot be used, look carefully for equally apt alternatives before choosing less apt ones. When choosing less apt candidate modalities, be particularly careful and creative in making them as usable as possible.

So far, we have addressed parsimonious modality candidate reasoning aimed to make sure that we have enough modalities for expressing the information to be expressed and that these modalities are as apt as possible. However, there are plenty of reasons why we might want to express, at least, part of the information to be exchanged in user–system interaction in several different modalities in parallel, sequentially or as alternatives. Here are some of them:
(1) Natural communication does it: the whole body expresses mental states, such as eagerness or depression, through speech content, prosody, tone of voice, facial expression, gaze, graphic and haptic gesture, head and body posture and more, producing an impression of sincerity. A single communicative act (Section 3.6.2) is often expressed through speech, facial expression and gesture at the same time, e.g.: "I don't know [eyes wide open, eyebrows raised] [forearms in front of torso, palms upwards moving outwards, shoulders moving upwards]". When expressed through speech, the same phonemic information is expressed both visually and acoustically, except for phonemes that cannot be visually distinguished. (2) Ordinary presentation does it, like when showing an image or a table and explaining it in text or

discourse, repeating important points in both modalities for emphasis or to ensure understanding and retention. (3) Teaching and training does it a lot, using repetition and elaboration in several modalities in order to lock up the information in the user's long-term memory. (4) Immersive, quasi-realistic presentation does it in imitation of natural perception, for instance by enabling acoustic, graphic, and sometimes even haptic access to the same objects and events. (5) Entertainment presentation does it by embellishing input and output in all sorts of ways. (6) Customisable systems may do it to fit different user preferences, environments of use, user profiles, etc. For instance, users may be offered the alternative of dictating text (acoustic or audiovisual spoken text input) or typing it in (haptic text input).

### 4.4.2 Relationships Among Modality Candidates

Section 4.4.1 illustrates how modality reasoning tends to draw heavily upon relationships between modalities. Even if we end up choosing a unimodal solution, this one should, at the very least, be based on consideration of which among several modality candidates is the more apt in the AMITUDE context, which implies consideration of modality relationships. And if we consider multimodal solutions, we should, at the very least, try to make sure that the chosen modalities are jointly sufficient for expressing the information to be exchanged between user and system and that there are no conflicts between them. In this section we take a systematic look at modality relations.

Table 4.4 shows eight common relations between (different) modalities. The reason why we speak about "relations" rather than "combinations" between modalities is that some relations in the table are not necessarily combinations, nor do they have to obtain in the same application. The table may still be incomplete but does offer a lot of developer's options. There is quite some literature on this subject already, including lists of advantages of using multiple modalities, e.g. Benoit et al. (2000), and early work on abstract typologies of modality combinations. Martin (1995) describes six types of potentially usable modality cooperation: complementarity, redundancy, equivalence, specialisation, concurrency and transfer. Nigay and Coutaz (1993) characterise multimodal systems in terms of levels of abstraction, use of modalities and multimodal fusion.

In Table 4.4, Column 1 names the modality relation and Column 2 explains it. We return to Columns 3 and 4 later.

*Complementarity* is the relation of expressing a single communicative act by expressing different pieces of information in several modalities, like when we use spoken discourse and graphic or haptic pointing to express "Put that [pointing] there [pointing]". If we don't point and only speak, the utterance is referentially ambiguous to the point of being meaningless; and if we only point, the whole point (sorry!) of the communicative act, and hence its meaning, is lost. Strict as it is, complementarity is quite common as suggested by these examples: a graphic, haptic or acoustic image of a woman accompanied by the label (in any medium) "Alice", provides information equivalent to, e.g. pointing to Alice's picture and saying "This

**Table 4.4**  Eight common relations between different modalities

| 1. Type of relation | 2. What it does | 3. Co-ordination | 4. Aimed at user groups |
|---|---|---|---|
| Complementarity | Several modalities necessary to express a single communicative act | Tight | Same |
| Addition | Add up different expressiveness of different modalities to express more information | Loose | Same or different |
| Redundancy | Express partly the same information in different modalities | Tight | Same or different |
| Elaboration | Express partly the same information in different modalities | Tight Loose | Same or different |
| Alternative | Express roughly the same information in different modalities | Loose None | Same or different |
| Stand-in | Fail to express the same information in a less apt modality | None | Same or different |
| Substitution | Replace more apt modality/modalities by less apt one(s) to express the same information | None | Special |
| Conflict | The human system cannot handle modality addition | Tight | None |

is Alice". Thus we find complementarity in labelled buttons; in haptic objects that express themselves in spoken keywords, like in "[Touching a virtual haptic object] 'door'"; maps with names on them; labelled graphs; etc. Note that complementarity cannot exist in just any modality combination but requires two or more modalities that have different and, indeed, complementary strengths in information expressiveness.

*Addition* is the relation of adding up information represented in different modalities in order to express all the information that needs to be expressed. If the modality candidates you've already got cannot express all of it, look for an additional modality to express the rest! Add sound bits to the slide show, images to the text, hands-on to the how-to-do advice. Note that modality addition does not always work and sometimes produces modality conflict (see below).

*Redundancy*, like Complementarity, is a pretty strict relation by which a communicative act expressed in one modality gets supplemented by expression of part or whole of the same information in another modality. Natural communication is replete with redundancy, as in audiovisual speech; redundancy is important in creating immersive interaction; we find it in sub-titled film and TV; etc. In some contexts, hand–arm pointing and other forms of pointing, such as gaze pointing, have been given a well-defined semantics, meaning, e.g. "What is this?", so that, when we point at something, the pointing itself carries this meaning. If we say at the same time "What is this?" there is perfect redundancy: we might either speak or point, and the message would be exactly the same (Bernsen 2006). Sometimes redundancy is partial, like when someone makes a spoken remark that is perfectly meaningful on its own, and accompanies the remark by a gesture that can only be understood based on the speech. Redundancy can only exist to the extent that the same information can be expressed in several modalities.

*Elaboration* is the phenomenon of using several modalities to bring the message across through repetition and variation. Show the image and describe it in speech, for instance, or show the text and elaborate on it in speech. Elaboration is common in GUI design when a single (stand-in, see below) modality is not sufficiently useable and a second is added to patch up the lack of information, like when a label is added to an image icon that few users are able to decode. Another form of elaboration is to provide icons for experienced users and offer novice users longer and more informative mouse-over keywords or even text.

*Alternative* modalities are typically used to cater for AMITUDE variations in user profile, user preferences, environment of use or device availability by offering more or less equally apt modalities for each variation, cf. examples in Section 4.4.1. The choice between alternative modalities may be through setup, customisation or automatic adaptation of the same application or through alternative applications.

*Stand-in* modalities incur loss of information and are typically used when a more apt modality that does not incur information loss, cannot be used for various reasons, such as lack of output real-estate (Section 4.4.1).

*Substitution* is like *alternative*, except that the substituting modality is less apt than the one it substitutes. Substitution is a key reason why multimodality could enable usability for virtually all people, because it enables more or less complete substitution of information representation from one modality to another that actually fits the target users who often have some form of disability.

Needless to say, those seven relations can fail for many different reasons, resulting in more or less unusable complementarity, addition, redundancy, elaboration, alternative, stand-in or substitution. At this point, too little is known about this large variety of cases, and we just highlight an important case.

*Conflict* is *addition* gone wrong because the human system cannot handle combination of the candidate modalities. You may have attended a presentation in which the speaker launches a demo featuring spoken language and then talks over the demo as if it were a non-acoustic video or presentation slide. GUI habits die hard! What happens is that the audience has difficulty following any of the simultaneous speech streams because the human system is unable to pay attention to two different streams of linguistic contents at the same time. A less serious conflict is pointed out by Nielsen who claims that, in general, it is best to minimise the use of graphics animation on web sites (although there *are* cases in which it can be useful, Nielsen 1999). The superior saliency of graphics animation compared to static graphics constantly "pulls at" the user's visual attention, distracting the user from inspecting the rest of the web page.

Table 4.4 Column 3 describes three different ways in which representations in modalities that we somehow relate to each other during development are being coordinated. *Tight coordination* (or micro-level coordination) means that the expressions in different modalities should be decoded together, as in the relations of complementarity and redundancy. *Loose coordination* means that the modalities form part of the same overall, or macro-level, representation or exchange of information, like images and text form part of this book. *No coordination* means that the modalities do not form part of the same overall representation or exchange.

Column 4 may suggest new ways of combining modalities. It says that complementary modalities are always aimed at the same user group(s). We suppose they have to be, because they must be decoded together as part of the same message, right? Substitution of modalities is aimed at special user groups – or might there be cases in which substitution is aimed at the same group? For all other modality relations, it seems that representations could serve different user groups. For instance, we might add visual speech to acoustic speech to help people in noisy conditions, but, by the same token, the application might then also come to benefit a new group of hard-of-hearing users who have trouble with speech-only output. Try to think of examples for all cases and compare with those at the book's web site.

### 4.4.3 Modality Combinations of Established Usability

Let's say that, using the rules in Section 4.4.1, we line up a number of modality candidates that can jointly represent the information to be exchanged between the system and its users. Furthermore, Section 4.4.2 helps make clear what kinds of relationships exist or could exist between those candidates and maybe suggests new modality candidates as well. What more can be done to support modality analysis?

One thing that would be good to have is a checklist of established modality combinations, that is, a list of combinations that have been massively tested and proved their usability with, primarily, large groups of ordinary, non-specialist users. Even if one of our modality candidate configurations belongs to this list, it might still turn out to have usability problems in the context of a particular application, but at least it would represent a shot at usable multimodality. It is useful to think of the list below as a list of *paradigms* of representation and exchange of information between user and system. Each paradigm has an unstated scope or represents a core set of successful and highly usable examples. If our system goes beyond this set, the paradigm may not be adhered to any more. We will see examples of this below and when analysing this book's Cases in Section 4.4.5.

Here is a short list of well-established stand-alone modalities and modality combinations. Use the taxonomy in Table 4.2 to decode them, if needed.

1. Dynamic graphic images input, as in camera surveillance.
2. Spoken discourse input, as in microphone surveillance.
3. Static graphic text and (1D, 2D or 3D) images output, as in books and web sites.
4. Static haptic text and (1D, 2D or 3D) images output, as in books and haptic device displays for the blind.
5. Static graphic text, keywords and maps, graphs or diagrams (compositional or conceptual) output, as in data graphics.
6. Dynamic graphic text and (2D or 3D) images output, spoken discourse, acoustic images and non-speech sound output, as in subtitled movies.

7. Haptic keyword, pointing and simple notation input, graphics output, as in simple search engines.
8. Haptic pointing and simple notation input, static and dynamic graphics output, non-speech acoustics output, as in many computer games.
9. Spoken discourse input/output, as in conversation over the phone.
10. Dynamic graphics image input/output, as in fun movement games for children.
11. Haptic body action input, dynamic graphic image output, as in VR surgery training.
12. Spoken discourse input, graphic (3D) or haptic (2D) pointing gesture input, static or dynamic graphics output, as in pointing to, and talking about, visible images, text or maths notation.
13. Spoken discourse input/output, haptic (2D/3D) pointing gesture and body action input, static haptic and graphic image output, as when the doctor examines the sprained ankle with his hands and asks if "this" hurts.
14. Situated dynamic natural input/output communication, including audiovisual spoken discourse, visual facial expression, gesture and body action, haptic gesture and body action, as in a brawl at the pub.
15. Situated dynamic natural input/output communication, including visual sign language discourse, facial expression, gesture and body action, haptic gesture and body action, as in a happy communion at the pub.

The list shows examples of various non-interactive input-only or output-only modalities and modality combinations (1–6), followed by paradigms of interaction (7–15), some of which only exist in human–human interaction so far. The interesting principle is that, if it works between people and can, in essence, be emulated by a system, it will work between humans and systems. The standard GUI is present as illustrated by simple search engines, like Google.

### 4.4.4 Combining Modalities – Science or Alchemy?

We discuss modality analysis at length because we believe it is crucial for HCI to put multimodal usability on solid foundations, or, at least, on the best foundations in town. One reason for the missing foundations has been the lack of a theory and taxonomy of unimodal modalities. However, there also seems to be a second, related reason.

Multimodality is often wrongly presented as something quite new (Section 4.1.1). Related to this view, we suspect, is an assumption that modality combination – the combination of unimodal modalities, no matter which – is a unique and non-analysable process that creates new emergent properties of representations. These properties cannot be predicted, or otherwise accounted for, from the nature of the constituent modalities and their joint interaction with the human system, i.e. with the way human learning, perception, central processing and action works. Each one of millions of possible modality combinations is a unique whole which can only be understood as such. If this is the case, modality analysis does not make sense. All the developer can do is select input and output modalities on a trial-and-error basis, finding out empirically if the multimodal combination works or not.

Our contrary view is that, since we have a theory of unimodal modalities, and *only because* of that, multimodal representation can be understood as constructed from unimodal representation, analogous to other constructive approaches in science – from elements to chemistry, from words to sentences, from software techniques to integrated systems. Like synthetic chemistry, modality combination is sometimes complex, but this does not preclude analysis and sometimes prediction of multimodal usability. Multimodal usability is a function of an ultimately transparent process of combining unimodal modalities and taking their relationships with the human system into account. Chemistry only began moving as a systematic science when the system of elements was in the making. Multimodal usability must be based on understanding of unimodal modalities.

In practice, modality analysis, candidate selection and usability prediction are supported by the following tools in this book, all presented above: the modality taxonomy (Sections 4.2.1 and 4.2.4), modality properties (Section 4.3.2), information channels (Section 4.2.5), modality aptitude (Section 4.4.1), modality relations (Section 4.4.2), knowledge of established multimodal combinations (Section 4.4.3) and general AMITUDE consistency analysis. In no case, however, will proper use of those tools make our system independent of CoMeDa cycles. We always need to test empirically that the modality combination actually works in its system and AMITUDE context. What the tools and their future extension into better tools can do in many cases, is to help avoid major surprises. Everything equal, the less is known about the modalities chosen, or about the chosen modality combination, including knowledge about their technical realisation – the more substantial the collection of usability information will have to be, and the larger the risk of surprises. For instance, if we choose a natural communication case from the list in Section 4.4.3, we are likely to get into various compromises with what is technically feasible today, so that the resulting system will need substantial empirical input and testing to become usable.

For more on the topic of this section, see Bernsen (2008).

### *4.4.5 Modality Analysis of the Cases*

To follow the modality analyses below, you may find it helpful to consult the Case design illustrations in Section 7.2.

*Sudoku.* The idea behind the Sudoku game is to demonstrate 3D graphic gesture input (Section 2.1). From an interaction point of view, 3D graphic gesture input is an elegant modality because it is device-free for the user: all the user has to do is perform natural pointing hand–arm gesture. This makes it a natural choice to add speech input, which frees the user from using, e.g. a keyboard device or pen pad for inputting written language. The speech input will be further specified in the design phase but must include the numbers 1–9 notation required by Sudoku, and probably has to include a couple of spoken commands as well. For output, the centre-piece will be a static graphic image Sudoku game board. Design will have to decide if we need to add to the display various static graphic image icons, possibly labelled with static graphic English typed labels. We might also need some English output messages, spoken or typed. In other words, we drop the standard GUI input modalities and devices in favour of interaction by situated speaking and pointing with reference to visible objects.

Is this multimodal candidate setup likely to be usable, given what we know about modalities? Note that the setup closely corresponds to Paradigm 12 in Section 4.4.3. However, similarity is *not* identity and may be dangerous for that reason, so let's look more closely. This time, rather than using spoken discourse input, we plan to use spoken number notation and some designer-designed spoken keywords. Both of these may create usability problems, cf. MPs 17 and 18 in Table 4.3. Moreover, is playing Sudoku by means of 3D pointing gesture sufficiently similar to the pointing-while-talking referred to in Paradigm 12 or is it something else entirely? It *may* be the latter, because you will need to point a lot when playing Sudoku! Third, Paradigm 12 mentions 3D graphic and 2D haptic pointing gesture as alternatives. We have chosen the former, not for reasons of superior usability but because we want to explore it – but might the latter be a more usable choice? Fourth, since we are clearly set to choose a "minimalist" modality combination, our target users might want to add modalities.

The pattern followed in the above, predictive modality analysis is to start from a closely resembling interaction paradigm known to be natural to people, spot the modality differences between paradigm and Case and analyse these by means of modality properties and task knowledge. To get an impression of the validity of the Sudoku modality analysis above, see Chapter 17 (Intermezzo 5).

*Treasure Hunt.* Compared to Sudoku, the Treasure Hunt game is considerably more complex and, as a whole, unsupported by any established interaction paradigm. We want to identify apt candidate modalities (Section 4.4.1) that can jointly make sure that the blind and the deaf-mute user can do their tasks.

*Output.* To provide equal access to the virtual environment (VE) in which game action takes place, we represent the VE as a static haptic 3D image for the blind user, and as a static 2D graphics image-enhanced map for the deaf-mute user, i.e. a standard 2D map with super-imposed images of points of interests like buildings, forests or graveyards. To help navigation, we annotate the graphics image map with static typed keywords for names and locations, and the haptic image with spoken keywords. Thus, when the blind user navigates the VE and arrives at a point of game interest, that point speaks to the user about itself in spoken keywords. We select similar candidate modalities for interior scenes, like when the user visits a house or a catacomb. We embellish the blind user's game by arbitrary non-speech sounds for colours of objects and use a simple arbitrary non-speech sound for signalling to the blind game partner that a step in the game has been successfully completed by the blind user or by the deaf-mute user. Correspondingly, the deaf-mute user visually watches messages arrive from the blind user or being successfully sent to the blind user.

The design phase might introduce spoken discourse output for the blind user in some cases, such as for starting the game by giving the user the first goal to achieve. When addressed by the blind user, the deaf-mute user will receive the message converted into graphics sign language produced by an embodied agent. When communicated to by the deaf-mute user, the blind user will receive the message converted into spoken keywords. The reason for using keywords rather than discourse is that keywords are sufficient for referring to points of interest in the VE. Finally, the deaf-mute user will be able to monitor the blind user's dynamically changing position on the static graphics VE image-enhanced map.

*Input.* The blind user will use haptic body action for moving around in 3D haptic space. Haptic notation will be used for acting on objects. Correspondingly, the deaf-mute user will use haptic pointing and haptic notation for navigation and object action, respectively, this time into a familiar static graphics VE output environment. When communicating to the blind user, the deaf-mute user will use (i) graphics sign language for linguistic messages and (ii) haptic body action for drawing a route onto the graphics VE map. This 2D drawing will be converted into 3D haptics and form part of the blind user's haptic VE map. When communicating to the deaf-mute user, the blind user will use spoken keywords.

How about that?! What we have here is a nice scheme for establishing correspondence between two alternative and partly substituting (Table 4.4) I/O modality worlds – the one of the blind user and the one of the deaf-mute user – in which all information available to, or produced by, one of the users is also available to the other, just *nearly always* represented in different modalities. In fact, the only case of using the same modality is that both users click on some device to produce haptic notation. This modality structure is useful for modality analysis, because we can analyse the usability of each player's modality "world" separately.

*Deaf-mute user.* The deaf-mute user's multimodal I/O world is familiar from computer gaming in most respects, cf. Paradigm 8 in Section 4.4.3. The deaf-mute user's world lacks non-speech acoustics, of course, and adds static graphic keywords on the VE map, sign language keywords input and drawing on a map. Drawing on the map is clearly apt for adding a route; sign language is apt for conveying keywords; and keywords on a map are apt for representing locations. As long as the keywords to be communicated refer to labelled points of interest on the deaf-mute user's map, they will cause no usability problems, provided the user is sufficiently proficient in sign language: all the user has to do is read a keyword from the map and express it in sign language. In conclusion, if the deaf-mute user is familiar with the sign language and has the dexterity required for the haptic input, this user's multimodal interface is likely to be usable in a basic sense.

*Blind user.* The blind user's multimodal I/O world is less straightforward for us to analyse, primarily because of our unfamiliarity with a 3D haptic VE speaking in keywords, and how this VE will work with blind users. Do blind people have a different sensitivity to 3D haptic information compared to the seeing? Do they have a better memory for it? Compared to the deaf-mute user's graphics VE, the blind user's haptic-acoustic VE is a substitution rather than an alternative

(Table 4.4). The deaf-mute user has at-a-glance access to the structure and contents of the graphics image map, whereas the blind user must laboriously build a memorised map of the VE by moving around in it. It's a fine idea of modality substitution, but we will have to study how usable it is in empirical CoMeDa cycles.

Spoken discourse is certainly apt for conveying game goals, and, as long as the keywords communicated to the blind user refer to labelled points of interest in the haptic VE, this *may* not cause usability problems. However, to the blind user, knowledge about a particular point of interest requires (i) having encountered this point during VE exploration, and/or (ii) managing to remember its label while searching for it and/or (iii) being able to find it. Since this is a computer game, (i) through (iii) might not be considered usability problems at all but, rather, part of the game challenge for blind users – at least as long as they don't create too much difficulty. The use of arbitrary non-speech sound for colours and game phases is a familiar cause of usability problems, cf. MP3 in Table 4.3. Again, the developers might argue that this is part of the game challenge.

*Maths.* The Maths system features natural communication Paradigm 14 from Section 4.4.3, except for I/O haptic gesture and body action, and visual gesture and body action output. Thus, the teacher will be a "talking face", which is a limiting case (no body) of an embodied conversational agent, or ECA (Cassell et al. 2000). Student spoken conversation with the teacher will be supported by something close to a classical GUI. To allow students exercise the typing of mathematical expressions, Maths will include haptic typed input rendered as static graphics output. To allow students to carefully study what the teacher says, Maths will include static graphic-typed output of everything the teacher says as well, cf. MP7 in Table 4.3. To enhance tacit observation of student affect through speech contents and prosody, visual facial expression, eye gaze and gesture, the system will use bio-sensors for monitoring heart rate and skin conductivity (Fig. 3.3). The static graphics output will include some labels/keywords.

Student–teacher conversation will be similar in kind to everyday human–human communication in classrooms and one-on-one teaching and training, teacher and student having full natural, situated communication, both of them writing mathematical expressions as well, and the teacher observing the student's interest, motivation and emotions. Still, there are differences, including the following: (i) the teacher is a talking head, not embodied; (ii) the system redundantly prints all that the teacher says; (iii) the student must wear bio-sensors; (iv) the system will fail to understand the student's natural communication input, affects and all, more frequently than a human teacher.

Re (i), we are not aware of findings to the effect that a missing body has negative usability effects in systems like Maths. Re (ii), we don't know if students would prefer speech output-only, or typed output-only, rather than having both. As for (iii), we don't know if there will be any negative usability effects from wearing the bio-sensor device. Re (iv), this is a major and complex usability risk. One fallback is all-typed student input. We don't know how usable this would be with spoken and/or typed teacher output.

In other words, the Maths system is a usability minefield, principally because of its goal of emulating so much of natural human communication. ECAs often have significant usability problems, cf. the discussions of ECA usability in Prendinger and Ishizuka (2004) and Ruttkay and Pelachaud (2004).

## 4.5  Input/Output Devices

Modalities and multimodality are about how abstract information can be physically represented in media and their information channels and in different forms called modalities. I/O devices form the third level of the abstraction hierarchy: abstract information → modalities → I/O devices. Whenever there is representation and exchange of information between user and system in some modality, the system needs I/O devices just like the user needs eyes, ears, a face, hands, etc. I/O devices raise usability issues of their own, so this section is about the device analysis part of AMITUDE analysis.

Some I/O devices are microphones, loudspeakers, data gloves, RFID tags, eye scanners, gaze trackers, graphics displays, cameras, controllers, keypads, force-feedback devices, bio-sensors and accelerometers. I/O devices rely on enabling technologies, such as graphics display technology for the hardware and computer graphics for the software, and may work with complex software systems, such as a webcam feeding into an advanced image-processing software package.

When discussing I/O devices, it is often a useful simplification to refer not only to the device itself but also to the technologies that enable the device to do some particular task, such as rendering speech prosody or tracking faces on realistic background clutter. There is an important point to this slightly unorthodox putting together of hardware devices and enabling technologies. In today's multimodal systems world, we may need any of the devices listed above, and many others, and we cannot always purchase exactly what we need. Instead, we may obtain some hardware and some software development platform upon which to build the capabilities our system needs. For instance, there is no top-quality, general-purpose speech recogniser for children's voices. To make a recogniser reasonably usable with children, it must be trained on data representative of the user population's voices and of the kind of language (vocabulary and grammar) they are likely to use during interaction. Furthermore, we may have to collect the training data ourselves. All of this requires CoMeDa cycles, and we address these issues in the methods and data handling chapters below.

The discipline that deals with fitting I/O devices to people is called ergonomics, or computer ergonomics more specifically, since ergonomics also addresses all manner of non-computerised equipment (like spades or door knobs) and object handling (e.g. lifting heavy objects). Computer ergonomics may be considered a special branch of HCI. While ergonomists are often medically trained people, the field also draws substantially upon psychology and hardware and software design, because ergonomists not only study existing devices and long-term effects of their use but also help making better, or new, ones.

### 4.5.1 Issues of Device Analysis

The goal of device analysis is to identify and select usable device candidates. It is tempting to view device selection as the final, nice and simple part of AMITUDE analysis, or as a formality we do after having identified our modality candidates. However, it's a dangerous simplification to view device analysis as having no constraining effects upon other AMITUDE aspects. I/O devices are full members of the AMITUDE club and may constrain other AMITUDE aspects as much as these may constrain the choice of devices. We must, of course, have some idea of the modalities to be used in order to look into devices, but once we do, it may turn out, e.g. that there currently is no device available for inputting or outputting the modality in question, in which case we must consider if we wish to build it ourselves or drop it. For instance, you may have a hard time locating a speech synthesiser that automatically generates emotional speech representing a range of different emotions. Today's good synthesisers can easily be configured (tagged) to generate fast or loud pronunciations, but that's a far cry from generating voices expressing anger, tension or hilarity.

Or suppose we want the system to see if the user's face looks happy or not, and then find out that this is only possible in a reasonably robust and usable manner if the visual background behind the user's face is of uniform colour and texture. In this case, we must either drop our facial-happiness-clues-spotting ambition, constrain the use environment specification, or build a usable facial-happiness spotter that does not rely on visual environment control.

Examples such as the above illustrate general issues created by devices during AMITUDE specification. Let's look at six common issues.

The emotional prosody example above is a case of *device unavailability* for modality reasons: given the modality candidate, no suitable device currently exists. We hypothesise that cases of device unavailability may exist for all AMITU(D)E aspects. In other words, (1) something in our specification of A, M, I, T, U or E requires a device that does not exist, is unobtainable or is prohibitive in other ways, so that we either have to build it or change our specification. Try to construct examples for all aspects and look at the examples at the book's web site.

The facial happiness example above is a case of *conditional device availability* for use environment reasons: we can have the device, but only if we constrain the use environment specification. We hypothesise that conditional device availability may exist for all AMITU(D)E aspects. (2) For each aspect A, M, I, T, U or E, we can have the desired device if we make our specification more restrictive. Try to construct examples for all aspects and look at the book's web site.

In other cases, the issue is, rather, one of *device proliferation*, i.e. (3) which one among many available devices to choose given the emerging AMITUDE specification? In the history of HCI, this question has stirred outbursts of ergonomic research from time to time. In the 1980s, for instance, people investigated manual input devices and their suitability for different types of task (Greenstein and Arnaut 1988, Mackinlay et al. 1990). Just try to produce hand-written text with a standard mouse! It's as awkward today as it was back then, and mainly due to the lack of precision control we have over the device. This kind of work may result in ergonomic standards, cf. MacKenzie (2003). Choosing among devices can be hard, especially if we include enabling technologies, as in "Can I build the user–system conversation I have in mind using Voice XML?" Sometimes it is advisable to spend a CoMeDa cycle on making careful comparison between candidate devices, such as among a range of speech synthesisers.

In a fourth class of cases, (4) the device exists and proliferation is not an issue, but *something militates*, or seems to, or may militate, against its use, as in "I want to build a system that monitors bio-signals from car drivers, but there is strong indication that drivers don't want to wear bio-sensors for reasons of personal comfort, task performance, or social fitting-in". If we cannot conceive of any way of packaging the bio-sensors so that car drivers accept wearing them, nor of embedding them in the car environment, we might drop the system idea or proceed in the hope that the problem will be solved in due course.

A typical case in multimodal research systems development is that of (5) *not knowing* if a device will be usable. The device may exist or have to be made in the project, but the issue is that of stretching the technology to achieve something that hasn't been done exactly like this before, with demonstrated, or at least measured, usability. The best thing to do is to assign a goodly amount of resources for investigating device usability as early as possible and to have a workable fallback strategy in case the device cannot be made usable.

A special case of device analysis concerns *simulation realism* in, e.g. VR or mixed-reality training simulators: (6) are the simulating devices jointly a realistic replication of what is supposed to be simulated? Many current car simulators, for instance, simulate the correspondence between analogue haptic driving input (steering) and visual output quite well, but fail to provide feedback on acceleration, deceleration, change of direction, road surface texture, as well as changes in noise level and noise composition due to changes in direction and surface texture. The issue is that the device should perhaps not be used for collecting certain kinds of data, because this will not reliably represent real driving.

There are other device issues, such as long-term health effects of using a device, which we will not go into here. The QWERTY keyboard layout from the late 1870s illustrates that devices can be too good for their own good and may have to be made less efficient. The QWERTY keyboard was developed to make typing so slow that the typewriter's type bars would not clash and jam during typing.

### 4.5.2 Device Analysis of the Cases

This section presents Case device analyses based upon the Case ideas (Section 2.1), the Case modality analyses (Section 4.4.5) and any other Case AMITUDE information (Chapters 3 and 4). We use the six points made in Section 4.5.1 as a checklist.

*Sudoku*. This system is, in fact, device motivated, aimed at demonstrating the usefulness of camera-captured 3D gesture. The game requires a reasonably large graphics display for pointing at while standing; stereo cameras and image processing for capturing 3D pointing arm–hand–finger gesture; a microphone setup for capturing the speech input; and a speech recogniser.

All required devices exist. Nothing seems to militate against their use. Since the spoken input will be just a few keywords, and we have excluded children's voices (Section 3.3.7), we expect that most speech recognisers will do and don't plan to make a comparative study of candidates. We might have a problem with standard number input, though, because recognisers tend to confuse short words more easily than longer words. The fallback is to use longer words, saying, e.g. "number eight" instead of just "eight". It is likely that the image-processing software will work properly only in a controlled use environment. This will be investigated and any necessary control will be imposed. Another key uncertainty is how usable the pointing gesture input will be for playing Sudoku. We don't have a fallback plan in this case: if the 3D pointing gesture input does not work for playing Sudoku, the project will fail.

*Treasure Hunt.* The deaf-mute user will have a graphics display, a mouse and a camera. The project will develop simple converters for (i) speech-to-sign-language, (ii) sign-language-to-speech, (iii) 2D analogue graphics-to-3D analogue haptics and (iv) a simple sign language recogniser. (i) and (ii) will only have to convert a small number of labels/keywords from one modality to another, and (iv) only has to recognise a couple of signs. (iii) must convert a single line. The blind user will use a loudspeaker, an analogue haptic force-feedback device with a button on it for exploring, and acting upon, the 3D haptic VE, text-to-speech, and a colour-to-sound converter. Given the simplicity of performance required of the new device programs, these are expected to be feasible to do, and so is the haptic VE. As for fallbacks, sign language I/O can easily be replaced by typed text I/O, whereas the fallback for the graphics-to-haptics converter is to find other game challenges. The really open issue is how usable the blind users will find the commercial haptic force-feedback device for exploring and acting upon the haptic VE.

*Maths.* The Maths system includes a GUI with graphics display, mouse and keyboard. In addition, the system has loudspeaker, microphone and special-purpose speech recognition for children's voices, including simple emotional–motivational prosody recognition, bio-sensors for monitoring heart rate and skin conductivity and a camera with project-made image-processing software for extracting simple facial expression and gesture cues to the student's emotional and motivational state. The fallback in case of severe usability problems with speech recognition is typed student input; and in case of problems with recognition of prosody, facial expression and gesture cues, asking the student. The speech recogniser will be identified through a comparative study.

The picture provided above may be reasonably representative of advanced multimodal systems development today. Referring to the numbered checklist points in Section 4.5.1, devices or their software are often being developed as part of the project (1); fallbacks in the form of more restrictive, less ambitious specifications are frequently required (2); comparative device evaluation is sometimes needed (3); and device usability often forms part of what the project aims to demonstrate (5). Comparing each device analysis to the rest of the AMITUDE model of use done for each Case, we found no factors militating against using the planned devices (4) – but that may change once we run CoMeDa cycles for testing the system model. Only Point (6) on simulation realism is not relevant to the Cases.

## 4.6  Key Points

This chapter completes the presentation of AMITUDE analysis by discussing modality and device analysis and illustrating both through Case analysis. As befits this book's title and the emergence of new modalities, modality combinations and novel multimodal applications, the presentation of *Modalities* has been particularly expansive. We have tried to convey a sense of how to work with modalities within a compact *taxonomy of modalities* in the *media of graphics, acoustics and haptics*. In addition, the chapter presents various tools and perspectives in support of creating and analysing multimodal combinations, including *modality properties, modality aptitude rules, modality relations* and a list of usable *multimodal combinations*. The section on *Devices* proposes a *checklist for device-related usability issues* for use in device analysis.

Looking at Chapters 3 and 4 together to conclude them both, their common goal is to introduce the *Concepts* part of CoMeDa (Fig. 1.2) in theory and practice. This we have done by, first, presenting the AMITUDE aspect as seven more or less structured sets of concepts for analysing the project goal and specifying an integrated model of use through holistic (constraint-based) reasoning. Second, by applying those sets of concepts to this book's Cases in *Case AMITUDE analysis*. Importantly, this has all been done in abstraction from important parts of the usability development process, so it's time to put usability work in a broader and more balanced perspective, starting with a summary of the Case AMITUDE analyses in Chapter 5 (Intermezzo 2) and continuing with the *Methods* part of CoMeDa work in Chapter 6 onwards.

## References

Benoit C, Martin J-C, Pelachaud C, Schomaker, L, Suhm B (2000) Audio-visual and multimodal speech-based systems. In: Gibbon D, Mertins I, Moore RK (eds) Handbook of multimodal and spoken dialogue systems. Kluwer Academic Publishers, Boston: 102–203.

Bernsen NO (1994) Foundations of multimodal representations. A taxonomy of representational modalities. Interacting with Computers 6/4: 347–371.

Bernsen NO (1995) Why are analogue graphics and natural language both needed in HCI? In: Paterno F (ed) Interactive systems: design, specification and verification. 1st Eurographics workshop, Focus on computer graphics. Springer: 235–251.

Bernsen NO (2002) Multimodality in language and speech systems – from theory to design support tool. In: Granström B, House D, Karlsson I (eds) Multimodality in language and speech systems. Kluwer Academic Publishers, Dordrecht: 93–148.

Bernsen NO (2006) Speech and 2D deictic gesture reference to virtual scenes. In: André E, Dybkjær L, Minker W, Neumann H, Weber M (eds) Perception and interactive technologies. Proceedings of international tutorial and research workshop. Springer, LNAI 4021.

Bernsen NO (2008) Multimodality theory. In: Tzovaras D (ed) Multimodal user interfaces. From signals to interaction, Signals and communication technology. Springer: 5–29.

Bernsen NO, Dybkjær L (1999a) Working paper on speech functionality. Esprit long-term research project DISC year 2 deliverable D2.10. University of Southern Denmark.

Bernsen NO, Dybkjær L (1999b) A theory of speech in multimodal systems. In: Dalsgaard P, Lee C-H, Heisterkamp P, Cole R (eds) Proceedings of the ESCA workshop on interactive dialogue in multi-modal systems, Irsee, Germany. ESCA, Bonn: 105–108.

Bertin J (1983) Semiology of graphics. Diagrams, networks, maps. Translation by Berg WJ. University of Wisconsin Press, Madison.

Bolt RA (1980) Put-that-there: voice and gesture at the graphics interface. Proceedings of the 7th annual conference on computer graphics and interactive techniques. Seattle: 262–270.

Cassell J, Sullivan J, Prevost S, Churchill E (2000) Embodied conversational agents. MIT Press, Cambridge.

Greenstein JS, Arnaut LY (1988) Input devices. In: Helander M (ed) Handbook of human-computer interaction. North-Holland, Amsterdam: 495–519.

Hovy E, Arens Y (1990) When is a picture worth a thousand words? Allocation of modalities in multimedia communication. AAAI symposium on human-computer interfaces. Stanford.

Johnson M, Lakoff G (1980) Metaphors we live by. University of Chicago Press, Chicago.

Jurafsky D, Martin JH (2000) Speech and language processing. An introduction to natural language processing, computational linguistics, and speech recognition. Prentice Hall, Englewood Cliffs.

Lakoff G (1987) Women, fire, and dangerous things: what categories reveal about the mind. University of Chicago Press, Chicago.

Luz S, Bernsen NO (1999) Interactive advice on the use of speech in multimodal systems design with SMALTO. In: Ostermann J, Ray Liu KJ, Sørensen JAa, Deprettere E, Kleijn WB (eds) Proceedings of the third IEEE workshop on multimedia signal processing, Elsinore, Denmark. IEEE, Piscataway: 489–494.

MacKenzie IS (2003) Motor behaviour models for human-computer interaction. In: Carroll JM (ed) HCI models, theories and frameworks. Towards a multidisciplinary science. Morgan Kaufmann, San Francisco.

Mackinlay J, Card SK, Robertson GG (1990) A semantic analysis of the design space of input devices. Human-Computer Interaction 5: 145–190.

Martin J-C (1995) Cooperations between modalities and binding through synchrony in multimodal interfaces. PhD thesis (in French). ENST, Orsay, France.

Mussio P, Cugini U, Bordegoni M (2001) Post-WIMP interactive systems: modeling visual and haptic interaction. Proceedings of the 9th international conference on human-computer interaction: 159–163.

Nielsen J (1999) Designing web usability. New Riders, Indiana.

Nigay L, Coutaz J (1993) A design space for multimodal systems: concurrent processing and data fusion. International conference on human-computer interaction. ACM Press, London: 172–178.

Oviatt S, Cohen P (2000) Multimodal interfaces that process what comes naturally. Communications of the ACM 43/3: 45–53.

Prendinger H, Ishizuka M (eds) (2004) Life-like characters. Springer Verlag, Berlin.

Ruttkay Z, Pelachaud C (eds) (2004) From brows to trust. Evaluating embodied conversational agents. Kluwer, Dordrecht.

Sutcliffe A, Kurniawan S, Shin J (2006) A method and advisor tool for multimedia user interface design. International Journal of Human-Computer Studies 64/4: 375–392.

Tufte ER (1983) The visual display of quantitative information. Graphics Press, Cheshire.

# Chapter 5
# Intermezzo 2: Status on Cases and Next Steps

This intermezzo summarises the AMITUDE Case analyses made in Chapters 3 and 4 to create AMITUDE models of use, or AMITUDE specifications, for the Cases (Section 5.1). We explain usability goals, requirements and evaluation criteria, and extend Case specification to include usability requirements (Section 5.2). Since the Case models of use appear to have been produced by pure thinking, Section 5.3 calls for the broader and more realistic perspective on usability work adopted from Chapter 6 onwards.

## 5.1 Case AMITUDE Models of Use

Tables 5.1, 5.2, 5.3, 5.4, 5.5, 5.6, 5.7 and 5.8 summarise the Case model of use analyses from Chapters 3 and 4. Note that task analyses have been added.

## 5.2 Case Usability Goals, Requirements and Evaluation Criteria

It is instructive at this point to take a close look at one of the AMITUDE models in Tables 5.1, 5.2, 5.3, 5.4, 5.5, 5.6, 5.7 and 5.8 and ask the question it's all about in this book: will the system specified be usable? Try to answer the question by consulting the decomposition of usability in Table 1.1. What do you get – that you don't know, right? You don't know if the system will work as specified, and it hasn't even been designed yet, so how could anyone tell? All we can say at this stage is that we are trying hard to do AMITUDE specifications of *usable* systems.

There is, however, a related question which we can, and should, address this early in development, namely, how could we tell whether the system is usable? We can tell by specifying *usability evaluation criteria* and in other ways to be discussed in Section 16.2. This is straightforward to understand and almost trivial: if we have a usability evaluation criterion, we can apply it to measure some aspect of system usability, right? But what we really want to know are two things: (1) Where do we get those criteria from, or how do we establish them in practice for our own system? And (2), why do we need them so early?

N.O. Bernsen, L. Dybkjær, *Multimodal Usability*, Human-Computer Interaction Series, DOI 10.1007/978-1-84882-553-6_5, © Springer-Verlag London Limited 2009

**Table 5.1**  Case development goals and status

| System | Sudoku | Treasure Hunt | Maths |
|---|---|---|---|
| Development goal | Research prototype for demonstrating useful visual 3D gesture + speech input | Research prototype for demonstrating blind/deaf-mute communication and collaboration | Research prototype for demonstrating a cognitive–affective basic maths tutoring companion for children |
| Status | Built by a colleague and students at ZGDV in Darmstadt, Germany, user tested by the authors | Built by colleagues at ITI-CERTH in Thessaloniki, Greece, user tested by the authors and a colleague from ITI-CERTH | Under development by one of the authors in collaboration with ITI-CERTH |

**Table 5.2**  AMITUDE Case specifications or early models of use – application type

| System | Application type(s) |
|---|---|
| Sudoku | Single-player, number puzzle computer game. Sudoku game. 3D-pointing gesture. Pointing gesture and speech for entertainment |
| Treasure Hunt | Two-player adventure computer game. Treasure Hunt game. Multi-user game. Games for people with disabilities |
| Maths | Affective learning. Intelligent maths/science tutoring for kids. Animated conversational agent. Spoken tutoring. Companions, friends. Edutainment for kids |

**Table 5.3**  AMITUDE Case specifications or early models of use – modalities

| System | Modalities |
|---|---|
| Sudoku | *Input:* English spoken notation and keywords, 3D visual pointing gesture<br>*Output:* 2D static graphics: image game board, image icons, possibly with English typed labels, possibly English typed text |
| Treasure Hunt | *Input, blind user:* 3D analogue haptic navigation, haptic notation for acting on objects<br>*Output, blind user:* 3D static haptic images (cityscape, landscape, in-house, underground), English spoken keywords, arbitrary non-speech sound, possibly English spoken discourse<br>*Input, deaf-mute user:* 2D analogue haptic pointing and line-drawing, haptic notation for acting on objects, 3D American sign language keywords<br>*Output, deaf-mute user:* 2D static graphics image map, static graphics English typed text, 3D dynamic graphics embodied agent producing American sign language |
| Maths | *Input:* English spoken conversation and/or English visual typed text conversation, visual English typed notation, haptic notation, visual facial expression, eye gaze, gesture, haptic heart rate, electrophysiological skin conductivity<br>*Output:* English spoken conversation, 2D static graphics English typed text conversation, notation and labels/keywords, 3D dynamic graphics face image showing facial expressions and eye gaze |

**Table 5.4**  AMITUDE Case specifications or early models of use – interaction

| System | Interaction |
|---|---|
| Sudoku | Two-way communication (deliberate) |
| Treasure Hunt | Two-way communication (deliberate). Computer-mediated human–human communication. Virtual action |
| Maths | Two-way communication (deliberate). Tacit observation (by a caring friend). Bio-sensing |

**Table 5.5**  AMITUDE Case specifications or early models of use – task

| System | User task, other activity, domain |
|---|---|
| Sudoku | *Task goal:* complete a Sudoku game<br>*Generic task*: add numbers onto game board consistent with the rules until game board is full<br>*Domain:* everything to do with Sudoku gaming, in particular, with computers<br>*Task analysis:* select to play a game. Select game difficulty. Insert numbers one by one. Optionally: delete or replace inserted number; reset game if player does not want to continue. Get congratulations when game is completed successfully. Stop or select new game<br>*Issues:* on-line help, external memory options, score-keeping, customisation, embellishments |
| Treasure Hunt | *Task goal:* two-user team collaborates over network to find hidden drawings. Task steps to be invented: Goals, steps, obstacles, rules<br>*Domain:* everything related to treasure hunting<br>*Task specification:* (1) blind user told to find red closet. Finds house with room containing red closet, assisted by spoken cues and musical sound colour codes. Told to go to the Town Hall. (2) Deaf user gets this message converted into sign language by animated agent. Blind user finds town hall and is told by mayor to go to the temple ruins. (3) Blind user searches temple ruins for inscription. (4) The enigmatic written message found is sent to deaf user as sign language. S/he figures out to go to the cemetery, finds key, reads inscription on key and performs sign language to tell blind user what the key is for. (5) Blind user gets instruction in speech, finds and enters catacombs, finds box and extracts map which is sent to deaf user. (6) Deaf user solves riddle on map, draws route on map and sends map to blind user with route converted into 3D groove. (7) Blind user haptically follows groove, enters forest, follows grooved forest path and eventually locates treasure |
| Maths | *Task goal:* understand and master basic multiplication<br>*Test task:* quasi-effortlessly multiply any two numbers between 1 and 10 and be right<br>*Domain:* everything to do with teaching basic maths to children<br>*Task analysis:* as new student, be screened for basic addition skills. Get user id. Use id to enter and leave teaching and training at will. Be taught basic multiplication. Train basic multiplication and multiplication tables. Receive help: error correction, error explanation, how to avoid. Receive scores, points and other progress indicators<br>*Issues:* tutoring strategy: how to organise teaching and training, how to personalise strategy. Affective strategy. Affect perception |

**Table 5.6** AMITUDE Case specifications or early models of use – user

| System | User |
|---|---|
| Sudoku | *Adults and adolescents:* familiar with the Sudoku game rules; able to visually read English; able to speak basic English; able to perform 3D pointing gesture; average levels (no major disorders) of speech, vision, dexterity, stamina |
| Treasure Hunt | *User 1:* adolescent or adult; visually disabled; average level of hearing; understands basic spoken English; can sense force feedback; can perform haptic input actions<br>*User 2:* adolescent or adult; hearing disabled; can visually read English; can produce American sign language; can draw lines; can do mouse clicking<br>*Both:* preferably some computer literacy, computer game experience and technology curiosity |
| Maths | *6–9 years old (second or third grade) who:* has English speaking and reading skills and limited accent; knows basic addition but not basic multiplication; has average levels (no major disorders) of speech, hearing, vision, dexterity |

**Table 5.7** AMITUDE Case specifications or early models of use – devices

| System | Interaction devices |
|---|---|
| Sudoku | *Input:* microphone and speech recognition, stereo cameras and image processing<br>*Output:* large graphics display |
| Treasure Hunt | *Input:* force-feedback device with clickable button, mouse, camera and image processing, speech recognition<br>*Output:* force feedback, loudspeaker, graphics display, text-to-speech |
| Maths | *Input:* microphone and speech recognition, keyboard, mouse, camera and image processing, bio-sensors for heart rate and skin conductivity<br>*Output:* loudspeaker and text-to-speech, graphics display |

**Table 5.8** AMITUDE Case specifications or early models of use – environment

| System | Environment of use |
|---|---|
| Sudoku | Public space. In-doors. Low/limited noise. No extreme lighting. Floor space. Spacious. Risk of equipment damage and theft |
| Treasure Hunt | In-doors. Low/limited noise. No extreme lighting. Chair and table |
| Maths | Ubiquitous use stand-alone or over the Internet. Low/limited noise. No extreme lighting. Use when socially acceptable |

We discuss (2) below. For now, believe us when we say that we need, from early on, a core set of usability evaluation criteria that have a crucial role throughout development. Now let's see how to establish this core set in several steps.

We build artefacts, including systems, for a purpose (Section 1.4.7). The high-level decomposition of usability in Section 1.4.6 states what it means for an artefact to serve its purpose well. In other words (Step 1.1), when we state the Case system goals (Section 2.1), we can to some extent *deduce* some high-level *usability goals*, such as that is should be fun to play the Sudoku system. And when we (Step 1.2) detail the Case system goals into factual Case requirements specifications in Section 5.1 above, we can to some extent deduce more specific *usability requirements* from those specifications. For instance, we state in the requirements specification that Sudoku will be played using 3D pointing gesture, which implies that pointing gesture must be easy to control by default. If there are no special reasons why pointing gesture must *not* be easy to control, we have the usability requirement "Pointing gesture must be easy to control". Sometimes usability requirements get sharpened so that they can serve directly as measurable *usability evaluation criteria*, e.g. "Test users should complete at least two games in 30 minutes".

In summary, there is nothing mysterious about where usability evaluation criteria come from or how to find out what, roughly, they should, or could, be about for a particular system. We start getting committed to them when fixing the system goal and continue to generate more, and more precise versions, of them, as we proceed through requirements specification and design. What we don't deduce, we contribute ourselves, such as exactly how to measure some property, e.g. ease of control of pointing gesture; exactly which measurement results (target values) to aim for; and exactly how many and which usability requirements to specify.

Table 5.9 shows usability requirements for the Cases. Usability requirements are no different from software requirements in general, except for specifically addressing usability. Like the AMITUDE model of use specification, usability requirements are part of the requirements specification for the system. A usability evaluation criterion specifies in quantitative or qualitative terms how to determine if a usability requirement has been met, cf. Section 16.2. Section 16.2 also shows that we have other ways of judging system usability than through usability evaluation criteria.

Now for (2), why do we need usability requirements so early? Because, without a set of early usability requirements turned into usability evaluation criteria, we will be working in the dark until the time when we, e.g. test the system with users and have to invent some evaluation criteria to make sense of the test data. This is sometimes done in the murkier waters of software engineering, and what typically happens is that the criteria get designed to fit the system as it happens to be, rather than trying to develop the system to fit requirements specified up-front. It can get even worse, i.e. when evaluation criteria are developed not only to fit the system but also for the – possibly few – aspects in which the system is not an abject usability failure. Terrible!

We discuss evaluation in Chapter 16 and apply the Table 5.9 Sudoku usability requirements when evaluating the system in Chapter 17 (Intermezzo 5). Note how the Maths User experience entry in Table 5.9 shows a different style of defining usability requirements, i.e. as a series of target quotes from system users. The Functionality row shows that the Maths prototype is the more ambitious of the three as regards usability, because the Sudoku and Treasure Hunt entries only speak of "basic functionality", meaning that test users must be able to play the game but might want different or additional functionality in order to find the system optimally useful. The Maths entry speaks of "adequate functionality", meaning that users should

**Table 5.9** Case usability requirements. EfM, ProdM, SafM and SatM refer to ISO standards as explained in Section 16.4.1

| System | Sudoku | Treasure Hunt | Maths |
|---|---|---|---|
| Technical quality | *EfM* Robustness: max. one crash or other disruptive error per 2 hours of interaction | *EfM* As for Sudoku | *EfM* As for Sudoku |
| Functionality | Basic functionality for playing Sudoku | Basic functionality for playing this kind of game | Adequate teaching and user modelling functionality *EfM* Good match between user-and system-perceived affect and motivation |
| Ease of use | *EfM* Pointing gesture easy to control *EfM* Speech input correctly understood *EfM* System easy to understand and operate *ProdM* Test users should complete at least two games in 30 minutes | *EfM* Haptic spoken navigation and haptic object action possible after brief instruction *ProdM* Complete game after 30 minutes max | *EfM* Near-walk-up-and-use with no instruction *ProdM* All students make good progress, 1/3 pass final tests after 10 hours *SafM* Safe to use for self-study by children |
| User experience | *SatM* Fun to play Sudoku this way *SatM* Would play again in, e.g. an airport | *SatM* Fun to play this kind of game, great perspectives *SatM* Challenge level is adequate *SatM* Would definitely play full, improved version | *SatM* "I like the teacher very much, she loves her job and the students, she can be tough but only when she has to, she can tell if I am having problems in class and then we talk about them and it helps. Some of her examples are fun and it's fun that one has to do a multiplication problem to choose something. It's also fun when she sets traps for us and that one can get many points by working hard" |

not want different or additional functionality. Thus, to satisfy the functionality requirements in the table, the Maths developers should expect to spend more resources on usability method application than the Sudoku and Treasure Hunt developers.

## 5.3 Towards a Broader Perspective on Usability Work

While Tables 5.1, 5.2, 5.3, 5.4, 5.5, 5.6, 5.7 and 5.8 show where we've got to in establishing a model of use for each Case, there are shortcomings in our presentation of how the tabled information was produced. Chapters 3 and 4 might suggest that AMITUDE models of use are produced by pure developer thinking, cf. Fig. 2.1. This is generally false and misleading! Typically, behind good early models of use lie not only lots of developer experience and discussion, but early application of many of the methods and other approaches we present from Chapter 6 onwards.

So we should have, cf. Fig. 5.1, (i) done Case usability workplanning from day 1, (ii) used the approaches needed to fix development goals, (iii) carried out usability requirements capture and then (iv) done AMITUDE and usability requirements specification. That's how good usability work is being done.

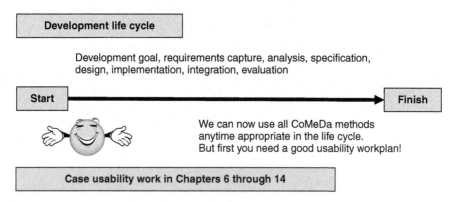

**Fig. 5.1**  How we should have worked on the Cases

# Chapter 6
# Common Approaches, Methods, Planning

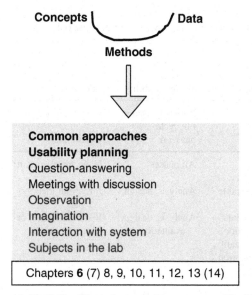

A CoMeDa cycle is a process of applying AMITUDE concepts and a usability method to collect usability data for analysis in order to improve system usability (Section 1.3.1). Having introduced the Concepts part of CoMeDa in Chapters 3 and 4, we move on to the Methods part on how to collect usability information. This chapter presents common informal usability information collection *Approaches* and introduces the more systematic usability *Methods* to be described in Chapters 8, 9, 10, 11, 12 and 13. We also describe two tools for managing usability: the general *Usability Workplan* and the more specific *Usability Method Plan*.

Section 6.1 describes common ways of collecting, or producing, usability information that we hesitate to call "methods" proper. Some of them were mentioned or even used as part of AMITUDE model of use case analysis in Chapters 3 and 4, summarised in Chapter 5 (Intermezzo 2). Section 6.2 introduces the broad range of methods for collecting usability information to be presented in Chapters 8, 9, 10, 11 and 12 and supported by discussion of how to work with users in the lab in Chapter 13. Section 6.3 presents the Usability Workplan, a tool that helps schedule which methods to use when in the life cycle. Section 6.4 describes the Usability Method Plan for detailed planning of each method application scheduled in the Usability Workplan.

N.O. Bernsen, L. Dybkjær, *Multimodal Usability*, Human-Computer Interaction Series, DOI 10.1007/978-1-84882-553-6_6, © Springer-Verlag London Limited 2009

## 6.1 Common Usability Approaches

The basic argument of this book is that a usable system is created by getting hold of enough of the right usability information and using the information well (Section 1.2.1). Some of the ways in which we collect or generate usability information have – contrary to methods (Section 6.2) – little or no well-established, general or systematic, prescriptive procedure to them, which can be learnt, forgotten, broken, followed to the dot, etc. We call these more informal ways *approaches* rather than methods and look at some of the most common ones in this section, cf. Table 6.1.

All approaches in Table 6.1 are probably familiar to most readers, and we have used several of them in this book already. We used *thinking* in establishing the Case AMITUDE analyses in Chapters 3 and 4; presented Modality *theory* in Chapter 4; and described the use of application types to access *related systems and projects* in Section 3.2. We now describe the approaches in more detail in Sections 6.1.1, 6.1.2, 6.1.3, 6.1.4, 6.1.5 and 6.1.6.

**Table 6.1**  Six common approaches for collecting usability information

| Approach | Usability data/information collected on | Primarily used in life cycle phase(s) | Conditions |
|---|---|---|---|
| *Thinking* | Creates ideas, constraints, etc. | All phases | None, always use it! |
| *Theory* | Knowledge applicable to the system | Analysis, design | If relevant theory exists |
| *Related systems and projects* and/or literature on them | Text 1 = ideas, goals, risks, specification, design, functionality, contents, evaluation results, methodology, etc. | Analysis, design, evaluation | If similar system or project exists |
| Directly relevant *empirical data* and/or literature about it | Data for analysis or other uses, results that can be transferred, training data, etc. | Analysis, design, implementa- tion, evaluation | If relevant empirical data or literature exists |
| *Descriptive sources* on one's own project | See Text 1 above | All phases | Unless no descriptive sources exist |
| *Experience* from related projects | See Text 1 above | Any phase | People are available with the experience |

## 6.1.1 Thinking

In usability development, "thinking" broadly refers to activities, such as using common sense, brainstorming, analysis, planning, reflection and consistency checking, problem diagnosis, maintaining a critical stance towards sources (literature, guidelines, code, this book) before and while using them, making sure that all steps required in following a method or data handling procedure have been taken, and properly so, drawing conclusions and making decisions. Thinking is essential to all life cycle phases and, for usability novices in particular, thinking is very much required for learning and for spotting one's own, possibly counterproductive, prejudices. Always think early about the next several steps ahead, leave them for a while and think again before acting. At the end of the day, it is only you and your team's thinking that can keep the project together and ensure that it moves in as straight a line as possible towards some meaningful goal.

Thinking is as much an approach to discovering and solving problems as to deciding that certain problems *cannot* be solved through developer thinking alone but require other sources and methods to be resolved. We used usability developer thinking with the Cases in Chapters 3 and 4, but we also realised the limitations of armchair thought, no matter how much experience it is based upon, when it comes to making a system fit real people. So, while the pitfalls of thinking hardly include thinking too much about issues that can be resolved by thought alone, they do include thinking too little and paying the price later, as well as trying to resolve issues by pure thought which should rather be solved by collecting usability data.

## 6.1.2 Theory

There are theories, and theory under development, for many topics of relevance to multimodal usability today and in future, including CoMeDa *Concepts, Methods* and *Data handling*. So it is not as if we enter a theoretical vacuum when generalising from GUI-oriented usability to multimodal usability and blending with people. Rather, we trespass onto a wealth of areas of theory development. You might, of course, get into something for which no theory exists yet, but chances are that someone has thought about your problem before and expressed those thoughts somehow. Some practical issues are the following: which kind of theory, when to approach theory and what to expect from it.

*Deep theory versus applied theory. Deep theory* is theory as it is being developed in a scientific discipline or across disciplines, including the humanities and the social sciences, aiming at first principles, structure, basic entities and mechanisms, generality and explanatory power. *Applied theory* is what we find in the literature when interactive systems researchers and developers have applied deep theory to make progress, either (i) in usability in general or (ii) with respect to a particular type of application. This book is of type (i). Type (ii) literature is mainly being produced by the communities around different interaction paradigms, cf. Box 1.2 in Section 1.4.4. Consult this literature! It may include operational information for your particular purposes. Contribute to it! Your system most probably is unique in several respects and we would all like to know about them.

*Prefer applied theory to deep theory when available.* Generally prefer applied theory produced by other developers to going straight to deep theory. For one thing, it is hard work to gain a footing in an unfamiliar scientific discipline. For another, applying deep theory to interactive system development tends to be hard as well. The theory "owners" – in psychology, sociology, organisation theory, conversation theory, film theory or whatnot – typically don't concern themselves with the kind of theory application we need, so you probably have to do it yourself. Someone has to do it, that's right, and their efforts are very much appreciated, but not necessarily you, unless you like it.

*A two-way street.* An interesting point concerns the applicability of deep theory. If you were to venture into deep theory in some domain, would you find what you need – say, some ready-made fragment of theory – and directly apply that fragment, for instance, by mapping the theory's entities onto entities in the application and then drawing the necessary inferences?This happens, of course. However, we believe that, quite often, you won't find a ready-made theory fragment which you can attempt to apply. Instead, you encounter one of these four cases: (1) You find conflicting theories, which is an important part of what science is all about, but what you actually need is solid, established theory. (2) You find entire disciplines that are not enthusiastic about grand theory at all, like anthropology, experimental psychology and conversational analysis. Some of them prefer to tell very detailed stories, others to do highly focused experiments, but it's unlikely that those stories and experiments address exactly the issues you need information about. (3) You find something that you believe *can* be applied directly, only to discover later on that the corner of reality which you are dealing with is richer than suggested or assumed by the theory. Our work on principles of cooperation in spoken dialogue is a case in point (Section 11.4). In fact, in that particular case we worked the other way around, first developing a set of principles of cooperativity and then trying to map this structure onto existing theory. The final case (4) is the one where you don't find anything at all relating to what you wish to understand. This is probably rare but, then again, the fact that something in science *relates* to our problem is far from ensuring its operational utility.

Case (3) probably is the important one. We believe that this happens rather frequently: there is theory all right, often good and solid too. But since its developers did not face the concrete problems we have as developers for usability, the theory was never developed to the point at which we can apply it directly. Consider communication acts (Section 3.6.2). Searle (1969) developed a theory of five basic types of speech act (see Section 15.5.5). However, for many interaction development purposes, we need more fine-grained distinctions that Searle did not provide. So far, this is like the cooperation principles case above. However, when it comes to theory of full communication acts, including coordinated speech, facial expression, gesture, gaze, posture, action, there is hardly any theory at all yet. Each of those modalities has been studied extensively, but their coordination into full communication acts has not. Suppose, e.g. that you are interested in applied theory on how to handle something as apparently limited as combined speech and pointing gesture input. All you are likely to find are early studies of the complexity of the problem (Landragin 2006, Bernsen 2006). Interestingly, it seems likely that the theory we need in this area will be based on major contributions from interactive systems researchers.

We are the ones who need the theory as soon as possible; we generate lots of data that can be used for theory development; and we develop the data handling tools (Section 15.5.6).

*Applied theory is cheap. If* we find reasonably established applied theory that can be used directly, we can make great strides at low cost. The conceptual work and the empirical work with people have been done, all we have to do is understand and apply. Note that theory is not only used to guide development, it's also used in theory-based evaluation to check if the theory has been followed in system model design, cf. Section 16.4.2.

### 6.1.3 Related Systems and Projects

Systems or projects similar to our own or otherwise related, and literature describing them, may provide valuable input on usability. We might find papers describing the usability goals and reasoning that went into a system having the same application type, task, domain or modalities as our own or come across a demo. We all tend to take a keen interest in discovering the usability – and other – strengths and weaknesses of competitor systems. Another use of information on related systems is when our system must be compatible with them in some respect.

### 6.1.4 Relevant Empirical Data, an ECA Example

It is also possible to come across raw empirical data that can help make our system usable, such as a corpus suited for analysing gestures in a similar context, or facial expression data for training our mental state recogniser. Data tends to be expensive to collect, difficult to get hold of and rarely straightforward to reuse, so those would be valuable resources should they turn up. When the data has been acquired, it must be handled properly, cf. Chapters 15 and 16.

Empirical data that can help improve system usability does not have to be raw data. In fact, compared to the chances of getting hold of reusable *raw data*, chances are higher of finding potentially useful empirical *data analysis results* in the literature. These are often found in the same papers as those discussed in Section 6.1.3. Let's illustrate this approach and highlight some pitfalls.

A key issue to be aware of in all kinds of transfer from one system to another – of reasoning, data or data analysis results – is the risk of comparing chalk and cheese. Suppose that the systems are aimed at different user groups. Does this difference make transfer invalid? It may, as may any other AMITUDE aspect difference, but this depends on the details, and you will have to decide for yourself.

In rare cases, the problem virtually disappears because the two systems are versions of the same system and differ only with respect to particular properties to be investigated. For instance, López et al. (2008) compare a speech-only (unimodal) version of a spoken dialogue system with an otherwise identical version in which the speaker is an embodied conversational agent (ECA). After testing both versions with users, one finding was that users were more impressed with the system's spoken dialogue in the speech-only version than in the ECA version. Since the spoken dialogue was identical in the two cases and since one would have thought that ECA-based systems are more technologically impressive than speech-only systems, the question is why did the users respond as they did? The authors propose this explanation: because the ECA behaves more like a human than does a disembodied unimodal spoken dialogue system, users unconsciously raise their expectations to the ECA's general similarity with a human, following which they are not particularly impressed with its spoken dialogue performance.

With any such finding, we should ask, first, is the explanation true? Second, if we go with the explanation, can it be transferred to our system? And third, if we decide that it can, which implications should we draw from it? In the present case, there is some consensus that the explanation is on the right track. If our ECA is more primitive than the one described by López et al. (2008), transfer might be invalid. If our ECA is similar to the one in the comparative experiment, we might consider making it more primitive so that users will find its appearance and non-verbal behaviour consistent with its spoken dialogue behaviour.

### 6.1.5  Descriptive Project Sources

All projects larger than Mickey Mouse size usually generate an accumulating document record, no matter whether they are student projects, granted research projects or commercial. Large parts of the usability information included in the record will be produced as a result of activities described elsewhere in this book – AMITUDE specification, usability workplanning, field studies, etc. – so the purpose of this section is simply to mention, for the sake of completeness, project sources on usability not discussed elsewhere. These may be early requirements specifications, project sketches, proposals, call for tender material and contract annexes, describing goals, approaches, requirements, risks, system and user quality goals, environments, interoperability, later changes to the requirements specification, developers' meeting minutes, domain descriptions, customer input, system documentation, technical test reports, review reports, change requests, problem lists, etc. Any such document may provide important usability information and should be taken into account when relevant.

### 6.1.6  Experience

Experience is always a valuable resource in building systems because it shortcuts the need for learning and may spare the project from risky trial-and-error activities. Even if the system is innovatively multimodal, many kinds of experience may come in handy for usability development, including experience with AMITUDE *concepts* analysis, experience with *methods*, including experience in working with users, experience in *data* handling, planning experience and experience from building similar systems. In the latter case, it is important to be aware of how far the similarities go and hence which experience is relevant. In the former cases, this book is to a large extent an attempt to make explicit lessons from more or less painful experiences to help others avoid trial and error.

Analogous with other parts of software engineering, choice among candidate methods for collecting usability information is often heavily influenced by methods already familiar to the developers. However, if, upon reflection, this book includes a more appropriate method that happens to be unfamiliar, we suggest to apply it anyway, starting from reading its description in the following. It's never too late to learn something new, and much trial and error can be avoided by getting into the right mindset and following a small set of common sense rules.

## 6.2 Methods for Usability

We now embark on the *methods* part of this book, which will keep us busy until Chapter 13. The goal of this section is to review all the methods we shall present so that readers can select methods of interest without having to read about them all. If you choose a method that requires working with users in the lab, you should read Chapter 13 as well.

Let's recall what these methods are for, how they are applied and what's in it for you. The methods are for collecting usability information that is needed for building a usable system and cannot be obtained in any other, often cheaper, way, such as by a common approach (Section 6.1). A method is applied as part of a CoMeDa cycle (Section 1.3.1), in which we use AMITUDE concepts, apply the method and handle the data collected. If you apply the methods you need, and do it properly, chances are that the system will fit the target users. If you don't, you will come to realise the old truth that the typical user doesn't have a clue about system code but is a master at revealing and spotting usability problems.

There is a multitude of methods out there for collecting various kinds of usability information. A *usability method* is a well-established procedure for collecting a particular kind of usability data in particular phases of the life cycle or even before it starts. Usability data, or usability information, is information that bears upon any component of system model usability as decomposed in Table 1.1.

Of the methods we shall present, some have their primary focus on *usability development*, some on *usability evaluation*. As shown in Chapter 16, however, all usability data analysis is intrinsically coupled with usability evaluation, so there cannot be any principled distinction between usability development and evaluation methods. Even proposing a development goal, like those for our Cases (Section 2.1), assumes evaluation, such as "People will like this system!" It is widely acknowledged that usability evaluation is integral to development and should be performed iteratively throughout the life cycle to find, and fix, as many problems with the evolving system model as early as possible, when it is maximally cheap to make larger changes. Note that several of the methods below have their origins in other sciences, such as psychology or the social sciences, and were imported into HCI.

Section 6.2.1 discusses user-centred design and links it to AMITUDE. Section 6.2.2 introduces the five groups of methods to be presented. Section 6.2.2 also introduces six differentiation factors that help express the relative importance of a method in a GUI context and a multimodal context, respectively. Sections 6.2.3, 6.2.4, 6.2.5, 6.2.6, and 6.2.7 review a group of methods each. Section 6.2.8 discusses which and how many methods to choose. Section 6.2.9 presents the template that will be used to describe each of the 24 methods in Chapters 8, 9, 10, 11 and 12.

## 6.2.1  Usability Methods Are User-Centred

Since users, as real people, are central to usability (Fig. 3.1), the user is always present one way or another – be it physically or only in the imagination – in usability methods. It is generally acknowledged that the involvement, from early on and throughout, of target users in development and evaluation is crucial to making the system fit the target users. This is the principle behind what is known as user-centred design (UCD). The ISO 13407 (1999) standard on human-centred design processes for interactive systems is the basis of many UCD approaches, cf. Fig. 11.16. The philosophy, which we express in terms of AMITUDE, is that the system must be developed with focus on how users work, what they need, what their skills are, etc. so that it will fit them when completed. This is in contrast to a development approach in which the system model mainly reflects the developers' ideas and, if the final system does not fit the users, they must adapt to it. The notion of user-centred design is a very broad one which carries none of the more partisan school-of-thought flavours, such as cooperative design or participatory design (Greenbaum and Kyng 1991, Nygaard 1990, Sharp et al. 2007).

Most UCD approaches suggest specific activities that should be completed at certain life cycle stages. The Usability Professionals' Association (UPA) has published a poster called *Designing the User Experience*, which shows a typical UCD process (UPA 2000). In this poster, the suggested UCD activities are ordered in four phases, as shown in Fig. 6.1.

It is useful at this point to look back and ahead in relation to the UPA UCD.

*Looking back* at this book so far, there is agreement with the user-centred ethos of Fig. 6.1. However, we need the AMITUDE framework to replace the partial AMITUDE analyses recommended in the figure. When a GUI is taken for granted, there is no need for modality and interaction analysis, and little need for application type and device analysis, reducing AMITUDE to aTUdE. Figure 6.1 corresponds to Section 6.1 regarding common approaches, except that commercial GUI-based development might also have an interest in empirical data analysis, cf. Section 6.1.3.

*Looking ahead* towards the method chapters and the Case designs in Chapter 7 (Intermezzo 3), we shall leave the neat commercial GUI world in which it is possible to recommend application of a particular set of methods to be applied, even in a particular order (Fig. 6.1), and enter the somewhat less well-organised world

| User-centred design activities | |
|---|---|
| **Analysis Phase** | |
| Meet with key stakeholders to set vision | Look at competitive products |
| Include usability tasks in the project plan | Create user profiles |
| Assemble a multidisciplinary team to ensure complete expertise | Develop a task analysis |
| | Document user scenarios |
| Develop usability goals and objectives | Document user performance requirements |
| Conduct field studies | |
| **Design Phase** | |
| Begin to brainstorm design concepts and metaphors | Conduct usability testing on low-fidelity prototypes |
| Develop screen flow and navigation model | Create high-fidelity detailed design |
| Do walk-throughs of design concepts | Do usability testing again |
| Begin design with paper and pencil | Document standards and guidelines |
| Create low-fidelity prototypes | Create a design specification |
| **Implementation Phase** | |
| Do ongoing heuristic evaluations | Conduct usability testing as soon as possible |
| Work closely with delivery team as design is implemented | |
| **Deployment Phase** | |
| Use surveys to get user feedback | Check objectives using usability testing |
| Conduct field studies to get info about actual use | |

**Fig. 6.1**   User-centred design activities in the development process as proposed by UPA. This list of activities is from UPA (2000) and reproduced with the permission of Nicole A. Tafoya

that also includes advanced research projects and multimodal usability. Below, we describe all methods mentioned in Fig. 6.1, as well as other methods, some of which are of particular importance to multimodal usability, and we revise priorities among methods to take the novelty of much multimodal work into account. Looking further ahead towards data collection planning and data handling, commercial GUI-based systems generally need these activities far less than multimodal systems do.

As an *exercise*, try to (i) find as many GUI-world cues in Fig. 6.1 as possible; (ii) match the common approaches (Section 6.1) with those in the figure; and (iii) match the methods in the figure with those reviewed later in this section. Compare with our findings at this book's web site.

## 6.2.2   Usability Methods Presented in This Book

Depending on the stage of development, there are often several methods to choose among for collecting missing usability information. Due to the large number of methods out there – many of which are very similar to each other – we do not intend to present an "exhaustive" set of methods. Our aim is to present a broad and diverse arsenal of methods that cover (i) end-to-end development and evaluation and (ii) all kinds of usability information (Section 1.4.6) and to discuss and illustrate methods in a multimodal context. This should enable selection of an appropriate usability method at all times, *especially if you are prepared to use a little ingenuity to twist one of "our" methods a bit when we haven't described exactly the method variation you need*. Methods have typical and less typical applications, and sometimes when we stretch the less typical ones, distinction between methods gets fuzzy, or thin, and a method may morph into another. For this reason, we often qualify statements about method use by words like "typically" or "normally".

This section introduces the methods by means of a simple and intuitive classification. While all methods serve to collect data that may subsequently be analysed and exploited (Chapter 16), they represent different approaches to data collection. Based on those approaches, the methods can be divided into five groups as follows, adding the number of methods in each group:

- Question-answering (6)
- Meetings with discussion (3)
- Observation (5)
- Imagination (5)
- Interaction with the system under development (5)

The tables in Sections 6.2.3, 6.2.4, 6.2.5, 6.2.6 and 6.2.7 preview each group, describing, for each method, its name, when in the life cycle it is typically being used, the kind of usability data collected and the kind of systems for which the method is relevant. Note that generalisations made in the tables are approximations for most of which exceptions exist or can be conceived.

The left-hand table column includes numbers between 1 and 6 or an asterisk (*). We discuss these codes in the method presentations. Their role is to offer an easy overview regarding the following issue. Today, most methods are being used in a GUI context. Since we discuss the methods in a wider, multimodal context, it is interesting to ask, for each method, if it is more important, or less important, in a multimodal context than in a GUI context or if the context makes no difference. If the context does make a difference, it is of interest to ask why. The list below shows the six *differentiation factors* we have identified so far as bearing upon the relative importance of a method in a GUI context and a multimodal context, respectively. If you are working on an innovative multimodal system, you might use the factors as filters in order to more easily zoom in on methods of importance to your project. Note that this is early work. There may be other factors, and the picture shown may be incomplete in other ways. The differentiation factors are as follows:

1. *Nature of the user–system interface*: in particular, GUI use of labelled icons and menus, the style of tacit interaction and the mostly static user interface is in contrast to the dynamic natural interaction in many non-GUI systems.

2. *User familiarity with the system type*: the less familiar the system type, the more information, illustration and, for some methods, hands-on interactive experience users need to be able to judge reliably. Otherwise, users will judge on the basis of what they imagine based on the insufficient information provided, which may have little to do with reality.
3. *Technology penetration*: GUI systems are everywhere today; multimodal systems are only emerging, so some methods may be mostly used with GUI systems today, although, in future, these methods might be used with all systems.
4. *How close to real-life deployment a system type is*: highly innovative and experimental systems are rarely close to deployment, and this makes a difference with respect to the relevance of some methods.
5. *The kind of data to be collected with users*: non-GUI systems tend to require collection of data of kinds not required for GUI systems, and collection of this data may require new methods. This is due to differences in the nature of the technology, many non-GUI systems aiming at automating people and their behaviours rather than serving as tools for people.
6. *General lack of knowledge (in experts and literature)*: for many innovative non-GUI systems, the knowledge required for applying a particular method does not exist yet. This generates a need for increased use of those methods that *can* be applied. Eventually, this is likely to create the knowledge so far missing.

Thus, it would probably be a waste of time to interview first-time test users about their expectations to the Treasure Hunt Game (Section 2.1), because they wouldn't have a clue about what to say before trying it, cf. factor 2. When we go from GUI-based to non-GUI systems, some usability methods gain in importance and others lose. If a method in the tables below is marked with an *, none of the differentiation factors apply. Further discussion can be found under the entry *Multimodal significance* in Chapters 8, 9, 10, 11 and 12, cf. the method template in Section 6.2.9.

### 6.2.3 Method Group 1: Question-Answering

When using a *question-answering method* from Table 6.2, we ask questions in an interview or a questionnaire. Depending on the method, questions may or may not relate to a system with which the questionees are about to interact or have just interacted. Question-answering methods are described in Chapter 8.

### 6.2.4 Method Group 2: Meetings with Discussion

In the *meetings with discussion* in Table 6.3, we meet and discuss with different groups of people who have an interest in the system. Meetings may or may not

**Table 6.2** Question-answering methods

| Question-answering | Primarily used in life cycle phase(s) | Usability data collected on | Which systems |
|---|---|---|---|
| *User surveys*: interviews or questionnaires[2] | Before project start. No interaction | Needs, opinions, attitudes, intentions, tasks, feedback | Familiar or easily explainable types |
| *Customers*: interviews or questionnaires[3,4] | Start of project. Analysis. No interaction | Requirements, goals, needs, preferences | Types that are being commercialised |
| *Domain experts*: interviews or questionnaires[5,6] | Analysis, early knowledge and scenario elicitation, initial design. No interaction | AMITUDE aspects in depth and in detail | All, provided that expertise exists |
| *Screening*: interviews or questionnaires with potential subjects* | Anytime. No interaction | Suitability as subject, given the goal or the specification | All types |
| *Pre-test* interviews or questionnaires[2] | First design done and onwards. Before interaction | User expectations to system. User facts and background | Types where a basis for user expectations exists or can reasonably be given |
| *Post-test* interviews or questionnaires[2,3,4,5,6] | First design done and onwards. After interaction | Experiences, opinions, suggestions. User facts and background | All types |

**Table 6.3** Methods based on meetings with discussion

| Meetings with discussion | Primarily used in life cycle phase(s) | Usability data collected on | Which systems |
|---|---|---|---|
| *Focus group* meetings[2] | Often some initial design done (at least some thoughts). No interaction | Ideas, attitudes, opinions, wants, needs | Types that can be clearly explained and understood by the participants |
| *Stakeholder* meetings[4] | From life cycle start to finish | Requirements, goals, needs, preferences, design, installation | All types |
| Workshops and other meetings involving *users or their representatives*[2] | Anytime, depending on purpose | Requirements, needs, opinions, preferences, feedback | All types |

involve interaction with a system under development. Methods based on discussion meetings are described in Chapter 9.

## 6.2.5 *Method Group 3: Observation*

Using the *observation methods* in Table 6.4, we observe people doing something of interest to making the system usable. The methods may or may not involve interaction with a system under development and may or may not involve interaction with the people observed. Observation is mainly done by human observers in real time in the field or in the lab. *Micro-behaviours*, as explained at the end of Section 4.2.4, are the actual details of the physical execution of human actions and other behaviours, such as how and how much the eyebrow moves when someone becomes surprised. In *macro-behavioural* observation, on the other hand, these details carry no interest, whereas the actions carried out do and the emotions and other mental states generated may. Observation methods are presented in Chapter 10.

**Table 6.4**  Observation methods

| Observation | Primarily used in life cycle phase(s) | Usability data collected on | Which systems |
| --- | --- | --- | --- |
| *Field methods, macro-behavioural*: field observation and learning through master–apprentice relationship[3] | Analysis, early design. No interaction with system to be developed Late evaluation. Interaction | All AMITUDE aspects, special attention to users, tasks and use environments | Primarily systems for organisations. People must exist who perform what's to be supported or performed by the system to be developed |
| *Field observation, micro-behavioural*[1,5,6] | Analysis, design, implementation. No interaction | Behaviour and communication details, central processing details | Systems perceiving, central processing and acting like people |
| *Category sorting*[5,6] | Early design. No interaction | Category structure inside people's heads | All systems |
| *Observation of users in real time* during user–system interaction[2,4,5,6] | First design done and onwards. Interaction | Behaviour, problems arising | Most types. Can be cumbersome for mobile systems in motion |
| *Human data collection in the lab* with people doing similar tasks or activities[1,5,6] | Analysis, design, implementation. No interaction with system to be developed | Macro- and micro-behaviour and communication details, central processing details | Systems perceiving, processing or acting like people. Training data for system components, e.g. speech recognisers |

## 6.2.6 Method Group 4: Imagination

We use *imagination methods* (Table 6.5) to analyse, specify, design and evaluate system functionality and user–system interaction. Imagination methods are described in Chapter 11.

## 6.2.7 Method Group 5: Interaction with System

Having users interact with a version of the system model and recording what happens is a rich source of usability data and can be done in many different ways as shown in Table 6.6. Interaction methods are described in Chapter 12.

## 6.2.8 Which and How Many Methods to Choose

Shocked by the number (24) of methods above? Don't be! Each method responds to specific and more or less common data collection needs which you might have some day soon yourself.

Which methods to use in a particular project, and how costly in resources using a particular method will be, depends on several factors. Before looking at these, a note about *counting* methods. While many methods can be used stand-alone, some typically come in clusters. For instance, if we do a lab test of the system with a representative user group, we might apply no less than five methods in the process: first, we screen subjects (Table 6.2); then, when they turn up in the lab, we give them a pre-test questionnaire (Table 6.2); make them interact with the implemented prototype (Table 6.6), during which time we observe them (Table 6.4); following

**Table 6.5** Imagination methods

| Imagination | Primarily used in life cycle phase(s) | Usability data collected on | Which systems |
|---|---|---|---|
| *Use cases and scenarios** | Specification and early design | Tasks or other activities | All types |
| *Personas** | Analysis, early design | Interactive behaviours of particular user types | All types |
| *Cognitive walk-through** | Early design and onwards | Interaction "logic", how human cognition handles the system | All types |
| *Guideline-based development and evaluation*[6] | Late analysis, early design and onwards | Conformity with guidelines | Types for which guidelines exist |
| *Standards*[6] | Late analysis, early design and onwards | Conformity with standards | Types for which standards exist |

**Table 6.6**  System interaction-based methods

| Interaction with system | Primarily used in life cycle phase(s) | Usability data collected on | Which systems |
|---|---|---|---|
| *Mock-up*: Low-fidelity and high-fidelity prototype[1] | Design | Coarse grained to medium detailed on interaction, intelligibility, functionality and user behaviour | Types which can be mocked up |
| *Wizard of Oz* (WOZ)[1,5] | First design done and onwards until full implementation available | Behaviour and communication details, central processing details, functionality, domain coverage | Types involving natural interaction |
| *Implemented prototype*[1,5,6] | First implementation and onwards | Behaviour and communication details, central processing details, functionality, domain coverage | All types |
| *Field test*[1,3] | System mostly implemented and close to final | Interaction patterns, functionality, domain coverage | All types that reach the field-testing stage |
| *Think-aloud*[1] | First design done and onwards | Structure and processing inside people's heads. Ease of use | Does not work for natural interaction systems |

which we give them a post-test interview (Table 6.2). This *lab test cluster* of methods is a single process, planned and executed as such, and if you do it twice, say, with a 1-year interval, you would have already done 10 usability method applications in the project.

Which methods to use very much depends on (i) the kinds of usability information required, but there are other factors as well, including (ii) if the project is research or commercial, highly innovative or less so, GUI-based or multimodal and (iii) the current development phase. If we are building a really innovative multimodal system like Treasure Hunt whose look-sound-and-feel is hard to explain, it probably makes little sense to use early methods which assume that people understand what interaction will be like. A more productive approach could be to start by using imagination methods that do not depend on the existence of guidelines and standards, because there probably aren't any (Table 6.5) and then proceed to interaction methods as soon as we have something – a small prototype, a design for WOZ simulation – for people to try out (Table 6.6). Note that interaction methods may be part of clusters, like the lab test cluster variation mentioned above.

A commercial project may be viewed as a far more downstream version of the research project, done, say, 10 years later. At that point, people may be familiar with the technologies used; guidelines and standards may have been developed; experts emerged; and there may be potential costumers around. Now we can consider using early surveys (Table 6.2), focus groups (Table 6.3) and guidelines and standards (Table 6.5), before proceeding to interaction methods (Table 6.6). For a comparative study of the changing pattern of method application from research to commercial development, see Dybkjær et al. (2005). We found that differences in usability evaluation objectives influence the number and kinds of usability evaluation methods applied.

Other factors influencing which methods to use are project (iv) technical and user quality requirements (Section 1.4.6), (v) team expertise in usability methods, (vi) scale, (vii) duration and (viii) budget.

Method application cost is an important factor. Cost depends on (i) method chosen, (ii) scale of method application, (iii) project technical and user quality requirements and (iv) scale and depth of data handling. Method application cost includes everything: planning, subject contact, subject recruitment, session preparations, sessions with people (customers, stakeholders, subjects, users), support staff, remuneration, travel and data handling. Imagination methods (Table 6.5) tend to be relatively cheap because the development team can apply these themselves. Some meetings (Table 6.3) are relatively cheap as long as one does not have to pay for people's time. Domain experts, if available, typically must be paid, sometimes handsomely (Table 6.2). Surveys are typically quite costly due to their size (Table 6.2). Cost also really tends to rise when subjects and users are to be involved and must be located, screened, invited, signed up, transported, hosted, tested, interviewed, remunerated, etc. (Tables 6.2, 6.3, 6.4 and 6.6). Data handling cost is often neglected, which is understandable as long as all we have to do is read through meeting minutes and scribble a couple of notes on what to do or modify. However, multimodal systems development often requires far more extensive (and costly) data handling, as we shall see in Chapters 15 and 16.

*Discount usability.* In view of the cost aspect of CoMeDa cycles in usability development, Nielsen (1993) proposed the idea of discount usability. His argument was the plain and simple one that a spot of usability work in industrial system development, such as application of a small set of usability guidelines and some simple CoMeDa practices, is better than none. To improve usability somewhat, we don't have to try to make sense of thousands of usability guidelines, organise user tests at every turn, perform endless psychological experimentation or wait years for an anthropologist to tell us work anecdotes from the hospital whose procedures we were supposed to automate.

An idea in the spirit of Nielsen's book is that it is normally better to run two or more small-scale evaluations using different methods, and preferably with some time in-between, rather than running one larger scale evaluation with a single method. One reason is that – in particular, early in the life cycle – we tend to find important problems in the first few evaluation sessions; if these problems are serious, there is no need to waste time on further testing before they have been corrected.

We normally want to evaluate system usability again when, in particular, serious errors have been remedied. A second reason is that no single method is able to reveal all kinds of usability errors, problems and weaknesses or suggest all kinds of requirements and design ideas. Two different methods may supplement each other and together help find more usability issues.

Chapter 7 (Intermezzo 3) discusses choice of usability methods for our Cases.

## 6.2.9 Method Presentation Template

The methods introduced in Sections 6.2.3, 6.2.4, 6.2.5, 6.2.6 and 6.2.7 are described in Chapters 8, 9, 10, 11 and 12, following the template shown in Table 6.7. The template was established iteratively by considering which information is generally useful to have in order to apply a usability method.

As for the individual methods, neither method name nor scope, description or type is uniform in the literature. We have established the method descriptions iteratively by (i) developing a list of candidate methods; (ii) drafting a description of each method; (iii) revising by consulting different descriptions of each method; and (iv) composing the list of methods presented, drawing upon own experience and sources we found relevant. We are to blame for any errors or omissions.

**Table 6.7**  Method description template

| Template sections | Explanation |
|---|---|
| Brief introduction | Brief description of what the method is about |
| When can you use the method and what is its scope? | When in the life cycle the method is most frequently used and the kind of systems the method may be used for? Note that the method may be useful in other life cycle phases as well. You will be the judge of that |
| Multimodal significance | Relative importance to GUI-based and multimodal development |
| How does the method work? | Brief general description of how the method works. Details are provided under planning and running |
| What is required for applying the method | People, equipment, materials, etc. |
| System/AMITUDE model | Required state of the AMITUDE model of use and of the system model more generally and possibly what the method contributes to it |
| Planning | What you need to prepare before applying the method? |
| Running | What to do and what to be aware of when applying the method? |
| Data | Which data is typically collected, how to post-process the data, what you may want to obtain from it and use it for? |
| Advantages and drawbacks | Advantages and disadvantages of using the method, sometimes compared to other methods |
| Example | One or more method illustrations |

## 6.3  Writing a Usability Workplan

Usability methods are like beads: you need a string for putting them together and make them useful as a necklace. The string that puts methods together and makes them useful, or even adequate, for the project is planning. For flexibility, it is best to break down usability planning into two steps. The first step schedules the usability work to be done in the project life cycle, including all activities to do with AMI-TUDE analysis, method application and data handling. This book probably is as flexible as can be as regards the *order* of life cycle development and evaluation activities (Section 1.2.2), but that just means that you have to order and plan them yourself. We call this step the *usability workplan* and discuss it in this section. The second step is a detailed plan for each method application and subsequent data handling. This is the *usability method plan* described in Section 6.4.

The usability workplan is part of the project plan that covers many issues other than usability. The usability workplan determines the scope of work aimed to advance usability development and test and measure conformance with usability requirements and evaluation criteria, eventually producing a system that satisfies them. A first, preliminary, plan should be written at project start. It is based on the budgeted amount of usability work and anything else about the project that's of relevance to usability. Budget, project goal and known usability requirements and risks together determine, in the preliminary plan, which methods to use when. The UCD in Fig. 6.1 may be viewed as a terse usability workplan.

If you have no separate usability budget, consider how important usability is for the project, the usability goals you need and want to achieve and any known risks. Maybe a number of usability requirements have been established from the outset. On this background, you estimate how much time to set aside for usability work since this is important to the usability workplan. Be aware that ambitious goals, high risks and a low budget are not a good combination. Quality costs!

The usability workplan, including its risk list, should be updated regularly to accommodate changes. We do not go into details about risk management in this book, see, e.g. DeMarco and Lister (2003), but stress that it is an important part of software development and highly relevant to usability work.

Workplan changes should be kept at a minimum in commercial projects, but we can never guarantee that we won't need an extra method or method change due to, e.g. changed priorities or new customer requests. In research projects, usability workplans tend to change more over time because it is difficult to predict from the start exactly what will be needed. A thorough workplan review should always be made when the workplan becomes based upon the AMITUDE specification and usability requirements as illustrated in Chapter 5 (Intermezzo 2).

In addition to describing a carefully selected set of usability methods to be applied in a particular order, the workplan may also include, e.g. deadlines and critical development issues. For instance, if the project has a fixed deadline, knowledge about the time it takes to apply a particular method and handle the collected data gives an absolute deadline for when to use some system interaction methods

(Table 6.6), which again fixes an absolute deadline for when to start preparations for applying the method.

Also, advanced multimodal projects typically have critical development issues, such as making some kind of multimodal mental state recognition work. Using the workplan and the criteria for recognition success, we can plan iterative application of a usability method for measuring recognition progress towards the criteria values and iteratively revise the plan should the target value prove more easy or difficult to achieve than expected. Should things turn, or remain, bad, we have early warning that now may be the time to adopt Plan B and drop the target for Plan A. "But isn't this a purely technical goal?" Well, it *might* be a purely technical goal if the project is solely about improving enabling technologies for signal processing and input fusion. However, if we are building an interactive multimodal system for real users to use for a purpose, then the quality of the system's mental state recognition and interpretation functionality becomes a usability requirement.

Never forget that the workplan and its time/effort schedule must be *realistic*. In fact, quite some information is required to decide which usability methods to use by when, including, at least the following: (i) how many and which resources to spend on usability, (ii) how much time and other resources application of a particular method requires in the project context and (iii) if there are any critical issues that require particular attention through method application. Description of these considerations and decisions forms part of the usability workplan. Note that sometimes a cost–benefit analysis is made to estimate to which extent usability activities, such as a particular CoMeDa cycle, are likely to pay off.

In *summary*, a usability workplan is a tool that defines the scope of the usability-related development and evaluation work – AMITUDE analysis, method application, data handling – needed to satisfy the usability requirements. The plan must be realistic as regards budget, time, team competence and other resources. Usability requirements form the basis of the workplan, which describes what to do when in order to be able to collect usability information, handle the data and make timely use of what its analysis implies. As the AMITUDE model of use is part of the system requirements specification, the usability workplan is part of the project time plan.

Each method scheduled in the usability workplan must be explained and detailed in a usability method plan.

## 6.4  Writing a Usability Method Plan

A usability method plan expands a method entry in the project-wide usability workplan (Section 6.3). In fact, a usability method plan includes preparations prior to method application, method application and subsequent data handling and analysis which we discuss in Chapters 15 and 16. "That's fine," – we hear you say – "but why more planning and paperwork?" Take a look at Box 6.1. The real point it makes is that even if we have carefully crafted a usability method plan for system evaluation, something will probably still go wrong, as illustrated for the Sudoku system test in Chapter 17 (Intermezzo 5). In other words, not to write a plan is asking for chaos. Let's generalise the text box message.

The are two main reasons why method planning is crucial. First, to ensure that exactly the usability information the project needs will be collected when the method is applied. If this part of the preparation goes seriously wrong, method application may be a waste of time and effort. Second, to avoid errors of method application that could affect data quality or quantity. Many usability methods are costly in time and effort. If method application does not produce the data needed, in contents, quality and quantity, reapplication may be necessary, which means a more or less serious loss of resources. Worse, the project time schedule might not allow method reapplication, in which case the project suffers a definitive loss of results that could affect system usability in all sorts of ways.

Note that a method plan is sometimes called test plan, evaluation plan, evaluation protocol or test protocol if its purpose is evaluation. We prefer *plan* to *protocol* because it emphasises the global nature of the planning required. And we prefer the more general *method plan* since we are dealing with both development and evaluation methods. In any case, make a detailed method plan every time you are going to apply a method from your usability workplan. The good news is that, once made, method plans can be reused to quite some extent.

A method plan sometimes covers a cluster of methods, such as a test of an implemented prototype with real-time observation, followed by a post-test questionnaire. See also the Case method plan example in Chapter 14 (Intermezzo 4).

In the following, Section 6.4.1 presents typical points in a method plan. Each of these points is addressed in more detail in Sections 6.4.2, 6.4.3, 6.4.4, 6.4.5, 6.4.6, 6.4.7 and 6.4.8.

## Box 6.1  Do a Usability Method Plan Next Time?

You and your colleagues spend three person weeks preparing and executing a user test over 3 days. On the final day, you discover that there was no agreement on who would operate the video cameras. As a result, there are no video recordings of user–system interaction. You have no record of what the users actually did as opposed to what your logfiles might show. Now, if this was the only mistake you committed in the absence of a method plan, you should feel lucky! Most probably, your sloppiness also resulted in events, such as that one-third of the users never showed up; a test machine had the wrong system version installed; some users never got anywhere because the system crashed immediately and there was no one present to fix it; and the interviewers could not find rooms in which to make the interviews, ending up in the crowded cafeteria with the subjects.

## 6.4.1 Method Plan Overview

The method plan describes everything to do with applying a usability method, from what the results of data analysis should be about, through all steps needed for applying the method properly, to answers to all practical questions about who is responsible for what, where, by when and how to do what. The purpose is to describe (i) method application or *data collection* and (ii) subsequent data handling, with so much care that everyone involved knows exactly what to do during data collection and everyone knows exactly what should be done about the collected usability data.

A method plan need not be a lengthy document – it just needs to have been carefully considered, which takes time to mature, especially if you are new to this kind of planning. If you reuse an earlier, successful method plan, *never* copy it mechanically even if you were the one who followed the plan. Even if there is no change of method, plan details tend to change, such as roles, participants, scenarios or equipments.

Typical points in a method plan are the following:

- *Purpose*: overall data collection goal;
- *Specific goals*: making sure to get the right data;
- *Avoiding priming*: in communication with data producers;
- *Subject recruitment*: making sure to get the right subjects;
- *Third parties*: people not from the lab, not developers, not users, if any;
- *Staff*: roles and responsibilities;
- *Location, equipment, other material, data handling, results presentation;*
- *Script*: for method application.

Note that since this list is meant to cover our 24 methods (Section 6.2.2) and more, some points do not apply to some methods. We recommend that you create your own preferred method plan structure, just never forgetting that it's all about the usability information that the method is planned to collect. When commenting on the points below, we sometimes refer to Chapter 13 for more detail. Chapter 13 discusses working with users in the lab and therefore deals with many of the method planning issues from the point of view of running lab sessions.

## 6.4.2 Data Collection Purpose

Always start by clearly stating the data collection purpose, e.g. to explore the workplace where the system will be installed; test if the system meets the specified usability requirements; or collect ideas about tasks people might want to do through spoken dialogue with their mobile phone. Clearly, the data collection purpose is a key factor in method selection in the first place, cf. Section 6.2.8.

### 6.4.3 Getting the Right Data

Having made the data collection purpose clear and selected the method, you must specify in detail what it is that you want to obtain knowledge about through analysis of the collected data. Note how method planning *starts* by reaching all the way to the crux of the data handling process, i.e. what can be learnt from the collected data through analysis. It is crucial to make the data collection purpose operational: if you don't carefully plan for the data to hold the usability information you need, the data will not necessarily include this information. In a slightly frivolous example, if you don't rig the implemented prototype test in such a way that subjects will exhibit certain emotions, such as by dropping spiders in front of them on camera, they probably won't. And then you'll get no data on the usability of your facial emotion recognition sub-system and hence not be able to apply any usability evaluation criterion specified.

Think about each method application as a way of asking specific questions: if you don't ask, you won't be told, and then the opportunity of asking will be gone.

### 6.4.4 Communication with Data Producers: Avoid Priming

No matter which method we use, there are always people involved who produce the usability information. These data producers may be just yourself – if you apply some imagination method (Section 6.2.6) – or meeting participants, test subjects, experts or others, depending on the method. Communication with the data producers is typically crucial for making sure to collect the right usability information: a questionnaire yields the right data only if it asks the right questions; a meeting only if it has the right agenda and sticks to it; a test subject only if provided with the right verbal or written instructions, tasks, scenarios or promptings, including, perhaps, the occasional spider; etc. Given the importance of data producer communication, method planning should devote ample time to carefully develop what will be communicated to the data producers and how. It is when communication goes wrong that you risk priming the data producers.

In the context of usability method application, *priming* is the general phenomenon of corrupting data by influencing data producers' behaviour. The whole idea of method application in a CoMeDa cycle is to collect usability information that can reliably be used for making the system usable. If data producers are influenced by something in the data collection process to produce information that reflects the process itself rather than properties of the system, this defeats the purpose of collecting data. All we have left is corrupt data, wasted resources and our prejudices that the data might have shaken, had it not been corrupt. This is bad, of course, and look at these two points: (1) The risk of priming attaches to all data collection methods where the data collector – you, for instance – is different from the data producer. This doesn't prevent you from making mistakes when applying, e.g. an imagination method yourself, of course. These mistakes just aren't called priming effects. (2) Causes of priming are endless and work behind the back of the honest CoMeDa cyclist. It is only dishonest data collectors who consciously try to corrupt the data by influencing the data producers. Take a look at Box 6.2.

Although the priming examples in Box 6.2 and Section 13.3.5 are from inter-action method applications (Section 6.2.7), they clearly suggest that priming could happen with any usability method that involves communication with data producers. Considerable work has been done on how to avoid priming when using, in particu-lar, question-answering methods (Section 6.2.3), and we will keep an eye on priming throughout the method chapters. A general piece of advice is that, as soon and as long as you are in the company of a data producer, consider yourself an *actor* in the service of incorrupt data and maintain an absolutely neutral stance towards the system model at all times. It does feel artificial to behave like this, but it may help avoid the spontaneity that gives you away and primes others.

## Box 6.2   Priming Subjects

We involve subjects because we want to collect data on how users behave vis-à-vis our system model. It follows that we don't want to influence – or prime – the way subjects behave in any way which could bias the data. Unfortunately, subjects may be primed in many different ways, and it is important to carefully plan each session with subjects in such a way that priming is avoided. Priming can be quite subtle and hard to spot as well.

Basically, whatever you *tell* subjects or give them in *writing* might cause priming effects in context. *Attitudes* can prime as well and so can *any* kind of deliberate and non-deliberate communication with subjects. If you are notice-ably excited about the wonderful system of yours that they are going to inter-act with, they will assume that you will be happy if they praise the system and avoid criticising it. If the experimenter instructs subjects in how to speak and point at the same time, it is natural to *demonstrate* what to do through a par-ticular example of speech and pointing interaction. No malicious intentions here, right? However, don't be surprised if the data shows that those subjects nearly always speak and point following the pattern shown to them by the experimenter, rather than following one of the many alternative patterns pos-sible (Martin et al. 2006). If you want subjects to speak spontaneously to the system, don't provide them with complete written scenario texts because they will simply read them aloud. If they do that, your hope of collecting sponta-neous interaction data goes out the window. One way of solving this problem is illustrated in Section 13.3.5. User spontaneity is often precious in data col-lection, and you may have to be smart to obtain it.

Related to priming is the fact that subjects *learn* from what they do during the session. They are smart, learn fast and draw their own conclusions, so they may have stopped being novice data producers long before the session is over.

### 6.4.5  Subject Recruitment, Third Parties

Some usability methods require subject recruitment in the sense of inviting people to act as data producers. The method plan should specify when and how to recruit how many users or subjects. As explained in detail in Section 13.2, recruitment may take considerable time and tends to cause more difficulty than first-time recruiters expect, so prepare for it well in advance.

Other methods require involvement of third parties, such as domain experts, expert evaluators or customers. The plan must include information about how many such people or organisations to involve, who they will be and how and when to get in touch with them. These people are likely to be busy, so you might ruin everything by acting too late relative to the date(s) on which the method will be applied.

### 6.4.6  Staff Roles and Responsibilities

A usability method has to be applied *by* someone, so method application planning involves assignment of roles and responsibilities, such as scenario or questionnaire designer, subject recruiter, experimenter (Section 13.4.7), observer (in the field or in the lab), system support, equipment support, making sure that data gets recorded and logged, domain expert, wizard, wizard's assistant, help desk operator, chairperson, meeting secretary, interviewer, data analyst and results presenter. This is a long list, not just because there are many different usability methods but also because application of a single method may imply 5–10 different roles. It is rare that a single person can do everything. Moreover, it is often advantageous to share method planning and execution, and for some methods this is a necessity, such as for Wizard of Oz simulations. For cost-effectiveness, each person involved should have the same role(s) throughout because it may be necessary to practice a given role, and some roles require a certain expertise.

In addition to assignment of roles, the method plan should include written instructions for each role about what to do, where, when, how, using which equipment and other materials and collaborating with whom. The role instructions may be separate from the common method application script (Section 6.4.8). If role training is required, such as for being able to apply a set of guidelines or acting as wizard, this must be planned as well. We recommend a meeting with the key support colleagues in which you go over the method plan together. Separate meetings with individual support staffers may also be needed to ensure a common understanding of their tasks during method application.

### 6.4.7  Location, Equipment, Other Materials, Data, Results

A usability method is being applied somewhere, using various equipment items, as well as general, method-specific and possibly other materials. See also the detailed discussion in Section 13.3.

*Location.* The location where the method will be applied could be anywhere – in a meeting room, downhill on skis, at a customer's production plant, etc. When you know the nature of the location and how long method application will take, you should ensure availability of a suitable location. This may be non-trivial to do, requiring meetings with the host organisation, if any, written permissions, reservations and more and may be impossible if you are running late.

*Equipment.* Make a list of the equipment that will be required. If some of it is not provided on location, bring it there. It is not good enough to make sure that the equipment is available when you are going to use it. Always set it up and test it before subjects or other participants arrive. If you are going to use the equipment outside the lab, test that it works before bringing it with you. Furthermore, during method application, support staff should check regularly that everything still works as intended, including, e.g. cameras, sound recording and logs.

*Other materials.* Each method planning process assumes and generates documentation – time plans, lists of workshop participants, subject instructions, etc. Some materials are basic to all or most methods, such as the system model and its AMITUDE model of use specification, when ready (Section 3.1). More special kinds of materials are sometimes needed as well, such as permission to make recordings in a certain environment, or forms signed by subjects to confirm their participation by informed consent and permit use of the collected data for specific purposes.

*Data collection, data handling, results presentation.* Method application *is* data collection, and it's clear from the above that a large part of the method plan describes how data collection is to take place. Data collection is followed by data handling, analysis and presentation of the results of data analysis. The method plan includes planning of data handling and results presentation, describing what will be done by whom and by when. We describe data handling and results presentation in Chapters 15 and 16.

### *6.4.8 Method Script*

The method script is a simple tool that draws upon, and refers to, the method plan items discussed above and schedules what will happen before, during and after method application. It describes where and when the method will be applied, who participates, who recruits subjects, which materials and equipment must be in place, the session schedule and subsequent data handling. For example, the script may describe date(s) and location(s) for the session(s), how many subjects will participate, who will recruit them, which information to give when contacting them, which equipment will be used, which material is needed during the session, how the session will proceed and what will happen to the collected data.

For ease of overview, include a checklist of what you need for the session, e.g. hardware, software and various kinds of materials, such as instructions to personnel involved, user instructions, scenarios and questionnaires.

A written script makes it easier to get input from others on correctness and completeness and serves to ensure process consistency if more people are involved in applying the method and preparing for it.

Chapter 14 (Intermezzo 4) shows an example of a method script.

## 6.5  Key Points

This chapter has introduced the core part of usability work that consists in collecting, or generating, usability information by means of various informal usability approaches as well as a careful selection of usability methods proper. A *Common Usability Approach* is a commonly used source of information that helps getting system usability right during development. A *Usability Method* is a well-established procedure for collecting usability data during the development process or even before its start. The methods presented in this book are of five categories: *Question-answering, Meetings with discussion, Observation, Imagination* and *Interaction with the system model*. A *Usability Workplan* defines, schedules and helps manage usability development and evaluation activities throughout the life cycle. A *Usability Method Plan* expands each method entry in the usability workplan and scripts in detail how the method will be applied and how the collected data will be handled.

## References

Bernsen NO (2006) Speech and 2D deictic gesture reference to virtual scenes. In: André E, Dybkjær L, Minker W, Neumann H, Weber M (eds) Perception and interactive technologies. Proceedings of international tutorial and research workshop. Springer, LNAI 4021.

DeMarco T, Lister T (2003) Waltzing the bears: managing risk on software projects. Dorset House Publishing Company, New York.

Dybkjær L, Bernsen NO, Dybkjær H (2005) Usability evaluation issues in commercial and research systems. In: CD-proceedings of the ISCA tutorial and research workshop and COST278 final workshop on applied spoken language interaction in distributed environments (ASIDE). Aalborg University, Denmark.

Greenbaum J, Kyng M (eds) (1991) Design at work: cooperative design of computer systems. Lawrence Erlbaum Associates, Hillsdale.

ISO 13407 (1999) Human-centred design processes for interactive systems. http://www.iso.org/iso/iso_catalogue/catalogue_tc/catalogue_detail.htm?csnumber=21197. Accessed 22 January 2009.

Landragin F (2006) Visual perception, language and gesture: a model for their understanding in multimodal dialogue systems. Signal Processing 86/12: 3578–3595.

López B, Hernández Á, Pardo D, Santos R, Rodríguez M (2008) ECA gesture strategies for robust SLDSs. In: Proceedings of the Artificial Intelligence and Simulation Behaviour Convention (AISB). Aberdeen, Scotland.

Martin J-C, Buisine S, Pitel G, Bernsen NO (2006) Fusion of children's speech and 2D gestures when conversing with 3D characters. Signal Processing Journal, Special issue on multimodal interaction. Elsevier.

Nielsen J (1993) Usability engineering. Academic Press, New York.

Nygaard K (1990) The origins of the Scandinavian school, why and how? Participatory design conference 1990 transcript. Computer Professionals for Social Responsibility, Seattle.

Sharp H, Rogers Y, Preece J (2007) Interaction design – beyond human–computer interaction. 2nd edn. John Wiley and Sons, New York.

Searle J (1969) Speech acts. Cambridge University Press, Cambridge.

UPA (2000) What is user-centered design? http://www.upassoc.org/usability_resources/about_usability/what_is_ucd.html. Accessed 4 February 2009.

# Chapter 7
# Intermezzo 3: Case Usability Workplan, Design

This intermezzo discusses Case usability workplanning in Section 7.1. Based on the Case AMITUDE specifications in Section 5.1, we take the next step and do some Case design, adding what in a multimodal world should probably be termed look-hear-and-feel to the Cases (Section 7.2).

## 7.1 Case Usability Workplans

We are now in a position to address usability workplan writing, introduced in Section 6.3, for the Cases. Since we have done the Case AMITUDE specifications without any usability workplan (Section 5.1), we would like to address two questions: (1) which among this book's 24 usability methods (Section 6.2) *might* we use from the start of each Case life cycle and until the start of Case design? (2) Which methods will or might we use henceforth?

(1) *Early (pre-design) methods that might have been used for the Cases.* Since all Cases are advanced multimodal systems, we would expect that some usability methods cannot be used early (pre-design) with much benefit because, e.g. a certain Case system is too unfamiliar to potential users, still belongs to advanced research far from deployment, customers and real stakeholders or is beyond available expertise, cf. the factors listed in Section 6.2.2. To check these expectations, let's look at the Cases in some detail, because the picture that will emerge is probably representative of advanced multimodal systems work today.

*Sudoku* is probably known to most people today, and it's primarily the speech-and-pointing interaction with the Sudoku system that is new, unfamiliar, in need of proof of concept, rather upstream of industrial development, and not clearly covered by available expertise. However, the interaction idea is natural and familiar, and hence, probably, easy to explain to potential users and others.

Given these points, it would seem un(der-)productive to have used the following early methods in order to establish the Sudoku model of use described in Section 5.1: micro-behavioural field observation (Section 6.2.5) because no one is doing the user task already in the way envisioned; guidelines or standards for speech and 3D pointing input (Section 6.2.6) because, to our knowledge, there isn't any consolidated guidelines or standards set except for the graphics output; experts in speech–3D pointing input (Section 6.2.3) because there aren't any; customer interviews (Section 6.2.3) and stakeholder meetings (Section 6.2.4) because it's hard to find customers or stakeholders prior to technology proof of concept. At best, we might find an entertainment company that might consider *acting* as customer and stakeholder.

On the other hand, macro-behavioural field methods (Section 6.2.5) might be used to find out how people play Sudoku on paper or over the Internet. Personas (Section 6.2.6) might describe users having different Sudoku expertise or differing in stamina.

The picture for *Treasure Hunt* is even more restrictive. Not only would it seem counter-productive to have used the methods listed as non-applicable for Sudoku above, and for similar reasons; this also applies to user surveys (Section 6.2.3), focus groups (Section 6.2.4) and macro-behavioural field methods (Section 6.2.5). The only early method uses would seem to be human data collection in the lab (Section 6.2.5), use cases and scenarios (Section 6.2.6) and involvement of a user group in user-centred development through meetings and workshops (Section 6.2.4), all of which could also be used in the Sudoku Case. Otherwise, it's all about getting the design done and implementing an early prototype for user testing (Section 6.2.7).

*Maths* is more like Sudoku rather than like Treasure Hunt as regards how many and which usability methods might be applied early and with benefit. User surveys (Section 6.2.3) would hardly yield much because of the unfamiliar technology. Guidelines or standards for maths self-tutoring for children (Section 6.2.6) don't exist, but do exist for the graphics and spoken dialogue parts of the system. However, a focus group meeting (Section 6.2.4) with teachers might provide input on tutoring contents, and it might be interesting to recruit a school as "customer" for making meaningful customer interviews (Section 6.2.3), stakeholder meetings and user workshops (Section 6.2.4). Expert interviews with teachers (Section 6.2.3) are clearly relevant, as are macro-behavioural field methods (Section 6.2.5), use cases and scenarios and personas (Section 6.2.6).

In conclusion, it *is* possible to apply, to varying degrees, usability methods early in advanced multimodal systems development, but highly innovative systems tend to reduce the number of applicable methods, shifting the emphasis somewhat onto "late" methods for interactive system model testing (Section 6.2.7).

(2) *Methods that might be used for the Cases from design onwards.* Figure 7.1 shows a usability workplan for the Maths system. As an exercise, try to draft workplans for Sudoku and Treasure Hunt, using the methods overview in Section 6.2. Figure 7.1 shows that method clusters (Section 6.2.8) will be used for Maths, and we have applied user test method clusters to the Sudoku and Treasure Hunt systems as well (Bernsen and Dybkjær 2007).

Figure 7.1 shows a Maths usability workplan sketch. Time to spend on method application (here measured in person weeks) includes preparation, application and data handling.

You might miss *screening* of potential subjects (Section 6.2.3). The reason is that subjects will be ordinary school children of the right age and background. Fitting this description is screening enough. We might have gone for a *macro-behavioural*

| Usability workplan | | | | |
|---|---|---|---|---|
| Project name: Maths | Workplan author: LD | | Date of plan v.2: 2008.12.02 | |
| Project calendar time: | 18 months | Project start date: | 2008.07.01 | |
| Total project resources: | 36 person months | | | |
| Usability work: | 12 person months total to be spent on common approaches, methods, data handling, and unforeseen issues arising. | | | |
| Development goal, cf. Table 5.1 | Research prototype for demonstrating a cognitive-affective basic maths tutoring companion for children. | | | |
| AMITUDE requirements: | See Tables 5.1–5.8 | | | |
| Usability requirements: | See Table 5.9 | | | |
| Methods planned | | | | |
| When | Method | | Person weeks | Done |
| Start month 2 | Use cases and scenarios. | | 1 week | x |
| Start month 2, overlap with use cases and scenarios | Personas: test of conversation design with different student types. | | 1 week | x |
| End month 2 | Expert interviews with 2 maths teachers. | | 3 weeks | x |
| Month 3 | Revisit use cases and personas. Extend use cases. | | 3 weeks | x |
| End month 3 | Category sorting to check understandability of faces; 10–15 school children. | | 2 weeks | x |
| Month 4 | Cognitive walk-through. | | 2 weeks | x |
| Month 6 | Interaction with console-based implemented prototype combined with real-time observation and post-test interview; 6 school children. | | 5–6 weeks | |
| Start month 8 | Human data collection in the lab: facial expression, gesture, bio-data for component training, 6 school children. | | 8 weeks | |
| Month 12 | Interaction with full implemented prototype, with real-time observation and post-test interview; 6 school children. | | 5–6 weeks | |
| Month 15-18 | Field test in school; 10–20 children. | | 8 weeks | |

**Fig. 7.1** Usability workplan skeleton for Maths system

*field study* of a maths teacher in class (Section 6.2.5) but chose to interview a teacher as domain expert instead. We might also have used our *guidelines* (Section 6.2.6) for cooperative spoken dialogue (see Section 11.4), but, since we made them, we are probably using them during implementation anyway. We might have used a pretest interview or questionnaire (Section 6.2.3), but this would hardly yield much because of the unfamiliarity of the technology. Finally, we might have applied early interaction methods (Section 6.2.7),but, having done rapid prototyping, we have gone for several implemented prototype tests instead, incrementally adding communication functionality between tests.

In total, our multimodal usability work on the Maths system draws upon some 10 usability methods, several of which will be used iteratively. This is – or should be! – typical of advanced multimodal research prototype development processes.

Note that there is micro-behavioural data collection in at least the following method applications: (1) expert interview: we ask the teachers about affective student micro-behaviours; (2) category sorting: we ask students to classify facial micro-behaviours; (3) interaction with implemented prototype: we collect data for analysis on students' spoken, facial and gesture micro-behaviours and (4) make notes about them during real-time observation; and (5) human data collection in the lab: we collect micro-behaviours for component training.

## 7.2  Case Design

This section describes the designs of the Sudoku, Treasure Hunt and Maths systems, based on their AMITUDE models of use (Section 5.1). Space does not allow discussion of design rationales – arguments pro and con design decisions (Carroll and Rosson 2003) – for the numerous specific design decisions made, but we hope that the designs themselves will stand out vividly from the descriptions and images. We refer to the designs in the methods and data handling chapters to follow.

### 7.2.1  Sudoku

*Design strategy.* Keep it simple: enable the user task but drop external memory options, score keeping, embellishments, etc. Limit online help to a single type of error display and customisation options to choice of game difficulty.

*Overall interaction design.* The main screen displays game board and labelled icons *new game* and *reset game*. The game board is a $9 \times 9$ square matrix built from nine separate squares each consisting of $3 \times 3$ little squares for holding numbers.

Figure 7.2 shows the main screen and a successfully solved game. Note that this and the following figures are from an implemented version of the game and not

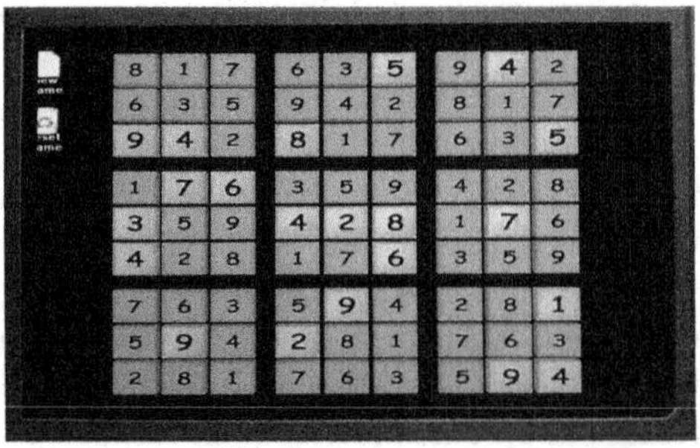

**Fig. 7.2**  A correctly solved Sudoku game

**Fig. 7.3** Levels of difficulty

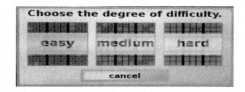

early design sketches. The proof of success in the figure is that all rows, columns and component 3×3 squares include all numbers from 1 through 9. To get started with the game shown, the player has pointed at the *new game* icon (top left-hand corner) to go to the auxiliary screen shown in Fig. 7.3 and customised the next game by pointing at the *easy* choice box. This choice yields a game board with 60 fixed numbers, so that the player must fill the remaining 21 squares. Careful inspection of the game board in Fig. 7.2 shows that the 60 *fixed numbers* are slightly smaller than the *inserted numbers* which, in addition, are shown in backlit squares. Fixed numbers cannot be altered during the game, whereas inserted numbers can. The alternative choices in Fig. 7.3 yield a start game board of 45 (*medium*) and 30 (*hard*) filled squares, respectively.

If the player feels in too much trouble during the game, pointing at the *reset game* icon beneath *new game* in Fig. 7.2 leads to the auxiliary screen shown in Fig. 7.4, which warns that proceeding with *reset game* means losing the current state of the game, leaving only the original, fixed game numbers.

If, according to the Sudoku rules, an inserted number (or several) is inconsistent with fixed or inserted numbers already present, the game board rows and 3×3 squares concerned are highlighted (in red) as shown in Fig. 7.5, where the left-most column includes both a fixed and an inserted number 9. In this example of the online help offered by the system, it is clear that the top-most number 9 must go because it's the only inserted number involved in the inconsistency. Note that the online help does not tell the player where the number should go. Thus, number 9 can go either into the top square in the second column from the left or into the third square from the top in this column. Putting the number in either of these locations will fail to

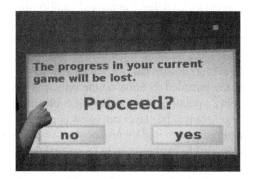

**Fig. 7.4** Restarting a game

**Fig. 7.5** The highlight in the
leftmost column indicates an
error

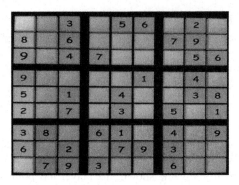

**Fig. 7.6** Congratulations
when a game has been
successfully completed

elicit error markup even though, since Sudoku games are supposed to be deterministic, only one of those squares can ultimately be the right one.

Finally, if the player has successfully solved a Sudoku puzzle, the congrats text shown in Fig. 7.6 appears.

*Number interaction, pointing and speaking.* During gameplay, the key user action is to insert a number into a game board square. To insert a number, the user must (i) point to a square that is empty or has an inserted number in it and (ii) speak a number between "Number one" and "Number nine". The temporal order of speaking and pointing is irrelevant, because the system will wait until it has received both a spoken key phrase and a pointing action before inserting the number in the square pointed to. To delete a non-fixed number, the player must point to the square and say either "delete this/that" or "remove this/that". To replace an inserted number with another, the player must point and say the new number.

To do a pointing input action, the player must stand by the line marked on the floor (not shown), face the screen and stretch arm and index finger to steer the cursor to the intended location on the screen. Thus, the player in Fig. 7.4 is not, in fact, doing a pointing input action but contemplating the screen while keeping the index finger ready. The player can speak at any time as long as the game is running. Spoken input is not required for producing system action in Figs. 7.3 and 7.4 but may be used redundantly or alternatively (Section 4.4.2) for starting a new game or resetting the game (Fig. 7.2).

## 7.2.2 Treasure Hunt

*Design strategy*. Create a 3D haptic virtual townscape and surrounding landscape in which to execute the seven task steps described in Table 5.5. Make sure that the blind user, who has the main role in the collaboration in the first system version, can retrieve clues sufficient to solving the task, including locate houses, rooms, room parts including closets of different colours, locate all other points of interest (town hall, mayor, temple ruins, inscription, catacombs, box, grooves, forest, treasure), open doors, closets and boxes and, throughout, get feedback on success and failure of actions done.

*Overall interaction design*. The blind user communicates with the system via a haptic force-feedback device shaped like a pencil (Fig. 7.7) in order to find an object or follow a groove. S/he is guided by whispers from objects touched upon, such as "house", "wall" or "closet". To act on an object found, such as opening a door or a box, the user clicks the button on the device. To provide feedback on action success, such as that a map has been found in a box, the system emits a beep when the result of a successful action is being sent to the deaf user. When the treasure has been located, the system congratulates the blind user through speech. Other than the challenge of haptically navigating the 3D environment, the system offers no designed obstacles for the blind player, except for rocks littering the grooves which the user must "climb over" to continue following a groove.

Before playing the game, the blind user must be trained in associating five different colours with five different musical sounds. Colours are used in the step when the blind user must find a red closet (Fig. 7.8). Figure 7.9 shows the gamescape map

**Fig. 7.7** Snapshot from the user test showing a subject, the haptic device, the laptop screen in front of the user and the video camera

**Fig. 7.8** The red closet to the right of the door. This picture from the Treasure Hunt system is used with permission of Kostas Moustakas

**Fig. 7.9** Map of the town and its environment with a path to the treasure area sketched by the deaf-mute. This picture from the Treasure Hunt system is used with permission of Kostas Moustakas

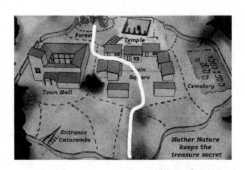

**Fig. 7.10** Grooved line map of the forest area visible in the top part of Fig. 7.9. This picture from the Treasure Hunt system is used with permission of Kostas Moustakas

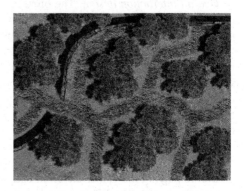

used by the deaf user to communicate with the blind user the path to the forest where the treasure is hidden. Figure 7.10 shows the forest area in detail.

### 7.2.3 Maths

*Design strategy.* (1) Specify session flow. (2) Specify student access to teaching and training as a function of student progress. (3) Specify overall contents per class. (4) Specify the teacher's personality – goals, attitudes, behaviour, etc. guided by the usability requirements in Section 5.2. (5) Write console-based, no-speech, typed text I/O first version of the program based on points 1 through 4. (6) Design and prototype first GUI-style version enhanced with teacher's animated face. (7) Add speech I/O. (8) Add emotion/attitude detection.

*Overall interaction design. Session flow* is specified with the following main tutoring components:

- Start of program:
    - student screening for basic addition skills required to start learning multiplication;
    - student selection and id (password) allocation.

- Main program phase:

    o a session runs from student login to student logout or to the student start-
      ing on a different class;
    o an ordered set of three classes teaching in-depth understanding of multi-
      plication;
    o each class session ends with an evaluation of how well it went, how much
      is still to be learnt and what the student needs to focus on;
    o training (sub-)sessions for training skills in (i) arbitrary two-factor,
      between-1-and-10 multiplication and (ii) multiplication tables. Training
      is heavily supervised for new students and students with difficulties and
      less supervised for more advanced students;
    o tests for entering a higher class;
    o exams to demonstrate mastery of basic multiplication;
    o end-of-session scores: the student gets a cumulative score for sharpness,
      skill and perseverance, which is compared to the scores of others;
    o end-of-session free-for-all where students can ask about the curriculum,
      what happened in class, comment on teaching and teachers, etc.

- End phase:

    o all exams passed, demonstrating mastery of basic multiplication.

We pass over the rather complex *student access* part.

The overall maths *contents* are as follows: *1st class*: Learn how to state and write multiplication problems; that multiplication is sort of different from, and sometimes more practical than, addition; that multiplication is analogous to jumping; special roles of 0 and 1. *2nd class*: Multiplication of small numbers (1, 2 and, in particular, 3); numbers can hide inside other numbers (because they are smaller); how to write multiplication problems; multiplication is more powerful than addition; multiplica-tion, like addition, is commutative (no use of the term, of course) and why this is useful in practice; special roles of 1 and 2. *3rd class*: Detailed teaching of the "big tables", i.e. the 4, 5, 6, 7, 8, 9 and 10 times tables, including similarities, differences and other relationships between them, which ones are harder and why, the "why" being explained in terms of a resting place analogy (i.e. products like $5 \times 4$, $5 \times 6$ and $5 \times 8$ end on 0 so that we can take a good rest, after which multiplication sort of restarts from scratch) and other tricks that may give a deeper understanding of numbers.

Figure 7.11 describes design principles for the *teacher's personality* and other-wise in the implemented console-based version. Note that the maths teacher, Mae "the matics", came to have three assistants, MultMachine, TableMult and AlMully-man, each having different roles and personalities.

Figure 7.12 shows MultMachine in conversation with a web site visitor. 3D Mae is shown in Fig. 10.3. See this book's web page for more illustrations.

| Design principles |
| --- |
| Only allow students in class who have the necessary maths qualifications: screen students, password protected access to class. |
| Install in the student basic understanding of multiplication through example, analogy, explanation, multiple problem views, comparison, and repetition. E.g. multiplication is like jumping (analogy). |
| Coach to automate multiplication skills. Done by two characters: MultMachine and TableMult. |
| Closely monitor problem solving, analyse, correct, explain if wrong, show what's right. E.g. be prepared to explain multiplication by 0 if not understood. |
| Closely monitor learning effort and progress, analyse and change strategy if learning is slow. Encourage the student. E.g. learn 4 times table before tackling higher numbers, do Class 1 perfect. |
| Closely monitor uncertainty, frustration, disappointment, boredom, and anger. React to alleviate. E.g. special sub-session on all about multiplying by 2. |
| Lead the tutoring as a whole but allow student freedom of choice and initiative when possible and meaningful. Following initial instruction and performance monitoring, the student can easily customise and modify levels of difficulty when working with MultMachine and TableMult. |
| Treat the student as a unique individual. Address each student by name. |
| Demonstrate comprehensive memory of what the student has done so far. |
| Consistently demonstrate love and moral authority. Mae is warm, motherly, all-forgiving but firm when the student, e.g. uses bad language, subtracting points from the cumulative score. |
| Show teacher as human and imperfect (except in maths). Tutoring is done by a team consisting of Mae, the teacher, who is human, MultMachine and TableMult, both machines, and AlMullyMan, human. Mae teaches classes, talks with the student at after-class free-for-all, and organises everything. MultMachine coaches free-style multiplication, TableMult coaches multiplication tables. AlMullyMan is old and grumpy, but remembers everything about every student and repeats a class if the student wants it repeated immediately. Each team member has its own personality. Team conversation is humorous and revealing about team members' attitudes towards one another, which induces students to take an interest in the team members and their relationships, leading to comments and questions in end-of-session free-for-all. |
| Use humour and surprise. |
| Add non-maths angles to the conversation. Non-maths, non-course-related topics are mainly to do with the team members, their personal characteristics and relationships. |
| Give rewards (in terms of points) for sharpness, skill and perseverance. |
| Use competitive structures from computer games when possible and justified. E.g. a student can always score higher than any other student has done so far, simply by repeating more classes or training more. The student's cumulative score is compared with those of other students at the end of each class, just before the end-of-class free-for all. Students can compete with themselves. |

**Fig. 7.11** Maths design principles

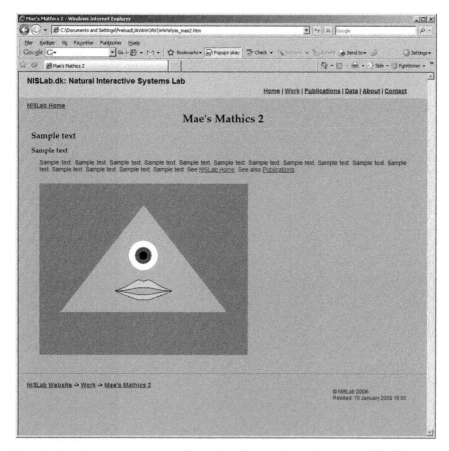

**Fig. 7.12** MultMachine in spoken conversation on the web

# References

Bernsen NO, Dybkjær L (2007) Report on iterative testing of multimodal usability and evaluation guide. SIMILAR deliverable D98.

Carroll JM, Rosson MB (2003) Design rationale as theory. In: Carroll JM (ed) HCI models, theories and frameworks. Towards a multidisciplinary science. Morgan Kaufmann, San Francisco.

# Chapter 8
# Question-Answering

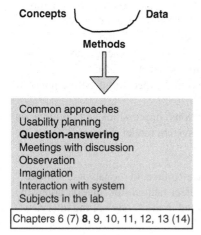

Concepts / Data

**Methods**

Common approaches
Usability planning
**Question-answering**
Meetings with discussion
Observation
Imagination
Interaction with system
Subjects in the lab

Chapters 6 (7) **8**, 9, 10, 11, 12, 13 (14)

In this first of five chapters on multimodal usability methods (Section 6.2.2), all methods presented make use of question-answering. Questions are being asked by members of the development team, answers are produced by potential or actual users, customers or experts. Question-answering is an excellent approach for collecting usability information when it is important to have many people answer a set of well-considered questions, and discussion is of little or no significance. Since all methods to be described make use of interviews or questionnaires, we first describe key aspects of interviews and questionnaires and then present six methods that make use of these techniques.

Sections 8.1 and 8.2 discuss purposes, varieties, techniques, data, advantages and disadvantages of interviews and questionnaires, respectively. Based on these two sections, and using the method description template in Section 6.2.9, Section 8.3 presents user surveys; Section 8.4 customer interviews and questionnaires; Section 8.5 expert interviews and questionnaires; Section 8.6 screening; Section 8.7 pre-test interviews and questionnaires; and Section 8.8 post-test interviews and questionnaires.

## 8.1 About Interviews

An interview (Doyle 2006, Robson 2002, Sharp et al. 2007, Stimson et al. 2003) is a dialogue in which one person, *the interviewer*, collects information from *respondent(s) or interviewee(s)* by asking questions.

N.O. Bernsen, L. Dybkjær, *Multimodal Usability*, Human-Computer Interaction Series, DOI 10.1007/978-1-84882-553-6_8, © Springer-Verlag London Limited 2009

### 8.1.1 Purposes

Interviews are a flexible instrument for collecting usability information anytime in the life cycle. Depending on purpose, the dialogue between interviewer and interviewee(s) takes slightly different forms. Key purposes of using interviews in usability development and evaluation include the following:

- *user survey* interviews which are often made independently of any particular development process (Section 8.3);
- *scenario elicitation* interviews in which customers or (potential) users are interviewed to elicit scenarios or other information needed in the early life cycle phases where goals are not yet very well understood (Section 8.4);
- *knowledge elicitation* interviews early in the life cycle, in which experts are questioned at length about domain- and task-relevant knowledge and processes with the aim of implementing this information in the system (Section 8.5);
- *screening* interviews for selecting subjects with the right background or skills, e.g. before performing a user survey or system test (Section 8.6);
- *pre-test* interviews for collecting user attitudes and expectations before interacting with a system model (Section 8.7);
- *post-test* interviews for collecting users' reactions, impressions and opinions on usability immediately after interaction with a system model (Section 8.8).

Interviews may be done over the phone or face-to-face, in the lab or elsewhere.

It is common to all or most interviews to collect factual information about the interviewee in addition to the information collected in the "body" of the interview.

### 8.1.2 Structured, Unstructured and Semi-Structured Interviews

Since an interview may be more or less structured, it is useful to distinguish between unstructured, structured and semi-structured interviews.

In a *structured interview*, each subject is asked the questions and presented with the answer options, and there is little or no conversation with the interviewee(s), except for clarification purposes. This is like a read-aloud questionnaire (Section 8.2), except that questionnaires are preferable for presenting complex answer options. You can figure out why from modality properties MP7 and MP8 in Section 4.3.2! A structured interview may work well when the information-collection goals are clear and enable formulation of a set of specific question–answer options.

An *unstructured interview* is much like a conversation based on the interviewer's plan for which topics to address during the interview. Topics may be raised through questions or in other ways. Typically, the plan, or topic list, is the same for all subjects interviewed, unless, e.g. different groups of users have used the system under different conditions, in which case the different conditions are often reflected in the topics raised by the interviewer. Unstructured interviews may be used in exploratory contexts, e.g. to elicit scenarios early in the life cycle.

A *semi-structured interview* mixes features from the structured and the unstructured interview. It often has a combination of specific question–answer options and broader questions that invite freestyle answers, and the interviewer can take the opportunity to ask follow-up questions in order to make the subject elaborate answers already provided. Otherwise, there is little or no conversation with the interviewee(s), except for clarification purposes.

No matter which interview form you choose, always run a couple of test interviews with colleagues or others to test if the questioning works as intended.

## 8.1.3  Closed Versus Open Questions, Priming Issues

In addition to interview structure, question format is an important instrument for getting hold of exactly the usability information needed from interviewees. Questions may be *closed*, i.e. have a pre-determined set of possible answers. This is the question type used in structured interviews and to some extent in semi-structured interviews. A yes/no question is a simple example, and one for which you don't have to write any pre-prepared answers. Other closed questions have larger numbers of pre-determined answers which might derive from the logic of the question itself or be defined by the interviewer and presented to subjects as constituting the range of answers to choose from. It is common knowledge that asking for the day of the week yields seven answer options. But if you want to know if the subject plays computer games less than 2 hours per week, between 2 and 10 hours or more than 10 hours, you must explain that these are the choices.

Questions may also be *open* with no pre-determined set of answers. This is the question type used in unstructured interviews and partly in semi-structured interviews. An example is when a subject is asked "How natural did it feel to handle the virtual walking stick?" This question focuses on naturalness – which you must be prepared to explain – but doesn't otherwise pre-define the subject's choice of answer. Like broader topics which do not have to be presented as questions, open questions often invite dialogue between interviewer and interviewee, the former seeking clear understanding of the subject's views on the question asked. Even if all other interview questions are closed ones, it is often a good idea to include an open final question asking if the subject has any additional comments.

If we want to be able to compare the information collected across subjects, we normally ask the same questions in the same order for all subjects. For this we choose a structured or a semi-structured interview to ensure that all or most questions are closed and conversation is avoided. Open questions in the semi-structured interview may be used to collect in-depth information about answers to closed questions, cf. Fig. 8.9, questions 6, 8, 15 and 20. Conversation during interviews, and changing the order of questions, creates different interview contexts for each subject and this may affect the data we want to use comparatively. Note that if you suspect that the order in which questions are asked may affect subjects' answers, you may counterbalance the effect by, e.g. asking half of the subjects your questions in one order and the other half in another order, cf. Section 17.1.3.

To *avoid priming* subjects (Section 6.4.4), act in a thoroughly neutral manner and behave uniformly when asking all questions of all subjects: no spin on questions, no leading questions, no revelatory body "language"! Note that being neutral is fully compatible with being friendly and relaxed. See Sections 8.2.2 and 8.2.3 for more on how to formulate questions.

Also remember that if a question or a topic is missing from your prepared list, or is not being expressed the way it should be, you will forever miss the subject's input on it. Never improvise during a structured or a semi-structured interview to patch up missing issues. If a vital question is missing, consider to include it before the next interview, cf. Section 13.4.6.

### 8.1.4 Running an Interview

Start the interview in a relaxed manner and keep it this way. Let the subject make any comments which may be on top of his/her mind before starting the interview proper. If not done prior to the interview, explain the purpose of the interview and what the data will be used for. Before closing the interview by thanking the subject, you may ask if there are any issues not covered by the interview that the subject would like to comment on.

Figure 8.1 advises on how to conduct a face-to-face interview.

In a *structured interview* you may simply read the prepared questions aloud. This ensures that all subjects are asked the questions in the same way and order. You have the initiative and you stick to the questions planned.

In a *semi-structured interview*, ask the questions and probe the subject further when required or planned to see if you can gather any additional information before moving on to the next question or topic. Be careful not to move on too hastily – you might miss an important comment.

If you run an *unstructured interview*, questions asked and topics raised by the interviewer are open, and there is no set of pre-defined answers to select from. Since this is a kind of conversation, the subject might take the initiative and touch upon topics other than those planned. Make sure to gently steer the conversation back to planned topics that haven't been addressed yet. Also remember to express yourself neutrally when generating questions on the fly, and make sure that all points on your agenda are covered in each interview.

Make notes throughout the interview. Note-taking, especially in unstructured and semi-structured interviews, burdens attention and memory to such an extent that it may be considered to divide the work between an interviewer and a note-taker who must be as capable as the interviewer in the topic of the interview. If the session is being recorded on audio or video, the interviewer or – better – a technician should monitor that the recording equipment is up and running.

| Steps to conducting an interview |
| --- |
| • Arrive early at the location where the interview is to take place. |
| • Try and ensure that the location is as quiet and as free of interruptions as possible. |
| • Ensure that you have all the equipment. |
| • Introduce anyone present to the participant. |
| • Assure participants that everything discussed will be confidential and ask for consent. |
| • Use clear and simple language. Allow participants time to think and speak. |
| • Reflecting people's answers back helps check that you understand what they are saying. |
| • Be a good listener and ask why and how. |
| • Check with the respondent that it is acceptable to continue an interview if it looks as though it may last longer than expected. |
| • Always collect demographic information such as age, gender and ethnicity. |
| • Do not give advice or answers that you are not in a position to offer. |
| • Tag and date any materials, including tapes, notes, maps or other items. |
| • Immediately after the interview reflect on what happened. Review any materials that have been produced. Are there any weaknesses in the way the interview was conducted? Were any topics missed? What new issues arose? |

**Fig. 8.1**  Steps to conducting a face-to-face interview from Stimson et al. (2003). Reproduced with the permission of Gerry Stimson

## 8.1.5 Data

Consider whether to record the interviews on audio or video. The advantage is that it is always possible to go back to the recorded data to clarify interpretation of notes made during the interview. However, it is time consuming to go through the interview record, and it's not always strictly necessary to have it. If you decide to record the interviews, make sure to have equipment that works as intended.

Data is your notes from the interview sessions and any recordings made. Handwritten notes must be typed for the record and in order to facilitate analysis which often involves several people. Some structuring of the notes may be required prior to data analysis, and it is often useful to enter questions and answers into a spreadsheet or use some other tool to create an overview. If you made recordings, you should consider if it's necessary to transcribe (part of) them. In most cases, this is hardly worth the effort – in particular if you have made good notes.

If you refrain from making notes during the interviews and prefer to rely on the recordings made, remember that this doubles the time spent on listening to the subjects. Making transcriptions takes even longer. Our general recommendation is to take notes and use the recordings only as a fallback source for when the notes are unclear on important points. If you analyse your notes in collaboration with colleagues, prepare to find that what's clear to you is not clear to others, or even that your notes are no longer clear to yourself.

See also Section 8.2.5 and Chapters 15 and 16 on data handling and analysis.

### *8.1.6  Advantages and Drawbacks*

Compared to questionnaires, interviews are more flexible, situated and personal, because you have the possibility to explain questions and ask for explanations of, and details on, interesting and important subject observations. This makes for richer results than those collected through a corresponding questionnaire. Also, an interview allows collection of more spontaneous feedback.

However, you need to be acutely aware of how you express yourself, both in order not to prime subjects and to make sure that you ask each of them for the same information. This makes interviewing harder and more exhausting than one might think. Moreover – and this is the downside of the flexible, situated and personal nature of interviews – no matter how careful you are, it is basically impossible to behave in exactly the same way towards each and every subject being interviewed. In addition, interviewing is quite time consuming, not least when it comes to analysing data from unstructured interviews.

Be aware that positive answers may sometimes be too positive, e.g. because subjects want to make you happy, don't view themselves as real, present or future, system users or are excited by ideas and perspectives rather than facts.

Note that over-the-phone interviews cannot include any graphics material, such as pictures, unless supported by, e.g. a web site.

## 8.2  About Questionnaires

A questionnaire (Dumas and Redish 1999, Hom 1998, Robson 2002, Rubin 1994, Sharp et al. 2007, Walonick 2004) is a structured list of questions used to elicit information from respondents in freestyle writing or by ticking off pre-defined answers. In principle, questionnaires are a relatively cheap means of collecting usability information.

### *8.2.1  Purposes*

Questionnaires can be used to collect usability information anytime in the life cycle. They are used for a large variety of purposes, such as *user surveys* (Section 8.3), *elicitation of scenarios* and other information from customers and (potential) users (Section 8.4), *knowledge elicitation* from experts (Section 8.5), *screening* of subjects (Section 8.6) and *pre-test* (Section 8.7) and *post-test* (Section 8.8) *questioning* of users. Thus, questionnaires are typically being used for the same purposes as interviews (Section 8.1), and a questionnaire is much like a structured or a semi-structured interview (Section 8.1.2).

Sometimes subjects are asked to fill in the questionnaire on the spot, sometimes there may be hours or days between the subject receiving and filling the questionnaire. In all cases, subjects have more time to reflect upon their answers than they have when answering questions in an interview.

A questionnaire may basically include three types of questions. First, there are *factual* questions. This could be demographic questions about the subject's age, gender, ethnicity, etc. that should always be included because the data may correlate in interesting ways with other information collected; questions on education, occupation, habits, knowledge, etc. as appropriate, such as whether the subject has done simulator training before and, if yes, with which kind of simulator; or factual questions about the subject's experience with your system, e.g. how many times the system crashed during interaction or whether the subject mostly used the touch screen or the mouse when given the choice.

Second, there are questions on subjects' *interests, beliefs or opinions*, like when a car manufacturers' organisation asks drivers to select from a list the communication services they might rather wish to make use of while driving.

Third, there are questions about subjects' *perception and evaluation* of a system they have used, such as whether they felt in control during interaction.

Depending on their purpose, some questionnaires include a mixture of all three question types while others are focused on a single type.

Like interview questions, questionnaire questions are open or closed (Section 8.1.3).

## 8.2.2 How to Design a Questionnaire

Specify in detail the information you want to collect and go from there to designing the questions that should help elicit this information as efficiently as possible. Specify how and for which purpose answers to each question will subsequently be analysed and used. This will help you get pertinent information rather than answers which you don't know what to do with.

Try to keep the questionnaire short. Ten pages of questions might easily scare people off before they even get started or they might give up halfway. Consider each question carefully. *Must* you know the answer or would it just be nice to know? If the latter, leave out the question. Be careful when expressing questions in writing. They should be clear and unambiguous and should not prime the user in any way (Section 6.4.4). Don't use jargon, technical or otherwise.

Give the questionnaire a meaningful title and a nice layout. Put an introductory message up front. Tell who you are and what the purpose of the questionnaire is. Include succinct instructions on how to fill the questionnaire. Encourage respondents to fill it and make clear that answers will be treated confidentially and that full anonymity is guaranteed. If there is a reward for filling the questionnaire, mention this explicitly. Rewards and an interest in the questionnaire contents are two factors that tend to increase the answer rate, especially if subjects don't fill the questionnaire at your premises.

It is crucial to use simple and direct language that is easily understandable. Figure 8.2 advises on issues to be aware of when asking questions, cf. Creative Research Systems (2007).

| **How to design and structure questions** |
|---|

- *Use neutral formulations.* Don't prime subjects. For example, you should not ask: "Were the error messages easy to understand?" but rather "Could you understand the error messages?" or "What did you think of the error messages?"

- *Don't ask double questions*, such as "Do you like A and B?" (or "Do you prefer P or Q?") unless A or B can be selected via, e.g. radio buttons. Otherwise, a subject who likes A but not B or who prefers Z would not know how to reply or might just say yes or no.

- *The question must accommodate all answers*, so don't use questions like: "Which computer do you have? 1. Apple Mac; 2. Dell PC". If you include answer options, these must exclude or complete each other. If you list a set of options for the subject to choose among (multiple choice), remember to include "other" or "none" so that subjects will always be in a position to answer.

- *A question must create variability* in the answers. Therefore, don't choose options so that you can predict that basically only one of them will be selected.

- *Don't take things for granted.* So don't ask a question like the following: "Are you satisfied with your computer: Yes or no?" Even today, some people don't have a computer.

- If you ask *questions to which the subject **doesn't know the answer immediately*** but will first have to investigate (e.g. "which part of your monthly budget do you spend on X"), many people will just give you an estimate which may mean large errors in the answers.

- It may be a good idea to *include a ì not applicable" or "don't know" option.* For instance, if you ask "Which type(s) of computer game do you prefer?", the subject may answer "not applicable" if s/he does not play computer games and have no interest in them, or a user may answer "don't know" if s/he has no particular preferences among the games s/he knows.

- Be careful when *using vaguely defined words* which may mean something different to different people, e.g. "the majority" or "most".

- Use only *well-known words* and only abbreviations you are sure everybody knows.

- *Consider if branching is really necessary*, i.e. having subsets of questions which should only be answered if some particular condition is met, e.g. owning a portable computer or having tried some particular program before. Branching may confuse the respondents.

- If you ask subjects to *put a list of items in prioritised order*, then don't put more than at most five items on the list. Lists of potential preferences to select from, on the other hand, may be quite long.

- *Avoid questions which are not clearly different from one another.* This kind of vagueness invites each subject to think hard about the intended difference in meaning, often generating different and spurious interpretations of the questions. Don't make subjects think hard about relationships among questions and hence about the consistency of their answers to them.

- *Group questions which are related.* Subjects do not necessarily work so much with the questions as to create a complete model of all of them and their relationships. Grouping questions makes it easier to get an overview of questions which are related to one another and hence to answer each of them as intended.

**Fig. 8.2**  Advice on how to design a questionnaire

It is often a good idea to include an "any other comments" question to prompt respondents for whatever comes to their minds that was not covered by the other questions.

Carefully consider the *order* of questions since it may affect subjects' answers. If you mention a particular kind of software in a question and later ask for software known to the respondents, s/he might mention that particular software simply because it was mentioned earlier. Accumulation of irrelevancies like this quickly makes subjects' answers worthless. Question order may also influence how easy or difficult it is to fill in the questionnaire. One rule of thumb – respecting the grouping constraint in Fig. 8.2 – is to put easy questions up front to encourage subjects to continue and leave difficult or sensitive ones until the end.

If a series of questions have the same answer options, such as good–medium–bad, good–medium–bad, etc., people tend to get used to them and think less about their answers as they move on. If you *must* have this long series of questions, try to ask them in a different order of different respondents so that it isn't the same questions that might be answered somewhat mechanically; or break the questions into shorter series with other questions in between; or modify question valence so that, instead of all questions being stated positively, some are stated negatively. Unless respondents are punch-drunk from having replied to too many similar questions already, the latter induces them to think more carefully about each answer. E.g. you might change the positive statement "The system's feedback was really good in error situations" to "When errors occurred there was no helpful feedback from the system". A respondent who agrees with the first statement should disagree with the second.

Let others test-drive, or comment upon, the questionnaire before you use it. This may reveal that some questions are ambiguous or unclear in other ways.

### 8.2.3 How to Ask a Question

There are several ways to ask a question. We describe three common ways below, see also Creative Research Systems (2007).

One way is to ask people to tick off one among a series of options. In *multiple-choice*, respondents tick off one from a list of explicit answers. Multiple-choice questions often take the form of *rating scale or agreement scale* questions which, e.g. ask people to rate a system by ticking off one from a set of options ranging from excellent to poor, cf. question 5 in Fig. 8.3. You may also use a *semantic differential scale*, where people rate something on, typically, a five- or seven-point scale with bipolar adjectives at each end, such as very good and very bad, cf. question 10 in Fig. 8.3. Or you might ask people to score their agreement or disagreement with some statement, for instance, on a scale from 1 to 5, where 1 is strongly disagree and 5 is strongly agree. The latter would typically be expressed on a *Likert scale*, cf. questions 7 and 8 in Fig. 8.3. Likert scales are quite common and typically use a five- or seven-point scale.

2. How many computers do you have at home:

3. What is your age?          <20    ☐

(check one box only)        20–40   ☐

                            40–60   ☐

                            >60    ☐

...

5. How would you describe your experience with web interaction in general? Would you say it is

very pleasant                          ☐

somewhat pleasant                      ☐

neither pleasant nor unpleasant        ☐

somewhat unpleasant                    ☐

very unpleasant                        ☐

...

|  | strongly agree | agree | neutral | disagree | strongly disagree |
|---|---|---|---|---|---|
| 7. It is often difficult to find what you are looking for on the web: | ☐ | ☐ | ☐ | ☐ | ☐ |
| 8. Spoken interaction is very useful: | ☐ | ☐ | ☐ | ☐ | ☐ |

...

10. Would you say that spoken interaction to control a car navigation system is

very attractive  ☐    ☐        ☐        ☐        ☐        ☐    ☐  very unattractive

...

12. Which advantages could you imagine that spoken input and output combined with web pages will have? (write as much text as you want)

**Fig. 8.3** Examples of questionnaire questions

A second way of asking questions is *numeric open-ended*, e.g. "How many hours per day on average do you play computer games?", cf. question 2 in Fig. 8.3. To close these questions, respondents are asked to choose between different ranges, such as none, under 2, 2–4 or more than 4, cf. question 3 in Fig. 8.3.

A third way of asking questions is through *open-ended* questions, in which questions are answered in written text, e.g. "Which improvements would you suggest?", cf. question 12 in Fig. 8.3.

### 8.2.4 Getting Questionnaires Filled

It's a very special interviewee indeed who refuses to answer the questions. Questionnaires are different, however, which creates a main problem for their use, i.e. how to ensure that one's questionnaire is being filled in by a number of people sufficient for collecting the usability information required? Since we are talking about the use of questionnaires for six different purposes (Section 8.2.1), and involving from a few respondents to thousands, the difficulty of getting a questionnaire (Q) filled in depends on, at least, the following factors:

- whether Q is to be filled at your premises as part of some session there or elsewhere;
- whether respondents have previously agreed to fill Q or have received an unsolicited Q;
- how interested respondents are in your system;
- how motivated respondents are by your communication about the system and by Q itself;
- how motivated respondents are by the rewards offered, such as a box of chocolate or participation to a lottery which might yield a larger reward, such as a holiday travel;
- how easy it is to fill and return the Q; and
- how persistent you are in following up and reminding respondents, preferably over the phone rather than via e-mail or letter, to return the filled Q both before and after the agreed or otherwise fixed deadline.

The best condition is (1) that respondents fill Q at your premises as part of their agreed schedule. This almost guarantees a 100% return rate, provided they have a pleasant environment to work in, ample time and a promise to get help if they have any questions. Since (1) is often impractical, the second best is (2) for respondents to have agreed or promised to fill Q. In themselves, promises yield only a low-to-modest return rate, especially if Q is filled after participation in some lab or field test or other session, rather than before. That's when you have to work hard on motivation through communication, rewards, making respondents feel personally involved or even part of the team, in some way, frequent gentle reminders, etc. (3) The difficult case is when respondents receive Q unsolicited and have no commitment whatsoever to fill and return it. This is when you may be looking at a return rate of maybe 5% which you have to work hard to increase to 15–20%, doing everything you can think of to motivate subjects to fill Q and make it as easy as possible for them to do.

The questionnaire return rate is always important and frequently crucial. This means that the number of respondents addressed or recruited must be based on the estimated return rate. If you need 30 respondents and estimate a return rate of 25%, you must recruit or address 120 subjects; and if the worst-case return rate is 12.5%, you should probably get hold of 240. Simple as it is, these maths come as a shock to many because 240 people, that's a lot of work! And if you reduce the target to 20 (worst case, 160 people needed), you may risk not getting enough data. In fact, all return rates lower than 100% may raise questions about data representativeness: maybe it was only the pensioners who, having lots of time, returned the questionnaire? As a rule, moreover, if you don't get enough filled questionnaires back, don't expect to have time to recruit additional respondents.

In field tests with hundreds of users, you might sample the user population rather than giving everyone a questionnaire, that is, if you have any means of contacting them in the first place, which you don't in the case of, e.g. anonymous downloads of your system. Also remember that you may get questionnaires back half-filled, especially if the questionnaire is long despite your best efforts to shorten it.

## 8.2.5 Data

The data is the filled questionnaires. If these are on paper, their contents should be entered into a database or a spreadsheet. If the questionnaire is available on the web, subjects' answers should automatically be saved in a database for, e.g. later spreadsheet import. There are tools that can help summarise answers to Likert-scale questions and others. Data may also be exported to statistical packages for running various statistics.

Which analyses you need to do depend on the use you are going to make of the data. Results should be nicely presented in, e.g. charts or diagrams along with brief explanations. Moreover, it is important that you try to make broader conclusions based on the data, always carefully considering which claims the data can and cannot support. See also Chapters 15 and 16 on data handling and analysis.

## 8.2.6 Advantages and Drawbacks

Questionnaires are a fairly cheap way to collect factual and subjective usability information, even from large numbers of respondents, in particular if available on the web so that people themselves can enter the data into a database. Other advantages include the following: (i) most people are familiar with general questionnaire style, having been exposed to various kinds of questionnaire from time to time; (ii) by using a questionnaire, you ensure that all those who answer respond to exactly the same questions, syntax and all; (iii) questionnaires can be filled anytime, anywhere; and (iv) there are tools that support interpretation of filled questionnaires.

Questionnaires tend to be more cost-effective than interviews if there are many questions or many participants who may even be geographically dispersed. Also, questionnaires may include pictures and footage, which over-the-phone interviews cannot (except if coordinated with a web site, and that's a challenge).

However, if you don't make sure that respondents fill the questionnaire before leaving the lab – or if you are not running a lab session in the first place – the answer rate is likely to be modest even if you work pretty hard to avoid it. Note also that if questionnaires are returned from outside the lab, you don't know, in principle, who filled them even if they carry the respondents' names.

Unlike answers to face-to-face interview questions, filled questionnaires don't come with intonation, gesture or facial expression, and there is no chance to ask for clarification or additional information unless respondents are interviewed afterwards. Unintelligible input will remain so.

If many respondents don't read well due to, e.g. dyslexia, semi-literacy, illiteracy or age, don't use a questionnaire. Also, remember that filling a sophisticated questionnaire on the computer can be difficult for many groups of people.

Be aware that favourable answers may sometimes be overly favourable, for instance, because subjects like the very idea of the system so much that this biases their perception of the actual system model they have interacted with.

## 8.3  User Survey

A user survey (Battey 2007, Creative Research Systems 2007, QuestionPro 2006, Robson 2002, UsabilityNet 2006, Walonick 2004) is an interview or a questionnaire-based method for asking *potential* users about their needs, attitudes, intentions and opinions concerning new systems and system ideas and for asking *actual* users about their satisfaction or problems with a certain system.

*When can you use the method and what is its scope?* Surveys are typically used with potential users before, or early in, the analysis phase and with actual users later on. Thus, if many users have used your system for a while, you could make a user survey to find out how satisfied they are and which problems they might have. If you wish to contact relatively many users, a user survey-by-questionnaire may be the only practical option. User surveys can be useful not only in commercial development but also in research. We have used them to, e.g. gauge interest in spoken dialogue systems among Danish private companies and public organisations, cf. the example in Fig. 8.4.

*Multimodal significance. Early* user surveys typically assume that potential users are reasonably familiar with the system or the system type addressed. Since this is often not the case for advanced multimodal systems, application of the user survey method early in the life cycle is biased towards use in GUI contexts, cf. Factor 2, *user familiarity with the system type* in Section 6.2.2. Even though the system is unfamiliar, it is sometimes possible to explain it rather straightforwardly in material attached to the survey so that respondents know what they are talking about when answering the questions. This is hard to do over the phone and runs significant risks of priming because the material provided may be users' sole source of information on the system. Still, that's what we did in the example in Fig. 8.4: we attached a small brochure on spoken dialogue systems to the survey questionnaire shown. This might also work for our Sudoku Case, whereas it would probably be presumptuous to explain Treasure Hunt and Maths in the way described (Section 2.1). Late surveys with actual users are not biased towards use in GUI contexts and could be used with all our Cases.

| Survey concerning a Danish version of a spoken dialogue system |
|---|

1.  Name of organisation: _____  Filled by: _____

2.  Trade

    ☐  County    ☐  Retail    ☐  IT    ☐  Financial sector

    ☐  Association (e.g. for    ☐  Publisher/newspaper    ☐  Insurance
        the disabled)

    ☐  Gas, water, heating,    ☐  Hospital    ☐  Municipality
        electricity

    ☐  Production industry    ☐  Administration    ☐  Transportation/travel (e.g.
                                                            taxi, ferry, bus)

    ☐  Other, which:_____

3.  Additional information about the organisation

    a.  Number of employees: ____ | b.  Estimated number of daily phone calls received:

    ☐  0-50    ☐  50-100    ☐  100-250    ☐  more than 250    ☐  Don't know

    c.  What do the phone calls concern?

    ☐  Switchboard and reception

    ☐  Customers' ordering of goods, materials, plans, tickets, etc.

    ☐  Reception of information/data from customers and/or suppliers

    ☐  Information to customers within well-delimited domains

    ☐  Other, which: _____    ☐  No tasks

    d.  How are customer calls handled for the moment in your organisation?

    ☐  Always via personal assistance    ☐  Via a touch-tone (voice-response) system
                                                 to the extent possible

    ☐  In some other way, please describe: _____    ☐  Don't know

4.  Only answer this question if your organisation uses a touch-tone system for the moment.

    a.  What are you using the system for: _____

    b.  Are you satisfied with the system:

    ☐  Yes    ☐  No    ☐  Don't know

    If no, please describe the dissatisfaction: _____

    c.  Did you investigate or receive input regarding what customers think of your system:

    ☐  Yes    ☐  No    ☐  Don't know

    If yes, what do they think: _____

    d.  Is it your perception that the present system will be able to handle the tasks you wish to
        deal with in the future:

    ☐  Yes    ☐  No    ☐  Don't know

5.  The following questions address whether a spoken dialogue system (SDS) will be useful and
    have a natural position in your organisation.

    a.  Which tasks do you think an SDS could optimise in your organisation?

    ☐  Switchboard and reception

    ☐  Customers' ordering of goods, materials, plans, tickets, etc.

**Fig. 8.4**  Survey questionnaire used to investigate market interest (translated from Danish)

☐   Reception of information/data from customers and/or suppliers

☐   Information to customers within well-delimited domains

☐   Other, which: _____        ☐   No tasks

b.   How many resources (persons) are today used in your organisation to handle those task you think an SDS may replace partially or fully? Please indicate estimated number of hours and minutes per day for each of the categories you have ticked off in question 5a.

| Possible task for an SDS | Estimate hours or minutes/day |
|---|---|
| Switchboard and reception | |
| Customers' ordering of goods, materials, plans, tickets, etc. | |
| Reception of information/data from customers and/or suppliers | |
| Information to customers within well-delimited domains | |
| Other, which | |

c.   Describe in few words which properties an SDS should have to be of benefit to your organisation (e.g. open 24 hours/day, handling routine-like tasks, cost reduction): _____

6.   Which importance will each of the arguments below have for a decision to optimise the handling of incoming calls in the organisation? (Put one tick per argument.)

| | Much impor-tance | Some impor-tance | Less impor-tance | No impor-tance | Don't know/not relevant |
|---|---|---|---|---|---|
| You can provide a **better service than today** (24 hours service, more user-friendly, reduced waiting time, etc.) | | | | | |
| You can **improve the organisation's image** | | | | | |
| You can **handle standard calls better and faster**, e.g. ordering of forms, tickets, etc. | | | | | |
| You can **better exploit personnel resources** | | | | | |
| You can **free personnel from boring repetitive work** and give them more exciting tasks | | | | | |
| You can ensure **current and systematic data collection for strategic planning** (marketing, decision support, etc.) | | | | | |
| **Other**, what: | | | | | |

7.   Will there in your opinion be a market within your trade for a Danish SDS?

☐   Yes                    ☐   No                            ☐   Don't know

8.   Do you want to receive additional information about the development of a Danish SDS?

☐   Yes                    ☐   No

9.   Might you be interested in participating in the development of a Danish SDS and in acting as the customer?

☐   Yes                    ☐   No

Note to public organisations: Please be aware that we may apply for financial support from Erhvervsfremmestyrelsen regarding joint projects between public and private organisations.

**Fig. 8.4**   (continued)

*How does the method work*? A set of questions of importance to possible or actual usability development activities is established and asked of potential or actual system users. The questions may be conveyed by surface mail, e-mail or the Internet or asked over the phone, in physical meetings or otherwise. In general, interview-based surveys are likely to produce better response rates than questionnaire-based surveys, but are more labour intensive: it is much easier to double the number of dispatched questionnaires than the number of telephone interviews.

*What is required for applying the method*? Potential or actual target users who may be anonymous or have to be identified or a representative user group selected among target users (Section 3.3.1). Both interviews and questionnaires can be run with anonymous subjects, such as when asking users of our system to anonymously fill in a questionnaire on the web or going to a museum to interview its visitors about a museum application we plan to build. Interviews require an interviewer, an interview script and, sometimes, recording equipment (Section 8.1.5). Questionnaire-based surveys require a questionnaire. From your point of view, electronic questionnaires are easier to handle than paper versions (Section 8.2.5).

*System/AMITUDE model*. There need not be a model (yet) if the method is used to collect information before project start – and there may never be one if the survey results are negative! If the survey is used to collect feedback, there must be an implemented model that respondents have had a chance to use.

*Planning*. Write a usability method plan based on items described in Section 6.4. Start from the purpose of collecting usability data (Section 6.4.2): what is it that you want to learn from the users this time? Some standard examples are the following:

• the potential market for the system you plan to develop;
• collecting modification wishes concerning your current system version.

Then operationalise the purpose (Section 6.4.3). This is a crucial step in usability method application: you want, say, to survey the potential market for spoken dialogue systems (Fig. 8.4). So, what exactly do you need to ask people about in order to do that? This may be about their experience with related touch-tone technologies, their attitudes towards technological innovation and much else besides. Then start the laborious process of turning information needs into an ordered series of linguistically expressed questions, using the advice in Section 8.1 or 8.2 and paying attention to priming avoidance (Section 6.4.4). You must decide whether to use a survey interview or a questionnaire, so consult their respective advantages and drawbacks in Sections 8.1.6 and 8.2.6.

Then it is time to consider user contact or recruitment. Unless you plan to address anonymous users, you will probably need to address a representative user group of some kind. This could be a representative group of target users (Section 3.3.1) or something more generic, like a representative set of organisations who might be interested in using the technology for some kind of application. There are companies specialising in helping with market surveys and databases that may support information seeking about potential user organisations.

Decide how many users you need based on resources available, the precision (confidence interval) needed and any other relevant factors in this particular case, cf. Sections 8.1 and 8.2. A small and representative sample will reflect the group from which it was drawn; a larger sample will reflect the target group more precisely. Note that doubling the number of users does not double precision. For instance, to double the precision you get from a sample of 250 users who actually respond to the survey, you would probably need 1000 users to respond. See Creative Research Systems (2007) for how to calculate sample sizes (follow the link to the "Sample Size Calculator").

If you send an unsolicited survey, it is far better to address *named individuals* than sending the survey to job titles like "the secretary" or "the product manager". See also Sections 8.1 and 8.2 on how to design and test interviews and questionnaires.

*Running.* See Sections 8.1.4 and 8.2.4 on how to do an interview and get a questionnaire filled.

*Data.* See Sections 8.1.5 and 8.2.5 on data from interviews and questionnaires and Chapters 15 and 16 on data handling and analysis. Analysis will often involve statistics. The purpose of an early survey may be to decide – based on answers to the individual questions – whether or not to develop a particular system or what kind of system to develop. Late surveys may look at, for each question, e.g. how many users complain and how serious they find particular problems. This may serve as a basis for deciding which changes to make to a system.

*Advantages and drawbacks.* The main advantage of user surveys is the opportunity to reach many users unsolicited or without prior contact and without having them come to you. An interview-based survey normally creates better and faster answer rates but is more expensive because someone has to absorb the refusals to participate, do the interviewing and note down the answers. Most expensive is the kind of interview in which you meet users. You often spend more time per interview than over the phone and may have to add travel time, not least if you go to several different places.

The main disadvantage is the risk of low return rates, in particular for unsolicited questionnaires, which may strongly affect data reliability. Even a medium return rate may yield strongly biased data. For example, don't call people at home during a workday to collect information on a multimodal system for home use. There will be a lot of people at work whom you fail to reach. Call in late afternoon or early evening like polling professionals do to avoid getting an overrepresentation of kids, unemployed and retired people who are not representative of the target group as a whole. Also note that people with low education or imperfect reading skills tend to have low response rates to written surveys.

*Example: Market interest survey questionnaire.* The questionnaire in Fig. 8.4 is from a survey from 2000 of the Danish market aimed at investigating interest in over-the-phone spoken dialogue systems. About 200 organisations from 13 trades (question 2) were extracted from a database and contacted by mail. This sample was representative with respect to factors such as trade differences, geographical spread across the country and company size. Organisations received the questionnaire, a cover letter and a folder explaining spoken dialogue systems. The return rate was 13.5% with no follow-up over the phone for which there was no time.


## 8.4  Customer Interviews and Questionnaires

Despite its title, the focus of this section is solely on collecting usability information about goals, needs, environment, time limits, etc. by interviewing a customer acquiring a system. This is what we refer to as a customer interview (Crow 2001, Bias et al. 2007). The reason is the pragmatic one that other forms of asking questions of customers through interviews or questionnaires are covered by other methods. To find out what your customers think of a system they are using or what potential customers want, think or do, apply a user survey (Section 8.3). And if you want to go to a customer to watch, talk and learn, apply the macro-behavioural field methods in Section 10.1.

*When can you use the method and what is its scope?* Customer interviews are made with one or a small number of real customers early in the life cycle to collect information that will feed into AMITUDE (Section 3.1) specification and design. If you develop off-the-shelf software and don't have powerful distributors as customers, you should rather consider using macro-behavioural field methods (Section 10.1) or a focus group (Section 9.1). Thus, customer interviews are typically business-to-business undertakings. They may be used in research projects as well if you have a particular customer (group) in mind and can find potential customers willing to act as such.

*Multimodal significance.* Customer interviews need customers. Since many advanced multimodal projects don't have customers yet – including our Cases (Section 2.1) – customer interviews are heavily biased towards GUI-based systems, cf. Factors 3, *technology penetration*, and 4, *how close to real-life deployment a system type is*, in Section 6.2.2. If you are working on a research system with no one even close to becoming a real customer, consider if a user survey might help collect information about potential customers (Section 8.3).

*How does the method work?* A customer interview is normally performed at the customer's premises. The typical aim is to capture information about particular AMITUDE (Section 3.1) or other system model aspects, for instance, because there is some uncertainty about the environment of use or it is unknown what is actually needed and what are the priorities. Questions must be to the point but also to some extent open-ended so that, on the one hand, the information retrieved is not too vague to be used in making informed specification and design decisions and, on the other, you don't limit the collected information unnecessarily.

*What is required for applying the method?* One or more customers, an interviewer, an interview script and, possibly, recording equipment (Section 8.1.5).

*System/AMITUDE model.* If a system model exists already, it will typically be in outline. The purpose of the method is to collect information that will help specify the model.

*Planning.* Write a usability method plan based on items described in Section 6.4, starting from the purpose of collecting usability data (Section 6.4.2). Operationalise the purpose (Section 6.4.3), for instance, by breaking it down into a series of headings and then adding more detailed issues under each. We have no idea about the details of your headings, of course, but since the customer interviews we describe deal with analysis and design for usability, you might use AMITUDE (Section 3.1) and the usability breakdown in Section 1.4.6 as framework to think in terms of. Then turn your information needs into an ordered series of linguistically expressed questions, using the advice in Section 8.1.

Typically, the customer organisation is known, but it may be necessary to identify the person(s) to talk to. Schedule the interview with the interviewee(s) well in advance, planning 1–2 hours per interview. Whom to talk to probably depends on what you want to know but, in large companies, it may be a challenge to identify the right people, i.e. those who actually have the information you are looking for. They may be managers, marketing people, support staff or others.

*Running.* See Section 8.1.4 on conducting an interview.

*Data.* See Section 8.1.5 on interview data and Chapters 15 and 16 on data handling and analysis. Data analysis typically focuses on retrieving as much AMITUDE information as possible from the collected data.

*Advantages and drawbacks.* A customer interview is an excellent, low-cost way of getting to thoroughly understand a customer's needs, preferences and requirements early in the project. This helps create a common understanding of the system and avoid misconceptions. See also 8.1.6 on advantages and drawbacks of interviews in general. Data reliability may be affected by factors, such as that customers don't always know what they want or they want something different in the next meeting.

*Example: Customer interview script.* Figure 8.5 shows a reconstructed excerpt from a customer interview script. We asked similar questions some 8 years ago in a small number of customer interviews aimed at identifying an organisation interested in being involved in the development and deployment of a spoken dialogue system. The customers we visited had expressed their interest in their responses to the survey questionnaire in Fig. 8.4. We did not bring a fully detailed and explicit written interview script at the time but took a more ad hoc approach during the meetings. We therefore missed some clear benefits of writing and using interview scripts, i.e. (1) we had no checklist of questions to ask and might have missed asking important questions; (2) we had no way of ensuring that the visited organisations were asked the same questions; and, very importantly, (3) we did not, prior to visiting the organisations, force ourselves to think through – in the way that having to create a complete, explicit interview script forces you to think – which information was essential for us to collect. In addition to asking questions, we explained spoken dialogue systems and what they can and cannot do and gave audio file examples. The

| Interview questions to customer regarding a spoken dialogue system |
|---|
| ... |
| • You have previously stated an interest in spoken dialogue systems (SDSs). Please describe what you think an SDS could be used for in your organisation. |
| • Which routine tasks are handled via the phone? |
| • How large a percentage of the total number of calls are calls concerning these routine tasks? |
| • How many of these calls are handled by a voice-response system and how many by a person? |
| • Which task(s) would you consider primary candidate(s) for being handled by an SDS and why? |
| • Please explain the work flow related to this/these task(s) in detail. |
| • Who are the users? |
| • In which ways do you expect that your organisation might benefit from an SDS handling this task/one or more of these tasks? |
| • How important are these benefits to your organisation? |
| • What are your primary concerns in introducing an SDS? |
| • How important are these concerns to your organisation? |
| • Have you measured user satisfaction for the task(s) we have discussed? If yes, what were the results? |
| • Which experiences do you have with SDSs? |
| • Which minimum requirements do you have to user satisfaction for an SDS? |
| ... |

**Fig. 8.5**  Reconstructed excerpt from a customer interview script

agreed purpose of the meetings was to determine if the organisation had the policies, expectations, tasks, users, etc. that would make it interesting for them to obtain such a system and realistic for us to deliver a satisfactory spoken dialogue system. This turned out to be the case for one organisation for whom we developed a frequently asked questions (FAQ) system (Section 3.4.3).

## 8.5  Expert Interviews and Questionnaires

Several of the methods we describe involve, or might involve, external experts in various capacities, such as when we study experts in the field (Sections 10.1 and 10.2), record them in the lab (Section 10.5) or get their help in applying guidelines (Section 11.4). The purpose of expert interviews and questionnaires is to draw upon AMITUDE expertise that's missing in the project team. Our concept of an expert is non-relative: it takes a lot of doing to become one, and once you are one, you are able to provide solutions with which other experts would often agree. If you are merely looking for a discussion partner who has done something similar to what you are up to, you are not looking for an expert in this sense.

*When can you use the method and what is its scope?* The method is mostly used relatively early in the life cycle when requirements and design are being analysed and specified, but it is perfectly possible to involve experts even earlier to investigate feasibility or later on during, e.g. multimodal fusion implementation, test data analysis or final system evaluation.

Expert interviews or questionnaires can be used to collect in-depth usability information about any AMITUDE aspect (Section 3.1) of any type of system, provided that the expertise actually exists and is available to the project. One aspect for which expertise is often available is task and domain. Thus if you want to, e.g. build characters that could blend with people as far as knowledge and reasoning about global warming or skills in dancing tango goes and are able to watch and correct users' misunderstandings or missteps, it might be a fine idea to ask an expert about the capabilities that the characters should have.

*Multimodal significance.* Both GUI-based and multimodal usability development can benefit from using expert interviews and questionnaires. Still, referring to our differentiation factors in Section 6.2.2, two differences may be noted. First, if you are into advanced multimodal system development, you may find that expertise does not exist or is prohibitively scarce, cf. Factor 6, *general lack of knowledge*. There may be expertise somewhere on multimodal virtual world navigation by the blind, cf. the Treasure Hunt Case (Section 2.1), but then again there may not, or the scarce expertise there is may not be available to us. To be sure, expertise may be aplenty, like for the Maths Case example in Fig. 8.6. Second, multimodal systems often need expertise on micro-behaviour, which is largely irrelevant to GUIs, cf. Factor 5, *the kind of data to be collected with users*.

*How does the method work.* If you need to pick the expert's brain in depth and don't have a quasi-complete set of precise questions lined up in advance – either because you lack the expertise to create one or because you need more of a discussion on several issues – you should run a rather unstructured interview, allowing for follow-up questions generated on the fly. This is probably the typical case. However, if you want to collect comparable information from several experts, you may want to use a questionnaire instead.

Note that questioning an external expert is often a semi-formal, one-shot affair, with priority on thorough preparation, precision and efficiency. This implies that life cycle timing is important: don't question the expert before you are ready! It's annoying to first find the questions that should really have been asked 2 months after questioning the expert. A phone or a video conference supported by web-based information may be a workable alternative to a face-to-face meeting.

*What is required for applying the method?* One or more experts. For interviews, an interviewer, an interview script and, possibly, recording equipment (Section 8.1.5). Alternatively, a questionnaire.

*System/AMITUDE model.* The system model may exist in outline or in more detail. The typical purpose of using the method is to collect information that will help make decisions and add relevant details to the AMITUDE model of use.

*Planning.* If expertise is scarce, start by making sure to have identified an expert, or several, who is prepared to help. Customers often have relevant expertise in their

| Questions about multiplication teaching to primary school maths teachers |
|---|
| 1. How old are children when they start learning multiplication: On average? |
| 2. In which grade: On average? Grade range? |
| 3. Which other kinds of basic arithmetic have they been taught before moving on to early multiplication: Addition? Subtraction? Other? Please explain. |
| 4. Do you teach early multiplication stand-alone or together with other basic arithmetic? Please describe. If together, please explain why. |
| 5. How many lessons do you spend on early multiplication, i.e. up to understanding and mastery of two-factor multiplication up to 10 x 10? How much calendar time? What determines that you move on? |
| 6. Which percentage of time in class is spent on (1) teaching using written material, your explanations and examples, and questions in class; and which percentage is spent on (2) training using oral and written exercises in multiplying numbers? |
| 7. Estimate the percentage of children who master early multiplication in the indicated calendar time. |
| 8. How do you tell if a child has learnt early multiplication? |
| 9. Which written material do you use? Please attach a copy. |
| 10. How do you explain early multiplication: As in the material? Using your own metaphors and other means? If the latter, please describe. |
| 11. Do the students have homework: which? |
| 12. Do the students use computers? If yes, what for? |
| 13. Do the students work in groups? If yes, what do they do? |
| 14. Do certain multiplication tables cause more problems than others? If yes, which? Why, do you think? |
| 15. Mention 1–3 issues that you consider crucial in children's learning of multiplication. |
| 16. Can you group under some description, possibly into different groups, children who do not succeed in learning early multiplication in the allotted time? Please describe each group. |
| 17. Do you use oral or written tests? If yes, please describe: Their purpose. The test(s). How you evaluate the results. |
| 18. Explain your criteria for leaving early multiplication and moving on: Is it simply timeout? Is there a test which reveals if the children have reached a certain average level? If yes, please describe the test and explain how you evaluate results. Other? Please explain. |

**Fig. 8.6** Draft questions on primary school maths teaching (translated from Danish)

organisation, but if there is no identified customer, you will have to look around for expertise. If you don't find any, choose a different method. If the expert is in a related business, make sure to take care of any confidentiality issues before presenting sensitive stuff.

If you find an expert, write a usability method plan based on plan items described in Section 6.4, starting from the purpose of collecting usability data (Section 6.4.2). Some examples of information to elicit are the following:

- task or domain knowledge that may help generate scenarios and use cases (Section 11.1) or verify domain and task details in the design;

- pros and cons of certain modality combinations, such as possible combinations of spoken discourse I/O and typed text I/O for the Maths Case (Section 2.1).

Then operationalise the purpose (Section 6.4.3), taking care not to exclude elicitation of important information by being too specific or too limited in what is being asked. Then turn information requests into questions, using the advice in Section 8.1 or 8.2. You must decide whether to use an interview or a questionnaire, cf. Sections 8.1.6 and 8.2.6.

*Running.* See Sections 8.1.4 and 8.2.4 on how to do an interview and get a questionnaire filled. Remember that the expert may not share your own expertise at all and that it may take some time to get onto the same page. We once asked a linguist – over the phone – how one addresses people in Italian. He answered that this depends on so many factors that we could forget about emulating what's going on. We convinced him by explaining exactly what we wanted to do, which was probably necessary in this case, and that took a long time. It is quite possible that, had we sent the expert a questionnaire instead, he might not have taken it seriously.

*Data.* See Sections 8.1.5 and 8.2.5 on data from interviews and questionnaires and Chapters 15 and 16 on data handling and analysis. Analysis of expert data typically involves information structuring followed by (i) thinking about feasibility, i.e. how could my system do this? (ii) Comparison with one's expectations, sometimes generating major surprises; and (iii) planning of what to incorporate into the AMITUDE model of use and the system model more generally, and how. If you ask several experts the same questions, you might sometimes be surprised by the extent of their disagreements, leaving you confused at a higher level than before.

*Advantages and drawbacks.* The main advantages of asking experts a systematic series of questions are that, once you have found available expertise, (1) it is simple to do in the sense that you have only the substance (the questions) to worry about; (2) you get it from the horse's mouth; and, best of all, (3) you can get usability information aimed at solving exactly your problems and no one else's. The expertise may even be given for free or for a small remuneration, out of interest for your project. Even if costly, if it's really needed, it's likely worth the cost. The main drawback, perhaps, is that experts sometimes disagree. See also Sections 8.1.6 and 8.2.6 on advantages and drawbacks of interviews and questionnaires in general.

*Example: Maths expert questionnaire.* Figure 8.6 shows a condensed layout of an excerpt from a questionnaire to experienced Danish school teachers teaching maths at primary school, cf. the Maths Case.

## 8.6   Screening Interviews and Questionnaires

Screening (Rubin 1994) is used to make sure that subjects have the right profile (Section 3.3.1) for participating in a session aimed at collecting usability information. Thus, screening is not primarily a method for *collecting* usability information but a tool that is frequently used prior to application of many of the methods we describe.

*When can you use the method and what is its scope?* Screening must be used if participants to a data collection session must have a specific profile, or the group of participants must have a specific composition, unless this can be ensured in other, simpler ways. If we need a representative user group (Section 3.3.1), e.g. screening is necessary unless the group composition we need has already been established in some other way. If all we need is a specific user profile, there will be more cases in which we don't have to do any screening ourselves, as described below. We might get the subjects through indirect screening, such as by recruiting school children in a particular grade and making sure with the school teacher and the parents that all children are fit to participate and allowed to do so, or we work with the people who simply happen to be present in the museum.

*Multimodal significance.* The need for screening would seem largely independent of whether the system to be developed is multimodal or GUI-based. Multimodal interaction and blending with people might need a larger variety of user profiles than does GUI-based interaction, but this is a small multimodal bias indeed, because screening is so very common. As for our Cases (Section 2.1), Sudoku required screening, cf. the example below, Treasure Hunt required indirect screening only, and so will the Maths system.

*How does the method work?* Based on the subject selection criteria – user profile, representative user group specification, other – identify potential subjects, contact them and use the criteria to select those you need. Selection is made through interviews or questionnaires and may be done in any of the ways described in Section 8.1 and 8.2, i.e. using mail, telephone, face-to-face, etc. as appropriate.

*What is required for applying the method?* Target users, a representative user group or others who fit the data producer profile. For interviews, an interviewer and an interview script. For questionnaires, a questionnaire.

*System/AMITUDE model.* The emerging system model is not directly part of the screening but lies behind the criteria for subject selection applied.

*Planning.* Even for screening it is advisable to write a usability method plan based on plan items described in Section 6.4. Start with the issue of identifying potential subjects, which may take time and be non-trivial, for instance, because they are rare, they are hard to convince or you need lots of them, cf. Section 13.2 on subject recruitment. Screening is used in combination with lab test methods (Sections 12.1, 12.2, 12.3, 12.5), real-time observation (Section 10.4) and pre- and post-test questioning (Sections 8.7 and 8.8). Subject recruitment is shared among methods in a cluster, whereas most other preparations must be done separately for each method.

Work on the subject selection criteria. If these cannot be imported from an existing AMITUDE model of use, they must be developed. After that, you need to develop a set of questions to potential subjects, answers to which can unambiguously reveal if the person meets the selection criteria. This is not rocket science but it isn't trivial either, because you cannot just ask, e.g. "Is your French good enough for testing my system?" Instead, you will often have to establish some facts about the person from which it can be deduced whether or not the subject meets some criterion. In the example, an interview could determine the quality of the person's French on the spot, but a questionnaire cannot. This example is a bit unusual, because the screening questions asked are typically the same, no matter if conveyed through an interview or a questionnaire.

Questions are typically concrete and to the point to avoid vaguely expressed freestyle answers that do not include the information we need, cf. Sections 8.2.2 and 8.2.3. No matter if you use an interview or a questionnaire, it should be brief. No need to waste more time than necessary with ill-fitting subjects – neither yours nor theirs.

You don't have to record a screening interview session. The potential subjects' answers should leave you in no doubt whether they are suitable as subjects or not.

Whether to choose interviews or use a questionnaire depends on so many factors that it is difficult to provide general advice. Brief telephone interviews are fine once you know whom to call, because they have a high return rate and you establish personal contact with subjects. A web-based questionnaire is useful not least for large subject populations who respond to your adverts in the press or elsewhere.

*Running.* See Sections 8.1.4 and 8.2.4 on carrying out an interview or getting a questionnaire filled.

*Data.* See Sections 8.1.5 and 8.2.5 on data from interviews and questionnaires. You should not spend much time on data analysis. With appropriate question design, it should be quick to decide from the answers whether or not a potential subject is suitable. If in doubt, leave the person out, unless the subjects you look for are rare. If you are composing a group of, e.g. representative users, it is quite possible that some of the profiles needed are missing from the first batch of potential users addressed, whereas other profiles needed turn out to be aplenty. Then you will have to contact more potential subjects.

*Advantages and drawbacks.* Usability data quality is to an important extent a function of who the data producers are. Screening is, therefore, a key instrument for ensuring quality data. Testing with the wrong subjects is like getting the wrong map when trying to get to some destination. See also Sections 8.1.6 and 8.2.6 on advantages and drawbacks of interviews and questionnaires in general.

*Example: Sudoku test screening.* Figure 8.7 shows the screening interview script we used when looking for subjects for testing the Sudoku Case system (Section 7.2.1). Sudoku is played by all kinds of users, including (not too small) children, adults and elderly people, male and female, novices, occasional players, highly skilled players and people with very different backgrounds. Having restricted our user profile to adults and adolescents (Section 3.3.7), we wanted a group of test subjects representing the user differences just mentioned, subject to the qualification that resources would only allow for a relatively small group of 10–15 users.

We aimed for reasonable gender and age balance, i.e. at least 40% males and at least 40% females, and approximately one-third of the subjects under 30 years old, between 30 and 50 and above 50, respectively. In addition, we planned to have four subjects at each of the following skill levels, with approximate gender balance at each level:

---

**User screening interview script**

The questions below will be asked to potential test subjects in order to determine if we need their participation and in which test user category.

**Name** What is your name?

**Age** How old are you?

**Gender** Are you male or female?

**Education** What is your education?

**Occupation** Which kind of work do you do?

**Knowledge of English** Is your knowledge of English = none, modest, average, good, very good?
**Game experience** Have you played Sudoku before?

*If yes:*

>    For how long have you played?

>    How much have you played?

>    Do you play regularly? *If yes:*

>>        How often do you play?

>    Have you tried to play Sudoku over the Internet?

>    Game strength: Describe the degree of difficulty of the games that you play and normally solve.

*If no:*

>    What makes you interested in participating in testing our Sudoku game?

**Experience with similar systems**

Have you tried systems which understand spoken input before?

*If yes:* Have you tried systems which understand spoken and pointing input before?

**NOTE**: Users with little or no Sudoku experience are characterised by only having played a little, if at all; not playing regularly; and not being good at solving Sudoku games other than quite easy ones.

---

**Fig. 8.7** Screening questions to potential Sudoku system test subjects

1. little or no experience in Sudoku but an interest in trying it (again);
2. some experience in Sudoku, has managed easy-to-medium-difficult games;
3. used to managing difficult Sudoku games.

As for ensuring subjects with different backgrounds, we stipulated the rather weak requirement that no more than two subjects must have the same profession.

Potential subjects were contacted over the phone or face-to-face and screened prior to recruitment on the basis of the interview questions in Fig. 8.7.

## 8.7  Pre-Test Interviews and Questionnaires

A pre-test interview or questionnaire (Dumas and Redish 1999, Rubin 1994) is used to collect usability information from subjects before they test the system model, cf.

Chapter 12. A typical purpose is to collect data on subjects' anticipations concerning the system, often in order to compare with post-test data (Section 8.8) collected with the same subjects.

*When can you use the method and what is its scope?* Pre-test interviews and questionnaires are used primarily before a lab user test that applies, e.g. the Wizard of Oz (Section 12.2) or implemented prototype (Section 12.3) method. Pretest interviews and questionnaires are not normally used with field tests (Section 12.4), partly because this would somehow conflict with the field test idea and the user's freedom to decide if and when to use the system and partly because you need access to the users beforehand and many field tests don't provide that.

The anticipatory usability information sought in pre-test questioning typically is about subjects' opinions about, and attitudes towards, the system (type), their expectations to the nature and quality of the interaction or their planned interaction strategies. This assumes that subjects are in a position to form reasonably qualified and concrete anticipations, either because they are familiar with the system type or because the system can be explained to them sufficiently well in connection with the interview or the questionnaire.

*Multimodal significance.* If the system is unusual, difficult to explain and unfamiliar to the subjects, pre-test interviews and questionnaires probably yield little data of interest. This suggests that the method is biased towards GUI-based systems, cf. Factor 2, *user familiarity with the system type*, in Section 6.2.2. On the other hand, if the system can be successfully explained to subjects, it may be interesting to get data on their anticipations because of the potential for finding significant discrepancies between anticipation and the reality found during the test. These anticipations may tell something about how the system (type) can be expected to be received in general, which may help determine how to best communicate about it.

As for the Cases (Section 2.1), we might have used the method with the Sudoku system as illustrated in Fig. 8.8, whereas a pre-test questionnaire would make little sense with the users (young children) of the Maths system. Even a pre-test interview would seem doubtful. For Treasure Hunt, the method would not be recommended due to the nature of the system.

*How does the method work?* A pre-test interview is made right before subjects interact with a system model. The interview is done over the phone or face-to-face, depending on where and how the test takes place. Interviews may be made with a single user, a pair, triple, etc. depending on, e.g. whether interaction is single- or multi-user. Note that multi-user interviews are generally more difficult to handle than single-user interviews. A pre-test questionnaire may be filled before the subjects come to the lab or once they are there.

When pre-test questioning subjects, the plan often is to compare the data with information collected in a post-test interview or questionnaire with the same subjects. To facilitate comparison, some or all of the pre-test interview or questionnaire questions are often repeated (with the necessary changes) in the post-test interview or questionnaire. Compare, e.g. Figs. 8.8 and 8.9.

---

**Sudoku pre-test interview script**

**Input and Output.** You should answer the following questions by simply picking a word or number from the following list: 1 = unsuitable, 2 = rather unsuitable, 3 = neither/nor, 4 = rather suitable, 5 = suitable. 1 (unsuitable) is worst, 5 (suitable) is best, and 3 (neither/nor) is right in between. [**NOTE:** type these metrics on paper and hand it to the subject, or write the metrics on a blackboard which is clearly visible to the subject]. The questions are about your input to the system and the system's output to you.

1.   How suitable do you imagine pointing input is for games like Sudoku?

2.   How suitable do you imagine spoken input is for games like Sudoku?

3.   How suitable do you imagine screen output is for games like Sudoku?

4.   How suitable do you imagine the combination of pointing and spoken input, and screen output, is for games like Sudoku?

**Functionality.** The next questions are about how you imagine to play the game.

5.   What will you be able to do by pointing?

6.   What will you be able to do by speaking to the system?

7.   Which information do you expect to have on the screen?

**User Experience.** The next questions are about what you imagine gameplay to be like.

8.   What will it be like to solve Sudoku games in the way described?

9.   Compared with Sudoku games on paper or on the Internet, which advantages and disadvantages do you see for the game you are going to try?

---

**Fig. 8.8**   Constructed pre-test interview script for the Sudoku Case

If sufficient subject background information has not been collected during screening (Section 8.6), it may be collected as part of a pre-test interview or questionnaire.

*What is required for applying the method?* Subjects who are target users or constitute a representative user group (Section 3.3.1). For interviews, an interviewer, a list of questions or topics, possibly recording equipment (Section 8.1.5). For questionnaires, a questionnaire and sufficient time and a quiet location to fill it.

*System/AMITUDE model.* Pre-test questioning assumes that subsequent interaction with the system model is planned. Any system model version will do as long as users are able to interact with it. Typically, a detailed version is used.

*Planning.* Write a usability method plan based on plan items described in Section 6.4. Start from the purpose of collecting usability data (Section 6.4.2). If you plan to use a pre-test interview or questionnaire, you will normally want to use a post-test ditto to obtain data for comparison. Moreover, the post-test questioning will typically be your main target. We suggest to first plan the post-test questioning, cf. Section 8.8, and then make the pre-test interview or questionnaire design correspond. This is done by lifting the substance of post-test questions which can meaningfully be asked before the test, into the pre-test set of questions, reformulating as necessary. Use the same order of questions and the same kind of closed or open questions. Typically, some post-test questions will be too detailed for being asked before having interacted with the system.

Identify subjects so that you can contact them and make an agreement with them, cf. Section 13.2. Note that pre-test questioning is used in combination with other methods, i.e. one of the lab test methods (Sections 12.1, 12.2, 12.3, 12.5) and, possibly, real-time observation of users (Section 10.4), screening (Section 8.6) and post-test questioning (Section 8.8). Subject recruitment is shared among methods in a cluster while most other preparations must be done separately per method.

Sort out any staff roles as interviewer, note-taker and responsible for recording equipment. See Chapter 13 for general advice on having subjects in the lab.

*Running.* Before answering anticipatory questions, subjects must be told enough about the system to be able to anticipate interaction with it, but not so much, we suggest, that they start analysing interaction in detail based on the information provided. Examples of how this works could be the system information that must be provided in order for pre-test questioning to make sense for the Sudoku system (Section 2.1) or the spoken dialogue system analysed in Section 3.4.2. For the Sudoku system, all we have to tell the subjects is that it's about playing Sudoku by pointing towards a screen and speaking a number or some other command. For the spoken dialogue system, all we need to say is that it's about making a flight reservation by talking to a machine rather than talking to a human.

The reasons why something this simple might work are that subjects (i) are familiar with the *task* in advance and (ii) understand what it means to *interact* with the system using the *modalities* described. This might work for the Maths Case (Section 2.1) as well, whereas we don't see it working for Treasure Hunt (Section 2.1) because subjects are not familiar with the Treasure Hunt task in advance nor, probably, with the kind of 3D haptic interaction used – it's not like feeling your way in darkness using your hands, for instance. See also Sections 8.1.4 and 8.2.4 on carrying out an interview or getting a questionnaire filled.

*Data.* See Sections 8.1.5 and 8.2.5 on data from interviews and questionnaires and Chapters 15 and 16 on data handling and analysis. Data analysis is often focused on comparing the pre-test data with the post-test data to see if, e.g. expectations were met, attitudes and opinions changed or any other discrepancy or similarity of interest to further system development can be revealed from the two data sets. Moreover, these data sets normally form part of a larger set of test data sources that should be analysed as a whole.

*Advantages and drawbacks.* Pre-test interviews and questionnaires are being used far less than their post-test counterparts (Section 8.8). The reason probably is that what's on offer is a chance to access users' technology preconceptions, and we don't always need to know about these. This knowledge, however, may be useful for adjusting communication about the technology and may provide important cues to the interpretation of post-test interview and questionnaire data. If people believe that we can do a lot with technology, they may be more easily disappointed when trying out what we have done; if they are sceptical, they may be positively surprised, and we can learn from the details if we are clever enough to elicit them.

See also Sections 8.1.6 and 8.2.6 on advantages and drawbacks of interviews and questionnaires in general.

*Example: Sudoku pre-test interview script.* The questions in Fig. 8.8 were constructed based on the post-test interview script for evaluating the Sudoku system in Fig. 8.9. The comments should be read aloud by the interviewer except for the note. Note that, prior to the interview, the subject must have a description of the system to be tested. Otherwise the questions will make no sense.

## 8.8 Post-Test Interviews and Questionnaires

The purpose of a post-test interview or questionnaire (Dumas and Redish 1999, Rubin 1994) is to collect usability information from subjects about the system they have just used in a test.

*When can you use the method and what is its scope?* Post-test interviews and questionnaires can be used after any system model user test, for instance, after the tests described in Chapter 12: mock-up (Section 12.1), Wizard of Oz (Section 12.2), implemented prototype (Section 12.3), field test (Section 12.4) and think-aloud (Section 12.5). Most of these methods are typically being applied in the lab. Note that post-test questioning requires access to the users, which may be difficult or impossible in the majority of field tests (Section 12.4). If, e.g. the system is being tested in some public space and you go there to hand out questionnaires, chances are that you will get few filled questionnaires back, no matter if you try to make people fill the questionnaire right away or ask them to return the filled questionnaire later on. In this case, you might get more data by making brief – like 3–5 minutes – interviews.

*Multimodal significance.* While the method is important to the development of usable interactive systems, no matter if these are GUI-based or multimodal, the overall significance of post-test interviews and questionnaires would seem higher for multimodal systems. The reason is that, as argued in Section 7.1, early application of some methods is infeasible for some advanced multimodal systems so that these systems first meet real people when being tested by them. This makes usability information collected through post-test questioning even more important, because there are fewer other ways to obtain usability data. It is in this sense that the present method is biased towards multimodal systems, cf. the following factors described in Section 6.2.2: *lack of user familiarity* (Factor 2) and *technology penetration* (Factor 3), *upstream of deployment* (Factor 4), *data collected with users* (Factor 5) and *general lack of knowledge* (Factor 6).

So if you are into advanced multimodality, watch this method! For this book's Cases (Section 2.1), iterative post-test questioning of subjects is an essential source of usability data. The biases just mentioned hold the most for Treasure Hunt, for which several methods in Chapters 8–12 are inapplicable (Section 7.1).

*How does the method work?* A post-test interview is made right after sub-jects have interacted with a system model when memory of the interaction is still vivid and can be expressed spontaneously. Interviews may be done over the phone or face-to-face. The former method is useful with geographically remote or dispersed field test users (Section 12.4). You may allow unstruc-tured discussion as part of a post-test interview (Section 8.1.2) but, typically, you would like to have a (semi-)structured part to get comparable data from all subjects.

Like the post-test interview, a post-test questionnaire is given to users right after having interacted with a system model. If interaction took place in the lab, users are typically asked to fill the questionnaire on the spot; if not, there may be hours or days between interaction and filling of the questionnaire, and there may be trouble getting all questionnaires filled and returned. In any case, users will have more time to reflect upon their answers than when answering questions in a post-test interview. For this reason, it may be a good idea to briefly interview the test subjects even if they will receive a questionnaire as well.

Post-test interviews may be made with single users, pairs, triples, etc. depending on, e.g. whether interaction was single- or multi-user or if the think-aloud method was used with two users interacting with a system model together (Section 12.5). Another option sometimes worth considering is to invite the same, or partially the same, subjects to participate in several system test iterations in order to collect data on progress made as perceived by the subjects.

If sufficient background information on subjects hasn't been collected during screening (Section 8.6) or pre-test questioning (Section 8.7), it should be collected as part of the post-test interview or questionnaire.

*What is required for applying the method?* Subjects who are target users or constitute a representative user group (Section 3.3.1) and who have interacted with the system model. For interviews, an interviewer, an interview script and, possibly, recording equipment (Section 8.1.5). For questionnaires, a questionnaire and, if it's to be filled in the lab under your control, sufficient time and a quiet loca-tion to fill it.

*System/AMITUDE model.* Any system/AMITUDE model version will do as long as subjects are able to interact with it, i.e. anything between an early mock-up and a close to final system.

*Planning.* Write a usability method plan based on plan items described in Section 6.4, starting from the purpose of collecting usability data (Section 6.4.2). Oper-ationalise the purpose and don't forget to collect data on any relevant usability requirement, cf. Section 5.2. It is useful to start by listing all the topics on which data must be collected, making sure not to forget any of them, and then specify more precise information needs per topic. Decide whether to use an interview, a questionnaire or a combination of both. Use the advice in Section 8.1 or 8.2 to turn your information needs into an ordered series of linguistically expressed questions.

Identify subjects so that you can contact them and make an agreement with them, cf. Section 13.2. Note that post-test questioning is used in combination with other methods, i.e. one of the lab test methods (Sections 12.1, 12.2, 12.3, 12.5) and, possibly, real-time observation of users (Section 10.4), screening (Section 8.6) and pretest questioning (Section 8.7). Subject recruitment is shared among methods in a cluster, while most other preparations must be done separately per method.

Sort out any staff roles as interviewer, note-taker and responsible for recording equipment.

Consult Sections 8.1.6 and 8.2.6 on the pros and cons of interviews and questionnaires. If the test takes place in the lab, plan to interview each subject or to hand each subject a copy of the questionnaire, right after their interaction with the system. Promise to be on standby if they have any questions while filling the questionnaire. Even if the interview is made over the phone, this should be done right after interaction. Make sure you have an agreement with the subjects to do so.

See also Chapter 13 for general advice on planning lab sessions.

*Running.* See Sections 8.1.4 and 8.2.4 on carrying out an interview and getting a questionnaire filled, respectively.

*Data.* See Sections 8.1.5 and 8.2.5 on data from interviews and questionnaires and Chapters 15 and 16 on data handling and analysis. Analysis typically focuses on extracting information that can help evaluate how close the system is to satisfying its usability requirements and make clear which improvements are needed. Chapter 17 (Intermezzo 5) presents an analysis report based on, among other things, the post-test interview script in Fig. 8.9. Typically, post-test interviews and questionnaires form part of a larger set of test data resources that should be analysed as a whole.

*Advantages and drawbacks.* Post-test interviews or questionnaires are very important in interactive systems development because there is no alternative to this way of collecting usability information on how the current system model works with real people. The method can be used iteratively in advanced multimodal systems development and is particularly important if several other usability methods don't apply. When used iteratively with representative user groups, the method helps steer even highly innovative development towards a really usable result.

The price of using the method is a significant total cost of planning, execution and data handling of a method cluster which typically consists of (i) running the test (Chapter 12) with users in the lab (Chapter 13), (ii) observing the test subjects (Section 10.4), (iii) post-test questioning (this section) and possibly also (iv) screening (Section 8.6) and (v) pre-test questioning (Section 8.7). All the collected data must be handled and analysed (Chapters 15 and 16). See also Sections 8.1.6 and 8.2.6 on advantages and drawbacks of interviews and questionnaires in general.

*Example: Sudoku post-test interview script.* The interview script in Fig. 8.9 was used in a semi-structured post-test interview during evaluation of the Sudoku Case system (Section 2.1). Except for the note, comments in the script are read aloud by the interviewer. Note that there are no questions about name, age, etc. because we already asked for this information in the screening interview (Section 8.6). The script illustrates several points about writing and using interview questions:

---

**Sudoku post-test interview script**

**Input and Output.** You should answer the following questions by simply picking a word or number from the following list: 1 = unsuitable, 2 = rather unsuitable, 3 = neither/nor, 4 = rather suitable, 5 = suitable. 1 (unsuitable) is worst, 5 (suitable) is best, and 3 (neither/nor) is right in between. [**NOTE**: type these metrics on paper and hand it to the subject, or write the metrics on a blackboard which is clearly visible to the subject]. The questions are all about your input to the system and the system's output to you.

1.   How suitable do you think pointing input is for games like the one you have just tried?

2.   How suitable do you think spoken input is for games like the one you have just tried?

3.   How suitable do you think screen output is for games like the one you have just tried?

4.   How suitable do you think the combination of pointing and spoken input, and screen output, is for games like the one you have just tried?

**Quality.** The next questions are all about how you think it was to play the game and communicate with it.

5.   To which extent did the system understand you when you pointed at something?

6.   How well did it otherwise work to use pointing input? Were there any problems? Which?

7.   To which extent did the system understand what you said?

8.   How well did it otherwise work to speak to the system? Were there any problems? Which?

9.   To which extent did the system understand combinations of speech and pointing input?

10.  How well did it otherwise work to use combined speech and pointing input?

11.  To which extent did you miss other ways (than pointing and speech) to input information?

12.  How easy or difficult was it to understand what to do from looking at the screen? Did you have any problems with some of what was shown on the screen? Which?

13.  To which extent did you miss other forms of output (than via the screen)?

14.  In general, how was it to use combined pointing and spoken input, and screen output, for interacting with the system?

15.  How easy or difficult was it to play the game? Did you have any problems playing? Which?

16.  To which extent did you feel in control when playing the game?

**Functionality**

17.  Do you think the system offered you all the functions you need for playing Sudoku, or did you miss anything? If yes, what? For instance:

   • anything missing from what you could do by pointing?

   • anything missing from what you could do by speaking to the system.

   • missing information on the screen.

   • other missing information.

This is important for us to know in order to be able to improve the game.

**User Experience**

18.  What do you think of solving Sudoku games in the way you just tried?

19.  Comparing with traditional Sudoku games on paper, or possibly with games on the Internet, what do you think are the advantages and disadvantages of the game you just tried?

20.  If you were to come across the system somewhere in a public space, would you play again? *If yes:* why? *If no:* why not?

**Fig. 8.9**  Sudoku post-test interview script (translated from Danish)

**FAQ post-test questionnaire**

Below you will find a number of questions which we would like you to answer. For the first
seven questions we ask you to tick off your answer on a scale from 1 (most positive) to 5 (most
negative) regarding your opinion on the spoken dialogue system we are developing. If you select
4 or 5 in any case, we are very interested in more detailed comments which you can write under
question 8. Any other comments you may have are also welcome here. Later this year we are going to test a new version of the system. If you are willing to participate again, please tick off
"yes" under question 9 and answer question 10. We will choose by lot ten winners of a box of
chocolate among those who send us their comments by filling in the questionnaire. If you want
to participate in the lottery, please remember to answer question 10.

|  | Questions | Most positive | 1 | 2 | 3 | 4 | 5 | Most negative |
|---|---|---|---|---|---|---|---|---|
| 1. | Was the system able to do what you expected? | Yes, indeed | | | | | | No, certainly not |
| 2. | Did you get the information you wanted? | Yes, I got all the information I wanted | | | | | | No, I got none of the information I wanted |
| 3. | How was it to navigate in the system? | Easy | | | | | | Difficult |
| 4. | What did you think of the help function (if you used it)? | I got exactly the help I needed | | | | | | It was of no use |
| 5. | What did you think of talking to the system? | It was convenient and efficient | | | | | | It was time consuming and not a good experience |
| 6. | Did the system understand what you said? | Yes, all the time | | | | | | No, not at any time |
| 7. | What did you think of the system's voice? | Nice and easy to understand | | | | | | Annoying and difficult to understand |
| 8. | Comments on your answers to questions 1–7 + any other comments. | | | | | | | |
| 9. | May we contact you later when we run a new evaluation? | Yes | | | No | | | |
| 10. | Optional: Name and address (including e-mail and/or phone number). | Name, address, e-mail, phone | | | | | | |

**Fig. 8.10** Post-test questionnaire used during development of an FAQ spoken dialogue system
(translated from Danish)

*You forget your own lessons.* This time we forgot to include a question we always
use, i.e. the final, almost mandatory "any other comments" question which sometimes triggers useful information.

*Questions may be too fine-grained.* Three question pairs (5+6, 7+8, 9+10) turned
out to represent too fine-grained and research-oriented distinctions which were not

shared by the subjects. Thus, several subjects tended to answer one when asked the other and then had no further comments to the second question.

*Unforeseen questions emerge.* During the test but too late, we realised that we were missing an important question, i.e. if the subjects found that they learnt anything during gameplay that made them change their interaction style.

*Example: FAQ post-test questionnaire.* The questionnaire in Fig. 8.10 was created, put on the web and used by us during the development of a commercial telephone-based spoken dialogue system for answering frequently asked questions on Danish holiday allowances, cf. Section 3.4.3.

## References

Battey K (2007) Survey questions and answer types. http://www.surveyconsole.com/console/showArticle.do?articleID=survey-questions. Accessed 17 January 2009.

Bias R, Butler S, Gunther R (2007) Customer interviews and profiles. http://theusabilityteam.com/customerinterviewsandprofiles.asp. Accessed 17 January 2009.

Creative Research Systems (2007) Survey design. http://www.surveysystem.com/sdesign.htm. Accessed 18 January 2009.

Crow K (2001) Customer interviews. http://www.npd-solutions.com/interviews.html. Accessed 17 January 2009.

Doyle JK (2006) Chapter 11: Introduction to interviewing techniques. http://www.wpi.edu/Academics/GPP/Students/ch11.html. Accessed 7 February 2009.

Dumas, JS, Redish, JC (1999) A practical guide to usability testing. Rev edn. Intellect Books.

Hom J (1998) The usability methods toolbox. http://jthom.best.vwh.net/usability. Accessed 19 January 2009.

QuestionPro (2006) Designing your online survey. http://www.questionpro.com/buildyoursurvey. Accessed 7 February 2009.

Robson C (2002) Real world research. 2nd edn. Wiley-Blackwell, Oxford, UK.

Rubin J (1994) Handbook of usability testing. John Wiley and Sons, New York.

Sharp H, Rogers Y, Preece J (2007) Interaction design – beyond human-computer interaction. 2nd edn. John Wiley and Sons.

Stimson GV, Donoghoe MC, Fitch C, Rhodes T with Ball A, Weiler G (2003) Rapid assessment and response technical guide. 9.4 Interviews. WHO, Geneva, http://www.who.int/docstore/hiv/Core/Chapter_9.4.html. Accessed 17 January 2009.

UsabilityNet (2006) User survey for design. http://www.usabilitynet.org/tools/surveys.html. Accessed 7 February 2009.

Walonick DS (2004) Excerpts from: survival statistics. http://www.suu.edu/faculty/wright/nfs4480/surveys.pdf. Accessed 19 January 2009.

# Chapter 9
# Meetings with Discussion

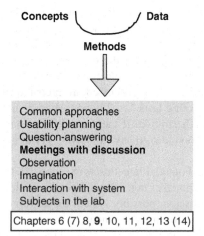

In this second of five chapters on multi-modal usability methods (Section 6.2.2), all methods presented focus on discussion between development team representatives, on the one hand, and customer representatives or potential or actual users, on the other. Three of the main strengths of discussions in meetings are to (i) generate and elaborate upon new ideas, (ii) collectively get deeper into the problems and issues facing the development project and (iii) help reach agreement and consensus. These virtues make discussions in well-prepared meetings a vital source of usability information. Moreover, meetings tend to be low cost.

Section 9.1 describes focus group meetings; Section 9.2 stakeholder meetings; and Section 9.3 more general-purpose uses of meetings and workshops.

## 9.1 Focus Group Meetings

A focus group meeting (Hom 1998, Nielsen 1997, Sharp et al. 2007, Silverman 2006, UsabilityNet 2006a) is a somewhat informal technique that helps collect information about potential users' ideas, attitudes, views, perceptions, wishes, needs, etc. concerning particular usability issues that are brought up for discussion. Focus group meetings are typically one-off.

*When can you use the method and what is its scope?* Focus group meetings help explore the system idea or model, typically at an early stage, such as early analysis, to help discover what potential users want from the system. In this case there is no interaction with a system model. However, focus group meetings can also be used for evaluating a system that the participants have used prior to the meeting, which may reveal problems, unfulfilled expectations, etc.

N.O. Bernsen, L. Dybkjær, *Multimodal Usability*, Human-Computer Interaction Series, DOI 10.1007/978-1-84882-553-6_9, © Springer-Verlag London Limited 2009

To our knowledge, most research projects do not use focus groups despite the fact that many of them might benefit a lot from an early focus group discussion with real people. You might walk away with a different and better system in mind!

*Multimodal significance.* Early focus group meetings yield reliable usability data only if the participants are able to rather quickly get a firm grasp of the system idea or model to be discussed. Since this may not be possible for some advanced multimodal system concepts, focus groups would seem somewhat biased towards GUI-based development, cf. Factor 2, *user familiarity with the system type*, in Section 6.2.2. Thus it would probably be futile to organise an early focus group meeting about our Treasure Hunt Case (Section 2.1). If we want subjects to discuss some unfamiliar and difficult to imagine modality combination, they may have to interact with the system first.

*How does the method work?* The idea is that participants have a structured discussion of topics arising from the application idea. A group leader is responsible for opening, moderating and closing the discussion. It is important to note that the goal is *not* consensus building. The goal is to collect all the different opinions, attitudes, etc. that exist in the focus group. Focus group meetings are not open brainstorming meetings either, because the issues to be discussed are prepared in some detail before the meeting. A typical meeting lasts $1\frac{1}{2}$–2 hours, which is not a long time, and calls for careful meeting orchestration. If there are different target user groups (Section 3.3.6), it may be a good idea to have a meeting per target group.

*What is required for applying the method?* Potential target users (Section 3.3.1), a skilled group leader, possibly a rapporteur who takes notes throughout the session (recommended), a script with topics for discussion, possibly system model representations and other materials, audio or video recording equipment.

*System/AMITUDE model.* In early uses of focus groups, an outline of the system model will often exist, and the purpose of the meeting is to collect usability information that will support decision on AMITUDE and other system model requirements and priorities. Late uses of the method assume an implemented model.

*Planning.* Write a usability method plan based on items described in Section 6.4. Start from the purpose of collecting usability data (Section 6.4.2). Use the purpose to guide the creation of a script with questions you want discussed and to help decide which additional material to include for illustration and discussion, if any (Section 6.4.3).

If a video, a demonstration or an example will be shown at the meeting, check in advance that it can be shown as planned. You may also want a brief questionnaire to be filled during the session. The questionnaire must of course be prepared in advance, see Section 8.2 on questionnaires.

Some 4–12 subjects must be recruited, see Section 13.2. It is important that the subjects take a real interest in the topics you want to discuss, so getting the recruitment right is important. You may want to use screening during the selection process, see Section 8.6.

An experienced group leader must be found who understands the goal of the meeting and is capable of chairing a group discussion well, keeping it on track and ensuring that everybody contributes. If you want to involve a rapporteur, this person must be found as well.

See also Chapter 13 for general advice on lab session planning.

*Running.* Create a good atmosphere. Have participants introduce themselves to get acquainted. The group leader is responsible for starting the discussion, keeping it flowing and maintaining focus on the issues to be discussed. An introduction telling what will be discussed, possibly supported by a demonstration or a video, is useful for kindling discussion. The group leader or – much better – the rapporteur should take notes throughout the session.

An informal discussion style probably works best. Try to make it fun! Encourage everyone to put forward opinions and thoughts and encourage interaction and group discussion. Try to avoid groupthink. Most importantly, ask the right questions in the right way. Questions should be non-directive and you should avoid yes/no questions. Remember that questions are supposed to be a stimulus to elicit further information from the data producers, cf. Fig. 9.1.

The meeting is closed by the group leader who thanks the participants for their time and possibly hands out rewards. See also Chapter 13 for general advice on conducting lab sessions.

*Data.* Data comprises meeting notes and any recordings made. At least the audio side of a focus group meeting should be recorded, but often video recording is used as well, which may be helpful for, e.g. checking subjects' tacit reactions to some

| How to phrase focus group questions |
| --- |
| • Give me a [picture, description] of... |
| • I'd like you all to [discuss, decide]... |
| • Tell me what goes on when you ... |
| • Describe what it's like to ... |
| • Tell me about ... Tell me more about that... |
| • Somebody sum this all up ... |
| • Let's see [pause] I'm having trouble figuring out how I should word this to my client... |
| • Give me an example. |
| • Explain to me ... |
| • Let me pose a problem ... |
| • I'm wondering what would you do if... |
| • What I'd like to hear about is how you are dealing with ... |
| • Ask each other to find out ... |
| • I don't think I'm getting it all. Here's what I've got so far, tell me what I am missing or not getting correctly ... |
| • So, it sounds like you're saying ... |
| • That's helpful. Now let's hear some different thoughts ... |
| • How might someone do that? |

**Fig. 9.1** Examples of how to phrase questions for discussion in a focus group. These questions are from Silverman (2006) and are reproduced with the permission of George Silverman

statements or questions. Make sure to obtain the necessary permissions to use the recordings, cf. Section 13.3.4. The data may or may not be transcribed, depending on its future use and the resources available, as reflected in the usability method plan. If data analysis must be kept at a minimum, ask the group leader, possibly in collaboration with the rapporteur, to write a short meeting summary, highlighting the most important results. See also Chapters 15 and 16 on data handling and analysis.

*Advantages and drawbacks.* Focus group meetings offer low-cost access to real people for discovering user needs and requirements that would be more costly to retrieve in other ways, such as by visiting users' homes or workplaces. The usability information collected may also be useful when developing questionnaire or interview questions or deciding what to test later on during development. When used for system evaluation, focus group meetings reveal what users think of a certain product and which priorities, preferences, attitudes and expectations they have regarding its future development.

Focus groups do not produce information about what users actually do with a given system, since they typically don't interact with the system during the meeting. The data collected may thus be inaccurate or misleading, because there is sometimes a major difference between what users *say* they do, or claim that they want, and what they actually do or need. If participants are not entirely familiar with the issues discussed, this adds unreliability to the data. There is, moreover, a risk of groupthink, i.e. some of the more dominant participants influence others to tacitly agree with them, although, in fact, they don't. They avoid putting forward their own views because they find this more convenient or are afraid to appear foolish.

*Example: Generic focus group questions.* Figure 9.1 shows examples of non-directive requests for information that may be used by the focus group leader.

## 9.2 Stakeholder Meetings

Stakeholder meetings (UsabilityNet 2006b) are typically held between customer representatives and people from the development team – all called stakeholders because they have professional interest in the system to be developed. A stakeholder meeting is often one in a series whose aims are to present, exchange information about, discuss and build common understanding and agreement about current status, requirements, functionality, other system model and AMITUDE-related (Section 3.1) aspects, deliveries, future processes and objectives.

*When can you use the method and what is its scope?* Stakeholder meetings can be used from project start and throughout the development process. A series of stakeholder meetings typically forms a central part of the collaboration with a customer during development.

The method's two primary limitations are (1) the large number of cases of off-the-shelf product development and (2) research projects. In the former case, if no stakeholders are available, focus groups (Section 9.1) and, sometimes, more permanent user groups following the project (Section 9.3) may be employed instead. Although most research projects have no real customers and end users, we have had good experience with meetings with potential stakeholders in advanced multimodal system projects, having received substantial advice on customers, company organisation and interest in the application, access to recordings of company–customer dialogues, etc. This requires that you find, e.g. an organisation that is a potential stakeholder and willing to take on a stakeholder role in your project, at least for a meeting or two.

A kind of very early stakeholder meeting is about whether to introduce a new technology in the organisation in the first place. We had such meetings with staff in a large public transportation company. As one meeting turned into several, we noticed that the number of stakeholders from the organisation kept increasing from one meeting to the next. If not before, we felt being taken seriously when the labour union representative began to attend, worried about the effects on employment of the new technology under discussion.

*Multimodal significance.* Since stakeholder meetings typically assume real customers, the method is generally more relevant to GUI-based development than to advanced multimodal system projects, cf. Factor 4 in Section 6.2.2, *how close to real-life deployment a system type is.* As many of today's non-GUI systems are experimental research systems, the business aspects will often be missing or present only in some abstract form. Stakeholder meetings thus tend to be biased towards GUI-based systems, and none of our Cases (Section 2.1) would probably be amenable to stakeholder meetings at this point.

*How does the method work?* A stakeholder meeting may last from less than an hour to a full day or longer and involves people who have knowledge about the intended uses and users of the system, such as the project manager, developers, end users, procurer representatives and people from marketing, training and support. Typically, a stakeholder meeting is a commitment that has important specific project consequences, rather than a loosely organised brainstorming event.

Note that the stakeholders you need to talk to are not necessarily present at the first meetings, all of them, but may first have to be identified and invited, e.g. a representative from a user group you didn't know would be using the system.

If a scheduled meeting is infeasible for some reason, consider interviewing stakeholders individually over the phone instead in order not to lose momentum. Note, however, that this excludes the vital elements of joint discussion and consensus building and may create problems for the project if allowed to continue for too long. Asynchronous group e-mail discussion is not a viable alternative.

*What is required for applying the method?* Stakeholders, a meeting facilitator, a rapporteur who makes a record of the meeting, a carefully prepared list of issues to be discussed (the agenda).

*System/AMITUDE model.* The system model may be at any stage of development depending on when in the life cycle the meeting takes place. The outcome of a stakeholder meeting helps steer its further development.

*Planning.* Make a usability method plan based on items described in Section 6.4, starting from the purpose of collecting usability data (Section 6.4.2).

Make the purpose operational (Section 6.4.3) by preparing the meeting agenda based on the usability information you want to collect and issues you want to discuss. Circulate the agenda to the participants prior to the meeting so that they can add or revise items and prepare themselves to actively take part in the meeting.

Decide upon date and time, invite the stakeholders, book a room. If there is a problem with date or time, try to move them.

*Running.* The meeting is led by the facilitator who manages the agenda. The facilitator must be careful to avoid that time is being wasted on long-winded discussions of minor issues. The rapporteur takes notes throughout the meeting and must be particularly careful to minute all decisions, conclusions and action points.

If it turns out that information is missing so that a decision cannot be made, it is important to agree on how the information can be found and how to proceed once it has been. In case of obscurity or disagreement during the discussion, you should get the issue sorted out during the meeting so that you have a basis for subsequent work. In general, keep the participants on their toes at all times or you risk missing essential usability information because you never asked for it.

*Data.* A stakeholder meeting typically produces a meeting record of issues discussed, action points, conclusions and decisions arrived at, possibly important arguments and observations, etc. Typically, stakeholder meetings are not recorded on audio or video. The meeting record (or the minutes), including all agreed decision and action points and conclusions, should be sent to the participants for confirmation. The usability data we need may be included in the meeting record or derived from our own notes.

See Chapters 15 and 16 on data handling and analysis.

*Advantages and drawbacks.* Stakeholder meetings are essential to the successful development of systems tailored to a particular customer. Without the continuous monitoring and information exchange they enable, there would be more failed projects and unusable systems around. Bringing stakeholders together early is a great opportunity to discuss and agree on AMITUDE and usability requirements before embarking on system design. Later stakeholder meetings help making necessary adjustments to keep the project on track.

What you get from using the method depends on your preparation of the list of issues for discussion and on how well managed the meeting is. If you forget to bring up an important issue, there is no guarantee that others will. If the facilitator is not careful, the discussion may get sidetracked, important agenda issues left undiscussed and decisions too hastily made. Stakeholders are not necessarily in agreement with one another nor with you, and they are not necessarily consistent from one meeting to another.

*Example: Generic stakeholder meeting issues.* Figure 9.2 lists questions and issues that are often relevant at stakeholder meetings. Note that many of the questions suggest an early meeting. Note also the GUI context. As an exercise, you might try to spot which AMITUDE aspects (Section 3.1) are being considered; which methods and other approaches; which usability requirements, and compare with our findings at the book's web site.

| Examples of questions for a stakeholder meeting |
| --- |
| • Why is the system being developed? What are the overall objectives? How will it be judged as a success? |
| • Who are the intended users and what are their tasks? Why will they use the system? What is their experience and expertise? |
| • Who are the other stakeholders and how might they be impacted by the consequences of a usable or unusable system? |
| • What are the stakeholder and organisational requirements? |
| • What are the technical and environmental constraints? What types of hardware will be used in what environments? |
| • What key functionality is needed to support the users' needs? |
| • How will the system be used? What is the overall workflow, e.g. from deciding to use the system, through operating it to obtaining results? What are typical scenarios of what the users can achieve? |
| • What are the usability goals? (e.g. How important is ease of use and ease of learning? How long should it take users to complete their tasks? Is it important to minimise user errors? What GUI style guide should be used?) |
| • How will users obtain assistance? |
| • Are there any initial design concepts? |
| • Is there an existing or competitor system? |

**Fig. 9.2** Examples of questions and issues that may be discussed at a stakeholder meeting. The questions are from UsabilityNet (2006b) and are reproduced with the permission of Nigel Bevan, manager of UsabilityNet

Figure 9.3 is from a project on a frequently asked questions (FAQ) spoken dialogue system which we developed for a customer together with a software company, cf. Section 3.4.3. The figure shows an agenda with nice brief discussion summaries and action points right after each agenda point. The agenda is from one of a series of stakeholder meetings called "steering committee meetings". There were three partners in the project. All partners were represented at stakeholder meetings by one permanent representative each. Other people participated as required, depending on

| Agenda/Summary |
| --- |
| 1.  Holiday allowance in general, in particular the information part, frequently asked questions. |
| 2.  Holiday allowance, guidance on payment.<br>See points on holiday allowance below.<br>**Action point:** LK checks whether holiday allowance forms may be submitted by fax. |
| 3.  Discussion of paper-based model of information system.<br>Was thoroughly discussed and resulted in an updated model. A wish list has been initiated. HD informed that the supplier has implemented a first version and made some tests. LD informed that the dialogues from the test are being transcribed.<br>**Action point:** The next version will be tested on Thursday or Friday this week – this time with employees from the customer. LD and DS will coordinate instructions and tests. |

**Fig. 9.3** Agenda and summary from a stakeholder meeting about a spoken dialogue system

the focus of the meeting. The meeting referenced in Fig. 9.3 included a person from the user side. Under point 2 there is a reference to "points on holiday allowance". The list of points summarises various aspects of holiday allowance discussed at the meeting and has not been included in the example to keep it short.

## 9.3  Workshops and Other Meetings with User Representatives

Whereas focus group (Section 9.1) and stakeholder (Section 9.2) meetings are specialised methods for collecting usability information through discussion, what we call *workshops and other meetings* are meant to cover other uses of meetings with discussion for collecting usability information with representatives of potential or actual users.

*When can you use the method and what is its scope?* Workshops and other shorter meetings can be used anytime in the life cycle, from requirements capture through interface design to feedback on the usability of user–system interaction and functionality based on a system demonstration. Hands-on experience is an excellent background for discussion.

The method can be used with all kinds of projects. Some research and commercial projects create a group of target users at project start and work with them throughout the life cycle, using workshops and other meetings as the main vehicle of collaboration. It is often an advantage, not least in research projects, to primarily involve highly motivated, articulate and rather computer-literate user representatives in order to generate goodly amounts of usability information in the early stages of exploring new technology.

*Multimodal significance.* No matter if the project is GUI-based or multimodal, the usability of its outcome stands to benefit from occasional or regular workshops and other meetings with real people. If the project is an innovative multimodal one which is, furthermore, rather unfamiliar to people, such as Maths and Treasure Hunt (Section 2.1), a one-off workshop or meeting may be futile due to *user unfamiliarity*, cf. Factor 2 in Section 6.2.2. In such cases, establishment of a more permanent group of user representatives who will follow the project is an option worth considering.

*How does the method work?* Workshops and other meetings range from open-ended brainstorming sessions to sessions having very precise aims and may be one-off or part of a series involving the same user representatives and developers throughout. The project impact of the usability data collected depends, among other things, on the timeliness of the meeting's goals, how well the project ideas and the system/AMITUDE model are presented, the qualifications and enthusiasm of the user representatives, the quality of the chairmanship and whether the user input appears reasonable and feasible within the frames of the project.

Workshops or meetings should be led by a facilitator, and someone should take notes. A session typically lasts from half a day to a couple of days.

Depending on their purpose, workshops and meetings can be run in many different ways. We will just mention one, i.e. affinity diagramming.

*Affinity diagrams.* One way to structure results in a brainstorming meeting is by using affinity diagramming, cf. SiliconFarEast (2004), Balanced Scorecard Institute (1996) and Sharp et al. (2007). This method is useful for soliciting user ideas early in the life cycle. Participants are given an exercise stated very briefly, such as "determine steps and issues involved in developing a portable virtual haptics system". Participants brainstorm and produce ideas, each of which is written onto, e.g. a post-it note that can be tagged to a wall or a board.

After the brainstorming, all notes are stuck onto the wall one at a time so that the notes get grouped naturally together. When all notes have been put up, participants are asked to give each group a name or a heading. For example, there could be a group on algorithms, one on application ideas, one on core functionality and one on devices. The affinity diagram is drawn by connecting the headings and groups with lines, or is simply apparent from the layout on the board.

*What is required for applying the method?* Potential target users (Section 3.3.1) or actual users, all of whom are capable and enthusiastic, and dare speak up in a group; a skilled meeting facilitator who knows the stuff to be discussed; a vigilant rapporteur to take minutes and make notes; an agenda, possibly a system model, possibly other materials to be presented, possibly a bunch of computers and software.

*System/AMITUDE model.* The system model may be at any stage of development. The outcome of the workshop or the meeting feeds into its further development, no matter when in the life cycle it is held.

*Planning.* Make a usability method plan based on items described in Section 6.4 and start from the purpose of collecting usability data (Section 6.4.2). Make the purpose operational (Section 6.4.3) by preparing the meeting agenda based on the usability information you want to collect and issues you want to discuss. Circulate the agenda to the participants prior to the meeting so that they can prepare themselves to actively take part. Prepare whatever you intend to present, such as slides, handouts, demos or maybe a questionnaire (Section 8.2). If you need others to make presentations, try to make sure that they prepare themselves as well.

If the meeting or the workshop is one-off or is to be the first in a series, participants must be identified, which is not necessarily straightforward to do. A dozen years ago, we spent several months locating computer enthusiasts on small Danish islands, who wanted to collaborate with each other and with us in a user-centred and participatory design process for building the Magic Lounge, a system for group meetings using chat and verbal conversation in parallel (Bernsen et al. 1998). Having identified the participants, you decide on date and time and invite them. If some participants are crucial to the success of the meeting, make sure that they can come before inviting the others. If the workshop lasts for more than a day, you may have to arrange for accommodation or, at least, information about accommodation and transportation. You may also have to arrange for lunch and dinner. Remember to book a room.

If there will be a hands-on session, make sure to have access to a room with enough computers and that the system model and anything else required is installed on them. An alternative is to ask the participants to bring their own laptops. In that case you must make the software available to them for installation prior to the workshop or make it available for download or on a CD at the meeting. In both cases, be prepared to discover that installation may not work smoothly for all. There is a risk of wasting time, in particular, if everybody must do installation during the workshop.

*Running.* A workshop or a meeting is led by a facilitator who is responsible for keeping the time schedule set in the agenda. Make sure that there is plenty of time for discussion of the key agenda items, because that's where you get the usability data it's all about. The rapporteur who is tasked with taking the minutes, therefore, has the key role of carefully including all comments made that potentially bear upon system usability. Minutes and notes should reflect what the users propose, prefer, like or what they miss or want changed, as well as any other important observation. A workshop or a meeting need not result in consensus nor in any particular conclusions. However, if conclusions are made or there is consensus about something significant, this should of course be recorded.

*Data.* The data produced at workshops or meetings is minutes and notes. If there has been interaction with a more or less implemented system model, there may also be logfiles or video recordings. Otherwise, workshops or meetings are not recorded on audio or video. Minutes should be sent to the participants for confirmation. Depth of data analysis depends on the significance of the meeting or its results. Any logfiles or recordings will normally be analysed. In how much detail they are analysed depends on resources and expected benefit. See Chapters 15 and 16 on data handling and analysis.

*Advantages and drawbacks.* A workshop or other meeting is an excellent opportunity to meet and discuss with real or potential users. Even if a hands-on session is included, the method is quite different from the test methods described in Chapter 12: it can be used early in the life cycle, before there is anything to test; it has time for discussion and exchange of experience; it typically needs capable participants, not a representative user group; and a meeting is relatively simple to organise, provided that you can find the right participants without too much difficulty. Reserved participants, a bad atmosphere, a weak facilitator unable to keep the time or an ill-prepared agenda may all result in a poor outcome.

A workshop can be relatively costly, depending on how many participants there are, its duration and not least where people come from. If you haven't prepared a workshop before, you are in for some tough time and steep learning, especially because you need meticulous preparation and execution to make the effort worthwhile in terms of the amount of usability data collected.

We have good experience ourselves with establishing a more permanent user group to work with, making them some sort of participants in the project and meeting them regularly. Note, however, that this is a heavy-duty approach in terms of meeting schedule, preparations, communication with participants and cost in terms of time, effort and money.

| Final agenda for NITE workshop, Pisa, 5–6 June 2003 | | | |
|---|---|---|---|
| **Thursday 5th June** | | **18–18.30** | SCORE: an ANVIL-Based Annotation Scheme for Multimodal Communication |
| **9.30–10.00** | Welcome address and presentation of meeting objectives | | |
| **10.00–11.00** | The NITE view | **20.00** | Joint Dinner in Pisa |
| **11.00–11.30** | Coffee break | **Friday 6th June** | |
| **11.30–12.30** | The NXT environment | **9.30–9.45** | Arrival |
| **12.30–13.30** | The Observer | **9.45–11.00** | Hands-on sessions |
| **13.30–15.00** | Lunch | **11.00–11.30** | Coffee break |
| **15.00–16.00** | The NWB workbench | **11.30–13.00** | Hands-on sessions continued |
| **16.00–16.30** | IDIAP Smart Meeting Room, Media File Server, A/V tracking, and modelling of multimodal interaction | **13.00–14.30** | Lunch |
| | | **14.30–16.00** | Structured discussion, reporting feedback from the morning session |
| **16.30–17.00** | Coffee break | **16.00–16.30** | Coffee break |
| **17.00–17.30** | Creating multimodal, multilevel annotated corpora using XML-based text technology | **16.30–17.00** | Concluding remarks and future plans |
| **17.30–18.00** | Gesture annotation using NITE tools | | |

**Fig. 9.4** Agenda from a workshop with (potential) users of multimodal annotation tools

*Example: Workshop agenda.* The agenda in Fig. 9.4 is from a workshop held in the European NITE (Natural Interactive Tools Engineering) research project on multimodal annotation tools. Presenters' names have been omitted but would typically be included in each presentation entry. The workshop was held late in the life cycle, and implemented tools were available for the user representatives to try. Some of the 10–15 participants were, in fact, already familiar with one of the tools, while others were novice users. Roughly, the first day was spent on presenting NITE software and other multimodal annotation tools, while the second day focused on hands-on sessions and on getting as much feedback from participants as possible. Among other things, they were asked to fill a questionnaire on the basis of their hands-on experience, and notes were taken during the discussions.

# References

Balanced Scorecard Institute (1996) Basic tools for process improvement. Module 4: affinity diagram. http://www.balancedscorecard.org/Portals/0/PDF/affinity.pdf. Accessed 18 January 2009.

Bernsen NO, Rist T, Martin J-C, Hauck C, Boullier D, Briffault X, Dybkjær L, Henry C, Masoodian M, Néel F, Profitlich HJ, André E, Schweitzer J, Vapillon J (1998) A thematic inhabited information space with "intelligent" communication services. La Lettre de l'Intelligence Artificielle 134–135–136 Nimes, France 188–192.

Hom J (1998) The usability methods toolbox. http://jthom.best.vwh.net/usability. Accessed 19 January 2009.

Nielsen J (1997) The use and misuse of focus groups. http://www.useit.com/papers/focusgroups.html. Accessed 4 February 2009.

Sharp H, Rogers Y, Preece J (2007) Interaction design – beyond human–computer interaction. 2nd edn. John Wiley and Sons, New York.

SiliconFarEast (2004) Affinity diagram. http://www.siliconfareast.com/affinity.htm. Accessed 18 January 2009.

Silverman G (2006) How to get beneath the surface in focus groups. http://www.mnav.com/bensurf.htm. Accessed 17 January 2009.

UsabilityNet (2006a) Focus groups. http://usabilitynet.org/tools/focusgroups.htm. Accessed 4 February 2009.

UsabilityNet (2006b) Stakeholder meeting. http://usabilitynet.org/tools/stakeholder.htm. Accessed 17 January 2009.

# Chapter 10
# Observation of Users

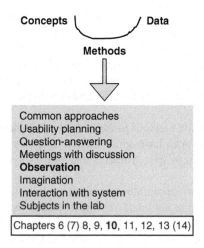

Concepts / Data

Methods

Common approaches
Usability planning
Question-answering
Meetings with discussion
**Observation**
Imagination
Interaction with system
Subjects in the lab

Chapters 6 (7) 8, 9, **10**, 11, 12, 13 (14)

In this third of five chapters on multimodal usability methods (Section 6.2.2), all methods presented capitalise on observation of users, but in very different ways. Focus of observation sometimes settles upon the user, sometimes on the context of use or on something produced by the user and sometimes on several of these. Moreover, observation may zoom in or out to capture very different types of events. In particular, zooming-in captures micro-behaviours of central importance to much of multimodal interaction and blending with people.

What's common and special to observation methods is not just that these methods are useful for finding out what people actually do in context. Observation is indispensable, because much of what it reveals is something which the people observed couldn't even tell us if they tried. Few people have a fully detailed picture of *what* they do from minute to minute at work or at home, and they have even less of an idea about *how* they do what they do in detail, how they react to events or how they think about things. Since we aim to fit systems to people, there often is no other way than to start by observing them.

Section 10.1 describes macro-behavioural field methods; Section 10.2 micro-behavioural field observations; Section 10.3 a generalisation of the card sorting method, which we call category sorting; Section 10.4 user observation during a system model test; and Section 10.5 human data collection in the lab.

## 10.1 Macro-Behavioural Field Methods

Field observation methods come under different names and descriptions but have so much in common for the purposes of this book that we present most of what

N.O. Bernsen, L. Dybkjær, *Multimodal Usability*, Human-Computer Interaction Series, DOI 10.1007/978-1-84882-553-6_10, © Springer-Verlag London Limited 2009

is done with them under a single heading. Methods range from field interview, contextual inquiry (Beyer and Holtzblatt 1998, Gaffney 2004, Alexander 2006, Hom 1998, Sharp et al. 2007, UsabilityNet 2006a) and field observation (Sharp et al. 2007, UsabilityNet 2006b) to ethnographic studies (Robson 2002, Sharp et al. 2007, Hom 1998), and we use the term macro-behavioural field methods to cover most of their uses. All are based on observing or interviewing people in the field in order to collect usability information on what they do in context, and how. The distinction between macro- and micro-behavioural (Section 10.2) field methods, on the other hand, seems to be our own.

*When can you use the method and what is its scope?* Macro-behavioural field methods are typically used early in the life cycle to investigate how potential users actually work or act "in the wild". Results are used to help generate AMITUDE (Section 3.1) requirements and design input for systems that will support or replace the tasks or other activities investigated in the field. The methods require that people exist who perform activities of interest to system development, no matter whether those activities are being computer supported or not. Although typically used when developing systems for organisations, the methods have a wider scope, and the people observed may be in their homes, at work or anywhere else, and don't have to be professionals at what they do.

The methods can also be used as evaluation methods in the late part of the development process when visiting target users who have some version of the system installed. In that case, the methods are used to spot problems that call for system model changes.

*Multimodal significance.* There are great opportunities for multimodal systems and systems blending with people to support or automate existing activities, including such that are being supported by GUI-based systems. For instance, development of two Case systems, Sudoku and Maths (Section 2.1), could be supported by usability data collected through macro-behavioural field methods with Sudoku players at home and maths teachers in class, respectively. Thus, even if the methods may be primarily used in GUI-based development today due to the *technology penetration* achieved by GUI-based systems, cf. Factor 3 in Section 6.2.2 – the balance is likely to change at some point.

*How do the methods work?* Macro-behavioural field methods are applied where people perform the activities of interest – at work, at home, onboard a ship, etc. Their traditional core is to observe, or "be" with, people without being noticed, because that's how to obtain "ecologically valid" data, but this may be supplemented with requests for clarification and explanation when the people observed are free to answer them, with interviews, and even with assuming the role of apprentice to the master of some activity. Ethnographic studies may take years, but it is important to stress that field methods can often be applied by only spending, say, 2–5 hours per person observed.

*What is required for applying the method?* Typically one observed person at a time, 1–2 colleagues from the development team, a script with issues on which to collect usability information as well as issues to inform the people observed about, possibly audio or video recording equipment, possibly one or more brief interview scripts (Section 8.1) or questionnaires (Section 8.2), possibly a permission (see Section 13.3.4).

*System/AMITUDE model.* The system model may exist in outline. The purpose of macro-behavioural field methods is typically to collect usability information that will support requirements specification, design decisions and model priorities.

*Planning.* Write a usability method plan based on items described in Section 6.4. Start from the purpose of collecting usability data (Section 6.4.2). Use the purpose to guide creation of a script with topics you need information about and questions you want answered either through observation or by asking them (Section 6.4.3): how is the physical environment; how is the psychological, social and organisational environment; who collaborates with the person observed; what is the person doing; which physical and information objects are close at hand; what are they being used for; what are the individual and social goals relating to the activities of interest; what would they like to change and how; etc.

If you are going to visit people at work, try to obtain information about the workplace before going there. This helps focus data collection planning. Always collect information about people, such as name, age, gender, education, work experience, any other item needed, either by making interviews or by asking them to fill in a small questionnaire. In both cases, questions must be prepared in advance.

Prepare what to tell people about yourself, your project, why you are visiting them, the plan for the visit and what you are going to use the collected data for. Write it down so that everyone gets the same information.

As a rule, observing five to six people with the same profile (Section 3.3.1) yields pretty solid data, but you may still get useful data even if there's only time to observe two to three people. Identify and contact the people you want to visit. If the activities you are interested in are being carried out by, e.g. people with two different profiles, you need to observe more people. Make an agreement with the individuals about the visit and remember that you probably need to make an agreement with management as well if they are employees in an organisation. You may also need an official permission (Section 13.3.4) from management, in particular if you are going to make video recordings. Make sure to visit on a normal day and not, e.g. on a day when nothing much is going on, although that's when people have more time for you.

Think about how to make people cooperate and have confidence in you, in particular if you plan to do a good deal of interviewing and not just act as a fly on the wall – such as by dressing like them and showing genuine enthusiasm for what they do. Being open about what you are doing is also likely to help. Still, remember that some people are easier to strike up a relationship with than others.

When planning the visits, keep in mind that it is tiring to spend several hours observing, so preferably don't plan to observe more than one person per day. It often pays off to be two people visiting. Two can capture more of what's going on than one, and it is hard for a single person to pay full attention observing while handling recording equipment at the same time.

Check all equipment and make sure to have everything you need, including, e.g. enough charged batteries. Note that equipment takes time to set up and may attract more attention than desirable. If you want to give users something to thank them for their time, remember to buy it, see also Section 13.2.6 on rewards.

*Running.* Try to establish a low-key and pleasant atmosphere around yourself so that people feel comfortable having you around. Start by telling about yourself, the project, the visit, the plan for the day, etc. Check if you are visiting on an average day or if there is anything special going on. The major part of your time should be spent observing and talking to the person in the use environment and learning how people do their tasks and other activities of interest. Keep an open mind and make sure to collect the data listed in your script.

Don't hesitate to ask questions and request explanations in order to fully under-stand people's background, role(s), task(s), environment of use, supporting equip-ment, etc., so as to better understand what they need from your system. Phrase all questions in a neutral manner to avoid priming. You're on stage, remember (Section 6.4.4)! Be courteous and aware of the situation. Don't interfere. If the person is talk-ing to a customer or negotiating the entrance to a busy harbour, it's probably a bad idea to interrupt.

Take copious notes throughout. The gentle way is by using paper and pencil rather than a laptop. Remember that the notes are very important even if you also make audio or video recordings. If you don't make such recordings, it may still be useful to take photographs of the use environment.

*Data.* Data includes notes from the visits, any interview notes and filled ques-tionnaires, any recordings and other material people may have given you. Since a visit may take several hours, you may end up with dozens of hours of recorded data. It is a good idea to use the notes as primary data source in order to reduce the time spent on data handling. Avoid having to transcribe the recordings, if possible, and only use them as back-up when the notes are confusing or insufficient.

If at all possible, type in and elaborate on all notes from a visit before making the next visit. This helps maintain an overview and discover missing information. As a minimum, write your overall impressions and brief conclusions. When the field study is over, you can then swiftly review the notes and present the team with first, tentative-but-general conclusions.

The task of data analysis typically appears somewhat tortuous: you (i) collect data in the field on how people carry out tasks or other activities that your system will eventually support or replace; (ii) analyse this data based on the AMITUDE framework (Section 3.1), sort-of-as-if you want to build an AMITUDE model of use of what is actually going on, imperfections and all; and then (iii) further analyse this model to extract requirements for the specification and design of a new system. The new system might do things very differently from how they are currently being done in the field, but field observation cannot tell you anything about that. All it can do is model what's actually going on in the workplace or elsewhere, including, of course, people's wishes for improvements of work flow, process, communication, etc. This is what we call a large data handling gap in Section 15.1. See also Chapters 15 and 16 on data handling and analysis.

*Advantages and drawbacks.* Macro-behavioural field methods provide a great opportunity to experience and understand what people actually do in their real environment when carrying out activities in some sense similar to those the system is intended to support or replace. This usability information cannot be obtained in any other way than through field investigation: what is going on in the wild generally cannot be reproduced in the lab, and we cannot simply ask people to tell what they do at work, at home, or elsewhere because they are not necessarily good at remembering and explaining the routines they follow every day and the detailed physical, psychological, social and organisational context in which this happens.

However, people may behave differently when outsiders are present, depending on how intrusive their presence is felt to be. It is crucial that users are cooperative and it is up to you to ensure it. Furthermore, real life has a lot of variability, so if the day of your visit is very slow or very busy, or if something special happens that takes most of the day, you risk getting the wrong model of use from your data.

Interviewing is more intrusive than pure observation and is more of a "time robber" for people. Conversely, observation is subjective and error-prone if you don't ask enough questions and verify your interpretations.

Macro-behavioural field methods are relatively costly because they are labour intensive. You must travel to one or several locations to visit people and spend hours with each of them, taking their time as well. Data analysis is often complex. Here, you can at least save time by having good notes and little need for consulting any recordings. Preparations can be heavy, too, especially, of course, if you are into monster challenges fraught with politics and other complications, such as the creation and use of electronic patient journals in hospitals, countrywide. Finally, it may be difficult to obtain the field study permissions needed.

*Example: Notes from use of a macro-behavioural field method.* Figure 10.1 shows excerpts from elaborated notes taken by one of the authors during field observation and interviewing at a travel agency. The aim of the visit was to learn how travel agents handle phone calls related to domestic flight tickets, including reservation, change and cancellation. The collected information was used in the specification of the spoken dialogue system discussed in Section 3.4.2. Among other things, we learned about the use environment, work processes and which information was

---

**Notes from a visit to a travel agency**

Seven travel agents answering customer calls share the largest room. ... Each employee has on his desk a telephone and an Ericsson (Nokia or ICL) terminal coupled to a mainframe, except for the secretary and two people handling group trips who have PCs. ... Books and material are also placed on the desks for convenience. Probably the most important book is the flight ABC which is a table of all flights. ... Material not often used is placed along the walls, alongside some of the hardware. On the first floor there is a telex, two fax machines, a printer which is used to print hardcopies of reservations, and a photocopier. ...

... A booking requires that the customer (typically a secretary) indicates at least the name of the organisation to which the invoice must be sent, departure and destination airports, date, approximate time, name of passenger(s) and, if a return ticket is required, date and approximate time of the return journey. Very often a customer profile exists for the passenger. ...Information on people who travel often is kept in a so-called customer profile system which is part of the Smart system. The customer profile system contains information, such as name, airline preferences, seating, ... so that it is not necessary to ask, e.g. how to spell the name of a passenger every time. ...

---

**Fig. 10.1** Excerpts of notes from macro-behavioural field observation at a travel agency (translated from Danish)

stored in a database. The latter gave us an idea of how to cope with travellers' names in the dialogue system.

## 10.2 Micro-Behavioural Field Observation

Like the macro-behavioural field methods (Section 10.1), micro-behavioural field observation is carried out in the field but with a very different focus and purpose. Whereas the former methods collect usability information on tasks or other activities, patterns of collaboration, workflow, etc., micro-behavioural observation focuses on the physical execution of activities and how it expresses the mind, i.e. on the micro-details of people's behaviour, cf. end of Section 4.2.5.

The special point about micro-behavioural field observation as opposed to micro-behaviour data collection in the lab (Section 10.5) is that field observation collects real-life behavioural data, i.e. data that, ideally, is in no way affected by factors to do with the data collection. There is a possible terminological confusion lurking here which we have better clarify: one can of course "go out in the field", that is, leave the lab and give subjects multiple instructions on what (not) to do before recording them. We discuss such cases in connection with micro-behavioural data collection in the lab and reserve the term micro-behavioural field observation for more or less pure, fly-on-the-wall observation of real-life behaviour.

*When can you use the method and what is its scope?* Micro-behavioural field observation is used early-to-mid life cycle to collect usability data for developing system abilities to recognise and understand any kind of human behaviour and generate emulation of human behaviour of any kind, from walking pensively to having a mad fit of anger. Micro-behavioural validity is essential to successful behaviour recognition, and humans are highly sensitive to whether gestures, facial expressions, verbal articulations, body movements or actions are micro-behaviourally valid or not.

However, since much of this data can be collected more easily in a controlled lab environment or similar, cf. Section 10.5, micro-behavioural field observation is primarily used when a more controlled and constraining method of data collection is impractical, insufficient or infeasible. In a simple example of *impractical*, while we might never succeed in persuading travel agent Smith to come to the lab and talk to his customers from there, he and his company might be perfectly willing to let us record his communication with customers at work. Illustrating *insufficient*, we need real-life, fly-on-the-wall data for testing the system on what it is ultimately up against in order to work unconstrained in the field. And, illustrating *infeasible*, if our vision system is to pick up rule violations in football matches, we need to observe real football matches.

*Multimodal significance.* Rarely relevant to standard GUI-based development, micro-behavioural observation is essential to multimodal systems for blending with people, because these systems need to model aspects of human perception, central processing, communication and action, cf. Factors 1, 5 and 6 in Section 6.2.2, *nature of the user–system interface, the kind of data to be collected with users* and *general lack of knowledge*, respectively. All our Cases need micro-behavioural observation data (Section 2.1) because they must recognise and understand human behaviour input, such as speech and sign language, and the Maths system, in particular, might need micro-behavioural data from the field. This data is being used in various ways to train, design and test the systems' components for recognising, understanding or generating speech, pointing gesture, sign language, facial expression and bio-sensor data.

*How does the method work?* Micro-behavioural field observation is almost fully based on recording of audio, video, electrophysiological and other data. Micro-behaviour is generally far too fast and complex to be perceived by humans in real time, which is why running horses were wrongly depicted for centuries without anyone being able to spot the errors. This implies that the actual observation to be done on the data, in fact, happens during data analysis rather than during data collection, cf. Chapter 16.

While it is perfectly standard for a macro-behavioural field method to note, for instance, that travel agent Smith in a friendly manner asks the user about the travel destination – the micro-behavioural interest in this exchange would be how, exactly, Mr. Smith's face and body posture express friendliness, which exact wording he uses to ask the question, which intonation he uses, which accent he has, which exact gestures he might do and how these micro-behaviours are coordinated in time. We use the term *micro* to highlight this focus on exactly how we do the things we do.

*What is required for applying the method?* Humans who fit the specified profile, recording equipment, one or two people in charge of making the recordings, possibly a consent form or other permission signed by the data producers or their organisation, allowing recordings to be made (see Section 13.3.4). Note that the subjects to be recorded may have many different relationships with the project. They may, of course, be target users or a representative user group (Section 3.3.1), but they are often people who are particularly good at producing the micro-behaviours we need to study in detail, or who can simply perform those behaviours. For example, if you want to make recordings of tango dancers, you must decide if you need professional dancers or if the local amateur dance club will do. It is not always necessary to be present to get recordings made. If, e.g. you can make an agreement with a company who will provide access to recordings of customer calls, all that needs to be done to record the calls is to set up equipment that can automatically log the calls during an agreed period. Note that the callers may have to be asked for permission to allow their calls to be recorded.

*System/AMITUDE model.* The system model will have been specified to some extent. The purpose of the method is to collect usability data in support of design specification or implementation.

*Planning.* Make a usability method plan based on items described in Section 6.4, starting from the purpose of collecting usability data (Section 6.4.2) and followed by purpose operationalisation (Section 6.4.3). Then specify the data producer profile and find out where to make the data collection. This may all be very simple to do if all one needs is a stack of Champions League football matches on video, but may be more complicated if, for instance, data recording focuses on behaviour details that require special equipment setup, putting markers on subjects, etc.

How many subjects and how much data are needed depends on data collection purpose and must be estimated from case to case based on available expertise. While a phone call is perhaps two minutes, a table tennis game or a class at school take much longer. However, keep in mind that data collection and analysis is time consuming and may easily be prohibitively expensive in resources. How many hours of human–human flight reservation data, recorded with how many different people, do we need to collect +95% of the linguistic constructs people use to book a flight in English? The answer is probably a hundred times more than you can afford to collect and analyse by hand!

It is often necessary to contact the people who are going to be recorded, or make an agreement with an organisation on when and how to make the recordings and get the necessary permissions. Make sure that recordings will be made at times when the behaviour you want to record is actually being produced. Prepare some information to give to subjects orally or in writing already when contacting them. At least you should tell subjects why they are important and inform about the purpose of the recordings, and what the data will be used for. If subjects must have a certain level of expertise, such as at least 3 years of teaching experience, you may have to screen them first, cf. Section 8.6.

Make sure to have all equipment, including, e.g. enough charged batteries. Check that everything works. If recordings are to be made in a difficult environment, it may be worthwhile to go there first to check how and where to best mount camera(s) and other equipment. Even then, plan to have ample time to set up and test the equipment on each recording day.

*Running.* Go to the recording location well in advance to put up equipment and make sure that everything works fine. We recommend that at least two people go there because this will make the recording operation so much more robust to the real-life incidents that are bound to happen. Try to make yourself received with friendliness and tolerance, and then try to become ignored and unobtrusive while recording. Note-taking is usually unimportant. If at all possible, sample-check the recordings right after they have been made to make sure that they are all right and nothing has to be adjusted.

*Data.* The recordings are your data. Since micro-behavioural field observation is about behaviour details, fine-grained data analysis is often needed. Analysis may require detailed annotation of the data in order to be able to extract the usability information of interest. This can be extremely labour intensive to do, so be careful when planning how much data to annotate in-depth. See Chapters 15 and 16 on data handling and analysis.

*Advantages and drawbacks.* Micro-behavioural field observation is unique in producing real-life data on human micro-behaviour details. If uncorrupted by priming and other factors due to the recording process, this data shows exactly how particular individuals carry out activities in real life. There isn't really any other way of getting this information, the best approximation probably being that of asking professional actors to perform as if they were real-life people, which is their job anyway. Still, it's not the same thing, although it is an option to keep in mind in case

| Collection of micro-behavioural field data: telephone-based spoken dialogues |
|---|
| In connection with the development of an over-the-phone spoken dialogue system in the flight travel domain in the early 1990s, we contacted a travel agency in order to collect recordings of real-life dialogues between a travel agent and customers. The purpose was to analyse the dialogues to obtain cues to how the system's dialogue should be modelled. |
| We agreed with the travel agency to send them the recording equipment, and they would then record relevant incoming calls during a particular period. For legal reasons, the travel agent always had to inform the caller that the dialogue would be recorded only if permitted by the caller. Recording only started once the caller had given permission. This is of course a weakness in the data since we cannot study how a dialogue starts. On the other hand, the data was very valuable even with the initial part of each dialogue missing, since there were plenty of other issues to study, such as order of information requested and given, how information received is being confirmed, and how process feedback is provided during human database look-ups. |
| The following excerpt is from one of the recorded dialogues between a customer (C) and a travel agent (A) based in Aalborg, Denmark. It shows the first part from recording start. The customer continues to book another ticket. |

| | |
|---|---|
| A: I'm just going to look up your profile. | A: Yes, at 7.20. |
| C: Yes. | C: 7.20. |
| A: And who is going to travel? | A: And this is the sixth, then. [PAUSE] I just |
| C: NAME. | have to enter the account number, you know, |
| A: NAME, and when does he want to depart? | when he needs it [the ticket] over there [in Copenhagen]. |
| C: At 7 tonight. | |
| A: From Copenhagen? | ... |
| C: From Copenhagen to Aalborg. | A: Third July from Copenhagen at 7 in the evening and from here on sixth July at 7.20. |
| A: And only one way? | C: Yes. |
| C: No, he'll return on Monday morning. | A: And the reference number is NUMBER. ... |

**Fig. 10.2** Collection of real-life spoken dialogues (dialogue translated from Danish)

real-life recordings are out of the question. Note that the use of actors for micro-behaviour data collection is a hotly debated issue. Note also that, once you start controlling data collection in the field in any way, it's no longer micro-behavioural field observation but data collection in the lab, cf. Section 10.5.

When people know that they are being recorded, this may change their behaviour, so there is always a question about data reliability, especially with small data sets.

*Example: Travel agent micro-behaviour.* Figure 10.2 describes collection of a set of spoken dialogues for the purpose of studying how callers and travel agents express themselves, and in which order they request or present information. Note that the *how* issue is a micro-behavioural one whereas the information presentation *order* issue is a macro-behavioural one. The collected data was used as input to the specification of the system described in Section 3.4.2.

## 10.3 Category Sorting

Category sorting is unique among the methods in this book because its sole purpose is to find out how people think or, more specifically, how they split up the world into conceptual categories. Categories are fundamental to representation and exchange

of information because they strongly influence how people classify and group items
of any kind. Thus, if we want our representations to be understood as we intend
them to be, we better adjust them to the recipients, which is, in fact, just a special
case of fitting systems to people. Category sorting is a generalisation of the card
sorting method used in GUI-based development (Spencer and Warfel 2004, Nielsen
1995, Lamantia 2003, UsabilityNet 2006c).

*When can you use the method and what is its scope?* Category sorting is typically
used to help sort out how to represent information in early design. The information
can be of any kind – we show a facial expression example at the end of this section. In GUI-based development, the method known as *card sorting* is applied in
attempts to reduce some key usability problems with classical GUI-style interfaces,
i.e. the problem of designer-designed static graphic labels and keywords (Section
4.3.2), and the related problem of static graphic icons. In both cases, the problem
is that labels/keywords and icons in menus, on buttons, and elsewhere, even when
put together as labelled icons, are multiply ambiguous, partly because each user is
able to interpret a single expression in different ways; partly because different users
tend to interpret the expression differently; and partly because the information to be
conveyed often is functional information that is particularly hard to convey in single
words or phrases. Some consequences are that users cannot easily find what they are
looking for because it's not where they expect it to be; cannot build a simple mental
model  (Payne 2003) of the information and hence have difficulty learning to use
the interface; and remain in a state of uncertainty and confusion.

One of the methods used to try to reduce the problem is to ask subjects to sort
a stack of cards, each card having a menu label or icon on it, into smaller stacks,
grouping related items together under a common heading label or icon, and sometimes also to point out unintelligible or ambiguous keywords or icons and propose
alternatives.

Generalising, what category sorting can do is to present any set of representations in any modality or modality combination and ask subjects to describe or crit-
icise each representation; group representations under given or created headings;
tell what's missing from a group or doesn't belong to it, or what sounds, looks or
feels odd, natural, likeable, ambiguous or disturbing, etc.; or anything else we can
think of using the method for. The method may be used whenever we have a set of
representations that we want subjects to sort or assess.

Note that working with this method typically requires a substantial amount of
analysis and creation of representations. Category sorting is not needed for the
domain part of an application if there already exists some broadly accepted classification which it makes sense to use, such as a set of categories from some part of
medicine. Even then, category sorting might be useful for the part of the interface
to do with system operation, which is not usually taught in medical school.

*Multimodal significance.* Category sorting addresses human categorisation in
all media and most modalities described in this book (Chapter 4) and would
seem important for mapping out all manner of human categorisation relevant to
blending-with-people systems. This suggests that the method might be more important to multimodal usability than to GUI-based usability, due to Factors 5 and 6 in

Section 6.2.2, i.e. the *kind of data to be collected with users* and the *general lack of knowledge*. Category sorting is applied to the Maths Case (Section 2.1) in the example at the end of this section. The method might also have been applied to Treasure Hunt in order to decide which sounds to use for representing which colours (Section 7.2.2). In the version we tested (Bernsen and Dybkjær 2007), the sounds were arbitrary and difficult to remember, and two of them were too similar to be easily distinguished. Using category sorting, subjects might have been presented with a list of sounds and asked to categorise them relative to the predefined set of five colours plus a "don't know" group. This might have produced a more usable set of sounds.

*How does the method work?* Provide each subject with a set of representations, or sorting items, in any modality or modality combination and ask them to perform their categorisation work, cf. above, either individually or in groups discussing how to solve the problem. If subjects are asked to categorise items into groups, you may run either an *open category sorting* in which the subjects themselves decide which and how many groups to create or a *closed category sorting* in which you have already established the groups and subjects have to allocate items to these groups.

*What is required for applying the method?* Target users or a representative user group (Section 3.3.1), an experimenter, representations to sort, possibly computers (corresponding to the number of subjects working in parallel), possibly video recording equipment.

*System/AMITUDE model.* A first version of the system model has been specified and design is starting or ongoing. The purpose of category sorting is to collect usability data in support of information representation design.

*Planning.* Make a usability method plan based on items described in Section 6.4. Start from the purpose of collecting usability data (Section 6.4.2). Operationalise the purpose by first creating or selecting the representations to be presented to subjects (Section 6.4.3). This is where to invest design energy in human–system information exchange, because the subjects aren't likely to provide much useful input beyond the representations they are being presented with and the issues they are being asked to address. So if those representations and issues aren't carefully prepared, method application may be wasted. Make the representations easy to handle, i.e. browse, inspect individually, compare, revisit, group or otherwise annotate, etc.

Second, write a script of subject instructions, so that all subjects receive the same information on what the exercise is about and exactly what they are supposed to do with the representations, how to handle the representations on a computer (unless you use physical cards) and what things should look like when they have finished their tasks. Each representation may be accompanied by questions, such as whether the subject understands the item or has alternative proposals, or how well it fits into some category. Be quite explicit on how subjects should handle "don't know" cases. It is generally preferable to offer subjects the option of saying "don't know" rather than forcing them to make categorisation decisions they aren't convinced about at all. Number the representations for ease of reference but make sure to randomise contents when presented to subjects. It is practical to give subjects simple forms to fill with their categorisation solutions, and some subjects might appreciate to have some way of making notes as well. Loading the filled forms into a database may save precious data handling time.

In the standard case, it is important to plan for subjects to have ample time to apply their considered judgment to the work. People spend quite different amounts of time on sorting a stack of items. As a rule of thumb, it takes about half an hour to sort 50 items. If the categorisation tasks are different from classical card sorting, make a test with a couple of colleagues to get an idea of the time required. Note that representations that include haptic or acoustic modalities are more time consuming to compare than graphic modalities, because the former must be inspected one at a time and remembered in order to make comparisons, whereas the latter can be visually compared side-by-side. Note also that cases might exist in which fast spontaneous categorisation is required.

Make sure to have pens and rubber bands ready if you use physical cards. Have a camera available for making pictures of how each subject has laid out the cards on the table. When using electronic representations, make sure to have enough computers. Put the representations on each computer and check that everything works. Be prepared to answer questions from subjects. Remember to book the rooms needed.

Our recommendation is to invite at least 15 subjects. See Section 13.2 on subject recruitment and Section 13.3 on other issues related to preparing a lab session.

*Running.* Subjects may arrive at the same time or at different times. In any case you should give them the prepared instructions either orally, on paper, or both, and then leave them to do their work so that they don't feel under any kind of pressure. However, it must be easy for them to get hold of the experimenter in case they have questions or when they are done. Make sure that solutions are photographed or saved on disk. See also Chapter 13 on issues related to running a lab session.

*Data.* The primary data consists of the results of the categorisation work, preferably stored in a database. If not, it is useful to enter the data for each participant into a spreadsheet or database so that you can easily examine the result patterns that have emerged. Subjects often agree in a good deal of the cases they are presented with. This agreement may be important or surprising in its own right, of course. Otherwise, the items deserving special attention are those on which there is little or no consensus as well as the proportion of "don't knows". If there is a large proportion of don't knows and disagreements all over the place, this may be an interesting analytic challenge for a theoretician, but, for the design you are creating, it probably means back to the drawing board to thoroughly redesign the representations and prepare a new category sorting exercise. See also Chapters 15 and 16 on data handling and analysis.

*Advantages and drawbacks.* Providing direct and focused access to how people categorise the world, category sorting is an excellent tool for revealing all manner of category strengths and weaknesses in the system's representation of information, including, e.g. everything from clarity and harmlessness through to obscurity and offence to fundamentalists, and all manner of relationships across categories. Moreover, the method is generally relatively cheap to use.

A potential drawback is that category sorting is AMITUDE context-free, so that the categories used and the results achieved, may not always be optimal in the actual

**Fig. 10.3**  Facial expressions from the Maths system subjected to category sorting

AMITUDE context (Section 3.1). Furthermore, results are sometimes ambiguous and hard to interpret, sending us back to the design analysis we came from.

The risk of doing group sorting is that individual perceptions may be lost in a collective consensus determined by the views and stamina of few subjects. The advantage is the group discussion.

*Example: Maths facial expression sorting.* Figure 10.3 shows a small example of category sorting from the Maths system (Section 2.1). The entire sorting process was carried out on computer. Eight files, numbered from 1 to 8, each contained a face. Subjects were asked to open the files one by one in any order and categorise the facial expressions. First, they were given the open task of classifying each expression using the most appropriate predicate they could think of. Next, they were asked to go through the images again, this time to solve the closed task of classifying each face as being either neutral, happy, annoyed or surprised. Classifications were entered into forms, each containing a table with the file name numbers and empty slots to fill. The forms also asked subjects to tick off on a 5-point scale from *very easy* to *very difficult*, how it was to make the classification. Finally, the forms invited subjects to write free-style comments on the open task and on the adequacy of the facial expressions in the closed task.

## 10.4  Observation of Users in Real Time

Observation of users in real time (Rubin 1994, Sharp et al. 2007) refers to the activity of observing subjects while they interact with some system model version. The goal is to collect usability information on user–system interaction while it's happening, typically in order to complement the data collected from logfiles and post-test questioning (Section 8.8) and create as complete a set of data on the inter- action as possible. The method closest to real-time user observation in this book's arsenal is the observation-oriented part of the macro-behavioural field methods (Section 10.1). Probably the main difference is that an observer using the former is expected to be familiar with the system interacted with, and with the plan for interaction, whereas an observer using the latter is out there in the unfamiliar "wild" and may be observing much else besides user–system interaction.

*When can you use the method and what is its scope?* Real-time observation can be used as soon as there is a system model with which it makes sense for users to interact. Among the five interaction methods described in Chapter 12, user obser- vation is frequently applied with the two prototype test methods, Wizard of Oz and think-aloud (Sections 12.1, 12.2, 12.3 and 12.5). For practical reasons, the method is used with lab sessions, including exported lab tests, like when an observer is seated in the back of the car while the subject is driving and interacting with a spoken car control system prototype. If, on the other hand, we are running an unsupervised field test (Section 12.4), observation becomes difficult or impossible since subjects may use the system whenever they want and normally do so in their own environment, such as at work or at home. Similarly, real-time user observation can be cumbersome if users keep moving around with their mobile applications.

*Multimodal significance.* Since user–system interaction tests are a *must* in usabil- ity development, user observation is, in principle, as important to GUI-based system testing as it is to multimodal systems testing. Still, we believe that there is a tendency for advanced multimodal system projects to need more lab tests or supervised field tests, make more use of iterative testing, and use more user observation than stan- dard GUI projects. This means that the user observation method has a slight bias towards multimodal development for usability, cf. Factors 2, 4, 5 and 6 in Section 6.2.2, i.e. *user familiarity* with the system type, *how close to real-life deployment* a system is, the *kind of data* to be collected with users and general *lack of knowl- edge*, respectively. Regarding our Cases, real-time user observation was used in the Sudoku and Treasure Hunt tests, cf. the example below, and will be used in all Maths tests as well.

*How does the method work?* Armed with pen and paper or a laptop, the observer watches the subject(s) interact with the system model and takes notes throughout the session on what the subject is doing and possibly why. Note that much of this information will not be apparent from any logfiles collected nor reported in any post-test question-answering. Note also, on the other hand, so to speak, that some forms of interaction are difficult to observe, such as the VR tactile interaction in the Treasure Hunt Case.

Observers, being human, have limited attention spans and limited working memories, so don't count on them to provide, e.g. exact quantitative information on what happened in a session or a complete account of what happened in a complex series of events. For this reason, it is good practice to record sessions on, in most cases, video in order to have the possibility to inspect particularly interesting parts later on.

*What is required for applying the method?* Target users or a representative user group (Section 3.3.1), an observer, a system model, pen and paper or a laptop, recording equipment.

*System/AMITUDE model.* Any model version will do as long as you can apply a method from Chapter 12 and subjects are able to interact with the system model.

*Planning.* Make a usability method plan based on items described in Section 6.4. Consider your general purpose of collecting usability data (Section 6.4.2) as being that of collecting data which could supplement data from other methods that have been planned, such as a post-test questioning (Section 8.8) and logfiles. Typically, this means that the observer must keep an open mind and avoid wasting attention on, e.g. counting events which are being counted more reliably in the log, or describing events that simply follow the test script. In addition, the nature of the system, or observations made in an earlier test, may give rise to special events to look out for.

Make sure to be familiar with the system model to be tested so that you know how the system works and maybe also where the potential stumbling blocks are. Similarly, good observer preparation requires thorough familiarity with the test script so that the observer knows what to expect at any point during the test.

Note that the observation method is often clustered with a lab test method, cf. Sections 12.1, 12.2, 12.3 and 12.5. The two methods would share the task of subject recruitment, whereas most other preparations must be done individually per method. See also Chapter 13 on working with subjects in the lab.

*Running.* By default, an observer should assume the role of a fly on the wall. Place the observer behind, and out of sight of, the subject or, better, behind a one-way mirror that enables full observation of the subject but not vice versa. In any case, the subject should be told about the observer's presence despite the fact that this information may influence interaction. Once known to the subject, the observer should be as unobtrusive as possible to avoid any additional interference.

Focus on what the user is doing. Preferably, somebody else should take care of any recording equipment. If you must take care of it, make sure to start the equipment, check from time to time that it is running and stop it at the end of each session. Use the breaks to ensure that there is enough tape, battery or whatnot for the next session.

Observation is not like taking the minutes of a meeting. It's rather like noticing all manner of unscripted details that may be of interest and making local and preliminary hypotheses and conclusions on the test. The observer watches the subject's non-verbal and verbal behaviour for signs of their mental states, what is difficult or easy, what goes wrong, how subjects cope, pauses, hesitations and re-starts, exclamations, help provided by the experimenter, test interruptions involving other staff, differences between the ways in which different subjects handle interaction, emerging interaction patterns, etc. Whenever something wrong or unexpected occurs and you have an idea why, make notes about your preliminary explanations and conclusions. See also Chapter 13 for general information on running a lab session.

*Data.* The data typically consists of notes, recordings and logfiles. In many cases, the recordings only serve as backup to be used in case the notes are insufficient or unintelligible on some point, or if some special event happened whose details might be of interest. In other cases, the recordings must be reviewed in total. This may simply be because the observer could not watch everything the subjects did during the test because of occlusion of their hands or faces; or it may be because the recordings serve as a main data source on subjects' macro- or micro-behaviour, cf. Chapters 15 and 16 on data handling and analysis. Typically, observation notes and test recordings form part of a larger set of test data resources that should be analysed as a whole.

If you wrote the notes on paper, type them into a computer. Elaborate on the notes and make them coherent and understandable for others. Having done this, go through the notes again to see which conclusions can be drawn with respect to the test itself, system evaluation and improvement of the system model. Then combine the notes with the other data resources produced.

---

**Observation notes from test of the Treasure Hunt system**

**Task 1 – Find red closet**

Has problems understanding temple ruins.

Is told that he must go into a house to find the red closet.

Searches for a long time. Finds houses but no doors. Doesn't stick to the houses.

It turns out that he thinks that he must hear a beep before he clicks on a house. He is told to just click to enter and that there are 4 houses one can enter and 4 one cannot enter. [In fact there are only 3 houses one can enter.]

Enters the right house but gets out through the door after clicking on it and after having clicked around and not found the closet. He only searched in one side of the room (where there is no red closet).

[Strangely, the system sometimes says "house" when the wall is touched from the inside, and sometimes it emits the tone for grey colour instead.]

Enters a new house – this time the one with the blue closet.

Now he sticks to the houses.

Exits and finally enters the house with the red closet again. Finds the closet and is told he needs to click.

This task took approximately 10 minutes.

**Task 3 – Go to temple ruins ... Task 5 – Go to catacombs ...**

**Task 7 – Follow grooved paths**

Moves the cursor around and doesn't at first discover the groove when passing over it. Is helped: try to find something you can follow and which goes in a certain direction. Seems to follow the groove but loses it again. Is helped, finds the groove and its end.

Gets the forest map and is told that he must imagine that the map is hanging on a wall (i.e. this is a – mostly – 2D object). He is told not to click this time but to find the path, go to its end, maybe then go to the other end (its start).

Finds the starting point but has difficulties following the path. Is told that the path has obstacles on it. Subject: this is when one thinks that the path ends.

Finds it after some time and with some help and then finds the treasure.

[The test with this first subject made us realise that we probably had to do a lot of coaching and explanation before and, mainly during, the gameplay.]

---

**Fig. 10.4** Typed and elaborated observation notes from an implemented prototype evaluation session with the Treasure Hunt system. Translated from Danish

*Advantages and drawbacks.* Observation of subject behaviour during interaction is an important source on everything from small system inadequacies to major flaws. Moreover, the method is cheap and simple to apply.

A potentially serious problem is that some subjects may feel disturbed and stressed, and change behaviour when there are people in the room other than themselves and possibly the experimenter. See above and Chapter 13 on useful steps to prevent subject stress.

*Example: Treasure Hunt observation notes.* Figure 10.4 shows an excerpt from elaborated observation notes made during the first implemented prototype evaluation session with the Treasure Hunt system (Bernsen and Dybkjær 2007). The original notes were made on paper by two observers, one of whom acted in the role of experimenter as well, and subsequently combined. Texts in square brackets are comments added by the observers. As it appears, it was necessary to help and advise the subject a good deal more than anticipated. See also the task specification in Section 5.1. For the full version of the notes, see this book's web site.

## 10.5  Human Data Collection in the Lab

Human data collection in the lab serves to collect usability information on human activity and behaviour – or macro- and micro-behavioural data – under controlled conditions. This is typically done in the laboratory, but it is perfectly possible to establish controlled conditions elsewhere, such as in a car, in the street, or in a borrowed surgery theatre. This is in contrast to human data collection in the field (Sections 10.1 and 10.2) where the whole point is to avoid having any controlling influence on the data collected. Typical purposes of collecting human data under controlled conditions are to create a data resource for component training, see, e.g. Speecon (2004), or for studying particular forms of activity and behaviour in depth, cf. the example below. Human data collection in the lab does *not* involve user–system interaction as in real-time user observation (Section 10.4).

*When can you use the method and what is its scope?* Controlled human data collection can be useful anytime in the life cycle, depending on what the data will be used for. Data for studying behaviour is often used early whereas training data is used during component implementation.

The scope of the method is any system whose capabilities of input recognition and understanding, central processing, or output generation can benefit from information on the appearance and behaviour of humans. Some such systems strictly require field data as opposed to data collected under controlled conditions, but there can be several reasons for using "controlled data" rather than field data. Possible reasons include that field data is of too low quality, too costly to collect, too complex for component training or other uses or contains unwanted noise or variability. In lab-like conditions, we can exert the control on data collection required for producing exactly the data we need for some purpose, subject only, of course, to ethical constraints. Thus, even if we could manage to control the conditions, we should not use subjects for collecting facial expressions of people whose parachutes terminally refuse to unfold.

*Multimodal significance.* Controlled human data collection is strongly biased towards multimodal development and systems blending with people, because standard GUI-based systems have little or no purpose for using the collected data, cf. Factor 1, *nature of the user–system interface;* Factor 5, the *kind of data* to be collected with users; and Factor 6, general *lack of knowledge*, in Section 6.2.2. The method is particularly important for building non-GUI systems that model aspects of human perception, central processing, communication and action. All our Case systems (Section 2.1) could benefit from training and test data recorded with humans in the lab.

*How does the method work?* Invite as many subjects as needed to the lab or "exported lab" environment. Instruct the subjects and let them carry out the activity on which you want to collect data while recording what they do. In the simplest case, subjects do nothing but get photographed for training and testing of, e.g. graphic face recognition algorithms. Otherwise, they may just walk; read words and sentences aloud; smile, look normal and look angry; discuss something in pairs; drive a particular route around town, maybe after having downed a six-pack; or do numerous prescribed gestures.

*What is required for applying the method?* Target users or a representative user group (Section 3.3.1), or just people suitable for data collection, an experimenter or several, recording equipment, a data collection script including instructions for the subjects, possibly a consent form (see Section 13.3.4).

*System/AMITUDE model.* If only an outline system model exists, the purpose of using the method is to collect data in support of requirements specification and design. If the system model is at implementation stage, the method is typically used to collect training data.

*Planning.* Write a method plan (Section 6.4), starting from the purpose of collecting usability data (Section 6.4.2). The range of possible purposes is unlimited but what's guaranteed is that it takes careful planning to obtain the right data no matter the purpose. If you get purpose operationalisation (Section 6.4.3) wrong, it's data collection all over again, which is why the data collection protocols (=method plans) for large human data collections run into hundreds of pages. So, analyse the key properties the data should possess to be adequate for the purposes it will be used for in data analysis or component training. Then design the data collection process, starting with what the human subjects should do to produce data possessing those properties; followed by design of the process itself, including number of subjects, subject profiles, subject instructions, staff roles, data collection equipment which may be anything from mikes and cameras through bio-sensors to body markers and RFID tags, etc. See Chapter 13 for details on planning lab sessions.

The number of subjects required may vary greatly. Professional training data collection often involves hundreds of subjects, whereas a few subjects may do for behavioural studies. It depends on the degree of reliability required. To be able to draw highly reliable conclusions from data analysis, or ensure representativeness of the collected data, make sure to collect a sufficient amount of data with a representative group of subjects. Note, however, that the more data you want to collect, the more costly the process becomes in terms of planning and preparation, the data collection itself, and, not least, subsequent processing and analysis.

By designing well, and informed by any constraints on resources and skills that the team might have, you make as sure as you can that the data actually exhibits the phenomena you need and in the quality required. Otherwise, see Box 10.1.

## Box 10.1 How Not to Do Human Data Collection

One of the authors was the subject in a component training exercise based on which the component would generate face and lip movement animation of the subject when giving a talk. Collection of allegedly phonetically rich audiovisual speech data was done by a data collection novice. The short sentences to be read aloud in front of a camera were presented in small-font dense text on pieces of paper, making reading hard, the more so because the sentences were very much alike. The subject instructions failed to hammer in the crucial what (not) to do's. The location was a tight lab corner with unstable equipment mounted on chairs, and people occasionally talking elsewhere in the room. The experimenter stood in the subject's line of vision throughout data recording, making expressive faces. The subject tried and sometimes failed to accurately read some 40 sentences from one of the paper sheets – which is far from sufficient even if those sentences were from a phonetically rich corpus – the reading being frequently interrupted by an increasingly frustrated experimenter offering re-phrased and new instructions. There was a sense of impatience and time pressure about the whole thing. Then, data collection was abruptly terminated because the experimenter felt that this data would be good enough and, besides, the more data, the longer the component training time, and "video data takes a lot of disk space".

It came as no surprise that the component did not behave very convincingly in the trial prior to the talk. An unplanned data re-recording had to be done at short notice, this time with a few more sentences, now double-spaced larger font on the subject's request; clearer and more insistent instruction; some focus on phonemes which did not seem present in the part of the corpus that had been read aloud the first time; in a quiet office but with no less than three people crowding in on the subject during data recording. Did the animation improve? Maybe a wee bit!

*Running.* Start with a bit of small-talk to make subjects feel relaxed and at ease before introducing the recording setup. Give them the prepared instructions and any other material, and time to look at it. Wire them up as needed and carefully instruct them, before data collection begins, about what to do and how. Even having done dry-runs with colleagues, you may still have to run a couple of tests with each subject to make sure that the setup works and the subject does as instructed, actually producing the intended behaviour. Typically, it's necessary, not least in data collection for component training, to carefully monitor each subject throughout, making sure that the subject does not get sloppy following instructions after a while. It is tedious to produce, e.g. substantial amounts of similar and contextually rather meaningless data for component training, and one's concentration may easily begin to fade. If this happens, interrupt data collection and instruct the subject again. Warn subjects about this problem up front but remember that each new instruction takes time to absorb and follow. Be unobtrusive during monitoring, don't stand in front of the subject and stare at him or her.

If at all possible, sample-check the recordings right after they have been made to make sure that nothing needs to be adjusted. If data collection takes days, weeks or months – we once conducted a 12-month exercise (Box 15.1) – take a deeper look at the data as soon as practically possible, such as by the end of day 1 and then regularly. If something's wrong, there may still be time to rescue the data collection effort. See also Chapter 13 for advice on running lab sessions.

*Data.* The recordings are the data, and it is often only when you are about to do the data handling that the real work begins, cf. Chapter 15. Which further processing the data needs depends on the intended use. It is often necessary to annotate the data in some way, when intended both for component training and for in-depth analysis. Component training programs typically need to know what the correct (component) output should be, and this means that, e.g. data for speech recogniser training must be transcribed. If the aim is not component training but to analyse behaviour in depth for practical or theoretical purposes, annotation of the phenomena of interest is very likely needed for easy extraction of information. An example of a practical purpose could be to extract the 10 most common gestures occurring in Italian politicians' public speeches in order to build an animated character of this kind. A theoretical purpose could be to understand the semantic contributions of eyebrow movements. See Chapters 15 and 16 on data handling and analysis.

*Advantages and drawbacks.* Controlled human data collection is extremely important to multimodal systems development for several reasons. First, the method enables collection of almost any kind of data on human behaviour and action. Second, with proper control we can produce data on time, to quality specification, with or without particular kinds of noise and with the specified variability and representativeness. Producing a similar data source in the field is often hard or impossible as well as more expensive. And, third, many of today's technologies are not yet sufficiently mature for being trained with uncontrolled field data even if this data exists and can be collected in sufficient quantity and quality. Developers of multimodal systems and systems blending with people make frequent use of controlled human data collection and are likely to use the method massively in future, until technologies have matured to the point of processing most kinds of uncontrolled data in the field.

Novices have a die-hard tendency to underestimate controlled human data collection – "You just start the camera or, even better, grab an already made TV program and look at it, right!?" Wrong. It's not just that large-scale data collection may take a year to do and involve several people full-time who may have to create, or at least meticulously follow, hundreds of pages of data collection design documentation. Even small-scale data collection, in addition to being difficult to get right, can be costly in preparation, execution and data handling.

*Example: Human conversation data collection.* When we began to work on the Andersen system (Section 3.4.5, Bernsen et al. 2004), we decided to create a small data resource for analysing verbal and non-verbal turn-taking behaviour in multi-modal human–human conversation. Since turn-taking is something people talking do all the time, you might think that it's easy to just snatch a bit of conversation from some film or TV programme, and correspondingly daft to create a resource from scratch. However, if you take a closer look at the films and TV programmes you have in mind, you will probably realise that the cameras rarely show both, or all, interlocutors at the same time. Most of the time, the cameras show only the person speaking and, more often than not, only that person's face in close-up, thus omitting both the interlocutor and lots of important detail on hand and arm gesture, body posture and orientation, etc. Gaze direction one cannot tell either because an image of the speaker's face doesn't show who or what the speaker is looking at. And since turn-taking negotiation involves the interlocutor spoken to as much as, or more than, the speaker, most of the time you have no idea of what the interlocutor is doing in order to grab the turn or signal not to want to have it yet.

Having looked around for some time and finding no re-usable resource that was adequate for our purpose, we ended up making our own human data collection in the lab. Two people discussed the floor plans of a new building to which we were going to move soon after the recordings were made. Three cameras captured (1) the first interlocutor, (2) the second interlocutor and (3) both interlocutors at a distance, respectively, including their immediate environment which may hold objects used in the conversation. A microphone on each person captured the speech. For ease of analysis, the three camera recordings were later mounted in a single synchronised video image frame as shown in Fig. 10.5.

In the terms of this section, the data collection purpose behind the data resource in Fig. 10.5 is an applied theoretical one: we wanted to study turn-taking mechanisms with a view to have Andersen use some of them in both input interpretation and output generation. Incidentally, the resource is also quite useful for analysing the combined use of speech and (mainly) pointing gesture, because the interlocutors discuss and point to the floor plans all the time. This point somewhat contradicts our maxim that, speaking generally, *a data resource is, at best, useful for a single purpose*, i.e. its original data collection purpose. Still, it's sometimes difficult to see what's being pointed at, and we could have done better had speech and pointing gesture been the data collection purpose. Finally, even if this data collection exercise was actually cheap, doing in-depth analysis of it is not since it's very time consuming.

**Fig. 10.5**  Three simultaneous camera recordings mounted in one image frame

# References

Alexander D (2006) Contextual inquiry and field studies. http://www.deyalexander.com/resources/uxd/contextual-inquiry.html. Accessed 19 January 2009.

Bernsen NO, Charfuelàn M, Corradini A, Dybkjær L, Hansen T, Kiilerich S, Kolodnytsky M, Kupkin D, Mehta M (2004) Conversational H. C. Andersen. First prototype description. In: André E, Dybkjær L, Minker W, Heisterkamp P (eds) Proceedings of the tutorial and research workshop on affective dialogue systems. Springer Verlag, Heidelberg: LNAI 3068: 305–308.

Bernsen NO, Dybkjær L (2007) Report on iterative testing of multimodal usability and evaluation guide. SIMILAR deliverable D98.

Beyer H, Holtzblatt K (1998) Contextual design: defining customer-centered systems. Academic Press.

Gaffney G (2004) Contextual enquiry – a primer. http://www.sitepoint.com/article/contextual-enquiry-primer. Accessed 19 January 2009.

Hom J (1998) Contextual inquiry. http://jthom.best.vwh.net/usability. Accessed 19 January 2009.

Lamantia J (2003) Analyzing card sort results with a spreadsheet template. http://www.boxesandarrows.com/view/analyzing_card_sort_results_with_a_spreadsheet_template. Accessed 19 January 2009.

Nielsen J (1995) Card sorting to discover the users' model of the information space. http://www.useit.com/papers/sun/cardsort.html. Accessed 19 January 2009.

Payne SJ (2003) Users' mental models: the very idea. In: Carroll JM (ed) HCI models, theories and frameworks. Towards a multidisciplinary science. Morgan Kaufmann, San Francisco.

Robson C (2002) Real world research. 2nd edn. Wiley-Blackwell, Oxford, UK.

Rubin J (1994) Handbook of usability testing. John Wiley and Sons, New York.

Sharp H, Rogers Y, Preece J (2007) Interaction design – beyond human-computer interaction. 2nd edn. John Wiley and Sons, New York.

Speecon (2004) Speech driven interfaces for consumer devices. http://www.speechdat.org/speecon/index.html. Accessed 6 February 2009.

Spencer D, Warfel T (2004) Card sorting: a definitive guide. http://www.boxesandarrows.com/view/card_sorting_a_definitive_guide. Accessed 19 January 2009.

UsabilityNet (2006a) Contextual inquiry. http://usabilitynet.org/tools/contextualinquiry.htm. Accessed 6 February 2009.

UsabilityNet (2006b) User observation/field studies. http://usabilitynet.org/tools/userobservation. htm. Accessed 6 February 2009.

UsabilityNet (2006c) Card sorting. http://usabilitynet.org/tools/cardsorting.htm. Accessed 6 February 2009.

# Chapter 11
# Imagination

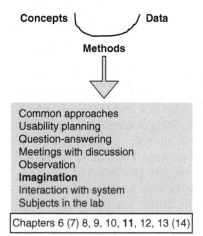

Concepts ⌣ Data

**Methods**

Common approaches
Usability planning
Question-answering
Meetings with discussion
Observation
**Imagination**
Interaction with system
Subjects in the lab

Chapters 6 (7) 8, 9, 10, 11, 12, 13 (14)

In this fourth of five chapters on multimodal usability methods (Section 6.2.2), none of the methods presented involves subjects or users. Instead, all methods draw upon the imagination and experience of the development team or external experts in order to reason about user activities, user types, user–system interaction or how to facilitate ease of use.

Section 11.1 presents use cases and scenarios; Section 11.2 personas; Section 11.3 cognitive walk-throughs; and Section 11.4 guidelines. The discussion of standards in Section 11.5 focuses on ISO/IEC's usability work methodology. This is not a usability method in our sense (Section 6.2) but, rather, comparable to this book as a whole.

## 11.1 Use Cases and Scenarios

Our presentation of the use cases and scenarios method began in Section 3.4 which should be read as background. Task or activity decomposition (Section 3.4.1) is used to analyse and specify what real users will actually do with the system. Focus is on functionality and interaction. Working with use cases is an integral part of task analysis as illustrated in Section 3.4.2.

A *use case* (Jacobson et al. 1992, Cockburn 2001, 2002, Malan and Bredemeyer 2001, Wikipedia 2009a) describes, at an abstract level, a piece of user–system interaction aimed at achieving some (sub-)goal, such as "input a destination" in a car navigation system, "book a one-way flight ticket" or "make Hans Christian Andersen tell about his life". Thus, depending on the chosen level of decomposition, a use case corresponds to what is described as a (sub-)task or other activity in Section 3.4.1.

N.O. Bernsen, L. Dybkjær, *Multimodal Usability*, Human-Computer Interaction
Series, DOI 10.1007/978-1-84882-553-6_11, © Springer-Verlag London Limited 2009

A *scenario* is a concrete instantiation of a use case (Section 13.3.5). In the examples above, scenario instantiations could be "Unter den Linden in Berlin", "a one-way ticket for David Carson from Copenhagen to Aalborg at 7.20 on 15 December 2009" and "find out why Andersen left his mother and his home town to go to Copenhagen at the age of 14".

*When can you use the method and what is its scope?* Use cases are specified as part of the requirements specification and further detailed during design, i.e. fairly early in the life cycle. A precondition for writing use cases is a task analysis as described in Section 3.4. Note that use cases are not well suited for capturing or modelling non-functional requirements, such as robustness and real-time behaviour.

When tasks are absent, only the domain provides constraints (Section 3.4.5) and users can often make a far wider range of inputs, making use case analysis more uncertain. Still, use case analysis is highly supportive of non-task-oriented systems.

*Multimodal significance.* No matter if the system is GUI-based or multimodal, usability is likely to benefit from application of use cases. Between the Case task analyses in Section 5.1 and the Case designs in Section 7.2, all our Case systems (Section 2.1) have benefited from use case analysis and design, cf. the Maths use case and scenario examples at the end of this section.

*How does the method work?* The process of task analysis described in Section 3.4.2, including the questions about *basic task*, *what else* and *is that all*, breaks down tasks into sub-tasks or use cases. Scenarios, being concrete instantiations of use cases, serve both to help discover use cases (or sub-tasks) during task analysis and to help analyse the complexity inherent in a use case. For instance, if the use case is *input a date* in natural language, it only requires production of a few different scenarios to realise that the system should be able to understand not only absolute date indications, such as "February fifth, 2010", but also relative ones, such as "tomorrow" or "this Friday", and it must be able to reject invalid and irrelevant dates, such as in "I want to book a single room for February thirtieth last year".

Use cases often start as brief descriptions in requirements analysis – corresponding to the *Summary* in Fig. 11.1 – and are further detailed during design analysis. Typical descriptive entries for writing use cases include those explained in Fig. 11.1 and exemplified in Fig. 11.2. Focus is on viewing (sub-)tasks or other activities from the user's point of view.

Use cases and scenarios may be created by development team members individually or as team work. Ideally, we should make use cases that jointly cover all possible user–system interaction. If interaction is complex, involving numerous possible sub-goals each having numerous possible scenario instantiations, this is impossible in practice, which means that we lose part of our overview and control of user–system interaction. In this case, at least make sure to include the most important sub-tasks or -activities.

*What is required for applying the method?* As much information as already exists on the system model, including any AMITUDE requirements specified (Chapters 3 and 4); development team members; a computer for typing use cases and scenarios. If you already made a thorough task (or activity) analysis (Section 3.4), this will

| Use case entries | |
| --- | --- |
| Use case name | Unique name indicating the purpose of the use case, e.g. transfer funds, negotiate meeting time, or make animated character feel pity and want to help you. |
| Summary | Brief description of the use case. |
| Actors | Who interacts with the system in this use case. |
| Preconditions | Conditions that must be true before it is possible to enter the use case during interaction. |
| Basic course of events | Main steps involved in carrying out the use case. |
| Alternative paths | Description of possible variations and exceptions if something goes wrong. |
| Post-conditions | Conditions that will be true after the use case has been achieved. |
| Notes | Any comments that did not fit into one of the above categories. |
| Author and date | Good for keeping track of versions. |

**Fig. 11.1**   Main entries in a detailed use case description

| Use case concerning free multiplication training | |
| --- | --- |
| Use case name | Train multiplication. |
| Summary | A user enters the free multiplication module, and is asked to multiply two numbers and state the result until s/he wants no more questions. |
| Actors | Student. |
| Preconditions | The user has done screening and two classes on basic principles of multiplication, and has passed the initial test for entering third class. |
| Basic course of events | Select free multiplication with MultMachine. |
| | Set max. product. If, e.g. max. is set to 50, the user is not given tasks beyond 10 x 5: one factor will be max. 10, the other max. 5. |
| | [1]The system provides a task. |
| | The user answers. |
| | The system provides feedback on correctness (including facial expression) and asks if the user wants a new task. |
| | The user answers. If yes, go to [1]. |
| | If no, the system provides answer statistics, evaluates the session, and proposes how to continue teaching and training (including facial expression). |
| Alternative paths | Max. product is not between 1 and 100. The user is made aware of the error and asked to provide a new max. |
| Post-conditions | The user may choose to enter the free training module again, possibly choosing another upper limit, or go to a point where other choices for training and teaching are available. |
| Notes | N/A |
| Author and date | Dybkjær 7 October 2008 |

**Fig. 11.2**   Fairly detailed use case description

form the basis for writing use cases. Otherwise, this analysis forms part of applying the use case method.

*System/AMITUDE model.* The model exists in outline. The purpose of use case analysis is to collect information that will support further requirements and design specification.

*Planning.* The main planning step is to collect all available information about the system model, AMITUDE specification progress and, in particular, task and domain analysis and specification, before getting started on imaginative use case and scenario development. Note that several of the typical points on usability method planning in Section 6.4 do not apply since we are not working with users or subjects. If the use case work will be done as a group exercise, you need to organise a developers meeting. It can be very productive for imaginative use case and scenario creation to interleave this work with some of this book's other methods, such as visiting potential users (Section 10.1) or inviting them for a meeting (Chapter 9) about what they would like to be able to do with the system and what they expect from it.

*Running.* Start with a task analysis (Section 3.4), unless already done. It is important to delimit the domain the system must operate within and identify core structures, such as basic task(s), sub-task order, if any, and user goals. As illustrated in Section 3.4.2, don't stop when having identified a couple of basic tasks. Continue to ask *what else?* to find new use cases and increase, through scenario analysis, your understanding of the richness of those you've already identified. Many find it helpful to start by thinking in terms of concrete scenarios (Section 13.3.5) which may then be turned into more abstract use cases. If you have made persona descriptions (Section 11.2), these may also support scenario and use case identification.

Note that frequently used tasks or other activities must be made easy to initiate and accomplish, although there may be exceptions for entertainment systems.

*Data.* Data comprises the use cases and scenarios that have been generated. These may require elaboration, in particular if noted down quickly in handwriting. Type the results and make sure that all use cases are represented at approximately the same level of detail. As soon as this has been done, they should feed into specification and design, possibly being further detailed in the design process. The two key questions in data analysis are the following: (i) is the set of use cases comprehensive enough? and (ii) for each use case, is the set of scenarios sufficiently complete? A firm and positive answer is not always available to these questions. See also Chapters 15 and 16 on data handling and analysis.

*Advantages and drawbacks.* Analysis and design of tasks (activities), use cases and scenarios is mandatory in system development. Adequate domain analysis, and adequate analysis and design of task–sub-task structure and task contents, is very important to the achievement of a successful system. This is probably because the adequacy, or the lack of it, can have major implications for most generic aspects of usability: functionality, ease of use and user experience (Section 1.4.6). Making use cases and scenarios forces us to think concretely and in detail about functionality and usability aspects of our system. Use cases and, in particular, scenarios (Section 13.3.5) are central to the application of many of the methods described in this book, including the other imagination methods (this chapter) and all user–system interaction methods (Chapter 12).

Despite having adopted, as far as possible, a systematic approach to use case writing, i.e. one guided by solid task analysis, there is always a risk that important use cases and scenarios have been overlooked. Discovering all possible and relevant use cases and scenarios, however, is often practically impossible. This is one of the main reasons why development is iterative and needs as much input from real people as it can get.

*Examples: Maths use case, use case diagram and scenarios.* Developers are often introduced to use cases via UML (Unified Modelling Language) (Booch et al. 1999). Use cases may be put together in a use case diagram for which the UML standard has a graphical notation. Use case diagrams are one of nine kinds of UML diagram. A use case diagram shows relations between actors (users) and use cases, cf. the example in Fig. 11.3. Note that an actor may be a human or another system.

Figure 11.2 shows a use case for free multiplication training, one of the tasks the student may undertake in Maths 3rd class, cf. Section 7.2.3. Figure 11.3 shows a use case diagram that includes the multiplication training use case plus others that form part of 3rd class. Figure 11.4 shows three scenarios that a user might perform in 3rd class. Note that the initial test must be passed before any of the other use cases in Fig. 11.3 can be entered. The third scenario is an instantiation of the use case in Fig. 11.2. Scenarios may be used for test purposes later. See Section 13.3.5 for more on scenarios.

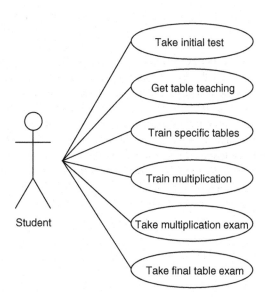

**Fig. 11.3** Use case diagram for student interaction with the Math system in 3rd class

| Maths scenarios |
| --- |
| 1. Take initial 3rd class test. |
| 2. Having passed initial 3rd class test, train the 7 times table. |
| 3. Having passed initial 3rd class test, train multiplication for 10 minutes using 80 as max. |

**Fig. 11.4**  Three scenarios relating to 3rd class of the Maths system

## 11.2 Personas

A persona (Cooper 1999, 2008, Calabria 2004, Pruitt and Adlin 2006, Sharp et al. 2007, Wikipedia 2009b) is a detailed description of a fictitious character who is an archetypical system user and thus represents a group of target users. A persona puts a personal face onto the otherwise abstract concept of a target user and may help figure out which needs, preferences, expectations, etc. to design for.

*When can you use the method and what is its scope?* Personas are specified by the development team in the analysis phase or during early design.

The method seems applicable to all systems except those tailored to one or very few people. In such cases it would not make sense to work with archetypical users (personas) rather than the real users.

*Multimodal significance.* No matter if you are developing a system that is GUI-based or multimodal, personas may be used to get a better grasp of the target users and which usability requirements this may imply or suggest. Thus, personas would seem rather unaffected by the differentiation factors in Section 6.2.2. We could have created personas from the Case user profiles in Section 3.3.7 and used these in the Case designs in Section 7.2, cf. the Maths persona example at the end of this section.

*How does the method work?* The method consists in writing, based on the target user profile and the analysis of the composition of the target user group (Section 3.3.1), a reasonably detailed, 1–2 pages description for each persona you decide to include. The description is a narrative that captures potentially relevant issues, such as behaviour, goals, wishes, skills, experience, attitudes, environment, age and gender. Like target user profile and target user group composition, persona creation may be based on information collected via, e.g. macro-behavioural field methods (Section 10.1), a market survey (Section 8.3), a focus group meeting (Section 9.1), a stakeholder meeting (Section 9.2) or a meeting/workshop with users (Section 9.3). If you don't have such data, you can still write personas but you do need background knowledge from somewhere about the target users.

It is common to distinguish between *primary* and *secondary personas*. A primary persona represents a target user group (Section 3.3.1) and is the design focus. If there are several target user groups, you need as many primary personas. A secondary persona represents an important sub-group in a target user group. The basic needs of a secondary persona can typically be met by designing the system for the primary persona plus some additions in the form of customisation options or online user modelling (Section 3.3.1). For example, the Sudoku Case system has a single target user group (Section 5.1) and hence one primary persona. From within the target group, we could then define three secondary personas, i.e. a novice, medium-level and expert player, respectively, and enable each of them to have fun using the system by offering a customisation option so that they can all select the game level difficulty they prefer. Or, in the Maths Case, we could imagine having two very different target user groups and hence two primary personas, i.e. a maths teacher and a student. The teacher might, e.g. add new exercises to the system while the student needs to practice multiplication, but not vice versa.

For each primary persona, the standard advice is not to have more than a couple of secondary personas. In all cases, try to delimit your efforts to a few personas so that you don't get overwhelmed and confused by too many small variations.

*What is required for applying the method?* A system AMITUDE specification, including a target user group analysis, cf. Section 5.1, one or more persons from the development team, a computer for typing the persona descriptions.

*System/AMITUDE model.* The system model probably exists in outline, and the AMITUDE model of use should be near-complete. The purpose of the method is to collect information that will support requirements and design specification.

*Planning.* Persona analysis doesn't require much planning in itself, except for gathering all the user information that has been collected already. Note also that several of the typical points on usability method planning in Section 6.4 do not apply since we are not working with users or subjects. If the persona work is to be done as a group exercise, you need to organise a developers meeting. Also, it can be very productive for persona creation to interleave this work with some of this book's other methods, such as those mentioned under *How the method works* above.

*Running.* Use the data and knowledge you have to help identify needs, behaviour patterns, attitude, skill level, etc. that may suggest creation of one or several personas. For each persona, decide if it's a primary or a secondary persona and why. A good way to start a persona description is to make a list of characteristics, cf. Figs. 11.6 and 11.7. Characteristics often included in persona descriptions are name, picture, age, gender, family, education, job, interests, goals, tasks/activities, needs, environment, computer literacy, computer and other equipment used, frequency of doing the task/activity which the system is meant for, barriers, expectations, preferences, etc. Note that the list is not exhaustive nor are items mandatory. Goals are important, though, including results that the persona wants to achieve and user experiences the persona prefers.

Many like to give their personas real names like John Dalrymple or Mary Jones while others find this ridiculous and use descriptive names instead, such as "the bright student" or "the lazy student".

Having made a list of persona characteristics, you can use the list for writing a narrative persona description. Be careful not to add too many and unnecessary details.

*Data.* Data is the persona descriptions. In development, analysing personas in the evolving AMITUDE model of use context may help identify missing functionality, facilitate scenario and use case writing (Section 11.1), help make decisions about contents and design and prioritise work – e.g. satisfying a secondary persona is not as important as satisfying a primary one. In evaluation, personas may be used as concrete body-and-mind individuals whom the system should fit. See also Chapters 15 and 16 on data handling and analysis.

*Advantages and Drawbacks.* Personas put faces on typical users and support development team members in understanding, sharing and applying a detailed picture of whom they are actually developing a system for. Many find personas helpful for purposes such as those described under data above.

Others, however, don't need explicitly described personas in order to do user-centred development and take into account the broad and concrete diversity of people who all fit the target user profile. Some argue that the use of personas risks locking the mind and prevents it from considering user diversity that's not present in the personas designed. It is also easy for some – developers and stakeholders alike – to get absorbed in irrelevant persona details, like "another name would be better" or "the hair colour is wrong". A persona that's not solidly based on data about target users may provide a wrong picture and so may a target user profile or a target user group analysis.

*Examples: One primary and two secondary personas for the Maths system.* Figure 11.5 describes a primary persona, Figs. 11.6 and 11.7 outline two secondary

---

**Paul, the average maths student**

**Personal details**

Paul is an 8 years old boy who lives with his parents and his two years younger brother in a house near Copenhagen in Denmark. He has his own room and so has his brother. His father is an account manager, his mother a nurse.

He is a lively and generally happy child, somewhat thin with rapid movements, blue eyes in a vivid face and light brown hair. His voice is often a little shrill when he becomes eager.

Paul likes to play football and he is fond of his Gameboy. He does not have his own computer but shares one with his brother. He has a couple of very good friends who he sees quite often after school and in the weekends – whenever it suits his parents.

**Computer literacy**

Both Paul and his brother play computer games from time to time but Paul has several other interests as well, so he does not feel it is a problem that he has to share the computer. He knows the basics about starting and stopping programs, and there are a few games he is quite familiar with. If he needs assistance, his father is normally happy to help and explain things.

**School and maths**

Paul attends primary school. He is fairly average in most topics except sports where he is above average. Going to school is ok. He is rarely teased, and he likes to play with classmates during the breaks.

He has five maths lessons per week distributed over four days. So far he has learned addition and subtraction, and soon he will start to learn multiplication. Luckily there has been little homework so far. He finds the maths teacher ok though not very entertaining.

Paul is reasonably active during the maths lessons although his teacher could sometimes wish for more. Paul does not care about that. His ambitions do not exceed the average and he has no intention of working towards a top 5 position or similar in class regarding maths. As long as he is not seen as being one of the blockheads and as long as his parents are kept reasonably happy, everything is fine with him.

He has heard that they will be using a computer system to which you can talk when they start learning multiplication. He hopes that he will not make a fool of himself when speaking to a computer. He would find it awful to be teased. Otherwise he is quite curious about the new system.

**Fig. 11.5** The primary persona for the Maths system

| David, the ambitious competitor |
|---|

**Personal details**

- 8 years, dark hair, brown eyes, pleasant face, tall, athletic, uses relatively few gestures
- lives with his parents and older sister in a house in a Copenhagen suburb
- has his own room
- good at sports in general, plays tennis and football, likes computer games

**Computer literacy**

- has his own computer
- plays computer games several hours per week, is on Messenger

**School and maths**

- attends primary school
- strong in most topics, including maths which is a favourite
- motivated by competition
- likes maths lessons; happily spends time on maths at home if he can get additional exercises
- parents always happy to answer questions and help
- goal is to be top in class in maths; strong competition from another boy and two girls
- heard about a new system at school that will help students learn multiplication
- looks forward to this – heard it should be like a computer game and that you can compete with the system; moreover you can also use it at home
- he is wondering if you can also compete with the others in class

**Fig. 11.6** A secondary persona for the Maths system

| Susan, the blockhead |
|---|

**Personal details**

- 8 years, small, blue eyes, blond hair, often looks a little sad, speaks relatively slowly
- lives with her divorced mother and two brothers in an apartment in Copenhagen
- shares a room with her older brother
- watches TV, plays with dolls and other stuff, not many friends

**Computer literacy**

- one computer in the family mostly occupied by the brothers
- not very interested in computers; has tried games a couple of times

**School and maths**

- attends primary school
- weak in maths and has little self-confidence
- not much help from her mother regarding school work
- often feels stupid in maths because she cannot answer the teacher's questions
- feels disliked by the teacher
- heard about the multiplication system they are going to use
- fears it because she is quite unfamiliar with computer games, but at the same time hopes that it will be more patient with her than the teacher and help her when she needs it without the whole class staring at her, and hopes that eventually she will learn some maths

**Fig. 11.7** Another secondary persona for the Maths system personas. The primary persona is Paul, an average maths student about to learn multiplication. His goals are to keep his average level, not to be seen as one of the blockheads or a fool and keep his parents reasonably happy with his results.

David is a secondary persona, sketched in bullet items in Fig. 11.6. David can use Paul's interface but needs something more to satisfy his ambitious and competitive nature. His goals are to become top in class and have even more fun in maths, possibly helped by the new system which he expects to be a combination of a maths teacher and a computer game.

Susan is another secondary persona, sketched in Fig. 11.7. She can use Paul's interface but needs something to help and motivate her due to her low self-confidence and general lack of talent in maths. Susan's goals are to avoid feeling disliked by the teacher, to get help without others knowing about it and to obtain a basic understanding of maths so that she doesn't always feel lost.

## 11.3 Cognitive Walk-Through

A cognitive walk-through helps evaluate system "interaction logic" as regards (i) how easy it is to use and (ii) the sufficiency of the functionality it offers, cf. Section 1.4.6. Focus is on users' cognitive processes when trying to get a task/activity done based on information provided by the system.

*When can you use the method and what is its scope?* Walk-throughs are typically made when the design has become detailed enough to express concrete interaction but before any substantial implementation. The method addresses human cognitive processes during interaction and helps evaluate the union of task logic and design logic. *Task logic* is factual issues related to the task(s) handled by the system, such as which are the sub-tasks and what is the task order, if any (Section 3.4). *Design logic* is issues related to interaction design, such as how to carry out the tasks or which meta-communication approach has been chosen. Meta-communication is communication about communication itself in order to recover from communication failure, e.g. clarifying an ambiguity or rephrasing something that was misrecognised. While task-oriented systems have both task and design logic, non-task-oriented systems have only design logic. However, since it's the union of task and design logic we test in a cognitive walk-through, the method can be used for both kinds of systems.

*Multimodal significance.* Cognitive walk-throughs were originally used for GUI evaluation but can be applied to all multimodal systems. This method would seem rather unaffected by the differentiation factors in Section 6.2.2. Cognitive walk-throughs could be made with all our Case systems (Section 7.2).

*How does the method work?* Let's start by describing the method's origins in the lively and complex golden age of HCI (Section 1.4.3): cognitive walk-throughs are based on the CE+ cognitive theory of exploratory learning. CE+ gets its *C* from CCT (cognitive complexity theory), its *E* from EXPL (a computer program intended to model the process of learning from demonstrations) and its + from the rest it's based upon, i.e. puzzle-problem literature and cognitive architectures, see Polson and Lewis (1990). Right! CE+ theory includes an information-processing model of human cognition and decision making, describing human–computer interaction in terms of four steps which, in most cases, are repeated several times. The user

1. decides on a goal to be achieved by using the system, e.g. to have a document spell checked;
2. scans the static graphic GUI interface (screen, keyboard), looking for available input actions, e.g. menus, buttons, command line input;
3. selects the action that seems most likely to lead to the goal;
4. carries out the action and evaluates the graphic on-screen feedback to find out if s/he came closer to his/her goal;
5. sets the next goal, etc.

The walk-through method is then used by evaluators as follows. Each step in the correct action sequence for a given scenario (Sections 11.1 and 13.3.5) is scrutinised, and the evaluators must then try to tell a plausible story about why the user would make the correct choice by asking the following four questions:

a. Will the user realise what the correct next step is to solve the task?
b. Will the user realise that the right action is available in the interface?
c. Will the user figure out that an available action is the correct next step?
d. If the user carries out the right action, will s/he realise that there was progress towards the goal?

These questions form the basis of an evaluation sheet prepared before running the test. The evaluation sheet – and the four questions – is used for each action to be carried out. See also, e.g. Lewis et al. (1990), Wharton et al. (1994) and Sharp et al. (2007).

The walk-through is not a prediction of the actions the user will actually choose. It's a test of whether there is a plausible story for making a correct choice at each step along the solution path in a scenario-based action sequence. If there isn't, the interface clearly has a problem. The walk-through may be applied as well in a less rigorous way than described above, using only a system model and some scenarios, but not an elaborate evaluation sheet. Based on the scenarios, you carry out an "interaction" with the system by walking though the system model step by step while pursuing your goals and considering each correct action. If anything is missing, confusing or otherwise problematic, you make a note of it. See also Rowley and Rhoades (1992) and Spencer (2000) for a more fast-paced and streamlined applications of the method.

Points 1–5 above are clearly GUI-centred, reflecting classical GUI-style deliberate interaction (Section 3.6.1) and are more or less meaningless with many other modality combinations. For instance, there is no freedom of perceptual inspection (Section 4.2.2) for scanning a thoroughly dynamic speech-only interface: there is nothing to scan! And scanning even of *static* haptics is a very different matter from scanning static graphics (Section 4.4.5). However, we believe that cognitive walk-throughs can be used widely for multimodal systems, as long as we forget about points 1–5 and stick to the more abstract points a–d above, as illustrated in the example at the end of this section. For instance, even if a user cannot scan a speech-only interface at all, the user can consider the next action to take based on the information the system has provided so far and to the extent that the user remembers this information.

A walk-through is typically carried out as a group exercise, evaluators trying to put themselves in the position of a user. They step through the system model based on scenarios and evaluate for each step how difficult it is for the user to identify and carry out the next correct action and how clear the feedback is.

A related method is the *pluralistic walk-through* in which the group of evaluators includes users and usability experts in addition to developers. The evaluators step through scenarios considering and discussing their actions and any related usability issues (Bias 1994, Sharp et al. 2007).

*What is required for applying the method?* A system model; evaluator(s) from the development team; a description of the target users, their knowledge and other relevant properties; scenarios; a list of correct actions required to perform each of the scenarios and achieve each of the goals with the present system model; optionally, a rapporteur. Note that a developer who has been heavily involved in the interaction design is likely to be too biased to apply the method.

*System/AMITUDE model.* The system model, including an AMITUDE model of use, typically exists as a detailed design specification. The model may be partially implemented but then only in an early version.

*Planning.* Make a usability method plan based on items described in Section 6.4. Start from the purpose of collecting usability data (Section 6.4.2). Operationalise the purpose by creating a set of representative scenarios and, for each scenario, a description of correct actions required to achieve the goal (Section 6.4.3). If you have made use cases (Section 11.1), you might select or construct one scenario per use case to obtain a suitable set. Describe the target user group composition in detail. Note that several of the typical points on usability method planning in Section 6.4 do not apply since we are not working with users or subjects.

If the work will be done as a group exercise, you need to organise a developers meeting. Appoint an evaluator or, preferably, a group of evaluators and, preferably, a rapporteur who takes notes. The rapporteur may participate in the evaluation. Furthermore, an evaluation sheet must be written. The evaluation sheet is used for making notes on each step taken during the walk-through, cf. the entry *How does the method work*.

*Running.* This should be straightforward based on the description under the entry *How does the method work*. Note, however, that it takes some training to become fluent in using the method with the right amount of unhurried care.

*Data.* Data comprises evaluation sheets and notes made by evaluators and rapporteur. If handwritten on paper, type sheets and notes on a computer. Sheets and notes should be analysed and turned into a document describing which changes are needed in the system model and why. See also Chapters 15 and 16 on data handling and analysis.

*Advantages and drawbacks.* A cognitive walk-through is rather cheap and fast because it can be done without involving external people, such as target users or experts. Method application yields a systematic evaluation of the system model – or selected parts of it – early in the life cycle, providing input on important classes of usability problems, i.e. ease of use and adequacy of functionality. Used well, the method provides a pretty good evaluation of the union of task and design logic of the system model, but limited by the scope of the scenarios used. The more representative the scenarios are of actual future system use, the more reliable the results.

You don't get data on how a representative user group would interact with the system nor on micro-behavioural interaction, user experience, error handling or whether target users would miss functionality.

*Example: Walk-through of a spoken dialogue system.* The following example is from a walk-through of a spoken dialogue system for flight ticket reservation (Bernsen et al. 1998a), see also Section 3.4.2. The primary target group is secretaries used to booking flights, but others may use it as well.

A walk-through was done based on scenarios like the one in Fig. 11.8 and a system model represented as graphs with states and transitions. Figure 11.9 shows a small part of the early system model. Correct actions for a given scenario correspond to a particular path through the system model graphs.

Since no static graphics are available, all the user can do is (i) listen to the spoken output, such as "Do you want anything else?" in Fig. 11.9, for available next steps

---

**Change of flight ticket scenario**

A ticket has been booked for Frede Olsen who has ID number 22. The ticket is for a travel from Copenhagen to Ålborg on Tuesday 27 October at 7.30 and back again on the same day at 17.25. The ticket reference number is 443. Unfortunately, Frede has turned ill and Axel Hansen, who has ID number 23, is going instead. Make the necessary changes. The customer number of the company is 111.

**Fig. 11.8**  Scenario used in a walk-through

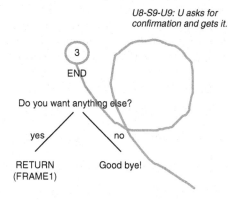

**Fig. 11.9**  System model annotated with a problem found in a walk-through

and actions, and (ii) remember any instructions the system might have provided earlier. The dialogue is mostly system-directed, prompting the user for the next input at each step. Thus, as long as the user realises that the information asked for in each step leads in the right direction and as long as the user possesses the requested information and understands that this is the case, we can provide a plausible argument that the user would make the correct next step and wait for feedback and new system initiative.

Towards the end of the dialogue based on the scenario in Fig. 11.8, the user has provided the ID number of the person who is going to travel instead of Frede Olsen and has been asked whether he wants to change anything else, to which he has answered "No". At this point, the task is completed from the system's point of view, and it asks the user if he wants anything else. However, the system has *not* provided proper feedback, so the user cannot know for sure if the requested change was actually completed. This makes it likely that a good many users will ask for confirmation rather than answer the system's question, cf. the annotated system model part in Fig. 11.9. The handwritten loop and associated note above the loop indicate that confirmation is missing in the system model.

We didn't use an evaluation sheet. Instead, we annotated the system model graphs whenever we found a problem in selecting the correct next action. The evaluation team was a mix of developers and subjects, almost like in a pluralistic walk-through.

## 11.4 Guideline-Based Usability Development and Evaluation

Guideline-based development seeks to make the system's design conform with a particular set of usability guidelines. Guideline-based evaluation assesses conformance.

*When can you use the method and what is its scope?* Guideline-based development and evaluation is used primarily during design and early implementation. As implementation proceeds, the system becomes increasingly difficult and costly to modify in the light of the findings made. On the other hand, not everything can be checked for guideline conformance before the system runs.

The method can be used when a set of guidelines is available for the application type to which the system under development belongs. In advanced multimodal systems research, there often isn't any set of guidelines dedicated to the application type at hand. Note that (i) since anyone can propose guidelines, not all guideline sets out there are well-founded and worth applying. Always check the scope and quality of the work upon which the guidelines are based. And (ii) guidelines don't always come labelled with the application types to which they apply. In particular, so-called general usability guidelines come with the claim that they are valid for all application types, which they are not. It's just that their GUI-oriented authors haven't quite discovered multimodal systems and may have ignored entertainment systems and other non-traditional application types as well. If you try to use them – which we don't oppose, we just recommend caution – keep in mind that the guideline authors probably never imagined a system like yours.

*Multimodal significance.* Since many usability guideline sets are based on development experience with a certain application type, it takes a while from the appearance of a new application type until there is sufficient experience with it to form the basis for early guideline proposals. This is why there is a lack of well-founded guidelines for many multimodal and blending-with-people application types and why guideline-based development and evaluation is biased towards GUI-based systems due to *general lack of knowledge*, cf. Factor 6 in Section 6.2.2. Regarding our Cases (Section 2.1), we can apply the cooperative dialogue guidelines in Figs. 11.12 and 11.13 to the spoken interaction part of each system. Other guideline sets might be applied to the screen output that all Cases have or to the standard GUI configuration part of two of the Cases. It should always be kept in mind, though, that guidelines developed for, e.g. spoken dialogue alone or standard GUI-based interaction alone, are not necessarily applicable wholesale to spoken dialogue or GUI-based interaction in larger multimodal contexts.

*How does the method work?* Guidelines are either based on theory or rules of thumb based on experience, summarising good practice in some application area defined by AMITUDE aspects. Whether used for development or for evaluation, guideline lists may be viewed as checklists. When used for evaluation, guideline application becomes analogous to data annotation, cf. Section 15.5.

Guidelines may be used by non-experts as well as experts, that is, unless they are so replete with theoretical concepts that it takes full understanding of the underlying theory to apply them. The non-expert always needs to spend some time getting familiar with a set of guidelines to be able to apply it appropriately.

In guideline-based evaluation, or *heuristic evaluation*, one or more evaluators go through the current system model, checking interface and interaction against a set of guidelines to find out which guidelines might be violated and how. It is a very good idea that several evaluators apply the guidelines. A single evaluator might miss too much – even experts miss out things. Each evaluator should do a separate evaluation and write down all findings with due reference to the violated guidelines and then negotiate the findings with the others.

If guideline-based evaluation is done by an external expert, this is often called an *expert review*. Contrary to novices, who simply try to apply the guidelines, experts are expected to evaluate the usability of the current system model based on solid experience and background knowledge of which the guidelines form part.

Let's briefly look at a concrete example of what it means to "go through the system model" with a set of guidelines in hand. The first guideline in Fig. 11.12 reads "Make your contribution as informative as is required (for the current purposes of the exchange)". This guideline applies, at least, to spoken, task-oriented, shared-goal dialogue. When applied for development, you carefully check each system output phrase as you write it, considering if it is sufficiently informative in the given context, i.e. provides the user with the information s/he needs to continue the dialogue appropriately. When the guideline is applied for evaluation, you evaluate each system phrase in context to see if it is sufficiently informative.

*What is required for applying the method?* A system model, guidelines, a development team (if guidelines are used for development) or one or more internal or external evaluators, frequently a set of scenarios of use.

*System/AMITUDE model.* The system model can be at any stage, ranging from an outline to a fully implemented system. If the model is primitive, the guidelines can be used to generate ideas for its more detailed elaboration. If fully developed, the guidelines are used to check if the system model conforms to them.

*Planning.* Make a usability method plan based on items described in Section 6.4 but note that several of the typical points do not apply since you are not working with users. Start from the purpose of collecting usability data (Section 6.4.2) and identify a candidate guideline set to apply. Make sure that the system or part of it is within the scope of the guidelines and take a close look at their empirical or theoretical basis: is the theory well-established or brand new and untested? Are the guidelines based on substantial and diverse empirical research or just being proposed based upon a single prototype development process? If the guidelines are worth applying with due caution, the guideline set constitutes the operationalisation of the data collection purpose (Section 6.4.3).

Train developers or evaluators in applying the guidelines by going through use scenario examples together and discuss the issues arising. Alternatively, identify and invite external expert(s).

Doing guideline-based evaluation can be demanding, and a session typically lasts 1–2 hours. More time is often necessary when the system is complex but, in this case, it is preferable to split the evaluation into several sessions, focusing on different system model parts or guideline subsets in each session.

If the system is walk-up-and-use (Section 3.2.3) or evaluators are familiar with its domain, they should be able to construct use cases and scenarios on the fly. If the evaluators are not familiar with the domain, give them a set of use scenarios, set size depending on interaction complexity. The scenarios show the evaluators the steps a user would have to perform to carry out typical tasks or other activities.

To ensure that the problems identified are passed on correctly, it is a good idea to plan for a post-evaluation data analysis meeting between evaluators and the developers who are going to fix the problems identified. Guidelines typically help identify usability problems but have little to say about how to fix the problems.

*Running.* When using guidelines for development, we don't run method application *sessions* like with most other methods. Rather, guideline application should become part of the way developers think.

In guideline-based evaluation, on the other hand, method application is session-based. It is important to get an overview of the system model and of the structure and flow of interaction before applying the guidelines. This is done by consulting available system model representations, such as a graph-based or hypertext-based model of the dialogue structure of the flight booking system described in Section 3.4.2 and using scenarios to figure out how they are supposed to work in practical interaction. Then you go through the system model, applying the chosen set of guidelines. If the guidelines are those shown in Figs. 11.12 and 11.13, you study each designed output phrase in context and evaluate it against the guidelines. This is done by either traversing every system output one guideline at a time or applying every guideline to a single output at a time.

The evaluator must make note of every potential problem found, referring to the violated guideline(s) and being as specific as possible as to why there is a problem. It is not enough to say that you don't like a particular feature. You may not like it, and you may be right that there is a problem, but this has nothing to do with applying an articulate set of guidelines. If there are several things wrong with some aspect, each problem should be noted and explained separately. This facilitates the work of those who have to think about how to fix the problems.

If the evaluator discovers something that appears questionable although not in conflict with the guidelines, this should of course be made note of as well.

If more than one evaluator is involved, they should have a consensus meeting after having finished their individual evaluations. At this meeting, findings and disagreements are discussed until consensus is reached.

*Data.* Although guideline application for development does not usually result in a specific data set, it might do so. This is done by writing a design rationale account of the work, describing for each major guideline-based design decision which guideline it was based upon and how.

The data from guideline-based evaluation is the findings made by the evaluator. If there is more than one evaluator, findings and conclusions should be made consistent, merged and redundancies removed. This data should be presented in writing to the developers responsible for making system improvements. It is also a good idea to have a data analysis meeting among evaluators and developers in which the data is presented and discussed. See also Chapters 15 and 16 on data handling and analysis.

*Advantages and Drawbacks.* Guideline application is relatively cheap and fast because it can be done without involving external people, such as target users or experts. Even with an external expert, and despite any fee that must be paid, the method is still relatively cheap. Otherwise, everything depends on the quality of the guidelines, their appropriateness for the particular system they are being applied to and the skills of those applying them. An evaluation using well-founded and appropriate usability guidelines provides information on the extent to which the system model design conforms to good practice or if there is something one should seriously consider changing to avoid potential usability problems.

Compared to a test with target users based on interaction (Chapter 12), guidelines (i) can often be applied at an earlier stage and (ii) may provide information that will not necessarily be obtained with interacting users. These are generally unaware of good practice, and a single user test cannot be expected to reveal all usability problems.

Guidelines, whether high-level generic or low-level particular, always have limited scope and coverage, and this transfers to guideline-based development and evaluation. When applying a set of guidelines, focus must be on exactly the areas they address. Any other usability issues will have to be found in other ways.

Note that even expert guideline-based evaluation might be tainted by the expert's attitudes and opinions. Usability experts do not always take a neutral stance towards multimodal interaction involving particular sets of modalities, and some are downright polemical against, e.g. spoken interaction or interaction involving animated characters. This is one reason for using more than one expert. Another is that different people tend to find different problems.

*Examples: Three different guideline sets.* There are very many usability guideline sets out there. Some are claimed to be general, whereas others are specifically aimed at particular application types. Many guidelines aren't widely used, e.g. because they are very limited in scope or lack solid empirical or theoretical foundations. *Style guides* are highly detailed and specific guideline sets mostly exist for GUI-based interfaces. For example, the Microsoft style guides for Windows applications are widely applied not only by Microsoft but also by Windows application developers in general. Style guides are often a company-wide standard, cf. Section 11.5.

We show three examples of guideline sets. The first two are widely known and purportedly quite general, i.e. Shneiderman's eight golden rules (Shneiderman and Plaisant 2005) and Nielsen's ten usability heuristics (Nielsen 1994a). The third example (Bernsen et al. 1998a) is far more specific, providing guidelines for system cooperativity in shared-goal, task-oriented, spoken dialogue applications (Figs. 11.12 and 11.13).

Figure 11.10 shows Shneiderman's rules. An interesting question of multimodal usability is how general these guidelines really are. The guidelines are deeply marked by good, old, task-oriented GUI interface design issues, which well fit the fact that their first version dates back to Shneiderman (1987). However, the updated version in Fig. 11.10 is as recent as 2005. The mention of help screens, colour, fonts, the delete command, visual presentation of objects, greying out menu items, entry fields, retyping, multi-page displays, window motion, etc. abundantly shows that this is not about general multimodal interaction. It's a surprise that, nevertheless, Guideline 2 appeals to universal usability – as if GUI-based systems could satisfy this requirement on their own.

The question is if, at some point in the future, we will see an equally small set of guidelines purport to address multimodal interaction in general, whether task-oriented or not. Possibly, the generalisations required might surpass meaningful guideline writing. For instance, referring to the numbered golden rules, system output consistency (1) may be a nuisance in conversational systems; closure (4) is for some sub-class of tasks only; error prevention (5) is not for competitive systems; reversal of actions (6) is not relevant in a computer game shoot-out and is often prohibited in simulators: You just "crash and die" if you do something seriously wrong. Being in control of the interaction (7) may damage entertainment and immersion. As for universal usability (2), is that the task of a single system or is it rather a mission for multimodal system developers in general, i.e. that of building systems for all users, including the blind and the physically disabled? Reasonable feedback is probably necessary just like in human–human communication. However, its informativeness (3) clearly depends on system purpose. A poker-playing interface agent should have a poker face, right? Finally, reducing short-term memory load (8) is

---

**Shneiderman's eight golden rules**

**1. Strive for consistency.** This rule is the most frequently violated one, but following it can be tricky because there are many forms of consistency. Consistent sequences of actions should be required in similar situations; identical terminology should be used in prompts, menus, and help screens; and consistent colour, layout, capitalization, fonts, and so on should be employed throughout. Exceptions, such as required confirmation of the delete command or no echoing of passwords, should be comprehensible and limited in number.

**2. Cater to universal usability.** Recognize the needs of diverse users and design for plasticity, facilitating transformation of content. Novice-expert differences, age ranges, disabilities, and technology diversity each enrich the spectrum of requirements that guides design. Adding features for novices, such as explanations, and features for experts, such as shortcuts and faster pacing, can enrich the interface design and improve perceived system quality.

**3. Offer informative feedback.** For every user action, there should be some system feedback. For frequent and minor actions, the response can be modest, whereas for infrequent and major actions, the response should be more substantial. Visual presentation of the objects of interest provides a convenient environment for showing changes explicitly.

**4. Design dialogs to yield closure.** Sequences of actions should be organized into groups with a beginning, middle, and end. Informative feedback at the completion of a group of actions gives operators the satisfaction of accomplishment, a sense of relief, the signal to drop contingency plans from their minds, and a signal to prepare for the next group of actions. For example, e-commerce web sites move users from selecting products to the checkout, ending with a clear confirmation page that completes the transaction.

**5. Prevent errors.** As much as possible, design the system such that users cannot make serious errors; for example, grey out menu items that are not appropriate and do not allow alphabetic characters in numeric entry fields. If a user makes an error, the interface should detect the error and offer simple, constructive, and specific instructions for recovery. For example, users should not have to retype an entire name-address form if they enter an invalid zip code, but rather should be guided to repair only the faulty part. Erroneous actions should leave the system state unchanged, or the interface should give instructions about restoring the state.

**6. Permit easy reversal of actions.** As much as possible, actions should be reversible. This feature relieves anxiety, since the user knows that errors can be undone, thus encouraging exploration of unfamiliar options. The units of reversibility may be a single action, a data-entry task, or a complete group of actions, such as entry of a name and address block.

**7. Support internal locus of control.** Experienced operators strongly desire the sense that they are in charge of the interface and that the interface responds to their actions. Surprising interface actions, tedious sequences of data entries, inability to obtain or difficulty in obtaining necessary information, and inability to produce the action desired all build anxiety and dissatisfaction.

**8. Reduce short-term memory load.** The limitation of human information processing in short-term memory (the rule of thumb is that humans can remember "seven plus or minus two chunks" of information) requires that displays be kept simple, multiple-page displays be consolidated, window-motion frequency be reduced, and sufficient training time be allotted for codes, mnemonics, and sequences of actions. Where appropriate, online access to command-syntax forms, abbreviations, codes, and other information should be provided.

---

**Fig. 11.10**  Shneiderman's eight golden rules of interface design (Shneiderman and Plaisant 2005). These rules are from Shneiderman/Plaisant, DESIGNING THE USER INTERFACE: PREVIEW, © 1998. Reproduced by permission of Pearson Education, Inc. and Ben Shneiderman

often important but not always. Increasing short-term memory load is good for confusing the user if that's what the system wishes to do, e.g. as part of a game. Our advice is that if you consider to apply the golden rules, think carefully about the relationship between your own system and task-oriented GUI systems.

| **Nielsen's ten usability heuristics** |
| --- |
| **1. Visibility of system status.** The system should always keep users informed about what is going on, through appropriate feedback within reasonable time. |
| **2. Match between system and the real world.** The system should speak the users' language, with words, phrases and concepts familiar to the user, rather than system-oriented terms. Follow real-world conventions, making information appear in a natural and logical order. |
| **3. User control and freedom.** Users often choose system functions by mistake and will need a clearly marked "emergency exit" to leave the unwanted state without having to go through an extended dialogue. Support undo and redo. |
| **4. Consistency and standards.** Users should not have to wonder whether different words, situations, or actions mean the same thing. Follow platform conventions. |
| **5. Error prevention.** Even better than good error messages is a careful design which prevents a problem from occurring in the first place. Either eliminate error-prone conditions or check for them and present users with a confirmation option before they commit to the action. |
| **6. Recognition rather than recall.** Minimize the user's memory load by making objects, actions, and options visible. The user should not have to remember information from one part of the dialogue to another. Instructions for use of the system should be visible or easily retrievable whenever appropriate. |
| **7. Flexibility and efficiency of use.** Accelerators – unseen by the novice user – may often speed up the interaction for the expert user such that the system can cater to both inexperienced and experienced users. Allow users to tailor frequent actions. |
| **8. Aesthetic and minimalist design.** Dialogues should not contain information which is irrelevant or rarely needed. Every extra unit of information in a dialogue competes with the relevant units of information and diminishes their relative visibility. |
| **9. Help users recognize, diagnose, and recover from errors.** Error messages should be expressed in plain language (no codes), precisely indicate the problem, and constructively suggest a solution. |
| **10. Help and documentation.** Even though it is better if the system can be used without documentation, it may be necessary to provide help and documentation. Any such information should be easy to search, focused on the user's task, list concrete steps to be carried out, and not be too large. |

**Fig. 11.11** Jakob Nielsen's ten usability heuristics. These heuristics are from Nielsen (1994a) and are reproduced with the permission of Jakob Nielsen

Figure 11.11 shows Nielsen's ten usability guidelines. Their first version is from Nielsen and Molich (1990) and Molich and Nielsen (1990), the revised version in Fig. 11.11 is from Nielsen (1994a, b).

We leave it to the reader to compare the details of Shneiderman and Nielsen's usability guidelines. This is an interesting exercise that demonstrates how difficult it is to write generic usability guidelines even for a particular sub-class of systems defined by a certain modality combination, task orientation and efficiency.

How about the multimodal generality of Nielsen's heuristics? It seems fair to say that they primarily address task-oriented systems and have been written with GUIs in mind, as witnessed by the many occurrences of the term "visible" and derivatives. Many multimodal systems have no visible output at all. Or, what about "undo" functionality: if you offend an animated friend, should there be an "undo" function? Apologising is not the same as "undo"! However, despite their advanced age, Nielsen's guidelines appear less GUI dependent than Shneiderman's and might be somewhat more easily applicable to non-GUI systems. We believe that there is useful advice for multimodal system developers in these guidelines if only you can find it, properly apply it to your system and ignore everything that militates against achieving usability for non-GUI and/or non-task-oriented systems. Depending on the application, you might have to ignore much of the advice provided in the heuristics, not just everything to do with visibility. For instance, you may not need to present information in a natural and logical order nor worry about speeding up interaction for expert users.

Figures 11.12 and 11.13 show a set of guidelines for cooperative, shared-goal, task-oriented, spoken human–computer dialogue. These guidelines are very different from those of Shneiderman and Nielsen: they (i) don't address GUIs at all; (ii) go to great length announcing the narrow scope within which they are claimed to be valid; and (iii) are not empirical rules of thumb but, rather, empirical rules backed by linguistic–pragmatic theory of cooperativity. In terms of AMITUDE aspects, the cooperativity guidelines target a particular *application type*, i.e. shared-goal, task-oriented systems, a particular *modality*, i.e. unimodal speech input and output, a particular type of *interaction*, i.e. deliberate, involuntary or unaware two-way communication in which user and system can be presumed to share a single goal throughout interaction, i.e. that of achieving the task as efficiently as possible.

| Aspect | Generic guideline | Guideline formulation |
|---|---|---|
| 1. Informativeness | GG1 | *Make your contribution as informative as is required (for the current purposes of the exchange). |
| | GG2 | *Do not make your contribution more informative than is required. |
| 2. Truth and evidence | GG3 | *Do not say what you believe to be false. |
| | GG4 | *Do not say that for which you lack adequate evidence. |
| 3. Relevance | GG5 | *Be relevant, i.e. be appropriate to the immediate needs at each stage of the transaction. |
| 4. Manner | GG6 | *Avoid obscurity of expression. |
| | GG7 | *Avoid ambiguity. |
| | GG8 | *Be brief (avoid unnecessary prolixity). |
| | GG9 | *Be orderly. |
| 5. Partner asymmetry | GG10 | Inform the users of important non-normal characteristics which they should take into account in order to behave cooperatively in spoken interaction. Ensure the feasibility of what is required of them. |
| 6. Background knowledge | GG11 | Take partners' relevant background knowledge into account. |
| | GG12 | Take into account legitimate partner expectations as to your own background knowledge. |
| 7. Meta-communication | GG13 | Enable repair or clarification meta-communication in case of communication failure. |

**Fig. 11.12** Generic guidelines for shared-goal, cooperative-spoken human–computer dialogue

| Aspect | Specific guideline | Guideline formulation |
|---|---|---|
| 1. Informativeness | SG1 (GG1) | Be fully explicit in communicating to users the commitments they have made. |
| | SG2 (GG1) | Provide feedback on each piece of information provided by the user. |
| 4. Manner | SG3 (GG7) | Provide same formulation of the same question (or address) to users everywhere in the system's interaction turns. |
| 5. Partner asymmetry | SG4 (GG10) | Provide clear and comprehensible communication of what the system can and cannot do. |
| | SG5 (GG10) | Provide clear and sufficient instructions to users on how to interact with the system. |
| 6. Background knowledge | SG6 (GG11) | Take into account possible (and possibly erroneous) user inferences by analogy from related task domains. |
| | SG7 (GG11) | Separate whenever possible between the needs of novice and expert users (user-adaptive interaction). |
| | SG8 (GG12) | Provide sufficient task domain knowledge and inference. |
| 7. Meta-communication | SG9 (GG13) | Initiate repair meta-communication if system understanding has failed. |
| | SG10 (GG13) | Initiate clarification meta-communication in case of inconsistent user input. |
| | SG11 (GG13) | Initiate clarification meta-communication in case of ambiguous user input. |

**Fig. 11.13** Specific guidelines for shared-goal, cooperative spoken human–computer dialogue

We developed the guidelines based on the lengthy process of creating, testing and revising our dialogue design for a flight ticket reservation system (Bernsen et al. 1998a), see also Section 3.4.2, and then realised, and later demonstrated, that a large subset of the guidelines were strictly identical to those proposed by Grice (1975) in his paper on conversational implicature. This gave a nice theoretical backing for that subset because Grice's results still stand when restricted to shared-goal dialogue. The guidelines are available on the web (Bernsen et al. 1998b), including examples of how they are applied.

The cooperativity guidelines represent a first approximation to an operational definition of system cooperativity in task-oriented, shared-goal interaction. Their purpose is to achieve the shared goal as directly and smoothly as possible. In other words, the idea is that, if developers follow the guidelines when designing a task-oriented spoken dialogue system, the system will behave with a maximum of cooperativity during the dialogue with the user.

Figure 11.12 shows 13 *generic* guidelines expressed at the same level of generality as the Gricean maxims of cooperativity in human–human conversation (affixed with an ∗) (Grice 1975). Each *specific* guideline in Fig. 11.13 is subsumed by a generic guideline and details a particular aspect of importance of it. The left-hand column characterises the aspect of interaction addressed by each guideline.

Do the cooperativity guidelines have a scope more general than stated above? We have not investigated this issue much yet. The limitations concerning task-orientation, shared-goal interaction and linguistically expressed system output would seem fixed. If your system does not have these properties, several of the guidelines will be inapplicable, at least. Apart from those limitations, it is possible that the cooperativity guidelines could be useful, more or less as a whole, for interactive systems using many different kinds of input/output modalities in addition to the linguistic (speech or text) output which they address, maybe even for GUIs augmented with non-standard GUI modalities.

Note that we have chosen not to distinguish among the terms *guidelines*, *principles*, *heuristics* and *rules*, having mainly used the term guideline in a broad sense. It is worth knowing that, while those four terms are sometimes used as equivalents, this is not always the case. The term "principles" is sometimes taken to mean something broader and longer lasting than "guidelines" that are taken to focus more narrowly on current technology. Shneiderman regards the golden rules as principles rather than guidelines. Nielsen calls his guidelines a list of heuristics and defines "heuristics" as a set of recognised usability principles.

## 11.5  Usability Standards

The term "standard" is used about documents that describe recommendations approved by a recognised body. A *de facto standard* has not been approved by a recognised body but has nevertheless become accepted as a standard through its widespread use.

International standards are normally developed by an expert group or committee, drawing upon standards, best practice or research developed in particular companies or countries. Well-known international standards organisations include the International Organization for Standardization (ISO), the International Electrotechnical Commission (IEC), the International Telecommunication Union (ITU), the Institute of Electrical and Electronics Engineers (IEEE) and the World Wide Web Consortium (W3C). These organisations produce standards on many different topics far from all of which are software related. Software-related standards address all aspects of software development, including, e.g. software life cycle processes, cf. IEEE 1074 (2006) and ISO/IEC 12207 (2008), and software requirements specification, cf. IEEE 830 (1998).

Some standards are *usability standards*, being related to usability development or evaluation in various ways. There are at least three very different kinds of usability standards: (1) *Complex usability work methodologies* complete with definitions, usability decomposition, a list of usability methods, evaluation criteria, other process stuff, etc. just like the one proposed in this book. An example is ISO/IEC 9126 parts 1–4 (2001–2004), which we will look at below. (2) *Guidelines* like those described in Section 11.4, e.g. the W3C web contents accessibility guidelines (WCAG) (W3C WCAG 2008) that provide recommendations for how to make web contents available to a wider range of people with disabilities. For example, one of the guidelines about perceivability recommends that text alternatives are provided "for any non-text content, so that it can be changed" into, e.g. Braille or speech. Each guideline is further broken down into more specific guidelines that provide details on, e.g. which techniques to use. For instance, for the guideline just mentioned there is a breakdown into different kinds of non-text contents and what to do in each individual case. The WCAG document also contains a section on requirements to WCAG conformance. (3) *Style guides*, i.e. design-related standards for writing documents, web pages and other software. GUI style guides may describe, e.g. shape and size of buttons, layout and contents of menus and design of dialogue boxes. An example is ISO/IEC 14754 (1999) on "Information technology – pen-based interfaces – common gestures for text editing with pen-based systems", which defines a set of basic 2D gesture input commands (select, delete, insert space, split line, move, copy, cut, paste, scroll and undo) and feedback for pen-based interfaces.

Usability standards, in other words, are at the same time a wide-ranging subject and something that's being very much addressed in this book already. Usability standard guidelines are applied just like the guidelines described in Section 11.4. We don't think that usability standard style guides require discussion in this book: they primarily exist in order to make developers do the same, implement interfaces and interaction in the same way rather than differently for each new application, which is good for the users as well, because they don't have to adapt to differently styled interfaces and interaction styles to the extent that the differences are made to disappear. However, style guides do *not* primarily exist in order to solve other usability problems – *Ctrl+V* may be the standard shortcut key for *paste* in all MS Office software and much other software but that's about its only claim to usability.

### 11.5.1 ISO/IEC Usability Work Methodology

In the remainder of this section, we illustrate the ISO/IEC usability methodology, partly because we want you to not only respect standards but consider applying them yourself, partly because comparison highlights the differences between a standards methodology and what's presented in this book. ISO and IEC have produced several well-known and highly usability-relevant standards. The other international bodies mentioned above have less focus on usability, and W3C is restricted to web technology – which becomes less of a restriction as time goes by. IEEE has, among others, standards for quality assurance but seems focused on technical aspects and functionality rather than user interaction and experience.

According to UsabilityNet (2006), standards related to usability may be categorised as being concerned primarily with the following:

- use of the product in a particular context of use (quality in use);
- user interface and interaction (product quality);

**Fig. 11.14** Model of quality in use. This figure, taken from ISO/IEC 9126-1: 2001 Software engineering – Product quality – Part 1: Quality model, is reproduced with the permission of the International Organization for Standardization, ISO. The standard can be obtained from any ISO member and from the web site of the ISO Central Secretariat at the following address: www.iso.org. Copyright remains with ISO

- process used to develop the product (process quality);
- capability of an organisation to apply user-centred design (organisational capability).

*Quality in use.* The ISO/IEC 9126-1 (2001) standard on "Software engineering – Product quality – Part 1: Quality model" is meant to help define and specify quality requirements. The standard defines quality in use as follows, cf. Fig. 11.14:

The capability of the software product to enable specified users to achieve specified goals with effectiveness, productivity, safety and satisfaction in specified contexts of use.

In this book's terminology, we notice the *User* and *Use environment* aspects and the notion of user goals in interaction. We also notice some kind of decomposition of usability, cf. Section 1.4.6. The four *quality-in-use* attributes are defined as follows:

*Effectiveness:* The capability of the software product to enable users to achieve specified goals with accuracy and completeness in a specified context of use.

*Productivity:* The capability of the software product to enable users to expend appropriate amounts of resources in relation to the effectiveness achieved in a specified context of use.

*Safety:* The capability of the software product to achieve acceptable levels of risk of harm to people, business, software, property or the environment in a specified context of use.

*Satisfaction:* The capability of the software product to satisfy users in a specified context of use.

A later ISO standard ISO/IEC 9126-4 (2004) "Software engineering – Product quality – Part 4: Quality in use metrics" includes examples of metrics for effectiveness, productivity, safety and satisfaction, i.e. usability criteria for measuring these quality-in-use attributes objectively and quantitatively. We present evaluation criteria in Section 16.4, where we also discuss the limited extent to which those four attributes apply to this book's Cases, cf. the annotation of the Case usability requirements in Section 5.2, Table 5.9.

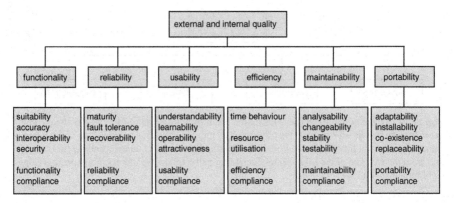

**Fig. 11.15**   Model of external and internal quality. This figure, taken from ISO/IEC 9126-1: 2001 Software engineering – Product quality – Part 1: Quality model, is reproduced with the permission of the International Organization for Standardization, ISO. The standard can be obtained from any ISO member and from the web site of the ISO Central Secretariat at the following address: www.iso.org. Copyright remains with ISO

*Product quality*. Quality in use is the user's view of quality. Quality in use is affected by the quality of the development process and by the product quality. Following ISO/IEC 9126-1 (2001), product quality can be evaluated by measuring internal and external quality attributes. Internal quality is "the totality of characteristics of the software product from an internal view" and external quality is the "totality of characteristics of the software product from an external view". Figure 11.15 shows how external and internal quality are categorised into six characteristics that again are divided into sub-characteristics.

Usability is defined as

> The capability of the software product to be understood, learned, used and attractive to the user, when used under specified conditions.

Usability has two roles according to ISO/IEC 9126-1 (2001), i.e. a detailed software design activity (cf. the definition of usability) and the overall goal of covering the users' needs (quality in use).

ISO/IEC 9126-2 (2003) and ISO/IEC 9126-3 (2003) include examples of metrics for measuring understandability, learnability, operability and attractiveness, e.g. time to learning to use a function, can users undo functions, do users respond appropriately to error messages, what proportion of functions is documented, what proportion of functions can be undone and what proportion of error messages are self-explanatory.

Several standards other than ISO/IEC 9126-1 (2001) also address aspects of product quality. These standards are not always focused on GUIs. Here are some examples: ISO 14915 (2002–2003) and IEC 61997 (2001) provide recommendations on multimedia interfaces. Static output modalities, such as text, graphics and images, and dynamic output modalities, such as audio, animation and video, are included. ISO/IEC 18021 (2002) presents recommendations on user interfaces for

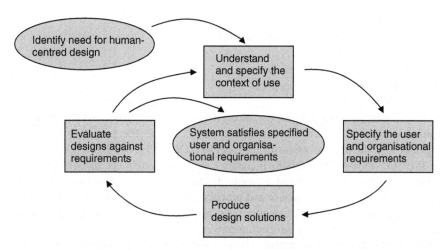

**Fig. 11.16**    User-centred design process. This figure, taken from ISO 13407: 1999 Human-centred design processes for interactive systems, is reproduced with the permission of the International Organization for Standardization, ISO. The standard can be obtained from any ISO member and from the web site of the ISO Central Secretariat at the following address: www.iso.org. Copyright remains with ISO

mobile tools like PDAs and smartphones, which can update or be updated from a database via a communication link.

*Process quality.* Development and evaluation is a process, and human-centred development processes are often recommended, cf. Section 6.2.1. ISO 13407 (1999) on "Human-centred design processes for interactive systems" explains the activities required for user-centred design. The process and main activities recommended by this standard are shown in Fig. 11.16.

ISO 16982 (2002) outlines the types of usability methods that can be used, including user observation (Section 10.4), questionnaires and interviews (Chapter 5) and think-aloud (Section 12.5). ISO/IEC 14598-5 (1998) provides guidance on the software evaluation process in terms of a step-wise procedure and draws on the quality characteristics expressed in ISO/IEC 9126-1 (2001), cf. above. Four main characteristics are defined for the evaluation process: repeatability, reproducibility, impartiality and objectivity. Main process activities include analysis of evaluation requirements, evaluation specification, evaluation design and plan, execution of plan and evaluation conclusion.

*Organisational capability.* ISO 18529 (2000) on "Ergonomics – ergonomics of human–system interaction – human-centred life cycle process descriptions" presents a usability maturity model which includes a structured set of human-centred design processes derived from ISO 13407 (1999) and a survey of good practice. Human-centred design processes should follow the following recommendations:

1.  ensure human-centred design content in system strategy;
2.  plan and manage the human-centred design process;

3. specify the user and organisational requirements;
4. understand and specify the context of use;
5. produce design solutions;
6. evaluate designs against requirements;
7. introduce and operate the system.

The usability maturity model can be used to assess the extent to which an organisation is capable of carrying out user-centred design. The model can be used together with the process assessment model in ISO/IEC 15504 (2003–2008).

ISO/IEC 15504 (2003–2008) includes a process assessment model that comprises a process dimension and a capability dimension. The model thus provides indicators of process performance and process capability. Processes that can be performed are divided into nine categories, i.e. acquisition, supply, engineering, operation, support, management, process improvement, resource and infrastructure and reuse. Process capability is measured on a six-point scale as incomplete, performed, managed, established, predictable or optimising. The scale expresses increasing degrees of capability of the performed process.

### 11.5.2  Comparison with This Book

The ISO/IEC usability work methodology illustrated in the previous section is not a usability method in the sense of this book (Section 6.2) but is rather comparable to this book as a whole, i.e. as a comprehensive methodology for working on usability in the life cycle. So, it does not make sense to discuss the ISO/IEC methodology in terms of our usability methods template (Section 6.2.9). Instead, let's ask: why not use ISO/IEC instead of this book?

Why not indeed! We share the underlying philosophy of human-centred development and evaluation, cf. Section 6.2.1, and our basic decompositions of usability are closely related, compare Table 1.1 and Fig. 11.15. In fact, for HCI novices, the primary reason for picking up this book before adopting ISO/IEC methodology is that the latter may be hard to do "cold", without any prior introduction to usability work. Second, although standards may be updated from time to time, standard production and updating tends to take a long time to do and is typically being done to reflect best current industrial practice within current industrial scope of application, and the latter is always behind the innovation curve. This means that new developments, which, at first, are of interest only to advanced research prototype development, may take a decade or more to become reflected in standards. Thus, obviously, the ISO/IEC methodology does not incorporate the generalisations of HCI aimed at in this book and summarised in Chapter 18. For instance, the ISO/IEC methodology does not include the full AMITUDE framework (Section 3.1), but only part of it, and the attributes of, and metrics for, effectiveness, productivity, safety and satisfaction described in Section 11.5.1 are only relevant for characterising and evaluating a subset of systems but not all systems, as illustrated for this book's Cases in Section 16.4.1.

# References

Bernsen NO, Dybkjær H, Dybkjær L (1998a) Designing interactive speech systems. From first ideas to user testing. Springer Verlag, Heidelberg.

Bernsen NO, Dybkjær H, Dybkjær L (1998b) Guidelines for cooperative dialogue. http://spokendialogue.dk/Cooperativity/Guidelines.html. Accessed 21 January 2009.

Bias RG (1994) The pluralistic usability walkthrough: coordinated empathies. In: Nielsen J, Mack R (eds) Usability inspection methods. John Wiley & Sons, New York: 63–76.

Booch G, Rumbaugh J, Jacobson I (1999) The unified modeling language user guide. Addison-Wesley, USA.

Calabria T (2004) An introduction to personas and how to create them. http://www.steptwo.com.au/papers/kmc_personas. Accessed 20 January 2009.

Cockburn A (2001) Writing effective use cases. Addison-Wesley, New York.

Cockburn (2002) Use cases, ten years later. http://alistair.cockburn.us/Use+cases2c+ten+years+later. Accessed 7 February 2009.

Cooper A (2008) Personas. http://www.cooper.com/journal/personas. Accessed 20 January 2009.

Cooper A (1999) The inmates are running the asylum. SAMS, USA.

Grice P (1975) Logic and conversation. In: Cole P, Morgan JL (eds) Syntax and semantics 3: speech acts. New York: Academic Press, 41–58. Reprinted in Grice P (1989) Studies in the way of words. Harvard University Press, Cambridge, MA.

IEC 61997 (2001) Guidelines for the user interface in multimedia equipment for general purpose use. http://webstore.iec.ch/webstore/webstore.nsf/artnum/027914. Accessed 22 January 2009.

IEEE 1074 (2006) IEEE standard for developing a software project life cycle process. Available via http://www.ieee.org/web/standards/home/index.html. Accessed 21 January 2009.

IEEE 830 (1998) IEEE recommended practice for software requirements specifications – description. Available via http://standards.ieee.org/reading/ieee/std_public/description/se/830-1998_desc.html. Accessed 21 January 2009.

ISO 13407 (1999) Human-centred design processes for interactive systems. http://www.iso.org/iso/iso_catalogue/catalogue_tc/catalogue_detail.htm?csnumber=21197. Accessed 22 January 2009.

ISO 14915 (2002–2003) Software ergonomics for multimedia user interfaces. Parts 1–3, http://www.iso.org/iso/iso_catalogue/catalogue_tc/catalogue_detail.htm?csnumber=25578. Accessed 22 January 2009.

ISO 16982 (2002) Ergonomics of human–system interaction – usability methods supporting human-centred design. http://www.iso.org/iso/catalogue_detail?csnumber=31176. Accessed 22 January 2009.

ISO 18529 (2000) Ergonomics – ergonomics of human–system interaction – human-centred life cycle process descriptions. http://www.iso.org/iso/iso_catalogue/catalogue_tc/catalogue_detail.htm?csnumber=33499. Accessed 22 January 2009.

ISO/IEC 12207 (2008) Systems and software engineering – software life cycle processes. http://www.iso.org/iso/catalogue_detail?csnumber=43447. Accessed 21 January 2009.

ISO/IEC 14598-5 (1998) Information technology – software product evaluation – part 5: process for evaluators. http://www.iso.org/iso/iso_catalogue/catalogue_tc/catalogue_detail.htm?csnumber=24906. Accessed 22 January 2009.

ISO/IEC 14754 (1999) Information technology – pen-based interfaces – common gestures for text editing with pen-based systems. http://www.iso.org/iso/iso_catalogue/catalogue_tc/catalogue_detail.htm?csnumber=25490. Accessed 21 January 2009.

ISO/IEC 15407 (2003–2008) Information technology – process assessment. Parts 1–7, http://www.iso.org/iso/iso_catalogue/catalogue_tc/catalogue_detail.htm?csnumber=38932. Accessed 22 January 2009.

ISO/IEC 18021 (2002) Information technology – user interfaces for mobile tools for management of database communications in a client-server model. http://www.iso.org/iso/iso_catalogue/catalogue_tc/catalogue_detail.htm?csnumber=30806. Accessed 22 February 2009.

ISO/IEC 9126-1 (2001) Software engineering – product quality – part 1: quality model. http://www.iso.org/iso/iso_catalogue/catalogue_tc/catalogue_detail.htm?csnumber=22749. Accessed 22 January 2009.

ISO/IEC 9126-2 (2003) Software engineering – product quality – part 2: external metrics. http://www.iso.org/iso/iso_catalogue/catalogue_tc/catalogue_detail.htm?csnumber=22750. Accessed 22 January 2009.

ISO/IEC 9126-3 (2003) Software engineering – product quality – part 3: internal metrics. http://www.iso.org/iso/iso_catalogue/catalogue_tc/catalogue_detail.htm?csnumber=22891. Accessed 22 January 2009.

ISO/IEC 9126-4 (2004) Software engineering – product quality – part 4: quality in use metrics. http://www.iso.org/iso/iso_catalogue/catalogue_tc/catalogue_detail.htm?csnumber=39752. Accessed 22 January 2009.

Jacobson I, Christerson M, Jonsson P, Overgaard G (1992) Object-oriented software engineering: a use case driven approach. ACM Press, Addison-Wesley, New York.

Lewis C, Polson O, Wharton C, Rieman J (1990) Testing a walkthrough methodology for theory-based design of walk-up-and-use interfaces. Proceedings of CHI: 235–242.

Malan R, Bredemeyer D (2001) Functional requirements and use cases. Bredemeyer Consulting, white paper, http://www.bredemeyer.com/pdf_files/functreq.pdf. Accessed 20 January 2009.

Molich R, Nielsen J (1990) Improving a human–computer dialogue. Communications of the ACM 33/3: 338–348.

Nielsen J (1994a) Ten usability heuristics. http://www.useit.com/papers/heuristic/heuristic_list.html. Accessed 21 January 2009.

Nielsen J (1994b) Heuristic evaluation. In: Nielsen J, Mack RL (eds) Usability inspection methods. John Wiley & Sons, New York.

Nielsen J, Molich R (1990) Heuristic evaluation of user interfaces. Proceedings of the ACM CHI conference. Seattle, WA: 249–256.

Polson PG, Lewis CH (1990) Theory-based design for easily learned interfaces. Human–Computer Interaction 5: 191–220. Lawrence Erlbaum Associates.

Pruitt J, Adlin T (2006) The persona life cycle: keeping people in mind throughout product design. Morgan Kaufmann Publishers.

Rowley DE, Rhoades DG (1992) The cognitive jogthrough: a fast-paced user interface evaluation procedure. Proceedings of CHI: 389–395.

Sharp H, Rogers Y, Preece J (2007) Interaction design – beyond human–computer interaction. 2nd edn. John Wiley and Sons, New York.

Shneidermann B (1987) Designing the user interface. Addison-Wesley, Reading, MA.

Shneiderman B, Plaisant C (2005) Designing the user interface. 4th edn. Addison Wesley, New York.

Spencer R (2000) The streamlined cognitive walkthrough method, working around social constraints encountered in a software development company. Proceedings of CHI: 353–359.

UsabilityNet (2006) International standards for HCI and usability. http://usabilitynet.org/tools/r_international.htm. Accessed 22 January 2009.

W3C WCAG (2008) Web contents accessibility guidelines 2.0. http://www.w3.org/TR/WCAG20/. Accessed 21 January 2009.

Wharton C, Rieman J, Lewis C, Polson P (1994) The cognitive walkthrough method: a practitioner's guide. In: Nielsen J, Mack R (eds) Usability inspection methods. John Wiley & Sons, New York, USA: 105–140.

Wikipedia (2009a) Use case. http://en.wikipedia.org/wiki/Use_case. Accessed 20 January 2009.

Wikipedia (2009b) Personas. http://en.wikipedia.org/wiki/Personas. Accessed 7 February 2009.

# Chapter 12
# Interaction with the System

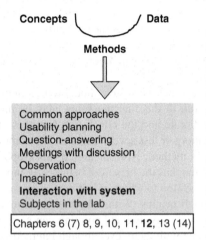

In this fifth and last of five chapters on multimodal usability methods (Section 6.2.2), all methods presented have users interacting with a system model prototype. A prototype is an experimental interactive model of the target system, or parts of it, that is used for data collection, testing or demonstration. This may be anything from a mock-up that only exists as a slide show to a fully coded and virtually completed system that is submitted to a final field test. If the prototype is partially or wholly unimplemented, it normally takes human intervention to make it interact with subjects. The methods presented include two very different uses of human-mediated interaction, two different sets of conditions for testing an implementation and a special method for studying information processing in subjects during interaction.

Section 12.1 describes interaction with a mock-up; Section 12.2 the Wizard of Oz (WOZ) method; Section 12.3 interaction with an implemented prototype; Section 12.4 field tests; and Section 12.5 the think-aloud method.

## 12.1 Mock-Up

Mock-ups range from low-fidelity to high-fidelity (unimplemented) prototypes (Dumas and Redish 1999, Nielsen Norman Group (year unknown), Sefelin et al. 2003, Sharp et al. 2007, Wikipedia 2008) and are used to collect early data on user–system interaction. In a low-fidelity prototype, the design is obviously preliminary, as only hand-drawn interface sketches are available, while the design of an unimplemented high-fidelity prototype may be near-final. A *storyboard* is related to mock-ups. It consists of a series of sketches illustrating how a user may step through a

N.O. Bernsen, L. Dybkjær, *Multimodal Usability*, Human-Computer Interaction Series, DOI 10.1007/978-1-84882-553-6_12, © Springer-Verlag London Limited 2009

task or other activity, cf. Sharp et al. (2007). However, a storyboard rather focuses on the process, i.e. what we imagine the user does and can do based on scenarios. A mock-up is meant to look-sound-or-feel like the system, and we want to learn about the interaction process by having users interact with it.

*When can you use the method and what is its scope?* The method can be used during design when nothing has been implemented.

Mock-ups have traditionally been used in a GUI context. With a bit of creativity, however, the graphics output may be supplemented, or even replaced, by spoken or other acoustic output, or even haptics. Likewise, input does not have to be standard GUI haptics but could include speech, camera-captured information or even bio-sensor data, as long as it's intelligibly represented to the participants in the situation. However, if the system handles complex interactive tasks, has complex multimodal I/O, has back-end data access, includes dynamic objects, assumes high-speed, high-precision performance or otherwise, mock-ups quickly become unwieldy. Then you might consider if it makes sense to mock-up part of the system (vertical approach), e.g. those parts you are most uncertain about or those which form the core of user–system interaction.

Mock-ups are basically limited by the fact that the system model representation is mocked up rather than implemented. Add to this that mock-ups may be more or less early, more or less refined and elaborate and the conclusion becomes that the system model representation imposes more or less severe limits on the usability information that can be collected with this method. Nevertheless, a mock-up can still provide valuable input which, in addition, has the benefit of being early input.

*Multimodal significance.* It is an open question to which extent mock-ups can be used productively beyond their standard GUI origins. Within those, system model representations made from paper, stored images, typing and pointing can generate meaningful usability data when users interact with them, even though interaction is more or less constantly mediated by human intervention. The mock-up method thus *may* have a rather strong bias towards GUI-based interaction due to the *nature of the user–system interface*, cf. Factor 1 in Section 6.2.2. But let's look at our Cases.

A mock-up of the Treasure Hunt system's (Section 5.1) 3D haptic virtual environment (VE), or part of it, might be done by building a 3D toy model with houses, a forest, etc. having the experimenter whisper spoken keyword feedback and having the blind user interact with a pencil rather than the hands, in order to better correspond to the haptic device used in the implemented system. It would be rather easy to mock up the hearing-impaired user's corresponding GUI-based VE, and the sign language I/O part could be included easily. The Sudoku game board could be mocked up on a flip-over chart or via a slide show projected onto a wall to which the user speaks and points using a laser pointer, post-it notes being used for holding numbers, cf. the example below. Part of the Maths system could be mocked up as well, such as the table training sessions, including pictures of what is going to become the animated face.

It could work, couldn't it? For instance, the Treasure Hunt mock-up might yield much-needed data on the amount and contents of the whispered spoken feedback required for smooth navigation in the haptic VE.

*How does the method work?* Target users interact with the mocked-up system and are usually given scenarios to carry out. Since there is no automated functionality, it is up to the experimenter and any assistant to handle all interactions, e.g. by taking care of output acoustics or speech or making changes to what the user sees on the "screen" by, e.g. adding and removing stickers. Note that the method can also be used for testing device mock-ups.

*What is required for applying the method?* An early system model, target users or a representative user group (Section 3.3.1), scenarios, an experimenter, possibly an assistant, possibly an observer (Section 10.4), recording equipment, other materials as needed, e.g. stickers or a pencil (i.e. a device mock-up) to point with.

*System/AMITUDE model.* The system model is at this stage available only as an interface with no underlying functionality. A sketchy interface is called a low-fidelity prototype, a more elaborate and detailed one is a high-fidelity prototype.

*Planning.* Make a usability method plan based on items described in Section 6.4. Start from the purpose of collecting usability data (Section 6.4.2): which kinds of data can be reliably collected with a mock-up at this point? Which parts of the system can be mocked up to produce reliable data? Operationalise the purpose to guide mock-up design and scenario creation and script how the session will proceed (Section 6.4.3).

Planning a mock-up user test involves a number of standard steps as described in Sections 13.2 and 13.3 on session preparation, including, e.g. subject recruitment. Try to have everything you need drawn, built, scripted, recorded and otherwise prepared in advance. Make a dry run with colleagues. It might turn into several! Note that a mock-up is often used in combination with other methods, such as screening, pre-test and post-test questioning (Section 8.6, 8.7 and 8.8) and observation of users (Section 10.4). Subject recruitment is shared among methods in a cluster, while most other preparations must be done individually per method.

Many applications draw on a database or other internal or external information sources. When using a mock-up, it is inconvenient to use a lot of data. On the other hand, the data used must be realistic. The trick is to design scenarios and give them to users. Scenarios help ensure that all parts of the system, or those of interest, are being tested and that we know in advance which data will be needed. We can then use stickers on data fields or have the right spoken output phrases ready when "running" the system with users.

*Running.* Section 13.4 explains issues to do and be aware of during a lab session. Specific to mock-ups is that the experimenter interacts closely with the user during the test. The user is typically asked to carry out scenarios by interacting with the system model. The experimenter is responsible for the timely and correct performance of any action required by the user's action and for explaining what happens, whenever needed. Since the experimenter must focus on system actions, it is useful to include an observer who makes notes on problems and other issues of interest. However, the experimenter may also make notes to the extent possible.

*Data.* The data comprises notes and session recordings. Typically, the notes are the primary data. If carefully made, they cover all main issues and there isn't much extra value in going through the recordings. The recordings are still valuable for checking up on any issues arising during data analysis. A crucial issue in data analysis is to distinguish clearly between results that can and cannot be extrapolated to interaction with an implemented system model version.

Often mock-up data forms part of a larger set of test data resources that should be analysed as a whole. See also Chapters 15 and 16 on data handling and analysis.

*Advantages and drawbacks.* Mock-ups are typically cheap and relatively fast to create and revise. Yet the information collected may be valuable, because we get it early in the design process. In fact, creating the mock-up can be an important step forward in itself because it makes an interface perceptually concrete that might so far have existed only as a text specification. Low-fidelity tests may demonstrate that important functionality and ease-of-use issues have been ignored or left underspecified, contributing to requirements generation and refinement, task or other activity analysis and allowing low-cost interaction experimentation. High-fidelity tests may provide substantial input on interface design as well.

Note that users may be more prone to criticising a system that does not appear very polished or clearly hasn't been implemented. This is, of course, an advantage, not a drawback.

The drawbacks are mainly that (i) the system is not real, so many things cannot be tested meaningfully, such as if the system crashes, how well it recognises and interprets user input or how fast it performs; and (ii) it takes careful preparation and

**Fig. 12.1** Testing a mock-up of our Sudoku system Case

data analysis to distinguish between usability information that *can* be reliably trans-ferred to system development and information that's merely an artificial product of the special conditions characterising the mock-up test.

*Example: Mock-up.* Figure 12.1 shows a mock-up of the Sudoku Case (Section 2.1). The game board is projected onto a wall. The user points with a light pen and speaks the number he wants to insert in the square pointed to. The experimenter recognises the number, writes it on a post-it note and sticks it to the wall.

## 12.2  Wizard of Oz

The Wizard of Oz (WOZ) method (Bernsen et al. 1998, Fraser and Gilbert 1991) is a powerful simulation technique for collecting usability information prior to imple-mentation or with a partially implemented system. In the latter case we call it a *bionic WOZ.* One or several human "wizards" simulate the system with users who believe that they interact with a real system.

*When can you use the method and what is its scope?* WOZ is used during design and implementation, primarily in the lab but also in "exported lab environments" where sessions take place outside the lab in, e.g. a car or as part of an exhibition or over the phone. In fact, WOZ can even be used in combination with a field test (Section 12.4) as we once did in a museum, cf. the example below.

WOZ is frequently used in spoken dialogue system development but has a far larger potential and has, in fact, been used to simulate many different types of multi-modal system. WOZ is particularly suited for developing systems that communicate with users in the natural interactive modalities used in human–human communi-cation, i.e. speech, gesture, facial expression, gaze, head and body posture, body action, etc. or that refer to what humans can see, hear, feel, taste, smell, etc. – because it is easy for human wizards to recognise, understand and produce infor-mation represented in these modalities in response to user input. Similarly, the more systems need to emulate human central processing, the more we would expect WOZ to become an integral part of system development.

During interaction, users must believe that they are interacting with a real sys-tem. This is technically easy to accomplish for spoken dialogue, i.e. by having the wizard communicate with the user over a loudspeaker or a telephone. The wizard can also fairly easily remote control other output aspects, such as simple graphics output, including simple animated character gesture and posture. Converting wiz-ard speech to animated talking head audiovisual speech output can also be done today but requires dedicated software. Converting a wizard's fully natural multi-modal communicative behaviour, attitudes, emotions and all into equivalent 3D ani-mated character or robot behaviour is a challenge for the next few years.

As for modalities and modality combinations other than those natural to humans, there is no intrinsic reason why a wizard could not simulate some of those as well. You have to use your imagination and sense of feasibility to determine whether it is desirable to try. Wizards are able to immediately understand very many dif-ferent kinds of user input represented in different modality combinations, such as speech and deictic gesture. However, few would be able to make sense of, e.g. dozens of simultaneous and continuous streams of "brainwave" EEG (electroencephalography) input.

*Multimodal significance.* There is hardly much point in using WOZ to simulate a standard GUI-based system because it uses few I/O modalities natural to humans. WOZ is biased towards multimodal systems, or system parts, that use natural human interaction. This means that the method is influenced by differentiation Factors 1 and 5, i.e. *the nature of the user–system interface* and *the kind of data to be collected with users*, cf. Section 6.2.2. The method is particularly important for innovative multimodal and blending-with-people systems.

Among our Cases, especially the advanced spoken conversation of the Maths system (Section 5.1) would be quite suitable for WOZ simulation.

*How does the method work?* One or more wizards simulate the detailed system design or parts of it. It is crucial to the reliability of the collected data that subjects interact without knowing that the system is partially or fully simulated.

*What is required for applying the method?* One or more wizards, an experimenter, possibly an assistant, possibly an observer (Section 10.4), target users or a representative user group (Section 3.3.1), a detailed system model representation that is easy for the wizard to follow, usually scenarios, recording and possibly logging equipment, possibly WOZ support tools.

*System/AMITUDE model.* A detailed draft of the system model, its contents, interaction structure and flow is required. Since the wizards may not be developers, it is important to tailor, or convert, the system model representation so that the wizards are able to use it in close to real time.

For simple systems, a graph representation may suffice, showing interaction structure and flow, and possible user input and corresponding system output. For more complex systems, the wizard would get lost in a graph representation and something else is needed, such as the hypertext in Fig. 12.3. You might draw the model on paper, but an electronic (e.g. hypertext, hypermedia) model is much to be preferred since (i) it allows the wizard to just click on a link to get to the next output and (ii) it allows tools support.

*Planning.* Make a usability method plan based on items described in Section 6.4. Start from the purpose of collecting usability data (Section 6.4.2). Use the purpose to guide creation of scenarios on which interaction with the simulated system will be based and make a script for how the session will proceed (Section 6.4.3). Usually, scenarios are used to ensure that all system parts will be tested.

WOZ session planning involves a number of standard steps as described in Sections 13.2 and 13.3 on session preparation, including, e.g. subject recruitment. Note that the WOZ method is often used in combination with other methods such as screening, pre-test and post-test questioning (Sections 8.6, 8.7 and 8.8) and observation of users (Section 10.4). Subject recruitment is shared among methods in a cluster, while most other preparations must be done individually per method.

Be aware that the wizard needs time to *train* because simulating a system convincingly in real time is no easy task. To the extent possible, the wizard must learn to act within the limitations of the system model, i.e. to simulate reduced (compared to what a human is capable of) input recognition, input understanding, reasoning, emotional reactivity, etc. corresponding to what the real system is likely to have. Output must be as specified in the system model, which, today, typically means that it must be fluent and presented in a thoroughly consistent fashion since we are not yet at the stage where systems are built to emulate, for instance, human disfluencies of expression. Ideally, the wizard must also be able to simulate misunderstandings and other system shortcomings with proper frequency and to improvise convincingly if there are gaps in the system model and the user produces input that was not planned for.

Several wizards may be required if, e.g. the system is complex and uses more than one input modality. For instance, if the input modalities are not effortlessly fusioned by humans, each wizard might be responsible for taking care of a different input modality. This makes their job simpler on the input side, but they might have to collaborate on the output side, which also requires training.

The wizard's job can be facilitated in at least two ways. One is to use an assistant. Don't task the wizard with acting as a calculator or doing other high-cognitive-load jobs that computers can do much faster! Let an assistant use a computer instead and present the result to the wizard. For example, the assistant may operate a database on a separate computer or make notes of relevant events, such as information provided by the user which may have to be used in confirmation feedback later on. The assistant may also make useful observations during the simulations and note them down.

A second way of making the wizard's life easier is to support simulation by electronic tools. For example, a data glove may be used to capture wizard gestures and render them to the subject. For speech, tools are not an absolute necessity but a convenience that should be carefully considered. Spoken output might be recorded in advance or sent through text-to-speech synthesis. In both cases, the wizard only needs one click to send spoken output to the user instead of having to read aloud the output with the risk of stumbling over words. The user's spoken input may pass through a speech recogniser to ensure a realistic level of misrecognition and non-recognition. Voice distortion may be applied to both input and output: when used on input, the idea is to make it easier for the wizard to misunderstand or fail to understand the input, given that no speech recogniser is used as front end. When distortion is used on output, the purpose may be to, e.g. have a male voice from a female wizard or ensure that the voice sounds somewhat mechanical and hence that users will not expect the system to possess full human capabilities. There are also tools that help wizards navigate the interaction structure and that log the interaction, cf. Fig. 12.4. Scenarios also work as tools for the wizard, allowing the wizard to know what to expect from the user. In all cases, wizard training is needed and the wizard must know the support tools well.

On the wizard's computer, nothing should be running during a session except the software in use. Audio and video recording should be done on a separate computer to avoid any interference with the wizard's task. The wizard should not have any other role than that of simulating the system. Thus, an experimenter is needed who is responsible for taking care of the users.

*Running.* Section 13.4 explains issues to do and be aware of during a lab session, e.g. when using WOZ. Make sure that the wizard is ready and that everything works when the session starts.

*Data.* WOZ simulation data normally comprises audio and possibly video recordings of user input behaviour and system output behaviour, notes and possibly logfiles from running system components. Depending on data collection purpose, the audio recordings may be transcribed and annotated, and logfiles may be annotated as well. Note that the wizard (and the assistant) will typically have a good idea of where the main problems lie. Data should be analysed to the extent considered necessary to determine how close we are to the goal and to make decisions on which system improvements to make. Often WOZ data forms part of a larger set of test data resources that should be analysed as a whole. See also Chapters 15 and 16 on data handling and analysis.

*Advantages and drawbacks.* Not a single line of code is required to run a WOZ session in which a subject interacts with something that feels like a real and quasi-complete system. And we get to collect much of the real-time interactive user behaviour data, which we would otherwise need an implemented prototype for collecting. We can collect data on the vocabulary, grammar and semantics that people use, their facial expressions and gestures as coordinated with the speech, etc. This strongly helps pinpoint problems rather early in the life cycle while it is cheap to make system model changes. Following data analysis, all we have to do is revise the design rather than the program code. The revisions can then be exposed to a new WOZ simulation and so on until the design has been perfected, after which we implement the result. No other usability method can do that.

A related advantage is the use of WOZ for focused experimentation through simulation. If we are uncertain about the effects on interaction of a particular system behaviour style or strategy, for instance, we can simulate alternative styles or strategies and leave it to subsequent data analysis to decide which approach to implement. This aspect of WOZ also allows researchers to collect human behaviour data unrelated to any particular system development process.

Successful use of WOZ strongly depends on how good the wizard is. Still, even well-trained wizards find it difficult to simulate in real time the levels of recognition, understanding, reasoning, emotional sensitivity, etc. which the implemented system will be capable of. This is partly because humans are capable of so much more than systems will be in the foreseeable future and partly because it is hard to predict the performance of many system components before they have been built and hence impossible to provide the wizard with realistic simulation performance targets. Also, WOZ tends to be fairly expensive because it involves substantial preparation as regards wizard training, team collaboration and tools and materials creation.

*Examples: WOZ set-up, WOZ system model representation and WOZ tool.* Figure 12.2 shows the field WOZ set-up used in testing the first complete conversation design of the Hans Christian Andersen system, a multimodal, blending-with-people, walk-up-and-use system for having conversation with the fairytale author (Bernsen et al. 2004). In the set-up shown, the wizard was placed in the basement of the Andersen museum in Odense, Denmark, using a hyperlinked document as

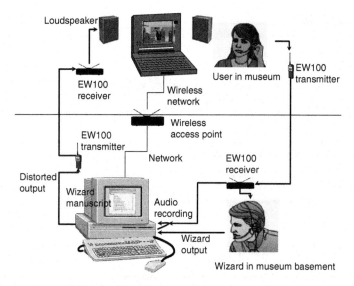

**Fig. 12.2**  A multimodal Wizard of Oz set-up in the field

navigation tool to quickly locate the output that should be provided in response to the user's input. The wizard also controlled a primitive Andersen animation on the user's screen, making wizard output multimodal. Two wizards took turns in recording around 500 conversations over 2 weeks. Since one wizard was female, voice distortion was used to render her voice indistinguishable from a male voice. Users were museum visitors who could use the system freely during their visit.

Figure 12.3 shows what a wizard's system model may look like, i.e. a hyperlinked html representation of a spoken dialogue system model fragment (mostly in Danish) facilitating wizard navigation. The model was used for development and evaluation of an FAQ (frequently asked questions) system on holiday allowance regulations and rules which most Danes must deal with (Section 3.4.3) (Dybkjær and Dybkjær 2004). The model backbone is a large number of so-called stories to be given in reply to a user's input. A story either asks a question to find out more about what the user wants or replies directly to a user question. The story shown is of the former kind, asking whether the user wants information about small amounts of money or about errors related to the amount of money paid. Most of the snippet shown deals with how to handle possible problems with the user's input.

Figure 12.4 shows a WOZ tool, DialogDesigner (Dybkjær and Dybkjær 2005), that supports navigation in a spoken dialogue model by showing the next possible transitions (bottom, left) that the wizard must choose among in the context of the user's *Input* (middle, left). When a transition has been selected, the corresponding system *Prompt* is shown in the text field above *Input*. The log on the right shows interaction so far. The tool has been used in development and evaluation of commercial spoken dialogue systems. The pizza ordering example shown was made for illustration only.

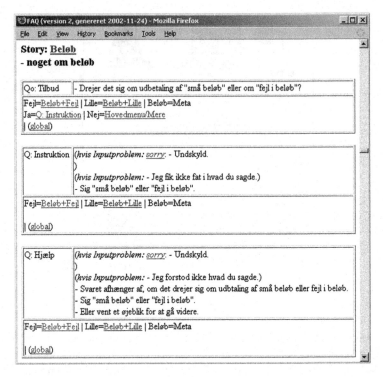

**Fig. 12.3**  Part of a system model used for WOZ simulation

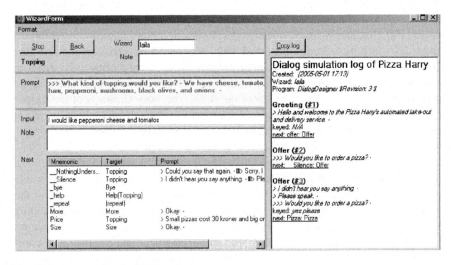

**Fig. 12.4**  An example of a WOZ tool

## 12.3 Implemented Prototype Lab Test

An implemented prototype (Wikipedia 2009) is an experimental model of the target system or parts of it. The prototype may be one of several milestone system versions and may be used, among other things, to explore the feasibility of a planned system, evaluate its usability or collect data for development purposes. In a lab test, the prototype is typically exposed to controlled and systematic testing of some or all of its present capabilities.

*When can you use the method and what is its scope?* A prototype may be implemented early in the life cycle in order to explore technical feasibility. Typically, these prototypes only implement parts of interest to feasibility, and they must be as fast and cheap as possible to produce. There need not be any user–system interaction involved, and we shall not discuss them further.

Horizontal or vertical implemented prototypes may be used in the design phase. A *horizontal* prototype has broad interface coverage but may have little functionality in place below the interface. A *vertical* prototype contains only a limited part of the interface, which, however, can be tested in depth (Nielsen 1993).

Full-scale implemented prototypes implement a detailed design, including interface and functionality, and are typically used in the middle and late project stages. Like WOZ-simulated systems (Section 12.2), an implemented prototype lab test may also be used in "exported lab environments", where sessions are conducted in, e.g. a car or at a shipyard but still under controlled lab-like conditions in which we decide when the interaction takes place and what subjects should do.

An implemented prototype is a very useful instrument for collecting usability data. Several new input/output modality combinations are not easily subjected to mock-up (Section 12.1) testing but require fast real-time interaction. And even the WOZ method (Section 12.2) has limitations that can only be overcome through implemented prototype testing. These points make implemented prototypes even more important for advanced multimodal system development. Moreover, implemented prototype lab tests can be carried out long before the system is fully implemented and stable enough to be made available for a field test.

*Multimodal significance.* No matter whether a system is GUI-based or multimodal, its usability will benefit from implemented prototype evaluation. Still, we believe, there is a clear tendency for advanced multimodal system projects to require more lab tests and make more use of iterative testing than do standard GUI projects. This implies that the implemented prototype method has a bias towards multimodal usability development, cf. Factors 1, 5 and 6 in Section 6.2.2, i.e. the *nature of the user–system interface*, the *kind of data* to be collected with users and general *lack of knowledge*, respectively. Regarding our Cases (Section 2.1), implemented prototype lab tests have been done for two of them and is planned for the third as well. We present results of testing the implemented Sudoku prototype in Chapter 17 (Intermezzo 5).

*How does the method work?* Typically, target users or a representative user group interact with the implemented prototype in the controlled lab environment of use, and interaction is based on carefully created scenarios designed to systematically expose all main aspects of the current system version to user interaction. This emphasis on control and systematicity – which may be more or less, cf. Section 13.1 – is common to all methods in this chapter except field tests (Section 12.4) in which users always decide for themselves which tasks or activities to carry out with the system and in which environment of use. Strictly speaking, the lab is not a necessary condition for having controlled and systematic test conditions, since these conditions can also be established outside the lab. In these cases, we speak about "an exported lab test".

Subjects may interact with the prototype alone or in the presence of others. For example, an observer may be present in the same room as the subject or – preferably – behind a one-way mirror (Section 10.4).

Note that prototypes also enable collection of data on users' interaction with hardware interfaces.

*What is required for applying the method?* An implemented system model, target users or a representative user group (Section 3.3.1), an experimenter, maybe an observer (Section 10.4), typically scenarios, recording equipment, typically logging facilities, any hardware devices needed for interaction with the system model.

*System/AMITUDE model.* An implemented version of the system model must be available, so that the user can interact with it and get a real impression of functionality and usability of at least part of the system.

*Planning.* Make a usability method plan based on items described in Section 6.4. Start from the purpose of collecting usability data (Section 6.4.2). Use the purpose to guide scenario creation and scripting of how the session will proceed (Section 6.4.3).

Planning of an implemented prototype lab session involves a number of standard steps described in Sections 13.2 and 13.3 on session preparation, including, e.g. subject recruitment. Note that implemented prototype testing in the lab is often used in combination with other methods such as screening, pre-test and post-test questioning (Sections 8.6, 8.7 and 8.8) and observation of users (Section 10.4). Subject recruitment is shared among methods in a cluster, while most other preparations must be done individually per method.

Careful scenario creation makes it possible to ensure that all parts of the system, those of special interest or those implemented, will be tested systematically.

*Running.* Section 13.4 explains issues to be aware of during implemented prototype sessions.

*Data.* Data from subjects' interaction with an implemented prototype in the lab comprises audio and video recordings of user input behaviour and system output and logfiles from system components. Often data from lab prototype testing forms part of a larger set of test data resources that should be analysed as a whole. See also Chapters 15 and 16 on data handling and analysis.

*Advantages and drawbacks.* The unique advantage of implemented prototype lab tests is that they enable collection of usability data on all aspects of system model design. In advanced multimodal system development, the first prototype lab test may be the first time ever that anything remotely like the current system has met real people. A running prototype is more effective, and even mandatory, for revealing certain usability problems compared to, e.g. a mock-up (Section 12.1) or a WOZ simulation (Section 12.2). Interaction brings the user face-to-face with the real look-sound-and-feel of the system and yields real system data rather than data on wizard behaviour.

The main limitation of this method – even in an exported lab environment – is the reverse of its controlled and systematic nature: we don't get to see what users would use the system for when given full control of it outside the lab. Users in the lab are under a sort of contract to do as they are told, and that quite often means a lot of acting and pretence: pretending to want to book a flight, pretending to want to know about Hans Christian Andersen's life, etc., all of which affects the reliability of the collected data in sometimes inscrutable ways.

Some collected data may only inadequately reflect properties of the final system. Almost by definition, a prototype is not a final system in the sense of fully possessing all the properties the final system is intended to have. This may not be an issue of components. The prototype may well possess all the components of the final system. However, it may still have, e.g. less knowledge than the final system, for instance, because it's a research prototype and there is no interesting research involved in providing the system with all the knowledge required to serve its purpose. This may mean that, while the prototype performs acceptably, the final system, if it were to be built, might still turn out to cause problems, e.g. because it has become unacceptably slow or does not scale up as expected in other respects. Thus, it is important to consider how missing or limited properties of the prototype might affect the results produced with the final system.

Having implemented a prototype, it is tempting not to throw away code that turned out not to be too good in the light of the usability evaluation made. However, it pays off to throw away bad code rather than trying to reuse it. Bad code often causes many problems later on.

**Fig. 12.5** An implemented prototype of a multimodal edutainment system

*Example: Implemented prototype.* Figure 12.5 shows a user interacting with the second and final implemented prototype of the Hans Christian Andersen system developed in the European NICE project 2001–2004. The primary target users, children and adolescents, visit the author in his study to have spoken conversation about his life, fairytales, person and study and use 2D haptic pointing gesture to indicate visible objects they want to hear stories about (Bernsen and Dybkjær 2005).

## 12.4  Field Test

A field test takes place in the target environment of use and with target users who decide for themselves when to use the system and what for. This implies considerable variation in our possibilities for collecting data and contacting users. Field tests serve in general to collect usability data on real-life system use for evaluation purposes or otherwise.

*When can you use the method and what is its scope?* Typically, field tests are carried out late in the life cycle when the system model is fully implemented, has been tested in the lab and is expected to be close to final. This notwithstanding, it *is* possible to carry out, e.g. WOZ simulations in the field as well, as we did for the Hans Christian Andersen system, cf. the example in Fig. 12.2.

Any system that is sufficiently mature can be field tested. Field testing is often a step towards commercialisation, and alpha and beta testing are, in fact, kinds of field testing. Even research systems are sometimes field tested, but many are not because they lack technical maturity or other necessary qualities.

*Multimodal significance.* A field test requires the system to be sufficiently mature and robust to endure real users. Since many research systems fail to reach a realistic field-testing stage before the project ends, the method is currently of limited use for multimodal systems due to Factors 1 and 3 in Section 6.2.2, i.e. the *nature of the user–system interface* and *technology penetration*. However, field testing must be expected to gain very much in importance as multimodal systems mature. Note that the method may be difficult or impractical if special, hard to get or install or expensive software or devices are required in multiple installations.

Since all our Case systems (Section 2.1) use such software or hardware, special precautions would have to be taken to field test them. Sudoku should be installed at some public location where many visitors could be expected to use it. The Treasure Hunt system might be installed at an institution for the blind and for the deaf mute where many potential users will be around. The haptic device used by the blind is expensive, which puts certain restrictions on the number of installations and on the locations at which the system can be safely set up. Maths field testing would probably require field testing over several weeks or even months in at least some 10–20 individual homes and maybe in schools as well.

*How does the method work?* A field test is carried out in an uncontrolled environment, which may be at home, at work, in a museum, in a hospital, at a kiosk, on a ship or anywhere else. We may or may not know where the system is being used and we may or may not know who the users are. The system may be installed on users' own computers, mobile phones or otherwise, on computers belonging to, e.g. a railway company or a museum or accessed over telephone or Internet and run on a server somewhere, and users are completely free to decide what they want to use the system for, how to interact with it, when, etc. This means, on the one hand, that we have no control over which system properties are being tested; on the other, we get to collect data on real tasks or other activities that someone wants or needs to do, which they are, how they are being done, when, how often, etc.

So the crucial issue in any field test is to collect data on system use, no matter the circumstances, which means that we must determine what are the possibilities in a given context, cf. the discussion under *Planning* below.

Field tests may have few or many users, take weeks or months and generate corresponding amounts of data. Contrary to a lab test (Sections 12.1, 12.2, 12.3 and 12.5), it may be impossible to ensure a representative user population. This problem may sometimes be compensated for by having a large number of users. Getting detailed information about users is often infeasible.

*What is required for applying the method?* A system model, target users, possibly logging, possibly tracking and recording equipment.

*System/AMITUDE model.* Typically, the system model is fully implemented and near-final. It must be so robust that users rarely need technical support.

*Planning.* Make a usability method plan based on items described in Section 6.4. Start from the purpose of collecting usability data (Section 6.4.2). Use the purpose to decide on the data to collect and how to collect it (Section 6.4.3). It is difficult to give general advice on how to operationalise data collection due to the broad diversity of field test contexts. In the following, we address issues that are relevant in some, or most, field tests, but you must decide yourself if and how they apply to your case.

If logging of system component interaction and system output is possible, do it because logfile data is good at revealing, in particular, usability information on technical quality and ease of use (Section 1.4.6). Logging may not work if you make the system available on the Internet free for download, because you will most likely have no chance to get hold of any logfiles. Also, if you are using WOZ, there is often nothing to log.

User input is also desirable if at all possible. Screen tracking software may help record what the user is doing on the screen. Audio recording of spoken interaction should be made, no matter if interaction is done over the phone or directly in front of the system. Without a recording of what the user actually said, as opposed to what was logged as speech recogniser output, there is no way to judge what the user said when analysing the data. This point seems valid for a large class of input processing technologies and seems to imply that, whichever the signals produced by the user, these signals should be recorded if at all possible. Thus, if we do a field test with image processing components, we need a video record of the input.

As for logfile creation, input recording makes sense only if we can get access to the files produced. In many cases this *is* possible – at least if there is not a problem in getting permission to make recordings. For example, we can get access to logfiles and recordings if the system is installed in an exhibition room or in a stationary place at work or at home, and we have either direct access to the computers or have an agreement with a system administrator or similar to extract logfiles and recordings and send them to us, cf. the example below. Difficult cases include, e.g. software made available for free on the Internet, and mobile applications also typically make video recording hard.

If you have access to communicate with users, like when developing an application for an organisation, you may ask users to report by e-mail any usability issues they come across or you may do a survey (Section 8.3) after they have used the system for some time. You may also have a chance to briefly interview users, e.g. if your system is installed at an exhibition or in some other public place where people come and where you can contact them after they have tried the system.

If you don't know the users and have no direct contact with them, you can ask them for an anonymous evaluation of the system. This can be done with telephone-based systems and systems made available on the Internet. You can also direct users' attention to a web-based questionnaire (Section 8.2) or leave questionnaire handouts next to, e.g. a kiosk. A web-based forum is yet another possibility where users can discuss your software and exchange experiences.

It is important to check the needs and possibilities for collecting data and any legal issues involved before running the field test. Be aware that you are not necessarily permitted to record dialogues or video record users without their knowledge, and if you have to tell them, unobtrusiveness is gone and you move closer to a kind of lab test.

If the system is not walk-up-and-use, you must ensure that user guide material or a manual can be made available to users when the test starts, e.g. online.

Test users may be found in various ways. If the system is, e.g. an over-the-phone system for customers, you install it on a server in the organisation that is going to use it and wait for users to call. You do not explicitly recruit them. Similarly, if you have developed some kind of kiosk intended for use by tourists, you put it up at, e.g. railway stations, central city squares or museums, depending on what you are allowed to do and what seems most relevant, and then you wait for users to show up and deliver data all by themselves. In other cases, you may have to explicitly recruit users and make sure that they have the system installed. In yet other cases, you make the software available for download on a web site and advertise it. It is then up to those who want to use it to download and install it.

*Running.* Make sure that the system is installed and runs properly on the equipment to be used during the field test or that it is made available for download and duly advertised. In some field tests, it is not someone from the development team who installs the system but someone at the user's or customer's site. However, it is still up to *you* to make sure that everything is working correctly, e.g. via remote access. You want field test data, not explanations why the field test failed.

If possible, frequently monitor all installed copies throughout the test to make sure that everything works fine and to collect the data produced so far. If the system has crashed or the tracking, logging or recording equipment has stopped working, you won't benefit much from the test because the data is gone.

If you run a forum, you may have to answer questions and otherwise provide feedback.

*Data.* A field test may provide various kinds of data, including logfiles, tracking data, audio and/or video recordings, incident reports or anonymous comments. Depending on the details we are interested in, we may have to annotate (part of) the data. If data is collected via other methods, such as interviews or questionnaires, this data should be analysed together with the rest of the test data. In all cases, focus of analysis is to find out if the system has weaknesses that must be looked into. See also Chapters 15 and 16 on data handling and analysis.

*Advantages and drawbacks.* A field test provides valuable data on how real users interact with the system in real life when carrying out tasks or activities of their own choice or which they need to carry out at work. Depending on the type of application, field testing may also provide information on how system software and hardware is being handled in the field (e.g. at a customer organisation), problems encountered in supporting proper running of the system in the field, user motivation and preferences and much more.

Field tests provide information that cannot be obtained in other ways, such as in an implemented prototype lab test with a representative user group (Section 12.3). Lab tests create artificial motivation for subjects to interact with the system, no matter if scenarios are used or not. Whatever the motivation of each subject might be in other respects, the baseline is that the subject has agreed to go to the lab and take part in a system test. The subject goes as promised, but the system being tested most often has no role in the subject's life. Subjects don't need, e.g. the flight tickets they book with the flight booking system they are testing, and they therefore basically don't care if, e.g. the tickets are valid for one day or another. They don't die or hurt other people if the simulated car they are driving crashes because they pay too much attention to the complex multimodal navigation system being tested, and they know it! To see how users with real motivation behave, we need a field test in which users use the system because it promises to do for them what they want it to do or what their work requires them to do.

In some cases, target users are actually not asked whether they would like to participate in a field test. They participate because the organisation for which they work installs the system on their computers. In other cases, people have a choice. Note that people who volunteer to participate in a field test often do so because they are interested in using the system for their own purposes, which is one of the reasons why a group of field test users is not necessarily representative of the target user population as a whole. The technology freak will jump to participate but this is not necessarily the case with other target users. Sometimes people other than the enthusiasts can be tempted to participate, e.g. by being offered to call the system at a reduced fee compared to using a human-operated service or by being offered a faster service by skipping the queue to human-operated service.

Unless very substantial amounts of data is collected, field testing often fails to deliver an all-round test of the system. Some parts of system functionality will be used quite frequently whereas others will be used rarely, if at all. Therefore, a field test cannot replace lab tests or other scenario-based test methods that allow us to expose any part of system functionality to user interaction or inspection. Another thing to be prepared for is that even quite small field tests may generate large amounts of data for analysis.

*Example: Field test of a pronunciation trainer.* Figure 12.6 shows a screenshot of the Danish Pronunciation Trainer (DPT), which was field tested at nine training sites – language schools and others – across Denmark during 4–5 months in 2004–2005 (Bernsen et al. 2006). The DPT is a tutoring application for language skills self-training. For such applications, usability testing actually involves two distinct tasks. One is to evaluate the user interface and user–system interaction, the other is to evaluate students' learning progress with the system. A learning progress evaluation exercise takes time because many students have to use the system for a longer period of time in order to collect data enabling assessment of their progress in learning whatever the system is teaching them. This is often hard to do in the lab for practical resource reasons of space, staff time, etc. In many cases, field testing is the only solution. Some of the lessons learned during the field test of the DPT illustrate aspects of field testing more generally.

Field test support is a challenge. The system was supposed to be kept running at nine training sites by local support staff who, in turn, were supported by us through an installation package, documentation, telephone, e-mails and visits to the four sites closest to NISLab. Local staff also had to send us the training logfiles produced. It turned out that only the four sites which received regular visits by us actually produced logfiles, which could be used for assessing student progress. The more remote sites either did not send any logfiles or sent too few logfiles for progress evaluation purposes.

Field users are really out of your control. A total of 88 students used the DPT, producing 800+ logfiles. Of these, 22 students produced a sufficient number of logfiles

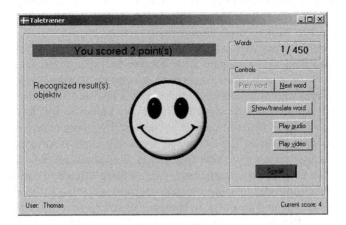

**Fig. 12.6** Screenshot of the Danish Pronunciation Trainer

for enabling progress evaluation. We never met the students, we had no opportunity to observe them during training, and we had little idea of how, if at all, they were being motivated to train with the DPT at each individual site. These conditions are very much like those of a commercial system which someone just gets hold of and uses out there.

The data is valuable. Despite the problems and conditions just described, analysis of the DPT field trial data provided rather convincing evidence that the system actually succeeds in improving the language pronunciation skills of adult foreigners trying to acquire a second language (Bernsen et al. 2006).

## 12.5 Think-Aloud

The idea of the think-aloud method (Dumas and Redish 1999, Hom 1998, NIAR 2004, Rubin 1994, Sharp et al. 2007, van Someren et al. 1994) is to have subjects speak what's on their minds during interaction, opening a "window" into the workings of each user's mind. Thus, instead of having to try to infer the interacting user's real-time mental processes from the non-verbal behaviour we can observe anyway, we ask the user to explicitly report what's going on.

*When can you use the method and what is its scope?* The think-aloud method requires a system model with which the user can interact. This model may be everything from an early mock-up to a close-to-final system. Thus, think-aloud can be used from quite early in the life cycle and onwards.

As for the method's scope, there are pretty strong limitations due to the interactive modalities involved. Since these limitations are complex, we can only highlight some main limitations and refer to good modality thinking for the rest, cf. Chapter 4. Since subjects need time to be able to carry out the interaction *and* speak about it, think-aloud works only with relatively slow and deliberate interaction. It's hardly suitable for, e.g. participants in a real-time virtual boxing match. Moreover, since thinking aloud is a form of natural human communication that involves the entire class of communication modalities associated with speaking, the method is incompatible with human–system interaction that involves the same class of modalities. The same applies if spoken think-aloud is replaced by sign language think-"aloud": it is hardly feasible to have gesture interaction with the system and think-"aloud" through sign language at the same time.

Think-aloud works for standard GUI-based interaction because of the static graphics output and the self-paced haptic input and works equally well if the graphics output is replaced or augmented by static haptics. Both the graphics and the haptics may, in fact, be dynamic as long as change is not too fast for thinking aloud during interaction. But then, again, don't expect users to speak aloud about other things when contemplating and executing handwriting or typing input, because those are linguistic modalities, and so is thinking aloud, and people aren't very good at producing two independent strands of linguistic representation in parallel.

Also, we suggest caution when considering to use think-aloud during interaction which requires the subject to spend significant attentional resources on highly

dynamic external tasks and events, such as real-traffic car driving, while interacting
with the system that is being evaluated. This may endanger safe driving, which is
already being challenged because the subject has to interact with some in-car system
while driving.

If the use environment is noisy, recording the subject speaking aloud may pose
technical problems but these can often be resolved.

*Multimodal significance.* Think-aloud works best when the user has time to deliberate between making information exchanges with the system, as in ordinary GUI or
static 3D haptic interaction. Thus, the method is affected by differentiation Factor 1,
i.e. the *nature of the user–system interface*, cf. Section 6.2.2.

Among our Cases (Section 2.1), both Maths and Sudoku have spoken interaction
in a key role, which means that think-aloud cannot be used. The blind user's interaction with the Treasure Hunt system, on the other hand, would be an excellent target
for applying think-aloud.

*How does the method work?* Think-aloud has its roots in experimental psychology and is a particular way for subjects to interact with the system model. The
user spontaneously thinks aloud during interaction, i.e. expresses in speech (or sign
language) what s/he is doing, trying, expecting, thinking, does not understand, emotional reactions, etc. The experimenter prompts the user if the user stops thinking
aloud. The application permitting, two users may be asked to interact with the system together. This often creates a more natural setting for thinking aloud because
the users simply communicate about how to solve the scenarios through interaction.
The method helps reveal problems encountered during interaction as well as how
users think about these problems and interaction more generally. It is the job of
the experimenter or the observer to make notes on anything of interest during the
session, including any preliminary conclusions.

*What is required for applying the method?* A system model whose modalities
are not incompatible with thinking aloud, target users or a representative user group
(Section 3.3.1), one or two users at a time, an experimenter, preferably an observer
(Section 10.4), warm-up material, scenarios, audio or video recording equipment.

*System/AMITUDE model.* The system model may be at any stage of development
ranging from an early mock-up to a fully implemented prototype.

*Planning.* Make a usability method plan based on items described in Section
6.4. Use modality analysis to assess if think-aloud is compatible with the modalities
used. Then start from the purpose of collecting usability data (Section 6.4.2). Use
the purpose to guide scenario creation and scripting of how the session will proceed
(Section 6.4.3).

Planning of a think-aloud session involves a number of standard steps described
in Sections 13.2 and 13.3 on session preparation, including, e.g. subject recruitment. Note that think-aloud testing is often used in combination with other methods
such as screening, pre-test and post-test questioning (Sections 8.6, 8.7 and 8.8) and
observation of users (Section 10.4). Subject recruitment is shared among methods
in a cluster, while most other preparations must be done individually per method.

Think about and, possibly, write down what to say to the subjects by way of introducing the method and prepare some warm-up exercises in addition to the scenarios

to be used. Thinking aloud, especially in its monologue (single-subject) variety, is not something most people are accustomed to doing. Most people *can* do it, however, once they are in the appropriate mindset. Remember to include time for the warm-up exercises in the session schedule.

*Running*. Make subjects feel comfortable and at ease. Nervous or stressed people are not good at thinking aloud, and people may feel embarrassed if they don't know how to solve a task which they feel they should be able to solve. Therefore, an atmosphere of confidence and trust is very important. Remember to offer subjects something to drink. A think-aloud session may take quite some time and be hard on the voice.

Start by explaining what is going to happen and what is expected. Give subjects a warm-up task so that you can demonstrate the method. Encourage them to ask any questions during the warm-up and explain that questions should not be asked during the session proper. Continue warming up until you are fully satisfied that the subject has understood that you are interested in everything to do with his/her way of solving tasks or doing other interactive activities, feels that it is feasible and okay to think aloud and is ready to start. This may easily take 15 minutes.

The experimenter should interfere as little as possible with the user's thought processes to avoid influencing them. Provide continuation feedback (like yes, OK, hmm) to show that you are listening. Don't interrupt if the user makes an error. If there is something you don't understand, make a note and clarify the issue right after the session. If, which often happens, you need to prompt a user who has stopped talking, often without noticing, you should *not* say, e.g. "tell me what you think" because this may be perceived as if you are asking for an opinion. Say, rather, "try to say everything that goes through your mind" or "keep on talking".

Note that expert users may have difficulty expressing why they do what they do. This may be because they don't want to share their knowledge or because they try to simplify things for the (wrongly assumed) benefit of the experimenter. More likely it's because much of what they do are automated skill-based actions which they are not used to thinking about any more. Once we have learned to ride a bicycle, we don't think about how we do it and find it hard to explain to others. It is easier to get verbal information from subjects who have not automated the problem-solving process and have to think hard about what they do.

*Data*. Data from a think-aloud session comprises any notes made and recordings of what the subject said and, if on video, did. Often data from a think-aloud test forms part of a larger set of test data resources that should be analysed as a whole. In particular, observation notes are often tightly integrated with the think-aloud data. Thus, if you transcribe the recordings (Section 15.5.3), it's a good idea to insert observation notes and any video-based observations along with what was said, e.g. "subject frowns, looks lost". Observations should be clearly marked so as not to be confused with the transcription. Interpretations are part of the subsequent data analysis. If you add interpretations to transcriptions and observations, they should be clearly marked as interpretations. See also Chapters 15 and 16 on data handling and analysis.

*Advantages and drawbacks.* Within its modality-dependent limitations, think-aloud offers a fantastic opportunity to look directly into the minds of interacting users. The method is fairly cheap, provides valuable data on user performance and users' assumptions, inferences, preferences, expectations, frustrations, etc. and informs about misunderstandings and confusing issues that cause errors or problems. We get data on users' mental models of the system (Payne 2003) and how they pursue the goals of interaction. This helps understand the actual reasons why users experience problems with the system. When developers try to solve the problems experienced by users, it can be a great advantage to know the central processing aspects of what triggered them.

Think-aloud data never fully represents a user's central processes, cognition, conation, emotion and all (Section 3.3), and its reliability is not beyond doubt either. Most of us find it somewhat unnatural to think aloud, and it can be exhausting to do for an extended period of time. Subjects forget to think aloud from time to time and must be prompted by the experimenter. Verbalisation takes time and competes with the mental resources dedicated to user–system interaction. Some people are very good at expressing themselves and describing a process, while others are less apt at this kind of verbalisation. The quality of the data depends on how good the subject is at verbalising the process. Children are generally not very good at thinking aloud. Moreover, the unnaturalness of the situation might make the subject behave differently from what this person would otherwise do when solving the same scenarios with the same system. Despite these drawbacks, think-aloud is a useful method when used within its scope of application as described above.

**Fig. 12.7** iPhone clock screen (world clock). The + at the top enables addition of a city name

| Transcription | Observation notes and analysis |
|---|---|
| | User looks at start page |
| What happens if I press the clock | One of the icons shows a clock. The user selects it and gets the "clock screen" |
| Start ... world clock it says at the bottom | |
| and Washington DC | Copenhagen and Washington DC are shown |
| It's not right here | |
| Ehmm which other options are there | Looks at the bottom of the screen again |
| Today ... press Washington ... nothing much happens | |
| I can add something | Has found the + (top right) |
| Yes, and if I now write Chicago here | |
| C – H – I – C – A – G – O | The user spells |
| Chocago ... how do you delete | |
| Well it is probably faster just to delete it | Does not find a way to delete the wrong o. Deletes all |
| Chicago ... here it comes | Having entered the first few letters, Chicago shows up on the menu among other options. The user selects it so that it appears on the same list as the original Copenhagen and Washington DC choices |
| There ... it is 9.54 today ... 9.55 | |
| In Copenhagen it is 16.55 and in Chicago it is now 9.55 | |
| It must mean that they are 7 hours behind us | |

**Fig. 12.8** Transcribed think-aloud protocol (*left*) with observation notes and analysis (*right*) (translated from Danish)

*Example: Transcription from a warm-up exercise with observer's notes.* Figure 12.7 shows an iPhone screenshot from a think-aloud exercise where the (Danish) user's task was to use an iPhone to find out what time it was in Chicago. Figure 12.8 shows the transcription (left) from the exercise. Observation notes and other comments are added to the right, facilitating, together with Fig. 12.7, understanding of what is going on.

# References

Bernsen NO, Dybkjær H, Dybkjær L (1998) Designing interactive speech systems. From first ideas to user testing. Springer Verlag, Heidelberg.
Bernsen NO, Dybkjær L (2005) Meet Hans Christian Andersen. Proceedings of the 6th SIGdial workshop on discourse and dialogue. Lisbon, Portugal: 237–241.
Bernsen NO, Dybkjær L, Kiilerich S (2004) Evaluating conversation with Hans Christian Andersen. Proceedings of LREC 3: 1011–1014. Lisbon, Portugal.
Bernsen NO, Hansen TK, Kiilerich S, Madsen TK (2006) Field evaluation of a single-word pronunciation training system. Proceedings of LREC, Genova, Italy: 2068–2073.

Dumas, JS, Redish, JC (1999) A practical guide to usability testing. Rev edn, Intellect Books.

Dybkjær H, Dybkjær L (2004) Modeling complex spoken dialog. IEEE Computer August, 32–40.

Dybkjær H, Dybkjær L (2005) DialogDesigner – a tool for rapid system design and evaluation. Proceedings of 6th SIGdial workshop on discourse and dialogue. Lisbon, Portugal: 227–231.

Fraser NM, Gilbert GN (1991) Simulating speech systems. Computer Speech and Language 5: 81–99.

Hom J (1998) Contextual inquiry. http://jthom.best.vwh.net/usability. Accessed 19 January 2009.

NIAR (2004) Think-aloud protocol. http://www.niar.wichita.edu/humanfactors/toolbox/T_A% 20Protocol.htm. Accessed 24 January 2009.

Nielsen J (1993) Usability engineering. Academic Press, New York.

Nielsen Norman Group (year unknown) Paper prototyping: a how-to training video. http://www.nngroup.com/reports/prototyping. Accessed 22 January 2009.

Payne SJ (2003) Users' mental models: The very idea. In: Carroll JM (ed) HCI models, theories and frameworks. Towards a multidisciplinary science. Morgan Kaufmann, San Francisco.

Rubin J (1994) Handbook of usability testing. John Wiley and Sons, New York.

Sefelin R, Tscheligi M, Giller V (2003) Paper prototyping – what is it good for? A comparison of paper- and computer-based low-fidelity prototyping. Proceedings of CHI: 778–779.

Sharp H, Rogers Y, Preece J (2007) Interaction design – beyond human-computer interaction. 2nd edn. John Wiley and Sons, New York.

van Someren MW, Barnard Y, Sandberg J (1994) The think aloud method: a practical guide to modelling cognitive processes. Academic Press, London.

Wikipedia (2008) Paper prototyping. http://en.wikipedia.org/wiki/Paper_prototypes. Accessed 7 February 2009.

Wikipedia (2009) Software prototyping. http://en.wikipedia.org/wiki/Software_prototyping. Accessed 7 February 2009.

# Chapter 13
# Lab Sessions with Subjects

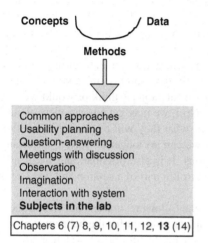

About half of the methods presented in Chapters 8–12 are based on lab sessions with users or subjects. This chapter supports those method presentations and the concrete usability method plans based on them, by describing how to deal with subjects before, during and after lab sessions. Note that lab sessions include supervised sessions that are exported to take place outside the lab in, e.g. a car or a museum. Some of the issues to be described are relevant also to usability methods that are not lab sessions in any sense, which is why so many method descriptions in the previous five chapters refer to the present chapter.

Section 13.1 reviews the methods that are typically applied in a lab setting and discusses the issue of micro-control over the lab session. Section 13.2 describes subject recruitment. Section 13.3 addresses lab session preparation with respect to equipment and materials, such as scenarios and consent forms. Section 13.4 discusses what to do and pay attention to while a lab test is running, from welcoming the subjects over training to help and improvisation. Section 13.5 describes post-session issues of debriefing and keeping in touch.

## 13.1 Lab Test and Development Methods. Micro-Control

Among the usability methods introduced in Section 6.2, 11 are typically applied with users or subjects in a lab setting: pre- and post-test interviews and questionnaires (Chapter 8), focus group meetings, workshops and meetings with users

N.O. Bernsen, L. Dybkjær, *Multimodal Usability*, Human-Computer Interaction
Series, DOI 10.1007/978-1-84882-553-6_13, © Springer-Verlag London Limited 2009

(Chapter 9), category sorting, real-time observation of users, human data collection in the lab (Chapter 10) and mock-ups, Wizard of Oz, implemented prototypes and think-aloud (Chapter 12). Of these, the following seven are primarily *user test methods:* pre-test interviews/questionnaires are used prior to a test, while post-test interviews/questionnaires are used after a test. During a test we may use Wizard of Oz, a mock-up, an implemented prototype and think-aloud and we may add observation of users to any of these. The remaining four methods, i.e. focus group meetings, workshops and meetings with users, category sorting and human data collection in the lab, are primarily *user development methods.* Unless explicitly stated, the issues addressed in the sub-sections of this chapter are applicable to all methods mentioned above.

Before going into detail about how to handle subjects in the lab, it is worth pointing out that most of the above *user lab methods* can be planned and applied with a larger or smaller degree of micro-control, which has important effects on the results of applying a method. Micro-control means planning in detail what will be done and how; less micro-control means leaving more details to subjects during sessions. With tight micro-control, we tend to get exactly the usability information we aim to collect, but we get little information about what subjects think or would want to do if given more leeway. With less micro-control, we may get a better view of subjects' attitudes, what is important to them or what they will do during interaction or otherwise when given some leeway, but we can no longer be sure to cover any specific amount of ground during the sessions. It is also possible, and frequently useful, to do both, i.e. having tight micro-control in part of a session and less so for the rest.

Some examples of tight micro-control are the following: nothing but closed questions in questionnaires or interviews; a complete protocol for the behaviour minutiae to be recorded; a set of scenarios that enable testing of all system parts; an extremely detailed meeting agenda. Examples of less tight control are the following: free brainstorming in a meeting or a workshop; subjects invent categories for sorting a given set of instances, instead of being given pre-defined categories; skeleton scenarios in which subjects are free to invent all necessary details; an all-open-question interview; high-level behaviour descriptions for which subjects must fill in all details.

The degree of micro-control aimed for in a particular lab session should be quite clear from the usability method plan (Section 6.4). In the following, we describe potential method plan issues relating to the fact that the method will be applied in the lab or in lab-like conditions outside the lab, and with target users or with a representative user group (Section 3.3.1). Some of these issues may be needed in plans for other method applications as well, even if no lab(-like) session is involved. We leave it to the reader to extract from this chapter what needs to be done in sessions with non-target users or when applying non-lab methods. To read more detailed accounts of lab tests, see, e.g. Rubin (1994) and Dumas and Redish (1999) from which this chapter has drawn inspiration.

## 13.2  Session Preparation – Subject Recruitment

Subject recruitment is about when, how and where to get the right subjects, how many of them you need and how to interact with them.

### 13.2.1  How to Select Subjects

A group of subjects or users can be composed in at least four different ways:

- all target users;
- a representative group of target users;
- a non-representative group of target users;
- non-target users.

It's fairly rare to have the chance to meet and work with all target users, but it does happen, in particular when the system is being tailor-made for a specific individual or a group of people. When it happens, target users and subjects become perfectly identical. Otherwise, there are three choices left.

The first choice is to use representative user groups  (Section 3.3.1) as much as possible and unless there are good reasons not to, because this yields the most reliable usability data. This is what we did – or tried to do – for the Sudoku Case (Chapter 17). Target users having different skills, backgrounds, age, gender, etc. may have quite different attitudes and conduct tasks or other activities with the same system in very different ways.

The second choice is to have just any group of target users, e.g. because the system, like Treasure Hunt (Section 5.1), is at such an early stage that a group of target users is good enough for finding a first batch of major usability problems or because it isn't possible to compose a representative user group yet.

The third, most questionable and sometimes most tempting, choice is to collect usability data with just any bunch of available people, such as university students or colleagues. University students have lots of good properties, being typically bright, curious, energetic, reasonably computer literate, easy to contact and persuade to participate – but often belonging to the target user group is *not* one of them. The same applies to our colleagues. It is not a good idea to have university students test a system for elderly people in their homes. Somewhat more generally speaking, university students and colleagues should primarily be used in two ways. First, for quick testing of system parts rather than full, integrated systems. It is often a highly repetitive process to test and revise system components, such as speech recognisers or image processing software. Second, they are helpful in all sorts of preparatory work, such as test driving an evaluation set-up before the real subjects arrive, testing an exploratory system concept which doesn't have a target user profile yet, first-time testing the system outside the development team.

To select target users, or a representative group of them, you must first do user profile analysis, cf. Section 3.3.6, and then possibly screen potential subjects, cf. Section 8.6. Remember that there may be several target user groups.


## 13.2.2 *Number of Subjects*

How many subjects to enrol for a development or evaluation session depends on, among other things, the following:

- how *reliable* results on usability should be: in general, the higher the reliability required, the more users are needed. Note that this is not true for meetings and workshops;
- how many *resources* are available for planning and executing the method and analysing the collected data: as a rule, the more resources you have, the more subjects you can afford to recruit. Note that this does not hold for meetings and workshops: having more participants doesn't imply more data (minutes);
- how *easy* it is to find suitable subjects willing, or allowed, to participate;
- session *duration*: if each subject generates roughly the same amount of data, as is the case with most lab methods mentioned in Section 13.1 apart from the two meeting methods, and if sessions are long, you may want fewer subjects than if sessions are brief, in order not to generate too large amounts of data for analysis;
- session *preparation*: if preparations are heavy on resources, it is preferable to collect data with more than just a couple of subjects, unless sessions are exceedingly long. The value of the data collected must be in some reasonable correspondence with the value of the time invested in preparations;
- if *statistically significant* results are needed: in general, this takes a considerable number of users to achieve and is irrelevant for meetings and workshops;
- if you are making a *comparative* study and need subjects for two (or more) different test conditions.


A guess would be that the number of subjects involved in most usability development and evaluation sessions range from 4 to 15. It is costly to involve subjects in larger numbers on an individual basis because of the time spent on them before and during the session as well as during data analysis, and meetings involving many users soon become unwieldy and unproductive. There is often a risk of diminishing returns, such as when a test with 12 subjects might identify 90% of the usability issues raised by the system model, whereas a test with 24 subjects might raise the percentage to only, say, 95%. It is therefore preferable to run several tests with fewer users and some development time in-between, rather than running a single large test. Three tests with four users each typically give more value for money than does a single test with 12 users (Nielsen 1993).

Still, more data produced on an individual basis by a representative user group is always better data. Professional data collection for component training sometimes requires several hundreds of subjects.

### 13.2.3  Where to Get Subjects

Where to find subjects depends entirely on the specified user profile. It is often necessary to be smart in order to recruit subjects corresponding to every wrinkle in that profile. Some approaches to consider are to contact or use the following:

- organisations for which the system is being developed;
- personal networks of the developers and other colleagues at work. Someone just might have a relative who is male, more than 50 years old, speaks the dialect spoken in Region X, Country Y, lives within commuting distance from the lab and is willing to participate;
- sports clubs and similar organisations inside which a call for subjects spreads efficiently through word of mouth. Age range may not be a problem – we once recruited a 76-year-old lady who was still active in a track-and-field club;
- professional organisations for target users, such as the hard of hearing;
- schools of all kinds, from pre-school through universities to lifelong learning;
- adverts at one's organisation's web site;
- publications – internal, newspapers, radio, TV and other media – that might publish on the project. It is often easy to sneak in a call for subjects into the journalist's copy, complete with web address, phone number, e-mail and all;
- public places like shopping malls, trains.

If none of this is useful, if all fails or nothing works within the time frame, you may have to consider advertising or using a recruitment agency. Depending on the number and profiles of the subjects, identifying potential subjects may take weeks or months and require numerous phone calls, e-mails, explanations, etc. Remember that company users spend company time participating and need acceptance from their boss.

### 13.2.4  Information for Initial Subject Contact

Initial and subsequent contacts with subjects may take many different forms, such as over the phone and in writing throughout (you never actually meet them); initial contact via a web site for signing up, followed by subjects showing up for screening or for the development or evaluation session itself; screening done over the web. In all cases, you need to inform them, at initial contact time, on what the session is about, what they are expected to do, etc. No matter whether the information will be conveyed orally or in writing, it is a good idea to write it down. This ensures that everyone is told the same story, facilitates iteration and improvement on what to tell and is good to have next time a similar kind of session is up. Consider to include at least the following kinds of information:

- for a development session: what will the subject be expected to do and why is this subject important;
- for an evaluation session: what kind of system will be tested, what will the subject be expected to do and why is this test person important;
- in which environment will the session take place (what should the user expect);
- duration of the session;
- phone number to call if the session is telephone-based, for cancellation or if the subject is delayed;
- e-mail and web site address: many subjects use e-mail, many will be curious to know more about your organisation and its work; and the web site may play various useful roles in working with subjects;
- address: if the user has to go to the lab, general openness;
- date and time of the session;
- what does the user get in return (if anything).

This, of course, is a minimum that assumes that subjects will be given additional information later on, such as on data confidentiality. Many subjects are curious and exited about participating, so if there is additional material, intelligible to them, on system and development goals, by all means include it unless there is a priming risk (Section 6.4.4).

Figure 13.1 shows a snail-mail letter sent to company users after their test participation had been agreed over the phone. The system model was a WOZ simulation (Section 12.2) of a telephone-based spoken dialogue flight booking system (Bernsen et al. 1998), see also Section 3.4.2. Thus, users did not have to come to the lab but conducted this "exported lab test" over the phone. This is a one-shot communication to subjects, which aims to tell them all they need to know in order to feel confident and informed when participating in the test. Note that, in this case, no rewards were dangled in front of the users. We were nicking company time.

The leaflet mentioned in Fig. 13.1 describes the flight reservation system and shows an example dialogue. We gave subjects this information because we believed that we had to tell them something about the system and what to expect. Talking to a computer over the phone was not a familiar thing to do in the early 1990s. In retrospect, the inclusion of an example was clearly an error. The system was intended to be walk-up-and-use, so people should be able to use it without having seen any examples. Furthermore, the example may have had a priming effect on those subjects who actually read the leaflet in advance.

### 13.2.5  Will All Subjects Show Up?

Don't forget that, despite their enthusiasm for trying the system or otherwise participating in a session, subjects have other obligations. Their calendars might be quite full, and it is necessary to make appointments well in advance of the session date,

---

**Introduction letter to subjects**

Dear NN,

Thank you very much for agreeing to spend your time on helping us test our system.

I enclose

- a leaflet describing the reservation system you are going to use;
- four tasks which we ask you to solve by calling the system;
- a questionnaire which we ask you to fill and return in the enclosed envelope after your interaction with the system.

It would be an advantage if you look at the enclosed before carrying out the tasks.

The purpose of the test is to collect data that will serve two purposes: (i) it will help us evaluate how well our reservation system works, in particular regarding the user interface, i.e. the dialogue between you and the system, and (ii) it will provide a basis for improving the system.

Your dialogues with the system will be recorded on tape so that we can analyse them to find the weaknesses of the system and try to make improvements. After the test, all references that may identify you will be deleted from the data in order to ensure your full anonymity.

The questionnaire is intended to help us find out what users think of the system. Maybe you find that there are problems and issues that need to be improved. We would very much like to know about such problems and issues, so that we can take them into account. Information given in the questionnaire will of course be anonymous in the same way as the audio recordings.

If you are in doubt about anything, or if there is anything you want to know more about, you are very welcome to call me at phone number *xxx*.

As agreed, we would like you to call our system on Thursday, 12 January, and carry out the tasks. I will call you when the system is up and ready to receive your call.

Best regards    Laila Dybkjær

---

**Fig. 13.1** An introduction letter to subjects (translated from Danish)

such as 2 months before. It is also useful to contact subjects 1 or 2 days before the session to remind them about the appointment. Even then, several might cancel at the last minute, simply not show up, not make the agreed phone call or otherwise not do what was agreed. The method plan (Section 6.4) must take this into account. One possibility is to have subjects on standby, ready to be called to come and fill a free test time slot or participate in a meeting or other session. Another is to make sure that, if all subjects show up, there will be more than strictly needed. A third is to simply recruit new subjects until there are enough.

## 13.2.6 Remuneration of Subjects

When we spend people's time, it is considered good practice to give them something modest in return. Be smart about what to offer subjects, considering their age, gender, culture, religion, etc. Some options are cinema ticket vouchers (in our experience, this works well with both children and adults – even with blind subjects); a box of chocolate; a bottle of wine; or even a relatively small amount of money. You may sometimes be required to cover travel expenses as well. If you make a lottery instead, drawing the winners from a hat, the winners get more, the losers get nothing, but people might appreciate.

## 13.3  Session Preparation – Material and Equipment

Typically, various items, described in the method plan (Section 6.4), must be in place prior to the lab session. Frequently used materials and equipment include:

| | |
|---|---|
| checklists | scenarios |
| the exact version of the system model to be tested or presented | subject training material (Sections 10.5, 12.5) |
| equipment: computers, video recorders, sound recorders, cameras, loudspeakers, microphones, large screens, tables, chairs | user guide, manual, other written support materials |
| | lab observation plan (Section 10.4) |
| videos, handouts, slide shows, other presentation materials | wizard instructions (Section 12.2) |
| | wizard support information (Section 12.2) |
| introduction and instructions to subjects | staff roles and instructions (Section 6.4.6) |
| meeting/workshop agenda (Section 9.3) | user debriefing guide |
| draft list of questions to address (Section 9.1) | interview script (Sections 8.6, 8.7 and 8.8) |
| categories to work on (Section 10.3); | questionnaire (Sections 8.6, 8.7 and 8.8) |
| consent form | water, soft drinks, sweets, food |
| | remunerations (Section 13.2.6) |

In the following, we address the points on the above list that are not followed by a reference. For the other points, please refer to the referenced sections.

### 13.3.1  Checklist for What to Do Before the Session

You want nothing to go wrong during the session that could jeopardise the amount and quality of the collected data. Checklists serve as reminders to everyone involved in organising and conducting the session. For example, you might have a checklist for what must have been done the day before sessions start, including entries like those listed below. Note that some things must have been done much earlier – subject recruitment, renewal of software licenses, ensuring that key staff will not be on holiday or, in case of an exported lab session, making sure that the environment where the session will take place is available, e.g. a car has been rented or a room in a museum is available and can be used for the purpose.

- Is the session environment available and ready?
- Is all hardware, including recording equipment, set up; does it work?
- Are extra batteries, tape, storage space, etc. available?
- Is all software installed in the right versions; does it run?
- Is everybody in the lab aware that session machines should not be touched from now on, unless something relating to the session needs fixing?
- Are all written materials for staff and subjects available and printed?
- Are other materials, like videos or questionnaires on the web, available and ready?
- Subject status: have they been reminded; are there any cancellations?
- Double-check environments and equipment – remember Murphy's law!

- Does everyone involved in the session know his/her role and what to do?
- Is the subject remuneration in place and does someone know where it is?
- Are soft drinks and candies for the subjects in place somewhere?

Note that if you want to make a comparative study, you need to prepare at least two different conditions under which to apply the method. These may relate to differences in, e.g. amount of instruction given to subjects, modalities available in the system model, category sorting task description or environment of use.

It is also useful to create a checklist for what to do on session day(s).

### 13.3.2 System Model, Software, Equipment

If the system model, implemented or otherwise, is the key component in the session, as when it is being evaluated (Chapter 12), make sure that the model is available in the planned version and ready for use.

Carefully go through everything needed for subjects to understand and interact with the system model: mock-up components, WOZ system model representation, computers, interactive devices, network connections, rooms, etc. Is everything ready and functional? Do you have spare equipment if something crashes? If not, what could happen? Test the complete set-up as it will be when subjects arrive. Carefully go through any logging and recording software and equipment. Check that the logging software actually logs the data as planned. Check audio and video recording equipment. Do you have sufficient disk or tape space to store the recordings? Are the batteries fresh and do you have spares?

This all takes time but is well spent in order to avoid panic and crises during the session day(s), including hasty problem fixes which you regret later when they turn out to have negative consequences for data handling or otherwise. Don't assume that someone else did something essential but check that it has been done.

It happens that the system model is not ready as planned on the day before the session. We all suffer from optimism. So we start firefighting, asking, e.g. can the system model be completed by the time the first user arrives tomorrow (if we all work overnight)? Can we simulate missing functionality or otherwise benefit from inserting a human in the loop? Do we have to simplify the scenarios? The ultimate question is whether to cancel the session at the last minute, and we don't want to face that one. The moral is: Exercise extraordinary realism when scheduling the session based on when the system model version is planned to be ready. If uncertain, rather add a couple of weeks unless this is absolutely impossible to do.

### 13.3.3 Presentation Material, Introductions, Instructions

Some lab methods, e.g. focus group meetings, often use discussion materials, such as videos, slides, drawings or paper printouts. Other methods, e.g. category sorting or human data collection, use material to be handled or otherwise used by subjects during the session. Check that it's all ready the day before. For videos, sound files, text files or anything else to be run on a computer or other electronic equipment, explicitly check that it runs on the actual equipment to be used and that your computer works with the data projector.

Verbal introductions to, and instructions for, subjects should be prepared in advance, and it is a good idea to write them down. Rehearse what you are going to say and make sure that everyone gets the same information in the same order. This may be important to the quality of the collected data. Print the stuff and bring the printed version to the session.

### 13.3.4 Consent Forms and Other Permissions

A consent form is a form signed by each subject, giving permission to use data collected during the session for purposes specified in the form. Be aware that this may be a legal minefield. The basic, internationally recognised principle is that of *informed consent*, i.e. that you must clearly, objectively and completely inform subjects about the purpose of the research, expected duration and procedures; possible risks, discomfort, adverse effects and side effects (if any); any benefits to the subject or to others that may reasonably be expected from the research; what the collected data will be used for; guarantee of anonymity for presentation purposes; how the data will be stored to ensure privacy protection, who will have access to it, in some cases when it will be destroyed; their right to decline to participate and to withdraw once participation has begun and the foreseeable consequences of declining or withdrawing; and whom to contact for questions about the research and research participants' rights.

Note that legislation differs in different countries. In Europe, relevant regulations include the Charter of Fundamental Rights of the EU and Directive 95/46/EC of the European Parliament and of the Council of 24 October 1995 on the protection of individuals with regard to the processing of personal data and on the free movement of such data. A basic and influential document on informed consent is the Helsinki Declaration adopted by the World Medical Association in 1964 and amended most recently in 2000.

Your intentions are pure, of course, we are sure you don't intend to harm subjects in any way! However, this is exactly when it is easy to be blind to what could happen and fail to think it through. It is always useful to think up a couple of worst-case scenarios and use these as background when designing the consent form. What happens if a subject breaks a leg when attending a session in your lab? Do you know exactly what you will be using the data recordings for in coming years? You never thought about it? Then think! Even if all you want is to use face-up video shots of subjects in conference presentations, following which you won't leave a trace anywhere – not even on the conference computer which held the presentation and video clips – this might be considered a violation of subjects' privacy, unless having been explicitly consented to in writing. It's *not* smart to act on the assumption that subjects will never find out.

We often need to collect personal information about subjects – address and other coordinates, age, habits, social environment, ethnicity, religion, even basic information about health. The consent form should guarantee that any use of this information will be thoroughly anonymised prior to publication.

For obvious reasons, children and young people are a special subject category. No parents want to see recognisable pictures or videos of their child in a web site report on the session, maybe complete with name, the area where the child lives or the school s/he attends, when and where the recordings were made, etc. To the extent possible, we always shoot videos of children and adolescent subjects from behind in order to not even possess data showing recognisable subjects. Don't ask the child to sign a consent form. The form should be directed to the parents who should sign it on behalf of each child or adolescent. Sometimes a meeting with the parents is required to smoothen the process, i.e. to present yourself, the team and what it does, describe the planned session, invite the parents to attend, describe data protection safeguards, etc. The parents will be all ears, basically positive, suspicious if you cannot make all facts, conditions and safeguards crystal clear. If you recruit underage subjects through their school, their teacher will often have to be involved in the process, which, in our experience, is a good thing. It is crucial not to put the teacher in a difficult position between the parents and the project. Inform the teacher about everything and make sure that s/he understands all issues to do with informed consent.

Figure 13.2 shows a draft of a parental consent form from a European research project, Today's Stories, in which children used small video cameras in their school environment to make synchronised recordings for creating little stories about their day at school (Panayi et al. 1999).

We need a different kind of consent or permission if we want to make, e.g. macro- or micro-behavioural field observation (Sections 10.1 and 10.2) in an organisation. You may have to sign a non-disclosure agreement to be permitted access to the organisation, including agreement to certain restrictions on the use to be made of the collected data or on the data you are allowed to collect. Make sure that everything is perfectly straight before starting any kind of data collection in an organisation.

## 13.3.5  Scenarios and Priming

Scenarios, or descriptions of tasks or other activities (Section 11.1), are often given to users in lab tests in order to test possible situations of use of the system model and introduce a certain degree of systematicity into the test process. Common approaches are to create scenarios that cover the capabilities of the system evenly or focus specifically on certain aspects of the interaction, for instance, because these aspects are suspected of causing usability problems. A basic problem in scenario design is to capture, in a limited number of scenarios, as much of the space of possible situations of use as possible.

| **Informed consent form** | |
| --- | --- |
| Project: XXX | Project No: XXX |
| Project Coordinator: XXX | Research Team: XXX |
| LAB NAME and ADDRESS | |
| NAME and PHONE of CONTACT PERSON | |

Participant's Name.........................................................................................................

Age: Years....................................Months....................................................

I...........................................on behalf of ...............................................

certify that the project "XXX" in which my child is to participate has been explained to me and that all of my questions have been answered satisfactorily. I voluntarily agree to allow my child to participate and understand that I may withdraw my child's participation at any time without penalty. I also give consent for the researchers to use personal information about my child in their work on the understanding that my child's anonymity and confidentiality will be respected, except in the case of certain types of electronic material. I understand that the results of this study will be used for review, analysis and dissemination to the academic research community and other interested parties through publications, presentations, and other electronic media. The information contained in these materials will not be used in any other public or commercial form without additional consent. I understand the reasons for and nature of the dissemination of outcomes from the project and I understand that I shall be kept informed.

The material will be collected according to the protocols submitted to the University ethics committee.

Copies of the protocols are held at the University.

I release the researchers from any liability connected with the use of these written, photographic, video and electronic materials.

I have spoken with my child named above, and as his/her parent/guardian, I believe that s/he is willing to be involved with this project.

Signature...................................................(parent/guardian)

Date...............................................................

**Fig. 13.2** A consent form from a project involving children as subjects

Scenarios are also used with user lab development methods, such as when target users invent scenarios in focus group meetings or other meetings or workshops in order to describe imagined situations of use.

In its standard meaning, a scenario is a particular interactive task. Not all systems are task-oriented, though (Section 3.4.5), and it is sometimes more appropriate to give subjects broader goals to pursue through interaction. An example is a collaborative conversational adventure game in which one of the players is instructed to behave as a difficult collaborator who tends to disagree with the goals of other participants, human and virtual. We call such instructions "scenarios" as well.

Scenarios for system model testing in the lab are typically designed by the development team. It *is* possible, though, to let subjects decide what they wish to do when interacting with the system model throughout. However, some drawbacks are that (i) interaction often fails to address all those aspects of system functionality that the developers want to address; (ii) comparison of user behaviour and performance becomes less systematic; (iii) it can be difficult or impossible to figure out what exactly the user is actually trying to achieve, if anything; and (iv) users sometimes feel lost trying to come up with scenarios when facing a system they don't know. On the other hand, a risk of using developer-designed scenarios is that important real-life task aspects, and other user-related constraints on interaction, are ignored, which may result in a sub-optimal system unless those problems are discovered in other ways. These pros and cons explain why it is sometimes preferred to use a mixture of developer-designed scenarios and more freestyle user interaction. For instance, the lab test might start in a first, freestyle condition which also allows the user to explore and play around with the system and then proceed to a second, scenario-based condition.

Scenarios may be presented to subjects orally or in writing. In most cases, a static graphics presentation is used, for instance, on a paper handout. Some advantages are that (i) all users receive exactly the same information; (ii) the user may return to the handout as often as s/he likes in case of uncertainty about what to do; and (iii) while users can only be expected to remember brief scenarios when orally presented, longer written scenarios do not present short-term memory problems. However, if all the user has to do is pursue some simple goal that is obvious in the context, no handouts may be required.

It is important to make sure that scenarios are unambiguous. If ambiguous, you can be sure that some users will interpret them in unintended ways.

A key problem with scenarios is that they are easily presented in ways that risk priming users (Section 6.4.4, Box 6.2). A classical case is that of using written or spoken scenarios as a basis for interaction that itself includes spoken or written input. It doesn't matter if the application is based on keyword commands or takes spontaneous spoken or written input – users always tend to reuse the scenario phrasings. The effect is that the collected data holds no micro-behavioural information about the spontaneous language (vocabulary, grammar, speech acts, etc.) people use in addressing the system. All that the data shows is that users are able to remember what they are told and capable of reading aloud. The test thus provides no help at all for designing the system's capabilities of spoken input recognition and understanding.

Figure 13.3 shows a scenario presentation that strongly primes spoken or written interaction. We can expect that most users will say "on Monday" when asked for the date and not, e.g. "the day after tomorrow", "on 16 January" or whatever else would be an equivalent, appropriate and perfectly ordinary date expression. Do you think that the time expressions are likely to prime subjects as well?

---

**Flight ticket reservation scenario (strongly priming)**

Jan Jensen who works and lives in Copenhagen is going to Aalborg on Monday to attend a meeting. He would like to get a ticket for the departure at 7.20 and back again at 17.45. Book his ticket.

---

**Fig. 13.3** Strongly priming scenario description

One approach to priming avoidance is to design more abstract and open-ended, text-based scenarios so that users are not primed by specific formulations and must provide most details themselves, cf. Figs. 13.4 and 13.5.

This approach works fine for relatively uncontrolled tests. However, if you want micro-control (Section 13.1), you must plan what will be tested exactly, and this cannot be done with open and abstract scenarios. We cannot, e.g. predict if the user, in the scenario in Fig. 13.4, will ask for a discount ticket or not, so we might end up not having the discount option chosen by any subject in any scenario and hence not tested at all. In a controlled test, the scenarios must describe the tasks to be performed in all necessary detail while, at the same time, avoiding that users repeat the phrases used. A good solution is to combine text and analogue graphics in describing the scenario, emulating more closely the real-life situation of a user who needs date and time information and looks up in a calendar or an agenda, looks at a watch, etc. Figures 13.6 and 13.7 show two different ways of indicating date and time in this way (Dybkjær et al. 1995). Note the difference in date information in the two figures. The date is indicated in boldface in the calendar in Fig. 13.6. In Fig. 13.7, the date is indicated on a days-of-the-week line starting with today in boldface and indicating the target date in boldface.

The point just illustrated for spoken interaction is valid far more generally and might be expressed like this: If subjects are to provide spontaneous micro-behavioural data, do not show them examples of this micro-behaviour. They will probably copy the examples. Show an image of someone pointing and they will point in more or less the same way. What to do? Tell them to point, use the interpretational scope of language (Section 4.2.2) and there will be nothing to imitate. Instruct them in modalities different from those they will use for input, and there will be nothing to copy.

| Flight ticket reservation scenario without details |
| --- |
| You live in Copenhagen. Your favourite uncle in Aalborg would love to see you during the Christmas holidays and has promised to pay for your flight ticket. Plan your trip and book your ticket. |

**Fig. 13.4** Open scenario description. Detailed decisions are left to the subject

| Abstract scenario descriptions |
| --- |
| 1. Try to get as much information as you can about the location where H. C. Andersen lives. |
| 2. Tell Andersen about a game you like. |
| 3. Can you find out which games he likes? |

**Fig. 13.5** Three abstract-goal scenario descriptions for interacting with a multimodal (spoken and pointing gesture input, spoken and graphics output), blending-with-people, non-task-oriented system

---

**Flight ticket reservation scenario using analogue graphics (1)**

Rikke Hansen from Copenhagen must travel to Aalborg as shown in the calendar and on the clock. Rikke is 10 years old. Book her ticket.

**JANUARY 2006**                                      FEBRUARY 2006

| M | T | W | T | F | S | S | **WEEK** |   | M | T | W | T | F | S | S | WEEK |
|---|---|---|---|---|---|---|---|---|---|---|---|---|---|---|---|---|
|   |   |   |   |   |   | 1 | 52 |   |   |   | 1 | 2 | 3 | 4 | 5 | 5 |
| 2 | 3 | 4 | 5 | 6 | 7 | 8 | 1 |   | 6 | 7 | 8 | 9 | 10 | 11 | 12 | 6 |
| 9 | 10 | 11 | 12 | 13 | 14 | 15 | 2 |   | 13 | 14 | 15 | 16 | 17 | 18 | 19 | 7 |
| 16 | 17 | 18 | 19 | 20 | 21 | 22 | 3 |   | 20 | 21 | 22 | 23 | 24 | 25 | 26 | 8 |
| **23** | 24 | 25 | 26 | 27 | 28 | 29 | **4** |   | 27 | 28 |   |   |   |   |   | 9 |
| 30 | 31 |   |   |   |   |   | 5 |   |   |   |   |   |   |   |   |   |

**Fig. 13.6** Scenario combining analogue graphics and text to convey key information which could prime the user if shown in the text modality only (example 1)

---

**Flight ticket reservation scenario using analogue graphics (2)**

Jens and Marie Hansen live in Copenhagen. They will attend a meeting in Aalborg as shown in the calendar which starts with today in boldface and shows the day of departure as the next day in boldface. The meeting starts and ends as shown on the two clocks. The flight takes about 35 minutes. The time to get from the airport to the meeting is about 45 minutes. Book their tickets.

M T **W** T F S S M T W **T** F S S

**Fig. 13.7** Scenario combining analogue graphics and text to convey key information that could prime the user if shown in the text modality only (example 2)

## 13.3.6 Guides, Manuals, Other Written Support

Lab tests often require written support material, on paper, on-screen or otherwise. Thus, interaction may have some form of complexity to it, which is not easily remembered from verbal instruction. Some systems are meant for specialists who may need hours of study before using the system in practice. Even if subjects come to the lab for the test, it is sometimes useful to make written material available in advance and ask them to study it before turning up. You won't like to handle subjects who turn up unprepared, so try to make sure that they come prepared!

A particular form of written support is the *user guide* that is meant to convey a working idea of how to interact with the system. A guide is typically rather brief and often includes a description of the system model and examples illustrating how to interact, as in the leaflet mentioned in the introduction letter in Fig. 13.1 (Section 13.2.4). If real users will receive a guide eventually, it is fine to have it tested by subjects. Otherwise, you should be keenly aware of any advantages the guide may give subjects compared to real users and consider how this may affect your data.

A more elaborate written support document is the *user manual*. If the final system will have a manual, it is a good idea to have subjects evaluate the current manual version together with the current system model. One way to do this is to make subjects read the manual in advance or at least take a look at it and keep it at hand during interaction.

### 13.3.7 Subject Debriefing Guide

A debriefing guide helps the experimenter remember what to ask or talk about when debriefing subjects. See also Section 13.5.1.

## 13.4 During the Session

From the moment subjects arrive and throughout the session, you or someone else on the team must know what to do, what to be aware of, and how to handle various situations that may occur. We discuss these obligations in the following.

### 13.4.1 Subjects Arrive

Don't let subjects wait. If they arrive one by one, schedule their arrival so that they can start immediately. Since there may be many subjects coming on the same day, this means that you have to stick closely to the schedule. The best way to ensure this is not to make the schedule overly tight. If you haven't tried this before, we assure you that everybody involved could use a breather every now and then in between taking care of new subjects. When they arrive, welcome them and make them feel comfortable in what is likely to be to them an unfamiliar environment populated by strange people. If they must wait a bit, make sure someone is there to talk to them.

Don't start firing instructions straight away, no matter if subjects arrive one by one or as a group. Some initial small talk is important to make them feel at ease. Make clear that their presence is appreciated and important to getting the system tested or to collecting information crucial to system development. Be aware of the priming risk (Section 6.4.4) from the start and consider yourself an actor, even if never contemplating yourself in that role. For example, your talk to test subjects about the system must not be perceived as if you believe that they are going to try something fantastic and unique, worldwide. If you do that, many of them will try hard not to let you down and to view the system as fantastic indeed. That's not what you need from subjects, you need reliable data. Note that priming may be an issue not only in a lab test context but also in relation to meetings and workshops.

## 13.4.2 Introduction and Instructions to Subjects, Subject Training

What to tell subjects by way of introduction largely depends on the method to be applied. Provide, at least, some practical details. Tell them in detail about the session plan and about any breaks. Inform them if the session is being recorded. If there are several subjects at the same time, let them introduce themselves so that you all get acquainted. Introduce subjects to anyone else who will be present in the room where the session takes place and explain their roles. If an observer will be observing the subject through a window or via a camera, tell the subject. If subjects are left on their own during the session, make sure that someone, typically the experimenter, is available, and tell them how to get in touch with that person. If there are time limits, tell subjects in advance how much time they have – for a scenario, for their work in a particular condition – and that they will be interrupted when time is up. Unless already done, make them sign the consent form, if any (Section 13.3.4), taking your time to explain it and answer questions.

You may want to give more details about the usability method you are using and what you want subjects to do. If they don't arrive at the same time, make sure that everyone gets the same information.

Lab test sessions often start with a training phase, because training may be required for at least four different reasons: test method, interactive devices, system model and manner of interaction.

*Test method.* Some methods require training or getting used to. To think aloud (Section 12.5), for instance, subjects must feel at ease thinking aloud before starting the data collection part of the session. Similarly, mock-ups (Section 12.1) are used following some collaborative procedure between subject and experimenter, and the user must be familiar with the procedure before data collection starts.

*Interactive devices.* Interaction by means of unfamiliar devices must, as a rule, be trained before data collection starts. If not, all we are going to capture initially will be, e.g. a user struggling with some 3D haptic device or trying to input 3D hand gesture code to control a mouse pointer on the screen, interrupted by the experimenter trying to provide instruction.

*System model.* Initial training must not be provided for running walk-up-and-use systems, of course, but many other systems require some amount of familiarisation before data collection begins – unless, that is, we specifically wish to study how subjects figure out how the system works. Rest assured that a brief initial familiarisation will not prevent users from encountering interface and interaction problems. Let subjects familiarise themselves based on what they are told; don't use planned scenario contents for illustration and don't demonstrate what to do if this means showing subjects micro-behaviours that may have a priming effect.

*Interaction manner.* Most people are familiar with standard GUI-based interaction. However, if subjects are expected to interact in ways unfamiliar to them, it is wise to start with a little training. Speaking to a system is a case in point. Many users need, first, to become familiar with wearing a carefully adjusted headset; second, to master system-specific conventions on when (not) to speak, such as pushing a button before talking or waiting for the virtual character to have finished its output; and third, to adjust the recording level by speaking a few words. But this is not the end of it, because the manner in which the user speaks to the system often matters a great deal. Typically, the user should speak naturally in terms of speaking rate and loudness; not speak more slowly if the system has failed to understand the input; not shout either; try to avoid disfluencies to a reasonable extent by planning what to say before speaking; and avoid speaking very long utterances. None of this has anything to do with input contents. It is your choice if you want to train the subjects in these things or not. If you don't, chances are that the speech recognition rate will be significantly lower. Your decision should depend on whether or not you expect real users to receive instruction and training. During training you can ask the subject to adjust speaking rate, volume and the rest of it, if that's what's needed to collect the right kind of data.

Like system testing, human data collection in the lab typically includes initial training. Most of the points made above are relevant.

This discussion about training is, in fact, about *data quality*. Unless the data *is* about the familiarisation process, high data quality assumes a process of training until everything works as it should. Many data collection efforts, whether made for usability testing or component training purposes, have been ruined due to far too little attention being paid to up front subject training.

If you expect to train the subjects, you must plan the training and possibly prepare training material. This might be, e.g. small tasks for familiarising subjects with thinking aloud or a few sentences to be spoken initially in a data collection session where the audio is being recorded and the lip movements tracked.

### 13.4.3 Carrying Out the Session

Be careful and attentive throughout the session. It is easy to misinterpret what you hear or see or to inadvertently influence what happens. Be fully aware of your own role and try to be neutral and unbiased. Never make subjects feel stupid.

Remember that not only what you say and don't say matters, but also your body language may influence subjects. For example, don't show surprise upon realising what users try to do with the system or expect from it. If you need to work on this, record a session with a colleague and analyse what you did right and wrong.

Maintain a relaxed atmosphere during the session, whatever happens. Remember that it is when things go wrong that your determination to remain unaffected is being tested, not when everything flows smoothly. Humour is fine but make sure to laugh with, not of, the subject.

If you are running a test, always remember that it's the system you are testing, not the user. If the user has problems, you can only blame the system, your pre-test instructions or your preconceptions about users.

Encourage subjects, implicitly and explicitly, to be themselves and not behave in ways which they believe you want them to. If you need to impose constraints on their behaviour during the session, explain why. For good or worse, each constraint imposed limits the information present in the data.

You will probably make errors when running sessions, especially if you are not very experienced or if your skills have become a tad rusty. Don't despair if you find out that you made an error. If the error may have influenced the subject or the data collected, make a note about it and carry on.

### 13.4.4  When and How to Help a Test Subject

Subjects sometimes need help during a test, although, as a general rule, we should not feel sorry for them when they struggle and shouldn't try to save them. By intervening, we risk losing important information about their problems and how they try to solve them. Only in the following cases it is OK to provide help:

- the user is very confused or totally lost;
- the user is very frustrated and close to giving up;
- the user seems to feel bad about doing something;
- certain cases of system incompleteness that stall interaction and data collection, such as a missing error message which leaves interaction dangling;
- a technical problem requires immediate solution for the test to continue, e.g. if the system crashes, a component loops or an interaction device malfunctions.

It is the experimenter's job to provide help in such cases. Make a note that the user received help, what the problem was and what kind of help was provided. The note may be made by the observer, if there is one.

Note that the above is based on the assumption that you have good reason to believe that the user has understood the instructions provided prior to the test session. If not, you have created a situation with no free exit. If you intervene, you get poor data; if you don't, you get poor data.

If something goes wrong and needs fixing, never blame the subject. Sometimes you simply have to repeat an instruction given earlier, because the user forgot. If the cause of the problem is not obvious, try to clarify by letting the user express what happens and what is confusing. Don't tell the user explicitly what to do. If the user is stuck, try to give helpful information little by little. A slight hint may be enough to get the user back on track. When helping the user, pay attention to later tasks or activities and the potential effects the help may have on the user's performance on these.

### 13.4.5  What Not to Say When Subjects Ask Questions

Be careful when subjects ask questions. You may easily reveal information that they should not have, e.g. because it might influence the data. One trick is to reverse the question and ask what the user believes. Another trick is to talk your way out of it.

Thus, if the user says "Did the others have this many problems?", you might answer "Did you have more problems than expected?"

There are, of course, many questions that you can safely answer straight away, such as if the subject asks during training if what s/he did was fine and in accordance with instructions or asks about the duration of the session.

When dealing with subjects, there are things one may sometimes feel tempted to say but, nevertheless, shouldn't say to them. Some examples of misplaced humour, irony, sarcasm, scolding and the rest of it are, cf. (Rubin 1994), the following:

- Don't say more than three times, "Remember that we are not testing *you*."
- Amazing, nobody did THAT before!
- Could we stop for a moment? I get so very tired seeing you struggle like that.
- I actually didn't mean that you can press *any* button.
- Yes, it is natural that experimenters cry during sessions.
- You are sure that you have used a computer before?
- I told you very clearly not to do that!


### 13.4.6  When to Deviate from the Method Plan

It may be necessary to deviate from the method plan. Cases like the following might justify deviation:

- Subjects don't understand the scenarios
  - o  revise the scenarios.
- Scenarios covering parts of the system functionality that should have been tested have been left out by mistake
  - o  try to include the parts in question if this can be done in a reasonably controlled fashion through scenario revision, addition or otherwise.
- The questionnaire or interview script includes infelicitous questions or misses important questions
  - o  change the questionnaire or interview questions.
- A subject does not show up
  - o  if needed, try to find another subject with the same profile and schedule that subject last if subjects arrive one at a time.

Many other cases than these happen in real life, of course. Do your method planning carefully and think about fallback options in order to avoid hazardous stopgap plan changes during the session or the data recording. In most cases of sudden method plan change, one or two things happen: (1) the schedule suffers, and subjects are being inconvenienced and (2) data split into two different data sets, one from before the error was discovered and one from when the problem had been fixed in what we hope is a reasonably rational and controlled manner. It can be hard to decide what to do with two partially different data sets. If the problem is fixed early and subjects arrive one by one, the bulk of the data may still be as desired and the net effect of the modification is that fewer subjects than originally planned were involved in generating this data. If the session is a group session, errors may strike harder because you may be left without any usable data for the part of the session affected by the problem.

### 13.4.7 The Experimenter

The experimenter, or session leader, has a key role during a lab session. The central task of the experimenter is contact with subjects: welcoming them, introducing what is going to happen, instructing them, helping them, performing the system's actions during user interaction with a mock-up, making the subject think aloud, etc. To fill the role well, the experimenter must be well prepared, act openly and friendly towards subjects and stay focused and attentive throughout.

The experimenter is not necessarily in the same room as the subject during the session but must always be within easy reach.

## 13.5  After the Session

We normally don't bid subjects farewell immediately after the session. It is common practice to debrief them, and there may be other issues to handle as well.

### 13.5.1 Subject Debriefing

Debriefing is an opportunity for telling subjects about issues we feel they should know about, such as that the Wizard of Oz-simulated system wasn't real (Section 12.2). It is also an opportunity for subjects to tell what is on their minds. This is particularly important after a test if there is no post-test interview or questionnaire, since the debriefing is then the only chance for subjects to utter their frustrations, ask curious questions, provide admiring comments they feel they *must* give, etc. Let subjects speak first and tell what's on their minds. Then you can start asking about more general things and eventually move towards specific issues. Focus on understanding problems and difficulties. Remember to be neutral.

If there is a post-test interview or questionnaire, debriefing may be done right after, being quite short in this case since subjects should by then have been able to offload their minds by answering the post-test questions. If you have questions to answers provided in a questionnaire, you may ask them during debriefing.

With meetings and workshops, "debriefing" is normally included as part of the session in the sense that one typically asks, towards the end, if there are any other issues to address. With category sorting and human data collection in the lab, debriefing is normally short as well and may take the form of small talk.

Whichever kind of session has been run, debriefing time is also time for handing out remunerations and reimbursements, making any future arrangements, etc.

## *13.5.2 Data Handling*

Data handling and analysis starts during, or immediately after, usability method application, cf. Chapters 15 and 16.


## *13.5.3 Post-Session Subject Contact*

Subjects are not necessarily ancient history after the session. If they must fill a questionnaire after having left the lab, you should monitor that questionnaires get returned and remind anyone who is running late. Some tests include subjects who have used an earlier system version before and have come back to give feedback on progress made and be compared with subjects who never used the system before. Some projects work with the same group of subjects from start to finish. Even if subjects are one-off by intention, it's a good idea to tell them that you might want to come back for more information later on and ask their consent.


## 13.6 Key Points

Nearly half of the usability methods described in Chapters 8, 9, 10, 11 and 12 are *user lab methods* in the sense that they are typically applied with subjects in a lab setting or exported lab setting. Some methods are lab test methods, others are lab development methods.

User lab methods may be applied in a *more or less micro-controlled* manner depending on the purpose of using the method.

When preparing a lab session, the main focus should in general be on *user recruitment* and on the *material and equipment* needed.

Being well prepared for the session includes knowing *how to deal with subjects* from the moment they arrive and throughout and awareness of the many things that may not work out exactly as planned.

Always *debrief* subjects and users before they leave the lab, making sure that all mutual commitments have been met or will be met.


## References

Bernsen NO, Dybkjær H, Dybkjær L (1998) Designing interactive speech systems. From first ideas to user testing. Springer Verlag, New York.
Dumas, JS, Redish, JC (1999) A practical guide to usability testing. Rev edn. Intellect Books.
Dybkjær L, Bernsen NO, Dybkjær H (1995) Scenario design for spoken language dialogue systems development. Proceedings of the ESCA workshop on spoken dialogue systems, Vigsø, Denmark, 93–96.
Nielsen J (1993) Usability engineering. Academic Press, New York.
Panayi M, Van de Velde W, Roy D, Cakmakci O, De Paepe K, Bernsen NO (1999) Today's stories. In: Gellersen HW (ed) Proceedings of the first international symposium on handheld and ubiquitous computing (HUC'99). Springer, Berlin, LNCS 1707: 320–323.
Rubin J (1994) Handbook of usability testing. John Wiley and Sons, New York.

# Chapter 14
# Intermezzo 4: Case Usability Method Plan

This fourth intermezzo illustrates Case method planning by presenting a usability method plan for testing the Sudoku system (Section 2.1). Since the test process involves a cluster of four methods, we describe these in order in a single method plan, i.e. screening interview (Section 8.6), lab test of implemented prototype (Section 12.3), observation of users (Section 10.4) and post-test interview (Section 8.8).

## 14.1 Data Collection Purpose

The primary purpose of collecting data is to evaluate the usability of the Sudoku system, cf. Section 1.4.6.

## 14.2 Getting the Right Data

Table 14.1 operationalises the data collection purpose, showing what to measure and how, i.e. by means of which usability method. All 20 table items will be addressed in a post-test interview, and 10 items (5–10, 12, 15–17) will be evaluated based on real-time observation of the test subjects as well. Questions 1–4 are closed Likert-scale questions, all other interview questions are semi-open or open. The phrasing of interview instructions and questions is shown in Fig. 8.9.

## 14.3 Communication with the Data Producers

Before subjects are invited to participate, they will be screened based on the questions in Fig. 8.7. We tell each of them that s/he is going to help us evaluate an electronic Sudoku game for about an hour, including about half an hour for introduction and gameplay and about 20 minutes for the subsequent interview. Remuneration will be two open cinema tickets. No transportation or other costs can be covered. The exact location of the test is described, and date and time will be agreed upon if the person fits into the representative user group to be established and is willing to participate. All invitees will be given an e-mail address and a telephone

N.O. Bernsen, L. Dybkjær, *Multimodal Usability*, Human-Computer Interaction Series, DOI 10.1007/978-1-84882-553-6_14, © Springer-Verlag London Limited 2009

**Table 14.1**  What to look for in the collected data

| What to measure | How to measure |
|---|---|
| *Appropriateness of modalities used* | |
| 1. Appropriateness of pointing input | Closed interview question |
| 2. Appropriateness of spoken input | Closed interview question |
| 3. Appropriateness of screen output | Closed interview question |
| 4. Appropriateness of modality combination for interaction | Closed interview question |
| *Quality of interaction* | |
| 5. Quality of pointing input understanding | Interview question + data from the interaction |
| 6. Quality of pointing input provision | Interview question + data from the interaction |
| 7. Quality of speech input understanding | Interview question + data from the interaction |
| 8. Quality of speech input provision | Interview question + data from the interaction |
| 9. Quality of combined speech gesture input understanding | Interview question + data from the interaction |
| 10. Quality of combined speech gesture input provision | Interview question + data from the interaction |
| 11. Missing input modalities? | Interview question |
| 12. Output interface intelligibility | Interview question + data from the interaction |
| 13. Missing output modalities? | Interview question |
| 14. Naturalness of interaction | Interview question |
| 15. Ease of interaction | Interview question + data from the interaction |
| 16. User in control | Interview question + data from the interaction |
| *Functionality* | |
| 17. Sufficiency of functionality | Interview question + data from the interaction |
| *User experience* | |
| 18. User satisfaction | Interview question |
| 19. Advantages and disadvantages | Interview question |
| 20. Play again? | Interview question |

number in case they need more information or have to send their apologies. For ease of communication, subjects are asked for their e-mail address and phone number as well.

Prior to using the system, each user will be given a brief introduction to the system by the experimenter who will

- tell that the expected use environment of the system is not at home but, rather, in places like a shop while waiting for someone to decide which clothes to buy, in airport terminals, train stations, at exhibitions;
- briefly explain the rules if the subject has not played Sudoku before;
- briefly explain and show what the buttons on the screen are meant for;
- demonstrate how to start a game, play and change to a new game;
- tell that the user is expected to try/play two games and start a third one;
- ask the user to select the easy, medium or hard game level (Section 7.2.1);

- explain and show how the experimenter will slide a piece of paper into the subject's field of view (not to interfere with camera and speech input), when s/he should change to a new game or change game level;
- explain that the user will not necessarily have finished a game when signalled to start a new game or end the session;
- clearly emphasise that this is not at all a test of the user's Sudoku skills but a test of how good the system is for playing the game in special environments.

The purpose of asking users to start a new game towards the end of the session is to collect additional data on this particular action.

*Exceptions*: should a subject go "cold" during gameplay, so that little or no interaction happens for a long period of time, the experimenter may signal change to a new game or even ask the user if the gaming level should be changed to an easier one. We don't get useful data if a user does not play. This will be done as follows: if the user seems to have run out of options and pauses for more than 3 minutes, or several times for longer than 2 minutes, the user will be asked to choose between selecting a new game or lowering the game difficulty level by one step.

*Priming note*: In order that we collect spontaneous data on the use of combined speech and gesture, the experimenter must be *extremely careful* when demonstrating how to talk and point. In the introductory demonstration, the experimenter must use all three possible forms of temporal combination of speech and gesture, i.e. (i) speak and then point afterwards, (ii) speak and point at more or less the same time and (iii) point, retract the hand and then speak. This must be trained in advance and must be natural when demonstrating the system.

## 14.4 Subject Recruitment, A Representative User Group

The user profile for the Sudoku system is described in Table 5.6.

Resources allow only a relatively small user group of 10–15 subjects, and we have decided to invite 12. We aim for a reasonable balance regarding gender, i.e. at least 40% must be male and at least 40 % female, and age, i.e. approximately one-third must be under 30 years old, between 30 and 50 and above 50.

Regarding Sudoku skills, we will divide subjects into three groups of four, each balanced with respect to gender, i.e.:

1. subjects who have little or no experience in Sudoku but have an interest in trying it (again);
2. subjects with some experience who have managed easy-to-medium difficulty games;
3. subjects used to managing difficult games.

Subjects are expected to play at a level corresponding to their skills and experience. We shall not consider subjects' educational background and age in other respects than for ensuring the age spread described and ensuring that there will be no more than two subjects having the same profession across all three groups.

To select test subjects according to the above criteria, potential subjects will be contacted over the phone or face to face and screened prior to recruitment. User screening instructions and questions are shown in Fig. 8.7.

## 14.5 Staff Roles and Responsibilities

We need people for the following pre-session roles:

1. someone who designs a set of screening interview questions, including instructions on what to tell potential subjects and guidelines on whom to recruit;
2. someone who designs a set of post-test interview questions, including instructions to subjects;
3. someone who writes instructions on what to tell subjects before they start using the system and how to help them if needed;
4. someone who contacts, screens and recruits users according to (1);
5. a technician who takes care of the technical set-up of the system and tests it, including calibration of the stereo cameras for capturing pointing gesture input;
6. a person who makes sure that recording equipment is available, fully functional and has been installed where the Sudoku system has been set up.

Roles 1, 2 and 3 will be iteratively handled by Ole and Laila, role 4 will be taken care of by Svend and roles 5 and 6 by Torben.

Users will arrive one by one. During the session, we need

1. someone who receives and takes care of the user when s/he is not in the test room;
2. an experimenter who has the contact with the user during the session;
3. a technician who maintains the system and checks it before each session;
4. a person who takes care of the video camera recording the subjects;
5. one or two observers;
6. one or two interviewers.

Role 1 will be taken care of by Svend, roles 3 and 4 by Torben and the remaining roles (2, 5, 6) will be shared by Ole and Laila.

## 14.6 Location, Equipment, Other Materials, Data, Results

*Location.* Test sessions are scheduled to take place in NISLab's usability lab over 2 days on Thursday 7 June and Tuesday 12 June. The expected session duration is about 50 minutes. Users are not expected to have to wait. If they arrive early, they will be put in a room where there will be coffee and something to read. The interviews will also take place in the relaxed environment of this room.

*Equipment.* The Sudoku game board is shown on a 42″ screen. The two cameras (DMK 21F04 from ImagingSource) are mounted at the ceiling. The user has a Logitech headset microphone for spoken input to a Microsoft SAPI 1.5 recogniser. A chalk line on the floor shows where to stand to allow camera capture of pointing gesture. Interaction (video and audio) is recorded on video recorder.

*Other materials.* Svend will maintain a schedule showing who will show up when.

*Data collection and data handling.* The data to be collected includes the following:

- video and audio recordings of user–system interaction. The video will show the user's hand/arm and the screen contents and will be shot from a position slightly to the left/right of, and behind, the user;
- observation notes produced by the observers during the sessions;
- interview notes written during the post-test interviews.

When test data collection has been completed, the data will be validated to make sure that it is, in fact, appropriate for the data analysis planned. A detailed plan for data markup and coding scheme creation will be specified by then.

*Results presentation.* An overview of the results of data analysis will be produced by augmenting Table 14.1 with overall results per evaluation criterion. The results will be explained in more detail per criterion and, to the extent possible and relevant, accompanied by suggestions for system improvements. If relevant, results will also be discussed in relation to each of the three test groups (Section 14.4).

## 14.7 Method Script

Before setting the plan in motion, it must be tested that the system is suitable for being exposed to the test. Roles and responsibilities are described in Section 14.5. Questions and instructions must be prepared well in advance.

Twelve test users must be recruited following the criteria described in Section 14.4. To minimise transportation costs we will recruit local subjects. However, although all subjects might be recruited among employees (researchers, administrators, support staff) and students at the university and still be in line with the criteria in Section 14.4, we will recruit at least four subjects from outside the university.

Based on the screening information in Section 14.3 and Fig. 8.7, Sudoku skills and interests will be assessed by asking to which group subjects consider themselves to belong: novice, intermediary, expert; how often they play Sudoku; for how long they have played; and, informally, at which level(s) of difficulty they prefer to play. They must know the numbers 1–9 in English. If a potential subject has a profile that is still missing according to Section 14.4, s/he will be invited. If not, we ask if we can keep him/her on standby in case of a no-show during the test.

   The test location is described in Section 14.6. We plan to have six 1-hour sessions per day, thus leaving sufficient time for each test so that no user has to wait.

   A session is expected to spend max. 5 minutes on system and task introductions (Section 14.3), followed by 25 minutes gameplay, followed by a 20 minute interview in a separate room. Gameplay will normally spend 12 minutes on playing Game 1, 1 minute for changing game and 12 minutes for playing Game 2, see also Section 14.3.

   The interview will be based on the instructions and questions shown in Fig. 8.9 and based on Table 14.1.

   Each user will receive two open cinema tickets in reward.

   The collected data will be handled as described in Section 14.6.

   *Checklist* of what must be completed before the first session starts and, in some cases, much earlier: roles distributed; screening interview questions done; post-test interview questions and instructions done; instructions to subjects on first contact done; instructions to users before gameplay done; 12 users recruited; test room booked; interview room booked; cinema tickets bought; candy and soft drinks bought and available in the interview room; system appropriateness tested; system set-up tested; recording equipment tested; instructions printed and rehearsed, inter-view questions and instructions printed.

# Chapter 15
# Data Handling

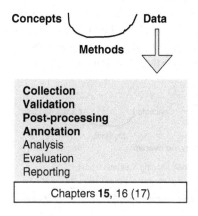

Concepts | Data

Methods

Collection
Validation
Post-processing
Annotation
Analysis
Evaluation
Reporting

Chapters **15**, 16 (17)

In this chapter we come, finally, to the third CoMeDa cycle phase (Section 1.3.1) in which we have to process the data collected with any of the 24 usability methods described in Chapters 8, 9, 10, 11 and 12 and backed up by Chapter 13 on working with users in the lab. In multimodal conceptual diagram terms, so to speak (Section 4.2.4), we now ask what happens to the data you stuffed into your box for analysis in Fig. 1.1. What happens is *data handling*, the processing of raw usability data through to presentation of the final results of its analysis. Results may be used for many different purposes, including improvement of the system model and, in particular, its AMITUDE part (Box 1.1), component training, theory development, decision to launch a project, etc.

Data handling actually begins with data collection planning and data collection which have been the topics of Chapters 6, 7, 8, 9, 10. 11, 12 and 13. In this and the next chapter, we look at the remaining steps in the data handling cycle. Chapter 15 is about the data handling steps that precede data analysis and add value to the raw data collected. Chapter 16 is about data analysis and evaluation and results reporting.

Section 15.1 presents the data handling cycle that's embedded in the CoMeDa cycle. Section 15.2 expounds on the amazing properties of data. Section 15.3 describes the different kinds of data you may have collected, and the book-keeping to be done before proceeding to data validation and data post-processing as discussed in Section 15.4. Section 15.5 gives an introduction to data annotation, including annotation schemes and annotation tools. Section 15.6 discusses coding procedures and coding best practice.

N.O. Bernsen, L. Dybkjær, *Multimodal Usability*, Human-Computer Interaction Series, DOI 10.1007/978-1-84882-553-6_15, © Springer-Verlag London Limited 2009

## 15.1  The Data Handling Cycle

Each usability method (Section 6.2) is applied in order to collect usability data. Anytime in the life cycle, we may select and apply a particular method or other approach (Section 6.1) to collect data on phenomena we need to understand better in order to build a usable system. It is tempting to believe that, once the data has been collected, it's over: we briefly look at it and then use it for whichever purpose we had in collecting it in the first place. We are not saying that this is *totally* wrong. It actually may happen, such as when, say, an expert (Section 8.5) looks at our system and comments that we need to measure gaze direction to provide appropriate feedback to the user, and we realise that, yes!, that's what we must do. The comment is a data point, and our action is to use it as it stands. However, even here there is something in between data and action, namely, the reasoning we do to realise that the expert is right. So, generalising enormously: between any data set, on the one hand, and action based on it, on the other, there is a data handling cycle in which the data is being processed before drawing conclusions on the impact of the data on the system model.

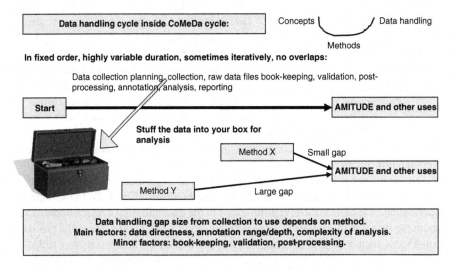

**Fig. 15.1**  The data handling cycle (*top part*) and data handling gaps (*bottom*)

The top half of Fig. 15.1 shows the data handling cycle that, in fact, envelops each usability method application. We might as well turn the cycle into the following principle right away:

> *Data Handling Rule No. 1:* No matter the data collection purpose and the method, always go through all steps in the data handling cycle.

The cycle starts with data collection planning, which is the core of the usability workplan (Section 6.3) and its associated method plans (Section 6.4). We apply a method by following the method plan we wrote for it, collect usability data and continue with the data handling cycle steps to be described in this and the next chapter, i.e. raw data files book-keeping, data validation, data post-processing, data annotation, data analysis and reporting. Once you get into thinking in these terms, you will see that it is surprisingly rare that one can skip even a single one of those steps.

The bottom half of Fig. 15.1 contributes another point to a model of the data handling process. We have seen in Chapters 6, 7, 8, 9, 10, 11, 12 and 13 how the methods described differ in many respects – typical life cycle phase(s), data contents and system type relevance (Section 6.2.2), cost, methodological detail and complexity, general frequency of use and more. The data handling gap shown in the figure is different. The size of the data handling gap is an estimated measure of the amount of transformation that data collected with a particular method must undergo during data handling before the result can be used for its purpose. This measure depends on the three major and three minor factors listed at the bottom of Fig. 15.1.

For instance, when the evolving AMITUDE model is being discussed at a stakeholder meeting (Section 9.2) and conclusions stated in the meeting minutes (= the collected data), the gap may be relatively small because: (i) *the data directness* is high since the conclusions are meant to be applied to the model more or less directly; (ii) *annotation* is not needed: the minutes are clear and to-the-point as they stand; (iii) *complexity of analysis* is low in this case, let's say, because we are dealing with straightforward additions to the AMITUDE model of use; (iv) *book-keeping* is simple – it's just an unambiguously named file in the project archive once the meeting notes have been (v) *post-processed* by being structured and typed; and (vi) *data validation* is straightforward in most cases: we send the minutes to the participants and make the necessary revisions based on their comments. On the other hand, if we go to some organisation to chart their existing work processes using a macrobehavioural field method (Section 10.1), and in preparation for introducing a new system which might radically change those work processes, data directness may be low and complexity of analysis high because it takes a great deal of reasoning about the new system to make use of the collected information at all.

We suggest the data handling gap notion as a useful tool for planning the data handling effort and allocating resources, and one which should be factored in already at the time of method selection. Note that gap size is independent of the amount of data collected. Typically, more data collected means more data handling work, of course, but that's often a quasi-linear factor. A large data gap size can act as a multiplier of the amount of work to be done, whereas a small gap size may act as a divisor. In addition, the existence of detailed written procedures for all data handling steps contributes greatly to the speed and efficiency of data handling.

## 15.2  The Nature of Data, Corpora, Data Resources

Before looking at the data handling process in more detail, let's marvel at some key properties of data. It is customary to speak about a (data) *corpus* or *data resource* which was designed for a particular purpose and collected at a specific point in time. Data is:

- *empirical, new knowledge:* collected from observation or logging of user behaviour during user–system interaction, from meetings or interviews with users or questionnaires given to them, from application of guidelines to a system model (no users involved), and even from observation and recording of humans and human–human interaction. The latter can be essential if too little is known, empirically or theoretically, about some class of interaction phenomena prior to system development. For instance, if we don't know how people's eyebrows move when they laugh or cry, and find nothing adequate about it in the literature, data collection and analysis may be the only way if realistic eyebrow movement is to be a feature of the system's output.
- *physically instantiated in some external form:* from meeting or observation notes on paper to videos and logfiles. "External" means that data is available in a form that is, in principle, accessible to everyone. What's only in your head is not data. Its external nature means that data can often be profitably transformed prior to, and in order to facilitate, analysis, preferably through some automated or semi-automated process, such as digitisation, feature extraction, filtering, file segmentation, file or schema format conversion, file compression, spelling correction, logfile pretty-printing, video frame mounting and many others;
- *unique:* never before collected with this particular group of people in these circumstances, with this particular purpose for this particular system model, etc.;
- *tacit and passive:* data only yields new information when analysed with particular questions in mind;
- *abundantly rich:* like an image worth more than a thousand words, a data set can yield information about more things than we want or need to ask about or can even think of asking about. So, it's crucial to ask the right questions;
- *limited by data collection purpose and methodology:* despite its richness, data only answers certain questions and does not answer all others. When data collection is over, all you have is the data. If you, e.g. omitted to capture some aspect of user behaviour during the test and this aspect turns out to be essential to evaluation, this is just bad luck and you have to start all over again. Another implication is that data is much harder to re-use than we tend to think. Even slight differences in data collection purpose, for instance, can render existing high-quality data sets useless, cf. Section 10.5 and Fig. 10.5. So, you need to determine the questions before collecting the data;
- *in need of validation:* once collected, data needs validation prior to exploitation. This is especially the case with data for training and test of components and systems. With large and expensive data sets, validation is often performed by an independent organisation who verifies that the data quality conforms with the standards imposed;
- *precious:* data collection, especially with target users or a representative user group (Section 3.3.6), is costly to do. Large data sets can be worth hundreds of thousands in any currency. Just as importantly, having to repeat a data cycle because of glitches in planning or execution is likely to upset many if not most development schedules and budgets;

- *scarce*, for two reasons: (1) Data is limited by purpose: there may be corpora out there that might help answer your questions without the need to launch a new data collection exercise, but it is also quite possible that none of them can answer exactly the questions you need answers to. (2) Special-purpose data is being collected in large quantities all the time, but companies and academics tend to hold tight onto their data for all sorts of reasons and often unreasonably. So, even if you have good reason to think that you could re-use someone else's data, you may find it impossible to get access to this data.

## 15.3  Raw Data Files, Data Book-Keeping, Meta-Data

Section 15.3.1 lists the raw data files collected with methods described in this book. Before processing the data it is important to do some book-keeping as described in Section 15.3.2. A special kind of book-keeping is the writing of meta-data, see Section 15.3.3.

### *15.3.1 Raw Data Files*

Collected data is represented in *raw data files*, i.e. files that have not yet been transformed, modified or annotated. Application of this book's methods may produce raw data files of the following kinds:

- *interview notes* from surveys and from customer, expert and subject interviews;
- *filled questionnaires* from surveys, experts and subjects;
- *minutes and notes* from meetings with focus groups, stakeholders and users;
- *observation notes* from macro-behavioural field methods and real-time user observation in the lab and in the field;
- *use cases, scenarios, persona descriptions, cognitive walk-through notes and annotations, guideline and standards application notes;*
- *audio and video recordings, photos* from focus groups, subject interviews, user meetings and workshops, macro- and micro-behavioural field studies, user–system model interaction, think-aloud and human data collection;
- *bio-sensor and ambient sensor readings* from lab tests;
- *categorisation results* from category sorting;
- *affinity diagrams* from meetings with users;
- *system and component logfiles* from lab tests and field tests;
- *comments* from field test users.

In terms of format, notes, comments, minutes, filled questionnaires, use cases, scenarios, annotations and affinity diagrams may be hand-written or typed; video, audio and static image files are preferably in common formats, such as avi or mpeg, vaw and gif, jpeg, tiff, etc.; logfiles are text files and so may sensor readings be.

Important points about raw data files are the following: (1) These files are your gold ore, they're all that's left of method application, and you must exploit their contents to make the data collection effort worthwhile. (2) Take good care of them: keep them, back them up, never modify the original file versions! If something goes wrong later on in the data handling cycle, you may have to return to the original raw data for a re-start. (3) Use the raw data more or less as-is for documentation, reporting and publication. (4) Remember that the raw data might be exploited for other purposes later on and that common file formats facilitate data post-processing and re-use.

## 15.3.2  Data Book-Keeping

If you are a data handling person, you may not have to read this and the next section; if not, you'll ignore them at your peril! For some method applications, all that's left are some pages of minutes or notes. Those cases are simple – so simple, in fact, that they tend to be ignored in discussions about data handling. In many other cases, method application will have left you with a goodly amount of data files. Once you start handling those files, and before you know it, the number of processed versions of the raw data files becomes significant. So, establish, from the very beginning, a strongly informative, i.e. clear, explicit, unambiguous and coordinated, *labelling policy* for the raw data files, informed by a reasonable file structure which makes clear where the file belongs. Label cross-referencing is important to clearly mark, e.g. which logfiles correspond to which video and/or audio file, for instance because all files represent various aspects of the same interaction. Then follow a systematic policy in labelling any file modifications, making it evident which files relate to which earlier file versions and in which way. This is basic version control at data file level.

If in doubt as to how much effort to put into data organisation and documentation up front, including meta-data, cf. below, consider the following points. (i) To have many raw data files from the same method application, lots of file versions related in time and otherwise, and several people working on the files in parallel, is a recipe for chaos unless everyone maintains a pretty rigorous file structure scheme throughout. A relatively small, 12-subject system model test easily generates 60 raw data files which will then get post-processed in various ways, annotated in different ways, analysed from several perspectives and results presented in various ways, etc. (ii) As emphasised in all method chapters, data collection is done in a context described in the usability method plan (Section 6.4) and associated documents, and all documentation of that context should follow the raw and processed data files throughout. (iii) Three months after method application – far earlier if you ask us! – all data handling details have been forgotten, and all you have to assist work on the data is the file structure and its documentation. (iv) This is, in fact, the situation of a newcomer who gets a copy of the data and its collection context in order to start working on it. Finally, (v) you will appreciate the work done when writing papers and next time you get into data handling.

### 15.3.3 Meta-Data

Meta-data is data about data, aimed to facilitate data handling and retrieval of relevant data sets from, e.g. the web. Meta-data is a key element in documenting raw data to oneself and others. There is no standard set of meta-data information items for raw data files, but a good model to keep in mind is the following: provide *all* the information that *you* would like to have about *somebody else's* data resource when trying to decide whether to use that resource. We suggest including everything relevant from among the following information items that have been found useful in many cases (Dybkjær et al. 2002). If other items are needed, just add them to the data documentation:

1. raw data referenced, file structure;
2. date of collection of raw data;
3. date of creation of meta-data;
4. name(s) of collector(s) of raw data;
5. name(s) of creator(s) of meta-data;
6. location of collection of raw data;
7. purpose of collection of raw data, modalities involved, etc.;
8. data collection method;
9. size of raw data (measured in, e.g. duration, number of interactions or Mb);
10. accessibility (free or fee, web site, contact information, forms to fill, etc.);
11. file technicalities: file format, compression information, other post-processing information, etc.;
12. recording setup description: environment, equipment, microphone, camera, sensor placements, constraints observed, etc.;
13. collection context description: questionnaire, interview script, meeting agenda, observation script, task, scenario, instructions, guidelines, standards, system model, etc.;
14. participants: numbers, roles (meeting participant, target user, representative user group, etc.), nationality, language, etc.;
15. if speech data: sampling rate, age and gender of each speaker, speakers' native language, geographical provenance, accents, social class, drinking and smoking habits, whether the speakers are known to each other, whether the speakers are practiced in the dialogue activity performed;
16. references to other raw data files which are important to the raw data described and to annotations of the raw data described;
17. references to literature, reports, etc., providing more details on the raw data or some aspect of it;
18. notes: anything else that should be mentioned.

Each time the data files are modified, add to the meta-data a description of the modifications made. In this way, anyone, including yourself, can come back to the data anytime and easily determine if it's of interest or not.

## 15.4   Preparing to Use the Data

Armed with a well-documented set of raw data files (Section 15.3), it is time to prepare the data for analysis, component training or otherwise. This section is about various preparatory steps that may be required.

### 15.4.1   Raw Data Validation

All raw data corpora must be validated prior to use. Validation makes sure that the collected raw data can actually be used for the purpose for which it was collected, and this requires checking various properties of the data. Which properties to check in a particular case depends to some extent on the data collection purpose, but, in general, validation ensures that the raw data is actually there in the *volume* required, has the *contents* specified, is of sufficient *quality* for specified purposes of post-processing, analysis or exploitation and is properly *labelled, organised* and *documented*. Volume, contents and quality may affect an additional factor, i.e. data *reliability*. To briefly illustrate: if we need 100 hours of good-quality data and managed to collect 25 hours only, we need more data; if one cannot clearly see subjects' eyes on the video, the data is not useful for studying eye gaze expression; if the microphone was low-quality, the speech data may be useless for recogniser training; and if 1/3 of the representative user group never showed up and were replaced by students, the data probably isn't representative any more.

Thus, data validation says, and asks: now that we have done the planned data collection, do we have what we need to proceed with data handling without any plan modifications, or do we have to collect more data, with better contents, of better quality or stronger reliability? Data validation is primarily meant to spot problems created during data *collection*, but nothing prevents data validation from finding errors in the data collection *design* as well.

Raw data validation can be more or less costly, formal and rigorous depending on the data and the exploitation purpose. Box 15.1 describes large-scale data collection and rigorous validation. In many cases, however, all we need to do is to make sure that the planned data is there and is readable – the workshop notes are there in full; one completely filled questionnaire per subject is there; the confirmed minutes are there; 10 use cases are there; the affinity diagram, the logfiles per subject, the categorised representations, etc.

### Box 15.1   Data Collection Story– Speech for Consumer Devices

Large-scale data collection for component training may take a year to do, involving several colleagues full-time who are required to first create, or at least meticulously follow, hundreds of pages of data collection design documentation. The collection of the Danish SPEECON (Speech-driven interfaces for consumer devices) corpus was such an exercise. SPEECON (Speecon 2004) was an EU-initiated project that became global later on and which has developed speech corpora for more than 20 languages of sufficient quality for training speech recognisers in recognising speech in different dialects, spoken by speakers of different age groups and gender, in different acoustic environments, such as cars of different sizes, offices, open-air spaces, living rooms, children's rooms and large populated indoor halls.

A total of 600 speakers were recruited by word-of-mouth from sports clubs and other organisations, ads in the printed press, ads smuggled into radio interviews, etc. Each speaker spent approximately 1 hour being instructed and producing for the record a mixture of read speech and spontaneous speech about fixed topics. Data validation followed a complex sampling protocol and was done by a professional validation company.

Although the data collection design was followed throughout, this design was not 100% complete, nor could it have been. For instance, we began data collection in September and happened to speak, in October, to colleagues in Stockholm who were busy doing the same exercise for the Swedish language. At some point they remarked on the undesirability of recording outdoors in winter, which we had not thought of, unfortunately. We ended up doing open-air recordings in February and March in Denmark, sometimes in close-to-zero degrees Celsius temperatures.

## 15.4.2 Raw Data Post-Processing

The physical and external nature of raw data (Section 15.2) offers endless opportunities for automated, semi-automated and manual raw data post-processing before using the data files. Post-processing is typically done in order to optimise data representation for a particular purpose of analysis or component training. The resulting post-processed data file may be of the following types, at least: *data combination*, combining information from separate data files as in the example in Fig. 10.5, combining interview or observation notes, etc., all without raw data loss; *data conversion* into a data representation that is informationally equivalent in the practical sense that all the information required by the data collection purpose is still there – but which represents the information differently in some way, such as in typed text rather than handwriting, in a different file format, in a segmented or compressed representation or in a re-structured set of notes which hasn't lost a single original formulation; or *data extraction* made to support focus on particular aspects of the data, such as in feature extraction and filtering for any number of purposes. Some data analysis support tools (or coding tools) support data transformation and feature extraction, cf. Section 15.5.6.

Is post-processed raw data still raw data? This is a terminological question that we suggest to answer in the affirmative. Post-processed data is raw data that has undergone one or several of the post-processing operations just mentioned. The real issue is the line between, on the one hand, post-processed data that preserves its raw data status even if there is information reduction, as in data extraction, and post-processed data where the post-processing involves raw data modification due to interpretation. Interpretation does something more to the raw data than the operations above which merely combine, convert or reduce, always by applying some general and mechanical procedure. A short summary of a workshop or interview, for instance, is an interpretation. There is nothing wrong with interpreted data as long as interpretation is always clearly marked as such, so that its soundness can be evaluated by others if necessary.

We illustrate a simple and practical form of data post-processing which combines representation layout conversion and data extraction in order to improve analytical focus. We call it *pretty-print*. When doing manual data analysis, it is possible to speed up work and reduce error at the same time if the data representation can be easily scanned for relevant information. Some claim to read XML text without being slowed down, and there are even those who happily read postscript. For many others, it is desirable to convert logfile text data into a special-purpose format that is optimised for its data analysis purpose and may filter out unnecessary detail. Figures 15.2a and 15.2b show a logfile and its pretty-print version, respectively, the latter having been designed to facilitate analysis and diagnosis of communication problems in spoken dialogue. The example is from the Danish Dialogue System project on flight ticket reservation (1991–1996) (Bernsen et al. 1998). The pretty-print enables the analyst to easily focus on (i) the contents of the spoken dialogue turns and (ii) resort to system component communication when required for diagnostic purposes. User and system utterances in Fig. 15.2b have been translated into English. Translation involves interpretation, so translation is another example of a process which no longer maintains the data as raw data. Note that the contents of Fig. 15.2a correspond to the first half of Fig. 15.2b. The rest of Fig. 15.2b shows how the dialogue continues and helps give a fuller picture of what the pretty-print looks like.

## 15.5  Raw Data Annotation

This section gives an introduction to the special world of raw data annotation, continuing from our present position in the data handling cycle: at this point, we have our post-processed raw data in place and are ready for the next data handling step. Remember that this chapter is about data handling for system model development and evaluation, component training and other purposes of a more scientific nature. In any case, the next step is *data annotation* – also called *data tagging*, *data markup* or *data coding*. Annotation is relevant to virtually all kinds of raw data and can be anything from highlighting key points in the minutes of a stakeholder meeting,

```
<u id="S3-29a" who="S" topic=customer> Oplys venligst kundenummer! </u>
<u id="U3-29a" who="C-3" topic=customer> Nummer <t type=cardinal value="4">fire</t>. </u>
<keyed which="U3-29a">nummerfire</keyed>
<recognised which="U3-29a" grammar="Number" score=0.000000>nummer fire</recognised>
<parse which="U3-29a">
          | Current parsecontext: grammarset:  Command
          |              Command Command Yesno Number
          | semantic objects:
          | actionso(action ActionSO) [action --NULL--]
          | yesnoso(choice BooleanSO) [choice --NULL--]
          | customerso(number IntSO) [number [ones ••• ] ]
          | Resulting Parse Tree # 0
          | Subgrammar[ 5 ]: Number
          | L:[s_9,sem={number={ones={number=4}}}]:
          |                {cat=s,stype=ellipse}.[
          |    L:[nummer_1]: {cat=n,nb=sing,semtype=id,
          |                     defs=indef, [ ••• ]
          | ]
          | set Slot number "4"
</parse>
<database type="query" modifier="CUSTOMER">
          | customer: 4 </database>
<database type="answer" modifier="STATUS">
          | status: DB_OK   </database>
<u id="S3-30a" who="S" topic=customer>kundenummer <t type=cardinal value="4">4</t></u>
```

**Fig. 15.2a**   Logfile excerpt

|          |         |                                             |
|----------|---------|---------------------------------------------|
| customer | S3-29a  | Please state the customer number!           |
| customer | U3-29a  | Number 4.                                   |
|          |         |                                             |
|          |         | keyed: numberfour                           |
|          |         | recognised [Number/0.000000]: number four   |
|          |         | semantics: number "4"                       |
|          |         | database [query/CUSTOMER]                   |
|          |         | database [answer/STATUS] DB_OK              |
|          |         |                                             |
| customer | S3-30a  | Customer number 4                           |
| persons  | S3-30b  | How many people will travel?                |
| persons  | U3-30a  | 2 adults and 2 children.                    |
|          |         |                                             |
|          |         | keyed: Twoadultsandtwochildren              |
|          |         | recognised [Persons/-76.000000]:            |
|          |         | okay nine and two children                  |
|          |         | semantics: number "2" choice "1"            |
|          |         |                                             |
| persons  | S3-31a  | 2 people                                    |

**Fig. 15.2b**   Pretty-print extraction, partly from the logfile in Fig. 15.2a

through marking up subject hesitations in conversation, to application of elaborate
sets of coding schemes to raw multimodal data.

The purpose of data annotation is to add value to a raw data file by creating markers or tags referring to phenomena of interest in the data, either through modifying
a copy of the raw data file itself or by establishing a separate file which is somehow aligned, temporally or otherwise, with the raw data file. The latter is called
*stand-off annotation* and is the more common approach. We are all familiar with
simple forms of annotation, such as insertion of square-bracketed comments into
prose text or pointers to errors in maths. More advanced data annotation is essential
for many purposes in multimodal systems development and its underlying theories,
such as analysing human behaviour, measuring to various usability evaluation criteria (Chapter 16) or training micro-behaviour recognisers. Some forms of annotation
can be automated or semi-automated, like syntactic part-of-speech tagging of a spoken dialogue corpus. However, there are still large numbers of phenomena in raw
data that must be annotated manually, which makes annotation costly and time consuming to do.

In what follows, Section 15.5.1 explains annotation and the use of coding
schemes by means of a familiar example. Section 15.5.2 lists various purposes
served by corpus annotation. Section 15.5.3 illustrates annotation using data transcription as an example and shows an example of a transcription tag set. Section
15.5.4 illustrates complex annotation of natural interaction. Section 15.5.5 takes
a look at established general coding schemes for blending with people. Coding tools that can greatly facilitate the annotation work are discussed in Section
15.5.6.

### 15.5.1  Bird Watching and Data Coding

As data annotation is very much like systematic bird watching, we explain the basic
notions using bird watching as an example, see Box 15.2.

### Box 15.2  Bird Watching Story

You are disembarking on a tiny uninhabited and unforested island, and your
task is to spend as long as it takes until you have found out how many birds
there are and of which kinds (or species).

As a support tool, *Tool-1*, you carry a list of candidate bird names on which
you will mark the numbers you observe of each kind. The list is divided into
three sections. Section 1 has form fields describing the name of the list itself,
who developed it, when this was done, based on which bird observation exercises and other sources it was done, etc. Section 2 has a number of form fields
to be filled by you, such as name, date and duration of exercise. Section 3 lists

the names of the birds it is expected that you may see. Next to each bird name is an empty field where you may write the total number of birds observed to be of this kind.

However, the list of birds' names won't help much unless you are a trained bird watcher, which, we assume, you are not. This is why you bring as a second tool, *Tool-2*, an excerpt from a multimodal field guide complete with pictures of each bird on your list, young, male and female, in flight and sitting, its name, little arrows pointing to distinguishing features of each bird, a piece of text describing the look-sound-and-feel of each bird and a name-indexed audio file with the sounds made by each bird. Tool-2 includes originator information like Tool-1.

You complete the job but have to admit defeat in two cases. In *Case-1* there is a flock of birds all of which seem to be of the same kind but which are not on your list and hence not described in Tool-2. You invent a dummy name for them and describe them as best you can. In *Case-2*, although you watch them intently for a long time through binoculars, you cannot tell if a couple of birds belong to one or the other among two of the kinds in your Tool-1 list.

Oh, we forgot to mention that you brought two friends who did the same exercise without exchanging any information with you or with each other. One of them is a novice bird watcher like yourself, the other is an expert. Upon returning from the island, you use the expert's list to check Section 3 in your own list, having entered your personal coordinates, the tools you used, and other information items in Section 2. You also compare your Section 3 with the results made by the second novice.

The story in Box 15.2 illustrates the basics of data annotation. In fact, bird watching *is* data annotation albeit of a special kind, because bird registration is normally done in real time rather than on the basis of recorded raw data that exists separately from the reality it represents (Section 15.2). Ignoring this difference, the detailed correspondences with data annotation terminology and concepts are

1. The island ecology is a *data corpus*. Your task or *coding purpose* is to annotate a particular *class of phenomena* in the data, i.e. birds rather than mammals, insects, plants, geology or micro-climate on this island.
2. The island visitors are *annotators* (taggers, coders) who represent different *levels of coding expertise* in coding the phenomena targeted in the story.
3. The kinds of birds are *types* of phenomena of a certain class; individual birds are *tokens* of types of phenomena.
4. Tool-1, the list of birds expected to be found on the island, expresses a *hypothesis* which, in the present case, is a scientific one, about the types of phenomena that will be present in the data.

5.  The list of bird names constituting the body of Tool-1 is the *tag list* for tagging the phenomena observed in the corpus. So if you see two herring gulls, herring gull being on the tag list, you might note "2 herring gulls, 2.09 PM". Or, for efficiency and speed, you might replace the full names of the birds by shorthand or acronyms for tagging each bird, such as HeG for herring gull. Tags consist of such more or less intelligible, simple notation.

6.  Tool-2, the field guide excerpt and audio file, is the *tag semantics* which explain how to identify each token in the corpus as belonging to a particular type.

7.  Jointly, Tool-1 Section 3 and Tool-2 constitute the body of a *coding scheme* for annotating phenomena of a particular class. We might call it the Island X summer bird coding scheme or something like that.

8.  The Case-1 missing bird type – supposing that the omission is, indeed, correctly spotted by the novice bird watcher rather than reflecting, e.g. the watcher's inability to correctly apply the tag semantics – is a *flaw in the hypothesis* about the class of phenomena to be annotated, that is, about which birds there are on Island X in the summer. Such flaws happen, and one purpose of data annotation is to improve hypotheses and theories about classes of phenomena. When investigating multimodal usability, we create new coding schemes all the time because many phenomena of interest have not been investigated to the extent needed for machines to handle them. *Some* coding schemes are based on solid, established theory or comprehensive corpus analysis. However, many new coding schemes are more or less strongly hypothetical, like, say, the list of birds expected to live or feed on the island in the story.

9.  The Case-2 birds that could not be classified unambiguously even after lengthy observation – supposing that the birds were on the list and could, in fact, be distinguished under the conditions of observation available – reveal a *flaw in the tag semantics*. Somehow, the producer of the tag semantics did not manage to provide clear and unambiguous identifying characteristics for several types of phenomena in the class. This often happens with new coding schemes and could mean different things, e.g. that the coding scheme producer was not sufficiently explicit in describing the tag semantics or that the underlying theory is immature or in trouble. In any case, the coding scheme is flawed because it cannot be communicated for unambiguous application by man or machine.

10. Having returned from the island, you filled Tool-1 Section 2 with coding *metadata*. The originator information included with Tool-1 and Tool-2 is meta-data as well. Meta-data information on coding schemes and coding files is essential for others who consider re-using a particular coding scheme. There have been many discussions on meta-data in general and on which information items to include. The following set of items is based on common sense and experience among the NITE partners (Dybkjær et al. 2002): reference to the coding file body; dates of creation, coding, revisions; names of coders and their characteristics; version number; reference to the coding scheme applied; references to the actual coding files or raw data referred to in the applied coding scheme; names of the (numbered) coders in the coding procedure (see Section 15.6);

purpose of creation; classes of phenomena and modalities annotated; history of coding procedure; notes; and references to literature, reports, publications, etc. More specialised information should of course be added as needed in the particular case.

11. You and your novice friend used the expert's observations as a *gold standard* with which to check the correctness of your observations. By comparing the gold standard with your own observation record, you can easily mark up the instances in which you made correct identifications, omissions (you found no bird of this kind) and false insertions (you found a bird of this kind that wasn't there) with respect to types and tokens, respectively. Gold standard codings are produced by expert coders and used for various purposes, such as training and progress evaluation of novice coders. However, don't expect to find a gold standard coding when you need one! Make it yourself.

12. When checking your coding against the coding made by your fellow novice coder, what you did was to work out *inter-coder agreement* on the corpus. Inter-coder agreement measures can provide information on several points. With coding non-experts, inter-coder agreement can provide information on the clarity and sufficiency of the tag semantics. With coding experts, inter-coder agreement provides crucial information on the maturity of the underlying scientific theory as well as on its applicability by machines. We are used to thinking that, clearly, if the coding experts cannot agree to any sufficient extent, we will hardly be able to train machines to apply the coding scheme with sufficient accuracy.

Finally, note that advanced bird watchers don't just count birds but study their behaviour in detail, just like we do when studying and annotating human behaviour.

## 15.5.2 Purposes of Corpus Annotation

Data corpora collected with usability methods are annotated for many different generic purposes, including to

- highlight and comment upon usability information in notes, logfiles and other data resources (Section 15.3.1). This is normally done rather informally and without using the annotation machinery described in Section 15.5.1, but it's part of a continuum with the following points:
- create annotated data resources for usability development and evaluation, technical component and system evaluation, component and system training, etc.;
- develop new coding schemes for known or new classes of phenomena;
- develop new theory about classes of phenomena and their interrelationships, which can be applied for usability purposes;
- test the adequacy and completeness of theories.

### 15.5.3  Orthographic Transcription: An Example

At this point we need an example, so let's illustrate annotation by means of a basic and very common form, namely, *orthographic* transcription of speech. You might need it in your next project for transcribing user input speech or other audio- or video-recorded human speech data. Suppose that a speech recogniser is part of a user test. In this case, we can save time by using the speech recognition logfile data and work on this data rather than typing in from scratch what the user said. We extract the logfile and produce the input speech transcription by listening to an audio record of what the user said, correcting the logfile for speech recognition errors. There are coding tools which can help (Section 15.5.6).

*Coding purpose.* So far so good, but now we come to a point that demonstrates in a nutshell why there is a whole world of annotation out there: even transcription requires annotation. Before transcribing the spoken input data, we need to know exactly what the coding purpose is. This could be to extract an improved recogniser vocabulary or linguistic data for improving the language model; classify the subject's spoken conversation contributions in various ways; study any among dozens of speech behaviour phenomena; link the speech to other communication events, such as gesture, or to external events that might influence the speech – in fact, there is an unlimited number of coding purposes even for speech transcription. So let us note instead a number of things that we may have to do, most of which depend on the specific coding purpose.

*Transcription instructions.* Almost no matter what the coding purpose is, the transcription should be made homogeneous and consistent by following a set of transcription instructions. This also applies when you do the transcription yourself. If you have two or more coders (transcribers) who are not provided with quite precise instructions, chances are that they will transcribe the same raw data file very differently. One might try to transcribe what was said "exactly" as it was said, sometimes writing, e.g. "I have" and sometimes "I've", depending on how the user spoke the words; some invent neologisms and non-words when trying to render the user's pronunciation, such as "I dooon't . . ." when the user is hesitating; punctuation will be different, use of capitals will be different, and so on. We cannot have any of that, especially, but not only, if a machine will be using the transcribed data. To avoid it, we must specify exactly how the transcription should be done to fulfil the coding purpose. It is good practice to request coders to use correct orthographic spelling of words throughout rather than inventing their own spelling because, in practice, this is the only way to ensure uniform transcription. But this is only the beginning.

*Transcription coding* is frequently used to mark up phenomena of importance to how utterances were spoken, what happens on the audio track in addition to the spoken utterance, etc. To this end, transcription instructions must be supplemented with a *transcription coding scheme*. An example is a scheme with the following set of tags and very brief tag semantics:

1. bn = background noise: non-speech sound;
2. bs = background speech: speech heard in the background;

3. fp = filled pause: with speaker-produced non-speech sounds in it;
4. fs = false start: the speaker starts to speak, pauses and then repeats or modifies;
5. hs = hesitation: the speaker hesitates in mid-word or -phrase;
6. mw = mispronounced word: incorrectly pronounced word;
7. os = overlapping speech: simultaneous speech from several speakers;
8. up = unfilled pause: silence;
9. uw = unknown word: not possible to determine which word this is.

A real applicable version of this coding scheme would have more extensive definitions of tag semantics, examples of each type of phenomenon to be annotated, indications of minimum durations of pauses, etc. The Text Encoding Initiative (TEI) has proposed guidelines for speech transcription, including an extensible and modifiable tag set (Sperberg-McQueen and Burnard 1994, 2004). Like many other speech transcription schemes, the coding scheme above is a variation on the TEI proposal. The precise tag set needed in each case depends on corpus contents and coding purpose. For instance, if we are to transcribe speech made by car drivers, we might want an *ee* tag for referring to external events, such as traffic events, which potentially affect the driver's speech. Other workers in spoken dialogue, such as conversational analysts, tend to use far more tags than those listed above in order to mirror even more closely what was actually said. It is perfectly possible to create tags for new types of phenomena, define their semantics and hence create new or extended coding schemes.

*Usability applications.* There are many reasons why a coding scheme like the transcription scheme above may be important to development for usability. For instance, the scheme includes several tags (e.g. *fp, fs, hs*) for marking up different kinds of disfluencies in the user's speech. Disfluency phenomena may reflect individual user differences but might also reflect *task* difficulty; sudden events in the *use environment*; age, gender and other *user* properties; interface or *interaction* design problems; difficulties in providing input in a particular *modality* or in several *modalities*; *device* problems; etc.

*Adding discourse context.* Transcribed *input* speech can be analysed for many purposes in itself. However, if transcription is based on the speech recogniser logfile, the spoken interaction context consisting of turns made by both user and system will be incomplete. Analysing this context is often a main purpose of having made the transcription in the first place. To be able to access more of the spoken discourse context, we may need to extract the speech synthesiser's output logfile as well, combine it turn-wise in proper temporal sequence with the transcribed input and maybe produce a pretty-print version of the whole thing to facilitate analysis as illustrated in Fig. 15.2b.

Orthographic transcription is universally used for the study of spoken interaction. A more specialised form of transcription is *phonetic* transcription by means of a phonetic alphabet, such as SAMPA (Speech Assessment Methods Phonetic Alphabet) (SAMPA 2005), to capture pronunciation details.

### 15.5.4  Multimodal Annotation, Blending with People

Orthographic transcription (Section 15.5.3) is often the first step in more complex annotation of speech corpora and multimodal corpora that include spoken interaction. It is difficult to exaggerate the importance of this huge class of annotations for future multimodal systems and systems blending with people.

To illustrate complex annotation of multimodal, natural interactive human–human conversation, suppose that, in the course of a conversation recorded on video, Speaker 1 (S1) says to Speaker 2 (S2): "The man bought these toys for his children [pointing to the toys]". This example was proposed by Edinburgh University in the NITE project (NITE 2005). We have inserted the example into the tiered coding presentation in Fig. 15.3.

In this figure, the acronyms before the first dash (-) in the left-hand column refer to the coding schemes applied as well as, in the bottom row, to time measured along

| Complex multimodal annotation | | | | | | | | |
|---|---|---|---|---|---|---|---|---|
| CS/t | ................................................................................................................................. | | | | | | | N/A |
| POS1.1-S1 | S | | | | | | | SC |
| POS1.2-S1 | | | VP hlem=buy | | | | | SC |
| SE1-S1 | frame=buy fo=agt | | | frame=buy fo=pat | | | frame=buy fo=ben | SC |
| POS1.3-S1 | NP hlem=man | | | NP hlem=toy | | PP prep=for hlem=child | NP hlem=child | SC |
| POS1.4-S1 | DT | NN | VBD | DT | NNS | IN | PPS | NNS | SC |
| POS1.1-S2 | | | | | | | | SC |
| POS1.2-S2 | | | | | | | | SC |
| SE1-S2 | | | | | | | | SC |
| POS1.3-S2 | | | | | | | | SC |
| POS1.4-S2 | | | | | | | | SC |
| C1-S1 | | | | c2 | | | c3 | SC |
| CoR1-S1 | anchor5 | | | | | | anaphor5 | SC |
| WL1-S1 | w30 the | w31 man | w32 bought | w33 these | w34 toys | w35 for | w36 his | w37 children | TC |
| ToBI-S1 | | | | H* | | | | H*L | SC |
| C1-S2 | | | | | | | | SC |
| CoR1-S2 | | | | | | | | SC |
| WL1-S2 | | | | | | | | TC |
| ToBI-S2 | | | | | | | | SC |
| GPC1-S1-R | | prep | stroke | hold | | retract | | TC |
| GPC1-S1-L | | | | | N/A | | | TC |
| GPC1-S2-R | | | | | | | | TC |
| GPC1-S2-L | | | | | | | | TC |
| GC1-S1-R | | g3-de, target=toys | | | | | | TC |
| GC1-S1-L | | | | | g4-di | | | TC |
| GC1-S2-R | | | | | | | | TC |
| GC1-S2-L | | | | | | | | TC |
| UL1-S1 | U5, the man bought these toys for his children | | | | | | | TC |
| UL1-S2 | | | | | | | | TC |
| DLC1 | main | | | | | | | TC |
| time | ................................................................................................................................. | | | | | | | N/A |

**Fig. 15.3**  Complex multimodal data coding

a common timeline in, say, milliseconds. Most of the coding scheme references are dummies. The reason for the relative emptiness of the coding representation in the figure is that most tags belonging to a particular coding scheme occur twice, once for each speaker, S1 and S2, as indicated after the first dash in the left-hand column. An exception is the DLC1 (Discourse-Level Coding 1) coding scheme in the second row from the bottom. DLC1 marks up the overall phases of discourse which are common to both interlocutors who are presently in the *main* discourse phase. Another exception is gesture coding where we need to code separately for each hand/arm of each speaker (see below).

Working our way upwards, we next find utterance-level coding (UL1), i.e. the orthographic transcription of what S1 said in utterance 5 (U5). Then we see from (visual 3D) gesture coding (GC1) that S1 gestured deictically, i.e. by pointing to the toys in gesture 3 (g3-de) which was performed with the right hand/arm as shown by the R in the left-most column. In the analogue coding representation of Fig. 15.3 in which horizontal distance represents time, we immediately perceive the timing of gesture g3 and that S1 also did a "discursive" gesture (g4-di) with the left hand/arm. In the more detailed gesture phase coding (GPC1) representation, the deictic gesture (g3-de) is analysed into four timed phases, i.e. preparation, stroke, hold and retraction of the hand/arm. The left hand/arm gesture, on the other hand (g4-di), does not have phases as shown by the N/A.

Higher up, the prosody coding based on ToBI (ToBI 1999) is used to annotate word stress in U5. Then follows a word-level transcription of S1's utterance, from which the utterance-level transcription (UL1) already mentioned has been derived. Each word has a numbered id. Referring to the common timeline at the bottom, we see, for instance, that S1 puts stress on the word "these" during the holding phase of the deictic gesture. The reason why some of the words have been put on shaded background is that they have been coded for co-reference. Co-reference relationships, being long-distance – jumping over words, phrases, even sentences – in the transcription, are hard to show in other ways. The co-reference (CoR1) coding scheme row shows that the phrase "the man" serves as co-reference anchor for the anaphor "his" which refers back to "the man". Both have the same id (5) to mark that they constitute co-reference cluster 5 in the corpus.

Above the co-reference coding tier we meet something highly symbolic of the future of natural interactivity coding, i.e. cross-aspect cluster coding scheme 1 (C1) which provides ids c2 and c3 for two *multimodal clusters* consisting of coordinated spoken object reference, prosody and/or gesture as described above. Then follows part-of-speech (POS) tagging and semantic (SE) tagging which describe the utterance syntactic semantically, using several steps to show that the words uttered realise the semantic *buy* frame which takes an agent, a patient and a beneficiary.

Finally, the right-most column shows which coding tiers directly refer to the timeline (TC or time-stamped coding tiers) and which piggy-back on those timed directly (SC or structure coding).

Some essential points can be made rather forcefully by reference to Fig. 15.3:

- Despite its complexity, the coding only shows tagging of a single utterance in what is possibly a much longer conversation.

- The coding only codes for a fraction of what's going on when S1 produces U5. No coding schemes have been applied for coding, e.g. S1's head posture and orientation, body posture and orientation, facial expression or gaze behaviour, several of which very likely changed dynamically during the utterance of U5. Moreover, U5 has not been transcription tagged as illustrated in Section 15.5.3 nor transcribed phonetically; the discourse has not been coded for, e.g. communicative acts, communicative style, politeness, rhetorical structure or speaker roles; and S1 has not been coded, in any modality, for the emotions, attitudes or other central processing expressions that may have been displayed acoustically and visually when uttering U5.
- Working with each tier (row) – or, more precisely, each single tier, pair or quadruple of tiers, depending on the coding scheme – requires familiarity with a particular coding scheme and its underlying theory as well as with general coding best practice. Some people are experts in, e.g. co-reference coding in exactly the same way as some are experts in bird coding (Box 15.2). No one is an expert in all types of coding scheme referred to in Fig. 15.3.
- We conjecture that all interactive modalities have several aspects that ultimately have to be coded using different coding schemes. Each aspect is defined by a class of phenomena that may occur in multimodal interaction. For gesture, for instance, the figure illustrates that gesture can be coded with respect to (i) the body part(s) doing the gesture, (ii) gesture types, such as deictic gesture, and (iii), for some types of gesture only, gesture phases. More on this in Section 15.5.5.
- The figure illustrates the fundamental and, for system developers and behavioural researchers alike, most challenging fact that the aspects of communication present in the data are interrelated in numerous ways. This is because multimodal human communication behaviour is intricately coordinated, time-wise and contents-wise. Only complex data annotation can capture these coordinated cross-aspect clusters of interrelationships between phenomena belonging to different aspects, such as between a pointing gesture and what is being said and facially expressed at the same time; between the topics of discourse and an interlocutor's changing emotions; between the stress put on a word and its semantic and discourse contextual meaning; etc.
- Timing, as represented by the common timeline, is crucial for capturing relationships between phenomena from different aspects.
- The figure shows that some aspects, which are, in some sense, basic, are time-stamped directly, whereas others, which represent higher-level analysis of aspects already time stamped, do not require independent time-stamping.

If needed, we can now offer an explanation why it is not possible today to look up a scientifically sound and well-tested coding scheme for every aspect of human interactive behaviour as well as for its coordinated relationships with any number of other aspects of human interactive behaviour. The theory isn't there yet in many cases, because (i) it is only now that we begin to need it in full detail, (ii) no single person is an expert in but a few coding schemes and their underlying theory, and (iii) adequate theory development is probably, in practical terms, beyond our capacity unless supported by efficient coding tools that allow us to easily build complex codings like the one shown in Fig. 15.3 and way beyond. For an example of complex coding with the Anvil coding tool (Section 15.5.6), see the "multimodal score" annotation in Magno Caldognetto et al. (2004).

### 15.5.5 Languages and Coding Schemes for Blending with People

Systems start to blend with people when they can understand or generate some of the micro-behaviours that people use when presenting and exchanging information with one another, like in the combined speech and pointing example in the previous section. This section takes the discussion one step further by taking a structural view of the general and established coding schemes and coding languages we would like to have for developing systems that blend with people. We zoom in on blending with people micro-behaviour in three steps.

*Level 1: blending with people at the level of information presentation and exchange* (Fig. 3.3). People present and exchange information with one another through *two-way communication, action* and *tacit observation* (they also measure each other's bio-signals, but we will ignore this in what follows).

*Level 2: blending with people at the level of modalities* (Table 4.2). In terms of the taxonomy, people who make two-way communication, action and tacit observation use multiple modalities, such as *speech, facial expression, gesture* and *body action.* Speech is acoustic and visual (or graphic); facial expression is visual; gesture is visual and/or haptic and may be acoustic as well, like when someone audibly slaps your shoulder while you're looking and haptically sensing the impact; and body action can be visual, acoustic and haptic.

While those two steps take us to familiar levels, Step 3 does not. However, the previous section gave us, at least, an *example* from the level we now get to:

*Level 3 exemplified: blending with people at the level of micro-behaviour annotation* (Fig. 15.3). This figure analyses a snapshot of two-way human–human communication, combined speech and pointing gesture micro-behaviour, into the following aspects: discourse phase; orthographic utterance; visual 3D gesture type; visual 3D gesture phases; prosody; orthographic word; co-reference; temporal coordination of visual 3D gesture, word and prosody; part-of-speech; and semantic frames. The accompanying text stresses that this is merely a sub-set of aspects of common, situated two-way communication, and that many more aspects might have been included in the analysis in Fig. 15.3. Moreover, virtually all coding schemes referred to in Fig. 15.3 are dummies.

So what it would be useful to present at this point is (1) a structured overview of Level 3 rather than just an example, and (2) some real and useful coding schemes and related initiatives for annotating multimodal, blending with people interaction. The problem is the structured overview. It doesn't really exist yet, so this will be tentative and somewhat sketchy.

*Level 3 structured: blending with people at the level of micro-behaviour annotation* (Table 15.1). Before discussing Table 15.1, let's state what we need in order to

**Table 15.1** Different levels of general coding schemes or coding languages for blending with people. Italicised examples are illustrated in the text

| Level/Modality | Speech/voice | Facial | Gesture | Body action |
|---|---|---|---|---|
| **UNIMODAL** | | | | |
| Non-semantic elementary | *Transcription coding*, all phonemes in many languages, all visemes in some languages, ... | *All facial muscles* | *All body parts* | All body parts? |
| Non-semantic structural | Morphology, part-of-speech, syntactic structure | ? | *Gesture phases* (some gesture types) | Body action phases (some body action types)? |
| Semantic high-level | *Voice types* | *Face types* | *Gesture types* | ? |
| Semantic lower-level | Morphemes, words, utterances, speech acts, ... | ? | Emblems in some cultures | Body actions: grasp, push, pull, lift, turn, kick, ... |
| **MULTIMODAL** | | | | |
| Global states | Multimodal cues to cognitive and conative states, emotions and moods, interpersonal attitudes, physical states, personality | | | |
| Coordination | Bimodal: audiovisual speech, speech and pointing gesture or pointing gaze, sign language gesture and facial expression ... Trimodal: ... n-modal ... | | | |

build usable systems capable of blending with people: we need general and established coding schemes, or more general representation languages or notations, for representing all micro-behavioural aspects of modalities like those listed at Level 2 above, i.e. visual and/or acoustic and/or haptic speech, facial expression, gesture and body action.

The need for something *general* – coding schemes, languages – means that we are not talking about highly specific coding schemes, such as one for annotating shoplifting behaviour in department stores. There are infinitely many possible coding purposes for annotating micro-behaviour, so there will never be ready-made coding schemes available for all possible purposes. If you have a special coding purpose, you may have to develop the required coding scheme yourself. However, we would like to have easy ways of doing that by being able to draw upon general coding schemes or languages. For instance, if we need to annotate 10 particular facial expressions, it would be extremely helpful to be able to draw on a coding scheme or language that enables representation of all possible facial expressions. Or, if we need the system to be able to respond to four different user emotions, it would be extremely helpful to be able to draw on a general way of annotating emotions. Thus, Table 15.1 is about general coding schemes or languages only.

The need for *established* general coding schemes, or languages, is equally self-evident. Creating and validating a new general coding scheme or representation language for gesture or emotion annotation, for instance, is, in fact, scientific theory-building work that may easily take years to do, so this is not what we typically consider to form part of system development. Several factors contribute to making a coding scheme established: it is based on well-established theory about a class of phenomena; it is a standard established by some standardisation body; it has become a widely used de facto standard; or it is simply widely used without significant problems no matter the theory underlying it, if any. If we adopt some existing but not particularly well-established coding scheme for coding phenomena in our raw data, the risk is that some phenomena are not represented in the coding scheme, which makes us coding scheme co-developers and users at the same time.

Table 15.1 splits according to four groups of modalities in the taxonomy: speech, facial expression, gesture and body action. However, the tentative part of the table are the categories in the left-hand column.

*Unimodal, non-semantic elementary* coding schemes or languages represent classes of phenomena that (i) have no particular semantics (or meaning) but (ii) are necessary for grounding all possible semantically meaningful phenomena. In other words, phenomena in this layer are necessary for enabling phenomena at higher layers because information must be physically instantiated by information channels in order to be represented or exchanged, cf. Section 4.2.5. This layer has several coding schemes or representation languages for speech, such as phonemic coding for acoustic speech, viseme coding for visual speech, transcription coding as illustrated in Section 15.5.3, and coding for the many other information channels of human speech, such as pitch, intonation, rhythm, duration, stress, volume, gender, age, voice quality and phonemic articulation. Visemes are the visual counterparts of phonemes in spoken language. Unfortunately, the correspondence is not necessarily complete, so that, for all or most languages, some different phonemes are accompanied by identical visemes.

Based on research by one of the early theoreticians of facial expression (Ekman 1993, 1999a, 1999b), the Facial Action Coding System (FACS) (DataFace 2003) starts from the fact that facial expression is being generated by facial muscles used in isolation or in combination to express our mental and physical state. FACS specifies Action Units (AUs) for representing the muscular activity of the 50+ muscles in the human face that produces momentary changes in facial appearance, cf. Fig. 15.4 from the FACS Manual (2002). This means that any possible facial expression can in principle be represented by FACS, including those that carry communicative meaning, those that don't, the weird ones and those that actual faces never do. FACS is thus theoretically complete.

Corresponding to basic speech and facial coding, basic gesture coding needs a language for systematically describing the physical dimensions along which the body and its parts can express gesture. This could be a 3D coordinate system focusing on the parts of the body which can be involved in gesture expression (i.e. all of them), and a language for expressing all possible physical movements constituting gesture, including body orientation; body posture (sitting, standing, stooped, etc.); head orientation and posture; left and right arm position; hand shapes; orientation and posture of other body parts; speed and movement trajectories of it all;

**Fig. 15.4** Muscles
underlying upper face action
units. Muscular anatomy
(*top*). Muscular action
(*bottom*). The pictures are
from Chapter 2 in the FACS
Manual (2002). They are
reproduced with the
permission of Paul Ekman
and Joseph C. Hager

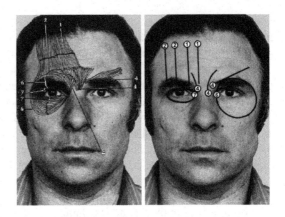

pauses and intervals between movement phases, etc. Figure 15.5 shows an early 2D physical description framework for capturing the dynamics of a gesturing torso, the lower part of the body being remarkably off-centre (McNeill 1992). A gesture coding scheme that covers more of this territory is FORM (Martell 2005). We consider it an open question whether the gesture coding language just sketched would be sufficient for expressing everything basic about body action. And we need, but don't seem to have in the state of the art yet, coding languages for facial expression and gesture corresponding to transcription coding for speech (Section 15.5.3) and able to express, e.g. pauses, false starts and occlusion in gesture and facial expression.

**Fig. 15.5** 2D reference
system for low-level gesture
annotation. This figure is
from David McNeill: Hand
and mind. © 1992 University
of Chicago, Fig. 3.1, page 89.
It is reproduced with the
permission of David McNeill
and University of Chicago
Press

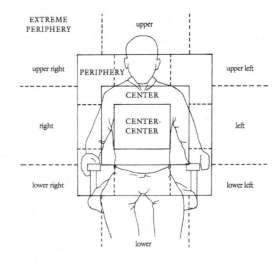

*Unimodal, non-semantic structural* is the next layer "upwards", and already this one is grounded in the non-semantic elementary layer discussed above. This layer is well-developed for speech, including, e.g. languages for expressing word morphology, part-of-speech and syntactic structure. We don't know if the facial expression domain includes such structures as well. The gesture domain does, however, in the form of the gesture execution phases illustrated for pointing gesture in Fig. 15.3. Possibly, the idea that some gesture types have execution phases could be transferred to some types of body actions.

*Unimodal, semantic high-level* languages and coding schemes exist for gesture in the form of a group of classical gesture types described by one of the early theoreticians of human gesture (McNeill 1992). Based on his work and that of others, some generally recognised 3D gesture types are

- *deictic* gesture through which we indicate – using hand pointing, head nods and otherwise – objects, events and processes and their aspects with a high degree of precision;
- *iconic* gesture in which we produce an analogue rendering, like an image sketch or simpler, of some spatio-temporal entity, as in the proverbial "The fish was huge [stretching both arms sideways to full length and bending the hands some] but the line broke!";
- *metaphoric* gesture in which we produce an iconic gesture from some source domain and want the interlocutor to interpret the gesture metaphorically as information about the target domain, as in "Then he exploded – boom! [stretching both hand-arms upwards and outwards to sketch an exploding substance]";
- *emblematic* gesture (or *emblems*) that work in communication in a way similar to conventional linguistic expressions or utterances, such as thumbs up, the terrible finger, V-for-victory, the affirmative head nod, a slap on the back, etc.;
- *baton* (or *beat*) gestures named after the music conductor's *baton*, i.e. typically repeated, rhythmic movements of the arms and hands, for instance in order to emphasise points made in speech. Politicians are often good at batons!

These gesture types would seem sufficiently well established for cautious practical coding scheme application. However, remember to have an *other gestures* category! We are still missing a really canonical (generally accepted, standard) 3D visual gesture coding scheme because questions remain about the completeness of typologies like the one above. For instance, does *emotive gesture*, such as banging one's fist on the table, fit into the typology? Is it a baton gone overboard? How about *metonymic gesture* (cf. Fig. 4.1)? Do we need a separate category for *mimetic gesture* (someone imitating the gesture micro-behaviour of someone else)? Moreover, even though much early gesture research was done with subjects sitting down, it seems clear that we may gesture with the entire body and any part of it. In fact, we communicate with the entire body, and this necessary generalisation of perspective might generate additional movement gesture types.

Nevertheless, this gesture typology seems to be the best there is at the moment. We might add the typology to the modality taxonomy in Table 4.2, expanding dynamic graphics gesture (12a2) at sub-sub-atomic level into 12a2a–e, comprising deictic, iconic and metaphoric gesture, emblem and baton, respectively. Like other modalities, the gesture types are rarely used for annotation as such: it's not very informative to code communication merely by tagging "one baton gesture", "one iconic gesture", or "one static graphic image", without including any contents, such as "pointing at the house" or "showing the diameter with rounded thumb and index finger". That's why we call coding languages, such as this one, "semantic high-level". These languages actually represent modalities.

So far, we have only discussed semantic high-level coding of gesture, because that's where our notion of semantic high-level coding comes from. Now let's ask if something similar exists for speech, facial and body action. This appears to be the case for facial expression: we can have *face emblems*, such as the deliberate eye blink (or wink); *face iconic*, such as mimicking open-mouthed astonishment; *face metaphoric*, such as showing that someone blew up; *eye gaze deictic*, when we point towards something using our gaze; and perhaps even *mouth batons*. Moreover, something similar exists for speech or, rather, voice, or "mouth or vocal tract-produced non-speech sound" as well: a wolf whistle emblem, for instance, means "how beautiful" (Massaro et al. 2005); we can speak iconically by speaking like someone; and use speech prosody as a baton.

*Unimodal, semantic lower-level* coding schemes and languages are where speech excels again. Morphemes, words, utterances, co-reference, topic and focus, speech acts, discourse structure and more all represent ways of getting at units of meaning that are being represented or exchanged. For instance, it is common to code for speech acts, i.e. the actions done by speakers when speaking the words they do. The basic theory is found in, among others, Searle (1969, 1983). However, Searle (1983) only theoretically grounds distinction between five basic speech acts: assertives ("the window is open"), directives ("open the window"), commissives ("I will open the window"), declarations ("I hereby declare this new bridge open for traffic") and expressives ("I love to have the window open"). For practical purposes of input analysis and output generation this tends to be insufficient, so most researchers write their own, more complex, task-specific dialogue act coding schemes, often picking and choosing from the influential DAMSL annotation scheme (Allan and Core 1997, Core and Allen 1997) that has been applied to, among other things, the Trains corpus (TRAINS 2000).

While there is a lot of languages for coding the semantics of speech behaviour, it is far less clear what we have for coding the semantics of facial expression and gesture. Are smiles and frowns semantic units like words? Hardly. As for gesture, it makes sense to make coding representation languages for representing the emblems of some culture and for coding deictic, iconic, metaphoric and baton gestures. Interestingly, human languages have thousands of verbs for describing body action semantic units, like "put", "move" or "open", and one approach to coding these might be to extend the frame semantics approach illustrated in Fig. 15.3.

*Global mental and physical states* – cognitive, conative, emotions and moods, interpersonal attitudes, physical states, personality – are being expressed in multi-modal or cross-modal fashion in all the modalities we are discussing, i.e. speech, facial expression, gesture and body action. Thus, for global states of people, each blending-with-people modality micro-behaviour only provides a *cue*, a factor to be taken into account together with others. Moreover, age, gender, personality, physical and psychological context and more, must be taken into account as well. That's how people are, and that's why global mental and physical state generation and recognition will be occupying research for many years to come.

Emotion interpretation and generation are considered important to many multi-modal and natural interactive systems. Today's researchers have been through the classic literature on human emotion, having lost a lot of naivety on the way, for instance with respect to the ease of recognising a person's current emotional state from the face alone. Facial expression only provides cues to emotion, and, arguably, facial emotion recognition on its own is rarely able to identify human emotion with any reasonable certainty. Humans put a happy face onto their sadness if their personality or the social context suggest that they do.

To capture a person's real emotion we need far more contextual information, i.e. what, in fact, happened to cause the emotion? – and information about the particular person, i.e. how would this person react? We also need to combine the perceived facial cues to emotion with other factors, such as speech prosody and the contents of what is being said if there is speech input, with gaze information and, possibly, gesture information as well, such as gesture speed and amplitude.

There is still disagreement over fundamental issues with respect to emotion, such as (i) the number of human emotions; (ii) whether emotions form a hierarchy based on a relatively small set of basic emotions, i.e. a short list of key emotions which are culturally universal and are all we really need in computing for a start, because the rest is detailed tunings and derivatives; and (iii) the descriptive parameters needed for characterising a particular emotion. Some classical discussions are Ekman (1999), Ortony et al. (1988) and Ortony and Turner (1990). Figure 15.6 illustrates emotion annotation using EARL (HUMAINE 2006), the HUMAINE Emotion Annotation and Representation Language, which is an XML-based language for representing and annotating emotions. The annotation can be done using, e.g. Anvil, cf. Section 15.5.6. In the Maths Case (Section 2.1), we plan to code facial training data using a pragmatic coding scheme which only codes for sadness, anger, happiness and other emotions.

*Multimodal coordination* coding schemes and languages. We will need to develop cluster coding schemes for all modality combinations that work well, cf. the list in Section 4.4.3.

We discuss relationships among modality candidates in Section 4.4.2 and would like to add a couple of observations on relationships among blending-with-people modalities.

*Facial expression and the others.* There is a sense in which facial expression is basic because it's always there. We may be awake without speaking nor gesturing

---

**Markup using EARL**

```
<emotion category="pleasure" probability="0.4" start="0.5"
end="1.02"/>

<emotion modality="voice" category="pleasure" probability="0.9"
start="0.5" end="1.02"/>

<emotion modality="face" category="neutral" probability="0.5"
start="0" end="2"/>

<emotion modality="text" probability="0.4" start="0.5" end="1.02"
arousal="-0.5" valence="0.1"/>
```

---

**Fig. 15.6**  EARL emotion markup

nor acting. However, the face and the gaze (Argyle 1988, Kendon 1990) are always there to "mirror the soul", to give cues to our mental and physical states through the use of facial muscles including eye environment muscles, gaze direction and pupil size. When speech, and not least speech prosody, gesture, including head and body posture, and/or body action get produced as well, we expect them to provide cues to mental and physical states consistent with the facial expression, which they don't always do, of course.

*Gesture and speech.* Regarding the relationship between gesture and other modalities, it is worth bearing in mind that, e.g. McNeill continuously stresses the close coordination relationship between gesture and speech. Gesturing without accompanying speech is done quite often, to be sure, but mostly in the case of emblems. An emblem is equivalent to some class of spoken utterances and hence can be meaningfully produced independently of accompanying speech. We have found that unambiguous deictic (pointing) gesture without accompanying speech occurs as well, but only, it seems, in a well-circumscribed class of cases in which the gesture has already been endowed – linguistically and typically through speech – with a clear semantics (Bernsen 2006). Figure 15.3 illustrates coordination between deictic gesture, speech prosody and semantics.

The implication seems to be that, if we want to annotate gesture in the data, we will typically have to code various aspects of speech as well. One reason is that speech and pointing gesture are typically used as complementary modalities (Section 4.4.2). Another interesting reason, McNeil points out, is that most types of gesture are deeply personal in various ways. Iconic and metaphoric gesture expressions, i.e. gestures which in various ways create a kind of real-time image of what they represent, are often invented on the spot by the person using them. Also, iconic, metaphoric and beat gestures are used with very different frequency by different people (McNeill 1992). The main reason why we understand these gestures when made by others is that we understand their accompanying speech. This is redundancy writ large, i.e. as applying to entire modality categories, cf. Section 4.4.2. From a tough interaction design point of view, interaction being exchange of information, we hardly need iconic, metaphoric and beat gesture at all because the accompanying speech is what expresses the necessary information! Or, we need those gesture types but mainly to make our animated characters *look* real.

*Conclusion.* To conclude this overview we would like to make two points. The first is that there is still much work to be done to establish general coding schemes for many classes of *unimodal* phenomena in the modalities discussed above. Progress will improve our abilities to develop multimodal applications that do not involve full natural human communication as input or output. For instance, we can easily think of many applications that only need input in a single modality, such as gaze pointing, spoken keywords or emblematic 3D gesture, together with whichever output modalities are appropriate.

The second point is that we are only beginning to respond to the fundamental facts that humans communicate (and interact with computers) with their entire body and mind, and do so through coordinated expression in multiple modalities. When dealing with natural multimodal human communication, it is ultimately artificial to only code for speech in isolation, facial expression in isolation, gesture in isolation, etc., no matter which particular class of phenomena is being coded in each case. Before we understand the complex multimodal coordination involved and the multiple modality relationships that are active in communication, we don't really understand human communication. Furthermore, it is only this comprehensive understanding of relationships between what is communicated through individual modalities that will enable machines to deal with very human communicative phenomena, such as insincerity, pretending, simulating, lying, irony, emotion concealment and terse humour. We need to establish and build on a new fundamental concept of a communicative act which is characterised in terms of the total set of modalities used.

## 15.5.6 Coding Tools

A coding tool is a tool for annotating data resources by applying one or several coding schemes. An annotation may reference raw data directly or reference other annotation layers which again reference raw data. The tool may include particular coding schemes and may support specification of new coding schemes. There may also be support for querying an annotated data resource and for applying statistics to annotated data. Not all coding tools have all of these properties, however. In more detail, a coding tool can be of great help in data annotation by helping to

- handle a range of common raw data file formats, allowing fine-grained manipulation of data represented in these formats, such as using millisecond and frame-by-frame navigation;
- time-stamp each phenomenon relative to a common timeline. Time-stamping is essential for analysing cross-modality coordination (Fig. 15.3) and many other temporal correlations in human behaviour, interactive and otherwise;
- create coding files (data annotation files) in a common format;
- enable specification of coding schemes in a common format;

- visually present data and data codings in ways which facilitate data analysis as illustrated in Fig. 15.3 which shows one among several styles of data and data coding presentation;
- facilitate coding and make it less error-prone by offering a coding palette corresponding to the specified coding scheme. Instead of typing in a tag manually, we select the tag from the coding palette and insert it at the relevant location in the coding file;
- support querying of the annotated data to extract information;
- support simple data statistics;
- enable data file import into the tool and data file export to other tools, such as statistics packages, with no need for cumbersome data conversions in between;
- support inclusion of meta-data with raw data files, coding schemes and coding files.

Several years ago, we made a survey of coding tools for natural interactive and multimodal data (Dybkjær et al. 2001, Dybkjær and Bernsen 2004). We found that, in the past, most researchers and developers had tended to make their own in-house coding tools which could be used for a particular coding purpose only. A few widely used coding tools had emerged as well, mostly addressing classes of relatively basic coding tasks, such as transcription coding (Section 15.5.3). In addition to these *special-purpose* coding tools, a number of more *general-purpose* tools were emerging at the time, i.e. tools that could support coding of phenomena in several modalities, such as spoken language and gesture. Today, there is still no fully general-purpose coding tool that supports all the tool functions listed above, enables coding for most conceivable coding purposes and enables customisation of data file presentation to suit any purpose of analysis.

The coding tools we looked at differed a lot with respect to other parameters, such as commercial/freeware/open source, robustness and the programming skills required for using them for new coding purposes. Some, following an ease-of-use philosophy, can be customised relatively easily for a range of purposes but tend to be fairly simple in what they can do. Others, following a coding toolkit philosophy, can be configured more broadly but only by programmers prepared to put in a significant amount of work to implement coding schemes, coding interfaces and any other missing module they need.

New tools keep appearing as do new versions of already existing tools, so we won't go into detail with any particular tool. Instead, we mention a few examples, including references to where to find more information about each tool and possibly download it. We stress that the tools mentioned are examples only and encourage you to look around on the Internet and in literature if you need a coding tool and if none of our examples seem to be just what you are looking for.

*Transcriber* (Transcriber 2008) is a special-purpose tool for orthographic speech transcription and transcription tagging, which provides a waveform view of the speech signal as well. Transcriber is open source and can be downloaded and used for free.

*Praat* (Praat 2009) supports both phonetic and orthographic transcriptions of speech, as well as speech visualisation, analysis and manipulation. Praat is open source and can be downloaded and used for free.

*The Observer* (Noldus 2009) is a commercial tool for annotating and analysing all manner of behavioural data captured in video files. The Observer also includes some elementary statistics.

*Anvil* (Kipp 2008) is a tool for annotating video files, originally developed for gesture annotation. Freely available for research but not open source, Anvil is probably one of the best current tools for annotating multimodal aspects of communication more generally. New coding schemes must be specified in XML. Otherwise, Anvil is ready to use. Anvil also offers the option to import intensity and pitch data from Praat which will then be displayed in a new tier.

The tools mentioned represent the coding in different ways. For instance, the Observer uses a vertical symbolic table format in which each entry is time stamped. Anvil uses a horizontal analogue timeline and horizontal tiers in which tags are aligned with the timeline, like in the representation in Fig. 15.3. Transcriber offers both a symbolic and an analogue view.

The *analogue view* makes it visually easy to directly relate and compare the timing of communication contributions in different modalities, whereas the symbolic view does not. On the other hand, the *symbolic view* of the spoken conversation in Transcriber provides a nice overview of a substantial fragment of the conversation, showing utterances in their conversation context. In analogue-view Anvil, it is hard to get an overview of what is being said in several consecutive conversation turns because the conversation contributions only occupy a single tier (row) in the data coding view interface, again like in Fig. 15.3.

As with nearly everything else in the data coding field, you should expect to spend some training and getting-used-to time with the tool before being able to use it, assuming that the tool you want to use runs on the platform of your choice and supports the data file formats you use.

*Annotation toolkits.* Another family of coding tools are programmers' kits rather than more or less ready-to-use coding tools. Like the latter, annotation toolkits are not universal because they have libraries and components with a particular coverage, such as aspects of linguistic annotation or aspects of video annotation. Toolkits assume programming experience, and you often have to develop entire components, including incorporation of the coding scheme you are going to use, to obtain a tool that is suitable for your purpose. On the other hand, if you can find a toolkit that already has at least some of the components you need, this is still better than starting to develop a tool from scratch.

Two Open Source toolkit examples are the Annotation Graph Toolkit (AGTK), a suite of software components for building tools for linguistic annotation of, e.g. audio and video files (AGTK 2007); and the NITE XML Toolkit (NXT), a set of libraries and tools for supporting annotation of text, audio and video files and including data handling, search and GUI components (NITE 2007, 2008).

*Alternatively.* As an alternative to dedicated coding tools and toolkits, you might settle for the good-old spreadsheet for annotating raw data. For instance, to study combined speech and gesture communication in the Sudoku (Section 2.1) test videos or in the data resource example in Section 10.5, we might copy orthographic transcription tagging made with Transcriber into a spreadsheet; watch, listen to and operate an independent video player showing the user's gestures; listen to what the user said; insert the observed gesture types and tokens into separate spreadsheet columns; symbolically describe temporal relationships between, e.g. onsets of speech and gesture; and then start coding for speech-gesture relationships. Counting of phenomena types and tokens in the data is done by hand or, better, by putting numbers into separate columns for automated counting. You may use shade (cf. Fig. 15.3) or colour coding to facilitate overview of the annotated data. The tags applied are in a separate open file. The coding is often research style and exploratory. This is clearly a sub-optimal procedure, but it does work for relatively simple multimodal and natural interactivity data coding.

## 15.6  Coding Procedure and Coding Best Practice

How would you have coded the birds in Section 15.5.1? Sat quietly somewhere unobtrusive, watching the birds, handling your tools to make sure to identify each bird correctly and making notes about the occurrence and number of birds of each kind? Suppose that you note the presence of two birds of kind A, then one B-bird, then three C-birds and then another A-bird. Are you sure that the last A-bird wasn't one of the two first A-birds? This is not always easy to determine. A more reliable procedure might have been to focus on a single species at a time, making sure to count all tokens of this type before moving on to code for the next kind of bird. Or, you might first count all birds on the small island somehow, and from then on focus solely on counting new arrivals.

Fortunately, when dealing with raw data as opposed to real-time behaviour, even though phenomena in video and sound files are transient, too, we have full control of the raw data display and can move back and forth frame-by-frame or millisecond by millisecond, repeating inspection of any part of the data as many times as required. For this reason, when going through the data, you might, with training, be able to look in parallel for all phenomena to be annotated following a single coding scheme. Even that may be too difficult in some cases, for instance if there are many types to look for; many tokens of each type; some tokens are hard to classify; types are related in complex ways relative to an individual token; or the coding needs high reliability. In such cases, it may be safer to go through the data file type by type. Another way of improving reliability is to go through the raw data file several times with the same focus, checking the correctness of annotations already made. This is advisable for all or most codings. A third coding procedure is to involve several annotators, like the bird watchers did in Section 15.5.1. The annotators would first annotate the data independently of one another, possibly doing several iterations each, and then compare annotations, returning to the data whenever a discrepancy is found between their codings and discussing the correct coding until they reach consensus in each case or decide that a case is undecidable. The latter may reflect back on the semantics of the coding scheme, the skills of the coders or the underlying theory. A more lightweight use of several coders is to have one coder do the annotation and the other(s) check it.

What annotators should never do is to try to apply several different coding schemes in parallel, no matter if a coding tool is being used or not. This procedure is bad coding practice because it will inevitably prove to be too strong a burden on the annotator's attention and memory, even if the annotator is an expert in several coding schemes. Always complete the coding with one coding scheme before proceeding to code the data using another coding scheme.

It is good coding documentation practice to describe, in the meta-data part of the coding file, the coding procedure that was followed in annotating the data, together with the coding skills of the coders (Section 15.5.1). The coding procedure followed and the skills of the coders are crucial indicators of the reliability of the coding made. No one wants to use, or re-use, coding files that are likely to be corrupt because the annotator has followed bad coding practice, and it may be hard going – and bordering on the fraudulent – to create interest in otherwise high-interest results that were achieved using questionable coding practice.

## 15.7 Key Points

This chapter has covered the data handling process up until the point where we are ready to analyse the data. Data handling starts with data collection, and *data collection planning* and *data collection* have, in fact, been the core topics of Chapters 6, 7, 8, 9, 10, 11, 12 and 13.

Collected data is *raw data* which may be of several different kinds. Typically, data collection yields substantial raw data, which means that *book-keeping* becomes important. Similarly, proper *meta-data* documentation of the collected data is crucial to future use. Before starting to work on or otherwise use the collected data, raw data must be *validated* to make sure that we have the amount of data we need and in the required quality. *Post-processing* of raw data may also be required to optimise data representation for the purpose for which the data will be used. For data collected with many of this book's methods and, not least, data on micro-behaviours for blending with people, the next step is *annotation*, preferably by means of *established coding schemes* and following *coding best practice*, possibly supported by a *coding tool*.

## References

AGTK (2007) Annotation graph toolkit. http://sourceforge.net/projects/agtk/. Accessed 21 February 2009.
Allan J, Core M (1997) Draft of DAMSL: dialog act markup in several layers. http://www.cs.rochester.edu/research/cisd/resources/damsl/RevisedManual. Accessed 21 February 2009.
Argyle M (1988) Bodily communication. London, Methuen, 1975. 2nd edn, Routledge.

Bernsen NO (2006) Speech and 2D deictic gesture reference to virtual scenes. In: André E, Dybkjær L, Minker W, Neumann H, Weber M (eds) Perception and interactive technologies. Proceedings of international tutorial and research workshop. Springer: LNAI 4021.

Bernsen NO, Dybkjær H, Dybkjær L (1998) Designing interactive speech systems. From first ideas to user testing. Springer Verlag, Heidelberg.

Core M, Allen J (1997) Coding dialogs with the DAMSL annotation scheme. Proceedings of the AAAI fall symposium on communicative action in humans and machines 28–35. Boston.

DataFace (2003) Description of facial action coding system (FACS). http://face-and-emotion.com/dataface/facs/description.jsp. Accessed 21 February 2009.

Dybkjær L, Berman S, Kipp M, Olsen MW, Pirrelli V, Reithinger N, Soria C (2001) Survey of existing tools, standards and user needs for annotation of natural interaction and multimodal data. ISLE deliverable D11.1. NISLab, Denmark.

Dybkjær L, Bernsen NO (2004) Towards general-purpose annotation tools – how far are we today? Proceedings of LREC 1: 197–200. Lisbon, Portugal.

Dybkjær L, Bernsen NO, Carletta J, Evert S, Kolodnytsky M, O'Donnell T (2002) The NITE markup framework. NITE deliverable D2.2. NISLab, Denmark.

Ekman P (1993) Facial expression and emotion. American Psychologist 48(4), 384–392.

Ekman P (1999a) Facial expressions. In: Dalgleish T, Power, M. (eds) Handbook of cognition and emotion, Chapter 16. John Wiley & Sons, New York.

Ekman P (1999b) Basic emotions. In: Dalgleish T, Power, M. (eds) Handbook of cognition and emotion, Chapter 3. John Wiley & Sons, New York.

FACS Manual (2002) Chapter 2: upper face action units. http://face-and-emotion.com/dataface/facs/manual/Chapter2.html. Accessed 21 February 2009.

HUMAINE (2006) HUMAINE emotion annotation and representation language (EARL). http://emotion-research.net/projects/humaine/earl. Accessed 21 February 2009.

Kendon A (1990) Conducting interaction. Cambridge University Press, Cambridge.

Kipp M (2008) Anvil: the video annotation research tool. http://www.anvil-software.de/. Accessed 21 February 2009.

Magno Caldognetto E, Poggi I, Cosi P, Cavicchio F, Merola G (2004) Multimodal score: an ANVIL based annotation scheme for multimodal audio-video analysis. Proceedings of LREC workshop on multimodal corpora, models of human behaviour for the specification and evaluation of multimodal input and output interfaces: 29–33. Lisbon, Portugal.

Martell C (2005) An extensible, kinematically-based gesture annotation scheme. In: van Kuppevelt J, Dybkjær L, Bernsen NO (eds) Advances in natural multimodal dialogue systems. Springer Series Text, Speech and Language Technology, 30: 79–95.

Massaro DW, Ouni S, Cohen MM, Clark R (2005) A multilingual embodied conversational agent. Proceedings of the 38th Hawaii International Conference on System Sciences, 296b.

McNeill (1992) Hand and mind. University of Chicago Press, Chicago.

NITE (2005) Natural interactivity tools engineering. http://nite.nis.sdu.dk. Accessed 21 February 2009.

NITE (2007) The NITE XML toolkit. http://www.ltg.ed.ac.uk/software/nxt. Accessed 21 February 2009.

NITE (2008) NITE XML toolkit homepages. http://www.ltg.ed.ac.uk/NITE/. Accessed 21 February 2009.

Noldus (2009) The Observer XT. http://www.noldus.com/human-behavior-research/products/the-observer-xt. Accessed 21 February 2009.

Ortony A, Clore A, Collins G (1988) The cognitive structure of emotions. Cambridge University Press, Cambridge.

Ortony A, Turner TJ (1990) What's basic about basic emotions? Psychological Review 97(3): 315–331.

Praat (2009) Praat: doing phonetics by computer. http://www.fon.hum.uva.nl/praat/. Accessed 21 February 2009.

SAMPA (2005) SAMPA computer readable phonetic alphabet. http://www.phon.ucl.ac.uk/home/sampa/index.html. Accessed 21 February 2009.

Searle J (1969) Speech acts. Cambridge University Press, Cambridge.

Searle J (1983) Intentionality. Cambridge University Press, Cambridge.

Speecon (2004) Speech driven interfaces for consumer devices. http://www.speechdat.org/speecon/index.html. Accessed 6 February 2009.

Sperberg-McQueen CM, Burnard L (1994) Guidelines for electronic text encoding and interchange. TEI P3, Text Encoding Initiative, Chicago, Oxford.

Sperberg-McQueen CM, Burnard L (2004) The XML version of the TEI guidelines. Text Encoding Initiative, http://www.tei-c.org/P4X/. Accessed 21 February 2009.

ToBI (1999) ToBI. http://www.ling.ohio-state.edu/~tobi. Accessed 21 February 2009.

TRAINS (2000) The TRAINS project: natural spoken dialogue and interactive planning. http://www.cs.rochester.edu/research/trains. Accessed 21 February 2009.

Transcriber (2008) A tool for segmenting, labeling and transcribing speech. http://trans.sourceforge.net/en/presentation.php. Accessed 21 February 2009.

# Chapter 16
# Usability Data Analysis and Evaluation

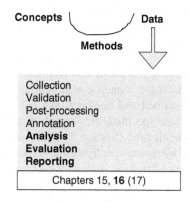

This chapter addresses the final, crowning steps of nearly all CoMeDa cycles, i.e. analysis of the collected usability data and reporting on results. The only exceptions are when we collect micro-behavioural data purely for component training purposes (cf. Sections 10.2 and 10.5) or collect user screening data (Section 8.6), in which cases there may be no real analysis, only data reporting. In all other cases of applying the methods described in this book, we apply the method *because* we need the results of data analysis.

The crucial role of data analysis is to identify, extract and reason about information in the data, which can help make system model usability *better* and/or tell us how *good* it has become. Those two italicised words demonstrate a very important point, i.e. that usability data analysis is intrinsically coupled with, or includes, usability evaluation. Due to its importance, we address usability evaluation separately after having discussed the data analysis process in general. Results reporting is discussed at the end of the chapter. To read an example of a data analysis report before continuing with the present chapter, see Chapter 17 (Intermezzo 5).

In the following, Section 16.1 presents a general model of usability data analysis, emphasising the support provided by the context of analysis and the dangers inherent in the non-rigorous nature of interpretation. Section 16.2, the first of four sections which focus on data analysis for usability evaluation, introduces evaluation arguments and criteria. Semi-nerdy Section 16.3 discusses the merits of quantitative, qualitative and other types of evaluation results and looks at various evaluation purposes. Section 16.4 broadens our perspective on the variety of usability evaluation criteria. Section 16.5 discusses usability evaluation in practice based on the Sudoku usability evaluation example in Chapter 17 (Intermezzo 5). Section 16.6 looks at how to report on analysis and evaluation results.

N.O. Bernsen, L. Dybkjær, *Multimodal Usability*, Human-Computer Interaction Series, DOI 10.1007/978-1-84882-553-6_16, © Springer-Verlag London Limited 2009

## 16.1  Data Analysis: Process and Issues

This section describes the context that supports data analysis (Section 16.1.1) and presents a general model of data analysis (Sections 16.1.2, 16.1.3 and 16.1.4) and preparation for action (Section 16.1.5) based on the results of analysis.

### *16.1.1  Context of Analysis*

Let's recapitulate the background of data analysis. In data handling cycle terms (Fig. 15.1), we first collect usability data by means of a usability method. The data consists of raw data file types like those listed in Section 15.3.1. The raw data files are then subjected to data book-keeping and meta-data description (Section 15.3), validation and post-processing (Section 15.4) and any annotation required (Section 15.5), following proper coding procedure (Section 15.6). We are now ready to analyse the data.

Assuming that data collection, validation, post-processing and annotation have proceeded more or less as planned – and this is a demanding assumption – most usability data analysis is pretty well circumscribed and does not take place in a vacuum at all. When the system model has been specified, the context of analysis includes (1) the *AMITUDE* model of use specification (Section 5.1); (2) *usability requirements* (Section 5.2); (3) the *usability workplan* specifying the data collection methods to use (Section 6.3); and (4) a *usability method plan* for each method, specifying the data collection purpose and generally organised with the sole aim of making as certain as possible that data satisfying this purpose actually gets collected (Section 6.4). Moreover, (5) when prepared and executed, the usability method plan involves and generates a smaller or larger amount of *documentation* that, together with the plan itself, is essential data analysis context. Finally, (6) other method applications may have taken place before the present one and may have generated relevant reports and other documentation as well. Here is a more detailed potential context list based on the discussion in this book:

- AMITUDE/system design
- AMITUDE/system specification
- Anomalies
- Architecture diagrams
- Categories to work on
- Checklists
- Consent form
- Data analysis reports
- Draft list of questions to address
- Early system documentation
- Equipment documentation
- Evaluation criteria
- Experimenter instructions
- Field observation plan
- Flow diagrams
- Open issues list
- Permissions
- Personas
- Questionnaire
- Scenarios
- Slide shows
- Staff instructions
- Standards set
- Subject training material
- System model
- User guide
- User instructions
- System model documentation
- Usability method plan
- Usability requirements

- Guideline set
- Interview script
- Lab observation plan
- Logfiles
- Manual
- Meeting/workshop agenda
- Meeting/workshop presentation

- Usability workplan
- Use cases
- User debriefing guide
- Video presentations
- Wizard instructions
- Wizard support information

To this may be added a different kind of context that includes literature for use during analysis, tools from pen and paper over spreadsheets to dedicated annotation tools, statistical packages, etc. It's only at the very early stages of system development that data analysis is missing substantial context. At these stages, the primary purpose of analysis is to accumulate and organise ideas that will eventually lead to a requirements specification, including an AMITUDE model of use.

In summary, we design and collect the data based on the project needs at the time and analyse it in the appropriate context based on the purpose for which it was collected. Most of the time, that's a pretty well-defined situation to be in. The situation is a bit less well defined, the less data directness there is (Section 15.1), of course, but that's partly a consequence of using certain methods, and it is a refreshing creativity challenge – isn't it? – to try to make sense of the system model potential in a set of brainstorming notes or field observation data.

So far, however, we are dealing with the ideal situation in which everything in the data handling cycle has been done best-practice and exactly according to plan. It often has not, which is why one of the items on the list above says *anomalies*. Anomalies are items on a list that we haven't mentioned before. These items describe everything that has *not* gone according to plan or has gone wrong in the method application and data handling process up to the start of data analysis. Sometimes the accumulating anomalies are so adverse that we never get to data analysis but must start afresh, like when we lost the video data somehow, messed around as in Box 10.1, or had planned to analyse turn-taking on the basis of a recorded discussion on TV, cf. the example in Section 10.5. At other times anomalies are less adverse, like when anomalies in subject recruitment make the data less reliable than planned, cf. Section 17.1.2.

Data analysis should always be done for the purposes for which the data was designed and collected. Nevertheless, it frequently happens that new analysis objectives come up and should be pursued as well, and it sometimes happens that a new objective can be pursued through analysis of data already collected rather than requiring new data. These objectives may reflect needs that unexpectedly arise during development or may be suggested by phenomena in the data resources themselves.

## 16.1.2  A General Model of Usability Data Analysis

We claimed in the chapter introduction that usability data analysis is intrinsically linked with evaluation. To see why, consider the following minimalist – very abstract – model of system development and evaluation. This model also explains another favourite claim in this book, i.e. that we do usability evaluation from day 1 and until we stop working on the system model.

We will expand the model several times, but let's start with the hazelnut shell view: all we do in development is two sets of binary operations, i.e. (O1.1) *Add or subtract* something with respect to the system model and (O1.2) address the question *What have we got?* Factoring in usability, we get this walnut shell view: (O2.1) *Add* something presumed usable to, or *subtract* something presumed unusable from, the AMITUDE model of use and (O2.2) address the question *Is what we have now usable – yes or no?*

To see how those operations can be performed as early as day 1, think about A proposing to B to build a speech-and-3D-pointing Sudoku system. That's an addition operation O2.1. Suppose that B reflects a bit and agrees that people might like the system. That's an affirmative operation O2.2! In fact, before proposing the idea, A probably did an affirmative operation with respect to the idea as well. If we call operations of type O2.1 *usability development* and operations of type O2.2 *usability evaluation*, we get the general picture that development and evaluation go hand in hand throughout the life cycle.

It is easy to factor usability methods (Chapters 8, 9, 10, 11, 12 and 13) and other approaches (Section 6.1) into the model: these serve to collect usability information to help us perform those operations. Once we have processed any raw data, it is the task of data analysis to answer "add" or "subtract", "yes" or "no".

To verify the model, take a look at the methods overview in Section 6.2.2. It appears that, in principle, all methods except user screening (Section 8.6) may help us perform *both* sets of operations. Select any method, such as a stakeholder meeting, and it is easy to imagine that the method could both evaluate the usability of some system property and suggest to add or remove a system property. This is why we have avoided any rigid division among this book's methods into usability development methods and usability evaluation methods. In summary, virtually all of this book's 24 methods may produce data that makes us add something presumed usable to the system model – in particular, to the AMITUDE model of use – or subtract something presumed unusable from the system model and answer "yes" or "no" to the question whether the current version of the model is usable.

Now let's replace those abstract model operations by a set of actual operations that we perform in usability data analysis. The following six should largely cover what is being done:

1. identify AMITUDE requirements and design ideas;
2. identify usability problems;
3. evaluate how the current AMITUDE model fits the target users in context;
4. evaluate usability development progress;
5. get as much operational information as possible on what should be modified in order to improve system usability;
6. assess the future potential of a technology.

When doing data analysis, we pursue some or all of the objectives above. In the example in Chapter 17 (Intermezzo 5), for instance, we primarily pursue (2), (3), (5) and (6). Moreover, in all cases the goal is to obtain as reliable results as possible. We get to reliability of analysis in Section 16.1.4 but note that, in general, reliability is a function of the reliability achieved in the entire data collection and data handling chain. Finally, note that the ultimate aim of analysis is *action* – to advance or improve specification or design, revise development plans if progress is too slow or too fast, fix or alleviate usability problems, take development into a new, more applied phase, take the system to the market, etc. It is only if the project dies as a result of analysis, or if the system will not be further developed or exploited for some other reason, that action on the results of analysis is not required.

Here follows a more complete model of data analysis prior to action:

- preliminary analysis and report, i.e. a short version of the following points;
- analysis of annotated data in context with aims (1), (2), (3), (4), (5) and/or (6) above;
- identification of implications;
- report on data collection, results and recommendations.

We discuss this model below but postpone reporting to Section 16.6.

### 16.1.3  Preliminary Analysis and Report

Following data collection, there is often pressure to report overall results and implications to colleagues straight away. Early reporting is facilitated by making a list of key observations during the data collection session(s). A first report might be based on this list, stressing, whenever required, that results are preliminary. If major decisions hinge upon those results, such as that an alternative design concept should be pursued or a major system modification set in motion, it is important to stress that final decision must await more detailed analysis. This analysis might be top of the list of what to do next when analysing the data in more depth.

In simple cases of method application, data analysis *ends* with an early report which might, e.g. simply consist of agreed and confirmed action points from a stakeholder meeting. In complex cases, data analysis may take weeks or months.

### 16.1.4  Data Analysis

Having emphasised in Section 16.1.1 how in a properly conducted, circumspect project, data analysis is pretty well contextualised most of the time, let's mention some more challenging aspects. First, revisit the nature of data in Section 15.2 and, in particular its properties of being tacit, rich and limited. At best, data only answers the questions you ask and, if you don't ask, data handling might as well not have happened at all. Second, how were you at literary/film/art analysis at school, i.e. at answering questions like "What does this book or movie or painting tell us about life, death, our times, the future and everything?" Did you like arts class? We hope so, because data analysis sometimes is like that: full of interpretation, conflicting evidence and demand for sound judgment and reasoning!

*How detailed?* Analysis should be as detailed as required by the data analysis purpose in the usability method plan, no more, no less, unless something unexpected comes up in the data or in the development context more generally. Thus, e.g. (i) carefully reflect on the confirmed minutes from an uneventful stakeholder meeting (Section 9.2) and take the necessary action, but do nothing special; (ii) apply the usability requirements (Section 5.2) to the Treasure Hunt test data but don't spend time on the test video recordings unless required for determining if the usability requirements are met; or (iii) make a global usability evaluation of the Sudoku Case by analysing the test data until all issues for which the data is found to provide evidence have been addressed. (i) is business as usual. If reflection on the minutes reveals something unexpected – are the stakeholders considering a brand new requirement that could upset the development plans and have severe usability repercussions? – the problem, or whatever it is, can rarely be solved by deeper data analysis but may require something else, like proactive developers discussion or a new meeting. (ii) *was* business as usual, and so was the global evaluation of the system. However, since the test plan turned out to be over-optimistic, it will be necessary to analyse the video data in order to improve test planning and subject instruction for the next user test, cf. the example in Section 10.4. (iii) is a recipe for potentially very detailed and prolonged data analysis, as illustrated in Chapter 17 (Intermezzo 5).

A common cause of plan change is when the analysis throws unexpected usability problems. For instance, we could not measure speech recognition rate in the Sudoku test data because of a rich bug (see Section 17.2.2). As a minimum, these problems must be diagnosed in order to explain their causes, but their occurrence may also lead to renewed annotation of data resources, for instance in order to more precisely assess the severity of a problem or to facilitate diagnosis by getting a more precise picture of how or why the problem occurs.

Analysis is usually faster and easier to do when there is little or no conflicting data. Thus, data from a focus group meeting (Section 9.1) with a rather unanimous outcome might be easy and fast to analyse. It is very different when the "overall message" of the data is far less clear than, or very different from, what was expected; when data interpretation encounters problems as to what the data "really means"; or when the planned data analysis opens up a new direction of analysis that turns out to be important to the project.

If no detailed data analysis is planned, what is often done is to go through the raw data looking for anything unexpected or unusual in order to consider if any of it has implications for system development. For instance, even if only a couple of users in a test population perform much worse than the rest, this could potentially mean that a significant fraction of the target users might have difficulty using the system.

*How reliable?* Data analysis, unless fully automated – and even then, until it is clear that automation works as intended – typically involves a larger or smaller amount of human interpretation, judgment and assessment. Different experts find different problems with the same system model. Humans disagree and make errors segmenting items, classifying them, counting them, estimating them, diagnosing them, applying criteria to them, prioritising them or judging them in other ways. Sometimes we have to change classification or modify criteria in mid-stream, increasing error probability. Novices tend to make more errors than the more experienced. Sometimes analysis can be partially automated, in particular if the raw data has been annotated so that a program can, e.g. count occurrences of certain phenomena. Remember to verify, using a small data sample, that the program actually computes what it is supposed to before applying it to the corpus. Some coding tools (Section 15.5.6) enable various kinds of information extraction. Automatic counting is an advantage, in particular, in case of large amounts of data, human counting being slow and error-prone.

The higher the reliability required, the more it is necessary to focus upon the exact procedure of data analysis; upon intersubjective control through having several analysts analyse the same data and discuss disagreements arising; upon training and upon having experienced or trained people rather than novices do the analysis. We have met these issues in connection with coding procedure already (Section 15.6). Reliability affects all or most aspects of data analysis. For instance, reliability is also at stake if you select to just listen to the audio track from a meeting or interview, making notes as you go along, rather than first transcribing the audio track and then analysing it. The latter procedure is the more reliable of the two, the former is the cheaper and might be sufficient in many cases.

We discuss the terrible issue of *evaluation bias* below (Section 16.5.3), but it should be pointed out that being biased towards certain outcomes of data analysis is potentially a general problem: just as we might want the system evaluation to be as positive as possible, we might interpret meeting minutes, expert reviews, field data or any other data corpus in ways corresponding more to our wishes and prejudices than to the actual facts expressed in the data. Given the amount of interpretation and judgment involved in data analysis, personal bias can have an easy time influencing results unless mental and methodological precautions are taken to prevent it.

*Annotation needed?* Detailed data analysis often requires elaborate annotation before the desired information can be extracted and evaluation criteria or other measures applied. However, as argued in Chapter 15, data annotation is relevant to virtually all the kinds of raw data listed in Section 15.3.1. So, the upshot is that we may well annotate the data according to plan before analysing it, but we might have to do more annotation once analysis has begun and we start seeing where it leads.

*Simple measurements* often form part of data analysis, particularly when evaluation criteria are being applied. How long does it take each user to complete the Treasure Hunt task (Table 5.5)? How many spoken dialogue turns does the user need to complete the flight booking task (Section 3.4.2)? How many words per utterance? If the amount of data is small, these counts could be done manually. However, if there is a substantial amount of data or if the data will be annotated anyway, simple counts like number of turns are better done automatically to ensure accuracy.

*Data statistics.* Results of data annotations and simple measurements feed into data statistics. Statistics are used to compute measures that characterise the data in terms of frequencies, distributions, scores, variability, etc. Examples are average number of errors per task or per user; rate of learning progress per training hour; modality preferences as related to gender, age or familiarity with the technology; percentage of users who completed a task within a set time frame; average Likert-scale rating of how much fun the system is; percentage of users who never gestured without speaking at the same time.

Simple descriptive statistics like those are often sufficient. However, to deliver statistically significant results you need inferential statistics. You should not use these more sophisticated kinds of statistics unless you are quite good at them. Otherwise, it is too easy to get them wrong and produce results that do more harm than good.

When mediated by some amount of interpretation, even qualitative data (see Section 16.3.3) can be subjected to statistics. For instance, free-text answers in open-question interview transcriptions (Section 8.1.3) might be categorised into negative, neutral or positive with respect to a particular topic, following which score rates can be calculated. This should be done separately by two analysts.

## 16.1.5 Problem Analysis: Identify Implications and Priorities

Reverting to our minimalist model in Section 16.1.2, we analyse usability data in order to determine how usable the current system model is, and what, if anything, should be added to, or subtracted from, the model to make it more usable. Once the data has revealed its secrets, we must decide what to do given what was found. Arriving at this stage is not always a linear process. It is often necessary to go back to the data to take another look to make sure what the basis for decision making really is. Remember that we are talking about data as varied in contents as listed in Section 15.3.1; coming in at any life cycle stage; and in projects ranging from the thoroughly familiar to the outrageously new. To move towards some general understanding of this process, we first look at two examples, one from usability evaluation and one from usability development, and then generalise a bit. In the first example, data analysis during evaluation of the current system model has identified a series of interaction problems, and we need to decide what to do about them. In the second, we have collected system model ideas from potential users and must decide what to do with them.

*Interaction problems analysis – an example.* Let's assume that we have done a first lab test of the spoken dialogue system described in Section 3.4.2. Based on usability requirements applied during data analysis, we find that several require-ments are not satisfied to the extent planned at this development stage. Time to task completion is much longer than specified in a requirement which states that 90% of the users should be able to successfully complete the scenario tasks within a certain time frame; the percentage of task failures is too high; and, in several cases, most users have difficulty understanding the meaning of what the system says. These problems are particularly prominent in certain specific scenarios among those given to the subjects. Diagnostic guideline application (Section 11.4) has revealed a series of output design problems. In most cases, test data diagnosis clearly shows what went wrong, i.e. which input steps were ignored or carried out in unexpected ways, which system states are missing and which output phrasings cause misunderstanding and confusion.

All problems identified must be organised along the same lines to support further analysis and decision making. In general, it is bad and risky practice to simply start fixing problems as they are found. The worst problems might be found last and, by then, there might be no time or other resources for fixing them. Moreover, what's a bad problem in the first place? Problem analysis and evaluation must include estimates of, at least

- *scope*: how widespread is the problem (how large a part of the system is affected);
- *seriousness*: how obstructive is the problem for user interaction;
- *frequency*: how often does the problem occur;
- *time and other resources* needed to fix the problem;
- *risk* related to fixing the problem.

We briefly look at these factors from an everything-equal perspective.

*Scope.* Problems affecting large parts of the system are usually more important to solve than problems relating to a single module only. For example, problems with output phrasing are normally local (output generation) problems, whereas a low-task success rate may be due to problems with several parts of the system.

*Seriousness.* Each identified problem may, e.g. be scored on a severity scale from 1 to 4 with the following interpretation:

1. problems that *prevent* the task or activity from being completed or otherwise prevent the system from serving its purpose, e.g. because the user cannot find the required functionality;
2. problems that are not prohibitive for carrying out the task or activity but which cause *serious delays* and *frustration*, e.g. due to missing feedback;
3. problems of *less usability significance*, e.g. a single term is used to refer to two different actions, which may be confusing to some users;
4. problems pointing towards *future work* and extensions, e.g. users' wish to have a real walking stick rather than a virtual one in a system teaching the blind to use a walking stick in a virtual environment.

From a seriousness perspective only, a problem that prevents users from completing a core task is clearly more serious than infelicitous phrasing of an output sentence which causes some users to become uncertain of what to do and ask for help.

*Frequency.* Frequently occurring problems command serious attention, highly infrequent problems are often less commanding. This enables a less serious problem to make its way up higher on the priority list than a more serious problem which is rarely observed.

*Time and other resources for fixing a problem, risk.* Assuming that there is a fixed amount of time and other resources available, a common situation is that not all identified problems can be fixed in the way we would like. So, prioritising becomes mandatory, and that's when it is important to be able to judge the resources needed for (i) finding a solution to fixing a problem and (ii) fix it. There are often trade-offs among different solutions, and "ideal" solutions often take longer and are sometimes more risky than less-than-ideal ones.

For each problem, we need to estimate the percentage of users affected and how likely it is that a user will actually experience the problem. Scope, seriousness and frequency together determine how critical a problem is and how much we should prioritise finding a solution. Even then, the estimated time this would take or the risk incurred could upset the priorities.

*Prioritising.* Having done the problems analysis, it is time to make recommendations for which problems to fix. This can be difficult to do. As problems are not always independent of one another, solution to one problem might interact with solutions to others, or might have side-effects and create new problems. Look at the widespread problems first, because they typically have larger effects. Discuss priorities among developers to get as many perspectives as possible. It is amazing how differently different people may view the same data. Use all sources of information, such as user priorities expressed in interviews and questionnaires.

Sometimes recommendations go higher up in the organisation. The actions finally settled upon may not be fully in line with the recommendations made, e.g. because management have plans for re-use of a particular component and therefore prioritise solutions of problems related to this component more than when the system is considered in isolation.

Even if no further development is planned, e.g. because the data is from the final evaluation of a research prototype, it is still important to identify and analyse problems to get an idea of the extent to which the project was successful. Note also that there is often no one-to-one mapping between data points and usability problems. A single data point may indicate several usability problems, and the same usability problem may appear in multiple data points.

*Interaction needs analysis.* Now suppose that the data is from a focus group meeting rather than from a system model test. Suppose that the system discussed is still a flight reservation system but this time based on spoken and 2D-pointing interaction via a web page and with an animated travel agent. Data analysis shows, say, that context-dependent help and combined acoustic and static graphic feedback appear to have high priority to nearly all focus group members, whereas animated face naturalness is not considered as important as expected. This suggests a couple of new system requirements and relaxation of an existing one.

Similar to the interaction problems analysis above, our analysis and evaluation of each identified issue must include estimates of, at least

- *scope*: which parts of the system will be affected by adding or subtracting the feature or system property implied by the requirement;
- *seriousness*: how important is it to users that the requirement is satisfied; how serious would an omission be;
- *frequency*: how often is the feature likely to be used or otherwise affect users' activities;

- *time and other resources* needed to add or subtract the feature;
- *risk* related to adding/subtracting the feature.

The items to be estimated are identical to those mentioned under interaction prob-lems analysis above. The crucial difference is that estimates are made on a looser and more fragile basis when no concrete system model is involved. For example, the actual importance of many features can only be estimated once there is a system model that can be tested with users. Omission of an important feature will manifest itself as a serious problem in interaction problems analysis.

*Problem analysis in general.* Let's try to generalise the interaction problems and needs examples just described to problem analysis of any usability data set, cf. the six usability data analysis operations listed in Section 16.1.2. Remember also that data analysis sometimes results in a clear picture, sometimes not (Section 16.1.4). Thus, a focus group (Section 9.1) might generate conflicting design ideas or point to features in need of further analysis; stakeholders (Section 9.2) might reveal problems with the specification as it stands; think-aloud (Section 12.5) might demonstrate serious user confusion; some component might be way behind schedule; a signal processing algorithm might not deliver as expected, causing interaction problems with the implemented prototype (Section 12.3); etc. In any case, it is necessary to

- organise, structure and analyse problems and candidate features;
- estimate their individual criticality based on scope, frequency and seriousness;
- find solutions to problems;
- estimate costs and risks for each problem solution and each candidate feature;
- prioritise proposed solutions and features.

We haven't presented any really detailed work on life cycle models in this book (Section 1.2.2), but those bullet points illustrate why several life cycle models emphasise risk analysis (Boehm 1989, Jacobson et al. 1999). We recommend to include, as part of risk management in the overall project plan, fallback solutions for development issues that are deemed to be high risk. When data analysis shows that the solution does not work, it's time to fall back on plan B.

*Inconclusive data.* With both development and evaluation data, it sometimes hap-pens that the collected data is inconclusive on important points: it might not be clear from analysis which solution users prefer or which solution their observed behaviour supports, if any; or it might not be clear if component progress is satis-factory because, e.g. (i) progress is not impressive and (ii) it was not possible to fix a progress target because the component does something completely new, such as recognising people's attitudes as distinct from their emotions. In such cases, possible actions are to collect new data as soon as possible, following a different data collec-tion protocol in order to bring the facts to light; intensify data collection following the original protocol in order to measure progress more frequently than planned; or fall back on a plan B.

## 16.2  Usability Evaluation

This section is the first of four discussing usability evaluation which is basic to all usability data analysis. Section 16.2.1 introduces the arguments, requirements and evaluation criteria involved in usability evaluation. Section 16.2.2 defines usability evaluation criteria in detail and describes the trade-off between precision and generality in usability evaluation.

### *16.2.1  Usability Arguments, Requirements, Criteria*

The picture we have from Section 16.1.2 is that we may think and reason about usability evaluation throughout the life cycle. This is fine as far as it goes, but it's too unsystematic and uncontrolled: we need to factor in the roles of applying usability methods and following more systematic usability evaluation practice. For this we need the notions of usability argument, usability requirement and usability evaluation criterion, so let's explain them.

*Usability arguments.* We use the term *usability argument* to refer to all informal usability evaluation made throughout the life cycle – in discussions, implicitly in proposals to add or remove something from the AMITUDE model, or based on other approaches (Section 6.1), including thinking and experience. What do these arguments appeal to? They appeal directly either to the top usability norms or goals defining usability in Table 1.1 or to more specific usability norms or goals that can be subsumed under these. An example of the latter is when someone says that the Sudoku gesture input (Section 5.1) is not yet good enough because it's still too difficult to control, implicitly appealing to the *ease of use* top norm in the table. In another example, suppose that we have a general system model idea of a spoken dialogue in-car system. A user survey shows that most car drivers would like to use in-car spoken dialogue for car navigation purposes. That's a (good) usability argument to the effect that users want this functionality, and, by referring to desired functionality, the argument directly appeals to the functionality part of our top usability goals in Table 1.1.

*Usability requirements.* Second, we have a more explicit instrument for preparing usability evaluation, namely, *usability requirements*, cf. Section 5.2. Usability requirements form part of the requirements specification, imposing requirements to system usability which are used to (a) steer development and (b) evaluate the system model based on data collected with usability methods.

A usability requirement may be of several different kinds. It may be a meta-requirement referring to a standard (Section 11.5) or a set of guidelines (Section 11.4), stating that the system should comply with those; a specialisation of the general usability norms (Table 1.1), such as that Sudoku pointing gesture should be easy to control (Table 5.9); or a quantitative measure with which the final system version should comply, such as that emotion recognition accuracy in the Maths Case (Section 5.1) should be at least 80%.

*Usability evaluation criteria.* Third, *usability evaluation criteria* (*metrics* in ISO terminology) are explicit criteria applied to data collected with usability methods, such as some of the methods presented in this book. A usability evaluation criterion may be identical to a usability requirement, or it may render a usability requirement operational as explained in the next section.

Confused? Don't be! We can summarise the message so far in two points:

1. Usability arguments, requirements and evaluation criteria are based on, refer to or specialise usability as defined in Table 1.1.
2. Based on data collected with a usability method, the system model is evaluated by a combination of usability arguments and usability evaluation criteria.

## *16.2.2  Usability Evaluation Criteria: The Evaluation Hierarchy*

Usability evaluation criteria are the most precise instruments in our evaluation tool-box. A usability evaluation criterion is a 3-point description of (i) *what* to measure; (ii) a measurable reference point or *target value* that is specified quantitatively or qualitatively; and (iii) *how* to measure.

Sometimes, not least in research prototype development (ii) cannot be specified with any quantitative accuracy because it is not known what could be a feasible and acceptable target value. For instance, prior to the first prototype test, our Sudoku usability requirements in Section 5.2 miss quantitative, as opposed to qualitative, target values for spoken input understanding and ease of pointing gesture control. The former just says, qualitatively, that speech input should be correctly understood, the latter that pointing gesture should be easy to control. However, since, in both cases, we are able to specify *what* to measure and *how* to measure it, these require-ments may still be turned into evaluation criteria by specifying the what and the how. In addition, many, if not most, qualitative target values are sort-of implicitly quan-titative, that is, we can tell when they are *definitely not* satisfied. For instance, the Sudoku system definitely doesn't understand spoken input correctly if the speech recognition rate is <90% correct keyword/key phrase recognition (assuming that <90% correct *recognition* translates into <90% correct *understanding*, which is plausible in this case).

*What to measure.* This is the self-explanatory part of a usability evaluation crite-rion, such as *spoken input understanding* or *ease of pointing gesture control*.

*Target value.* We are so used to thinking that "measured values" are quantitative and that criteria application yields quantitative results, that it is important to repeat that the target value of a usability evaluation criterion can be *either* quantitative or qualitative. We all love quantification, but it is worth contemplating that the top usability goals in Table 1.1 are not quantitative but qualitative ones, and that, as a matter of fact, there are a lot of target values in usability evaluation that we cannot currently quantify, at least not in an objective way (see Section 16.3). Sometimes we *can* operationalise a qualitative usability requirement into a quantitative and objective measure. For instance, after our first lab evaluation of the Sudoku system (Chapter 17), we might be able to establish a reasonable quantitative measure of ease of pointing gesture control which could form part of the usability requirements for the second version of the system and help guide its development.

*How to measure.* The *how* of an evaluation criterion is the method to use in measuring to the target value. The how must be specified because it is typically possible to measure the same *what* in very different ways (using different *hows*). This doesn't mean that they are all equally trustworthy, though. In the Sudoku speech understanding example above, measurement made with a well-trained user, like a developer who knows exactly how to pronounce the spoken commands in order to be recognised – might yield a recognition rate of +98%, whereas measurement with a large group of representative users in the lab might yield a 91% average, and a field test might yield an 88% average. Why would we put more trust in the 91 or 88% range than in the 98% in this case?

Note that the question whether the current system model is doing well or not is an altogether different one. If the test reported above is the final test, the system wouldn't seem to be doing too well; but if the test was made earlier, the system might be ahead of plan as regards speech understanding. As an alternative or supplement to the just described, *objective quantitative evaluation* of speech recognition, we might do *subjective quantitative evaluation* by asking the users how they would rate speech understanding on a 7-point scale from "very good" to "very bad". In this case, our target value could not be specified as a percentage but would have to be some average user score, such as the one corresponding to "very good".

Our definition of an evaluation criterion is close to the ISO/IEC 9126-1 (2001) (Software engineering – product quality) standard's definition of the term *metric* as "the defined measurement method and the measurement scale". The terms (evaluation) "criterion" and "metric" often seem to be used interchangeably in the literature. Also according to ISO/IEC 9126-1 (2001), a *measure* is "the number or category assigned to an attribute of an entity by making a measurement". Abstract stuff, right?

*The usability evaluation hierarchy.* Let's also link to ISO/IEC 9126-1 (2001) concerning an important general point about evaluation, i.e. the *usability evaluation hierarchy*. The top of this hierarchy is our usability decomposition in Table 1.1, which breaks down usability first into technical quality and user quality, and then breaks down user quality into the components functionality, ease of use and user experience. Similarly, in Fig. 11.15, ISO/IEC 9126-1's top node "External and internal quality" subsumes usability which it broken down into understandability, learnability, operability and attractiveness.

What's common to those high-level goals is that (i) they are slightly different articulations of the tip of an enormous iceberg which we call the usability evaluation hierarchy and (ii) we cannot meaningfully evaluate to this tip directly by means of evaluation criteria. Think about what would happen if we replaced all our tiresome low-level usability evaluations by a single criterion, i.e. evaluate the usability of this system on a 7-point scale from 1 "absolutely unusable" to 7 "absolutely usable" and got an average score of 4.9. See the problem? There is little information and no action here. We don't have the foggiest idea about what to do to improve system usability! That's why we measure things like speech recognition rate or time to task completion instead, even though they sit way down in the evaluation hierarchy. By evaluating lower down in the evaluation hierarchy, we gain data precision and action potential: if the speech recognition rate is 91 and should be 98, we know rather precisely what to aim for. What we lose, on the other hand, is being close to the top usability goals it's all about. So, when we have found, e.g. an average time to task completion of 3 minutes, we may be doing fine in this particular respect, but it really doesn't follow that our system is usable in all other respects. We still have two increasingly general, and therefore harder, questions to answer: (1) How is task performance overall, not just the time to task completion but also number of errors made, user satisfaction with doing tasks, etc.? and (2) How is system usability overall? Many different evaluation criteria and arguments may be needed to answer these two questions, each providing a small piece of the usability truth we're after.

It rather follows that any comprehensive usability evaluation of a system model needs to apply several – could be dozens of – usability criteria. On the other hand, it is unrealistic to apply all applicable usability evaluation criteria in a single evaluation exercise, even in research projects with particular focus on usability evaluation. This means that we need to select the criteria to apply from among a larger set of potentially useful criteria.

However, don't misunderstand when we speak about *selecting* evaluation criteria. It is often possible to select among criteria to apply, but, in many cases of innovative development, it is necessary to first *create* or *define* criteria before applying them, simply because those criteria are novel. Suppose that we need a criterion for gesture interpretation robustness when the system is faced with gesture disfluencies (Section 15.5.5). We don't know about any metrics for this phenomenon but they will appear sooner or later. Measuring system robustness with respect to speech disfluencies is already common.

Data analysis objectives (2) on usability problems, (3) on fitting users and (5) on operational information (see Section 16.1.2) should always be top priorities when selecting, defining and applying evaluation criteria. (3) pushes us towards the top-level goals or norms of the evaluation hierarchy, trying to get the overall picture of the system's usability. However, without (2) and (5) we cannot act much based on the evaluation results, because the information collected is not sufficiently detailed and operational, so (2) and (5) push us towards the bottom of the evaluation hierarchy in order to get as much detailed information as possible about each system characteristic.

## 16.3  Types of Evaluation Results and Purposes, Semi-Nerdy Stuff

Usability evaluation must be carried out in such a way that results are repeatable, reproducible, impartial and objective, cf. Section 11.5.1. Whoever gets the *what* and the *how* right when making an evaluation should arrive at the same results. These norms are pretty obvious because, without them, why spend resources on tests and other demanding evaluation activities instead of just inventing, subjectively, the results we like best?

This section looks at various aspects of evaluation and results. Section 16.2 mainly used an average percentage as example of an evaluation result, and it *is* tempting to consider that honest-to-God quantities like this one constitute the only or, at least, the best kind of results. However, it is important to understand why it is both necessary and useful to work with different kinds of evaluation results, and useful to keep in mind that evaluation may have a whole range of different, more special purposes. Section 16.3.1 discusses evaluation results as related to either design issues or technical issues. Section 16.3.2 is about objective versus subjective evaluation, and Section 16.3.3 is about quantitative versus qualitative evaluation. Section 16.3.4 describes different evaluation purposes and their relations to the software life cycle.

## 16.3.1  Technical Issues Versus Design Issues

If it survives that long, a system model goes through the stages of being an idea, specified, designed and built. For brevity, let's call everything to do with the three former for *design issues*, and everything to do with the latter *technical issues*. We can then say that we evaluate either the design or the technical implementation (or both). To see the difference, consider two interfaces which both make users run away. The first uses bright yellow text on turquoise background, the second has speech recognition that doesn't work. We have two usability problems here. The first one is a design problem that calls for a design change. The second is a technical problem because, say, the design idea of having speech recognition is fine and achievable, it just hasn't been properly realised yet.

It is for the above reason that the Sudoku usability evaluation in Chapter 17 (Intermezzo 5) has a section on technical issues. This is standard, and, moreover, it is standard to put this section early in the evaluation report. The reason is that subjects do not bother about the distinctions we are now discussing. If they encounter, e.g. a technically trivial but highly annoying system loop, this will influence their entire evaluation of the system. Therefore, put the technical issues up front in test reports, because they describe the context within which the subjects have experienced the system's design. And, even more importantly, try to get rid of all avoidable technical issues before a user test. It only takes a couple of seriously disruptive ones to ruin the value of the test data. This is also why our Case usability requirements invariably include a robustness requirement (Section 5.2).

## 16.3.2  Objective and Subjective Evaluation

Usability evaluation today is a mixture of objective and subjective evaluation in a special sense of these terms which should not be confused with the general meanings of "objective" and "subjective" defined at the start of this section (Section 16.3).

*Objective evaluation* is typically done by internal evaluators or by an external evaluation team. The goal of objective evaluation is to arrive at results that are independent of the personal opinions of users or subjects. *Subjective evaluation* typically represents users' non-expert, personal opinion of some property of the system, of the system as a whole or, less frequently, of some component.

A frequently asked question is whether objective evaluation is somehow "better" than subjective evaluation. In fact, as argued in the following, users' subjective evaluations, as collected following best evaluation practice, are essential to usability evaluation and are likely to remain so in the foreseeable future. For instance, it is standard practice to collect speech recogniser word error rate (WER) data, because WER tells something about the accuracy of speech recognition, which, in its turn, may be assumed to be an important factor in subjects' subjective evaluations of the system as a whole. However, we cannot *predict* subjects' evaluations of the system as a whole from the WER nor from any other known combination of objective measurements. If we could, we wouldn't need to collect users' subjective evaluations any more, but we still cannot. And it's the subjective evaluations that determine if people want to use the system, buy it, update their current system version to get a new and hopefully better one, etc. If you look at the usability Table 1.1, you'll see that two of the four entries, i.e. what users *want* and *user experience*, are subjective, and *ease of use* clearly has a subjective aspect as well. Even *does it work?* has!

Nevertheless, the dream remains of being able to compute users' subjective evaluations – what they want, how they will experience the system, etc. – from objective measurements without having to bother with subjects at all.

### 16.3.3 Quantitative and Qualitative Evaluation

We are used to thinking that objective is quantitative and subjective is qualitative, but no: both objective and subjective evaluations may be quantitative or qualitative.

*Quantitative evaluation* consists in expressing evaluation of the system in quantitative terms. When *objective*, quantitative evaluation is the result of either (i) applying some criterion, such as WER, that is independent of users' personal opinions, or (ii) expressing expert judgment quantitatively.

*Subjective* quantitative evaluation may take different forms: (i) users may express their opinions as quantitative scores of some kind, such as scoring the naturalness of an animated agent's eye movements at 4 on a 5-point scale. We consider such scorings quantitative, even if, as is often the case, each grade is defined in words as well, such as "5 = indistinguishable from a human voice". (ii) Users may express what they remember from the interaction in quantitative terms, such as when a user says that s/he asked for help six times. (iii) An evaluator may quantify users' opinions in some way, such as when finding that 80% of the test users preferred their camera-captured hands over the 3D mouse for on-screen navigation. While the calculation itself is, of course, objective, the 80% still express users' personal opinions.

*Qualitative evaluation* is expressed in a non-quantified way. When *objective*, qualitative evaluation consists in estimating or judging some property by reference to expert standards and rules, such as when finding that there is a lack of appropriate feedback in certain situations. *Subjective* qualitative evaluation consists in estimating or judging some property by expressing non-expert opinion qualitatively, such as when finding the eyebrow movements of a talking head unnatural.

Most of this is useful for something. Be careful regarding quantities remembered by subjects: if something is important to them, they may exaggerate the number of times it occurred, and vice versa, so better measure the quantities in other ways. An objective expert opinion may be extremely valuable when the purpose is to judge system aspects that are costly, rather difficult and/or quite complex to evaluate in other ways. Such evaluations are typically expressed in qualitative terms. We often prefer subjects' qualitative evaluation to their, equally subjective, quantitative evaluation because the former provides us with the more detailed information. Compare, e.g. a subject's Likert-scale *4* to a detailed response to an interview question, complete with responses to follow-up questions. Which of those would you prefer for evaluating the naturalness of an animated character's facial behaviour?

### 16.3.4 Five Different Evaluation Purposes

*What* to measure (Section 16.2.2) is closely related to evaluation purpose. Often distinction is made between *diagnostic evaluation* which focuses on finding usability errors and their causes; *performance evaluation* of how users perform with the system; *adequacy evaluation* which measures how well the system fits the users more generally; *comparative evaluation* which compares two or more systems, or system versions, in some respect; and *progress evaluation* which compares test results made with subsequent versions of the same system. A particular usability evaluation exercise may have any or all of these purposes.

*Diagnostic evaluation* primarily uses objective measures – quantitative, qualitative, both. Measures typically relate to user–system interaction problems, e.g. types of interaction problems, number of interaction problem types and tokens or seriousness of interaction problems of a particular type. The latter is important for prioritising which problems to fix immediately, first, or at all, and should be accompanied by an estimate of the effort needed to fix the problem, cf. Section 16.1.5. Depending on the nature of the problem, diagnosis may have to look for technical causes, causes due to the system's design or other causes, such as the use environment or even the user. An example of guidelines for preventing interaction problems is shown in Figs. 11.12 and 11.13. Subjective measures may be used as well, such as asking users about any interaction problems they might have experienced.

*Performance evaluation* primarily uses quantitative objective measures. Some common examples are time to task completion, number/percentage of correctly completed tasks, time spent on errors, time spent on manual or help desk or number of incorrect choices. A usability expert might use qualitative measures upon having tested the system, such as when writing an evaluation report describing the problems found. Subjective measures may be used as well. For instance, it is not uncommon in post-test interviews and questionnaires to include questions on the users' opinion of their performance with the system.

*Adequacy evaluation* typically uses both objective and subjective, quantitative and qualitative measures, as illustrated in the adequacy evaluation of the Sudoku Case reported in Chapter 17 (Intermezzo 5). Sometimes key adequacy evaluation criteria are included in the usability requirements, such as when the requirements specification specifies a final user test in which a group of X users, recruited in such-and-such a manner and composed in such-and-such a way, should have a task success rate of, say, 98%.

*Comparative evaluation* may use both objective and subjective measures, quantitative or qualitative, and is familiar from the many evaluations of products on the market published by consumer magazines and other organisations. This form of evaluation is generally complex to do in a scientifically sound manner, because different systems tend to differ in many ways and have different strengths and weaknesses. Typically, objective and quantitative comparison is made on key aspects of user performance, such as task success rate, or system or component adequacy, such as of the 3D pointing gesture recogniser. To enable meaningful comparison, all systems are evaluated under as similar conditions as possible, using, e.g. the same input data set, the same set of scenarios, the same target user group, use environment, etc.

So-called *evaluation campaigns* aim at driving system performance by means of comparative and competitive evaluation. In other cases, compared systems only differ in a single important respect, and it is this difference that is the topic of comparative evaluation. For instance, it is common in multimodal systems research to have subjects interact with the same application using different modalities and interaction devices, such as speech-only and speech + 2D haptic pointing gesture, and then compare their performance and subjective impressions.

*Progress evaluation* is a special kind of comparative evaluation of great interest to developers. Measures could be any of the measures used for diagnostic, performance and adequacy evaluation, since progress evaluation just requires that the same measure be applied to two different, typically subsequent, system versions in order to compare the results.

It is clear from their descriptions that those purpose-related evaluation types are not orthogonal at all. Rather, they reflect the many different purposes that might be served, even at the same time, by a particular evaluation exercise, such as a test with a group of representative users. In a multimodal system research project, we typically want to do all of them.

*Life cycle relations*. Focus tends to be on diagnostic evaluation in early development followed by adequacy evaluation later on. This is a natural continuum, from ironing out interaction problems at all levels from early on to testing the extent to which the system meets the usability requirements and fits the users as a whole. Diagnosis and adequacy are involved throughout, it's only the emphasis that changes. There is a twist to this standard view. Requirements analysis in early development is replete with evaluation reasoning about whether or not to include particular system properties of features. This reasoning is influenced by issues like feasibility and realism-given-resources, but we hardly have criteria for the core of it: we bet that the feature should stay or go, and then try to find out how right we were when doing adequacy evaluation of the system model later on.

Performance evaluation is equally important throughout the life cycle, i.e. from the time when performance measurements can be made at all. Many performance measures only make sense when there is an implemented system model. For instance, it makes no sense to measure interaction speed as long as speech recognition is done by a human wizard (Section 12.2). Progress evaluation may be done as soon as two comparable system models have been tested, including models as early as mock-ups (Section 12.1). Progress evaluation using Wizard of Oz enables the project to make substantial headway without writing code. Comparative evaluation can be made from early on as well, like in scientifically orchestrated, iterative evaluation campaigns. Comparative evaluation of system versions using different modalities is typically done as early as possible to determine which version to continue with and which one to throw away.

## 16.4  Types of Evaluation Criteria

We discuss where usability evaluation criteria come from in Section 5.2. Their primary source is usability requirements intended to make sure that the AMITUDE specification and design will fit the target users. If necessary, usability requirements are operationalised into evaluation criteria in the method plan (Section 6.4). In other words, we select or define evaluation criteria based on the requirements specification, as illustrated in Section 5.2. Note, however, that the usability requirements in Table 5.9 are a relatively meagre source of evaluation criteria because all systems are research prototypes about to be evaluated for the first time. A second evaluation would very likely include more, and more precise, criteria for each system because, by then we would know much more about what the potential problems are, what to measure, how to measure and which target values to aim for.

The aim of this section is to broaden our view of the huge variety of evaluation criteria out there. As an example, this book's web site shows the comprehensive set of evaluation criteria that was applied to the Andersen system (see Section 3.4.5).

### *16.4.1  Common Evaluation Criteria from ISO Usability Standards*

Section 11.5 mentions several examples of standards related to usability evaluation. A frequently quoted standard is ISO IEC 9126 on "software engineering – product quality". Part 1, "quality model" (2001), which defines *quality in use* in terms of four characteristics, i.e. effectiveness, productivity, safety and satisfaction (Fig. 11.14). Part 4, "quality in use metrics" (2004), proposes a basic set of metrics (evaluation criteria) for each of the four characteristics:

*Effectiveness* metrics (EfM) include task effectiveness, task completion and error frequency. These metrics focus on measuring the extent to which the users' goals were achieved, not on how they were achieved.

*Productivity* metrics  (ProdM) include task time, task efficiency, economic productivity (how cost-effective is the user), productive proportion (proportion of the time the user performs productive actions) and relative user efficiency (compared to an expert). These metrics measure resources spent relative to achievements.

*Safety* metrics (SafM) include user health and safety, safety of people affected by system use, economic damage, and software damage. These metrics focus on risk and harm issues.

*Satisfaction* metrics (SatM) include satisfaction scale, satisfaction questionnaire and discretionary usage (proportion of potential users that choose to use the system). These metrics are intended to assess users' attitudes.

Each metric is defined in more detail in the standard document, including how to interpret results. However, before applying those criteria, it is important to make sure that they are actually applicable to the system at hand, as we will now illustrate.

We have annotated the Case usability requirements with the four characteristics above in Table 5.9 and summarised the results obtained with the Sudoku system in Table 17.4. Except for the functionality requirements, the annotation *might seem* to work surprisingly well in view of the fact that, in particular, the productivity characteristic and the illustrated effectiveness metrics are strongly related to work-oriented systems. One would have thought that games like Sudoku and Treasure Hunt have little to do with productivity because, as long as it's fun, who cares about productivity? Similarly, if it's fun, who cares about task effectiveness?

Things are not what they seem, however, because the game *ProdMs* in Table 5.9 were not aimed to measure gameplay productivity at all. Their purpose was to ensure that the subjects would produce a sufficient amount of *test data* on all phases of gameplay because, clearly, we weren't likely to learn much from analysing obser-vation, logfile and video data showing a subject who, having chosen a Sudoku game that proved too difficult, would stare at the game board for 30 minutes without inserting a single number. That's why the experimenter, in both the Sudoku and the Treasure Hunt tests, was instructed to get things moving if subjects had been stuck for some time. So, the game *ProdMs* in Table 5.9 are productivity metrics all right, but they are artificial constructs made to ensure data production rather than measure system usability in terms of game productivity.

In general, productivity criteria are only marginally relevant to game evaluation, i.e. you might not want to launch a game that no one can complete, nor a game so easy that people get bored more or less immediately – whereas effectiveness criteria are relevant to all or most systems. This is not because all systems are task-oriented, as ISO assumes, but because they measure whether or not users achieve their goals in interacting with the system. Yet, again, there's a snag.

Suppose that we measure on some computer game we just played, using the ISO effectiveness metrics above, i.e. task effectiveness, task completion and error fre-quency, and find very high task effectiveness, 100% task completion and a very low error frequency. Excellent, right? Moreover, suppose that, to drive home the good news, we also ask subjects in a post-test interview or questionnaire how easy they found their tasks, and they unanimously answer "very easy". Super, no? However, before we triumph, we might want to make sure that this doesn't all mean "It was much too easy to play this boring game, never again!" Possibly, game applications initially need low task effectiveness and task completion and high error frequency to be fun.

ISO claims that, to evaluate quality in use, it is normally necessary to use at least one metric for each of the four characteristics mentioned. Note that we don't have any safety metrics for two of the games in Table 5.9 because it is hard to think of any, nor, probably, would we have had any productivity metrics outside the lab test environment. ISO also points out that

> The choice of metrics and the contexts in which they are measured is dependent on the objectives of the parties involved in the measurement. The relative importance of each metric to the goals should be considered. For example where usage is infrequent, higher importance may be given to metrics for understandability and learnability rather than quality in use.

Metrics for evaluating external and internal quality (Fig. 11.15) can be found in ISO IEC 9126 Parts 2 and 3 (2003), including metrics for understandability and learnability. ISO/IEC 9126-2 mentions learnability metrics, i.e. criteria for measuring *learning to use* a system, such as ease of function learning (how long does the user take to learn to use a function), ease of learning to perform a task in use (how long does the user take to learn how to perform the specified task efficiently), effectiveness of user documentation and/or help system (what proportion of tasks can be completed correctly after using the user documentation and/or help system), effectiveness of user documentation and/or help system in use (what proportion of functions can be used correctly after reading the documentation or using help systems), help accessibility (what proportion of the help topics can the user locate), help frequency (how frequently does the user have to access help to learn operation to complete his/her task) and (from ISO/IEC 9126-3) completeness of user documentation and/or help facility (what proportion of functions are described in the user documentation and/or help facility). Note that target values depend on system purpose, target users and possibly much else. If the system is intended for walk-up-and-use, the measured learning times should be basically zero, and there should be no need for documentation or help functionality.

Learnability criteria are quite different from criteria for measuring *student learning* in tutoring, training and teaching systems, such as our Maths Case (Section 2.1). The student must first learn to *use* the system, of course, but, after that, we need to measure student learning progress, course completion and more, cf. the student learning usability requirements for the Maths system in Table 5.9. Student learning criteria tend to be rather complex, because it is often necessary to start by measuring the student's baseline knowledge or skills in order to measure learning progress at all; then measure learning progress over a period of days, weeks or even months; then measure test performance; and then, months later, measure what it's all about, namely, long-term retention of what was taught.

Finally, ISO IEC 9126-4 lists a set of properties that metrics preferably should have in order to deliver valid results, including *reliability, repeatability, reproducibility, availability, indicativeness, correctness* and *meaningfulness*. This list is useful when you establish your own metrics.

In conclusion, (i) be prepared to define your own criteria when required and (ii) never treat an established evaluation framework as gospel when preparing to evaluate the usability of innovative multimodal systems or non-standard application types: as it turned out, we could use precious little of the ISO quality in use metrics above for evaluating the Sudoku game.

## 16.4.2 Other Kinds and Sources of Criteria

So far, we have said that evaluation criteria come from usability requirements, which in their turn are built from system, and in particular AMITUDE, requirements. In this process of building system, AMITUDE and usability requirements, useful help can be had from a range of sources.

*Criteria from evaluations of similar systems.* It is useful to look for similar systems that have been subjected to usability evaluation and to study criteria used and results reported. If you find a relevant system S, note these three caveats: First, assess how similar S is to your own system. Differences might be reflected in a different choice of evaluation criteria. Second, look at the usability requirements for S and not just at its purpose. If the developers of S primarily evaluate system purpose, and what you are after is to evaluate to particular usability requirements, or vice versa, the criteria might have to be different in the two cases. Third, and sadly, don't expect top quality in all usability evaluation descriptions. As paper reviewers, we continue to see sloppy usability evaluation reports accompany what might or might not be exciting new multimodal systems. Typically, low-quality evaluation reports don't quite tell which the criteria were, how they were applied, who and how many the users were, what, exactly, the results were and what the significance of those results is. One sometimes has the impression that, the poorer the report, the happier are the authors about the results of the usability evaluation of their system.

*Guidelines as evaluation criteria.* Usability guidelines typically describe characteristics which it is desirable that a system has or does not have, so it's an obvious idea to try to make evaluation criteria out of them. For instance, we have used the guidelines in Figs. 11.12 and 11.13 as a set of usability evaluation criteria for counting the number of cooperativity error types in a spoken dialogue system (Bernsen et al. 1998a, b).

Before specifying in detail what to measure, how to measure and a possible target value for applying a set of usability guidelines as evaluation criterion, take these precautions: (i) make sure that the guidelines are relevant to the system at hand. Guidelines are established with particular kinds of system in mind, such as GUI-based applications, speech-based systems or work-oriented systems and may be more or less irrelevant to systems of a different nature. (ii) Look at how high in the evaluation hierarchy the guidelines are. For instance, Shneiderman's and Nielsen's guideline sets in Figs. 11.10 and 11.11 may be viewed as expansions of our top-level *ease of use* norm (Section 1.4.6) downwards in the evaluation hierarchy (Section 16.2.2). This means that these guidelines are still pretty high up in the hierarchy, which suggests that it might be difficult to operationalise each of them into an evaluation criterion. For instance, Shneiderman and Nielsen both have a guideline on *error prevention*, and it certainly seems true that, for many systems, it is desirable that as few errors as possible occur during interaction, making error prevention a desirable characteristic. So the real difficulty in turning this guideline into a usability criterion seems to be to define how to measure error prevention in a system. Remember, the definition should enable anyone familiar with the issues to arrive at the same evaluation result for a given system.

*Theory-based evaluation criteria.* Especially in research prototype development, particular system characteristics may implement details of a theory – about social interaction, conversation, affective learning, whatever – whereupon it becomes part of usability evaluation to measure the extent to which the theory actually works or has been successfully implemented in the first place.

Suppose that the theory is from social science and concerns strategies for conflict resolution through spoken dialogue. Roughly, the theory says that people tend to follow one of three strategies, i.e. to either (i) talk about something else, (ii) attack the interlocutor's assumptions and formulations or (iii) listen and constructively seek to reach a compromise (Traum et al. 2008). As far as this theory is concerned, the development aim is to build a system for training human interlocutors in making the system pursue strategy (iii) and avoiding getting caught up in (i) or (ii). In this case, theory-based evaluation must analyse human–system negotiations and score them according to whether each move made by the human is conducive to making the system adopt strategy (iii) or not. Thus, one criterion could be number of interaction exchanges that can be categorised as belonging to (i) or (ii). Another criterion could be the rate of successfully resolved conflicts.

*New usability evaluation criteria.* In multimodal systems development, we sometimes have to define evaluation criteria for measuring something that hasn't been measured before, not even in kind. This can be relatively easy to do, like when the system is supposed to distinguish user sadness from anger, and we want to collect subjective data on how well it works. A questionnaire or interview question, or several, might do the job. It is often a greater challenge to develop criteria for objectively and quantitatively measuring the system's success in distinguishing user sadness from anger. In particular, how do we establish that the user is sad or angry during interaction in the first place? We are all fallible experts on the emotions of others, and, for some emotions, we are just as fallible as regards our own.

The criterion just mentioned probably is insignificant for interactive multimodal systems in general. The point is that we continue to need new evaluation criteria for all sorts of purposes. Some of these will become important general contributions to usability evaluation. For instance, a sound and general metrics for evaluating the quality of a system's spoken conversation would be relevant to all manner of future spoken and multimodal conversational systems. First attempts at such metrics have already been made (Traum et al. 2004). Another example of a complex evaluation criterion is for measuring the general quality of combined spontaneous speech and pointing gesture input understanding. In this case, the theory is far from ready yet (Bernsen 2006).

## 16.5   Usability Evaluation in Practice

The Sudoku evaluation in Chapter 17 (Intermezzo 5) shows what a usability evaluation report may look like, anomalies and all. In this section, we try to nuance the picture of usability evaluation presented so far in order to demolish any one-track mental model of evaluation you may have left after what has been said so far. It may be useful to read Section 17 (Intermezzo 5) before reading Section 16.5.3.

### *16.5.1  Sudoku and Other Evaluations*

Let's start by locating the Sudoku evaluation in the space of usability evaluations scoped by this book. The Sudoku evaluation is a (i) first (ii) general (or adequacy) (iii) lab test-based usability evaluation with (iv) a representative user group of (v) an innovative multimodal and (vi) relatively simple, (vii) implemented (viii) computer game (ix) research prototype.

Points (i) – (ix) locate the evaluation in that space, so let's see what else we can find in the space.

Point (i) *first* could have been *second, third, . . ., commercial beta off-the-shelf* or *one-of-a-kind-tailored* instead, in which case we would have known much more about what and how to measure and would have applied a larger number of objective and quantitative criteria. It is typical of a first user test that one discovers new important things to measure and more precise measurements of known properties.

Point (ii) *general (or adequacy)* could have been *diagnostic, performance, comparative* or *progress* instead, cf. Section 16.3.4, or just plain *selective*. An adequacy evaluation with a representative user group is the biggest deal we can make, comparable only to a large-scale field test. Both research and more downstream systems are often evaluated more selectively because, e.g. some AMITUDE properties are low priority; something did not work at all in the last test and must be firefighting-tested as soon as possible; or the usability of everything else is under control already. In research, we are under no obligation to polish everything to perfection, so we might, e.g. opt for basic quality in static graphics and graphics animation, while putting as many resources as possible into optimising the usability of speech and gesture interaction. Another reason for selective evaluation is that not all assumptions and decisions made during requirements and design analysis may be equally well founded. Those that are less well founded need special monitoring, often including selective usability evaluation to find out if a component will be usable at all, what the performance targets should be, what subjects think of it, etc.

Point (iii) *lab test* might instead have been *any imagination method* (Chapter 11), a *late survey* (Section 8.3), an *expert evaluation* (Section 8.5) or a *field test* (Section 12.4), and the actually used *post-test interview* could have been a *questionnaire* instead (Section 8.8), or there might have been a *pre-test interview or questionnaire* as well (Section 8.7).

Point (iv) *representative group of users* might instead have been just any group of target users, as in the Treasure Hunt Case test we did, cf. Section 3.3.7 and Bernsen and Dybkjær (2007), or even colleagues or students. This choice strongly affects data reliability and general interest in the data collected, especially if test subjects were colleagues or students.

Point (v) *innovative multimodal* could have been *well-thumbed standard GUI-based*, in which case we would have been able to benefit from a large apparatus of standards, guidelines, detailed style guides, etc. in doing the evaluation.

Point (vi) *relatively simple* could have been *complex*, in which case our already long evaluation report might have run into +100 pages.

Point (vii) *implemented* could have been *mocked-up* (Section 12.1) or *simulated* (Section 12.2), in which case we would have missed performance evaluation with key system components, i.e. combined speech recognition and pointing gesture.

Point (viii) *computer game* could have been loads of *other application types*, which strongly influences the kinds of evaluation criteria that are relevant (Section 16.4).

Point (ix) *research prototype* might have to be modified depending on the value of Point (i)!

## 16.5.2 Task Success: An Example Usability Evaluation Criterion

A usability evaluation criterion has a target value and specification of what and how to measure (Section 16.2.2). The *target value* often cannot be meaningfully (or non-arbitrarily) fixed in early system model tests, but may become crucial to deciding if the system is ready for exploitation and subsequent commercialisation.

To illustrate what it takes to specify the *what* and the *how* to measure for an objective and quantitative usability evaluation criterion, Box 16.1 shows the task success rate criterion as it might be used for the spoken dialogue system in Section 3.4.2, as well as a variation of the criterion that might be used for the FAQ system in Section 3.4.3. The example illustrates how it takes deliberation, precision and awareness of priming risks to specify the what and the how. Counting is not just counting!

### Box 16.1 Task Success Rate

Task success is an important objective/quantitative metric for task-oriented systems. The idea is to have users perform a number of tasks with the system and measure the percentage of successfully completed tasks. As usual, we need to think carefully about the various parameters involved in these metrics, such as

*When to use*. Task success is key to task-oriented systems, so, somehow, we look for how well users are able to accomplish tasks with the system each time we test the system model with users, no matter at which development stage the system model is. However, if we want to measure the task success rate to get a first reasonable estimate of what the task success rate of the final system might be, we must have most of the system model simulated or up and running.

*What to measure*. We want subjects to carry out *representative tasks* and measure the percentage of such tasks successfully accomplished. The more representative of real system use the tasks are, the more informative the measured task success rate is of what can be expected of the final system version. In a lab test, tasks are typically defined by us and given to users in the form of scenarios. In this case, the problem is to specify a representative set of tasks for users to carry out. In a field test, users determine what the tasks will be, and we may not be able to ensure that users constitute a sufficiently representative group.

*Representative user group*. The task success metric only yields reliable data with a representative group of users.

*How to measure*. A task for an over-the-phone flight booking system could be specified in a scenario like the one in Fig. 13.7.

Like many others, this task requires a series of user–system interactions even when everything works smoothly and no additional interaction is required to solve any problems arising. To measure if a particular task performance is successful, we measure whether or not the user manages to book a flight according to the specifications provided by the user. Note that we do *not* measure the success of individual user actions. The task is accomplished successfully if the user eventually books the flight asked for. If the user asks for a flight with specifications different from those in the scenario – which happens, of course – the metric uses what the user actually asks for and not what's in the scenario. If the user fails to book the flight, hangs up, tries again and succeeds, we must decide if this and the previous call count as a single task success, or if the fact that the user phones the system again means that a new task is being addressed based on the same scenario, and following a previous task attempt that failed. Our decision must be described as part of our description of the task success criterion, and, to remove any ambiguity about our results, we should measure and report how many task successes were preceded by hanging up and re-trying.

There is another class of tasks that needs a slightly different approach to task success measurement. An FAQ system, for instance, like the one described in Section 3.4.3, does not enable something like following a *series* of mandatory and optional dialogue steps. Rather, the goal is to successfully answer one or several user questions based on the system's FAQ knowledge. Since each question and its correct answer is independent of all other questions, as witnessed by the facts that a user might: (i) ask any one question and ignore the rest, (ii) ask any number of questions in any order and (iii) succeed in getting correct answers to some questions but fail to get correct answers to others – task success must in this case be measured at action level for each individual question–answer pair by looking at whether the question gets appropriately answered or not.

Interestingly, this latter approach to measuring a system's (sub-)task performance can also be applied to systems like the flight booking system above. What we measure in this case is not task success but *sub-task completion rate*, which is likely to yield far more detailed information on which parts of the system work well and which ones seem to have various difficulties. Also, assuming a running system model, the metric of sub-task completion per time interval can be used to measure efficiency.

*Knowing the user's current task goal.* This is essential to task success metrics application. If we don't know what the user is up to, we cannot determine if the user achieves the goal. Scenarios help, because we can normally assume that the user has understood the scenario, and, if this is not good enough, we can ask how a user interprets a scenario. Spoken input, and language input more generally, also helps because, in most but not all cases, we can tell what the user is up to from what the user says, types, expresses through sign language, etc. This is how we determine if a user has misunderstood a scenario. If neither scenarios nor language input is used, it is important to make sure that the users' task goals are known sufficiently well in some general way in order for application of task success metrics to make sense.

*What is not being measured.* The task success metrics illustrate well why we need several different usability criteria. There are several task success metrics, and no result arrived at by using them carries much information about the many other things we would like to measure, such as how efficient, easy, smooth or enjoyable user–system interaction is.

### 16.5.3  Sudoku Evaluation: General Points

In Section 16.5.1 we located the Sudoku evaluation reported in Chapter 17 (Intermezzo 5) in a multi-dimensional evaluation space and briefly described what else there is in that huge space. In this section, we focus on general points illustrated by the Sudoku test, primarily points on early implemented prototype adequacy evaluation.

1. *The system must be ready for the type of evaluation planned.* It was, fortunately. We had returned an earlier version that wasn't ready for user testing, but we weren't prepared for the massive impact of the number-in-the-wrong-square bug. It didn't show up much in our internal trials prior to the user test.

2. *Handle the collected data as described in Chapter 15.*

3. *Collect all analysis context documentation,* cf. Section 16.1.1.

4. *Make a complete list of anomalies,* cf. Sections 16.1.1 and 17.1.2. The best laid plans … – yes, despite them, and our best efforts, things went wrong, most seriously with respect to the representativeness of the subject population. Make sure that the anomalies are available when preparing the next user test method plan.

5. *The first user lab test produces a wealth of usability information.* This is clear from Chapter 17 (Intermezzo 5). We look at what to do about the information in the next points.

6. *Start by creating some basic data statistics,* cf. Sections 17.1.4 and 17.1.5.

7. *Analyse any technical issues in the data,* cf. Section 16.3.1. These help establish a picture of what the users were up against when interacting with the system model, cf. Section 17.2. Any technical issue arising is likely to influence subjects' evaluation of the system and should therefore be kept in mind throughout data analysis. Diagnose the technical issues while you're at it.

8. *Combine information from different data sources during analysis.* We do this a lot in Chapter 17 (Intermezzo 5), combining quantitative and qualitative, subjective and objective data in order to get as much information as possible on each identified usability issue, and drawing freely upon real-time user observation data, video data, post-test interview results (we had no logfile access) and context documentation. However, don't get lost in counting everything under the sun in the video data! You can't do it anyway because it's too rich, and you will have plenty of counting to do once you start uncovering the usability issues demonstrated or suggested by the data.

9. *Analyse usability requirement satisfaction.* This provides a bottom line for how the system model stands, cf. Section 17.6.

10. *First-time usability requirements are likely to be insufficient.* This is clear from Chapter 17 (Intermezzo 5). Arguably, requirements to a first user test *must* be insufficient if we are dealing with something really new. Insufficiency can be of several kinds, including (i) requirements that should be made quantitative but must remain qualitative until the first user test, because meaningful quantitative target values cannot be specified and (ii) requirements that aren't there but should have been.

11. *Organise the remainder of the data analysis.* What we had to support structuring of the Sudoku user test data analysis was primarily: (i) the usability requirements (Section 5.2); (ii) the interview questions (Fig. 8.9) and the more or less explicit evaluation priorities reflected in them; and (iii) our observation notes from the test itself. This is fine, and typical, too, providing a good start for what else to look for in the data. AMITUDE (Section 3.1) and a definition of usability (Section 1.4.6) can be used to support systematic looking as well. However,

it is also extremely important to let the data "speak" for itself and disclose new issues, even though this inevitably increases work on the data. And remember that, having left the solid ground of evaluating to usability evaluation criteria based on usability requirements, we are on our own and have to use the evaluation criteria and arguments (Section 16.2.1) that turn out to be required by the data.

12. *Carry out the remainder of the data analysis.* This is the really hard part of the work, mainly because of five factors: (i) *data richness*: open or semi-open interview data goes all over the place, and a single user remark may raise, or address, several usability issues. We need to keep track of that. (ii) *Numbers* matter a lot in a representative user group, so we need to keep track of how many users said or did what with respect to every single point of interest. (iii) *Sub-profiles*: *who* said what is almost as important as *how many*, because the user group is typically composed of sub-profiles according to, e.g. gender, age, background or experience, and it may matter a lot whether some issue is being judged very differently by different sub-groups. This must be kept track of, like when we found that the subjects who did not anticipate playing Sudoku in airports were primarily those who did not play Sudoku regularly anyway. (iv) *Semantics*: what, exactly, did users say on Point Umpteen? Subject X said that she would *definitely* play Sudoku in an airport. Subject Y said that he *might perhaps* play Sudoku in an airport. Did X and Y say the same thing or didn't they? To keep track of that, we must create categories of answers ad hoc. It's terribly easy to fudge up data analysis by ignoring important differences of semantics. And (v) *correlations*: see next point.

13. *Correlations in the data.* We look for correlations in at least two ways: (1) by computing correlations between known entities in the test, like a particular subject sub-profile, or a subset of scenarios given to some of the subjects, and something – could be most anything – in the data. We may do this because we want to test a hypothesis or simply to see what the results turn out to be. (2) By attempting to make explanatory sense of something in the data, which, we sense, sticks out somehow, like all subjects being more or less happy having copious conversation with the system, except for a single user who hates it. Why? Oh, that was the subject whose two weak spoken input attempts the system did not understand!

   This example may be insignificant, but it illustrates an important form of correlation, i.e. between subjective and objective data. The correlation may be one of confirmation, like when, in the Sudoku test, some subjects find interaction strenuous and others do not, and video analysis shows that the former tend to keep their arm raised throughout while the latter lower the arm after each series of moves. Once we have identified the correlation, we can predict the subjective interview response from objective video observation, and, at some point, we don't need the subjective data any more.

   However, contradictions or "tensions" between the two data sets frequently occur as well, for instance when a subject remembers the interaction as very different from what it actually was. Such inconsistencies, whether real or, ultimately, only apparent, should be further explored. An example of contradictory results from the evaluation of the second Andersen prototype (Section 3.4.5) is the following: did the user speak and point at the same time? "Yes!" the user says. According to the logfile, however, this was not the case. What we found by further data exploration was a correlation between those "inconsistent users" and those who had the language of interaction (English) as second language. The native English speakers actually did use speaking and pointing at the same time as well as saying that they did. Try to think about this finding.

In a large class of cases, it does not seem possible today to establish any strong correlation between objective/quantitative criteria, on the one hand, and subjective criteria (whether quantitative or not) on the other. It is simply not clear to which extent we are measuring the same thing when we measure "it" subjectively and objectively. For instance, it is hard to objectively quantify how much fun the system is, how immersive and absorbing, or how motivating to use for long-term training; how trustworthy, polite or likeable an animated character is; how natural is its gesture or speech; or how impressive its knowledge or its output graphics. When properties like these are important, there currently is no other way to evaluate them than by eliciting subjective user opinions, supplemented or supported, to the extent possible, by related objective/quantitative measurements.

Correlating objective–objective or subjective–subjective data may yield important results as well. The danger of explanatory correlations, causal or otherwise, is that the proposed explanation may be spurious.

14. *Sharpen, and increase the number of, usability requirements to guide work in preparation of a second user test* (or other method application). For the Sudoku system, in particular, we need quantitative minimum or maximum target values for pointing gesture control (min), speech recognition (min), speech understanding (min), no-effect speech input (max), cursor jitter (max), correlation between cursor position, screen object activation and activation feedback (100%) and deterministic games (100%). And we need new requirements to the perceptible differences between fixed and inserted numbers, optimisation of screen object activation delays, game loading process feedback, temporal order of speech and pointing, several points on graphics quality, adequacy of gameplay functionality, i.e. what to add to the existing minimal functionality, if anything, and interaction consistency.

15. *Take results into design.* Another part of the Sudoku data analysis results goes into discussion of design revisions. Should the system provide acoustic spoken or non-speech feedback? How? Should it have an undo function? Should it provide more help provided that this help is customisable? Etc. Some subjects proposed these features or expressed concerns that could be met by introducing them, others wouldn't have them. Or, should we postpone some or all design changes because the test user group was not really representative? Or should we implement our best bet for some of those features and make sure that they are carefully evaluated in the next user test?

16. *Judgment and its pitfalls.* Sound judgment is, of course, required throughout data analysis. The most important decision following a first prototype is: is this something or not? We believe that the Sudoku system is worth taking further in application-oriented research in order to see how good it could become in a next development phase. However, the real judgmental question is on what is this relatively-low-risk-but-optimistic judgment based? It is based on (a) *Rich data* (on a relatively simple system). (b) *Substantial data handling work*, including pretty thoroughly analysed usability test data. (c) *A good system idea*, i.e. evidence in the data that users want to use the system for entertainment in airports and other public locations. The subjects who said that, i.e. the large majority of the Sudoku aficionados among the subjects, represent thousands if not millions of aficionados even though the subject population was not representative of all possible users. (d) *Overall usability concept is right and complete*: there is pretty strong evidence in the data that the usability of the overall multimodal design concept is rather close to being right and complete and that the many improvements required, which encompass most aspects of user–system interaction, are all in matters of detail. Ironing these out should remove user uncertainty and provide for smooth interaction. We know what we will get if the system gets perfected. (e) *Clear technical feasibility*: the prototype proves the concept, and we are pretty convinced that it is technically feasible to achieve key performance targets for pointing gesture control and speech understanding. There is a lot of judgment in here! Are we wrong? Take a look at Chapter 17 (Intermezzo 5) and judge for yourself.

Where there is a lot of judgment, there is big room for error. If you cannot confirm the five italicised statements above for your own system, you are in some kind of trouble, and the right thing to do is to draw the implications whichever way they may lead. "No" to (a) means little action based on the data, more data collection and probably work on methodology improvement. "No" to (b) means little action and more data handling work. "No" to (c) suggests doing something else. "No" to (d) means back to design. "No" to (e) means technical experimentation or doing something else.

This is where temptations start, and they don't have to be conscious nor knowingly pursued.

The easiest way out is *owner's positive bias*. This is a simple form of data analysis in which you only look hard for one thing in the usability data, namely, confirmation that your system is GOOD! It doesn't matter in which way, as long as it's positive or, at least, not negative. It doesn't matter how little data you have collected or how inadequate your data handling methodology has been, there will be something positive in there, no doubt. You don't need to care about (c), (d) and (e) above at all. And while you're at it, you might as well spend the time saved on data handling on finding explanations why the data is poor. Try blaming the subjects: they never showed up, didn't listen to instructions, fudged system installation in the field test, never returned the logfile data, made suspicious excuses for pulling out, did not fill in the questionnaire, etc. Sorry! Please don't be like that.

Another important judgmental risk factor is *subjects' positive bias*. Test subjects, being only human, are known to cherish nice ideas and rosy future perspectives to the point of ignoring manifest flaws in the tested technology. So, don't put too much into subjective scorings and interview answers that might be influenced by dreams and cannot be cross-checked through correlations with objective data. Articulate subject visions, on the other hand, may provide great insight, as we saw with one of the Treasure Hunt test subjects, cf. Bernsen and Dybkjær (2007).

## 16.6 Reporting the Results of Data Analysis

A report on the results of data analysis is the crown on every CoMeDa cycle, and, in a very real sense, if it's not reported, it never happened. Depending on the data collection method applied, you may only need a fraction of the items below.

We already looked at *data documentation* and the crucial role of meta-data in protecting future data accessibility. Proper meta-data description serves to document the data collection process, the raw data files and any post-processing of these (Section 15.3). Similarly, any coding scheme-based data annotation gets documented in the coding file meta-data (Section 15.6). These best-practice steps enable easy extraction of data handling information for reporting purposes. As for *data analysis*, full reporting includes description of the data analysis procedure followed, presentation of results and recommendations justified by reference to the results, cf. the Sudoku evaluation report in Chapter 17 (Intermezzo 5).

From context documentation as listed in Section 16.1.1, data documentation and a comprehensive data analysis report, it is straightforward to produce reports for various purposes on the entire process of method selection, method application and data handling. Reports may serve as records, communication tools, tools for driving and guiding work to be done, basis for publications, etc. A report might include the following main sections:

- *executive summary*: overview of methods, procedures, results and recommendations;
- *method*: data collection method(s), data collection preparation, set-up, user profiles, collection process, raw data files, any anomalies during data collection;
- *procedures*: raw data handling procedures, data analysis, any anomalies;
- *results*: quantitative and qualitative results: what was found in the data;
- *recommendations* in the light of results; what should be done, discussions and explanations; make it easy to get an overview of the most important points;
- *appendix*: key data collection material, cf. the list in Section 16.1.1;
- *references*: any other material used;
- *acknowledgements*: people involved, support received.

*Method*. Sources include usability workplan (Section 6.3), usability method plan (Section 6.4), raw data meta-data (Section 15.3.3), other documentation from the list in Section 16.1.1, including anomalies: if the anomalies list is empty, *everything* must have gone exactly according to plan! Many method details matter to judging results reliability, not least how the data producers (subjects, experts, developers, etc.) were selected.

*Procedures.* Sources include coding file meta-data (Section 15.6), data analysis report (above) and the anomalies list (Section 16.1.1). Reporting on procedures followed – how results were arrived at, cross-checked, alternative interpretations rejected, etc. – is crucial because it allows others to judge the reliability and credibility of results. If the results presented are extraordinary in some way, and procedures are not carefully described and convincing, the professional reader will presume that the authors probably messed up their data handling and analysis.

*Results.* This section should have two parts at different levels of detail: an overview that allows fast access to the most important results and conclusions, and a section with more detailed results, including cross-references to raw data.

*Recommendations.* This section may have two parts: a summary of overall recommendations and a section providing more detail, including discussion and justification of the recommendations made. Deficient reasoning in this part may be the first sign of a project that is going to fail. Consider a split into short-term and long-term recommendations. If there are areas where further investigation is needed, this should be clearly pointed out. Be thorough and address all identified issues.

*Appendices, references:* The more sensational, economically significant, risky or controversial the findings and conclusions reported are, the stronger and more complete should be the supporting documentation.

Note that the reporting format just described is somewhat more formal and stand-alone than the Sudoku report in Chapter 17 (Intermezzo 5), which is supported by entries elsewhere in this book.

## 16.7 Key Points

This chapter has continued presentation of data handling from Chapter 15 by discussing data analysis and results reporting. *Data analysis* can start once raw data has been collected, validated, post-processed and annotated as appropriate, and must be done for the *purpose* for which the data was collected and in the appropriate *context* that accumulates over time in terms of specifications, plans, documentation, etc.

*Usability evaluation* is integral to, and a basic part of, analysis, based on usability *arguments* or on usability *evaluation criteria* derived from usability *requirements*. Different kinds of evaluation criteria were presented, including common criteria from ISO. We drew a general picture of what *evaluation* may be like *in practice* based on the Sudoku evaluation in Chapter 17 (Intermezzo 5). Finally, common sections were proposed for *reporting results* of data analysis.

## References

Bernsen NO (2006) Speech and 2D deictic gesture reference to virtual scenes. In: André E, Dybkjær L, Minker W, Neumann H, Weber M (eds) Perception and interactive technologies. Proceedings of international tutorial and research workshop. Springer, New York: LNAI 4021.
Bernsen NO, Dybkjær H, Dybkjær L (1998a) Designing interactive speech systems. From first ideas to user testing. Springer Verlag, Heidelberg.

Bernsen NO, Dybkjær H, Dybkjær L (1998b) Guidelines for cooperative dialogue. http://spokendialogue.dk/Cooperativity/Guidelines.html. Accessed 21 January 2009.

Bernsen NO, Dybkjær L (2007) Report on iterative testing of multimodal usability and evaluation guide. SIMILAR deliverable D98.

Boehm BW (ed) (1989) Software risk management. IEEE Press, Piscataway, NJ, USA.

ISO/IEC 9126-1 (2001) Software engineering – product quality – part 1: quality model. http://www.iso.org/iso/iso_catalogue/catalogue_tc/catalogue_detail.htm?csnumber=22749. Accessed 22 January 2009.

ISO/IEC 9126-2 (2003) Software engineering – product quality – part 2: external metrics. http://www.iso.org/iso/iso_catalogue/catalogue_tc/catalogue_detail.htm?csnumber=22750. Accessed 22 January 2009.

ISO/IEC 9126-3 (2003) Software engineering – product quality – part 3: internal metrics. http://www.iso.org/iso/iso_catalogue/catalogue_tc/catalogue_detail.htm?csnumber=22891. Accessed 22 January 2009.

ISO/IEC 9126-4 (2004) Software engineering – product quality – part 4: quality in use metrics. http://www.iso.org/iso/iso_catalogue/catalogue_tc/catalogue_detail.htm?csnumber=39752. Accessed 22 January 2009.

Jacobson I, Boosch G, Rumbaugh J (1999) The unified software development process. Addison-Wesley, New York.

Traum D, Robinson S, Stephan J (2004) Evaluation of multi-party virtual reality dialogue interaction. In: Proceedings of LREC, Lisbon, Portugal: 1699–1702.

Traum D, Swartout W, Gratch J, Marsella S (2008) A virtual human dialogue model for non-team interaction. In: Dybkjær L, Minker W (eds) Recent trends in discourse and dialogue. Text, Speech and Language Technology Series 39: 45–67. Springer, New York.

# Chapter 17
# Intermezzo 5: Sudoku Usability Evaluation

This intermezzo illustrates data handling and reporting as described in Chapters 15 and 16. The example used is our evaluation of the Sudoku Case system (Section 2.1) based on data collected in a lab test at NISLab on 7 and 12 June 2007 and first reported in Bernsen and Dybkjær (2007). This example involves application, according to the usability method plan in Chapter 14 (Intermezzo 4), of the following cluster of methods: user screening (Section 8.6), implemented prototype lab test (Section 12.3), real-time user observation (Section 10.4) and post-test interview (Section 8.8). The purpose of the evaluation was to have a representative user group play Sudoku games in order to assess (a) how usable the technology is at the present stage, (b) what could be done about the usability problems identified in the test and (c) how promising the technology is for the future. Point (a) includes evaluation of the system based on the usability requirements established in Section 5.2.

A global usability evaluation, such as the one described in this intermezzo, evaluates how the system model, primarily its AMITUDE specification and design, fits users in context. The evaluation report may be structured in different ways, cf. Section 16.6. We have chosen to illustrate a format that might be re-usable for other multimodal system evaluations, i.e.: start with (1) description of data handling and basic data analysis (Section 17.1); then present analyses of (2) all technical issues relevant to usability (Section 17.2); (3) appropriateness of individual modalities and modality combinations, of multimodal interaction as a whole and of the information exchanged during interaction (Section 17.3); (4) other functional issues (Section 17.4); (5) the closed questions in the interview (Section 17.5); and finish with (6) main conclusions, including a summary of the extent to which the system satisfies its usability requirements (Section 17.6).

## 17.1 Data

This section looks at the data analysis context, anomalies and issues arising from data collection, data validation and simple statistics on users and their gameplay.

N.O. Bernsen, L. Dybkjær, *Multimodal Usability*, Human-Computer Interaction Series, DOI 10.1007/978-1-84882-553-6_17, © Springer-Verlag London Limited 2009

### 17.1.1 Context of Data Analysis

It is useful to review the data analysis context that has been presented in this book, cf. the list in Section 16.1.1. The context includes the Sudoku system idea (Section 2.1), AMITUDE specification (Section 5.1), usability requirements (Section 5.2), design (Section 7.2.1), usability method plan (Chapter 14), including data collection purpose (Section 14.1), what to measure and how (Section 14.2), communication with data producers (Section 14.3), recruitment of subjects (Section 14.4), staff roles and responsibilities (Section 14.5), practicalities such as location, equipment, various material, and decisions on data collection, data handling and results presentation (Section 14.6), and a script for the test (Section 14.7), the screening interview script (used as example in Section 8.6), and the post-test interview script (used as example in Section 8.8). In what follows, we refer to this context as needed.

### 17.1.2 Anomalies

The test proceeded as planned except for the following anomalies compared to the method plan in Chapter 14 (Intermezzo 4):

1. A subject was planned for the first test day but came on the second day instead.
2. Session average time, including user interview, turned out to be 55 minutes, which was longer than planned and too close to the 60 minutes scheduled for each user. This created some stress among the staff involved in the test.
3. In the before-gameplay instructions to subjects on how to speak and point, we opted for a solution different from the one described in the note on priming in Section 14.3. We simply did not show the subjects how to speak and point, as this was felt to be the safer option for avoiding priming. Instead, we told subjects that they could speak and point in any temporal relationship.
4. For Subject 1, the interviewer forgot to ask questions 1–4 as closed questions (Section 8.8).
5. For Subject 1, the interviewer forgot to ask the any-other-comments question (Section 8.8).
6. More serious is the fact that the user population turned out to be less representative than planned, see Section 17.1.4.

### 17.1.3 Interview Questions: Three Issues

The post-test interviews (Section 8.8) included four Likert-scale questions (1–4). As an experiment, half of the subjects were asked these questions at the start of the interview, whereas the other half were asked the questions after question 16. We conclude that those four questions seemed hard to get across when asked at the start of the interview, because they deal with "systems *like* the one you've just tried". At this point, just coming back from the system trial, people have a hard time abstracting from this particular system when addressing the closed questions. It would seem preferable to ask those four questions after questions 5 through 16 have been asked. At this point, people have off-loaded their comments on the trial and are ready to think about multimodal gameplay more generally.

It also appears that several interview question pairs (5+6, 7+8, 9+10) represent too fine-grained and research-oriented distinctions which are not shared by subjects, so that several subjects tended to answer one when asked the other.

During the interviews, and due to comments made by one subject in particular, we realised that an additional question would have been productive. This was whether subjects learnt anything during gameplay that made them change their interaction style. It was too late to include the question at the time.

### 17.1.4  User Statistics

Potential subjects were screened over the phone or face-to-face in order to compose a user group that met the requirements described in Section 8.6. Table 17.1 shows the composition of the test subject population. Gender balance is fine with fifty–fifty male and female subjects. Regarding proficiency (at least according to the subjects themselves), the balance is also as planned, i.e. one-third beginners, one-third medium experienced players and one-third experienced players.

Age distribution is less in accordance with requirements. Average age is around 36 due to overrepresentation of young users in their early twenties and thirties. Only three users are over 50 and none are in their late thirties or forties. This unbalanced age distribution is probably related to another, more serious, inadequacy of representativeness in terms of occupation/education. No less than eight subjects are university students, including one PhD student, and most of them study natural science,

**Table 17.1**  The Sudoku test users

| Subject No. | Age | Gender | Occupation/education | Sudoku proficiency |
|---|---|---|---|---|
| 1 | 24 | Male | Medical student | Beginner |
| 2 | 23 | Male | Medical student | Beginner |
| 3 | 60 | Male | Lecturer in computer science | Experienced |
| 4 | 76 | Female | School teacher, retired | Beginner |
| 5 | 33 | Male | Economist | Medium |
| 6 | 30 | Male | Biomechanics/physical education student | Experienced |
| 7 | 23 | Female | Mathematics/physical education student | Experienced |
| 8 | 23 | Female | Mathematics/religion student | Medium |
| 9 | 31 | Female | PhD student in biology | Medium |
| 10 | 22 | Female | 1-year science student | Medium |
| 11 | +50 | Female | Medicine | Beginner |
| 12 | 31 | Male | Engineering student | Experienced |

medicine or engineering. If we include the remaining four subjects, three of these are academics as well. In fact, the shortest education represented among the subjects is that of the school teacher. In summary, this is a poor representation of the population of Sudoku players that appears to comprise people having a wide range of educational backgrounds and professions.

The required age division has to some extent been met. The problem is that the first age group (17–29 years) includes five users aged 22–24 and the second age group (30–49 years) includes four users aged 30–33, which is not a good spread within either age interval. The third age group (50+ years) includes three users with a much better age distribution (+50, 60 and 76, respectively).

Subject recruitment was handled by the person who normally does subject recruitment at NISLab, and does it well, usually following a screening script such as the one used in the present case.

The overrepresentation of young subjects may be ascribed to the fact that so many students were recruited. It was not the intention to recruit more than, at most, two students no matter their line of study. However, our formulation "no more than two test persons with the same profession" was clearly not interpreted in the sense intended. Furthermore, only three subjects came from outside the university. It turned out that the majority of subjects were found by announcing the Sudoku test in the daily university newsletter which is distributed in the university canteens and elsewhere, and which is being read almost uniquely by students and university staff. This was an easy way to recruit subjects but also a way likely to lead to the unrepresentative sample we had. The lessons learnt are that we should have supervised the recruitment process more closely than we did and that our subject requirements are not always as clear to others as they are to ourselves.

For the test results, the failed subject recruitment means that we did not have a representative user group and that the results cannot be claimed to be valid for the large group of target users.

### 17.1.5  Game Statistics

Table 17.2 shows the user test game statistics based on test video analysis. The table shows in detail the causes of the 16 (48.5%) games that were not completed. Otherwise, these stats quite nicely match the user-self-declared Sudoku game profiles in Table 17.1: the self-declared beginners chose the easiest game level, at least for a start. The self-declared medium-level players stuck to the medium game level. And the self-declared experienced gamers all tried to play at the hardest level but only two of them managed to complete a difficult game. The two others (subjects 3 and 7) retreated to the medium level after some struggle. In seven cases, subjects gave up because the system gave them problems as discussed in Section 17.2. Interaction clearly failed on the evaluation criterion that subjects should complete at least two games in 30 minutes (Section 5.2).

**Table 17.2**  Game statistics

| Game data/Subject No. | 1 | 2 | 3 | 4 | 5 | 6 | 7 | 8 | 9 | 10 | 11 | 12 |
|---|---|---|---|---|---|---|---|---|---|---|---|---|
| *Games started* | | | | | | | | | | | | |
| Total per player: * + ** below | 3 | 4 | 2 | 2 | 3 | 2 | 3 | 2 | 2 | 3 | 4 | 3 |
| Grand total: 33 | | | | | | | | | | | | |
| *Games completed* | | | | | | | | | | | | |
| Easy | xx | xx | | x | | | | | | x | x | |
| Medium | | | | | x | x | x | xx | | xx | | x |
| Difficult | | | | | | x | | | | | | x |
| Total per player* | 2 | 2 | 0 | 1 | 1 | 2 | 1 | 2 | 0 | 3 | 1 | 2 |
| Grand total: 17 = 51.5% | | | | | | | | | | | | |
| *Uncompleted games: problems* | | | | | | | | | | | | |
| Game too difficult: subject changes to easier level | x | x | | | | | x | | | | | |
| Game too difficult: subject asked to select easier level | | | x | | | | | | | | | |
| Problems: gives up and selects new game at same level | | | | | x | | | | x | | xx | |
| Problems: resets game (same level) | | | | | | | | | | | | x |
| Game reset by mistake | | | | | | x | | | | | | |
| Game stopped due to crash | | | x | | | | | | | | | |
| Total per player | 1 | 1 | 2 | 0 | 2 | 0 | 1 | 0 | 1 | 0 | 2 | 1 |
| Grand total: 11 = 33.3% | | | | | | | | | | | | |
| *Uncompleted games: time's-up* | | | | | | | | | | | | |
| Total per player | 0 | 1 | 0 | 1 | 0 | 0 | 1 | 0 | 1 | 0 | 1 | 0 |
| Grand total: 5 = 15.2% | | | | | | | | | | | | |
| *Uncompleted games: totals* | | | | | | | | | | | | |
| Total per player** | 1 | 2 | 2 | 1 | 2 | 0 | 2 | 0 | 2 | 0 | 3 | 1 |
| Grand total: 16 = 48.5% | | | | | | | | | | | | |

## 17.1.6 Data Validation

In quantity, the test data collected was as planned, including a set of observation notes from subjects' gameplay, 12 complete test videos and two sets of interview notes, made by the interviewer and the observer/experimenter, respectively.

In quality, one test video has noisy background throughout but everything said by the subject can be heard. In the test videos, it is sometimes hard to distinguish certain numbers on the Sudoku game board. While this is not an obstacle to video analysis in other respects, it does make it difficult or impossible for the analyst to do one particular thing, i.e. to "play ahead" of the user and keep track of the non-elementary errors made. However, this is outside the scope of the planned system usability evaluation and has no adverse effects on the evaluation presented here.

## 17.2 Technical Issues

Research prototypes are rarely technically perfect. Even in a usability test report, it is crucial to list the main technical problems encountered during the test as these affect user performance and tend to "colour" users' experience with the system as recorded in the post-test interviews.

### 17.2.1 Robustness

The system behaved robustly, with not a single crash during 5–6 hours of testing. Windows crashed once, ending the test with Subject S3 a few minutes early, cf. Table 17.2. The crash was probably due to overheating and was countered by increasing machine ventilation. After re-boot, cursor movement was somewhat jittery for a while. Thus, overall, the system satisfies the robustness requirement in Section 5.2. The only other technical problem was a microphone that hampered speech recognition of S8 until the mike was adjusted after about 5 minutes of gameplay.

### 17.2.2 Speech and Pointing

*Pointing precision.* Pointing precision is the ease of placing the cursor on a screen object, such as a game board square (Section 7.2.1) and keeping it there for as long as it takes to perform some action, such as inserting a number. The requirements to pointing precision are determined by the following facts: (1) that some users want to play fast and need a corresponding amount of cursor control; (2) that most users get tired in their arm/hand if they play at length with their arm and index finger stretched out towards the screen, as a result of which they may lower the arm or the hand/finger may start shaking; (3) that all users need an acceptable minimum of pointing precision and absence of cursor jitter in order to feel in control during gameplay; and (4) the size of the screen objects pointed to.

Several subjects expressed difficulty with pointing precision in the post-test interviews, referring to the factors mentioned above – finger/hand shaking (S1, S11), arm lowered (S2), cursor jitter (S4, S5), or more generally (S6, S9) – and a single user (S7) was observed to fail to insert a number in the intended square due to imprecise pointing. As for square size, S2 remarked that the squares should not be smaller than those used in the test.

In conclusion, since the game is intended for public locations and users are expected to play for limited amounts of time, such as $\frac{1}{2}$ hour, the pointing precision at present, given adequate camera calibration, would appear to be minimally acceptable for the general user. Both during our observation of subjects playing and when playing ourselves, it seems that pointing can be done with reasonable precision and a negligible amount of jitter, provided that the arm/hand/index finger is stretched out towards the screen. Also, there is always the possibility of increasing the size of the game board. This can be done easily while awaiting further improvement in pointing precision.

*Number Ends Up in Wrong Square (NIWS)*. The NIWS issue arises when a spoken number unintendedly ends up in a wrong square. This is probably the most serious technical problem in the present system version.

A spoken number may end up in a wrong square in a variety of situations. The typical situation is when the user points to a square, makes sure that it highlights and speaks a number which, however, fails to appear in the square. Most users then repeat the number one or more times – on the videos we observed up to 6–7 repetitions – while keeping the square highlighted. At some point the user gives up temporarily and moves the cursor out of the square in order to lower the arm, relax and try again. In this phase, either before the arm/hand/finger is lowered sufficiently for the cursor to disappear from the screen or when the arm/hand/finger is raising to point to the square again, the cursor passes through another square which highlights and shows the number spoken earlier. Now the user must remove this (in most cases) wrongly inserted number before getting back to the original square to retry to insert the number there. Even worse, the square into which the number was wrongly inserted was not empty but contained a previously inserted number which has now been overwritten. Sometimes the user could not remember the previously inserted number and had to try to work out what that number might have been in order to start getting back on track. Worse still, one user failed to notice the wrong insertion and suffered later on in the game. A variation of the scenario is when the cursor inadvertently errs into an adjacent square into which the spoken number gets inserted.

The causes of NIWS remain somewhat obscure. One part, clearly, is the design decision to enable spoken number entry in any temporal relationship with pointing. If a number could be entered only as long as a square is highlighted and active, the problem could not arise in the first place. The number spoken would be erased from memory as soon as the square became inactive. However, we classify this issue as technical rather than as a design decision effect, because there is a problem in the implementation. If the failed insertion of a spoken number into a highlighted square is due simply to the fact that the number is not being recognised – it is not being *mis*recognised because no other number gets inserted in the highlighted square – then this exact number would not end up in a different square later on. For that to happen, the number must have been recognised correctly. We suspect a missing-thread problem in system inter-module communication: the recogniser generates a queue of recognised numbers, and the first of these gets printed onto the screen when the main thread finds the time.

All subjects encountered NIWS, often several times, 83 times in total, with significant individual differences. None of the subjects seemed to find a way to avoid the problem, which is also hard to do: you might try to "sneak out" the cursor from the game board by moving it through a series of fixed numbers, avoiding all empty squares and squares containing inserted numbers, but this is hard to control and isn't always possible; or you might fold the index finger and retract the hand/arm along an axis perpendicular to the screen, so as to avoid any further cursor movement, but this is a complex, unnatural and not necessarily successful way to avoid the problem. The problem disrupts gameplay and causes frustration, annoyance and incomprehension to all.

A peculiar NIWS variation was when a subject gave up on inserting a spoken number into square S(n), lowered the arm, raised it again and pointed to S(n) anew, whereupon the number got inserted before the user managed to repeat it. Three subjects commented on this issue, and we estimate that about 2/3 of the users experienced it at least once. So maybe NIWS ought to be called *number in unintended square* instead (NIUS).

*Speech Recognition.* We mentioned that all subjects had the experience of failing to get a spoken number inserted into the square pointed to, even after repeating the number several times, and that this could not always be an issue of speech recognition failure.

On the other hand, it did happen – some times for most users, many times for several – that they were misrecognised by the system, which would insert a number different from the one actually spoken. For the users who had most difficulty being recognised, there was often a pattern to the misrecognitions. For instance, S4, S6 and S7 had some difficulty getting "number three" understood, whereas S9 had severe problems inserting a "4" which was nearly always recognised as a "5". In fact, the test notes show that all numbers except "9" posed problems for some subject. In addition, several subjects had difficulty removing numbers by saying "delete this/that" or "remove this/that". In a couple of cases, the subject went so far as to reset the game after failing to remove a misrecognised number. The worst case, though, was probably S9 who almost inevitably failed to insert "4" and ended up avoiding squares that needed a 4 in order not to lose yet another struggle with the system. This was the main reason why S9 failed to complete even a single game (Table 17.2). On the other hand, several subjects who had few speech recognition problems concluded that the system's speech understanding was "perfect" (S3) or that "The system understood me fine" (S10).

As illustrated, misrecognition, especially when repeated, is disruptive to gameplay. It must be kept in mind, though, that all subjects were native Danish speakers and none were native English speakers as well. One cannot off-hand blame an English speech recogniser for performing less than perfectly when exposed to more or less strong accents. We did not do any detailed phonetic evaluation of the quality of subjects' English, but our impression is that the number of misrecognitions made per subject is largely in proportion to the strength of their Danish accent. Moreover, none of the subjects listed, neither directly nor indirectly, the system's speech recognition quality as a reason for not playing with the system again. Even the unfortunate S9 who failed to complete any game mainly because of recognition problems, said afterwards that she just had to practice a more correct pronunciation. The experimenter demonstrated how the system would respond correctly to a properly pronounced "4" and she then repeated the pronunciation with success herself.

The facts are that a total of 23 positive cases of misrecognition were found in the video corpus, whereas the corpus shows a total of 300 speech input events to which the system did not respond, the large majority of which occurred when subjects kept repeating a number to no effect until the number eventually ended up in the wrong square, cf. above. Of those 323 events, S9 was involved in no less than 107, i.e. one third. We believe that the majority of those no-response events are linked to the missing-thread problem hypothesised above.

On this buggy background, it is hard to score the speech recognition quality with any accuracy. The subjects weren't deterred but the combined number of misrecognitions and no-response events is way too high.

### 17.2.3 Other Issues

*Issues involving the squares.* Observation of the game board squares during gameplay raises two issues that seem to reflect simple bugs: (1) an empty square does not activate (highlight) or takes some struggle to activate by, e.g. moving the cursor back and forth over it. The same square may work fine later in the game, so the problem always seemed to be temporary; (2) a square seems to be highlighted without being pointed to.

Issue (1) occurred a dozen times, always causing frustration because it was impossible to insert a number into a non-highlighted square. It disrupts your game if you are unable to insert the number you are presently focused on inserting. In most cases, subjects would continue trying for quite some time to insert the number they had in mind rather than moving on to other squares and numbers.

Issue (2) occurred quite frequently, one or several squares appearing to be permanently highlighted. This would happen both with squares that had not been pointed to during the game and squares into which a number had been inserted by the subject. While this problem is only minor, it may cause uncertainty in the user regarding which square the user is actually pointing to, given that two neighbouring squares are highlighted at the same time. No subject commented on the issue.

*Sudoku generation algorithm.* The system uses a simple algorithm for generating a new game. The algorithm starts from a simple completed game and permutes the game board rows while preserving correctness. What the algorithm does not do, or does not do perfectly, is check if the generated game has a unique solution, which Sudoku players are used to expecting and which acts as an implicit game rule, cf. Section 3.2.2. Thus, S5 ended up with multiple possible solutions and didn't seem to know what to do until the experimenter suggested that he simply select one of them. S6, the best player among the subjects, ended up in a similar situation. He realised what was the matter after a while, and then chose one of the possible solutions. S6 confirmed this after the test and said that he had never met a Sudoku that did not have a unique solution. The solution to this problem is to include a unique-solution test in the game generation algorithm.

## 17.3 Modality Appropriateness

Modality appropriateness evaluation is a qualitative analysis of test data that can form part of the usability evaluation of any interactive system. As long as everybody used standard GUIs, there was little reason for making an evaluation of this kind because – where would people go if the evaluation made them unhappy with the standard GUI? However, with the proliferation of modality combinations, modality appropriateness evaluation could be a major component of usability evaluation, as illustrated in this intermezzo.

We split appropriateness evaluation into three parts. The first part evaluates the individual modalities and their combinations (Section 17.3.1). The second looks at how the multimodal combination works as evidenced by the test data (Section 17.3.2) and the third looks at any required changes to the information represented in the system's modalities (Section 17.3.3). Device issues are included when relevant.

## 17.3.1  Component Modality Appropriateness

This part of the analysis has a common format: just replace the following modalities with your own. In the Sudoku Case, component modality appropriateness concerns the usability of combining spoken notation and keyword-based speech input, 3D visual pointing gesture input, 2D static graphic images, labelled image icons, and text for playing Sudoku (Section 5.1). The issues are whether

1.  existing modalities should be replaced by others, or removed;
2.  existing modalities should be maintained on certain conditions to be specified;
3.  additional modalities are required

given the data (Section 17.1), the A(M)ITUDE specification (Section 5.1) and design (Section 7.2.1), the usability requirements (Section 5.2) and arguments by reference to usability (Section 1.4.6).

*Keyword-based speech input.* The system uses a particular atomic-level input speech modality, i.e. keywords and key phrases which have been fixed by the developers (Section 7.2.1). Any other spoken input will either not be recognised or be misrecognised. This general approach suffers from familiar problems and limitations. To play the game at all, users must first learn or otherwise be informed about which keywords are allowed. Second, the more keywords, the more difficulty users will have learning what to say to the system. In principle, this is unsuitable for walk-up-and-use systems, but then again, the Sudoku system has not been claimed to be "pure" walk-up-and-use. Rather, it's the intended use environment that seems to require something close to walk-up-and-use. In particular, it is not clear at this point how real users will be informed about the keywords that must be used. What is clear is that users must be told somehow, because it seems unlikely that most of them would be able to figure out on their own which keywords to use. A simple solution could be to list the keywords in small-font text on the main screen (Section 7.2.1). In the user test, the experimenter in his introduction told the users what the keywords were in order to let the test data show how easy it was for the subjects to remember them.

Speech input, despite the recognition problems caused by Danish accent (Section 17.2), was broadly regarded by subjects as useful for the Sudoku game and other, comparable games, such as chess, in the intended use environment of public locations.

Regarding the use of keywords, subjects managed quite well to stick to the vocabulary they had been told to use. The few exceptions were that S5 forgot several times to say "number" before the integer; S10 tried once to say "erase this" to no effect; the disfluency in S11's "remove . . . ahmm . . . this" may have been due to difficulties in remembering what to say; and several subjects forgot at one time or other to add "this" or "that" to the "remove" or "delete" commands. No user complained that the spoken keywords were difficult to remember despite the fact that each subject had only been told them once.

In comparative terms, one subject (S10) found that speaking was easier than using drag-and-drop-numbers selected from a palette in Sudoku on the Internet.

In the test, input speech was captured by a headset microphone. Two subjects (S1, S10) pointed out that this was not an optimal solution because the headset is cumbersome to wear. In a public setting it would probably be advisable to use a lapel microphone instead as this is likely to be more acceptable to users.

We conclude that it is acceptable to use the small number of spoken keywords needed for the application.

*Alternatives to speech input.* For very different reasons, three subjects entertained ideas of removing speech input or replacing speech with a different modality. S7 found it "funny", "daft", "strange" and "difficult to get used to" to speak to a game machine. This seems to be a clear case of a "too exotic for me" user preference. As an alternative, and in order to make the game more physical and active than it already is, S6 suggested that users point to a square and then select the number to insert by jumping onto a numbered field in a palette on the floor. Similarly, S9 suggested to replace speech by pointing to a palette and then pointing to the game board. The suggestion was made in order to solve S9's massive problems controlling that the spoken number ends up in the intended square (Section 17.2.2).

*3D pointing input.* Most subjects found 3D pointing useful for playing Sudoku and similar games in public. Seven subjects pointed out that 3D pointing with the arm/hand/finger fully stretched is only suitable for playing for limited periods of time. It's hard, and takes concentration, to keep the arm/hand/finger still when pointing to a particular square; it is hard to keep the arm up for a longish stretch of time; and it's a problem to keep the arm straight.

These points are obviously correct. Yet comparison of the players on video shows an interesting and potentially mitigating factor: from the very start, several players displayed a style of calm and controlled gestural play, with full cursor control. While the other subjects tended to keep the arm up and pointed towards the screen for long periods of time, these players would put down the arm while scanning the game board for the next empty square to fill. The difference, we suggest, is that some subjects intuitively do what all or most others can *learn* to do.

In addition to adopting a more relaxed gaming style, there is another thing one can do to make playing less strenuous, namely, to change arm from time to time.

S6 found that it is good to use either arm for pointing. Several subjects began to do so at some point. However, S9 pointed out that changing arm for pointing is not necessarily a relaxing thing to do. People typically have a "leading eye" for aiming at something. If the arm is changed, it gets in the way for the "leading eye" (you don't change eye when you change arm), whereupon the body starts leaning to one side to avoid arm/hand occlusion and to actually see what is being pointed at. This explains why S9 tended to adopt a somewhat contorted position when pointing with her left arm. Try it out yourself!

*Alternatives and additions to 3D pointing.* 3D pointing input and its combination with speech input are the most innovative aspects of the Sudoku game. This means that these aspects are liable to go against established user habits and preferences. Moreover, some subjects felt it tiring to stand still, arm outstretched, for a long time and there's the NIWS problem (Section 17.2.2). These factors led to several proposals for alternatives or additions to 3D pointing.

Referring to physical exertion, S7 preferred a different pointing gesture sub-modality, i.e. 2D haptic (touch screen) pointing, to the present game style which he found annoying rather than relaxing. Similarly, S3 said that gaming would be more stable with a touch screen, and S6 mentioned the touch screen alternative as well. In fact, 2D haptic pointing is a perfectly viable alternative, i.e. to have a large touch screen for playing Sudoku in public. Moreover, like 3D visual pointing, 2D haptic pointing is done without the need for additional input devices. This argument may, in fact, be the strongest argument against installing 3D pointing Sudoku games in public locations.

S1 suggested augmenting the number of input modalities by adding a haptic modality to 3D visual pointing by using "a pen instead of the finger so that one could click". It is not clear whether this suggestion merely reflects the subject's habit of using a mouse for pointing-and-selecting, or whether it also reflects that the user does not feel in full control of number insertion through 3D pointing and speech. Similarly, S3 said that the system might have featured double-clicking instead of just pointing. However, when asked why, he simply said that he misses the clicking, suggesting that he is just unaccustomed to a graphics output domain into which one doesn't have to click to make things happen. However, echoing S1, S7 said that she prefers a touch screen – which may also use haptic code input – to standing with the arm in the air, saying "Did I click or not?". This at least *suggests* a feeling of not being in control. Also S9 would like to be able to click on something when there is a problem.

Yet another haptic pointing input modality was suggested by S4, i.e. to use a long pointing stick. It may be noted that S4 was particularly affected by cursor jitter following the system crash. Her suggestion seems to reflect a genuine control problem which, however, is not characteristic of the system in its normal state.

Suggesting to replace 3D pointing by a stick may seem exotic (or archaic), but still does address problems with the system at hand. Other modality alternatives proposed by subjects fall into the different category of being irrelevant for the application. S5 pointed out that it's less physically demanding to use a pencil or mouse rather than 3D gesture, and S9 found that it is better to use the mouse for pointing because 3D pointing is annoying. While criticisms of the system should be taken note of, and have been discussed above, those alternative suggestions are irrelevant because the present game is *not* being proposed as an alternative to, or replacement of, traditional ways of playing Sudoku.

*Keyword-based speech + 3D pointing input.* Although raising many issues concerning the details of spoken and 3D pointing interaction, none of the subjects directly questioned the *combination* of speech and 3D pointing input. This acceptance of the speech and 3D pointing modality combination is hardly surprising, because it's an extremely useful one which humans naturally employ all the time. Speech is notoriously bad at disambiguating spatial reference (Table 4.3) and attempts to do spatial reference through speech therefore tend to be replete with disfluencies as shown by Oviatt in numerous papers, e.g. Oviatt and Cohen (2000). It is possible, of course, when playing Sudoku to say, e.g. "Row number five column number three insert number seven", avoiding the use of pointing altogether. But pointing is just so much more convenient for supplying the spatial reference part of that statement, which is why we combine speech and pointing as often as we do. Emphasising the naturalness of this modality combination, S3 said that combined speech and pointing input is a great help for users unaccustomed to the keyboard.

When discussing the number-in-the-wrong-square problem (Section 17.2.2), we saw that the problem might be (almost) completely solved if the system would only enter spoken numbers into squares that are highlighted at the same time. The cost of this solution is to remove the opportunity to speak and point in any temporal order. Since we know from experience and from the scientific literature that humans sometimes speak and point "out of sync", even when speaking and pointing are complementary parts of the same communicative intent, this cost might seem to constitute a serious sacrifice of interaction naturalness. On the other hand, human communication is complex. We should not take for granted that reported findings of different temporal orderings of speech and pointing during interaction with computers can be generalised to all interactive tasks. How did the subjects actually speak and point?

In fact, the test videos show that all subjects consistently played by pointing and speaking *at the same time*, despite the fact that they were clearly told that they could speak and point in any temporal order. Even more specifically, they would first make sure that they saw the highlighting feedback from the square they pointed to; then make sure that the cursor remained stably pointed at this square; and only then speak the number to be inserted. And then, while keeping the square highlighted, they would verify that the number got inserted and that it was the right one (no misrecognition), before finally moving the cursor elsewhere or lower the arm. In other words, speaking was invariably "temporally encapsulated" inside a pointing gesture. S12 gave words to this approach, saying that he preferred to point and speak at the same time.

*Static graphics output.* The system's static output graphics consist of four displays: a main screen and three separate text displays, see Section 7.2.1. These representations were generally found to be simple, clear and easy to understand. The screen size was judged to be fine by one subject with no remarks to the contrary by the others. S2, S11 and S12 said that the red error indications are good, and only one (S7) mentioned the possibility of removing them. S2 remarked that the size of the squares should not be smaller than what was used in the test.

*Adding acoustic output.* To users familiar with computer games, it may seem rather obvious to consider adding acoustic output – speech or non-speech sound – for various purposes. The subjects proposed a number of additions mostly in order to improve the system's entertainment value – or decreasing it, depending on one's preferences.

S1 mentioned adding non-speech sound output but did not specify. S5 suggested using acoustic warnings instead of, or together with, the red highlighting of surface mistakes. S6 suggested an "AAUGH!" message for this purpose. S6 and S12 felt it would be fun to have a fanfare or a "YES!" when a game has been successfully completed. Reflecting user uncertainty during interaction, S6 suggested to have "little sounds" signalling that the system has recognised a spoken input number. Some had contrary preferences. S7 said that non-speech sounds can be irritating and that it's good that no sound is being output, e.g. in case of error. Similarly, referring to the system's graphics-only output, S8 remarked that it is "good that there is nothing else. Sound is irritating when you have to think, like in the 'Who wants to be a millionaire' TV show".

These comments suggest that the issue of using redundant acoustic output in some computer games and entertainment systems, at least, is a controversial one.

*Adding dynamic graphics output.* The main screen requires static graphics for representing the game board, because the players need freedom of perceptual inspection to plan their next move (Section 4.2.2). However, this does not exclude use of dynamic graphics for other purposes. S5 suggested that team competition, in particular, might have a timer showing for how long the user has been playing. If the timer were to run on-screen, this would be a case of dynamic graphics.

### 17.3.2 Gameplay Using Speech, Pointing and Graphics

In this section we look at the system's I/O modalities as a whole and how subjects viewed their appropriateness for playing Sudoku and similar games. The subjects had many different viewpoints on these issues. To keep focused, we start by noting that, in our view, the key issues are (i) how suitable is the modality combination for the system's primary purpose, i.e. to enable Sudoku gaming in public locations; and (ii) how subjects view the suitability of the modality combination for playing not only Sudoku in this kind of environment but also other, comparable board games, such as chess.

It is less interesting to compare the system with playing Sudoku on the Internet or on paper because the system is not meant to replace, or compete with, these ways of playing the game. Unsurprisingly, subjects, and especially the avid Sudoku gamers among them, had lots to say about the differences between the system and the traditional ways of playing the game, as well as about their preferred set of modalities, but this is comparing apples and carrots. We summarise subjects' remarks on these issues below but the remarks remain tangential to a functional evaluation of the system on its own premises. Still, some comparative claims actually do reveal a subject's views on the prospects of the system, for instance when the subject grants that the system is as good as using pencil and paper. This is revealing, because we take for granted that playing pencil-and-paper Sudoku is a well-tested and successful way of playing the game, as testified by its popularity among the millions of players across the world who play every day.

Several subjects were quite happy with the way the system worked during their test sessions. S1 (not a regular player) and S4 found playing "relatively easy" and S1 said that all the functionality needed was there: for deleting numbers, etc. S2 appreciated the error correction functionality as well. S3 found playing easy and said that it was his own mistake if there were problems. It is easy to get a new game and easy to delete a number in case of mistakes (S7).

Let us first look at the suitability of the system's modality combination for gaming in public.

*Playing in a public location.* Subjects provided substantial input on gaming in airports, train stations, shops and other public locations. Four said that they might use the system if they came across it in a public location and had time to spare. S3 said that, although he wouldn't play Sudoku in this way himself, others might well want to. In fact, he felt that the combination of speech and pointing input (and, we assume, static graphics output) is good for chess and many other games. Similarly, S9 found the system's I/O modality combination useful for many different purposes. S9 pointed out that one tends to sit a lot during air travel and that it would be fine to stand up and point in an airport. S5 said that if there are spectators, they can better follow the game on the screen than if it's being played on a newspaper page. Given the fact that three of the subjects were not really interested in playing Sudoku in any form, this data provides evidence that there might be considerable interest in using the system in public locations.

Several found that the system has social entertainment potential. S5 said that it might be used for team competition in game arcades, or people could play together in, e.g. a family competition. S12 compared Sudoku gaming in public with popular games, such as dart or billiard, and wished to use the system for competing in a similar way. S1 felt that the system might be used as a party game; S2 said that it would be better if two people could play against each other; and S10 found that the system was better suited for entertainment with several people present. Adding up, eight subjects adopted the idea of using the system in public.

Subjects also had concerns with respect to playing in public, however. S1, not a Sudoku player, would not like to play Sudoku in public but would be happy to play Trivial Pursuit instead. S4 would not play in public because spectators might interfere with her game. While S5 had nothing against onlookers, he did not want them to take too much interest in his gameplay. S12 noted the risk that spectators might talk over the spoken input. This is true and raises the issue of appropriate microphone setup for public gaming. A lapel mike might work provided that spectators can be relied on not to speak too loudly during someone else's game to avoid that the microphone captures the background speech. S6 pointed out that speaking while gaming in public locations might irritate others. This is also true. The challenge is to play where others aren't expecting a quiet environment.

*Comparisons.* Here follow those of the subjects' comments which, although comparing the system with other ways of playing Sudoku, include general points of interest on public gameplay.

*Optimal combination.* S1 found the system's interactive modalities an optimal combination for playing Sudoku. *As good as on paper.* To S4, using the system is more or less as good as solving Sudokus in the newspaper. *Children.* S5 remarked that children might prefer the tested game over pencil and paper. This point might be related to the following: *Gets the body active.* Like S9, S6 said that it's fine to involve the arm and the body. "It's good to get the body active". S8 found the game more physical and more immersive or engaging than playing in a [Sudoku game] book. "Adrenalin increases a bit when your body is involved in this way. This game is more fun than the Internet. Great fun". However, before we get too exited about physical training prospects, it's worth noting a comment from S9 who argued that the game setup requires a more action-oriented game – it's more relevant for more movement-oriented games. Similarly, S6 found the technology well suited for games more physically active than Sudoku. *Larger screen than on the Internet.* S5 found that, compared to playing over the Internet, it's good to have a larger screen "so that you don't need glasses".

In the following, subjects compare with more traditional ways of playing Sudoku. S2 found the system better than paper in that errors are shown immediately. S4 pointed out that the system, unlike paper Sudoku, does not require pencil and eraser because you can automatically delete a wrongly inserted number. Moreover, you never end up with paper completely filled with (support) numbers and notes (which damages the overview necessary to complete the game successfully). S2 found gaming a bit clumsy and slow compared to paper gaming, and S7 concurred with respect to the slowness. However, she found gaming fun as entertainment, confirming the system's potential for public gaming. S2 also pointed out that touch screen pointing + palette number selection would be faster. S3 insisted that Sudoku requires paper and pencil and did not like to play on a screen. S4 preferred to do crossword puzzles.

### 17.3.3 Information Appropriateness

In this section, we assume the system's modalities as-is and ask whether the information exchanged with users in those modalities is necessary and sufficient for playing Sudoku:

1. should information in any modality be supplemented by more information; or
2. should information actually provided in any modality be removed?

Note that information includes both input and output. In the following, we make no distinction as to how strongly a subject insisted on some information issue. There is a continuum in the way subjects phrase their suggestions, of course, and degrees of conviction can be important. However, given the small and not very representative test subject population (Section 17.1.4), it matters more to evaluate the merits of subjects' ideas than to scrutinise individual subject conviction. Still, ideas brought up by several subjects independently may warrant serious consideration.

Most information remarks concerned gaming support functionality.

*Undo, backtracking* as a spoken command with static graphics feedback. Sudoku players are familiar with the problems arising when discovering that an earlier number insertion was wrong. At this point, it is often impossible to remember the sequence of steps taken after the wrong number insertion, which means that one's game has been ruined. In view of the electronic nature of the tested game, four subjects (S3, S6, S7, S12) suggested to add an *undo* function which could help backtrack to the point at which the wrong number had been inserted, erasing the numbers inserted since then. This function, three of them added, should be executed solely through speech, without any pointing.

*Error indications* as static graphics text elicited by speech and/or pointing. *Undo* is an example of the many help and support functions that could be included in electronic Sudoku games. The present system provides one of these. It signals – by colouring the relevant row, column, or 3×3 field red (Section 7.2.1) – that an inserted number is identical to another number in that row, column or 3×3 field. Subjects were divided as to whether the system should offer additional help in identifying wrongly inserted numbers. S5 said that it would be useful to be able to switch on and off a function that signals non-obvious mistakes (the system would use its knowledge of the correct solution to evaluate each inserted number), and S11 wanted "more information on errors". However, the other subjects who addressed this type of function warned against it. S9, while happy with the red error indications, said that the system should not identify "deep" errors because that would make the game too easy; and S12 felt that even if a "deep" error function were optional, its very existence might tempt him and others to use it, destroying the real challenge of gameplay. Instead, S9 suggested a *help* function that would offer to insert the next number when a player got stuck. S6, on the contrary, warned against a *help* function because it is easy to be tempted to use the function too much or too early. S7 even argued that, had the game worked better, it shouldn't even highlight surface errors. She is probably referring to the NIWS bug (Section 17.2.2). Her remark is supported by the fact that very few surface errors (=7) were observed during 5–6 hours of test gameplay. Several subjects did make "deep" errors, though, and these caused quite some grief later on in their respective games.

*Game notes* as static graphic numbers inserted through pointing and speech. Sudoku players play the game in different ways and develop personal strategies for success. A common problem for most players is working memory load, especially when the game difficulty level goes up. When this happens, you find yourself doing all manner of calculations over which numbers might fit into a certain row, column, 3×3 field or block of 3×3 fields. Having done those calculations and concluded that none of the numbers can be inserted right away, the difficulty is to remember the results for use later in the game when more numbers are present. Many players use external memory support, writing possible numbers into the squares, writing them in the paper margins, etc., and often suffer later on when all this write-up obscures the numbers on the game board, or when they must erase or overwrite numbers that didn't work or which have been inserted. Top players therefore tend to use external memory sparingly, if at all. If you play on paper, you are free to invent any external memory system you want, and some Internet Sudoku sites offer various kinds of external memory functionality.

The present game version doesn't offer any note-taking functionality, and it is therefore to be expected that some of the subjects wish to have such functionality added, partly because they are used to having it and partly because it actually does off-load working memory. S7 remarked that "Paper makes it possible to insert possible numbers into the squares. Here I need to keep everything in my head". S7, S9 and S12 missed being able to insert possible numbers in the squares. S10 wanted both this opportunity and the option of inserting possible numbers in the margins for playing games more difficult than those she played during the test. S11 needed the margin support for difficult gaming as well. S3, who strongly prefers paper-and-pencil gaming, mentioned that he writes possible numbers in the squares and erases them later on.

From a technical point of view, in-square notes and margin notes are easy to add. From a usability point of view, however, the former may seem preferable because it would take a considerable amount of screen real-estate to impose some clear structure onto the margin notes which users might want to make. This is probably why we haven't seen any margin note functionality on Internet Sudoku sites whereas several sites feature in-square note functionality.

*Other acoustic input information.* Some subjects wished to add various spoken commands. S1 pointed out that the system's input command language vocabulary is quite limited and said that it would be more fun if more words could be used. S4 mentioned possible addition of a *move* command for moving an inserted number somewhere else. S6 mentioned the obvious point that it would be nice to have a system version with Danish speech recognition. Reflecting the long delay when loading a new game, S6 suggested to use a spoken command for choosing a new game instead of having to wait so long. Loading time will not be positively affected by a spoken command, however.

## 17.4 Functional Issues

In this section we discuss the functional issues identified in the test. A functional issue is not a technical problem, it's a design solution or a combined result of design decisions, which turns out to be questionable for some reason. This does not mean that every functional issue raised must be resolved through re-design and further development, but it does mean that the developers should take a hard look at their system and ask if it could be made better.

*Slow response time.* Even though one subject felt that the system reacts sufficiently fast to speech and pointing, with no disturbing delays, several others had remarks on delays in response to input. In a system like this, "real-time behaviour" is a fuzzy notion and you have to build in delays for various reasons. That's why we classify slow response time as a functional issue.

According to S3, "One has to get used to the fact that the system takes some time to discover that the finger has moved". S6 said that pointing is a bit slow due to the time it takes for the system to respond: the system cannot keep up when you have spotted a pattern and have 4–5 numbers to put in. S6 clearly attributed the delayed response to delays in pointing processing since he proposed to accelerate *new game* loading time by speaking instead of gesturing. He is right that the pointing gesture has a built-in delay but wrong in believing that speech would speed up loading time. S7 said that the system is very slow in reacting to pointing, S11 that the system was slow sometimes. S10 diplomatically said that it "sometimes took longer than others" for the system to understand speech + pointing.

A user's experience that response time is too slow either generally or for certain input actions, can be due to many different observations made during interaction. To mention some: (i) several subjects tried repeatedly to insert a number in a particular square without success; (ii) some squares did not highlight almost immediately; (iii) when subjects selected a new game, it took an estimated 10–20 seconds for the system to load; (iv) subjects often spent longer than strictly necessary to make sure that the intended square was highlighted and that the cursor was stable inside the square before speaking a number; and (v) fast-playing users may feel hampered by the fact that there has to be a certain minimal activation delay for any pointable screen object lest it becomes too easy to accidentally activate the object just by passing the cursor over it.

Of these factors, (i) is related to the NIWS problem (Section 17.2.2), so this is not necessarily a speech recognition or pronunciation problem; and even if it were a problem of one of these kinds, it's not a response time problem. (ii) is not a response time problem either, it's a bug. (iii) is a very particular response time problem since it only occurs when loading a new game. (iv) is not a response time problem. Moreover, (iv) can be alleviated through training in using the system efficiently. For instance, S5 said that, in retrospect, he might have spoken earlier once he had highlighted a square, rather than re-checking that the highlighting stayed in place before speaking. Finally, (v) is a response time problem if a user feels it is one. However, it's a necessary one and the only real issue is to calibrate the response time so that it becomes as small as possible without enabling users to activate anything by accident.

In conclusion, it is not clear to us that the system does have a real response time problem except for game loading time, and the uncertainty effects of this one can be mitigated, cf. next section.

*Uncertainty and lack of control during interaction.* Removing user uncertainty is an important goal in most interaction design. Uncertainty about what to do at a certain point during interaction, whether to do anything at all, whether the system actually did get the latest input, etc. – militates against the user's feeling of being in control of interaction and negatively affects user experience. Several features of the current system version tend to create user uncertainty.

*User background.* Sometimes uncertainty may be a function of a user's background. It is only to be expected that technology to which users have never been exposed before, creates uncertainty in and of itself. In many such cases, we believe, nothing can nor should be done about uncertainty. The technology is new, people are not yet used to it, and that's that. You don't put a horse in front of a functioning car even if some drivers miss one.

*Missing the click.* S1, S3 and S7 all "miss the click", and at least S7 comes close to expressing uncertainty. S7 asks: "What makes it choose – the pointing, speech, both?", which may be interpreted as yet another expression of uncertainty (rather than intellectual curiosity). S7 also asked if it is necessary to keep the hand pointed at a square for some time. S9 expresses lack of control and its effects directly, saying that she would like to click on something when there is a problem, adding that "one feels helpless, and this is something one is not used to". The situation S9 is referring to is when the spoken number fails to be inserted in the intended square and the subject is out of control with respect to (a) what is going on, (b) if it will be possible to insert the number in the next attempt and (c) whether the number will end up in some other square. Her helplessness shows how important it is to remove the NIWS problem (Section 17.2.2).

*Loading a new game.* S9 says that she doesn't know what to do when waiting for a new game to be loaded; S7 became visibly impatient; and S11 became uncertain when nothing happened. Uncertainty may be compounded by another factor, i.e. that subjects don't know – despite being told in the introduction to the system – if they should speak in addition to pointing when choosing a new game level, choosing a new game or resetting the current game (Section 7.2.1). After all, they have to speak *and* point to insert a number, and it may not be obvious to them that those other functions do not *require* both pointing and speech and that the developers therefore have chosen pointing-only for activation – except for choosing to play a new game where speech and pointing are equivalent alternatives. Especially when loading a new game, but also when resetting a game or choosing a new game, we observed several subjects trying to speak the contents of the labels that were visible at the same time. They would say "New game" when pointing at the *new game* icon or "Yes" when confirming that they wish to proceed to load a new game and acknowledge that the game just played will be lost (Section 7.2.1). The levels-of-difficulty screen (Section 7.2.1) may make it harder to simply read aloud the chosen game difficulty level, so we observed several users (e.g. S6) start talking free-style to the system or even mumbling comments and questions in Danish.

*Inconsistencies.* Is the problem just noted, i.e. not knowing when to speak in addition to pointing, an *inconsistency* in the interaction design? It is probably too early to judge because we first need a paradigm, or a set of guidelines, for what is consistent design of pointing and speech input. Intuitively, however, this is not inconsistent, in so far as users are only expected to speak in addition to pointing when speech-only or pointing-only cannot do the job. Moreover, the test videos indicate that subjects mostly did understand this, since many of them would first start speaking to the *Proceed?* screen when nothing happened in response to their pointing. However, it clearly *is* inconsistent design to enable alternative speech and pointing for choosing to play a new game but not for other similar commands.

*Icons.* Another potential cause of user uncertainty concerns the labelled icons *new game* and *reset game* in the top-left corner of the screen (Section 7.2.1). There are two problems: (1) the icons are partly hidden behind the screen frame and only partly visible; and (2) when moving the cursor up there, you might easily hit the lower one (*reset*) before getting to *new game*. Issue (1) is a relatively simple matter of ensuring that the game display fits standard screens. Issue (2) is more interesting.

S5 mistakenly pointed at *reset game* instead of *new game* and got the game he had just played rather than a new game. And, when observing the players, we noted that some went overboard trying not to make the cursor pass through *reset* on its way to *new game*. Neither the user nor we know if there is an activation delay when pointing at these icons (ensuring free passage for a cursor that just passes by the icon), but a user who has seen his numbers end up in the wrong place (Section 17.2.2) is likely to be wary of passing the cursor through *reset* on its way to *new game*. The same applies to game level selection (Section 7.2.1). As S7 asked, what happens if, in trying to select a particular game level, the pointing hand (i.e. the cursor) passes over some other active field in the menu?

*Remedies.* Some modifications that might alleviate the user uncertainties noted above are, first, to solve the NIWS problem (Section 17.2.2) which seems to be the most important cause of user uncertainty during gameplay by far. Second, the game loading time issue should be solved by providing process feedback during the loading of a new game: through an on-screen message, output speech or otherwise. Third, it might be considered to provide low-volume non-speech sound feedback on (i) successful square activation in addition to the current highlighting whose reliability as indicator of square activation (i.e. the readiness of a square to have a spoken number inserted into it) we are not sure about; and/or, as, in fact, suggested by S6, on (ii) the fact that the system has received, and is trying to recognise, spoken input. Whether or not any of this feedback should be added might be made dependent on how successfully NIWS gets solved. Even if the problem gets solved, uncertainty will remain in some cases, such as when a user fails to be recognised in many attempts in succession when trying to input a spoken number. Eventually, if the problem cannot be removed, an error message might be included, such as the system saying or displaying "I'm afraid that I have difficulty recognising you". Fourth, it must be ensured that activation-through-pointing of squares, icons and text fields can only be done when the cursor has pointed at any of these for a certain amount of time, so that subjects will not accidentally activate anything in the graphics output domain.

We don't know what S6 was referring to when remarking that the screen (graphics) quality "could be improved" but there are several candidates. One is the *reset game* and *new game* icons, cf. above; another, the "falsely highlighted" squares. A third candidate is the levels of difficulty screen that is fuzzy and blurred in parts (Section 7.2.1).

*Display functionality*. The fixed numbers on the game board are smaller than those inserted which, in addition, appear on a slightly lighter background (Section 7.2.1). We assumed that all subjects would notice. S8 found the size difference good because it is useful when one has to remove a number (fixed numbers cannot be removed). However, S4, S5 and S11 failed to notice the differences and tried to remove fixed numbers when in trouble. Moreover, it seems clear that at least S11 did not discover that this was impossible to do.

The evidence thus suggests that, either, not all subjects discovered the visible differences between fixed and inserted numbers, or that they failed to understand the meaning of those differences. We suggest making the difference between fixed and inserted numbers so conspicuous that it is immediately perceived by virtually all first-time players. In this particular case, we believe that almost every user will manage to interpret, e.g. a conspicuous difference in size or colour between fixed and inserted numbers correctly, because one would probably have to search extensively to find a Sudoku user who is not familiar with the distinction between fixed and inserted numbers: the former define the current game and you just don't try to remove them when in trouble! After all, nearly all game players know that one is not allowed to change the game rules when in trouble.

It is probably for reasons such as those just mentioned – i.e. if you perceive a clear visual difference you will understand its pragmatic meaning – that we expected all users to understand the pragmatic meaning of the clearly visible red coloured rows, columns and 3×3 fields that appear when a surface error has been made (Section 7.2.1). To our surprise, S11 did not get the meaning of the red colour even though she clearly perceived its sudden appearance. "[I was uncertain] when part of the board turned red. I postponed the red problem for later. [I] didn't understand the red in the beginning", she said. This observation could be a reason for introducing spoken output so that the system would say, for instance, "Uh-oh, you made a simple mistake". Alternatively, we might, in this particular case and even if S11 were representative of a relatively large number of users out there, which we don't know at present, leave it to users' natural intelligence to discover the pragmatic meaning of the red colour.

*The language issue*. We saw that S6 requested a Danish version of the system (Section 17.3.3). The only subject who had a problem understanding the on-screen text was S4 who didn't understand the word "proceed" (Section 7.2.1) and was helped by the experimenter. A Danish system version would also be likely to remove many of the speech recognition problems caused by subjects' Danish accents. Clearly, if the system is for public use it should include dedicated speech recognition for the country in which it is being installed. A system for an airport might use English or, even better, a choice of the planet's major languages, in which case a user would have to start by selecting the language of interaction.

*Learning and walk-up-and-use*. How close is the system to walk-up-and-use, to being usable without any instruction in how to use it?

The system is not walk-up-and-use because it does not teach, or even list, the Sudoku rules but assumes that users know them already. Is it walk-up-and-use for people familiar with the rules? No, but before looking into why, it may be noted that there probably never was a walk-up-and-use system that used new and unfamiliar modality-device combinations, such as for 3D pointing and input speech. The system uses both of these, to many users, new and unfamiliar technologies. In 10 years, the situation will probably be very different but, for now, subjects need instruction in how to play: how to stand at a pre-defined distance from the screen; point with arm/hand/index finger stretched; use English; use specific keywords; mount and use a microphone. This may seem a lot of instruction but, arguably, most of it will be commonplace when this kind of system is used in public locations, so that eventually users only need to be informed about the input keywords. If these are displayed on-screen, the system will have become walk-up-and-use.

Walk-up-and-use, however, does not imply that users don't have to learn to become good at using a system. This need for training-by-use may be a nuisance in utility systems but may actually be an asset for an entertainment system. The subjects, none of whom had used combined speech and 3D gesture before, began to learn how to use the system well when they started to play. This process is not just one of discovering exactly how to point and speak but may also involve abandoning, or modifying, preconceptions about what computers can and cannot do or understand, GUI habits, habits from playing Sudoku on paper or on the Internet, etc.

Let us look at the data collected on subjects' continued learning process during gameplay. As S6 said, playing Sudoku in this way took some getting-used-to.

*Speaking to the system.* S4 found that it was fine to talk to the system once you got into it. Since subjects were not told how to speak, they had to learn by themselves, starting from whichever assumptions they might have had initially about how one speaks to a machine. Thus, S5 learned during the game that it wasn't necessary to speak so loudly. It would appear that S5 initially believed that machines need "special treatment" in terms of speaking differently compared to speaking to humans. S5 then discovered that this was not necessary and, presumably, relaxed more when speaking to the system from then on. S9 observed that "One has to learn to speak in the right way". After having spoken to herself in Danish once and, as a result, turned a correct "7" into a "4" and getting red colour as well, S11 (mostly) stopped speaking to herself during gameplay.

*Pointing.* S8 noted that it takes time to learn that there is some latency time when pointing. At some early point in the game, S5 started using both arms interchangeably for pointing. S6 noted that it takes some getting-used-to to lower the arm when it is not needed. S8 would have liked to be able to both point and click but found that the designed way to play the game is OK when you get used to it.

*Speaking and pointing.* S5 believed, in retrospect, that he might have spoken earlier once he had highlighted a square, rather than re-checking that the highlighting stayed in place before speaking.

*Graphics output.* By the end of the game, S11 may or may not have learned what the red error colouring means. We don't quite know.

*Gaming as a whole.* At the end of the session, S8 felt in control "after having got used to it". S9 said that speech + pointing "would work better if I became a routine user". S11 "realised very soon how it worked". S12 said that it was simple enough when you first understood the system. He had to get used to the absence of mouse or pencil. After that it was OK.

## 17.5 User Interviews: Closed Questions Overview

The four Likert-scale questions in the post-test interviews (Section 8.8) addressed not only the Sudoku game but, more generally, the appropriateness of speech and pointing gesture input and static graphics output in similar games. Subjects were asked to answer the questions on a scale from 1 to 5 with 1 = unsuitable, 2 = rather unsuitable, 3 = neither/nor, 4 = rather suitable and 5 = suitable. Since S1 was not asked the questions in this way (Section 17.1.2), S1's answers are omitted from Table 17.3.

**Table 17.3** Appropriateness of the Sudoku game modalities. Shaded background indicates subjects who were asked the four questions late in the post-test interview. All other subjects were asked the questions at interview start (white background)

| Subject # | Pointing input | Spoken input | Screen output | Combination of the three |
|---|---|---|---|---|
| 1 | – | – | – | – |
| 2 | 4 | 3 (slow) | 5 | 3 |
| 3 | 1 (4–5 for chess) | 4 | 4 | 1 (4–5 for chess) |
| 4 | 4 (stick instead) | 4 | 5 | 4 |
| 5 | 4 | 3 | 5 | 3 |
| 6 | 4 | 4 | 4–5 | 5 (3 in concrete game) |
| 7 | 4 (in public locations) | 2 (funny) | 5 | 3 (speech is funny) |
| 8 | 3 | 4 | 4 (useful that inserted numbers look different) | 4 |
| 9 | 2–3 (imprecise, annoying with outstretched arm, mouse better) | 4 (when it works) | 4 | 3 (4 if more action-oriented) |
| 10 | 4 (missing note function) | 3 | 5 | 4 |
| 11 | 4 (requires holding hand straight) | 4 | 3 (sometimes slow) | 4 (missing note function) |
| 12 | 4 | 4–5 (for Sudoku, 3–4 for chess) | 5 | 4 (2–3 in noisy environments) |
| Average (first) | 3.1 | 3.4 | 4.2 | 2.8 |
| Average (later) | 3.83 | 3.75 | 4.75 | 4.0 |
| Average (total) | 3.5 | 3.6 | 4.5 | 3.45 |

Table 17.3 shows that subjects who were asked the modality appropriateness questions at interview start, scored all four questions lower on average than subjects who were asked the questions later in the interview. It is possible that first letting users talk about their experience with the concrete game influenced the way they answered the more general evaluation questions.

## 17.6  Conclusions

Table 17.4 concludes on our usability requirements from Section 5.2. The table contents may be viewed as a rough-and-ready summary of the large amount of more detailed information presented in the data analysis.

Possibly the main conclusion to be drawn from the test is that computers that can see are ready for board gaming. The system's main technical problem, the number-in-the-wrong-square bug (Section 17.2.2), can be solved, of course. Analysis suggests a design change as well, i.e. to drop the goal of enabling pointing in all temporal combinations with speech (before, simultaneously with, after). Video data analysis strongly suggests that users are not likely to miss the options of pointing before or after speaking, because none of the test subjects used these options. In addition, we hypothesise that fixing the number-in-the-wrong-square bug will make speech recognition minimally acceptable, at least, for gameplay.

The test suggests that the system uses an appropriate modality combination for its purpose. The closest competitor seems to be one that replaces visual 3D pointing by haptic 2D touch screen pointing but otherwise preserves the advantages of the tested

**Table 17.4**  Results on the Sudoku usability requirements

| Usability requirement/criterion | Result |
| --- | --- |
| Technical quality: robustness: max. one crash or other disruptive error per 2 hours of interaction | OK, Section 17.2.1 |
| Functionality: basic functionality for playing Sudoku | OK, no contrary evidence in the data |
| Ease of use: pointing gesture easy to control | Pointing precision minimally acceptable, Section 17.2.2 |
| Ease of use: speech input correctly understood | Too many recognition problems of unknown origin, Section 17.2.2 |
| Ease of use: system easy to understand and operate | Yes: input vocabulary (Section 17.3.1), output graphics (Section 17.3.1) No: no-effect speech input (Section 17.2.1), number in the wrong square (Section 17.2.2) |
| Ease of use: subjects should complete at least two games in 30 minutes | Not OK, Section 17.1.5 |
| User experience: fun to play Sudoku this way | Yes: most subjects, arguably, Section 17.3.2 |
| User experience: would play again in, e.g. an airport | Yes: +half the subjects, roughly, Section 17.3.2 |

system, i.e. of being based on the natural human communication ability of speaking and pointing, and of not requiring a haptic input device (separate from the screen). A deeper reason why the replacement makes sense is that the Sudoku system does not strongly require capturing of 3D arm/hand action, because all that the cameras have to process is a pointing gesture that produces 2D screen coordinates. It is only when pointing gestures become replaced or supplemented by other gesture types (see Section 15.5.5) and, even more generally, arm/hand actions, such as grasping a virtual chess piece and putting it down on the game board, and innumerable others – that visual 3D gesture/action technology moves beyond what can easily be done with standard haptic 2D touch screen gesture.

The Sudoku system also sits on another fence, i.e. it's physical all right but does not really qualify as a physical game. In this, however, stand-up Sudoku gaming resembles many popular games like dart or billiard, so there does not seem to be any obvious reason why Sudoku gaming should be made more physically demanding than it already is. Moreover, more than half of the subjects said they might use the system if they came across it in a public location and had time to spare. These subjects were all Sudoku players as opposed to the three subjects who weren't really interested in playing this game, and there were only one or two of the Sudoku players among the subjects who did not envision using the system. On the other hand, it should also be noted that the test did not manage to change the minds of those who were not Sudoku enthusiasts already.

As for instruction and learning requirements, subjects were given minimal instructions on how to play and, despite unfamiliar interaction technologies, playing and improving gameplay turned out to be well within the abilities of users, such as those selected for the test. The only exception seems to be the English language which the native Danish speakers had to use in the test. An important qualification should be noted, however, and that is the lack of representativeness of the test user population, as discussed in Section 17.1.4.

## References

Bernsen NO, Dybkjær L (2007) Report on iterative testing of multimodal usability and evaluation guide. SIMILAR deliverable D98.
Oviatt S, Cohen P (2000) Multimodal interfaces that process what comes naturally. Communications of the ACM 43/3: 45–53.

# Chapter 18
# Multimodal Usability: Conclusions and Future Work

In this final chapter, we take stock of two key purposes in writing the book: has multimodal usability become reasonably simple to grasp as a whole (Section 18.1)? And, how did generalisation of traditional GUI-oriented HCI work out? What have we demonstrated (Section 18.2)? Section 18.3 looks at needs, highlighted by the argument of this book, for future work in multimodal HCI.

## 18.1 Simple to Grasp?

We very much hope so. Overall, developing a usable system is simply about understanding AMITUDE, usability (the concept) and the language of fitting and conducting proper data collection planning, method selection, usability data collection, data handling and analysis. Having analysed the data, we hopefully know more about the usability of the current system model and might modify it in some way.

The devil is still around, to be sure, instigating temptation and confusion. It may be tempting to select too few usability methods for the kind of system addressed, or to be biased when analysing and interpreting the data. And confusion can have many sources. Systems are becoming more complex by the month, and some are beginning to behave a little like people. This book's usability method descriptions must be interpreted rather flexibly in order to find an optimal version of some method, or even an optimal combination of methods, for the given situation; micro-behaviour annotation is a new challenge to many; and sometimes new coding schemes or usability evaluation criteria must be developed from scratch.

Don't be tempted, and don't treat the messages in this book as gospel. We may or may not be wrong on particular points. Moreover, our descriptions of methods, other approaches, techniques, usability methodology as a whole are inevitably a bit too rigid for practical usability development work in the real world where every new development project is different from all others in innumerable ways. So, prepare to see through the rigidity and the simplifications; prepare to be as creative as new modality combinations and systems blending with people demand, and everything else to do with making the system usable becomes a matter of methodical work.

N.O. Bernsen, L. Dybkjær, *Multimodal Usability*, Human-Computer Interaction Series, DOI 10.1007/978-1-84882-553-6_18, © Springer-Verlag London Limited 2009

## 18.2  Nerdy Stuff: Generalisations of HCI Made in This Book

We set out to explore and demonstrate several much-needed, and, indeed, over-due generalisations of Human–Computer Interaction (HCI) theory and practice. The common goal of workers in HCI is to contribute to making systems fit their users, i.e. people. Generalisation requires a baseline to generalise from, and we have taken this to be more or less standard WIMP GUI-based human–computer interaction theory and practice that has dominated HCI for some four decades. It's still dominant – at web sites, on mobile phones, consoles and PCs used for work and gameplay – although an increasing number of new output and input modalities has been signalling the need for a broader approach to system usability for a while.

What did we find and demonstrate? Let's list and comment on the generalisations demonstrated in this book. We begin with generalisations of HCI contents (Section 18.2.1) and then move upstairs in the formal scientific edifice to methodology (Section 18.2.2) and, finally, framework and theory (Section 18.2.3).

### *18.2.1  Generalised Scope of Contents for Multimodal HCI*

There is no doubt that multimodal HCI has a far broader scope and far more and more diverse contents than its classical GUI predecessor. What's interesting is that scope and contents must be generalised in several different dimensions which imply, or are implied by, one another, i.e.

1. *From more or less standard WIMP GUI-based interaction to multimodal inter-action.* This is an enormous generalisation, because the WIMP modality com-bination (Windows, Icons, Menus, Pointing) is just one among thousands or millions of others, depending on how one counts. And modality theory (Sec-tion 4.2) does offer several ways of counting quite precisely. Another way of making this point is that it marks transition from largely ignoring modalities – if everything is WIMP, what's the point of discussing modalities at all? If it always rains, or the sun always shines, who needs meteorology? – to putting modalities up there centre stage when developing usable systems.
2. *From the computer as tool to blending with people.* Another huge generalisation. While WIMP interaction is much like a turbo version of pre-computer interaction (knobs, dials, typewriters, watches), we are entering a future in which systems are increasingly able to perceive, do mental processing, communicate and act like people, or what we have called fifth-generation technology, 5GT. This raises entirely new requirements to usability work and is intimately related to multi-modality.
3. *From human–computer interaction to representation and exchange of informa-tion between humans and computer systems.* This is a much overdue concep-tual update of traditional and prototypical interaction, i.e. deliberate, planned and often routine work into static graphics workspace (Fig. 3.3). We don't mind

keeping the term "interaction", but its interpretation as equivalent to prototypical interaction is clearly inadequate and has been so for a long time.

4. *From macro-behaviour to behaviour.* This is yet another huge generalisation. We hope to have made the point forcefully that multimodal usability and blending-with-people work has a voracious appetite for micro-behavioural data, coding schemes and tools, hence this generalisation which says that behaviour may be viewed both macro- and micro-behaviourally. GUI-based HCI has little or no need for micro-behavioural data, but if we want the system to understand an iconic gesture in a context of stressing a particular spoken phrase, to generate an embarrassed face or do zillions of other things that people do every day, we better study exactly how these behaviours are being made by people.

5. *From usability method application to the usability data handling cycle.* While points 1–4 above are honest-to-God generalisations, the present point might as well be considered a change of point of view – dramatic, perhaps, for those who, like the authors, never thought like this before, natural for those who did. Working in multimodal usability requires an appropriate stock of concepts properly understood through practice, as emphasised in the idea of CoMeDa cycles. And then this work requires efficient practice of the data handling cycle, from method selection through data collection, processing, and analysis, to results reporting. HCI was always about data, of course, but we consider the data handling cycle an important generalisation because multimodal usability and blending with people requires radically new work on, in particular, micro-behaviour data annotation. The data handling cycle hasn't been very visible in HCI so far for the same reason that modalities and micro-behaviours weren't.

On all five points, generalisation is explained as *extension of scope of contents*, i.e. as a need to address a much wider diversity than before – with respect to modalities (1), system capabilities (2), information presentation and exchange (3), behaviours (4) and data (5). Because of these extensions, multimodal usability needs to build new theory, such as modality theory (1); import new theory, such as theory about all aspects of people (2); embrace new technical domains, such as bio-sensing (3); fuse with new communities, such as the micro-behaviour data annotation community (4); and learn new methodologies, such as for micro-behaviour data handling (5).

## 18.2.2 Generalised Methodology for Multimodal HCI

In the theory of science, we would expect drastic extensions of scope and contents to carry, potentially, some amount of higher-level extensions with them. So let's ask whether, compared to GUI-based usability, the far larger diversity of multimodal usability can, or should, be addressed by the same methodology as before or if it calls for *methodological generalisation or extension* as well. We continue the list of generalisations by reviewing the methodologies presented.

6. *Standard GUI data collection methods re-prioritised.* The large majority of this book's 24 methods are already being used in some form for WIMP GUI-based development. For each method in this majority, we discuss if there are differences in the method's applicability and relevance to the development of, on the one hand, familiar GUI-based technologies, and, on the other, advanced multimodal research prototypes. The many differences identified are expressed in terms of differentiation factors (Section 6.2.2) in the *multimodal significance* entries in method Chapters 8, 9, 10, 11 and 12 and illustrated for the Cases (Section 7.1). Most differences are important to the method selections to be made by multimodal developers in present years, but are expected to go away when multimodal systems move downstream and turn mainstream, cf. Section 6.2.2, so that users become familiar with the systems, technology penetration grows, systems are being deployed and expert knowledge about them increases.

7. *Standard GUI data collection methods generalised.* We generalise card sorting to category sorting for multimodal use (Section 10.3).

8. *New multimodal usability methods.* We describe three methods of particular relevance to multimodal development and virtually none to WIMP-based ditto, i.e. micro-behavioural field observation (Section 10.2), human data collection in the lab (Section 10.5) and Wizard of Oz (Section 12.2). In addition, we add to standard HCI the methods and techniques of micro-behaviour coding (Section 15.5), modality analysis (Chapter 4) and general data handling (Chapters 15 and 16).

9. *A new general methodology for HCI.* When planning the present version of this book, and motivated by an interest in creating a unified view of multimodal usability work, or of multimodal HCI, we concluded that HCI methodology is all about data handling, including data collection.

As expected, we see that the massive extension of contents from GUI-based to multimodal HCI demonstrated in this book and described in points 1–5 above is accompanied by changes in relative importance of different usability methods; generalisation (in a single case) of individual methods; emergence into prominence of non-GUI-relevant methods; and, ultimately, by re-definition of the methodology of HCI as data handling. Conversely, these methodology-level changes themselves suggest that we are dealing with a rather substantial paradigm shift in HCI and usability work.

### 18.2.3 Generalised Framework and Theory of Multimodal HCI

A third and final question is if the generalisations of contents and methodology described in the two previous sections involve generalisation at the lofty level of framework (or approach) and theory.

10. *Approach, framework.* We propose a simple, because high-level, framework for multimodal HCI. It is that practical HCI work essentially consists in making three things work well together, i.e. (a) iterative development of an AMITUDE model of use, (b) data handling methodology and understanding of the language of fitting and (c) understanding of the notion of usability and related notions of usability requirements, arguments, evaluation criteria and the evaluation hierarchy. We submit that this framework is a reasonable approximation to the truth of the matter, comfortable and easy to explain and understand. As usability developers, we aim to collect the usability data we need, analyse it to assess and improve the model of use, and, having worked in a methodologically sound manner throughout, end up with a usable system. Or, if usability analysis demonstrates likely infeasibility of our project, we stop.

11. *Theory.* Befitting this book's special focus on generalising usability and HCI from a primary concern with GUI-based systems and interaction to addressing multimodal systems and interaction in general, we have primarily focused on describing modality theory as necessary theory underpinning HCI. Had there been any useful and usability-oriented taxonomies out there of application types, tasks, user profiles, devices or use environments, we would have presented them, but there are not.

12. *Usability.* With respect to usability, we have focused on (i) proposing a high-level decomposition of the concept (Section 1.4.6); (ii) generally describing "the" evaluation hierarchy underneath (Section 16.2.2) – nobody really knows if all more specific usability concepts can be subsumed and nicely hierarchically organised under the top of the usability iceberg described in Section 1.4.6; and, for illustration, (iii) discussing various attempts at capturing some of "the" usability hierarchy's next-to-top level through guideline sets or ISO standards (Sections 11.4, 11.5.1 and 16.4.1). None of this is cut in stone for multimodal use. It is incomplete and sometimes GUI-derived or -tainted, but still useful as far as it goes, if you are careful. It would be simple to add a couple of general normative concepts more to our decomposition of usability in Section 1.4.6, like *good performance* or *nice aesthetics*. Too simple, in fact, because where are the principles behind adding exactly these norms rather than others? In this area, like so many others of multimodal usability, there is still a lot of work to do.

Do points 10–12 amount to a new framework for HCI? We don't know and it matters far less than the generalisations described in the two previous sections. Was there "a" framework at the same level of generality before, so that a meaningful comparison can be made in the first place?

Still, the answer probably must be "yes" in some sense, because the generalisation described in this book is as substantial as it is. It's from (a) a small family of input/output modality combinations characterising standard GUI-based interaction, to all modalities and their combinations; and (b) computing for technology generations 1GT through 4GT to the inclusion of fifth generation technology (5GT) for automating people, cf. Section 1.4.2. That's not an interaction paradigm shift like those that keep happening almost every month, demanding the attention of the HCI community, cf. the examples in Box 1.2. That's rather two technical revolutions combined.

## 18.3 Future Work

We have hardly spoken about the community angle of generalising HCI as demonstrated in this book. However, generalisation clearly implies a need for the HCI community to join forces with communities in data handling and annotation, multimodal

Table 18.1  Needs for future work in multimodal HCI

| Generalisation | More work needed on |
|---|---|
| 1. From more or less standard WIMP GUI-based interaction to multimodal interaction | Modality description, properties, aptitude, relationships, taxonomy extension to the media of taste and smell. New modality combinations. Usability prediction |
| 2. From the computer as tool to blending with people | Model human central processing. Map from micro-behaviour to central processing and vice versa |
| 3. From human–computer interaction to representation and exchange of information between humans and computer systems | Model complete spontaneous natural multimodal communication acts |
| 4. From macro-behaviour to behaviour | Establish general representation languages and coding schemes for all levels of human communication and action. More free public-domain micro-behaviour data collections for analysis and component training |
| 5. From usability method application to the usability data handling cycle | Appraisals of this view |
| 6. Standard GUI data collection methods re-prioritised | New ways of using early usability methods with new, hard-to-explain modalities and combinations |
| 7. Standard GUI data collection methods generalised | Guideline and standard proposals for new modality combinations and for general usability, if possible |
| 8. New multimodal usability methods | Improved data collection for mobile and ubiquitous interaction and field testing |
| 9. A new general methodology for HCI, i.e. data handling | Better special-purpose and general data coding tools. Better understanding of when to add properties to, or subtract them from, the system model |
| 10–12. Approach and framework, theory, usability | More adequate and principled decomposition of usability at top and next levels. All modalities and modality combinations treated equal in HCI |

systems development, blending-with-people systems and multimodal signal processing. This is plainly necessary, because generalised multimodal HCI needs more work on several fronts, and some of this work must be done by those communities. Table 18.1 uses the 12-point structure of the previous sections to describe obvious challenges for which justification can be found in this book.

# Abbreviations

| | |
|---|---|
| ACM | Association for Computing Machinery |
| AGTK | Annotation Graph ToolKit. Coding tool |
| AI | Artificial Intelligence |
| AMITUDE | Application type, Modality, Interaction, Task, other activity, domain, User, Device, Environment of use. Part of this book's framework |
| ATM | Automated (bank) Teller Machine |
| AU | Action Units |
| CCT | Cognitive Complexity Theory |
| CHI | Computer–Human Interaction. Annual International Conference |
| CoMeDa | COncepts, MEthods and other approaches, DAta handling. Part of this book's framework |
| DAMSL | Dialogue Act Markup in Several Layers. Coding scheme |
| DPT | Danish Pronunciation Trainer |
| EARL | Emotion Annotation and Representation Language. Markup language |
| ECA | Embodied Conversational Agent |
| EEG | Electro-EncephaloGram |
| FACS | Facial Action Coding System |
| FAQ | Frequently Asked Question(s) |
| GG | Generic Guideline |
| GUI | Graphical User Interface |
| HCI | Human–Computer Interaction |
| HUMAINE | HUman–MAchine Interaction Network on Emotion. European research network 2004–2007 |
| ICT | Information and Communication Technologies |
| IEC | International Electrotechnical Commission |
| IEEE | Institute of Electrical and Electronics Engineers |
| I/O | Input/Output |
| IPR | Intellectual Property Rights |
| ISLE | International Standards for Language Engineering. EU–US research project |

N.O. Bernsen, L. Dybkjær, *Multimodal Usability*, Human-Computer Interaction Series, DOI 10.1007/978-1-84882-553-6_BM2, © Springer-Verlag London Limited 2009

| | |
|---|---|
| ISO | International Organization for Standardization |
| ITU | International Telecommunication Union |
| LNAI | Lecture Notes in Artificial Intelligence. Springer series |
| LNCS | Lecture Notes in Computer Science. Springer series |
| LREC | Language Resources and Evaluation Conference |
| MP | Modality Property |
| MR | Mandatory Rule in Section 3.4.3 |
| NICE | Natural Interactive Communication for Edutainment. European research project 2001–2004 |
| NITE | Natural Interactivity Tools Engineering. European research project 2001–2003 |
| NIWS | Number ends up In Wrong Square. System problem Section 17.2.2 |
| Nm | Nanometre |
| NWB | NITE Workbench for Windows. Coding tool |
| NXT | NITE XML Toolkit. Coding tool |
| PC | Personal Computer |
| PDA | Personal Digital Assistant |
| Q&A | Question-Answering methods or systems |
| R&D | Research and Development |
| RFID | Radio Frequency IDentification (tags) |
| RT | Rule of Thumb in Section 3.4.3 |
| SAMPA | Speech Assessment Methods Phonetic Alphabet |
| SC | Structure Coding |
| SDS | Spoken Dialogue System |
| SG | Specific Guideline |
| SIMILAR | Taskforce for creating human–machine interfaces SIMILAR to human–human communication. European research network 2003–2007 |
| SMALTO | Speech Modality Auxiliary Tool |
| SMS | Short Message Service on mobile phones |
| TC | Time-stamped Coding |
| TEI | Text Encoding Initiative |
| ToBI | Tones and Break Indices. Prosody transcription system |
| UCD | User-Centred Design |
| UML | Unified Modelling Language |
| UPA | Usability Professionals' Association |
| VE | Virtual Environment |
| VR | Virtual Reality |
| W3C | World Wide Web Consortium |
| WCAG | Web Contents Accessibility Guidelines |
| WER | Word Error Rate in speech recognition |
| WIMP | Windows, Icons, Menus, Pointing. The standard GUI components |
| WOZ | Wizard of Oz simulation method |
| WYSIWYG | What You See Is What You Get (in GUI output) |

# Index

**A**

Abstraction focus, 78
Acoustic representation, 86
Acoustics, 72, 76, 90
Acting, *see* Action
Action, 37, 38, 62, 355
Action units, 53
Actor, 143
Adequacy evaluation, 368
Ad hoc assignment of meaning, 78
Aesthetics, 417
Affective computing, 11, 32
Affective learning, 32, 37
Affinity diagram, 205
Alarm signals, 85
Alerts, 85
Ambient intelligence, 11
AMITUDE analysis, 110
AMITUDE model of use, 18, 26–31, 67, 121, 354
Analogue
    acoustics, 83
    coding representation, 333
    graphics, 83
    haptics, 84, 88
    modalities, 73
    modality families, 81
    representation, 78
    signs, 797
    view, 345
Anaphor, 333
Andersen system, 51, 229, 270–271, 276, 370
Annotation, 317, 345
    Graph Toolkit, 345
    stand-off, 326
    symbolic view of, 345
    toolkits, 345
Annotator, 327
Anomalies, 353, 388

Anthropology, 124
Anvil, 345
Application type, 27, 31–33, 114
Application type analysis, 31
Arbitrary meaning, 76
Arbitrary modalities, 74, 85
Aristotle, 37
Artefacts, 15–16
Attention, 36
Attitude, 334
Attractiveness metrics, 258
Audiovisual speech, 82
Availability of evaluation criteria, 370
Awareness, 36

**B**

Bar graphs, 84
Barge-in, 78
Basic task, 45
Basic task means-ends analysis, 45
Baton gesture, 340
Behaviour, 415
Beyond interaction, 59
Bio-interaction, 11
Bionic Wizard of Oz, 267
Bio-sensor data, 60
Bird watching story, 326
Blending with people, 10, 51, 60, 61, 62, 332–335, 415
Blending with people micro-behaviour, 335
Blind users, 41
Body, 38–39
Braille, 41, 82
Brainstorming meeting, 205

**C**

Card sorting, 218
Car navigation task, 50